Metalwork
Technology and Practice

Eighth Edition

Metalwork
Technology and Practice

Eighth Edition

Victor E. Repp, Ed. D.
Professor of Manufacturing Technology
College of Technology
Bowling Green State University
Bowling Green, Ohio

Willard J. McCarthy
Associate Professor, Emeritus
College of Applied Science and Technology
Illinois State University
Normal, Illinois

GLENCOE

Macmillan/McGraw-Hill

New York, New York   Columbus, Ohio   Mission Hills, California   Peoria, Illinois

METALWORK TECHNOLOGY AND PRACTICE, Eighth Edition

Send all inquiries to:
GLENCOE DIVISION
Macmillan/McGraw-Hill
3008 W. Willow Knolls Drive
Peoria, IL 61614-1083

ISBN 0-02-676460-1

Printed in the United States of America.

5 6 7 8 9 10   VHJ   99 98 97 96 95 94

Howard Davis: Technical Illustrator

Masco Corporation: Cover Photo

PREFACE

Metalwork Technology and Practice provides a comprehensive introduction to metal fabrication technology. It is intended as a textbook for entry level courses that provide laboratory experiences in metal fabrication. It also may be used as a reference book in metal product manufacturing courses or exercises.

For the Eighth Edition, each unit has been revised as needed to reflect current practice. The application of mathematics and science to metal processing has been emphasized, and a new Section on Metal Product Manufacturing has been added. The product section has also been revised and expanded, and now includes several new products designed for production on numerically controlled machine tools.

The traditional features of the book have been retained. The reading level is as low as practicable for a metalworking technical book of this level. Technical terms are in boldface type, and a list of them is provided at the end of each unit. A glossary of technical terms is also provided at the end of the text to aid student development of technical vocabulary. The review questions at the end of each unit also provides students with a convenient way to check their knowledge of each topic.

Measurements are given in U.S. Customary Units followed by S.I. Metric equivalents in brackets. Career sketches and vignettes of significant metalworking accomplishments, introduced in the Seventh Edition, are also continued as popular and educational features of the book.

Acknowledgement and appreciation are gratefully expressed by the publisher and author of the Eighth Edition to the people who provided helpful criticism and suggestions for the text, and to the industrial organizations that provided technical information and illustrations. Further comments and suggestions from metalworking instructors using this textbook are most welcome.

6

CONTENTS

10   *Contents*

PART

1

Introduction

As a three-time winner of the "Teacher of the Year" award, Gerald Mason has a firm hold on the interest, affection, and respect of his students and supervisors. At various times during his 27 years as an Industrial Technology Instructor, Gerald's city, school district, and state have each awarded him that high honor.

It all started for Gerald when he was a boy and used an old dining room table to mount some woodworking machines, a single electric motor, a line shaft, and a set of pulleys. He has been interested in almost anything mechanical ever since. To his basic high school education, he added several vocational courses—welding, machining, and auto mechanics. Then he earned a BS degree in Education and a MA degree in Industrial Education.

Now Gerald, who teaches metalworking in one of the largest school districts in his city, is sharing his interests with his students. In addition to learning the metalworking skills, Gerald and his students study safety precautions, discuss metalworking procedures in industry, do market surveys for metal products, and examine publicity for job openings.

Charles Zilch

Gerald seldom rests, even in the summer. He helps an Industrial Arts Club raise money to buy extra equipment for the classroom. The students have sold 20 can crushers and 40 computer tables that they made on their assembly lines. The money they raised was spent for a computer-controlled typesetter and several other teaching tools.

From Gerald, students learn that metalworking technology is a "good, steady area for future work and an excellent skill for both careers and hobbies."

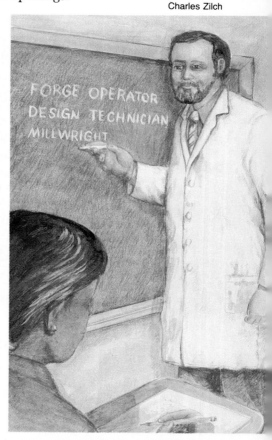

Gerald Mason
*Industrial Technology
Instructor*

UNIT 1

Careers in Metalworking

Metals are used in thousands of different ways and in thousands of different products and structures. People who work with metals design and make the smallest, largest, fastest, most beneficial, and most unusual things we use. In industries that process metals, and manufacture or service metal products, they work at many different jobs. A knowledge of metalwork can lead to a career in this important, growing industry.

1-1 Learning About Metalwork

Learning to work with metals in an educational setting is the best way to discover how much you like metalwork, Fig. 1–1. Educational courses in metalworking are carefully designed to provide controlled learning experiences. They provide the knowledge and develop the ability needed to work safely with metals, metalworking tools, equipment, and machinery.

The laboratory experiences in your coursework and the information in this textbook will introduce you to a wide range of activities in metalworking.

The metalworking industry is very large and diversified. It offers many exciting careers in the design, manufacture, marketing, and servicing of metal products.

Fig. 1-1 Metalworking in the school laboratory may spark your interest in a metalworking career. (Manual High School, Roger Bean)

1-2 Factors To Consider in Selecting a Career

It is entirely possible that you will live and work for 30 to 50 years after completing your formal education. Your living, home, pleasures, happiness, and success will depend to a large extent on the satisfaction and amount of income your job provides. Before making a career choice, it is important to know everything you can about the occupation that you plan to make your career. You will want to get answers to the following questions:

1. How much schooling or college education is required?
2. Will the occupation still exist when you finish your education?

3. How well does the occupation pay?
4. Is steady employment available?
5. Is the work dangerous?
6. Is there opportunity for advancement?
7. What is the chance of starting your own business?
8. What other opportunities, such as teaching, might be available?

To get answers to these questions, ask your parents, teachers, guidance counselor, and relatives about them. Read all you can about the occupation, beginning with information you will find in this unit. Furthermore, a good source of information concerning all types of careers, including metalworking careers, is the **Occupational Outlook Handbook.** This book is brought up-to-date every two years by the U.S. Department of Labor. It is available in many school or public libraries.

1-3 Classification of Occupations

An **occupation** is the kind of job or work at which a person is employed to earn a living. Occupation means the same as **job** or **vocation.** Many kinds of occupations can become rewarding careers.

Because of space limitations, only the descriptions of the more common metalworking occupations are included in this book. A complete listing is provided in the Dictionary of Occupational Titles. It is also published by the Department of Labor and is available in many libraries.

The amount of education and training required for different metalworking occupations varies widely. The training period may range from several days to five years or longer. For example, a drill press operator may be trained to perform simple drilling operations with a small drill press in several days. On the other hand, four years is generally required for training an engineer or a machinist.

General Classifications

Metalworking occupations are broadly classified by the knowledge, kind of skill, and

length of training needed to perform the required work. The following occupational classifications are commonly used:

1. unskilled workers
2. semiskilled workers
3. skilled workers
4. technicians
5. technologists
6. engineers.

These general occupational classifications will be explained in the following sections.

Unskilled Workers

This classification includes workers who require little or no special training for the tasks they perform. This classification includes laborers who handle and move materials manually, floor sweepers, and others who require little training or application of knowledge. The percentage of unskilled workers in the labor force is decreasing and will probably decrease further in the years ahead.

Semiskilled Workers

This classification includes workers requiring some special training. The training period for semiskilled jobs may range from several days to as much as one year. Examples of semiskilled metalworking jobs include assembly line workers, machine tool operators, inspectors, maintenance mechanics, and punch press operators.

Machine tool operators are generally included in the semiskilled classification. This group includes drill press operators, lathe operators, milling machine operators, and operators of nearly every kind of specialized production machine tool. Machine tool operators are generally employed to operate one kind of machine tool. As the operators become skilled, they can perform all of the operations that can be performed on one machine.

Because the skill and required training varies, semiskilled workers are further classified for job promotion and pay purposes. It is common practice to classify machine tool operators as **Class A, Class B,** or **Class C** operators. The Class A operator possesses more knowledge, skill, and experience than the Class B or Class C operator.

High school or vocational school metalwork or machine shop classes provide valuable experience not only for securing employment but also for advancing more rapidly as a machine tool operator. This kind of experience is also valuable in securing employment in many other kinds of semiskilled jobs in the metalworking industry.

1-6 Skilled Workers

Workers in this classification include those employed in the skilled trades. A trade is a job that generally requires from two to five years to learn. A person generally learns a skilled trade through a combination of shop instruction, classroom instruction, and on-the-job training. The classroom instruction includes **mathematics, blueprint reading, technical theory, science,** and instruction in any other subject required for the trade.

Examples of skilled trades among the metalworking occupations include the following: machinist, layout worker, tool-and-die maker, instrument maker, boilermaker, welder, sheet metalworker, molder, and heat-treater. Descriptions of these trades, the nature of the work involved, and educational training requirements are explained in Section 1–7.

A **tradesman** (a level of skill identified by trade unions), also called a **craftsman,** must be able to perform all of the tasks that are common in the trade. For example, a **machinist** is a skilled worker who must be able to set up and operate the machine tools used in the trade. The machinist must know shop mathematics, blueprint reading, and the use of precision measuring tools.

Methods of Learning a Trade

Apprenticeship is a highly recommended method for learning a skilled trade. An **apprentice** is someone who is employed to learn a trade, usually in an apprentice training program. See Fig. 1–2. The length of the apprenticeship training period may vary for different trades, anywhere from two to five years. The apprenticeship period for becoming a machinist or tool-and-die maker, for example, is usually four years.

To qualify for apprenticeship training in a skilled metalworking trade, you must generally be a high school graduate or have equivalent trade or vocational school education. You must have better-than-average mechanical ability. High school or vocational school graduates are frequently in demand as apprentices for skilled metalworking trades. However, they must have a good background in science, mathematics, English, drafting, and metalworking.

An apprentice is paid while learning a trade. A graduated pay scale is provided so that earnings increase as experience increases. On completion of the apprenticeship, the apprentice becomes a **journeyman.** A journeyman is a worker who has met minimum qualifications for employment as a skilled tradesman.

Fig. 1-2 *An apprentice program often provides "one-on-one" instruction from a journeyman machinist.* (Cincinnati Milacron)

A certificate is issued upon completion of the apprenticeship training program. This document is recognized by employers and labor unions throughout the country as qualification for entrance into the trade. The new journeyman must continue studying the tools, processes and procedures in the trade to become more highly skilled and to advance further.

The **pickup method** is a second way to acquire the broad knowledge and experience required for employment as a skilled tradesman. This method involves working in one occupational area until sufficient knowledge and experience are obtained to qualify as a skilled worker.

Workers who choose to learn a skilled trade by the pickup method will find that it usually takes longer than serving an apprenticeship. Frequently they must attend vocational or technical schools to learn blueprint reading, shop mathematics, and technical theory of the trade they are learning.

It is becoming increasingly difficult to learn skilled metalworking trades by the pickup method. The apprenticeship method is recognized as a more efficient method for learning a skilled trade.

1-7 Descriptions of Occupations

The following descriptions of skilled and semiskilled metalworking occupations are arranged in alphabetical order.

Aircraft-and-Engine Mechanic

An aircraft-and-engine mechanic inspects, repairs, and overhauls airplanes. The person must be able to use hand tools, run basic machine tools, and use precision measuring instruments. Some of the work is greasy and dirty, and some work has to be done outdoors.

Aircraft-and-engine mechanics should have a high school education and must attend a technical institute. They will learn engine theory, electricity-electronics, sheet metalwork, welding, and other subjects needed in

the trade. It takes two to four years to learn the trade.

To qualify for employment in jobs that require an **FAA** license, an aircraft-and-engine mechanic must pass tests given by the **Federal Aviation Agency.**

The airplane mechanic must guard against gasoline fumes, explosions, and the danger of inhaling poisonous carbon monoxide gas.

Auto Body Repair Mechanic

Auto body repair requires such metalworking skills as spot welding, arc welding, flame cutting, soldering, and riveting. Skillful use of straightening and smoothing tools is also required to be able to restore damaged bodies to like-new condition. Formal training in auto body repair can usually be obtained at vocational schools.

Boilermaker

The boilermaker assembles prefabricated parts made of **iron** and **steel plates** to make boilers, tanks, and machines. A boilermaker can also repair these assemblies. The boilermaker must drill and punch holes, use machines for cutting and bending the plates, drive hot **rivets,** and read **blueprints.**

Boilermakers work at the site where the boiler, tank, or machine is to be assembled. They must be skilled in using tools and equipment for installation and repair. There is the danger of being burned by hot boilers and rivets. It takes about four years as a helper to become a boilermaker.

Coremaker

A coremaker makes **cores** used to form holes or hollow parts in **castings.** Coremaking is described in Unit 32. The coremaker should learn mathematics and also learn how to read blueprints. A person may learn the trade in a foundry during an apprenticeship of about four years. The coremaker's job is closely related to the **molder's** trade.

Diemaker

The diemaker makes metal forms or patterns, called **dies,** that are used in **punch**

Fig. 1-3 *An expert machinist used a precision boring machine to make several hundred holes in this nuclear reactor core. Each hole was located precisely within a few ten-thousandths of an inch.* (Litton Industries, Inc.)

presses to stamp out forms in metal. Automobile fenders and other sheet metal parts are made with such dies. Diemakers can set up and run all standard machine tools. They must read blueprints, make **sketches,** use **layout tools,** and measure with **micrometers** (Fig. 1-3).

Diemakers use most of the information in this book. They must have good eyesight to make fine measurements. Diemakers should have at least a high school education. They will learn the trade and progress faster, however, if they are technical school or trade school graduates and are good at mathematics and drafting. It takes four to five years to learn the trade as an apprentice.

A diemaker is seldom without work and is one of the last persons to be laid off. The diemaker's, **diesinker's** and **toolmaker's** trades are closely related.

Diesinker

The diesinker makes **drop forging dies** that are used in **drop hammers** to hammer hot steel into the desired shape.

The diesinker must have good eyesight, read blueprints, make sketches, use layout tools, and measure with micrometers. A diesinker should have the same educational preparation as the diemaker.

Forge Operator

A forge operator runs a **forging press,** on which automobile axles, wrenches, etc. are forged. The forge operator must have a knowledge of iron and steel and must be able to read blueprints. He or she should have at least a high school education and must be strong and healthy. The work is hot, heavy, dirty, and noisy. The danger of being burned by hot metal is always present.

Gagemaker or Instrument Maker

The gagemaker, sometimes called an **instrument maker,** makes and repairs all kinds of gages and is a type of **toolmaker.** To do this a person must be able to set up and run any machine in the shop. Good eyesight is required to make accurate measurements. The gagemaker must read blueprints, make **sketches, lay out** the work, and use most of the information in this book.

The worker will learn the trade much quicker and progress faster as a technical school or trade school graduate. It takes at least four years to learn the trade.

Heat-treater

A heat-treater is one who performs heat-treatment operations on steel and other metals. A knowledge of how to **harden, temper, case-harden, anneal,** and **normalize** metal is required. This work is usually learned by working in the heat-treating department of a factory. A heat-treater should have at least a high school education. The work is hot and there is danger of being burned by hot metal and hot liquids. The heat-treater must sometimes guard against poisonous fumes.

Inspector

An inspector examines materials, parts, or assemblies while they are being made or immediately after they are finished (Fig. 1-4). Inspectors must be expert at reading blueprints and using all kinds of measuring tools and gages. An inspector should have at least a high school education.

Jeweler

The jeweler makes high-grade jewelry of platinum, gold, and silver. This work requires good eyesight, even though much of it is done while looking through a magnifying glass. The jeweler must know how to run a **jeweler's lathe** and other small hand and machine tools. The jeweler should have a high school or trade school education and learn the trade as an **apprentice.**

Layout Worker

A layout worker reads the dimensions given on blueprints. Then, with fine measuring and marking tools, the layout worker draws lines and marks on the metal surface to show where to cut or form the metal. Knowl-

Fig. 1-4 *At this plant in Spain, cans are manufactured to tolerances as low as 50 millionths of an inch. To control production quality, these technicians continually inspect and measure sample cans.* (National Can Corporation)

Fig. 1-5 *Computer software is used to give precision control to many machining operations. Some machinists operating these machines may need special knowledge of such programs.* (Hewlett Packard Company)

edge of mathematics, how things are made in the shop, and the properties of various metals is essential.

The layout worker is a diemaker, diesinker, machinist, toolmaker, or sheet metalworker who is chosen to do layout work for the other workers.

Machine Operator

A machine operator earns a living by adjusting and running only one machine, therefore becoming **specialized** in the operation of that machine. If machine operators run **drill presses,** they are **drill press operators;** if they run **lathes,** they are **lathe operators.** There are also **planer operators, milling machine operators** (Figs. 1-5 and 6), and **grinding machine operators.**

A person can learn to run some of these machines in three to six months. However, it may take a year or more to become expert on some of them. A machine operator should have a high school education and should be able to read blueprints and micrometers.

Fig. 1-6 *This machine operator is responsible for the precision drilling of holes.* (CBI Industries, Inc.)

There is the danger of being cut by sharp tools and sharp metals. Some of the work is greasy and dirty. This job is related to the machinist's, described below.

Machine Setup Workers

The machine setup worker specializes in getting machine tools ready for operation, and instructs machine operators in their use. He or she keeps an eye on the machines run by the machine operators, and keeps them adjusted. The machine setup worker may be a fully qualified machinist or may have learned how to set up these machines while employed as a machine operator. An ability to read blueprints and to use all kinds of measuring tools and gages is required.

Machinist

Machinists make precision metal parts, and repair and construct machine tools. They can set up and run standard machine tools (Fig. 1-7), read blueprints, make sketches, use layout tools, and measure with micrometers.

A machinist uses most of the information given in this book.

Good eyesight is essential, because the machinist must make fine measurements. A machinist must also have superior judgment of **depth** and **distance,** and also have good **coordination.** A high school education is preferred. The trade will be learned quicker and progress made faster if the machinist is a technical school or trade school graduate. It takes four years to learn the trade as an apprentice. There is the danger of being cut by sharp tools and metal, and some of the work is greasy and dirty.

Maintenance Mechanic

A maintenance mechanic is skilled in working with machines and in shaping and joining materials by using tools and instruments. **Preventive maintenance** is a major part of the job. Maintenance mechanics inspect equipment, oil and grease machines, and clean and repair parts, thus **preventing** breakdowns or work delays.

Fig 1-7 *This machinist is turning a part for a liquid storage tank. The numerically controlled machine required an investment of several hundred thousand dollars.* (CBI Company)

Metal Patternmaker

The metal patternmaker is a machinist who makes the **metal patterns** that are used to make molds in the **foundry.** These patterns are prepared from metal stock or from rough **castings.**

It takes about four years to learn the trade as an apprentice. The work is interesting and usually steady.

Metal Spinner

A metal spinner forms bowls, cups, trays, saucers, vases, pitchers, and other circular shapes by pressing flat pieces of sheet metal over forms that turn on the **lathe. Metal spinning** is explained in Unit 31. The metal spinner must have manipulative skill, be able to read drawings, and should have a high school education. There is danger of being cut by sharp tools and metals.

Millwright

A millwright moves and installs heavy machines and equipment in shops, and constructs any special foundation for them. The millwright must read blueprints and **lubricate, dismantle,** or **repair** the machinery installed. A person should have at least a high school education, and may learn the trade as an apprentice.

Molder

The molder makes **molds** of various materials for making metal castings. The molder should have a high school education and know how to read blueprints. It takes about four years to learn the trade as an apprentice.

The work may be hot, dusty, and dirty. There is the danger of being burned by hot metal and sparks. The molder's and **coremaker's** trades are closely related.

Plumber

The plumber installs and repairs sewer and drain pipes, water pipes, gas pipes, meters, sinks, bathtubs, showers, faucets, tanks, and similar equipment.

Plumbers should have a high school or trade school education, must learn mathematics, read blueprints, and know something about building construction in general. The work is often dirty and disagreeable. It takes five years to learn the trade as an apprentice. To obtain a license, an apprentice must pass a state examination. The plumber's, **pipefitter's,** and **steamfitter's** trades are closely related.

Polisher and Buffer

A polisher and buffer uses abrasive belts, discs, or wheels to smooth metal, and buffing wheels to polish metal. The work is usually learned on the job. It is dusty and dirty work.

Sales Representative for Machines, Tools, or Materials

A person selling machines must often know how to demonstrate their use, and must be able to answer any questions about them. It is also necessary to know how they are made.

A sales representative for machines or tools has often worked at a trade such as **diemaker, diesinker, machinist,** or **toolmaker** and often is a college graduate. Sales personnel must also know something about advertising, how to show or display goods, and how to write contracts for the things they sell. They must have a knowledge of the goods made by their company's competitors to compare these goods with those they are trying to sell. There are courses in **salesmanship** that can be studied. The salesperson must be neat and pleasant, must speak good English, and must know when to talk and when to be silent. Some sales personnel travel over a large territory, and are away from home for long periods.

Sheet Metalworker

A sheet metalworker makes and repairs such things as furnace ducts, furnaces, ventilators, signs, eave troughs, metal roofs, metal furniture and lockers, and automobile and airplane bodies, which are made out of **sheet metal.** Work may be done in a factory, on buildings, or on ships.

Fig. 1-8 *Many sheet metal workers are needed to build aircraft bodies. While the techniques are specialized, aircraft sheet metalworkers use the basic principles of assembling and fastening sheet metal.* (Boeing)

Toolmaker

The toolmaker makes and repairs all kinds of special tools, cutting tools, **jigs,** and **gages.** Because these are measured with fine instruments, the toolmaker's eyesight must be good. The toolmaker can set up and run all standard machine tools. He or she must read blueprints, make sketches, use layout tools, and measure with micrometers. The toolmaker uses most of the information in this book.

Toolmakers should have at least a high school education, but they will progress faster if they are technical school or trade school graduates. Knowledge of mathematics and drafting is necessary. It takes four to five years to learn the trade as an apprentice.

There is the danger of being cut by sharp tools and metals. The toolmaker's, **diemaker's, diesinker's,** and **gagemaker's** trades are closely related.

Sheet metalworkers must know how to **rivet, solder,** and read blueprints. They should have a high school or trade school education, know **geometry, drafting,** and how to make **patterns.** This trade takes three to four years to learn.

Spring and fall are the busy seasons for outdoor work. Factory work is more steady. The work is noisy at times, and there is the danger of falling from high places and of being cut by sharp edges of metal. The sheet metalworker must also guard against **lead poisoning,** caused by solder made of **lead** and **tin.** The sheet metalworker's and **tinsmith's** trades are closely related (Fig. 1-8).

Structural Steelworker

You have seen the great steel frames that form the skeletons of large buildings or skyscrapers. Fastening the many steel beams and frames together is called **structural steelwork** (Fig. 1-9). You may have seen a structural steelworker stand on a steel beam and swing high in the air. The structural steelworker also builds bridges and ships on which the big parts are **welded** or **riveted** together. Blueprints must be read, and it is necessary to be a careful and strong outdoor worker and a good climber. There is the danger of falling from high places.

Fig. 1-9 *Structural steel workers assemble girders and beams used in commercial and industrial buildings. They join the structural shapes with welds, rivets, or bolts.*

Tool Programmer, Numerical Control

A tool programmer analyzes and schedules the operations involved in machining metal parts on **numerically controlled** machine tools. Numerically controlled machine tools process parts automatically, with little effort or control on the part of the machine tool operator (Fig. 1-10).

The tool programmer reads and interprets the blueprint of a part to be machined. Then, the programmer analyzes and lists on a **program sheet** in proper sequence, the machine operations involved in machining the part.

The programmer must indicate (1) the kinds of operations to be performed, (2) the tools to be selected and used, (3) the correct cutting speeds and feeds, and (4) when cutting fluids are to be used. Hence, a tool programmer must have a good knowledge of mathematics, blueprint reading, and machine shop operations. With large, complex, multipurpose machine tools, a knowledge of a **computer-assisted programming language** is necessary.

Welder

The welder joins metal parts by melting the parts together with the use of the **oxyacetylene welding process,** the **electric-arc welding process,** or with other welding processes (Fig. 1-11). A highly skilled welder knows how to use a number of different welding processes, and is able to weld many different metals.

The welder should know about different metals and how to read blueprints. A beginner can learn to do simple welding jobs in a few hours. However, becoming skilled in welding with several different processes may take from six months to several years. There is danger of being burned by the torch or hot metal. Welders must be **licensed** in many states.

The welder is very important in industry today and will continue so in the future.

1-8 Technicians

Technician occupations are among the fastest growing in the United States. Technicians are workers whose jobs often require the application of scientific and mathematical principles. They usually work directly under scientists, engineers, or industrial managers. Industry needs several technicians for every professional engineer (Fig. 1-12).

In general, the educational requirements for technicians include high school graduation and two years of post-high school training. This kind of technical training is available in many types of schools, including technical institutes, junior colleges, community colleges, area technical schools, armed forces schools, and extension divisions of colleges and universities.

Technician occupations generally require technical education and training that ranks between the requirements of the skilled tradesman and those of the technologist. Technicians usually possess more knowledge of drafting, mathematics, science, and technical writing than a skilled craftsman. However, they are not expected to know as much about these subjects as technologists or engineers.

Fig. 1-10 *This numerically controlled laser measuring machine is being checked by an experienced technician.* (Hewlett Packard Company)

Fig. 1-11 *This welder is arc welding a tank to be used for liquid storage.* (CBI Company)

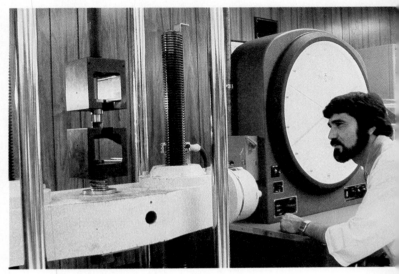

Fig. 1-12 *Using a standard tensile test machine, this technician subjects an aircraft engine bolt to a force of 600,000 pounds.* (Fairchild Industries)

Technicians usually train in only one area of technology, such as the following: mechanical technology, tool technology, industrial or manufacturing technology, aeronautical technology, automotive technology, civil engineering technology, metallurgical technology, instrumentation technology, and safety technology. Technicians usually are not required to perform as skilled craft workers; however, a knowledge of skilled trade practices and procedures is often required. The following descriptions are for technicians in metalworking industries.

Aeronautical Technicians

Technicians in this area assist engineers and scientists with problems involving the design, production, and testing of aircraft, rockets, helicopters, missiles, and spacecraft. They aid engineers by preparing layouts of structures, collecting information and making calculations, checking drawings, and performing many other duties.

Industrial Technicians

Industrial technicians are also called **manufacturing technicians** or **production technicians.** Industrial technicians assist industrial engineers, manufacturing engineers, and tool engineers in a wide variety of problems. They are particularly important in **metals manufacturing industries.**

They assist engineers with problems concerning the efficient use of employees, materials, and machines in the production of goods and services. These problems may involve plant layout, development and installation of special production machinery, planning the flow of raw materials or parts, developing materials-handling procedures, and controlling inventories. Industrial technicians are also concerned with time-and-motion studies, analysis of production procedures and costs, quality control of finished products, and packaging methods.

Instrumentation Technician

The instrumentation technician assists engineers in designing, developing, and making many different kinds of special measuring instruments and gages. Such instruments and

Fig. 1-13 *Some small parts must be precisely manufactured. Here, parts specifications are carefully checked by the technicians in the background. This technician in the foreground performs a visual spot check.* (Battelle Pacific Northwest Laboratories)

measuring devices are used for automatic regulation and control of machinery; measurement of weight, time, temperature, and speed of moving parts; measurement of volume, mixtures, and flow; and recording of data.

Mechanical Technician

Mechanical technicians assist engineers with problems involved in the design and development of machine tools, production machinery, automotive engines, diesel engines, and other kinds of machinery. They also assist engineers in making sketches and drawings of machine parts; estimating material and production costs; solving design problems involving surface finish, stress, strain, and vibration; and developing and performing test procedures on machines or equipment.

When making performance tests, technicians use many kinds of measuring instruments and gages (Fig. 1-13). They also prepare written reports of test results, including graphs, charts, and other data concerning the performance and efficiency of the equipment.

The **tool designer** is a well-known specialist who works in mechanical technology. The **tool design technician** designs tools, jigs, fix-

tures, and holding devices for many kinds of production machines. This specialist may also supervise others in making the tools.

Metallurgical Technician

Metallurgical technicians test samples of metals for their **chemical content, hardness, tensile strength, toughness, corrosion resistance, durability,** and **machinability.** They also assist **metallurgists** in developing improved methods of extracting metals from their **ores** and in the development of new metals and **alloys.**

Technologists

The occupational classification of **technologist** is a category of professional worker ranking between the engineer and the technician. Technologists are graduates of four-year colleges, where they receive academic preparation in **mathematics, physics, chemistry, engineering, graphics, computer programming, business organization,** and **management.** Many of the technologist degree programs require one or more periods of on-the-job work experiences called **internships.** The internships provide valuable professional experiences impossible to obtain in the classroom.

Engineering technologists are prepared to serve in positions of **engineering support.** With the work of the engineer becoming more and more theoretical, technologists are taking over much of the practical, or **applied,** work. The technologist may be called upon to do the on-site surveys, mathematical computations, design studies, laboratory experiments, and other tasks once performed by engineers. With technical and managerial abilities beyond those of the two-year technician, the engineering technologist may also supervise a staff of technicians.

Industrial technologists are employed either in technical positions or in positions of **middle management.** Some types of positions open to industrial technologists include department head; personnel manager; training

Fig. 1-14 *This quality control technician is checking the quality of this rolled aluminum sheet.* (Reynolds Metals Company)

Engineers specialize in one or more kinds of engineering, such as **mechanical, electrical,** or **chemical** engineering. Many kinds of engineers design metal products, develop and supervise the manufacturing procedures and processes for metal products, and specify the metals to be used in the products they design. Following are some kinds of engineering in which engineers must know and understand the properties of metals and metalworking processes:

1. *Architectural engineers* design all types of buildings. These may range from small homes constructed largely of wood, to factories and large buildings constructed of structural metals and masonry.
2. *Aeronautical* and *aerospace engineers* develop new designs for aircraft, missiles, and space vehicles (Fig. 1-15).
3. *Civil engineers* design highways, bridges, dams, waterways, and sanitary systems.

Fig. 1-15 *These aircraft engineers are working on the design details of a new aircraft. The model helps them visualize how it will look and function when built.* (Textron, Inc.)

director; technical writer; labor relations director; production manager; plant and product designer; and specialist in quality control, facilities planning, cost estimating, and time studies (Fig. 1-14). They may also work in the area of sales as a manufacturer's representative, sales engineer, product analyst, or sales manager or in various capacities in advertising, purchasing, sales and service.

1-10 Engineers

Engineers plan, design, and direct the building of roads, bridges, tunnels, factories, office buildings, waterworks, dams, mines, automobiles, aircraft and spacecraft, ships, railroads, power plants, electrical appliances, electronic equipment, radio and television stations, machinery, and engines. A college education is required to obtain an engineering degree. Engineers must be knowledgeable in **mathematics, drafting, physics,** and **chemistry.**

4. **Electrical** and **electronics engineers** design and develop electrical machinery, electrical switches, controls for machines and appliances, radios, televisions, automatic controls for industrial machinery, electric power generators, and many other electronically controlled products.
5. **Marine engineers** develop new designs for commercial and military ships, submarines, and other types of marine equipment.
6. **Mechanical engineers** design many different kinds of machines, appliances, and mechanical equipment for industrial and consumer use.
7. **Metallurgical engineers** develop and improve methods of extracting metals from their ores, refining them, and preparing them for practical use. They also develop new **alloys** with new properties.
8. **Tool and manufacturing** or **industrial engineers** generally start with the model, or **prototype,** of a product created by a **product engineer.** They analyze and plan the industrial processes needed to economically manufacture the product. They design the special manufacturing machines, equipment, assembly lines, and any packaging system required. They also supervise the construction and installation of the machines and equipment needed for production, and they organize the work force. Finally, they supervise and control production through manufacturing and assembly operations to the finished and packaged product.

REVIEW   REVIEW   REVIEW   REVIEW   REVIEW

WORDS TO KNOW

apprentice	heat-treater	metallurgist	skilled worker
boilermaker	inspector	metal patternmaker	steamfitter
carbon monoxide	instrument maker	metal spinner	structural
coremaker	jeweler	millwright	steelworker
diemaker	journeyman	molder	technician
diesinker	layout worker	pipefitter	technologist
engineer	lead poisoning	plumber	toolmaker
forge operator	machine operator	polisher	trade
foundry	machine setup	semiskilled worker	unskilled worker
gagemaker	worker	sheet metalworker	welder
	machinist		

REVIEW QUESTIONS

1. List several factors that you should consider in selecting your occupation.
2. List several school subjects that are generally needed to learn a trade or become a technician, technologist, or engineer.
3. List several kinds of semiskilled metalworking jobs.
4. What is the length of the training period for semiskilled metalworking jobs?
5. List several skilled metalworking trades.
6. In what two government publications can you find further information about skilled trades or occupations?
7. Describe the apprenticeship method of learning a trade.
8. What is a journeyman?
9. What education is required to become a technician? A technologist? An engineer?
10. List several kinds of work done by (1) technicians, (2) technologists, (3) engineers.

UNIT
2
Introducing Metals

What are metals? Usually they are shiny, solid materials that conduct heat and electricity. They come from ores that are mined from the earth, then melted and refined to separate each metal. Except for mercury, most metals are solid and hard at room temperatures.

2-1 The Importance of Metals

Metals are essential to the conduct of our daily lives, to our industrial society, and to our national defense (Fig. 2-1). Metals are everywhere around us. They are widely used in the manufacture of aircraft and spacecraft, automobiles, buses and trucks, railroad cars, bicycles and motorcycles, and ships and submarines. Structural steel and other structural metals are used in the construction of roads, bridges, tunnels, and buildings.

Many metals are used in the construction of home appliances. These include familiar labor-saving devices such as stoves, washing machines, clothes dryers, and dishwashers—and convenience items such as toasters, refrigerators, furnaces, and air conditioners. Also included are entertainment items such as radio and television sets, stereo phonographs, tape recorders, cameras, and projectors.

Metals are used extensively in the manufacture of hand tools, portable power tools, machine tools, farm and manufacturing machinery, and roadbuilding equipment. Sports equipment such as fishing reels, pleasure boats, outboard motors, golf clubs, and guns also make use of metals. Valuable or precious metals are often used in making coins, jewelry, tableware, and cutlery.

Fig. 2-1 *Metalworking and metal products are important in every part of modern life.*

transportation　　　　　Ogden Corp.

construction

Metalworking and metal products are important to . . .

Allegheny International

manufacturing

Fairchild Corporation

energy

Combustion Engineering, Inc.

communication

Fairchild Corporation

Florida Power & Light Co.

our daily lives

Talley Industries

Norris Industries

defense

Fairchild Corporation

2-2 Properties of Metals

Metals have different characteristics, called **properties.** When an engineer selects the metals for a product, he selects them on the basis of their properties.

Metal properties fall into three groups:

(1) *Chemical properties* are characteristics of the chemical composition of metals and their chemical reactions to other metals. **Corrosion resistance,** for example, is the ability to resist rusting (oxidation) or other chemical actions. Gold, stainless steel, aluminum, and copper are much more corrosion-resistant than iron and steel.

(2) *Physical properties* are characteristics of metals when they are not being acted upon by outside forces. Color, density, weight, and electrical and heat conductivity are physical properties. Density is expressed as the weight in grams of one cubic centimeter of material (the mass per unit volume). Conductivity is the ability to absorb and transmit heat or electricity.

(3) *Mechanical properties* are characteristics exhibited by metals when outside forces are applied to them. Metalworkers must have an understanding of the mechanical properties of metals when they make or shape metal products.

Fig. 2-2 *Drill rods are removed from a heat treating furnace. The heat treatment is being done to stress relieve the rods.* (Allegheny International)

2-3 Mechanical Properties

Metalworkers are often concerned with the following mechanical properties of metals and how they affect their work.

Hardness means resistance to penetration by other materials. Steel, for example, is much harder than lead or pure aluminum. Hardness may be increased by cold working such as bending, hammering, or rolling at room temperature. Hardness may also be increased or decreased by treating the metal in different ways with heat (Fig. 2-2).

Hardenability is the property of a metal to harden uniformly and completely. A metal with poor hardenability will harden on its surface only, while its center will be left relatively soft.

Brittleness refers to how easily a metal will break with little or no bending. Hardened tool steels and gray cast iron are brittle compared to unhardened steels.

Ductility is the property of a metal to be bent, rolled, or otherwise changed in shape without breaking. Metals high in ductility include soft steel, copper, and aluminum. They can be drawn into fine wire and rolled into thin sheets without breaking.

Malleability permits a metal to be hammered or rolled into shape without breaking. Most malleable metals are ductile. A few metals, such as lead and malleable cast iron, cannot be stretched very far without breaking and are therefore not ductile.

Toughness in metal refers to its ability to withstand sudden shock without breaking **(fracturing).** A metal high in toughness will usually bend or deform before fracturing.

When steel is made extremely hard by heat treatment, it loses much of its toughness. Cutting tools hardened by heat treatment will usually break before they bend very much. However, a special kind of heat treatment, called **tempering,** reduces hardness and increases toughness.

Toughness is often more important than hardness. For example, it is more important for steering knuckles, springs, axles, and other critical auto parts to rank high in toughness than to rank high in hardness.

Machinability refers to the ease with which metals may be **machined,** or cut by a machine tool (Fig. 2-3). **Machinability ratings** are expressed as a percentage in comparison with AISI 1112 steel, which is rated at 100%.

AISI stands for the American Iron and Steel Institute, a trade association of companies that sell or work with iron and steel. The AISI develops and sets ratings or standards for making, selling, and using different kinds of iron and steel.

Fusibility enables a metal, when in its liquid state, to join easily with another liquid metal. Metals high in fusibility are usually high in **weldability** (Fig. 2-4). Welding is discussed in Unit 26.

Strength is the resistance of a metal to deformation (Fig. 2-5). **Tensile strength** is resistance to being pulled apart. **Compressive strength** is resistance to being squeezed together. **Shear strength** is resistance to cutting or slicing forces. **Torsional strength** is resistance to twisting forces.

Elasticity is the ability of a material to return to its original size and shape after the external force causing a change in shape has been removed. **Elastic limit** is the maximum load per square inch or square centimeter that can be applied to a material without forcing it to change shape permanently.

Fatigue is the characteristic that causes a metal to fracture (break) under a repeated load that is well below the tensile strength of the metal. Parts subjected to repeated bending or vibration sometimes break because of **fatigue failure.**

Fig. 2-3 *Facing, a common machining operation, is done on a lathe. A cutting fluid helps the cutting action of the tool bit. Metals rated high in machinability can be cut more easily, leaving a smoother surface than with harder, tougher metals.*

Fig. 2-4 *The fusibility of metal, or the ease with which it may be melted, affects the strength of its welds.*

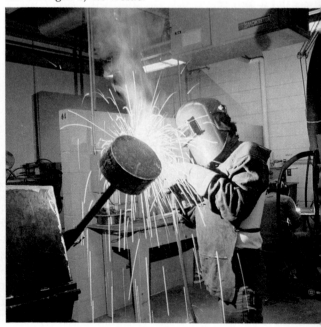

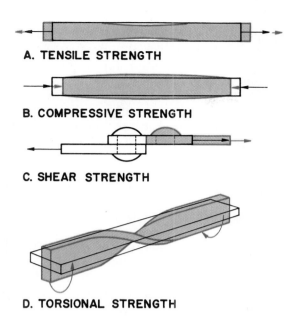

A. TENSILE STRENGTH

B. COMPRESSIVE STRENGTH

C. SHEAR STRENGTH

D. TORSIONAL STRENGTH

Fig. 2-5 *Types of strength in metals. The colored views show what happens when the stress on a metal exceeds its strength.*

2-4 Classification of Metals

Metals are classified as **pure metals** or as **alloys.**

Pure Metals

A pure metal is a single chemical element that is not combined with any other chemical element. A chemical element is a fundamental substance that cannot be decomposed (broken down) by chemical reaction into substances of simpler composition. The earth is made up of more than 100 elements.

Pure metals are generally too soft, low in strength, or low in some other desired property to be used in many commercial applications. Thus, their use in the pure state is limited to laboratory experiments and a few construction applications.

Metals may be further classified as either **ferrous** or **nonferrous** metals. The word "ferrous" is derived from the Latin word "ferrum," which means iron. The main element in all steel is iron. Thus, all steels are called ferrous metals. Examples of nonferrous metals are aluminum, copper, lead, tin, and zinc.

Alloys

The properties of a pure metal can be changed by melting and mixing one or more other pure metals with it. This process produces a new metal which is called an **alloy.** Nonmetallic elements may also be included in alloys. An alloy may have characteristics very different from the pure metals from which it was formed. Stainless steel is a familiar alloy composed of steel, nickel, and chromium. It is strong, tough, and much more corrosion-resistant than plain steel (Fig. 2-6).

The many kinds of alloys may also be classified as either **ferrous alloys** or **nonferrous alloys.** Alloys are named after the main, or **principal,** metal, called the **base metal.** Thus, steels that are intentionally alloyed with nickel, chromium, or tungsten are called steel alloys. When aluminum is alloyed with other metals, **aluminum alloys** are formed. Other metals may also be added to copper to form **copper alloys** or to zinc to form **zinc alloys.**

Fig. 2-6 *Space shuttles and the equipment necessary to launch them contain more than 45 basic metals in several thousand different alloys.* (Morton Thiokol Inc.)

2-5 Selection of Metals

Engineers, product designers, technicians, and skilled workers in metalworking occupations must understand the properties of various metals and their alloys. This knowledge is important to the intelligent selection and processing of metals for each product. For example, various aluminum alloys are used in the construction of spacecraft, aircraft, small engines, lawn furniture, storm windows, and small boats. Aluminum alloys are desirable for these products because they are lightweight, corrosion-resistant, and strong. The

---

TECHNOLOGIES AND PRACTICES

Showing Off: A Ladder to the Sky

For forty years (1889-1929), the Eiffel Tower in Paris was the tallest structure in the world. Today it is still one of the tallest towers. It was built to show off the new materials and methods used during the first century of the Industrial Revolution. The "new" material was iron. Iron had been used for many years for tools and weapons, but never before had an iron project as great as the Eiffel Tower been attempted.

The tower is named for Gustave Eiffel, the engineer who built it as part of the Paris International Exposition of 1889. The Exposition was a type of industrial fair with exhibits and demonstrations spotlighting new inventions. In the early stages of planning the fair, France's Minister of Commerce and Industry proposed a grand 1000-foot-tall [305 meters] structure that would be a symbol of France's pride and prosperity. A contest was held to find a suitable design. Eiffel's design was chosen after he convinced the Minister that a stone structure of that height would be impractical.

After his design was chosen, Eiffel had only two years to finish the tower. He had to plan every detail carefully and devise whole new building methods to make the grand idea a reality.

One major design problem was to determine the type of metal to be used. Eiffel could choose either cast iron, steel, or wrought iron for the tower's girders. Cast iron was too brittle and lacked tensile strength. Steel was lighter and more flexible, but Eiffel feared that steel's greater elasticity would produce too much sway in high winds. The wind was a very important factor to consider when building a tower that would reach 984 feet [300 meters] into the sky.

Eiffel chose wrought iron as the best material for the 7300 tons [6,636 metric tons] of metal used in the tower. It combined strength with rigidity and still was relatively light.

Eiffel completed the tower in time for it to be used as the entrance to the Paris Exposition. At that time, it was seen as an engineering marvel. While other structures may climb higher today, the Eiffel Tower still stands as a symbol of great technological advances.

(French Government, Tourist Office)

manufacture of tools used for cutting metals requires steels that can be hardened by heat treatment. Steels of this type include plain carbon and alloy **tool steels.** Files, hacksaw blades, drills, chisels, thread-cutting dies and many other cutting tools are made of tool steels.

More than 20,000 different kinds of metal are now available for use in manufacturing. There are hundreds of different grades of structural steels, alloy steels, tool steels, and specialty steels. More than 350 different aluminum alloys and more than 300 copper alloys are also available. Many other kinds of nonferrous alloys are in current use. In fact, there are more than 100 different metals used in the manufacture of a modern automobile.

In other chapters in this book, you will learn more about the different metals, their properties, and how they are produced. At this time, however, it is important to know that there are many different kinds of metals. Each kind of metal was developed to provide certain properties needed in the production of various metal products. You will want to know the principal properties of the common metals when you design and construct metal products in your metalworking course.

REVIEW REVIEW REVIEW REVIEW REVIEW

WORDS TO KNOW

AISI	density	fusibility	shear strength
alloy	ductility	hardenability	temper
base metal	elastic limit	hardness	tensile strength
brittleness	elasticity	machinability	tool steel
compressive	fatigue	malleability	torsional strength
strength	ferrous metal	nonferrous metal	toughness
corrosion resistance	fracture	properties of metal	weldability

REVIEW QUESTIONS

1. List ten important products made entirely or largely from metals.
2. Name the three groups of metal properties.
3. Name two principal ways of increasing metal hardness.
4. Name two metals considered to be brittle.
5. Explain the difference between ductility and malleability.
6. In what kinds of metal parts is toughness more important than hardness?
7. What is meant by fusibility in metals?
8. Name and explain each of the four kinds of strength metals may have.
9. What happens to a metal when its elastic limit is exceeded?
10. What are the causes of metal fatigue?
11. Why are pure metals of limited usefulness?
12. How does an alloy differ from a pure metal?
13. Explain the difference between ferrous and nonferrous metals.
14. What is meant by the base metal in an alloy?
15. How many different kinds of metals are now available? Why are there so many?

UNIT

3

Personal Safety in Metalworking

Working safely with metals can be divided into two main topics of concern:

1. protection against personal injury, and
2. prevention of damage to tools, equipment, and machines.

Safe use of tools, equipment, and machines will be dealt with in the units in which these items are discussed. This unit is about personal safety.

When working with metals, you must take great care to avoid personal injury. Solid metals are hard materials that often have sharp edges. Hot, sharp metal chips produced in cutting operations can burn and cut (Fig. 3-1). Grinding wheels can throw abrasive particles into unprotected eyes. Rotating tools and workpieces can catch loose clothing and hair (Fig. 3-2). Harmful rays from electric

welding arcs can burn unprotected skin and eyes. Liquid metals can spatter and cause painful burns (Fig. 3-3).

A careless worker can be painfully injured or cause others to be injured. Workers who work safely can avoid being injured. They must dress properly, follow correct work procedures, and work well as a team with fellow workers.

3-1 How To Dress Safely

1. Maximum eye protection requires the wearing of clean, properly fitted safety glasses with side shields, goggles, or a face shield approved by the National Safety Council (Fig. 3-4). State laws require everyone to wear eye protection in school shops,

Fig. 3-1 *Protect yourself against hot, sharp chips produced by the cutting tools of metalworking machines.* **Never pick up chips with your hands.**

Fig. 3-2 *Long, loose hair can get caught in machinery.* **Keep it in a cap or tie it back securely.**

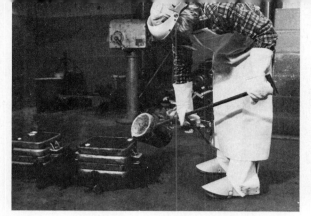

Fig. 3-3 *Handle hot liquid metals carefully and wear the correct safety clothing.*

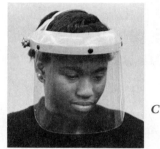

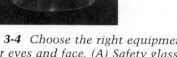

Fig. 3-4 *Choose the right equipment to protect your eyes and face. (A) Safety glasses with side shields. (B) Goggles. (C) Face shield for full-face protection.*

laboratories, and factories. **Your eyes cannot be replaced. Protect them at all costs.**

2. Close-fitting clothing made of hard, smooth-finished fabrics should be worn. Such fabric will not catch easily on sharp edges or rotating tools. Fuzzy sweaters are especially bad and should only be worn under a hard-finished shop coat or jacket.

   Long shirt sleeves should be close-fitting or rolled up past the elbow. Neckties should be removed or tucked into the shirt. A close-fitting apron or shopcoat will protect street clothes from the usual grime of metalworking (Fig. 3-5).

3. Feet should be protected against hot, sharp chips, heavy falling objects, and hot liquid metals. Safety shoes are best (Fig. 3-6), but ordinary leather shoes offer considerable protection. **Canvas shoes and open-toed sandals offer no protection and should never be worn when doing metalwork.**

4. **Always take off all jewelry before working with metals.** Wrist watches, rings, necklaces, and bracelets can get caught on equipment and cause serious injury.

Fig. 3-5 *Dressing safely for metalworking.*

SHORT HAIR OR WEAR A SMALL CAP
SAFETY GLASSES WITH SIDE SHIELDS
NO SWEATER
SCARF OR TIE TUCKED BETWEEN THE 1ST AND 2ND BUTTONS
SLEEVES ROLLED UP OR CUT OFF ABOVE THE ELBOWS
NO TORN POCKETS
CLEAN APRON THAT FITS CLOSELY AROUND THE BODY
NO WRISTWATCH, RING, OR GLOVES
APRON HANGS DOWN TO THE KNEES
STRONG APRON STRINGS TIED AT THE BACK
SAFETY SHOES

STEEL REINFORCEMENT

Fig. 3-6 *Safety shoe with steel-reinforced toe.*

5. Long, loose hair can be caught in **rotating tools.** Wear long hair under a close-fitting cap or tie it back tightly.

6. **Never wear gloves when operating metal-working machines.** They are easily caught in moving parts and may cause serious injury to the hands. (Workers **must** wear gloves, however, when handling hot materials or containers and when arc welding.)

3-2   Safe Work Practices

General

1. Get approval from your instructor or supervisor before using any equipment.
2. Make it a habit to stop, look, and think in unfamiliar situations. **When in doubt, ask your instructor or supervisor for help.**
3. Give serious and undivided attention to your work.
4. Do not walk through restricted areas marked by barriers or floor markings.

With Machinery and Machine Tools

1. Be sure all safety devices are in place and working correctly before using any machine or equipment.
2. Be sure to tighten workpieces and cutting tools securely in machine tools, so that cutting pressures cannot loosen them (Fig. 3-7).
3. Always keep hands away from moving machinery.
4. Never use your hands to stop moving machines or parts such as a lathe or drill press chuck.
5. When closing electric switches, use the insulated handle if available. Avoid touching the metal parts of the switch or switch box.
6. Never leave a running machine. Someone else may not expect it to be running and may be injured by it.
7. Always stop a machine before making measurements with tools that may catch in the machinery, such as a caliper.

Fig. 3-7 *Cutting tools and workpieces must be tightened securely for safe operation.*

Fig. 3-8 *Mark out-of-order equipment with a blue sign.*

8. Always stop machines to adjust, clean, oil, or repair them. When making hazardous repairs, disconnect the machine from its power source so that it cannot be turned on.
9. Disconnect out-of-order equipment and identify it with a blue sign (Fig. 3-8) as recommended by the National Safety Council.
10. When changing speeds on a cone pulley drive system, wait until the machine comes to a **full stop** before shifting the belt.
11. Replace projecting setscrews on rotating equipment with flush setscrews.

Fig. 3-9 *Learn to lift heavy objects by using the strength in your legs,* ***not your back.*** (Manual High School, Roger Bean)

Fig. 3-10 *Brushing is a safe way to remove sharp chips.* ***Never pick up chips with your hands.***

With Shop Materials

1. Handle materials carefully to avoid being cut.
2. Do not touch metal you suspect is hot. Test it first by sprinkling a few drops of water on it.
3. Get help in lifting or moving heavy pieces of metal or machine parts. Remember to lift with your legs, not your back (Fig. 3-9).
4. Get help also when handling long pieces of metal, so as to avoid injuring someone or damaging equipment.
5. Return large pieces of metal to their proper storage racks immediately after cutting off the pieces needed.

With Scrap and Waste

1. Use a brush, a piece of cardboard, or a stick to sweep up or push away sharp metal chips (Fig. 3-10). **Never use your hands.**
2. Never use compressed air to blow metal chips from a machine or work station without approval.
3. Keep aisles clear of small metal pieces, chips, and other waste. These are hazards to safe travel.
4. Keep floors clear of oil, grease, and other liquids that could cause someone to slip and fall.

With Other Students or Co-workers

1. Always try to be alert, patient, courteous, and willing to help. This is especially necessary in school shops where you may have to wait to use a tool or get help from your instructor.
2. When working with someone, agree **beforehand** on how the work will be done and who will do each part so that there will be no confusion that could lead to injury.
3. Do not disturb someone who is actively involved in operating a machine or other potentially hazardous equipment. You may cause them to make a mistake which could cause an accident.

3-3 Safe Use of Hand Tools

The improper use of hand tools frequently results in personal injury. The following safe work practices should be followed when using hand tools:

1. Use the right tool for the job to be performed.
2. See that tools and your hands are clean and free of grease or oil before use so that the tools can be held firmly.

3. Cutting tools should be sharp when using them. Dull tools cause accidents because they require greater force to use them. Dull tools also leave jagged edges that may cut someone.

4. Sharp-edge tools should be carried with their points and cutting edges pointing downward.

5. Heads of cold chisels and punches should not be allowed to mushroom or crack; they should be properly dressed or repaired.

6. When using a chisel, always chip in a direction which will prevent flying chips from striking others.

7. Choose the correct size and type of wrench for the job and use it properly. You can injure your knuckles or hand if the wrench slips.

8. When using a file, be sure that it is equipped with a snug-fitting handle. Otherwise, the sharp tang on the file could injure your hand.

9. When you hand tools to others, give them with the handle first (Fig. 3-11).

10. Always report damaged tools to the instructor. Damaged tools can cause injuries.

11. Tools should always be wiped free of grease or dirt after use and then returned to the proper storage place.

Fig. 3-11 *When you give a tool to someone, always offer it handle first. The scriber being handed to the student in this picture is needle sharp and hard enough to cut steel.*

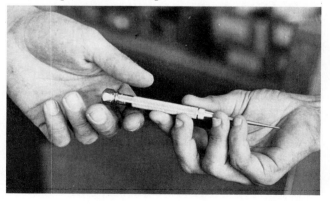

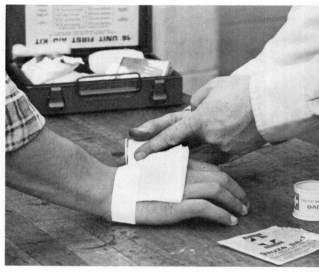

Fig. 3-12 *Get first aid for injuries* **right away.**

3-4 First Aid

1. Always notify the instructor immediately when you or another student are injured, no matter how slight the injury.

2. Get first aid as soon as possible (Fig. 3-12). It is good practice to let slight or moderate cuts bleed for a few moments before stopping the flow of blood. Free bleeding carries infectious particles out of the wound. **Severe cuts or bruises should receive the immediate attention of a doctor.**

3. Burns should also be treated promptly. A first-degree burn is one in which the skin is merely reddened. In a second-degree burn, the skin is blistered. In a third-degree burn, the skin is charred. Treat first-degree burns with applications of ice or cold water. Then apply a sterile dry bandage. **Second- and third-degree burns should receive a doctor's attention immediately.**

4. If you are concerned about an injury or an illness, don't be foolishly brave and "tough it out." Get professional help as soon as possible.

Fig. 3-13 *Always store oily rags in approved* **metal containers.**

3-5

Fire Prevention

1. Learn the location of the nearest fire alarm as well as the nearest fire exit.
2. Learn the location and use of fire protection equipment in the building. Fire extinguishers which use a **dry chemical** or **carbon dioxide** should be readily available at all times.
3. Place oily rags or waste in proper metal containers (Fig. 3-13). This guards against possible fire from **spontaneous combustion.**
4. Always close containers of inflammable materials such as paints or oils after use. Return them to their proper metal storage containers.

REVIEW REVIEW REVIEW REVIEW REVIEW

WORDS TO KNOW

abrasive particle	carbon dioxide	mushroom heads	safety glasses
arc welding rays	extinguisher	rotating tools	safety shoes

REVIEW QUESTIONS

1. What are the state laws on eye protection in school shops, laboratories, and factories?
2. Why shouldn't sweaters or loose clothing be worn while a person is around machinery?
3. What kinds of shoes offer best foot protection for metalworking?
4. Why is long hair a potential hazard around machinery?
5. Why shouldn't jewelry be worn when working with metals?
6. Why is it a good rule not to try to get the attention of a person who is operating a machine until that person has finished the particular operation or process being worked on?
7. Describe a simple way to test whether a piece of metal is too hot to pick up with bare hands.
8. Why should oil or grease be removed from the floor or cleaned from hand tools?
9. List two safety rules or safe practices regarding first aid and the reporting of injuries.
10. Why is it important that oily rags be stored in metal containers?

PART

2

Getting Acquainted with Metals

Safety precautions have always played a major role in metal-working. But it is only recently that educators have offered courses leading to degrees in industrial safety. Deborah Pisoni is one of three safety administrators for one of the largest and most versatile steel mills in Pennsylvania. She began her preparation with a B.S. in Physical Education. Many of her courses, particularly first-aid, drew her attention to accident prevention. So she decided to continue her schooling until she earned an M.A. in Safety Management.

The steel mill where Deborah works covers 727 acres. Different departments handle steel from its manufacture to its processing into products such as pipe, steel coils, and beams. Deborah has to be familiar with the safety aspects of all operations.

Deborah works mainly in the tubular pipe division of the steel works. The job is both physically and mentally demanding. She may walk from furnace to furnace and climb ladders to check cranes. She writes reports on her findings. And she may be "on call" after hours.

Steelmaking has great potential for industrial accidents, but Deborah feels that steel plants have actually become very safe places. The emphasis on safety, from management to employees throughout the mill, has never been greater. Should a serious accident occur, she or a co-worker is immediately called to the scene to discover the cause. Most of the injuries are minor and are caused not by machinery but by a worker's lapse in concentration. Deborah's biggest challenge is to motivate workers to be always alert.

She has been with the company seven years and is pleased to report a noticeable reduction in the number of accidents. She feels that enthusiasm, creativity, and concern for people are the basic qualifications for safety administrators.

Deborah Pisoni
Safety Administrator

UNIT

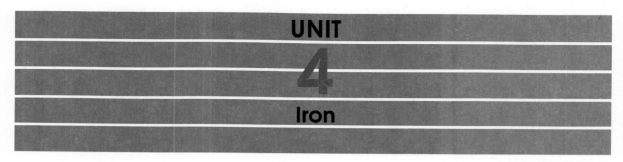

4

Iron

Iron is our most common and most useful metal. About 5% of the earth's crust (by weight) is iron. The chemical symbol for iron is Fe. Iron melts at 2795°F [1353°C] and boils at 4892°F [2700°C]. Its density is 7.9, which means that one cubic centimeter (one milliliter) of iron weighs 7.9 grams, and that its mass is 7.9 times that of water. The purest iron comes from the sky in the form of meteors. Pure iron does not rust in water; iron rusts because it contains impurities. Pure iron is seldom used in industry because it is too soft for most work. It is so soft that it can be scratched with the fingernail.

Iron is used in three forms:
1. Cast iron
2. Wrought iron
3. Steel.

The first two forms are explained in sections 4-2, 4-4 and 4-5; steel is explained in Units 5 and 6.

Fig. 4-1 *An open pit iron ore mine. Some of the largest machines and trucks in the world are used in this type of mining.* (Republic Steel Corporation)

4-1

Iron Ore

Iron ore is not pure as it comes from iron mines (Fig 4-1). Most of the iron ore in the United States is found in the mines of Michigan and Minnesota, known as the **Lake Superior Region** or **Mesabi Range.** Iron ore is also mined in Alabama and imported from foreign countries.

At first, iron ores were rich enough in iron to be used just as they were mined. Now, however, the rich deposits have been exhausted, and we must use iron ores with a much lower iron content.

Low-grade ores, such as **taconite** (consisting of two iron compounds plus quartz) are enriched in processing plants near the mines. This process begins with the separation of excess rock material from the ore. First, the ores are crushed to a fine powder. Magnetic separation removes those particles with high iron content. The iron-rich powder is then mixed with powdered coal to form pellets of rough ball shape. Finally, the pellets are baked to make them hard enough to keep their shape during handling and shipping.

Iron ore is carried from the mine processing plants in railroad freight cars to the loading docks on the Great Lakes. The ore is dumped into bins holding several carloads each. From these bins, the ore is dumped into large *ore boats*, which can carry up to 33,000 tons [30.030 t, metric tons] of ore. An ore boat can be loaded quickly, in less than three hours (Fig. 4-2). These boats then carry the ore to Chicago, Gary, Detroit, Cleveland, and other steelmaking cities along the Great Lakes. Modern boats have their own unloading equipment. These conveyors empty the boats in about five hours.

4-2

Pig Iron

Making **pig iron** is the first step in the purifying of iron and the making of steel. Pig iron is produced when the impurities are burned out of iron ore in a **blast furnace.** It is called a blast furnace because a blast of hot air is forced into it near the bottom. A blast furnace looks like a tall chimney on the outside, 50' to 100' [15 to 30 meters] high (Fig. 4-3). It is a large, round, iron shell from 20' to 30' [6 to 9 meters] in diameter, covered on the inside with special bricks or clay that can withstand great heat (Fig. 4-4). Each blast furnace has four or five giant stoves that heat the air.

Fig. 4-3 *A blast furnace for making pig iron.* (American Iron & Steel Institute)

Fig. 4-4 *A cross-section of a blast furnace. (A) stove, (B) blast furnace, (C) skip car, (D) slag ladle, (E) ladle for molten iron, (F) firebrick furnace lining.*

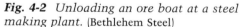

Fig. 4-2 *Unloading an ore boat at a steel making plant.* (Bethlehem Steel)

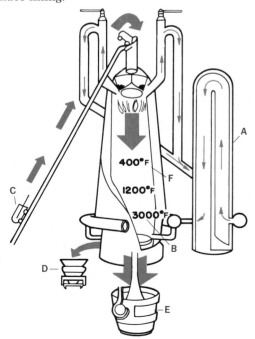

It takes about 2 tons [1.8 t] of iron ore, 1 ton [0.9 t] of coke (a purified form of coal), ½ ton [0.45 t] of limestone, and 4 tons [3.6 t] of air to make 1 ton [0.9 t] of pig iron. The iron ore, coke, and limestone are dumped into the top of the blast furnace, which holds about 1000 tons [909 t]. The burning coke and the blast of very hot air melt the iron ore. The limestone mixes with the ashes of the burnt coke and with the rock and earth of the iron ore. The mixture forms a waste that is called **slag.** Because the molten iron is heavier than the slag, it drips to the bottom of the furnace.

The furnace is emptied (called tapping) through a tap hole at the bottom. The melted iron flows out into a ladle for transfer to a steel furnace or into a trough and then into iron **pig molds** (Fig. 4-5). The slag, which floats on top of the melted iron in the blast furnace, is drained off through a separate hole. The blast furnace works continuously, and is tapped every 5 to 6 hours.

Pig iron is very hard and brittle. It is used in making cast iron, wrought iron, and steel.

Fig. 4-5 *Pig iron being poured into a pig casting machine.* (American Iron & Steel Institute)

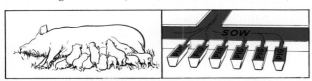

Pig iron contains about 93% pure iron (by weight) and from 3% to 5% **carbon.** The remainder is **silicon, sulfur, phosphorus,** and **manganese.**

Silicon is a chemical element found in rocks. It gives hardness to iron.

Sulfur is a yellow, flammable nonmetal. Excess sulfur and phosphorus weaken iron and steel. Too much sulfur makes these metals weak and brittle, causing cracks. Modern steel mills attempt to remove all impurities, including carbon and they carefully add elements as needed. A little sulfur is added to some steels for better machinability.

Phosphorus is a poisonous, active nonmetal. It causes brittleness and coarse grain in iron and steel.

Manganese is a grayish white metal, hard and brittle. It resembles iron but is not magnetic. It is used in making steel.

4-3

Cast Iron

Cast iron is pig iron that has been remelted and poured into a mold. The iron cools in the shape of a useful machine part or article. An object made this way is called a casting. Much pig iron is used to make cast iron castings.

4-4

Kinds of Cast Iron

There are several different kinds of cast iron. The properties of the different kinds of cast iron vary to a large degree. The amount, form, and arrangement of the carbon content in the iron make the difference. The carbon content may range from about 1.7% to 6% by weight in different kinds of cast iron. However, most grades of cast iron have carbon content ranging from about 2% to 4.5%. When broken, cast iron has a crystal-like grain structure at the fracture. The following are several common kinds of cast iron.

Fig. 4-6 *The feeder drive pulley of this combine is made of gray cast iron.*

Gray Cast Iron

One basic type usually contains from 1.7% to 4.5% carbon. It melts at about 2200°F [1204°C].

Most of the carbon in gray cast iron is in a **free** state. It is scattered in the form of **graphite** flakes throughout the crystalline grain structure of the metal. This arrangement of carbon makes the cast iron brittle. Thus, it fractures easily from sharp blows. It has a gray crystalline color where fractured. The gray color is due to the tiny flakes of graphite mixed in with the grains of iron.

Gray cast iron is the cheapest kind of iron. It is used to make large pipes, steam radiators, water hydrants, frames for machines, and other machine parts. It is used for products or parts that must be large and heavy but in which impact strength is not very important. Gray cast iron can be machined easily (Fig. 4-6). Several different grades of gray cast iron are available, each having different properties.

White Cast Iron

White cast iron is so named because of its white, crystalline color at the fracture when broken. White cast iron is made by rapidly cooling the molten pig iron. The carbon content usually ranges from about 2% to 3.5%. Most of the carbon in white cast iron is in a **chemically combined** state. It forms a very hard substance called **cementite,** or **iron carbide** (Fe$_3$C). White cast iron is so hard that it cannot be machined except by grinding. Its direct use is limited to castings requiring the surfaces to withstand abrasion and wear. The major use of white cast iron, however, is in making **malleable** cast iron.

Malleable iron is cast iron that has been made soft, tough, strong, and malleable. It generally has about a 2% to 2.6% carbon content. When white cast iron is heated at a high temperature for 100-120 hours, it is converted to malleable iron. This **heat-treatment** process, called **malleableizing,** takes place in a heat-treatment furnace. Metal is **malleable** if it can be hammered into different shapes without cracking. Heat-treatment changes the arrangement of the carbon from its combined state as **cementite** to free carbon. At the prolonged high temperature the free carbon comes together to form clusters or globules. The surrounding iron then becomes soft and machinable. Malleable castings are less brittle than gray or white cast iron castings, and have many of the tough characteristics of steel, which are described in Unit 5.

Several different grades of malleable iron are available. They are used for making tough castings for automobiles, tractors, and many kinds of machinery parts.

Ductile Cast Iron

Ductile cast iron is also known as **nodular iron** or **spheroidal graphite iron.** The carbon in ductile iron, like that in malleable iron, is in the free state. It is in small, rounded lumps of carbon clusters called nodules. The iron surrounding the tiny balls of graphite is soft, tough, and machinable.

Ductile cast iron is produced very much like gray cast iron. Magnesium alloys and certain other elements are added to a ladle of gray iron before it is poured into molds to make castings. These additives and proper heat treatment cause the carbon in the molten iron to form balls or nodules as it cools and becomes solid.

Ductile cast iron has properties similar to malleable iron. It is tough, machinable, and possesses many of the characteristics of steel. It is used for making tough castings for automobiles, farm machinery, and many other kinds of machinery.

Standard handbooks for machinists have information about different kinds and grades of cast iron.

4-5 Wrought Iron

Wrought iron is pig iron from which most of the carbon has been removed. It contains only about 0.04% carbon. Wrought iron was the most important structural metal before the development of the Bessemer steelmaking process. The metal was tough, easily formed, and corrosion-resistant. It was widely used for fences, horseshoes, nails, chain, lamps, and door hardware. It has been largely replaced with the use of hot-rolled low-carbon steels.

REVIEW REVIEW REVIEW REVIEW REVIEW

WORDS TO KNOW

blast furnace	gray cast iron	malleable iron	sulfur
carbon	heat treatment	manganese	taconite
cementite	iron ore	phosphorus	white cast iron
ductile cast iron	iron carbide	pig iron	wrought iron
free carbon	low-grade ores	silicon	
graphite	magnetic separation	slag	

REVIEW QUESTIONS

1. Where is iron ore found in the United States?
2. What is taconite? Describe how it is processed.
3. What is pig iron? Why is it so named?
4. Describe the furnace and the process for making pig iron.
5. What is cast iron? What is it used for?
6. What is gray cast iron and what is its chief use?
7. What is white cast iron and what is its chief use?
8. What is malleable iron? What is it used for?
9. What is ductile cast iron and what is it used for?
10. What is wrought iron? What was it used for?
11. What metal has largely replaced wrought iron?

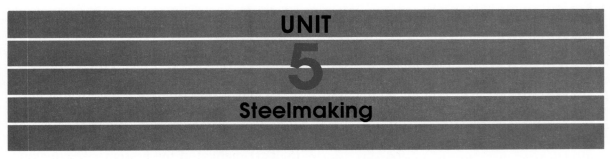

UNIT
5
Steelmaking

Steel is iron that contains carbon in different amounts, from 0.05% to about 1.7% by weight. Its carbon content is between that of wrought iron and cast iron. Steel is more **dense** than cast iron (that is, the iron and carbon in steel are packed closer together). It can be polished to a mirror finish. Steel can be made many times stronger and harder than cast iron and almost all other metals.

You will recall that pig iron contains from 3% to 5% carbon. Steel is made by refining pig iron, that is, by taking out some of the carbon and other impurities. Large quantities of steel scrap are also used—recycled—in steelmaking. Each batch of new steel is usually a mixture of pig iron and steel scrap.

Steel companies produce hundreds of different kinds of steel. They also make steel in various shapes.

This unit describes the basic methods of making steel with the Basic Oxygen Process, the Open Hearth Process, and the Electric Furnace Process.

This unit also describes the ways steel producers shape steel into mill products. These are sheets, plates, rods, bars, beams, and other structural shapes. Figure 5-1 shows the steelmaking process, from iron ore to finished steel mill products.

Unit 6 discusses the different kinds and grades of steel in greater detail.

Fig. 5-1 *How steel is made. After blooms, slabs, and billets are made, specialized rolling mills further process these basic forms into many different standard shapes.*

ten iron through a water-cooled lance that enters through the top of the furnace, (Fig. 5-2.) The end of the lance is positioned about 5 feet [1.5m] above the metal. As the oxygen is blown through the pig iron, the excess carbon and other impurities are rapidly burned off, changing the pig iron into steel.

The use of pure oxygen enables the chemical composition of the steel to be controlled very accurately. Therefore, BOP steel is of very high quality. Also, the use of pure oxygen results in higher furnace temperatures, thereby shortening the time required to convert the pig iron to steel. A BOP furnace can produce about 300 tons [272 t] of steel an hour. Most steel produced in the United States is made by the BOP process.

Fig. 5-2 *Oxygen lance in position ready for blowing oxygen into a basic oxygen furnace.* (Bethlehem Steel)

5-1 The Basic Oxygen Process (BOP)

To make steel from pig iron, it is necessary to remove carbon and other impurities. In the BOP, pure oxygen is blown into the mol-

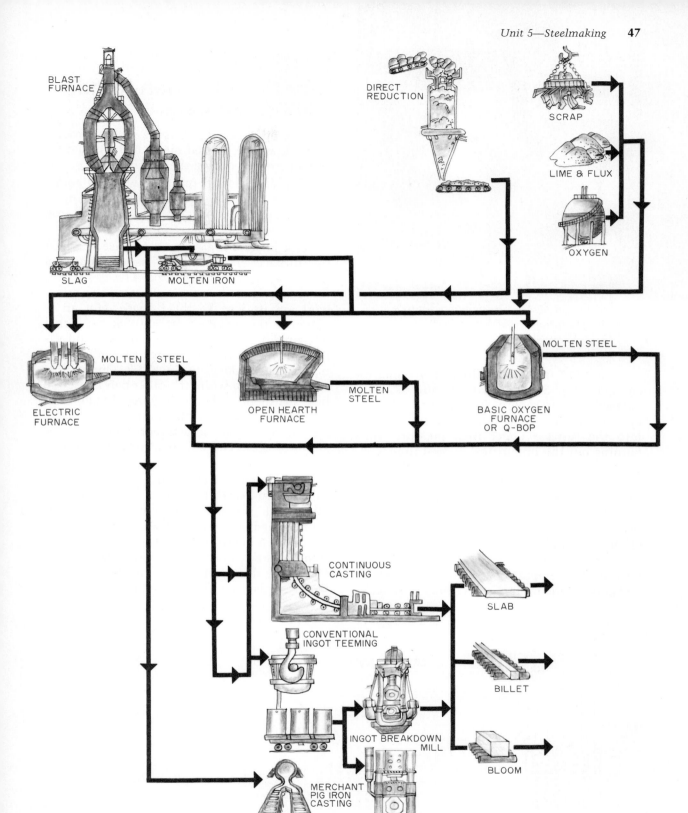

BLAST FURNACE

DIRECT REDUCTION

SCRAP

LIME & FLUX

OXYGEN

SLAG

MOLTEN IRON

ELECTRIC FURNACE

MOLTEN STEEL

OPEN HEARTH FURNACE

MOLTEN STEEL

MOLTEN STEEL

BASIC OXYGEN FURNACE OR Q-BOP

CONTINUOUS CASTING

SLAB

CONVENTIONAL INGOT TEEMING

BILLET

INGOT BREAKDOWN MILL

BLOOM

MERCHANT PIG IRON CASTING

HOT FORGING

Fig. 5-3 *Liquid pig iron being poured into a basic oxygen furnace.* (Bethlehem Steel)

The BOP furnace is tilted on its side for charging, (Fig. 5-3.) Molten iron and scrap are charged into its mouth. It is then tilted to an upright position, and pure oxygen is blown into the furnace under high pressure, thus burning out the impurities. Burned lime, converted from limestone, is also added to the furnace with the oxygen to increase the removal of impurities. When the impurities have been burned out of the molten iron, the necessary elements (such as carbon, nickel, chromium, and others) are added to meet the specifications for the steel required. The furnace is then emptied by tilting it on its side and pouring the molten steel into a large ladle.

5-2 The Open-Hearth Process

The open-hearthprocess is a slow process that allows the melted metal to be tested for carbon content during the heating.

The open-hearth furnace, which is somewhat like a baker's oven (Fig. 5-4), holds up to 200 tons [181.4 t] of metal. Pig iron and iron and steel scrap are charged into the furnace.

Hot air and a gas flame are used to heat the furnace. The furnace has two pairs of rooms with open brickwork. The gas passes through one of the rooms, heating the brickwork on its way to the furnace. Hot air is blown to the furnace from another room that has already been heated. The hot air and gas flame combine in the furnace to make a very hot flame [3,000 F, or 1,649 C]. One pair of rooms is heated while the other pair is used to heat the metal. When it becomes liquid, samples of the white-hot metal are taken, cooled, and analyzed. Any adjustments to the composition of the metal are then made before it is poured.

Steel made in an open-hearth furnace is called open-hearth steel. It is used for beams, rails, bolts, screws, shafts, etc. It is also used for making high-grade tool steel. An advantage of the open hearth furnace is that heavy scrap iron and steel, as well as pig iron can be used. However, the open-hearth process has been largely replaced with the basic oxygen process.

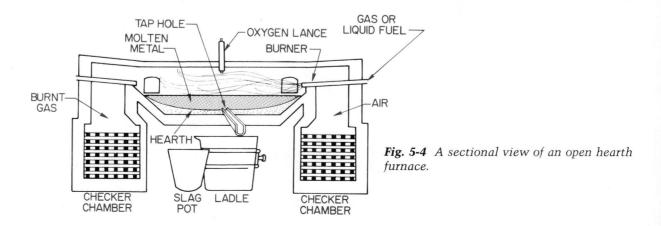

Fig. 5-4 *A sectional view of an open hearth furnace.*

A. UPRIGHT POSITION

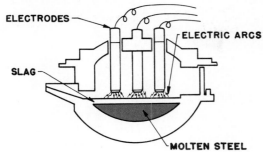

ELECTRODES

ELECTRIC ARCS

SLAG

MOLTEN STEEL

B. POURING POSITION

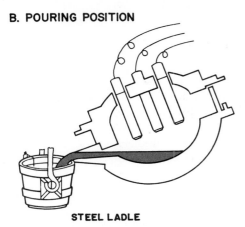

STEEL LADLE

Fig. 5-5 *Sectional views of an electric arc furnace.*

Fig. 5-6 *The electric furnace is widely used for producing steel alloys. (American Foundry Association)*

5-3 The Electric Furnace Processes

The *electric arc process* (Figs. 5-5 and 5-6) is used when close control of temperature and exact amounts of alloying elements are important. Higher temperatures can be reached with the electric arc furnace than with other steel-making furnaces. Electric arc furnaces are good for making high-carbon steel, steels alloyed with metals that have high melting points, and stainless steels.

Powerful electric arcs bridge the air gap between large carbon electrodes and the metal to be melted. (The metal serves as the other electrode.) The arcs produce the heat required to melt the metal. 100% iron and steel scrap can be used. Temperature control is very good. This makes possible very close control of the grain structure of the steel.

Electric induction furnaces (Fig. 5-7) greatly enlarged in recent years, have capacities up to 250 tons [225.7 t]. They are used for making small batches of high-quality steels or remelting metals for making steel castings. The intense alternating magnetic field of the furnace makes the steel heat up to its melting point.

Fig. 5-7 *An electric induction furnace. (Ajax Magnathermic)*

5-4 High Technology in Steelmaking

The use of computers, lasers, robots, and other high technology devices in steelmaking is rapidly increasing. Only a few examples can be given here due to space limitations.

Lasers are used in many ways in the production of steel sheets. They are used to measure sheet width and thickness, inspect flatness and finish, and control the alignment of the sheet as it is being rolled.

At Armco Steel, scanned beams from several high power lasers provide a 10% improvement in the magnetic properties of sheet steel used in electrical transformers. The laser treatment occurs at line speeds of 300 to 400 feet/min [91.44 to 121.92 meters/min]. A computer is used to adjust the laser power and scan rate to changes in line speed.

Another laser application is the measurement of refractory (insulating material) wear inside BOP furnaces. By using this technique, one company reports an increase of 5% in the number of heats from one of its furnaces, and a saving of 2% in refractory costs. While these numbers are small, the savings are not.

In iron making, the moisture content of coke charged into the blast furnace is measured with a nuclear gage. The moisture content must be known because it has considerable effect on the weight, and therefore amount, of coke charged into the furnace. This in turn effects the fuel economy of the blast furnace and the chemical composition of the pig iron.

A new type of mill roll has been developed for use in removing waves or buckles in heat-treated steel sheet. The roll is "inflated" (bulged) slightly with hydraulic pressure as needed in order to control sheet flatness. This type of roll lasts much longer between re-grindings than solid rolls.

The roll is used with a computerized flatness measuring and control system. The computer displays the shape of the sheet on a screen as it emerges from the rolling mill, and automatically adjusts the roll shape to produce better flatness.

Fig. 5-8 *Robot applying identification numbers to steel coils.* (Bethlehem Steel)

Robots are also appearing in steel mills. In one simple application, a robot is used to paint identifying numbers on rolls of steel sheet (Fig. 5-8).

5-5 Shaping Steel into Mill Products

When liquid steel is tapped from the steelmaking furnaces, the flow is directed into large ladles. The liquid steel may receive further treatment while it is in the ladle. This is called secondary steelmaking or ladle metallurgy. Further refining in the ladle may be done to adjust its chemical composition or to precisely control its pouring temperature.

From the ladle, the liquid steel is either poured into large ingot molds (Fig. 5-9) or into a continuous casting machine (Fig. 5-10). After cooling and removal from an ingot mold, the inside of the ingot may be white-hot while the outside is only red hot. To make the ingot ready for rolling, its temperature must be uniform throughout. Thus, ingots must be reheated in a gas furnace called a **soaking pit.**

Fig. 5-9 Steel being poured or "teemed" into ingot molds. Ingot sizes range from 100 pounds [45 kg] to 6 tons [5.5 t]. The dimensions of a common ingot size are 2' × 2' × 6' [.6m × .6m × 1.8m]. (Bethlehem Steel)

During the slow reheating process, the surface of the ingot develops a heavy layer of oxidized steel called **scale.** The scale is broken off and lost during the rolling process.

In continuous casting, the liquid steel is converted directly into a semi-finished slab ready for rolling into plates or sheets (Fig. 5-10). Considerable cost savings result from elimination of ingot reheating and handling. Also, continuous casting yields up to 15% more finished steel compared with the ingot-based process. It has been estimated that the cost savings resulting from use of continuous casters is an average $50 per ton [$55 per t].

About 60% of American steel output is now continuously cast.

Hot-Rolled Steel

After steel has been cast into ingots or slabs, they are reheated almost white-hot in a soaking pit (Fig. 5-11).

Fig. 5-10 A continuous casting machine for converting liquid steel directly into slabs, billets, or blooms. (American Iron & Steel Institute)

Fig. 5-11 Ingots must be reheated before they can be rolled. The furnace used for this is called a soaking pit. (American Iron & Steel Institute)

The steel is then rolled to shape in rolling mills (Fig. 5-1). Smooth cylindrical rolls are used to make flat sheets from slabs. **Sheet steel** is thinner than .250″ [6.35 mm]. **Plate steel** is .250″ [6.35 mm] thick or more.

Grooved rollers are used to press hot steel into smaller sizes and shapes. Round, square, and rectangular bars of all sizes are made. Structural shapes such as angle, channel, and I-beams are commonly made, as well as railroad rails.

After cooling, hot-rolled steel has a thin, black, hard skin or crust, which is called **scale.**

Cold-Rolled Steel

Cold-rolled steel is made from steel that has already been hot-rolled. The hot-rolled steel is a little larger than the final size of the cold-rolled steel. Thus, it is reduced a small amount by the cold rolling.

The bars or rods of hot-rolled steel, when cold, are first put in water containing **sulfuric acid.** This **pickling** solution removes the scale from the surface of the steel. After pickling, the sulfuric acid is washed off first in pure water, then in **lime water,** which is lime mixed with water. It stops the acid, which may still be on the steel, from eating further into it. The water evaporates and leaves a deposit of lime on the steel. This deposit keeps the steel from rusting until it can be rolled.

When dry, the bars are rolled while cold between highly finished rollers under great pressure. This rolling gives the bars a smooth, bright finish and a very exact size. They are then called cold-rolled steel and are often used without any more finishing or machining.

Cold-Drawn Steel

Cold-drawn steel is also made from hot-rolled steel that has been cooled and pickled. The size of the bar or rod is reduced a small amount at a time by **drawing** (pulling) the cold steel through drawing dies. The steel is drawn through smaller and smaller dies until the required diameter is obtained (Fig. 5-12).

A **wire-drawing die** (also called a **drawplate**) is used for drawing wire, as shown in Figures 5-12 and 5-13.

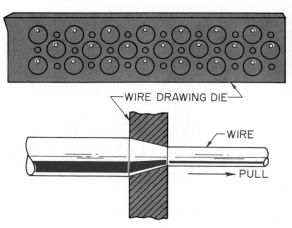

Fig. 5-12 *A die for drawing wire.*

Fig. 5-13 *A machine for drawing wire.*

Pipe and Tubing

Welded pipe and tubing are made by drawing a flat strip of metal through a bell-shaped die (Fig. 5-14). The joint is welded after the forming operation. Seamless pipe and tubing are made by piercing a hot bar of metal. After piercing, the pipe or tubing is drawn through dies to the desired size.

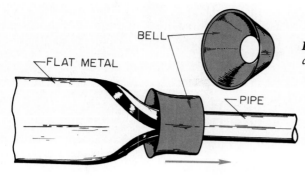

BELL

FLAT METAL

PIPE

Fig. 5-14 *Drawing a flat strip of metal through a bell-shaped die to form a pipe.*

REVIEW   REVIEW   REVIEW   REVIEW   REVIEW

WORDS TO KNOW

basic oxygen
  process
charging
cold-drawn steel
cold-rolled steel

continuous casting
drawplate
electric arc furnace
electric induction
  furnace

hot-rolled steel
ingot
mill
open-hearth furnace
pickling

scale
soaking pit
wire-drawing die

REVIEW QUESTIONS

1. What materials is steel made from?
2. What is the difference between pig iron and steel?
3. Describe the process of making steel.
4. What is an ingot?
5. Describe the open-hearth process of making steel.
6. How is steel made in the electric arc furnace?
7. What kinds of steel are made in the basic oxygen furnace? Open-hearth furnace? Electric furnace?
8. What is hot-rolled steel?
9. What is cold-rolled steel?
10. What is cold-drawn steel?

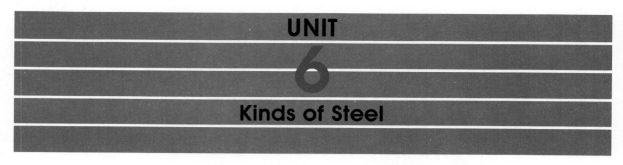

UNIT 6

Kinds of Steel

There are two main kinds of steels: **plain carbon steels** and **alloy steels.**

Plain carbon steels are divided into three main groups: **low-carbon steel,** also known as **mild steel; medium-carbon steel;** and **high-carbon steel.**

There are many kinds of alloy steels. The properties of each depend on the other elements (usually metals) that are added to the steel.

Low-Carbon Steel

Low-carbon steel by weight contains .05% to .30% carbon. Table 6-1 shows the carbon content of low-carbon steel and other plain carbon steels. Low-carbon steel is made in the basic-oxygen and open-hearth furnaces. Low-

Table 6-1

Carbon Steels and Their Uses	
Percent by weight of carbon in steel	**Uses**
Low-Carbon:	
0.05-0.20	Automobile bodies, buildings, pipes, chains, rivets, screws, nails.
0.20-0.30	Gears, shafts, bolts, forgings, bridges, buildings.
Medium-Carbon:	
0.30-0.40	Connecting rods, crank pins, axles, drop forgings.
0.40-0.50	Car axles, crankshafts, rails, boilers, auger bits, screwdrivers.
0.50-0.60	Hammers, sledges.
High-Carbon:	
0.60-0.70	Stamping and pressing dies, drop-forging dies, drop forgings, screwdrivers, blacksmiths' hammers, table knives, setscrews.
0.70-0.80	Punches, cold chisels, hammers, sledges, shear blades, table knives, drop-forging dies, anvil faces, wrenches, vise jaws, band saws, crowbars, lathe centers, rivet sets.
0.80-0.90	Punches, rivet sets, large taps, threading dies, drop-forging dies, shear blades, table knives, saws, hammers, cold chisels, woodworking chisels, rock drills, axes, springs.
0.90-1.00	Taps, small punches, threading dies, needles, knives, springs, machinists' hammers, screwdrivers, drills, milling cutters, axes, reamers, rock drills, chisels, lathe centers, hacksaw blades.
1.00-1.10	Axes, chisels, small taps, hand reamers, lathe centers, mandrels, threading dies, milling cutters, springs, turning and planing tools, knives, drills.
1.10-1.20	Milling cutters, reamers, woodworking tools, saws, knives, ball bearings, cold cutting dies, threading dies, taps, twist drills, pipe cutters, lathe centers, hatchets, turning and planing tools.
1.20-1.30	Turning and planing tools, twist drills, scythes, files, circular cutters, engravers' tools, surgical cutlery, saws for cutting metals, tools for turning brass and wood, reamers.
1.30-1.40	Small twist drills, razors, small engravers' tools, surgical instruments, knives, boring tools, wire drawing dies, tools for turning hard metals, files, woodworking chisels.
1.40-1.50	Razors, saws for cutting steel, wire drawing dies, fine cutters.

carbon steel is used for forge work, rivets, chains, and machine parts that do not need great strength. It is also used for almost every product that was once made of wrought iron.

Some low-carbon steel is **cold-rolled** between highly polished rollers under great pressure. This improves its tensile strength, and gives it a very smooth finish and exact size. It is then called **cold-rolled steel.**

6-2 Medium-Carbon Steel

Medium-carbon steel has more carbon and is stronger than low-carbon steel. It is also more difficult to bend, weld, and cut than low-carbon steel. It contains .30% to .60% carbon. Medium-carbon steel is used for bolts, shafts, car axles, rails, and other parts or tools that require strong metal. (See Table 6-1.)

Medium-carbon steels are frequently hardened and **tempered** by heat treatment. These steels can be hardened to a Rockwell-C hardness of 40 (medium hard) to 60 (very hard), depending on the carbon content and the thickness of the material. Unit 94 describes the Rockwell hardness test.

6-3 High-Carbon Steel

High-carbon steel, also known as **carbon tool steel,** contains between .60% and 1.50% carbon. The best grades of this steel are made in electric furnaces. High-carbon steel is called tool steel because it is used to make such tools as drills, taps, dies, reamers, files, cold chisels, crowbars, and hammers. (See Table 6-1.) It is hard to bend, weld, and cut.

High-carbon steel becomes very hard and brittle when it is hardened. The more carbon a steel contains, up to 0.80%, the harder it can be made. Hardness of Rockwell 60-66 can be attained.

High-carbon steel is rolled to the desired shape and is often ground to provide a smooth finish. Round bars that are accurately ground to standard drill sizes are called **drill rod.** Drill rod is used for making such tools as drills, reamers, taps, and punches. It is also used to make **dowel pins.** Dowel pins are used in die making to keep metal parts accurately aligned with each other.

Free-machining carbon steels are especially made to have high machinability. **Resulfurized carbon steels,** which have sulfur added in amounts from .08% to .33%, have much better machinability than plain carbon steels. The resulfurized steel designated AISI 1112 is given a machinability rating of 100%. Other steels are rated in comparison with AISI 1112 steel, as described in Section 2-3. For example, AISI 1012, a plain low-carbon steel, has a machinability rating of only 53%.

Lead is sometimes added to further improve the machinability of resulfurized steels. The percentage of lead added is small. Only about one third of a pound of lead for each hundred pounds of steel [151 grams per 45 kg] is used. Some leaded free-machining steels have machinability ratings as high as 300%.

A new free-machining steel alloy, DK1210, does not contain lead. It is capable of cutting speeds equalling or exceeding leaded steels and provides longer tool life. The alloy contains 0.10% bismuth and has a slightly higher sulfur content than the other free-machining steels.

Free-machining steels are used in automatic lathes for the high-speed manufacture of cylindrical and threaded parts.

Table 6-2 indicates some properties of several types of steel that are frequently used in industry and in metalworking classes.

6-4 Alloy Steels

Alloy steels are made by combining steels with one or more other elements. These elements are usually metals. They are intentionally added to obtain properties that are not found in plain carbon steels. Alloying may increase the following properties:

Table 6-2

Physical Properties of Steels

AISI no.	Condition of steel	Tensile strength (psi)	MPa	Brinell hardness*	Machinability rating (B 1112 = 100)
C 1018	Hot-Rolled	69,000	475.7	143	52
C 1018	Cold-Drawn	82,000	565.4	163	65
B 1112	Cold-Drawn	82,500	568.8	170	100
B 1113	Cold-Drawn	83,500	575.7	170	130
Ledloy 375	Cold-Drawn	79,000	544.7	155	220
C 1045	Cold-Drawn	103,000	710.2	217	60
C 1095	Hot-Rolled	142,000	979.1	293	—
C 1095	Water-Quenched at 1450° F, (788° C) Tempered at 800° F; (427° C).	200,000	1379.0	388	—

*Brinell Hardness is a standard measure of hardness that works best on metals that are not extremely hard. The steels measured here range from low to medium Brinell hardness.

1. Hardenability
2. Machinability
3. Strength through heat treatment
4. Strength as manufactured
5. Corrosion resistance
6. Wear resistance
7. Retention of hardness and strength at high temperatures.

The most important of the above properties are increased hardenability, corrosion resistance, and retention of hardness and strength at high temperatures. Most steel alloys must be heat-treated to develop their best properties.

There are three classes of alloy steels: *constructional alloy steels, alloy tool steels,* and *special alloy steels.*

Constructional alloy steels. These steels are used for such parts as shafts, gears, levers, bolts, springs, piston pins, and connecting rods. This group of alloys also includes steels used in the construction of bridges, auto frames, railroads, buildings, and ships. The constructional alloy steels have a relatively low alloy content as compared to alloy tool steels. Total alloy content of these steels ranges from 0.25% to about 6%.

Alloy tool steels. Alloy tool steels are used in making cutting and forming tools. They are used for high-quality drills, reamers, milling cutters, threading tools, punches, plastic molds, punch press tooling, and wrenches. Most alloy tool steels must be hardened in oil or air. Therefore, they are often referred to as oil-hardened or air-hardened tool steels. Generally, they harden more deeply than plain carbon tool steels and are more shock-resistant.

The total alloy content of alloy tool steels ranges from 0.25% to over 38%. There are hundreds of alloy tool steels. They are classified into different categories according to their basic properties. Each category has many grades. See Table 8-2.

Special alloy steels. Special alloy steels are designed for extreme service requirements. They include steels with very high heat, corrosion, or wear resistance. Included also are steels that get tougher and harder with use, such as those needed for power shovel teeth, tractor lugs, and rock crusher jaws.

Effects of Alloying Elements

About 26 elements are used, alone or in combination, in making alloy steels. The following paragraphs describe how the most important alloying elements affect the properties of steel.

Chromium, also known as **chrome,** gives hardness to steel, and toughens it. It also makes the steel's grain finer and causes the steel to resist rust, stains, shocks, and scratches. Chromium steel is used for safes, rock crushers, and automobile bearings.

Chromium is the basis for **stainless steel,** which contains from 11% to 26% chromium. It has a lasting, bright, silvery gloss. Following is a list of some important uses for stainless steel:

sinks	ball bearings
tabletops	fine measuring tools
tableware	and instruments
pots and pans	moldings
cutting tools	automobile parts
plates for false teeth	valves for airplane en-
dental tools	gines

Cobalt is an important metal used in making cutting tool alloys. (These alloys include high-speed steels, cast alloys, and cemented carbides.) The outstanding property of cobalt is its ability to improve the hardness of cutting tools when they are hot or even red-hot. Such properties are called the **hot-hardness** or **red-hardness** of cutting tools. Cutting tools with high cobalt content retain their hardness up to a dull red heat. Cobalt also improves wear resistance. Cobalt content in high-speed steels ranges from 5% to 12%. In cast alloys, it is used in amounts from 35% to 55%.

Cobalt is also alloyed with aluminum and nickel to make powerful **Alnico** permanent magnets.

Manganese is a hard, brittle, grayish-white metal. It purifies and adds strength and toughness to steel. Manganese steel remains hard even when cooled slowly. It is so very hard that it is difficult to cut, so it is usually **cast** into shape. **Wear** makes the surface harder. Manganese steel can stand hard wear, strain, hammering, and shocks. It is used for the jaws of rock and ore crushers, steam shovels, chains, gears, railway switches and crossings, and safes.

Molybdenum is called "Molly" for short in steel mills. A silvery white metal, it adds strength and hardness to steel, and allows it to stand heat and shocks. Molybdenum steel is used for automobile parts, high-grade machinery, wire as fine as 0.0004" [.01 mm] in diameter, ball bearings, and roller bearings.

Nickel adds strength and toughness to steel. Nickel steel does not rust easily and is very strong and hard. It is also **elastic;** that is, it can stand vibration, shocks, jolts, and wear by bouncing back to its original shape. It is used for wire cables, shafts, steel rails, automobile and railroad car axles, and **armor plate.** Nickel is also used with chromium to make **stainless steel.**

Tungsten is a rare, heavy, white metal that has a higher melting point than any other metal. Tungsten adds hardness to steel. It gives steel a fine grain, and allows steel to withstand heat. Tungsten is used as an alloying element in tool steels, high-speed steels, and in cemented carbide. It is also used in armor plate.

Vanadium is a pale, silver-gray metal. It is brittle and resists corrosion. Vanadium gives steel a fine grain, as well as toughness and strength. Vanadium steel can withstand great shocks. It is used for springs, automobile axles and gears, and other parts that vibrate when in use.

Chromium-vanadium steel is hard and has great **tensile strength.** It can be bent double while cold and is easy to cut. Chromium-vanadium steel is used for automobile parts such as springs, gears, steering knuckles, frames, axles, connecting rods, and other parts which must be strong and tough but not brittle.

High-Speed Steel (HSS)

High-speed steel, also known as **high-speed tool steel,** is another type of alloy steel. Its carbon content may range from about 0.70% to 1.50%. Several different grades are available. It generally contains one or more metals such as **chromium, vanadium, molybdenum, tungsten,** and **cobalt.** The first four of these elements are carbide formers. They combine with carbon to form carbides such as chromium carbide and vanadium carbide. These carbides are very hard and wear-resistant; therefore, they make good cutting tools.

Cobalt is not a carbide former, but it increases the **red-hardness** of the cutting tool. Thus, the tool retains its hardness at high temperatures. High-speed steel cutting tools retain their hardness without significant softening at temperatures up to about 1100°F [593°C]. This temperature is indicated by a dull, red heat. On the other hand, plain-carbon tool-steel cutting tools start to soften significantly at temperatures above 450°F [232°C].

High-speed steel is made in an electric furnace. It is used for cutting tools such as drills, reamers, countersinks, lathe tool bits, and milling cutters. It is called high-speed steel because cutting tools made of this material can be operated at speeds twice as fast as those for tools made of plain carbon tool steel. High-speed steels cost two to four times as much as carbon tool steels.

REVIEW   REVIEW   REVIEW   REVIEW   REVIEW

WORDS TO KNOW

alloy steels	free-machining	low-carbon steel	nickel
chromium	carbon steel	manganese	stainless steel
cobalt	hardenability	medium-carbon	tungsten
dowel pins	high-carbon steel	steel	vanadium
drill rod	high-speed steel	molybdenum	

REVIEW QUESTIONS

1. List the three groups of plain carbon steel together with their range of carbon contents.
2. Name several uses for each of the three groups of plain carbon steels.
3. What is done to steel to make it free-machining?
4. What is an alloy steel?
5. Why is steel alloyed?
6. Name the three classes of alloy steels and give several uses for each.
7. List each of the alloying elements discussed, together with its principal benefit when alloyed with steel.
8. What is high-speed steel? What is it used for? Why is it called high-speed steel?

UNIT
7

Nonferrous Metals and Their Alloys

Nonferrous metals and their alloys are those that contain no iron. This unit deals only with the important nonferrous metals that serve as bases for alloying with other metals. In contrast, Unit 6 discussed several important nonferrous metals that are used for alloying with steel.

7-1
Aluminum

Aluminum is a brilliant, silvery-white metal. The chemical symbol for aluminum is Al. It is the third most abundant element and one of our most useful metals. Although aluminum costs four or five times as much as iron or steel, it weighs only about one-third as much, with a density of 2.7. It also machines much faster (two to three times deeper cuts at cutting speeds twice as fast as those used for steel). It costs less to transport, is quite maintenance free, and has a natural surface beauty.

Aluminum is a good conductor of electricity and heat, and it reflects heat when highly polished. It can be drawn into very fine wire, spun or stamped into deep forms, and hammered or rolled into foil sheets as thin as 0.00025″ [.00635 mm].

Aluminum melts at 1220°F [660°C]. However, the temperature for casting aluminum in molds is usually 1300°F [704°C] to 1500°F [816°C]. This is about one-half the temperature required for casting iron or steel, making aluminum castings cheaper to produce.

Fig. 7-1 *An Arkansas bauxite mine.* (Reynolds Metals Company)

Refining Aluminum

Aluminum is made from an ore called **bauxite.** Important deposits are in Arkansas, Washington, Oregon, and Jamaica. It usually is mined in open pits (Fig. 7-1), then refined where cheap electrical power is available. One-sixth of the earth's crust is aluminum ore, but it is difficult to extract the pure metal.

Crushed bauxite is changed chemically, or refined, to aluminum oxide, a white powder also called **alumina** (Fig. 7-2).

Aluminum is obtained from alumina by removing the oxygen in alumina in a process called **smelting** (Fig. 7-3). (In smelting, an ore is heated until it melts. Often a chemical change also takes place, and metal is separated from the ore.)

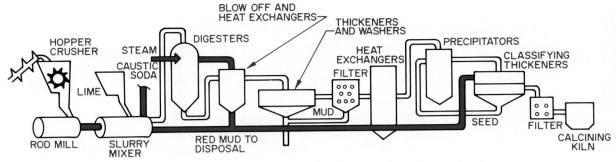

Fig. 7-2 *The refining process for changing bauxite to alumina.*

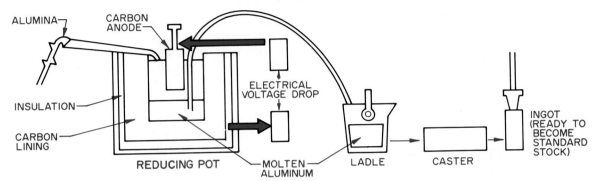

Fig. 7-3 *The smelting process for converting alumina to metallic aluminum. Electricity in the reducing pot passes from the carbon anodes, the positive electrodes, through the electrolyte to the carbon lining, where the aluminum deposits. The lining serves as the cathode or negative electrode.*

Fig. 7-4 *Aluminium is fabricated into standard shapes. (A) Aluminium logs are cast. (B) Tubing is extruded. (C) Sheet (and plate) is rolled. (D) Wire is drawn. (Reynolds Metals Company) (ALCOA)*

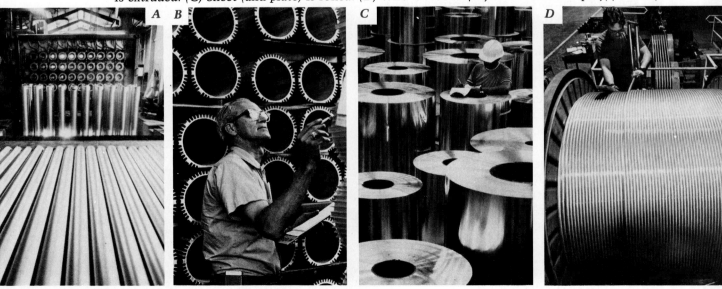

In large tanks called **reducing pots,** electricity passes from carbon electrodes, which are positive, through a mixture of alumina and molten **cryolite** (sodium aluminum fluoride). The reducing pots are also lined with carbon, which acts as the negative electrode and completes the circuit (Fig. 7-3). The electric current heats the mixture, and molten aluminum is deposited at the bottom of the tank, where it can be drained off.

After smelting, the metal is often alloyed, then cast, rolled, or **extruded** into many shapes (Fig. 7-4). The rolling mills that process aluminum are similar to mills that process steel. The shapes produced are also the same: sheets, plates, bars, rods, and wire. The rolling processes may have a dozen or more different steps (Fig. 7-5).

Extrude means to push heated material through a die to form a long strip in that shape. Extruding is much like squeezing toothpaste from a tube (Fig. 7-6). Many nonferrous alloys are formed into different shapes by the extrusion process.

Aluminum Base Alloys

Pure aluminum is too soft for many uses, but more than 350 alloys have made it ideal for many purposes. Some of the common uses for aluminum alloys are aircraft and rocket parts; bodies for railroad cars, trucks, and trailers; pistons, blocks, and heads for engines; window frames; cooking utensils; and foil and collapsible tubes for packaging.

Fig. 7-5 *This is one of the rolling mill processes: plate making. Below, a diagram of the important steps. Right, an ingot enters the hot-rolling mill.* (Aluminum Association)

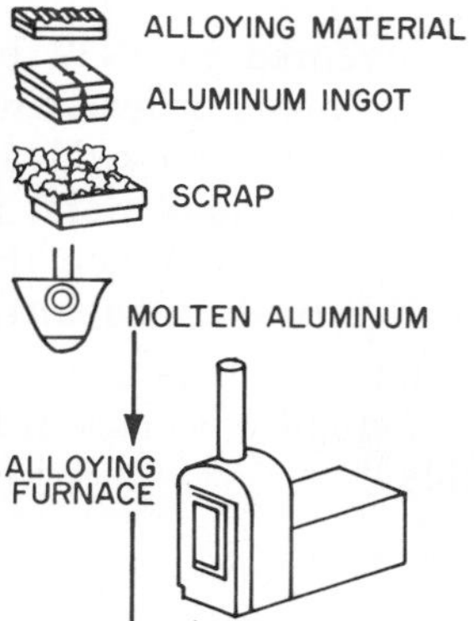

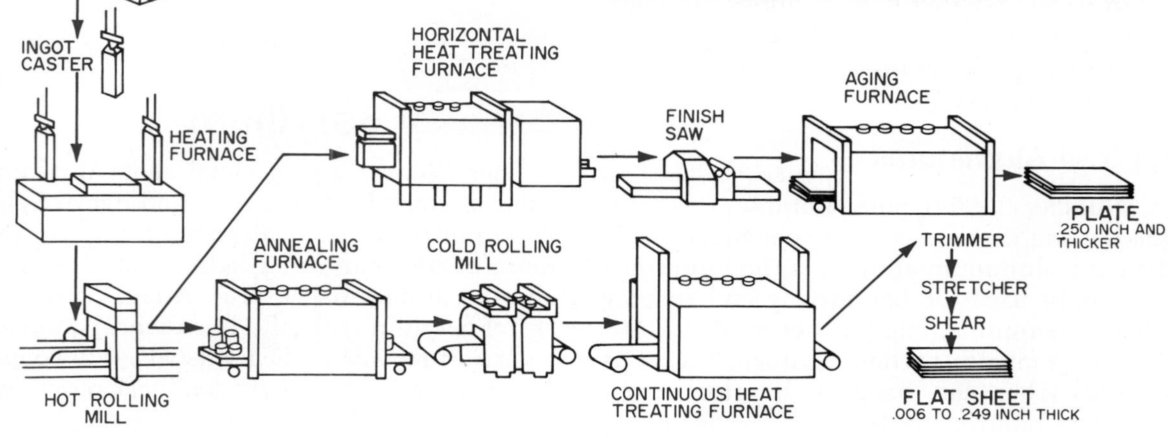

ALLOYING MATERIAL

ALUMINUM INGOT

SCRAP

MOLTEN ALUMINUM

ALLOYING FURNACE

INGOT CASTER

HEATING FURNACE

HORIZONTAL HEAT TREATING FURNACE

FINISH SAW

AGING FURNACE

ANNEALING FURNACE

COLD ROLLING MILL

TRIMMER

STRETCHER

SHEAR

PLATE
.250 INCH AND THICKER

HOT ROLLING MILL

CONTINUOUS HEAT TREATING FURNACE

FLAT SHEET
.006 TO .249 INCH THICK

Fig. 7-6 *A heated billet is squeezed through a die to produce this extruded shape.* (Aluminum Association)

Other metals added to pure aluminum greatly improve its physical properties. The metals commonly alloyed with aluminum include copper, zinc, magnesium, manganese, nickel, chromium, lead, bismuth, iron, and titanium.

The tensile strength of aluminum is one property that can be improved by heat treatment. Tensile strength varies from about 13,000 psi [89.6 MPa] for pure aluminum to about 81,000 psi [558.5 MPa] for special hardened alloys.

In Table 7-1 four typical alloys are compared with soft and hardened steel. The melting point of aluminum and other metals is given in Table 7-2.

Typical Aluminums

Number 1100-0 pure aluminum is soft, ductile, and more resistant to chemical attack than any aluminum alloy. It is the form most commonly used for hammering and shaping when maximum strength is not needed. However, it gradually becomes hardened as it is worked. When this happens, it must be **annealed** to remove the hardness. Annealing is

done by heating the aluminum to 650°F [343°C] (indicated by the heat at which blue carpenter's chalk turns whitish) and then allowing the heated metal to air-cool slowly. Annealing softens the aluminum and makes it tougher.

Number 2024 is often used for structural or machining applications. Number 6061 is used for a number of applications that require high tensile strength and good welding properties, such as railings and protective guards. Number 7075 is used for aircraft and other work where the highest strength is required. These three are strong, heat-treatable alloys.

Metal suppliers furnish data books and charts that list the alloys, meanings of number designations, properties of the alloys and recommended applications. Refer to these data books for more complete information.

7-2
Babbitt

Babbitt metal was invented in 1839 by Isaac Babbitt. It is an alloy made of **lead, tin, copper** and **antimony.** There are two kinds of babbitt. When the base or **principal** metal is lead, it is called **lead-base babbitt.** When the base metal is tin, it is called **tin-base babbitt.**

Babbitt metal does not rust. It is used for bearings in machines and engines because it is strong, tough and durable.

7-3
Beryllium

Beryllium is a gray metal about the same color as steel. It is expensive and lightweight. Beryllium is more heat-resistant, harder, and more brittle than other light metals, such as aluminum and magnesium. A small percentage of beryllium, usually less than 2%, makes a very strong alloy when it is added to copper or nickel. Its light weight and heat resistance are valued in aerospace applications.

Table 7-1

Physical Properties[1] of Aluminums

A.A. no.[2]	Old no.	Hardness brinell	Tensile strength (Psi)	MPA	Cold work-ability	Machin-ability	Weldability Gas	Arc	Spot	Corrosion resistance
1100-0[3]	2S	23	13,000	(89.6)	A+	D	A	A	B	A
2024-T36[4]	24S	130	73,000	(503.3)	E	B	D	B	A	B
6061-T6[5]	61S	95	41,000	(282.7)	C	B	(Good after heat-treating)			
7075-T6[6]	75S	150	76,000	(524)	D	B	D	D	B	B
C1018 Hot-Rolled Steel		143	69,000	(475.7)						
C1095 Tempered Steel		388	200,000	(1379)						

[1]Code for working properties: A = excellent, B = superior, C = good, D = poor, E = not recommended.
[2]That part of the Aluminum Association Number following the hyphen denotes the amount and kind of temper treatment used in manufacture.
[3]No. 1100-0 is 99% pure soft aluminum.
[4]No. 2024 contains 4.5% copper, 1.5% magnesium, and 0.6% manganese.
[5]No. 6061 contains 1.0% magnesium, 0.6% silicon, 0.25% copper, 0.25% chromium.
[6]No. 7075 contains 5.6% zinc, 2.5% magnesium, 1.6% copper, and 0.3% chromium.

The first of our space capsules used a heat shield of beryllium. Pure beryllium is also used in nuclear reactors.

SAFETY NOTE

Since beryllium dust is toxic, workers are required to wear respirators while machining it. The machines they use are equipped with vacuum dust collectors.

7-4 Cast Alloys

A number of cast alloys have been developed for use in metal-cutting tools. Some brand names include Stellite®, Rexalloy®, Armaloy®, and Tantung®. Cast alloys are metals composed of the following elements: cobalt-35% to 50%, chromium-25% to 35%, tungsten-10% to 20%, nickel-.01% to 5% and carbon-1.5% to 3%. Small amounts of other elements are sometimes added. Since cast alloys do not contain iron, they are not steels. They are very hard and cannot be machined, except by grinding.

Table 7-2

Melting Points of Metals

Metal	Degrees Fahrenheit	Degrees Celsius
Solder, 50-50	400	204
Pewter	420	216
Tin	449	232
Babbitt	462	239
Lead	621	327
Zinc	787	419
Magnesium	1204	651
Aluminum	1218	659
Bronze	1675	913
Brass	1700	927
Silver	1761	961
Gold	1945	1063
Copper	1981	1083
Iron, Cast	2200	1204
Beryllium	2323	1273
Steel	2500	1371
Nickel	2646	1452
Iron, Wrought	2700	1482
Titanium	3047	1675
Tungsten	6150	3399

The cast alloys are used as tips on cutting tools, as removable tool bits in lathe toolholders, and as inserts in tool-holders and milling cutters. They retain their hardness at high temperatures, up to about 1500°F [816°C]. Cast alloy cutting tools may be operated at cutting speeds 50% to 75% faster than those of high-speed steel cutting tools.

Metal Fabrics: Real Permanent Press

Don't throw away that pop can! It could be used in your next pair of pants. Crazy? Not really. The fashions of the future may well use aluminum for fabric. The idea of metal clothes isn't as strange as it sounds. Metal has been used for all kinds of wearing apparel for centuries.

One of the first uses was armor, used for protection more than 2,000 years ago. **Chain mail** had many small rings of metal hooked together like a knitted sweater and was a popular form of armor in the Middle Ages. France's Napoleon III (1808-73) considered outfitting his armies in armor made of a newly discovered "precious" metal, aluminum. Frederick VII of Denmark (1808-63) commissioned his armorers to make him a special helmet of aluminum and gold.

Soldiers and kings weren't the only people to use metal wearing apparel. A poncho worn in Peru in the 1200s had a section completely covered with small squares of thin sheet gold. In Finland, a woven wool mantle worn by a housewife around 1100 had a border of small tubes of brass worked into a braid. Besides being decorative, the tubes added strength to the mantle. Silver and gold were worked into the lace handkerchiefs of the ladies of Queen Elizabeth I's court of the 1500s.

Today, aluminum material is used for spacesuits and for specialized suits for firefighters, race car drivers, and other professionals in dangerous occupations. This up-to-date "armor" is still primarily used for protection.

What about widespread use of metal clothes? A Paris designer has used aluminum in a velvet coat to show how metal fabrics can be used in high fashion. The age of aluminum fabric for everyday use has not yet arrived. But the practical benefits may soon make aluminum clothes a reality.

Consider the high cost of heating entire buildings and homes. It may someday be more economical to "heat" and "cool" a person through the use of aluminum clothing. What's more, these clothes can be recycled. So while we may still recycle pop cans, we may also someday be trading in used clothing to be recycled into next year's fashions!

7-5   Copper Base Alloys

Copper is the oldest metal known to man. It is a tough, reddish-brown metal. Deposits of **copper ore** are found in Arizona, Michigan, Montana, and Utah. It is sold in the form of wire, bars, plates, and sheets.

Copper is the second-best conductor of electricity. Copper is used for electric wires and cables. It is also used for water heaters, radiators, pipes, kettles, window and door screens, and roofing.

In art metalwork, copper is used for bowls, vases, and trays. Copper hardens when hammered, but it can easily be softened by heating to a dull red heat and quenching in water.

Today there are about 300 copper-base alloys. One of these, beryllium copper, is copper to which a small amount of beryllium has been added. This very tough alloy is used for corrosion-resistant springs. Because it is non-sparking, it is used for wrenches and other metal objects in plants that manufacture explosives.

Most copper-base alloys are brasses and bronzes. Both alloys are closely related, although bronzes are generally harder than brasses. **Brass** is chiefly an alloy of **copper** and **zinc. Bronze** is chiefly an alloy of **copper** and **tin.** However, both brass and bronze often include other metals such as lead, phosphorous, nickel, antimony, aluminum, and manganese.

Silver is also alloyed with copper in several special alloys. **German silver** contains about 50% **copper,** 30% **zinc,** and 20% **nickel.** It is used in costume jewelry as a relatively inexpensive substitute for real silver.

Gold

Gold is a precious, heavy, beautiful, bright yellow metal. Pure gold is too soft for general use and is therefore alloyed with copper, silver, or other metals.

Gold can be hammered into very thin sheets called **gold leaf,** which is much thinner than the thinnest tissue paper. The art of covering something with gold leaf or gold powder is called **gilding.**

Gold is used mostly for jewelry, coins, and fillings in teeth. United States gold coins were made of 90% gold and 10% copper. Since gold does not corrode, an important use is for coating electrical switch contacts in computers and other electronic devices that require high reliability.

The purity of gold is measured in karats. Pure gold is 24 karats. An 18-karat gold ring is made of 18 parts by weight of gold and 6 parts by weight of some other metal. Jewelers abbreviate karat as k: for example, 14k gold.

White gold, a silvery metal used for jewelry, contains 15% to 20% nickel. The nickel content changes the color of the metal to silver.

Green gold has a greenish cast and is also used for jewelry. Fifteen karat green gold, for example, is 15 parts gold, 8 parts silver, and 1 part copper.

Lead

Lead is a very heavy, bluish-gray, poisonous metal.

> **SAFETY NOTE**
> Persons working with lead must guard against a disease called **lead poisoning.** Do not handle lead with bare hands or breathe the fumes from the overheated molten metal.

Lead is the softest metal in general use. When freshly cut, it is very bright; this brightness soon disappears when exposed to the air. Water and air, however, have less effect upon lead than most other metals.

Lead is used in auto batteries and is alloyed with tin to make solder and pewter. **White lead,** a pigment used in making some paints is made from lead. A small amount of lead added to other metals improves their machinability.

Magnesium and Its Alloys

Magnesium is a silvery-white, light, malleable metal that is much lighter than aluminum. It is abundant in nature but is always alloyed with another metal because of its high cost and low tensile strength. Magnesium may be alloyed with zinc, silicon, copper, nickel, manganese, iron, or tin. It is usually alloyed with aluminum to which it contributes strength and heat resistance.

In its pure form magnesium burns easily, giving off an intense white light, so it must be handled with care.

SAFETY NOTE
Special care also must be taken when machining magnesium. Dull tools can create enough frictional heat to ignite small magnesium chips.

Magnesium is used chiefly where light weight is important. For this reason it has many applications in transportation vehicles, especially in aircraft, missiles, and space vehicles.

7-9

Nickel Base Alloys

Nickel is a hard, tough, shiny, silvery metal. It does not rust and can be polished to a bright silvery finish. It is used for **plating** iron and brass to improve appearance (Fig. 7-7). Nickel plating may be used under chromium plating on trim for automobiles and appliances. Nickel is also used to toughen steel. The five-cent coin (a nickel) is made of one part **nickel** and three parts **copper.**

There are about 60 nickel-base alloys, with nickel contents ranging from about 62% to 99%. Elements alloyed with nickel include copper, aluminum, iron, silicon, manganese, chromium, titanium, and tungsten.

Monel metal is a white metal containing about two-thirds **nickel** and one-third **copper,** with small amounts of other elements. It is strong, tough, rust-resistant, and silvery. Monel metal is used for chemical and cooking equipment, motor boat propellers, nonmagnetic parts of aircraft, valve stems, and valves and pipes used for carrying corrosive liquids.

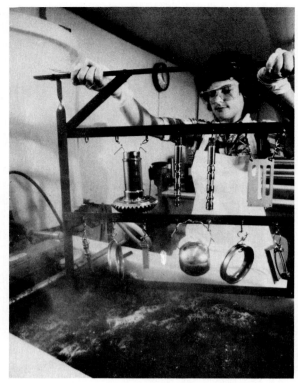

Fig. 7-7 *Nickel plating is being applied here to a variety of metal objects in a plating process test.* (Stauffer Chemicals)

Nickel is the base metal used in alloys for jet and rocket engines, and space vehicles. Such metals must have high strength and be able to resist high temperatures. Inconel®, Rene 41®, Hastelloy®, and Waspaloy® are some of their brand names.

7-10

Pewter

Pewter is a silvery white metal. It is made of 92 parts **tin,** 5 parts **antimony,** and 3 parts **copper.** Other grades of pewter contain a little more or less tin. The lower grades contain some **lead.**

Pewter is also called **Britannia metal** because it was first made in Britain. It is used for tableware, buttons and clasps for clothing, and other ornamental work.

7-11 Silver

Silver is a beautiful, shiny, white metal. Pure silver is very soft. For most commercial uses, it must be alloyed to make it harder and stronger. It is used for ornamental work, jewelry, tableware, mirrors, and coins. United States silver coins formerly contained nine parts silver and one part copper.

Sterling silver is silver with copper added to make it harder. It is used for tableware and jewelry.

Silver is the best conductor of electricity. It is used for bearings in aircraft and diesel engines because it has a higher fatigue rating than any other bearing material. Photographic film also uses large quantities of silver.

7-12 Tin

Tin is a shiny, silvery metal. "Tin cans" are made of steel coated with tin. The tin is actually less than 1% of the weight of the can. Tin does not rust.

Very few articles are made of pure tin. It is used in making **bronze, babbitt, pewter, solder,** and other alloys. When used, it always whitens the resultant metal and increases its hardness.

Tin is soft and can be rolled into very thin sheets. Tinfoil can be made as thin as .0002″ [.005 mm]. It was long used for wrapping tea, tobacco, drugs, cheese, candy, etc., to keep away air and moisture. Because tin is expensive, **aluminum foil** and plastic are now used. Tubes such as those used for toothpaste once were made of tin.

Tin plate, sheet steel coated with tin, is used for pots, pans, cans, pails, and metal roofing. It is often incorrectly called "tin." "Copper" kettles, used for cooking, are coated with tin to keep the copper from entering the cooked food.

7-13 Titanium and Its Alloys

Titanium is a silvery-gray metal with high strength and heat resistance. It weighs about 44% less than steel alloys, yet its tensile strength is equal to or greater than common structural steel alloys. Temperatures up to 800°F [427°C] do not weaken titanium, and it will tolerate temperatures up to 2000°F [1093°C] for short periods of time. Because of these properties, it is used for many supersonic aircraft parts, which are exposed to high degrees of vibration and heat.

Titanium is relatively **inert** (that is, it does not react chemically with many other substances). Thus, it is used to replace bone and cartilage in surgery. It is also used as a liner for pipes and tanks in the food-processing industries.

There are about 30 titanium alloys. The chief alloying elements are tin, aluminum, zirconium, manganese, molybdenum, vanadium, chromium, and columbium.

7-14 Tungsten

Tungsten has the highest melting point of all metals, 6098°F (3370°C). It is used chiefly as an alloying element in steels, see Unit 6-4, and for making **tungsten carbide.**

Tungsten carbide, also known as **cemented tungsten carbide,** is the hardest metal made by man. It is made by heating, or **sintering,** powdered metals, including tungsten, cobalt, and carbon in a mold. (Sintered metals are heated and fused together without melting.) Tungsten-carbide metal-cutting tools retain their hardness at temperatures as high as 1700°F [927°C] without significant softening. Such tools, known as **carbide tools,** cut two to four times faster than high-speed steel. Tungsten carbide is widely used for wire-drawing dies and other die making.

7-15

Zinc Base Alloys

Zinc is a brittle, bluish-white metal. It is used as a coating for iron and steel for protection against rust. Coating with zinc is called **galvanizing.** Some galvanizing is done by dipping the metal into molten zinc. As the zinc cools, it forms into **crystals,** which make the spotted pattern on **galvanized steel** (Fig. 7-8). Galvanizing is also done by **electroplating,** which produces a tightly bonded, smooth coating of zinc that provides superior paint adhesion.

When galvanized steel is heated, it produces a coating of zinc-steel alloy. The result is called **galvannealed metal.** These coated metals are used for wire fences, metal roofing, water tanks, water pipes, buckets, automobile frames, signs, and other products that must resist corrosion.

Zinc is also used in **German silver, brass, bronze,** and **dry cell batteries.** Like copper and brass, zinc hardens when hammered. It can be softened by heating and slow cooling.

Fig. 7-8 *Galvanized steel. The spangled surface pattern results when the zinc coating is applied by dipping.* (American Iron & Steel Institute)

There are 16 standard alloys of zinc. Zinc-based alloys are widely used for making die cast engine blocks for small gas engines, housings for small engines, carburetors, parts of typewriters, car door handles, and parts of portable electric tools.

REVIEW REVIEW REVIEW REVIEW REVIEW

WORDS TO KNOW

alumina	cast alloys	green gold	sintering
aluminum	cemented tungsten	karat	smelting
anneal	carbide	lead	sterling silver
antimony	copper	magnesium	tin
babbitt	extrude	monel metal	tin plate
bauxite	galvanized steel	nickel	titanium
beryllium	galvannealing	pewter	tungsten carbide
brass	German silver	reducing pot	white gold
bronze	gold	silver	zinc
	gold leaf		

(Review Continued)

REVIEW QUESTIONS

1. What is aluminum? What are its important properties? List several important uses.
2. Describe copper. What states is copper mined in? What are its important properties and uses?
3. What is brass? What is it used for?
4. What is bronze? What is it used for?
5. Describe zinc. What are its main uses?
6. Describe magnesium. What are its important properties and uses? What hazard is involved in machining it?
7. Describe nickel. List several uses for it.
8. What is titanium? List its major properties and uses.
9. What are the cast alloys used for?
10. What is babbitt metal? What is its major use?
11. What is beryllium? What is it used for?
12. What are the chief properties and uses of gold?
13. What is lead? How is it used?
14. What is pewter used for?
15. What are the chief properties and uses of silver?
16. Describe tin. What is it used for?
17. Describe how tungsten carbide is made, and name two main uses.

UNIT

8

Metal Designation and Identification

Metal manufacturers make thousands of different alloys, and continue to develop new ones. This has made it necessary to develop standard alloy numbering and marking systems for efficiency in specifying, ordering, and inventory control.

8-1 Steel Numbering Systems

Two major steel numbering systems have been developed, one by the **Society of Automotive Engineers** (SAE), the other by the **American Iron and Steel Institute** (AISI). Both systems use four-digit code numbers to identify the basic composition of plain carbon and alloy steels. Certain alloys have five-digit code numbers.

The first digit of the number usually indicates the basic steel type as follows:

1. carbon
2. nickel
3. nickel-chromium
4. molybdenum
5. chromium
6. chromium-vanadium
7. tungsten
8. nickel-chromium-molybdenum
9. silicon-manganese.

The first two digits together identify a series of metals within the basic alloy group. The second digit often, but not always, indicates the approximate percentage of the main alloying element. The third, fourth, and fifth digits indicate the amount of carbon content. Two examples of code numbers in the SAE/AISI steel numbering system are:

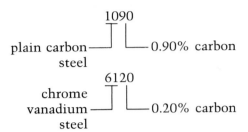

Table 8-1 gives the series numbers and the types of steel they identify. These numbers are called "series designations."

Many steels of constructional grade are made to certain hardenability standards. The letter H is used after the SAE/AISI number to identify this type of steel, for example, 1340H. More information on H steels can be found in standard engineering handbooks.

A special system is used for designating commonly used tool and die steels. There are seven main groups of these steels, some containing several subgroups. Each group is designated by a letter, followed by numerals for each specific tool steel (Table 8-2).

8-2   Aluminum Numbering Systems

Wrought aluminum alloys are designated by a four-number code. The first digit identifies the main alloying elements as follows:

1. aluminum of 99% or greater purity (no alloying element)
2. copper
3. manganese
4. silicon
5. magnesium
6. magnesium and silicon
7. zinc

Table 8-1

Series Designations in SAE-AISI Steel Code

Series	Types		
10xx ..	Nonsulphurized carbon steels		
11xx ..	Resulphurized carbon steels (free machining)		
12xx ..	Rephosphorized and resulphurized carbon steels (free machining)		
13xx ..	Mn 1.75%		
*23xx ..	Ni 3.50%		
*25xx ..	Ni 5.00%		
31xx ..	Ni 1.25%	Cr 0.65%	
33xx ..	Ni 3.50%	Cr 1.55%	
40xx ..	Mo 0.20 or 0.25%		
41xx ..	Cr 0.50 or 0.95%	Mo 0.12 or 0.20%	
43xx ..	Ni 1.80%	Cr 0.50 or 0.80%	Mo 0.25%
44xx ..	Mo 0.40%		
45xx ..	Mo 0.52%		
46xx ..	Ni 1.80%	Mo 0.25%	
47xx ..	Ni 1.05%	Cr 0.45%	Mo 0.20 or 0.35%
48xx ..	Ni 3.50%	Mo 0.25%	
50xx ..	Cr 0.25, 0.40 or 0.50%		
50xxx ..	C 1.00%	Cr 0.50%	
51xx ..	Cr 0.80, 0.90, 0.95, or 1.00%		
51xxx ..	C 1.00%	Cr 1.05%	
52xxx ..	Cr 1.00%	Cr 1.45%	
61xx ..	Cr 0.60, 0.80 or 0.95%		
	V 0.12%, 0.10% min., or 0.15% min.		
81xx ..	Ni 0.30%	Cr 0.40%	Mo 0.12%
86xx ..	Ni 0.55%	Cr 0.50%	Mo 0.20%
87xx ..	Ni 0.55%	Cr 0.05%	Mo 0.25%
88xx ..	Ni 0.55%	Cr 0.50%	Mo 0.35%
92xx ..	Mn 0.85%	Si 2.00%	Cr 0 or 0.35%
93xx ..	Ni 3.25%	Cr 1.20%	Mo 0.12%
94xx ..	Ni 0.45%	Cr 0.40%	Mo 0.12%
98xx ..	Ni 1.00%	Cr 0.80%	Mo 0.25%

*Not included in the current list of standard steels.
Abbreviations:
C   Carbon   Mo Molybdenum
Cr Chromium   Ni Nickel
Mn Manganese   Si Silicon
                               V   Vanadium

8. an element other than mentioned above
9. unassigned.

The second digit indicates control of impurities in the production of the metal, with 0 indicating no control. Nine indicates the highest degree of control. In the 1000 series, the last two digits indicate aluminum purity in hundredths of a percent over 99%. In other series, the last two numbers identify different alloys used within the series.

Table 8-2

Unit 8—Metal Designation and Identification **71**

Tool and Die Steel Designation System

Code	Designation
W	Water-hardening tool steel
S	Shock-resisting tool steel
O	Cold-work tool steel, oil-hardening
A	Cold-work tool steel, medium alloy air-hardening
D	Cold-work tool steel, high-carbon, high-chromium
H1-19	Hot-work tool steel, chromium types
H20-39	Hot-work tool steel, tungsten types
H40-59	Hot-work tool steel, molybdenum types
M	High-speed tool steel, molybdenum types
T	High-speed tool steel, tungsten types
L	Special-purpose tool steels, low-allow types
F	Special-purpose tool steels, carbon-tungsten types
P1-19	Mold steel, low-carbon types
P20-39	Mold steel, other types

Table 8-3

Aluminum Temper Designations

Code	Designation
F —	as fabricated
O —	annealed (wrought alloys only)
H —	strain-hardened (wrought alloys only)
	H1, + one or more digits, strain-hardened only
	H2, + one or more digits, strain-hardened, then partly annealed
	H3, + one or more digits, strain-hardened and stabilized
W —	solution heat-treated only, unstable temper
T —	thermally treated
	T2, annealed (casting alloys only)
	T3, solution heat-treated and cold-worked
	T4, solution heat-treated
	T5, artificially aged
	T6, solution heat-treated and artificially aged
	T7, solution heat-treated and stabilized
	T8, solution heat-treated, cold-worked and artificially aged
	T9, solution heat-treated, artificially aged, then cold-worked
	T10, artificially aged and cold-worked

Most aluminum alloys are made in several degrees of hardness. To indicate this hardness, a **temper designation** follows the alloy number, separated by a dash. The temper designations are given in Table 8-3. Thus, alloy 1100-0 indicates an aluminum of 99% purity that has been **annealed;** 2011-T3 indicates an aluminum/copper alloy that has been **solution heat-treated** and **cold-worked.** Aluminum casting alloys are designated by a separate three number system.

8-3 Other Metal Numbering Systems

Other numbering systems now in use include a three-digit system for copper and a three-digit system for stainless steel. Metal producers use separate systems for designating cast irons, zinc alloys, magnesium alloys, titanium alloys, super-strength space-age alloys, and precious metals. Metal designation has become complicated because more than one numbering system is often used for each type of metal.

To simplify this problem the SAE and **ASTM (American Society for Testing and Materials)** created **The Unified Numbering System for Metals and Alloys (UNS).** The UNS uses 16 numbered series for identifying certain metals and alloys. The UNS numbers consist of a single letter followed by a five-digit number (Table 8-4).

When possible, the UNS uses numbers from the old systems. For example, aluminum alloy 1100 has the UNS number of A91100,

Table 8-4

Unified Numbering System for Metals and Alloys

Code	Designation
Axxxxx	Aluminum and aluminum alloys
Cxxxxx	Copper and copper alloys
Exxxxx	Rare earth and rare earthlike metals and alloys
Fxxxxx	Cast irons
Gxxxxx	AISI and SAE carbon and alloy steels
Hxxxxx	AISI and SAE H-steels
Jxxxxx	Cast steels (except tool steels)
Kxxxxx	Miscellaneous steels and ferrous alloys
Lxxxxx	Low-melting metals and alloys
Mxxxxx	Miscellaneous nonferrous metals and alloys
Nxxxxx	Nickel and nickel alloys
Pxxxxx	Precious metals and alloys
Rxxxxx	Reactive and refractory metals and alloys
Sxxxxx	Heat- and corrosion-resistant stainless steels
Txxxxx	Tool steels, wrought and cast
Zxxxxx	Zinc and zinc alloys

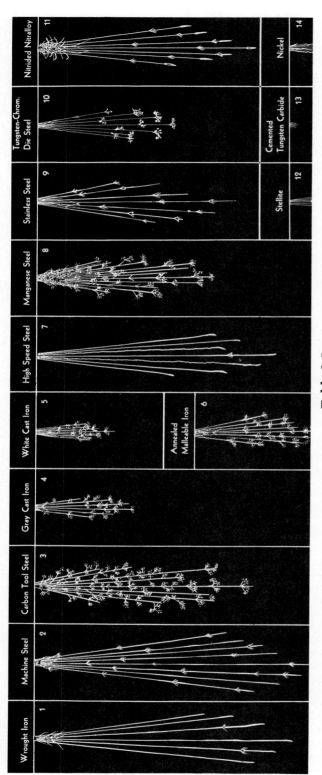

Table 8-5

Characteristics of Sparks Made by Grinding Metals

Metal	Volume of stream	Relative length of stream, in. (mm)†	Color of stream close to wheel	Color of streaks near end of stream	Quantity of spurts	Nature of spurts
1. Wrought iron	Large	65 (1651)	Straw	White	Very few	Forked
2. Machine steel (AISI 1020)	Large	70 (1778)	White	White	Few	Forked
3. Carbon tool steel	Moderately large	55 (1397)	White	White	Very many	Fine, repeating
4. Gray cast iron	Small	25 (635)	Red	Straw	Many	Fine, repeating
5. White cast Iron	Very small	20 (508)	Red	Straw	Few	Fine, repeating
6. Annealed malleable iron	Moderate	30 (762)	Red	Straw	Many	Fine, repeating
7. High-speed steel (18-4-1)	Small	60 (1524)	Red	Straw	Extremely few	Forked
8. Austenitic manganese steel	Moderately large	45 (1143)	White	White	Many	Fine, repeating
9. Stainless steel (Type 410)	Moderate	50 (1270)	Straw	White	Moderate	Forked
10. Tungsten-chromium die steel	Small	35 (889)	Red	Straw*	Many	Fine repeating*
11. Nitrided Nitralloy	Large (curved)	55 (1397)	White	White	Moderate	Forked
12. Stellite	Very small	10 (254)	Orange	Orange	None	
13. Cemented tungsten-carbide	Extremely small	2 (51)	Light Orange	Light Orange	None	
14. Nickel	Very small**	10 (254)	Orange	Orange	None	
15. Copper, brass, aluminum	None				None	

†Figures obtained with (12″) 305 mm wheel on bench stand are relative only. Actual length in each instance will vary with type of grinding wheel, pressure and speed. *Blue-white spurts. **Some wavy streaks.

and 1090 plain carbon steel is designated by the UNS number of G10900. Additional information on metal numbering systems can be found in engineering handbooks.

8-4 Color Code for Steel

The ends of steel bars are usually painted with one or more colors at the steel mill. The color or colors identify the type of steel in each bar. However, not all steel producers use the same color code. Therefore, to correctly identify the kind of steel by the color on it, you must know what company made the steel and what the company's color code is. The wholesaler that supplied the metal can usally provide this information.

When you cut a piece of stock from a bar, always start from the unpainted end. Then, the steel can be identified for future use.

8-5 Spark Testing

Sparks fly off when steel is put to a grinding wheel. Often they can identify the general type of an unknown steel. Each kind of steel produces a different color and volume of sparks. Thus, a steel of unknown composition can be roughly identified when its sparks match those of a known kind of steel.

Some practice is required to correctly identify steel by spark testing. The pressure used in grinding all the pieces should be the same. The color and volume of sparks produced should be studied carefully and compared to those shown in Table 8-5.

The volume of sparks depends on the carbon content. Wrought iron, produces very few sparks. High-carbon steel produces many sparks. Careful study of spark patterns 1-3 in Table 8-5 will help in identifying low-, medium-, and high-carbon steels.

REVIEW REVIEW REVIEW REVIEW REVIEW

WORDS TO KNOW

Aluminum Association (AA)
American Iron and Steel Institute (AISI)

American Society for Testing and Materials (ASTM)
color code

Society of Automotive Engineers (SAE)
spark testing

temper designation
Unified Numbering System (UNS)

REVIEW QUESTIONS

1. What does the first digit identify in the SAE/AISI steel numbering system?
2. What do the third and fourth digits tell in a four-digit SAE/AISI steel number?
3. What does the letter H mean when used with an SAE/AISI number?
4. Explain the system used to designate tool and die steels.
5. Describe the numbering system used for wrought aluminum alloys.
6. What is the system used to identify different degrees of hardness in aluminum alloys?
7. Why was the Unified Numbering System developed? How is it different from other metal numbering systems? How is it the same?
8. Why do steel producers paint the ends of steel bars different colors? What problems does this present to the users?
9. Explain how some unknown metals can be roughly identified by spark testing.

PART
3
Planning

When Bill Harold began work as a young draftsman at a large electronics firm, he immediately set out to discover what that firm wanted in a draftsman. He began watching the procedures that would be required for the type of work he wanted to do. Bill then set deliberate work goals. It wasn't long before he began to move up in the company. In his 45 years there, Bill progressed from draftsman to head draftsman with almost 150 others reporting to him. Then he moved to head production and then design engineer. From his early days when Bill might make a drawing of a simple motor part, he might now design an intricate part to be used in a space exploration vehicle.

Bill had a solid background for such advancement. He attended a vocational high school for four years. There he got basic experience in shop work, pattern-making, geometry, and science. He even designed and made a punch press in his final year. Moreover, Bill's drafting teacher was excellent, and that was the subject he followed in college. The creative skill required to turn an idea or written words into a pictorial sketch appealed to Bill very much.

In his earlier drafting years, Bill did a lot of manual drafting. But with the coming of computers, very few engineering drawings are now made that way. Bill was trained to use a CAD system, then he set up and supervised the computer-aided drafting (CAD) operations and procedures at his company.

Bill advises students to make a "nice looking drawing" and take the time to double check their dimensions. Most of all, Bill says, "Be proud of your work!" It would seem that Bill has every right to be proud of his.

Bill Harold
Production Project Engineer

Charles Zilch

UNIT
9

Reading Drawings and Making Sketches

Drawings of several types are used by product designers, engineers, technicians, and skilled workers. **Pictorial drawings** are often used at the design stage because they show how the product will look in three-dimensional form. Such drawings often start out as sketches on an engineer's or designer's sketch pad (Fig. 9-1). They may also be drawn electronically with a Computer-Aided Design or Computer-Aided Drafting (CAD) system (Fig. 9-2).

The designer usually makes many different pictorial sketches of a product before finding the best design. Pictorial sketches of drawings, however, usually do not provide all the information needed to make the product.

Production drawings are usually orthographic (multiview) drawings that provide detailed front, top, and side views of the product. These drawings are also called engineering or **working** drawings.

9-1 Working Drawings

A working drawing gives all the information needed to make a product (Fig. 9-3). It enables workers in different factories to make the same objects to the same specifications so that the parts are **interchangeable.** Automobile and aircraft parts are made in different parts of the country; yet when assembled they fit together and work properly. The working drawing makes this possible.

Working drawings must show the following:

1. Shape of every part of the object.
2. Sizes of all parts.
3. Kind of material.
4. Kind of finish.
5. How many pieces of each part are needed.

Working drawings are made according to a language understood by engineers and skilled workers. They are the manufacturing language of the entire industrial world.

To be able to read a working drawing, you must learn the meaning of the different kinds of lines, symbols, dimensions, and abbreviations it shows. You also need to understand how the different views of the object are related to each other.

9-2 Views

On a working drawing, each view usually shows the outline or shape of the object as seen from the front, top, and right or left side.

Fig. 9-1 *A designer made this pictorial sketch of the space shuttle during its development.* (Hewlett Packard)

TECHNOLOGIES AND PRACTICES

From Blackboards to Computers

In 1907, car manufacturer Henry Ford came up with the idea to design the Model T. He told one of his drafters about it this way: "Joe, I've got an idea to design a new car. Fix a place for yourself on the third floor, way back, a special room. Get your (drawing) boards up there and a blackboard and we'll start work on a new model." During the long hours of the designing process, Mr. Ford would place himself in a favorite rocking chair and have the boards with the new designs arranged so that he could get a good look at everything.

Today at Ford Motor Company the "special rooms" are not filled with blackboards and chalk but with cathode-ray-tubes (CRTs) and light pens. These are the main tools used in Computer-Aided Design (CAD). One thing remains the same: designers today, just as in Henry Ford's time, want to get a look at everything from every angle.

When design is begun on a new car, a clay model is made to determine the surface details. This data is put into a computer. Designers then work with the computer through the use of cathode-ray-tubes to produce three dimensional structural drawings.

The designer, or operator, sits in front of the CRT, which looks like a television set. The computer does much of the routine work of drawing lines and figuring ratios. The operator uses keys attached to the "tube" console to call up previous designs and parts from the computer's memory banks. Then, he or she uses a light pen to draw on the displayed design. The computer picks up the signals given by the pen and places lines on the design.

The three-dimensional drawing can be enlarged, reduced, and turned in the CRT "space." This way the operator can see the product from any angle. Designers can thus analyze their designs and make changes quickly.

Ford Motor Company began using Computer-Aided Design in the late 1960s. With the increased demand for high performance products with fuel efficient engines, greater analysis of performance factors has been needed. Use of computers in design therefore increased greatly in the late 1970s. Today more than 700 designers at Ford use CAD extensively to produce and analyze new designs.

Computer-Aided Design is used also by thousands of other companies nationwide.

Fig. 9-2 An engineer at a typical CAD work station.

To show an object completely, two or more views are usually needed. A few objects, such as a ball, can be described with only one view. No more views than are necessary should be drawn. It will help you to understand the relationship of these views if you imagine that the object is in a glass box (Fig. 9-4) with the views drawn on the front, top, and side of the box. When the box is unfolded, the views will be the same as on a working drawing. A working drawing of a **cylinder** needs only two views, the **front view** and **top view** (Fig. 9-5) because the front view of a cylinder looks the same as its side view.

Inch	mm
1/4	6.35
1/2	12.7
2 1/2	63.5
3.000	76.2
5.000	127
6.500	165.1

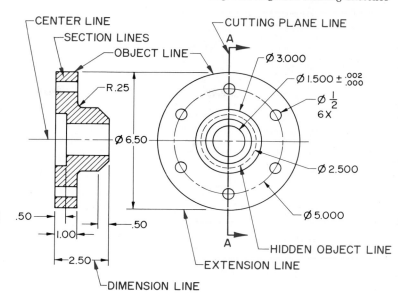

Fig. 9-3 *Working drawings convey the information skilled workers need to make the products we use. The metalworking industry could not function without working drawings.*

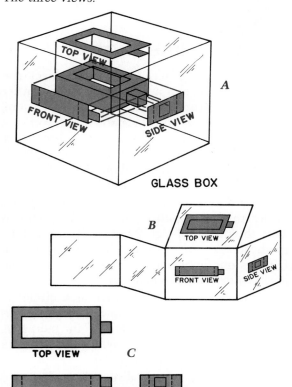

Fig. 9-4 *Imagine that the object you want to draw is inside a glass box. (A) Viewing the object through the glass box. (B) Unfolding the box. (C) The three views.*

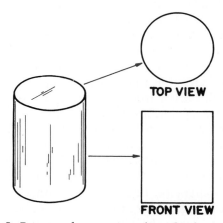

Fig. 9-5 *Front and top views of a cylinder.*

9-3 Lines on Working Drawings

The different kinds of lines used on working drawings are shown in Figure 9-6. They are also identified in the working drawing in Fig. 9-3.

An **object line** is a thick line used to show all edges that can be seen.

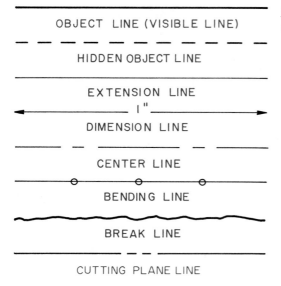

OBJECT LINE (VISIBLE LINE)

HIDDEN OBJECT LINE

EXTENSION LINE

DIMENSION LINE

CENTER LINE

BENDING LINE

BREAK LINE

CUTTING PLANE LINE

Fig. 9-6 *Lines used for making working drawings.*

Bending lines are light lines with a small circle drawn by hand at each end of the line. These lines show the places where sheet metal is bent to form parts of an object like the sides of a box.

A **break line** is an irregular line. It is used to show that a part of the object is broken off.

Section lines are light parallel lines drawn across a surface that has been cut away. The lines are usually slanted at 45° to the horizontal object line of the drawing.

A **cutting plane line** is a bold line like an object line. It shows the location of a **sectional** or **cutaway** view on an object. It is drawn with long dashes of 3/4 to 1-1/2 inches [19 to 38 mm]. The long dashes are separated by two 1/8″ [3 mm] dashes that are separated from each other and from the long dashes with a 1/16″ [1.5 mm] space.

A **hidden line** is an object line that is hidden in a particular view. It is made of dashes that are 1/8″ [3.2 mm] long and 1/16″ [1.6 mm] apart. It is used to show hidden edges, just as if you could look right through the object.

An **extension line** is a thin line. Extension lines are drawn from the edges of objects in the drawing that are to be dimensioned. Note that the extension line does not touch the object; it should start about 1/16″ [1.6 mm] from the object and extend about 1/8″ [3.2 mm] past the arrowhead on the **dimension line.**

A **dimension line** is also a thin line. It is drawn between the extension lines about 3/8″ [9.5 mm] from the object. The **dimension,** or measurement, is placed in the opening in the middle of the dimension line.

The distance from one hole in an object to another is dimensioned as the distance from the **center** of one hole to the **center** of the other. **Centerlines** locate the centers of circles or arcs. They are also used to show the **axis** of an object and to locate slots. (The **axis** of an object is a line through the object's center around which the object can rotate.) A centerline is a thin line made up of alternating 1″ [25.4 mm] lines and 1/8″ [3.2 mm] lines, separated by 1/16″ [1.6 mm] spaces. A centerline is drawn **horizontally** and **vertically** through the center of every circle and arc.

9-4   Dimensions

Dimensions give the size of the object, the location and size of any holes in it, and other important features of the object. Dimensions are the most important parts of a working drawing for metal workers. The **dimension lines** and dimensions are drawn as in Figure 9-6. **Arrowheads** should be about 3/16″ [4.8 mm] long and touch the extension lines.

The **diameter** of a circle should be given rather than the **radius** (Fig. 9-7). It is shown after the diameter sign Ø with a leader and arrowhead that points to the circle's centerlines. Dimensions between holes should always be given from **center to center.**

The size of an **arc** (a part of a circle) is shown by the letter R, followed by the number that specifies the length of its radius. A leader is drawn with an arrowhead that points to the arc's centerlines (Fig. 9-7).

Always give **overall dimensions** that give the total length, width, and height or thickness of the object (Fig. 9-3). A dimension should be repeated only when there is a special reason for doing so. If the space is too small for a dimension, use one of the ways shown in Figure 9-8.

Dimensions are most often read from the bottom or right side of the drawing. Some companies have all their drawings dimensioned so they can be read from the bottom of the sheet (Fig. 9-3). Make fractions of an inch with a **horizontal line,** as 1/2″, 3/4″. When all dimensions are in inches, the **inch marks (″)** can be omitted. **Metric dimensions should always be in millimeters.**

9-5 Metric Dimensioning

When drawings are dimensioned in the International System of metric measurements, the same rules generally apply as when they are dimensioned in the U.S. customary system (Fig. 9-9). The American National Standards Institute recommends that drawings dimensioned in millimeters carry the following note:

UNLESS OTHERWISE SPECIFIED
ALL DIMENSIONS ARE IN MILLIMETERS

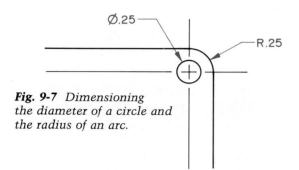

Fig. 9-7 *Dimensioning the diameter of a circle and the radius of an arc.*

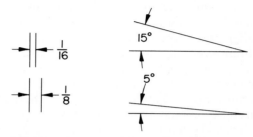

Fig. 9-8 *Dimensioning for small spaces.*

Fig. 9-9 *Metric dimensioning.*

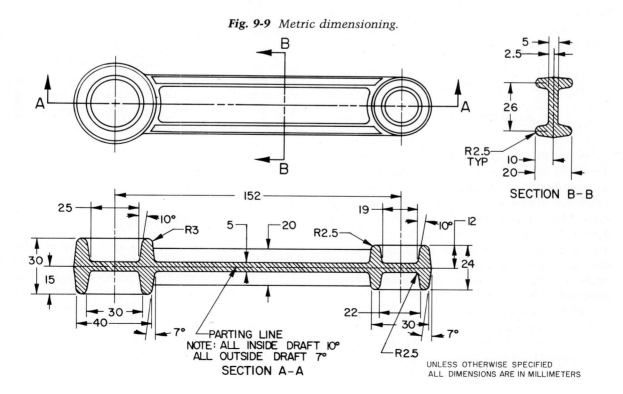

SECTION B–B

NOTE: ALL INSIDE DRAFT 10°
ALL OUTSIDE DRAFT 7°
SECTION A–A

UNLESS OTHERWISE SPECIFIED
ALL DIMENSIONS ARE IN MILLIMETERS

If drawings dimensioned in inches are to be used outside of the United States, they should carry a similar note:

UNLESS OTHERWISE SPECIFIED
ALL DIMENSIONS ARE IN INCHES

ANSI recommends that metalworking drawings be dimensioned in only one system. They should not be dual dimensioned in both systems.

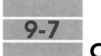

9-6 Tolerances and Allowances

Tolerances are acceptable variations in a dimension. They indicate how much larger or smaller the dimension on the part can be without affecting how well the part will fit in the final product. Tolerances are usually indicated on the drawing immediately after the dimension (Fig. 9-3). The use of ± indicates a **bilateral** tolerance; that is, the dimension may be either larger (+) or smaller (−) by the amount of tolerance stated, such as 1.25″ (31.75 mm) ± .005″ (0.13 mm). A **unilateral tolerance** allows variations to be made in only one direction. It is indicated by placing a zero after either the + or − sign, such as:

$$1.375'' + 0$$
$$- .005''$$
or
$$34.93 \text{ mm} + 0$$
$$- 0.13 \text{ mm}$$

Sometimes tolerances are not shown on the drawing. In these cases, common practice in metalworking assumes that if the dimensions are given with a **fractional part of an inch**, as ¾″ [19.05 mm], the tolerance is understood to be ± ¹⁄₆₄″ [0.4 mm]. (Metric dimensions are never given as fractions). For **decimal inch dimensions** without tolerances, such as .750″ [19.05 mm], the tolerance is understood to be ± .005″ [0.13 mm].

Allowance is a term used in precision machining to indicate the amount of acceptable clearance between mating parts (parts that fit together). Allowances may be **positive** (space between parts) to allow for a **sliding**, or **running, fit.** They may also be **negative** (no space between parts) to provide for an **interference,** or **force fit.** Allowances are determined by the dimensional tolerances given for each of the mating parts.

9-7 Cross Sections

The part of a working drawing that shows the object as if part of it had been cut away is called a **cross section** or simply a **section.** It shows the inside shapes of holes and the thickness of parts (Fig. 9-3). The cut surface is usually shown by **section lines.**

9-8 How Drawings Show Screw Threads

Two ways of showing **external** screw threads are shown in Figure 9-10. **Internal** screw threads (such as those on the inside of a nut) are shown in Figure 9-11. The note, ½″ - 13 UNC, means that the thread is ½″ in diameter and has 13 threads per inch and the kind of thread is **Unified National Coarse.** Threads are always right-hand threads unless the note includes the initials LH, meaning left-hand. Units 19-21 give more information about threads and threading.

9-9 Lettering

Notes are often necessary to give all the necessary information on a working drawing (Fig. 9-3). These should be lettered neatly and plainly so that the lettering can be read easily by everyone. Freehand lettering is a worthwhile skill for anyone who makes industrial sketches or drawings. Table 9-1 gives a list of standard abbreviations and symbols used on drawings.

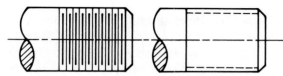

Fig. 9-10 *Two time-saving ways of showing external screw threads.*

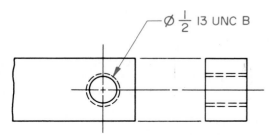

Ø $\frac{1}{2}$ 13 UNC B

Fig. 9-11 *The usual way of showing internal threads.*

Table 9-1

Abbreviations and Symbols Used on Drawings

'	Feet, or Minutes
"	Inches, or Seconds
°	Degrees
±	Plus or minus, more or less
c	Centerline
Ø	Diameter
R	Radius
□	Counterbore or spot-face
V	Countersink
↧	Depth
P	Pitch
RH	Right Hand
LH	Left Hand
USF	United States Form
USS	United States Standard
SAE	Society of Automotive Engineers
Thds.	Threads
NC	National Coarse
NF	National Fine
UNC	Unified National Coarse
UNF	Unified National Fine
CS	Carbon Steel
HRS	Hot-Rolled Steel
CRS	Cold-Rolled Steel
HSS	High-Speed Steel

Scale of Drawings

Oftentimes, an object is too large to be drawn full-size. In such cases, the drawing is reduced or **drawn to scale.** It may be drawn half-size, quarter-size, or even to a smaller scale. On a half-size drawing, for example, 1" = 2" [25.4 mm = 50.8 mm], and on a quarter-size drawing, 1" = 4" [25.4 mm = 101.6 mm]. However, the dimensions are placed on drawings the same as if the drawing were full-size. If the drawing is other than full-size, the scale that is used must be given in a note on the drawing.

Freehand Sketching

Sometimes it is necessary to make a part so quickly that there is no time to have an engineering drawing made. Or, only one part is to be made, as for testing the first, experimental prototype of a product before the de-

sign of the part is fixed. In this case it would be a needless expense to make a drawing. Very often the worker in the shop also has ideas about the design of an object. In such cases a sketch or freehand drawing can be quickly made using only paper and pencil. A sketch of a bracket is shown in Figure 9-12. Sketches should be as carefully made as a working drawing, giving all the information needed to make the part. And they should be neat so they can be read easily by others.

Sketching Lines

The straight edges of a paper pad may help a worker sketch straight lines. By using a finger as a guide along the edge of the pad (Fig. 9-13), the worker can produce a fairly straight line.

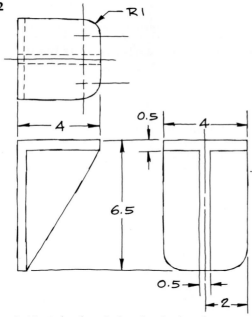

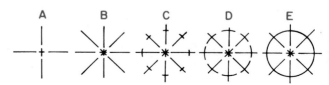

Fig. 9-12 *A freehand sketch of a bracket.*

D. Draw short **arcs** through the marks.

E. Finish circle.

Another easy way to sketch circles is to use two pencils like a **compass** and turn the paper under the pencils. Figure 9-15 shows how to sketch a circle this way. Large circles may be sketched by turning the paper under the pencil and middle finger (Fig. 9-16).

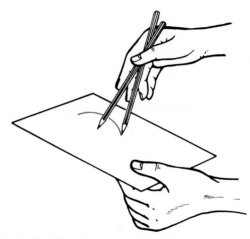

Fig. 9-14 *Steps in sketching a circle.*

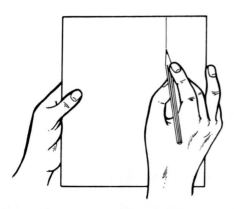

Fig. 9-13 *Sketching a line near the edge of the paper.*

Fig. 9-15 *Sketching a circle with two pencils.*

Fig. 9-16 *Sketching a circle by using the middle finger as the pivot and rotating the paper.*

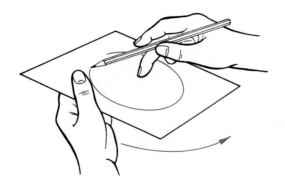

9-13

Sketching Circles

One way to sketch circles is shown in Figure 9-14:

A. Draw **centerlines** through the point that is to be the center of the circle.

B. Draw two **diagonal** lines.

C. Mark the **radius** of the circle on each of the lines.

REVIEW   REVIEW   REVIEW   REVIEW   REVIEW

WORDS TO KNOW

allowance	diameter	full-size drawing	section lines
axis	dimension	hidden line	sketch
bending line	dimension line	object line	symbol
blueprint	dual dimensioning	overall dimension	tolerance
break line	end view	pictorial drawing	top view
centerline	extension line	radius	visible line
cross section	front view	scale drawing	working drawing
cutting plane line			

REVIEW QUESTIONS

1. What are pictorial drawings? Why are they used?
2. What are working drawings? Why are they important?
3. What views of an object are shown in a working drawing?
4. Describe the basic lines used on working drawings.
5. Name two systems of measurement used in dimensioning metalworking drawings.
6. What is an overall dimension?
7. What is a cross section?
8. What is the difference between tolerance and allowance?
9. Where and how are tolerances shown on working drawings?
10. What is meant by a scale drawing? How is the scale indicated on the drawing?
11. Why is the ability to make freehand sketches useful?

UNIT 10

Product Planning

Manufacturing industries plan carefully for every item they make, whether a tin can or a space satellite. Design engineers work out the ideas and design for each product, and drafting departments make working drawings for every part. Engineers select the proper materials for the parts. Cost estimators calculate costs to the third or fourth decimal place. Then, purchasing agents buy the materials at the lowest possible market prices. Manufacturing and tool engineers, technicians, and skilled workers assemble the tools, equipment, and machinery needed to manufacture the product. They also plan each manufacturing step to get the most economical production. As you plan your product, you will learn to do many of the same things done in industry.

10-1 Making a Product Plan

Before attempting to construct a product of your own design, you should carefully prepare a **product plan.** A product plan contains all the information needed for successful construction of the product. A good plan includes the following information:

1. A working drawing of the product, carefully sketched freehand or even drawn in final form with drafting instruments. A pictorial sketch or drawing can also be used (Fig. 10-1).
2. A bill of materials (see Section 10-2).
3. A list of the steps for making the product, placed in the right order.
4. Approval of your instructor (if required) before making the product.

It is easier to prepare the product plan if you use a **plan sheet** designed for the purpose. A plan sheet of the type shown in Fig. 10-2 may be used, unless your instructor provides you with a different one. The working drawing should be attached to the completed plan sheet, thus completing the product plan.

Fig. 10-1 *Working drawing of a desk-top pencil holder.*

10-2 Bill of Materials

You must have the correct metal before you can make a metal product; therefore, it is necessary to know how to specify and order metals. The working drawing gives all of the information needed to make a bill of materials. The bill of materials made in the proper form (Fig. 10-2) should show:

1. The parts of the product, identified by names, numbers, or letters.
2. The number of pieces needed for each part.
3. The size of the standard stock needed (thickness, width, length).
4. The shape and the kind of material.
5. The standard parts used in the product.
6. The unit cost of the material (the cost per pound, per foot, per square foot; or per kilogram, per meter, per square meter, etc.).
7. The total cost of the materials.

10-3 Standard Parts

A **standard part** may be made by several companies. No matter which company makes it, the part is always the same. Five or six standard bolts of the same size are identical,

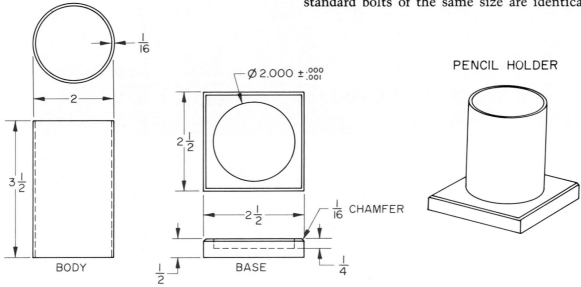

Product Plan

Name _Tim Johnson_ Grade _9_
Product _Desk-top pencil holder_ Hour _2_
Source of product idea _shop product idea file_

Estimated Time _2 hours_   Actual Time _3 hours_   Approved _Mason_

Bill of Materials

Part	No. of Pieces	Size			Material	Unit Cost (Per sq. ft., lb., etc.)	Total Cost
		Thickness	Width	Length			
Body	1	$\frac{1}{16}$" wall	2" Dia.	3$\frac{5}{8}$"	2024−T4 Alum.	$ 1.80 /ft.	$ .47
Base	1	$\frac{1}{2}$"	2$\frac{1}{2}$"	2$\frac{5}{8}$"	2024−T351 Alum.	$ 3.84/ft.	$ .84

Manufacturing Steps

Total Cost _$1.31_

Body:
1. Wrap tubing with 1100-0 aluminum strip and center it in lathe chuck.
2. Face off end. 3. File off sharp corner. 4. Satin finish outside of tubing with aluminum oxide cloth. 5. Turn piece around in chuck. 6. Mark 3½" Length with sharp pencil; face off extra metal. 7. File off sharp corner. 8. Satin finish rest of tubing. 9. Remove body from lathe chuck. 10. Deburr inside edges with scraper or abrasive cloth.

Base:
1. File off sharp edges of cut block. 2. Mount it in milling machine vise and carefully mill smooth finish on one end. 3. Turn workpiece around in vise. 4. Make light reference cut and measure. 5. Mill extra metal from block with one or more cuts and remove from vise. 6. File off sharp edges. 7. Using layout fluid, 8. mark layout lines ¼6" (16 mm) parallel each edge of top. 9. Mill chamfers. 10. Remove block from vise. 11. Mark center of block and 12. center punch. 13. Use wiggler to center base in independent chuck. Use 1100-0 aluminum strips to protect base. 14. Machine hole with facing cuts, not quite to full diameter but to full depth. 15. Carefully bore the hole to final size. 16. Remove base from lathe. 17. Wrap aluminum oxide abrasive around file, and satin finish chamfers and sides by draw-filing.

Assembly:
1. Use arbor press or vise to lightly press fit (force) tubing into hole in base. 2. If parts fit loosely because hole is oversize or tubing polished too small, glue parts with epoxy abrasive. 3. Cut 2 3/8" (60 mm) felt square and glue to bottom with rubber cement.

Fig. 10-2 *A form like this product plan may be used for planning your product. This is a completed form for the desk-top pencil holder shown in Fig. 10-1.*

even though they are made by as many different companies. Other types of hardware, such as nuts, rivets, screws, washers, and other fasteners that are made to standard sizes and shapes are also standard parts. Use hardware catalogs to get information about standard parts and materials.

10-4 Meaning of "Standard Stock"

Standard stock is the material that is used in the manufacture of finished products. Steel as it comes from the steel mill is standard stock. The term "standard stock" also means that the metal wholesaler carries a supply, or stock, of different kinds of metals of many different sizes and shapes. Manufacturers can save money by using standard kinds and sizes of metals that are produced at the mill to certain dimensions. Common shapes of standard stock are shown in Figure 10-3.

10-5 Measuring Standard Stock

Remember that the size given on the bill of materials is the size of the standard stock that you will **order.** The size given on the

working drawing is the **finished** size. The size of any part as given on the working drawing must have added to it the extra metal that is needed for finishing the object to size (Fig. 10-4). Standard stock is **specified** or described, as follows:

Flat Sheet or Strip

Thickness × width × length, for example:

⅛" × 1¾" × 4¼" [3 × 44 × 108 mm]

Hexagonal and Octagonal Bar

Distance across flat sides (flats) × length, for example:

1¼" × 4¼" [32 × 108 mm]

Round Bar

Diameter × length, for example:
2" Dia. × 4¼" [50 mm Dia. × 108 mm]

Square Bar

Thickness × width × length, for example:

1" × 1" × 4¼" [25 × 25 × 108 mm]

Structural Shapes

Overall cross-sectional dimensions × shape × wall thickness × length, for example:

Angle Beam:
1½" × 1½" angle × ³⁄₁₆" wall × 36" [38 × 38 mm angle × 4.76 mm wall × 914 mm]

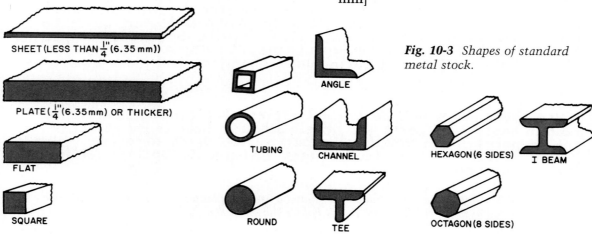

Fig. 10-3 *Shapes of standard metal stock.*

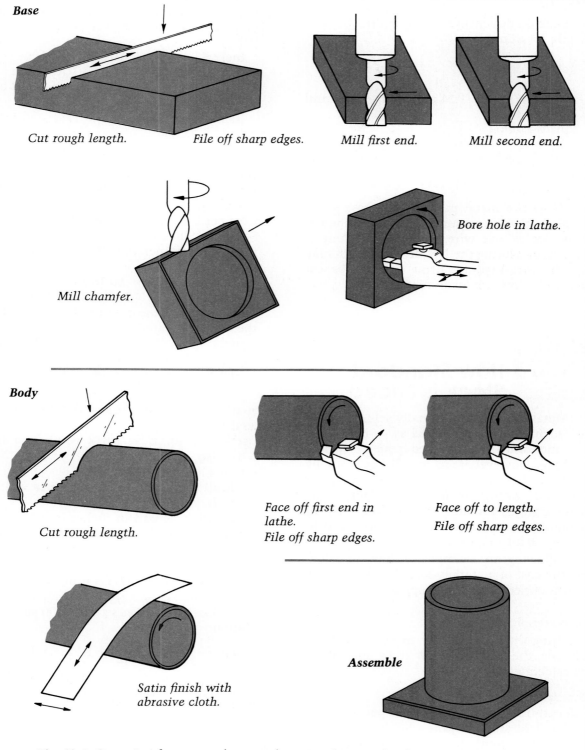

Base

Cut rough length. File off sharp edges. Mill first end. Mill second end.

Mill chamfer.

Bore hole in lathe.

Body

Cut rough length.

Face off first end in lathe.
File off sharp edges.

Face off to length.
File off sharp edges.

Satin finish with abrasive cloth.

Assemble

Fig. 10-4 *Operational sequence for manufacturing the parts for the pencil holder. The standard stock must be machined to the part dimensions given on the working drawing.*

Tubing

Outside dimensions × wall thickness × length, for example:

Round Tubing:
⅞″ Dia. × .049″ wall × 12″
[22 mm Dia. × 1.24 mm wall × 305 mm]

Square Tubing:
1″ × 1″ × .062″ wall × 18″
[25 × 25 mm × 1.57 mm wall × 457 mm]

The length of metal needed to make a **scroll** or **spiral** may be measured by first making the shape out of soft wire, then straightening it out and measuring the length. The length may also be measured by using dividers as explained in Unit 13, Section 13-6.

10-6   How Standard Stock Is Priced

Metal wholesalers normally sell all metals by weight. Prices are quoted as so many dollars and cents per hundred pounds. School suppliers, however, tend to sell bar stock by the lineal foot, sheet materials by the square foot, and casting metals by the pound. The prices charged for materials in your shop or laboratory very likely follow the pricing policies of school suppliers.

Following are examples of how to calculate the cost of materials according to the way they are priced by school suppliers.

For material sold by length:

Using the pencil holder in Fig. 10-1 as an example, the cost of the bar stock and tubing are calculated as follows:

General Formula:
length in feet (meters) × cost per ft. [m]
A. Standard stock required for base: 1 piece ½″ [12.7 mm] × 2½″ [63.5 mm], 2⅝″ [66.67 mm] long.
Cost per foot [meter]: $3.84 [$12.60]

Solution: Since the length required is less than a foot [meter], find the cost per inch [mm] by dividing the cost per foot by 12 [1000]:
Inch: $3.84 ÷ 12 = $0.32/in
Metric: $12.60 ÷ 1000 = $0.0126/mm
Then multiply the cost per inch [mm] by the length required:
Inch: .32 × 2⅝ = .32 × 21/8 = 6.72/8 = $.084
Metric: .0126 × 66.67 = $0.84

B. Standard stock required for the body:
1 piece 2″ [50.8 mm] Dia. × 3⅝″ [92.08 mm] long
Cost per foot [meter]: $1.80 [$5.91]
Solution: Since the length required is less than one foot [meter], first find the cost per inch [mm]:
Inch: $1.80 ÷ 12 = $0.15/in
Metric: $5.91 ÷ 1000 = $0.0059/mm
Then multiply the cost per inch [mm] by the length required:
Inch: $0.15 × 3⅝ = .15 × 29/8 = 4.35/8 = $0.54
Metric: $0.0059 × 92.08 = $0.54

For material sold by the square foot (meter):
General Formulas:
Cost = # of sq. ft. [sq. m] × cost per sq. ft. [sq. m]
To find # of sq. ft. [sq. m]:
1. Multiply length in ft. [m] times width in ft. [m], or
2. Multiply length in inches [mm] times width in inches [mm], then divide by 144 [1,000,000].
Example: Find the cost of a sheet of galvanized steel 11″ [279.4 mm] × 15″ [381 mm].
Cost: $0.65 per sq. ft. [$7.00 sq. m]
Solution:
Inch: $\frac{11 \times 15}{144} = \frac{165}{144} = 1.146$ sq. ft.
1.146 sq. ft × $.65/sq. ft. = $0.74
Metric: $\frac{279.4 \times 381}{1,000,000} = \frac{106,451.4}{1,000,000} =$ .1064514 sq. m
.1064514 s. m × $7.00/sq. m = $0.75 (the 1 cent difference is due to rounding)

All materials sold by weight:
General Formula:
 weight in pounds [Kg] × cost per pound [Kg]
Example: Find the cost of a ¾ lb. [0.34 Kg] zamac casting.

Cost: $0.87/lb. [$1.914/Kg]
 Solution:
  Inch: ¾ × 0.87 = 2.61/4 = $0.65
  Metric: 0.34 × $1.914 = $0.65

REVIEW   REVIEW   REVIEW   REVIEW   REVIEW

WORDS TO KNOW

distance across flats	angle	I-beam	spiral
bill of materials	channel	octagon	standard part
product plan	hexagon	tee	standard stock
scroll			

REVIEW QUESTIONS

1. What is a product plan, and what information is generally included on it?
2. What is a bill of materials, and what information should be on it?
3. Where may the information be found for making out a bill of materials?
4. What is meant by "standard stock"?
5. What are standard parts?
6. Should the size given on the bill of materials be that of the standard stock or of the finished part? Why?
7. Explain how the length of a curve or scroll can be measured.
8. What is the cost of 16″ [406 mm] of ½″ [12.7 mm] dia. 1018 steel rod that is priced at 15¢ per foot [49.2¢ per meter]?
9. Figure the cost of 8¾ pounds [3.98 kg] of ¼″ [6.35 mm] 1012 steel plate that is priced at 12¢ per pound [26.4¢ per kilogram].
10. Find the cost of 520 sq. inches [.33 sq. meters] of 22 gage sheet metal that is priced at 24¢ per square foot [$2.58 per square meter].

PART

4

Measuring and Laying Out

Pierre Wilson first became interested in metalwork as a member of a Future Engineers club in junior high school. He decided early that he could earn his living best in a skilled trade. In high school, he was given the opportunity to take part in a four-month "internship" program with a large milling plant. Pierre successfully completed the internship and has been at the plant now for three years.

He is progressing through a four-year technician apprenticeship and has learned the properties of a variety of metals and the functions of different milling machines. His major duties are to measure and lay out the company's products. In his work, he uses both plain micrometers and vernier measuring instruments.

Pierre says that though he could certainly "add and subtract," he found that using a micrometer was not as easy as it seemed. The first time he measured a part, the instrument read 1.872". To check himself, he measured again. The second reading was 1.879". Soon he discovered that the difference was caused by the way he was holding the instrument and applying pressure. After "a lot of practice," he learned to handle it properly. His measurements are now consistently accurate. A customer may send a broken shaft to the plant. Pierre carefully measures it and draws a blueprint for a new part.

Pierre continues his formal education at night school, where he works toward an associate degree as a Machinist Engineering Technician. Highly motivated since an early age, he is moving steadily and rapidly toward his goal of becoming a skilled metalworker.

Pierre Wilson
Apprentice Mechanical Technician

UNIT 11

Linear Measurement

Accurate measurement is the key to the production of interchangeable parts and mass production of metal products. Every part of a product must be accurately made to the size and shape specified by the designer. Parts that are not made accurately will not fit properly with other parts of the product. As a result, the finished product may not work properly or it may wear out sooner than it should.

Good workmanship depends greatly upon accurate measurement and layout work. Therefore, learning to read and use the common measuring and layout tools is important in metalworking. These tools are presented in Units 12-14, after linear measurement is explained here.

11-1 Linear Measurement

The United States is the last industrialized nation to continue using the inch system of **linear** (straight line) **measurement.** However, gradual adoption of the modern form of the metric system, the **International System of Units** (abbreviated SI) has begun. Many large corporations have converted completely or in part to the **SI Metric** system of measurement. Many companies are dimensioning their drawings in SI metric (millimeter) units. It is important, therefore, to learn both systems of linear measurement.

11-2 The U.S. Customary, or Inch, System

The inch is divided into the **common fractions** of ½", ¼", ⅛", ¹⁄₁₆", ¹⁄₃₂", and ¹⁄₆₄" (Fig. 11-1). With practice, parts can be measured accurately to ¹⁄₆₄th of an inch using steel rules having 1/64th graduations (Fig. 11-2). Steel rules are also made with **decimal fractions** of an inch such as ¹⁄₁₀" and ¹⁄₁₀₀" (Fig. 11-3).

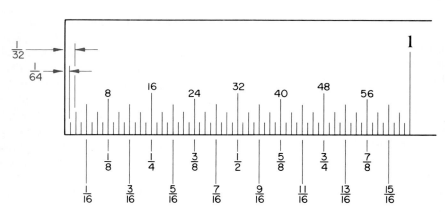

Fig. 11-1 The common customary inch rule divisions.

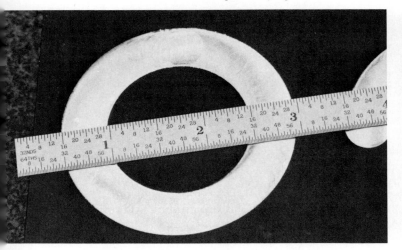

Fig. 11-2 *A steel rule (actual size) with 1/32″ graduations along the top edge and 1/64″ graduations along the bottom edge.*

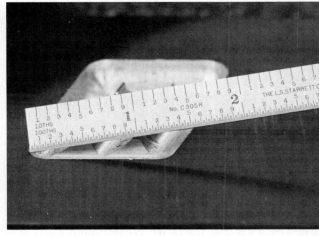

Fig. 11-3 *A rule marked in decimal fractions of an inch (actual size). The smallest division on the upper scale is .100″, on the lower scale .010″.*

Decimal fractions of an inch, however, are normally written on technical drawings in the following way:

$$\text{one tenth inch} = \frac{1}{10} = 0.100''$$

$$\text{one hundredth inch} = \frac{1}{100} = 0.010''$$

$$\text{one thousandth inch} = \frac{1}{1000} = 0.001''$$

$$\text{one ten-thousandth inch} = \frac{1}{10,000} = 0.0001''$$

Measurement of common fractions with a steel rule frequently cannot provide the accuracy required. Therefore, precision measuring instruments, such as **micrometers** and **verniers,** have been developed that measure accurately to $\frac{1}{1000}''$ and even $\frac{1}{10,000}''$. (These are described in Unit 14.) Since these instruments measure in decimal fractions, it is important to learn the **decimal equivalents** of the common fractions.

Decimal equivalents. The decimal equivalent of a common fraction may be found by dividing the numerator of the fraction by its denominator.

Example: ½ = 1 ÷ 2, or
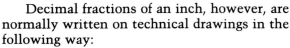

Table 11-1 gives the decimal equivalents of all the common fractions of an inch, together with their equivalent in millimeters.

> ***How big is one-thousandth of an inch?*** To give you an idea of .001″ (½₁₀₀₀″), this paper is about ³⁄₁₀₀₀″ thick, and thin tissue paper is about ¹⁄₁₀₀₀″ thick. A hair on your head is about ³⁄₁₀₀₀″ thick.

11-3
SI Metric System

The SI Metric system is a **base ten,** or **decimal,** system. Its units of measurement are related to each other by **powers of ten.** Each of the main units can be changed to a unit of more convenient size, when desired, by multiplying or dividing by powers of ten. Table 11-2 lists the names of several basic SI metric units, their symbols, and their relationship to each other. It is important to learn the metric symbols because they are used whenever metric measurements are written or printed. The same symbol is used for singular and plural.

Table 11-1

Fractional and Decimal Inch and Millimeter Equivalents

4ths	8ths	16ths	32nds	64ths	To 4 places	To 3 places	To 2 places	Milli-meters
				1/64	.0156	.016	.02	.397
			1/32		.0312	.031	.03	.794
				3/64	.0469	.047	.05	1.191
		1/16			.0625	.062	.06	1.588
				5/64	.0781	.078	.08	1.984
			3/32		.0938	.094	.09	2.381
				7/64	.1094	.109	.11	2.778
	1/8				.1250	.125	.12	3.175
				9/64	.1406	.141	.14	3.572
			5/32		.1562	.156	.16	3.969
				11/64	.1719	.172	.17	4.366
		3/16			.1875	.188	.19	4.762
				13/64	.2031	.203	.20	5.159
			7/32		.2188	.219	.22	5.556
				15/64	.2344	.234	.23	5.953
1/4					.2500	.250	.25	6.350
				17/64	.2656	.266	.27	6.747
			9/32		.2812	.281	.28	7.144
				19/64	.2969	.297	.30	7.541
		5/16			.3125	.312	.31	7.938
				21/64	.3281	.328	.33	8.334
			11/32		.3438	.344	.34	8.731
				23/64	.3594	.359	.36	9.128
	3/8				.3750	.375	.38	9.525
				25/64	.3906	.391	.39	9.922
			13/32		.4062	.406	.41	10.319
				27/64	.4219	.422	.42	10.716
		7/16			.4375	.438	.44	11.112
				29/64	.4531	.453	.45	11.509
			15/32		.4688	.469	.47	11.906
				31/64	.4844	.484	.48	12.303
					.5000	.500	.50	12.700

4ths	8ths	16ths	32nds	64ths	To 4 places	To 3 places	To 2 places	Milli-meters
				33/64	.5156	.516	.52	13.097
			17/32		.5312	.531	.53	13.494
				35/64	.5469	.547	.55	13.891
		9/16			.5625	.562	.56	14.288
				37/64	.5781	.578	.58	14.684
			19/32		.5938	.594	.59	15.081
				39/64	.6094	.609	.61	15.478
	5/8				.6250	.625	.62	15.875
				41/64	.6406	.641	.64	16.272
			21/32		.6562	.656	.66	16.669
				43/64	.6719	.672	.67	17.066
		11/16			.6875	.688	.69	17.462
				45/64	.7031	.703	.70	17.859
			23/32		.7188	.719	.72	18.256
				47/64	.7344	.734	.73	18.653
3/4					.7500	.750	.75	19.050
				49/64	.7656	.766	.77	19.447
			25/32		.7812	.781	.78	19.844
				51/64	.7969	.797	.80	20.241
		13/16			.8125	.812	.81	20.638
				53/64	.8281	.828	.83	21.034
			27/32		.8438	.844	.84	21.431
				55/64	.8594	.859	.86	21.828
	7/8				.8750	.875	.88	22.225
				57/64	.8906	.891	.89	22.622
			29/32		.9062	.906	.91	23.019
				59/64	.9219	.922	.92	23.416
		15/16			.9375	.938	.94	23.812
				61/64	.9531	.953	.95	24.209
			31/32		.9688	.969	.97	24.606
				63/64	.9844	.984	.98	25.003
					1.0000	1.000	1.00	25.400

Table 11-2

Metric SI Units

Property		Unit name	Symbol	Relationship of units
	Length	millimeter	mm	1 mm = 0.001 m
LINEAR		centimeter	cm	1 cm = 10 mm
MEASURE		decimeter	dm	1 dm = 10 cm or 100 mm
		meter	m	1 m = 100 cm or 1000 mm
		kilometer	km	1 km = 1,000 m
	Area	square centimeter	cm^2	1 cm^2 = 100 mm^2
SQUARE		square decimeter	dm^2	1 dm^2 = 100 cm^2
MEASURE		square meter	m^2	1 m^2 = 100 dm^2
		are	a	1 a = 100 m^2
		hectare	ha	1 ha = 100 a
		square kilometer	km^2	1 km^2 = 100 ha
		milligram	mg	1 mg = 0.001 g
MASS		gram	g	1 g = 1,000 mg
		kilogram	kg	1 kg = 1,000 g
		metric ton	1	1 t = 1,000 kg

Fig. 11-4 **A** *One meter, the basic unit of length in S.I. Metrics, and* **B** *one yard, a linear unit in the U.S. Customary system.* **C** *The sizes of inches and millimeters are compared at right.*

We are mainly concerned here with the basic SI Metric units of linear measurement. The **meter** is the basic unit of length. It measures 39.37″, roughly equal to the yard (Fig. 11-4). The meter is divided into **decimeters** [0.1 meter], **centimeters** [0.01 meter], and **millimeters** [0.001 meter]. **It has been agreed worldwide that metric dimensions on technical drawings for metalwork will be given in millimeters.**

Most metric rulers and tapes are divided into millimeters, abbreviated "mm," and are numbered at every 10 mm mark (Fig. 11-5). 300 mm rules are used instead of the familiar 12″ rules, and 150 mm steel rules replace the 6″ pocket rule. Precision steel rules are available with graduations as fine as 0.5 mm [½ mm] (Fig. 11-6).

A full range of metric micrometers and verniers are available for making measurements finer than ½ mm. Unit 14 explains how to read these instruments.

11-4 Use of Conversion Tables

Conversion tables are included in this book for convenience in converting dimensions in inches to dimensions in millimeters. Table 11-3 can be used for converting decimal parts of an inch to millimeters. Thus, if the metric equivalent of a decimal figure such as .835″ is desired, it may be found by using the following procedure:

$$0.8'' = 20.32 \text{ mm}$$
$$0.03'' = 0.762 \text{ mm}$$
$$\underline{0.005'' = 0.127 \text{ mm}}$$
$$0.835'' = 21.209 \text{ mm}$$

Table 11-1 lists fractions of an inch, their decimal equivalents, and their equivalents in millimeters. With this table, the metric equivalent of a common fraction, for example ⁵⁄₁₆″, can quickly be found to be 7.938 mm. (If great accuracy is not required, this would be rounded off to 8 mm.)

By using Table 11-1 and Table 11-3 together, the metric equivalent of any measurement in inches may be quickly obtained.

Useful inch-metric equivalencies to know. For calculating inch-metric equivalencies, it is useful to know the following:

$$1'' = 25.4 \text{ mm}$$
$$.001'' = 0.0254 \text{ mm}$$
$$1 \text{ mm} = 0.03937''$$

Table 11-3

Conversion Table
Decimal Parts of an Inch to Millimeters

Inches	Millimeters	Inches	Millimeters	Inches	Millimeters
0.001	0.025	0.01	0.254	0.1	2.54
0.002	0.051	0.02	0.508	0.2	5.08
0.003	0.076	0.03	0.762	0.3	7.62
0.004	0.102	0.04	1.016	0.4	10.16
0.005	0.127	0.05	1.270	0.5	12.70
0.006	0.152	0.06	1.524	0.6	15.24
0.007	0.178	0.07	1.778	0.7	17.78
0.008	0.203	0.08	2.032	0.8	20.32
0.009	0.229	0.09	2.286	0.9	22.86
				1.	25.40

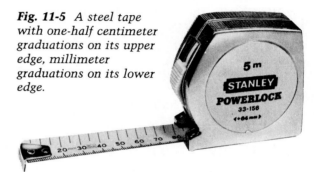

Fig. 11-5 *A steel tape with one-half centimeter graduations on its upper edge, millimeter graduations on its lower edge.*

Fig. 11-6 *A precision 150 mm steel rule with 1 mm and 0.5 mm graduations.*

REVIEW   REVIEW   REVIEW   REVIEW   REVIEW

WORDS TO KNOW

base ten	decimal equivalent	inch system	powers of ten
centimeter	decimal fraction	linear measurement	SI Metric system
common fraction	decimal system	meter	U.S. Customary
conversion tables	decimeter	millimeter	system

(Review Continued)

REVIEW QUESTIONS

1. Write the decimal equivalents of ½″, ¼″, ⅛″, ¹⁄₁₆″, ¹⁄₃₂″, ¹⁄₆₄″ to the nearest ¹⁄₁₀₀₀th of an inch. Say them.
2. Write the decimal equivalents of ⁴⁷⁄₆₁″, ¹³⁄₃₂″, ¹⁹⁄₆₁″, ¹⁵⁄₁₆″, ⅞″. Say them.
3. Write the following numbers: six hundred twenty-five thousandths; three hundred ninety-three thousandths; seven thousandths; sixteen thousandths; one half-thousandth; one quarter-thousandth; one ten-thousandth.
4. The answer to a problem is .225″. What is the nearest decimal equivalent that can be measured with a steel rule?
5. How thick is the paper in this book? Write it. Say it.
6. Why is it becoming more important to know the metric system of measurement?
7. What is the basic unit of length in the metric system? How long is it in inches?
8. How are metric rulers and tapes usually graduated and numbered?
9. What is the smallest unit of metric measurement usually found on precision steel rules?
10. Change the following fractions of an inch to millimeters:
    A. ³⁄₁₆
    B. ¼
    C. ⅜
    D. ¹⁹⁄₃₂
    E. ⁴⁵⁄₆₄
11. Convert the following decimal parts of an inch to millimeters:
    A. .720
    B. .315
    C. .019

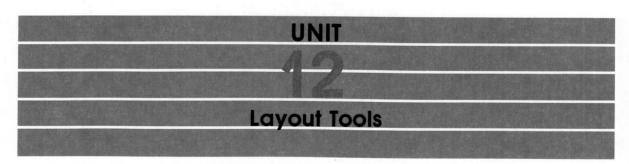

UNIT 12

Layout Tools

Layout work is the marking of lines, circles, and arcs on metal surfaces. It is the transferring of information from a **working drawing** to metal surfaces to show the location and amount of metal to be cut away. In many ways, laying out on metal is similar to making a **mechanical drawing** on paper.

The tools used for doing layout work are called **layout tools.** They are used by many skilled metalworkers: tool and die-makers, gage makers, layout workers, machinists, metal patternmakers, sheet metalworkers and structural steel workers.

Surface Plate

A surface plate is a large iron or granite plate with a very flat surface (Fig. 12-1). It provides an accurately flat surface on which to

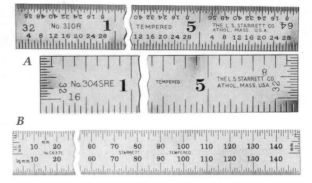

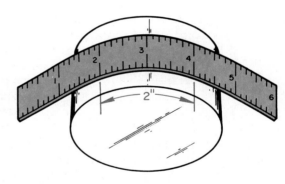

Fig. 12-1 Using a surface plate of black granite to help measure a workpiece accurately.

Fig. 12-2 Steel rules used in layout work. (A) U.S. Customary inch rules. (B) A metric rule. (L.S. Starrett Co.)

place the workpiece. Precision layout tools can then be used to accurately mark the layout lines needed on the workpiece.

The surface plate is an expensive piece of equipment. It should be used with care so that its finished surface will not be nicked or scratched. A small nick may keep the work or layout tools from lying perfectly flat and could cause errors in the layout. When the surface plate is not in use, the finished surface should be protected with a **wooden cover.** Iron surface plates should be kept lightly oiled to keep them from rusting.

Fig. 12-3 Measuring with a flexible rule.

12-2
Steel Rules

Steel rules (Fig. 12-2) are made in many lengths, widths, and thicknesses. The most commonly used steel rule is 6" [150 mm] long but lengths to 4' [1200 mm] are common. Because steel rules are used to make accurate measurements, they should be handled with care.

A thin, springy rule called a **flexible steel rule** is used to measure curves (Fig. 12-3). The use of a **hook rule** is shown in Figure 13-2. Unit 11 explains the **decimal rule,** and the **shrink rule,** used by patternmakers, is explained in Unit 32. More information about measuring with a steel rule can be found in Unit 13.

12-3
Combination Set

The combination set (Fig. 12-4) includes a **square** (or **combination**) **head, center head, bevel protractor, spirit level, steel rule,** and **scriber.** The rule, or **blade,** may be fastened quickly to each of the first three. The beginner should ask the instructor how this is done so that the small parts are not lost or damaged.

Figures 12-5, 13-3, 13-6, and 13-7 show a few of the uses of the steel rule when the square head, bevel protractor, or center head is

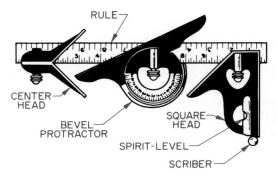

Fig. 12-4 *A combination set.*

fastened to it. **The combination square** is the most often used part of the combination set. It has many uses (Fig. 12-5; also Figs. 12-21 and 13-6). Note that 45° and 90° can be measured with it. Its **squareness** should be tested as shown in Figure 12-10.

The **center head,** because it forms a **right, or 90° angle,** may be used to extend a line around a corner (Fig. 12-6).

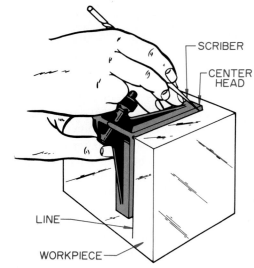

Fig. 12-6 *Using a center head to extend a line around a corner.*

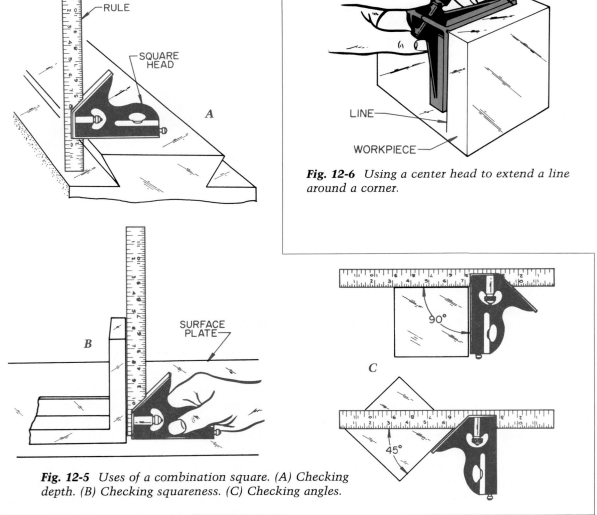

Fig. 12-5 *Uses of a combination square. (A) Checking depth. (B) Checking squareness. (C) Checking angles.*

With the steel rule fastened to it, the center head is called a **center square.** It is used to find the center of circles. See Fig. 13-7.

The **bevel protractor** (Fig. 12-7) is divided into **degrees** and with the rule fastened to it, any **angle** can be measured (Fig. 13-3).

A **spirit level** is usually fitted into the **bevel protractor** and the **head** of the combination square to help in **leveling** the work or setting it at an **angle.**

Test the squareness of any square by placing the **beam** of the square against a straight edge (Fig. 12-10). While holding the square in this position, mark a line along the edge of the blade with a scriber. Then turn the square over as shown by the dotted lines and see if the blade lines up with the first line.

12-4

Solid Steel Square

This square has a fixed blade (Fig. 12-8). It is more accurately square than the combination square, which, if its sliding parts are worn, may become inaccurate. The uses of the solid steel square are shown in Figure 12-9.

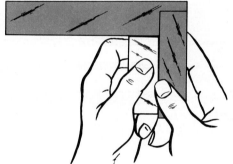

Fig. 12-7 *Setting work at an angle with a spirit level on a bevel protractor.*

Fig. 12-9 *Using the solid steel square to check squareness.*

Fig. 12-10 *Testing the squareness of a square.*

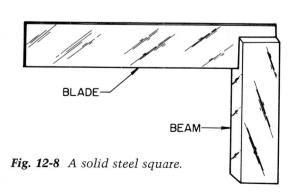

Fig. 12-8 *A solid steel square.*

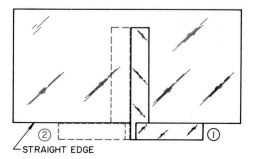

12-5 Scribers

Scribers are hardened steel marking tools that have sharp needle-like points (Fig. 12-11). They are used to scratch, or **scribe,** lines on metal.

12-6 Dividers

Dividers are two-legged steel instruments with hardened points (Fig. 12-12). Their size is measured by the greatest distance they can be opened between the two points. Thus, 6″ [152 mm] dividers open 6″ between the points. Dividers are used to scribe circles and arcs (Fig. 13-9), to lay off distances (Fig. 13-10), and to

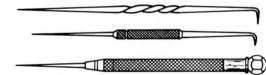

Fig. 12-11 *Scribers.*

measure distances. (See also Figs. 13-11, 13-12, and 13-13). On many steel rules, the graduations are cut deeply enough to allow dividers to be set from them (see Fig. 13-8).

12-7 Trammels

A large circle or an **arc** may be scribed with a tool called a **trammel** (Fig. 12-13). It is sometimes called a **beam compass** or **beam trammel,** and may also be used to measure distances in the same way that dividers are used.

12-8 Outside Calipers

An outside caliper is a two-legged steel instrument with its legs curved inward (Fig. 12-12). Its size is measured by the greatest distance it can be opened. It is used to measure the outside diameters of round objects and to measure widths and thicknesses of materials (Fig. 12-14). The distance between the legs is then measured with a rule (Fig. 12-15).

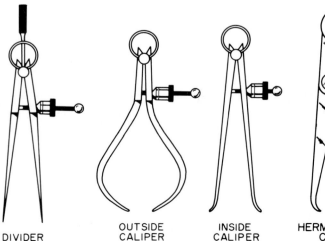

DIVIDER   OUTSIDE CALIPER   INSIDE CALIPER   HERMAPHRODITE CALIPER

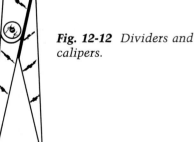

Fig. 12-12 *Dividers and calipers.*

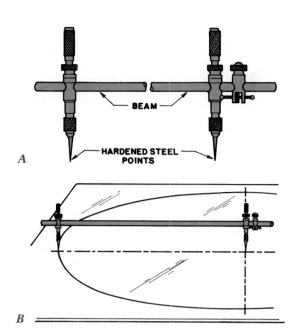

BEAM

HARDENED STEEL POINTS

A

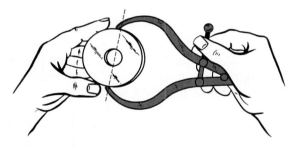

B

Fig. 12-13 *Trammels are used in the layout of large arcs and circles. (A) Parts of a trammel. (B) Using a trammel to scribe a circle.*

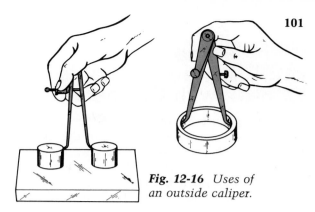

Fig. 12-16 *Uses of an outside caliper.*

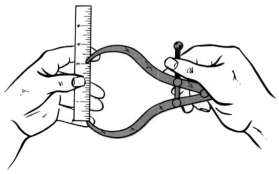

Fig. 12-14 *Using an outside caliper to measure an outside diameter.*

Fig. 12-15 *Setting or measuring an outside caliper against a steel rule.*

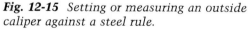

FLAT SURFACE

Fig. 12-17 *Setting or measuring an inside caliper against a steel rule.*

To set an outside caliper to a certain size, place a finger behind the end of the steel rule to keep the leg from slipping off. Then, set the other leg of the caliper to the size wanted (Fig. 12-15).

12-9

Inside Calipers

An inside caliper is a two-legged steel instrument with its legs curved outward (Fig. 12-12). It is used to measure the diameter of holes or to measure spaces (Fig. 12-16). The distance between the two legs is then measured on the rule (Fig. 12-17).

To set an inside caliper to a certain size, hold the end of the steel rule against a flat metal surface and then set the caliper (Fig. 12-17).

12-10 Fine Measurements with Calipers

Fine measurements with calipers depend upon the sense of **touch,** or **feel,** in the finger-tips. The caliper should, therefore, be held gently with the fingertips. Its legs should be moved slowly until both of them just touch the inner or outer sides of the object being measured. It is very easy to spring or bend the legs, thus obtaining a wrong measurement.

12-11 Transferring a Measurement from One Caliper to Another

To transfer a measurement from an inside caliper to an outside caliper, or vice versa, hold the caliper which already has the measurement in one hand and the caliper to be set in the other hand. Adjust the caliper to be set to the size of the one that already has the correct measurement (Fig. 12-18).

12-12 Hermaphrodite Calipers

The hermaphrodite caliper has one pointed leg like a divider and one bent leg (Fig. 12-12). It is used to find the center on the end of a round bar (Fig. 13-21), and to scribe lines **parallel** to the edge of a workpiece (Fig. 13-22).

12-13 Punches

The **prick punch** is a sharply pointed tool of **hardened steel** (Fig. 12-19). It is used to accurately define points to be **center-punched** as well as to put small **punch marks** on layout lines so they will last longer.

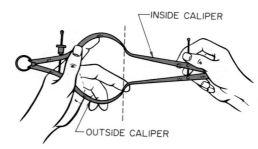

Fig. 12-18 *Transferring a measurement from one caliper to another.*

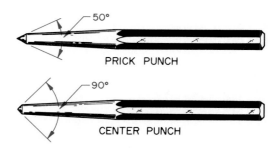

Fig. 12-19 *The difference between a prick punch and a center punch.*

The **center punch** looks like a prick punch (See Fig. 12-19). It is usually larger than the prick punch and has a 90° point.

The center punch is used to make prick punch marks larger at the centers of holes that are to be drilled, hence the name center punch.

12-14 Machinist's Hammer

The **head** of a machinist's hammer has a ball-shaped end, a **peen;** thus it is called a **ball-peen hammer** (Fig. 12-20). The face and peen are hardened steel; the steel in the middle, which surrounds the eye, or hole, for the handle, is left soft. The heads of machinist's hammers weigh from 1 ounce [28.35 grams] to 3 pounds [1.36 kg]. For layout work, a hammer weighing from two to six ounces [58 to 85 grams] should be used.

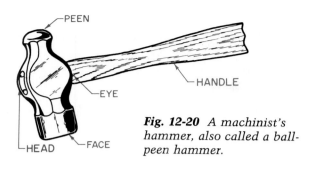

Fig. 12-20 *A machinist's hammer, also called a ball-peen hammer.*

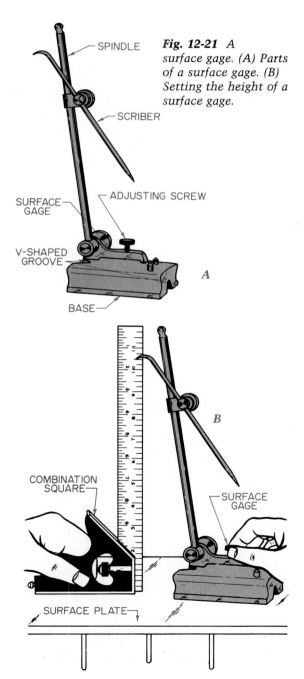

Fig. 12-21 *A surface gage. (A) Parts of a surface gage. (B) Setting the height of a surface gage.*

Surface Gage

The **surface gage** has a heavy, flat **base** carrying a **spindle** that may be set at any angle (Fig. 12-21A). Clamped to the spindle is a **scriber,** which may also be set at any angle or at any height. The **adjusting screw** is used for fine setting of the scriber. The height of the point of the scriber may be measured with a rule (Fig. 12-21B). The surface gage is used either to scribe layout lines or to measure heights (Fig. 12-22). The V-shaped grooves at one end and at the bottom make it useful on or against round work.

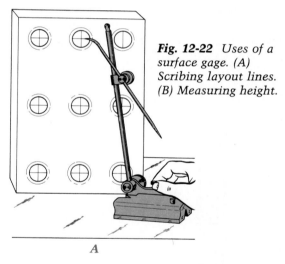

Fig. 12-22 *Uses of a surface gage. (A) Scribing layout lines. (B) Measuring height.*

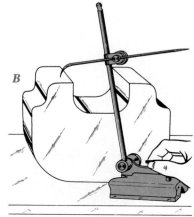

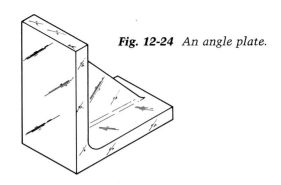

Fig. 12-24 *An angle plate.*

Vernier Height Gage

The **vernier height gage** (Fig. 12-23) may be used for the same kinds of layout work as the surface gage. It is a precision layout tool that utilizes beam graduations and a special movable scale called a **vernier** or **vernier scale.** The vernier height gage can provide positioning of the scriber to an accuracy of one-thousandth of an inch [0.025 mm]. Unit 14 explains how to read vernier scales.

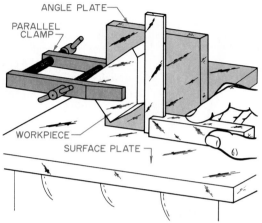

12-17

Angle Plate

The **angle plate** has two surfaces that are at 90° to each other (Fig. 12-24). It is often necessary to clamp a workpiece to an angle plate (Fig. 12-25) to work with it.

Fig. 12-25 *Using a parallel clamp and an angle plate in layout work.*

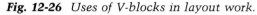

Fig. 12-26 *Uses of V-blocks in layout work.*

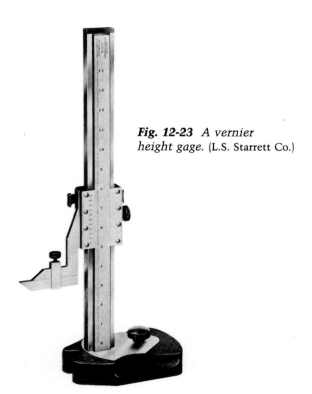

Fig. 12-23 *A vernier height gage.* (L.S. Starrett Co.)

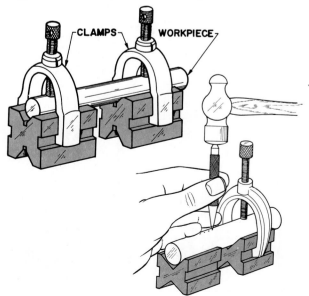

12-18 Parallel Clamp

The **parallel clamp**, also called a **tool-maker's clamp** is often used to hold parts together or to hold the work against an angle plate while laying it out (Fig. 12-25). Keep the jaws **parallel** to the surfaces of the workpiece being clamped.

12-19 V-Blocks

Blocks of steel with V-shaped grooves (Fig. 12-26) are used to hold round work for laying out. These **V-blocks** are usually made in matched pairs and come with clamps to hold the workpiece in the 90° V-groove.

REVIEW REVIEW REVIEW REVIEW REVIEW

WORDS TO KNOW

angle plate	dividers	outside caliper	surface plate
ball-peen hammer	graduation	parallel clamp	toolmaker's clamp
beam compass	hermaphrodite	prick punch	trammel
bevel protractor	caliper	right angle	V-block
center head	hook rule	scriber	vernier height gage
center punch	inside caliper	solid steel square	
combination set	machinist's	spirit level	
combination square	hammer	surface gage	

REVIEW QUESTIONS

1. What kind of work is layout work?
2. What is a surface plate used for?
3. How should the surface plate be protected when not in use? Why should it be protected?
4. What kinds of graduations are found on inch steel rules? Metric steel rules?
5. Name the parts of the combination set.
6. What two angles can be measured with a combination square?
7. Why is a solid steel square more exact than a combination square?
8. What is a scriber? What is it used for?
9. What are dividers? What are they used for?
10. Describe a trammel. What is it used for?
11. Describe an outside caliper. What is it used for?
12. What is an inside caliper used for?
13. Describe the hermaphrodite caliper. What is it used for?
14. What is the difference between a prick punch and a center punch? What is each used for?
15. Describe the surface gage. What is it used for?
16. What is a vernier height gage used for?
17. What is an angle plate? What is it used for?
18. Describe the V-block. What is the main use for V-blocks?

UNIT 13

Layout Techniques

The layout worker uses layout tools to transfer information accurately from working drawings to the work material. Any mistake in the layout means that the workpiece may be made incorrectly. Mistakes made in layout cause waste, either in labor or materials, and are therefore very expensive. Check and recheck all layout work against the working drawings before cutting or other work begins.

Fig. 13-1 *Two ways to apply layout fluid.*

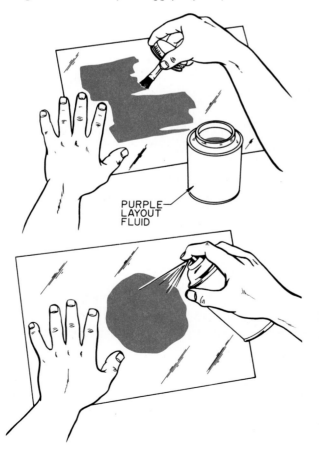

PURPLE LAYOUT FLUID

13-1 Coloring Metal for Layout

The first step in layout work is to color the surface on which you will draw the lines. This is done so that the scribed lines will show up more clearly than lines scribed on the bare metal. **Layout fluids** of different colors are made especially for layout work. The metal is first rubbed clean and then the fluid is brushed or sprayed on (Fig. 13-1). It dries quickly. Use steel wool or alcohol to remove the dried layout fluid after finishing the workpiece.

13-2 Measuring with Steel Rules

To measure with a steel rule, put the **edge** of the rule against the work so that the lines on the rule touch the work (Fig. 13-2). The **graduation** lines on the rule have a certain width. Always measure to the center of a line. Measure from the 1″ mark or from the 10 mm mark on a metric rule because the end of the rule may be worn.

13-3

Scribing Lines

After the layout fluid has dried on the metal surface, the layout can be made. To draw a straight line, place the steel rule, **square,** or **bevel protractor** in the correct posi-

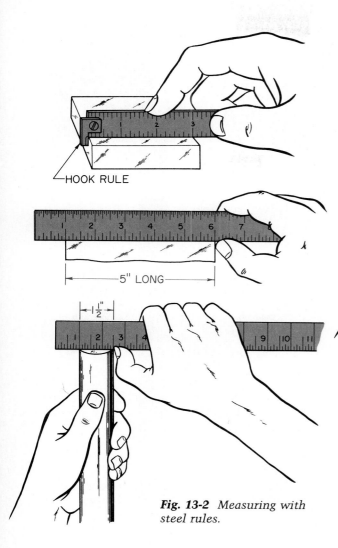

HOOK RULE

5" LONG

Fig. 13-2 *Measuring with steel rules.*

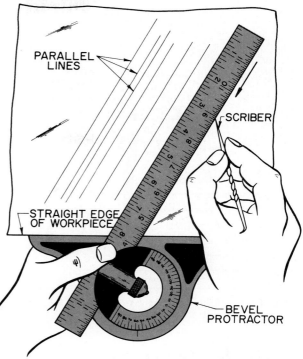

PARALLEL LINES

SCRIBER

STRAIGHT EDGE OF WORKPIECE

BEVEL PROTRACTOR

Fig. 13-3 *Scribing 57° lines, using a bevel protractor.*

RULE — SCRIBER

WORKPIECE

Fig. 13-4 *When scribing lines, slant the scriber so the point follows the lower edge of the rule.*

tion and hold it against the work with one hand (Fig. 13-3). Use a sharp scriber and be sure to lean it to one side so that the point will draw along the lower edge of the rule (Fig. 13-4).

13-4 Prick-Punching

The layout fluid and the scribed lines of a layout may wear off if the workpiece is handled much. The lines may be **prick-punched** to make them last longer. The point of the prick punch should be placed exactly on the line, held squarely on the surface, and struck lightly with the hammer (Fig. 13-5). The prick-punch marks should be closer together on curved lines than on straight lines.

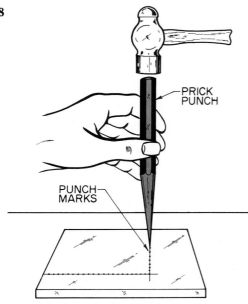

Fig. 13-5 *Prick-punching a line.*

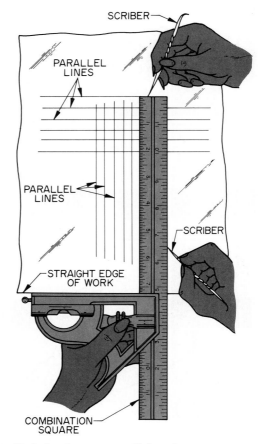

Fig. 13-6 *Laying out parallel and perpendicular lines with a combination square when the work has only one straight edge.*

Fig. 13-7 *Using a center square to find the center of a round workpiece.*

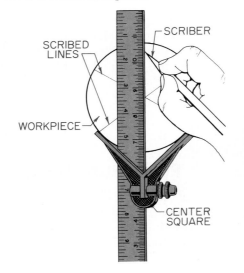

13-5 Using the Combination Set for Layout

The **combination square** is very useful for laying out lines that are either parallel to or **square with** a straight edge (Fig. 13-6). It is also useful for marking or checking 45° angles (Fig. 12-5).

The **bevel protractor** makes it possible to lay out or check an angle of any size (Fig. 13-3).

The **center square** may be used to find the center of a round piece of metal. Three lines about 60° apart should be drawn as in Figure 13-7.

13-6 Using the Dividers for Layout

Setting the dividers to a certain size is shown in Figure 13-8. To make a circle, set the dividers to the size of the **radius,** half the **diameter** desired. The V-shape of the steel rule graduations helps to set the points of the dividers accurately.

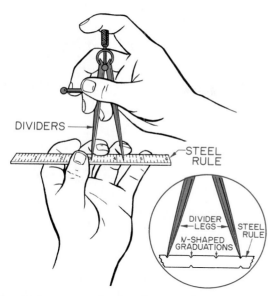

Fig. 13-8 *Setting the dividers to a known dimension.*

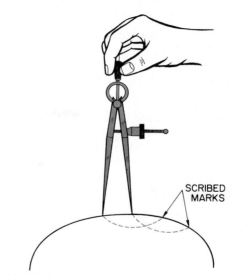

Fig. 13-10 *Laying out equal distances with the dividers.*

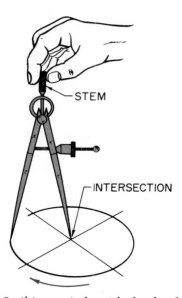

Fig. 13-9 *Scribing a circle with the dividers.*

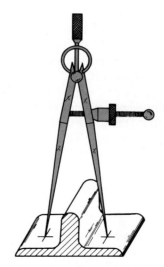

Fig. 13-11 *Measuring distances with the dividers.*

To scribe a circle with the dividers: Hold the dividers by the **stem** (Fig. 13-9). Place the point of one leg in the prick-punch mark at the intersection of the layout lines. Then swing the other leg in a circle.

Laying out equal distances with dividers is shown in Figure 13-10.

Measuring with the dividers: Each leg is placed at the intersection of two layout lines (Fig. 13-11). A steel rule is then used to measure the distance between the divider points. The dividers are useful for obtaining measurements that cannot be made directly with a steel rule.

Figure 13-12 shows how the dividers are used to measure the approximate length of a **curve** or a **scroll**. This is done by setting the dividers to a known distance, say 1″ [25 mm].

Then, step it off along the **center line** of the curve or scroll and count the number of steps. When a metal curve is bent, the outside of the metal stretches and the inside squeezes together, but the center-line does not change.

Finding the center of a circle: Put four small prick-punch marks on the **circumference.** Then, with the dividers set as near as possible to the **radius** of the circle, scribe four arcs (Fig. 13-13). The center of the circle is equally distant from each of the four arcs.

Sometimes the center of a circle is in a hole. To find the center of a hole, cut a piece of soft wood to fit across the hole (Fig. 13-14). A tack or a small piece of tin, with corners bent down like spurs, is then driven into the wood. The center may then be found with the **center square** or **four-arc method.**

Finding the center of an arc: Suppose that the arc **XY** in Figure 13-15 is already on the metal surface and that it is necessary to locate its center. To find the center of the arc:

1. Place three prick-punch marks **A, B,** and **C** anywhere on the arc **XY.**
2. With the dividers, scribe three arcs of the same radius from points **A, B,** and **C.**
3. Scribe lines **DE** and **FG** through the **intersections** of the arcs. The intersection at **O** is the center of the arc **XY.**

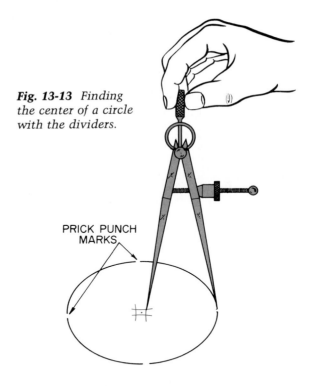

Fig. 13-13 *Finding the center of a circle with the dividers.*

PRICK PUNCH MARKS

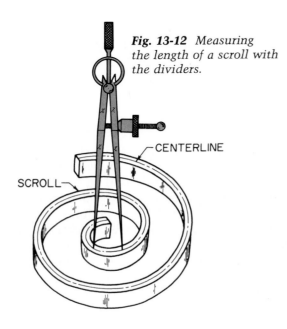

Fig. 13-12 *Measuring the length of a scroll with the dividers.*

CENTERLINE

SCROLL

Laying out parallel lines with the dividers: Suppose that the line **AB** (Fig. 13-16) is already on the metal surface and that it is necessary to draw the line **CD** parallel to **AB** and at a given distance from it:

1. Place small prick-punch marks at **E** and **F** near the ends of line **AB.**
2. Set the dividers to the distance that the two lines are to be apart.
3. With one leg of the dividers set at **E,** draw the arc **GH.**
4. With the same setting of the dividers and with **F** as a center, draw the arc **KL.**
5. Draw the line **CD tangent** to the arcs **GH** and **KL,** that is, touching each arc at one point.

The line **CD** is parallel to the line **AB** and is the given distance from **AB.**

Laying out a perpendicular line from a point to a line: Lines that form **right angles** (90 degrees) with each other are called **perpendicular lines** (Fig. 13-17). Suppose that the line **AB** and the point **C** in Figure 13-18 are already on the metal surface and that it is necessary to draw a perpendicular through point **C** to line **AB:**

1. Prick-punch point **C** lightly.
2. With the dividers set at any distance and with **C** as a center, scribe arcs crossing the line **AB** as at **D** and **E**.
3. Prick-punch lightly at **D** and **E**.
4. With **D** and **E** as centers, scribe arcs that cross at **F**.

The line drawn through the points **C** and **F** is perpendicular to the line **AB**.

Laying out a perpendicular line through a point on a line: Suppose that the line **AB** in Figure 13-19 is already on the metal surface and that it is necessary to draw a **perpendicular** through the point **C**, which is on line **AB**:

1. Prick-punch point **C** lightly.
2. With the divider set at any distance and with **C** as a center, scribe arcs crossing the line **AB** as at **D** and **E**.
3. Prick-punch lightly at **D** and **E**.

Fig. 13-16 *Laying out parallel lines with dividers.*

Fig. 13-17 *Perpendicular lines (all angles are 90°).*

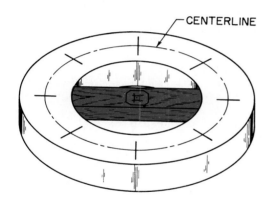

Fig. 13-14 *Bridging a hole to locate its center.*

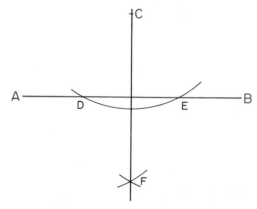

Fig. 13-18 *Drawing a perpendicular line from a point on a line, using dividers.*

Fig. 13-15 *Finding the center of an arc with dividers.*

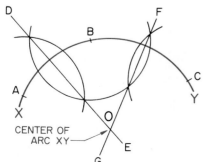

Fig. 13-19 *Drawing a perpendicular line through a point on a line, using dividers.*

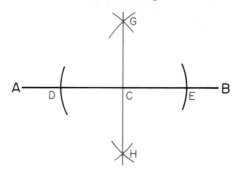

4. With **D** and **E** as centers and with the dividers set at a greater distance than before, scribe arcs that cross at **G** and **H**.

The line drawn through the points **G** and **H** also passes through the point **C** and is perpendicular to the line **AB**.

Bisecting an angle: Bisect means to cut or divide into **two** equal parts. Thus, to bisect an angle means to divide the angle into two equal angles.

Suppose that the angle **AOB** in Figure 13-20 is on the metal surface and it is necessary to bisect it:

1. Prick-punch lightly at **O**.
2. With the dividers set at any distance and with **O** as a center, draw arcs intersecting the angle lines, as at **C** and **D**.
3. Prick-punch lightly at **C** and **D**.
4. Then with **C** and **D** as centers, draw arcs that cross each other, as at **E**.

The line drawn through the points **E** and **O** bisects the angle **AOB**.

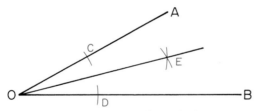

Fig. 13-20 *Bisecting an angle with dividers.*

13-7 Using the Hermaphrodite Caliper

Finding the center on the end of a round bar: Set the hermaphrodite caliper to the approximate radius of the bar and scribe four arcs (Fig. 13-21).

Laying out parallel lines: The caliper is first set the proper distance from the edge to the line to be inscribed. Hold the bent leg against the edge of the work and as the caliper is moved along, the pointed leg draws a line on the surface parallel to the edge of the work (Fig. 13-22).

Fig. 13-22
Scribing lines parallel to an edge with a hermaphrodite caliper.

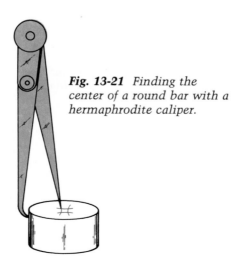

Fig. 13-21 *Finding the center of a round bar with a hermaphrodite caliper.*

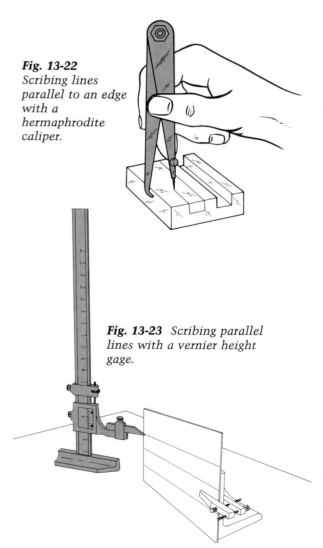

Fig. 13-23 *Scribing parallel lines with a vernier height gage.*

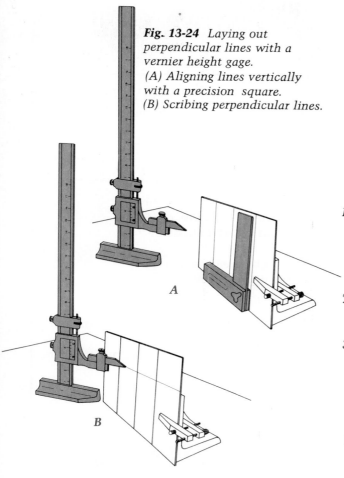

Fig. 13-24 *Laying out perpendicular lines with a vernier height gage.*
(A) Aligning lines vertically with a precision square.
(B) Scribing perpendicular lines.

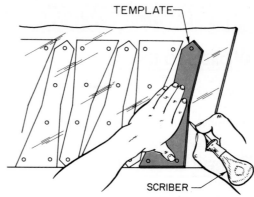

Fig. 13-25 *Laying out work with a template.*

2. Set the vernier to the correct reading for the first line and scribe it. (Vernier reading is covered in Unit 14.)
3. Reset the vernier to the reading required for the next line and scribe it. The line will automatically be parallel to the line already drawn. If more parallel lines are needed, continue as in Step 3.

Layout of perpendicular lines:

1. First lay out the lines required in one direction, following the procedure outlined for parallel lines above.
2. Turn the workpiece and, using a precision square, align the lines vertically (Fig. 13-24). Clamp the workpiece in this position. Any line now drawn parallel to the surface plate will be perpendicular to the lines already scribed.

13-8 Laying Out Lines with a Vernier Height Gage

Layout of parallel lines: The vernier height gage is always used on a precision flat surface such as a surface plate. Hence, all lines drawn by its scriber as it is moved across the flat surface will be parallel to that surface (Fig 13-23). To scribe parallel lines on a workpiece accurately, use the following procedure:

1. Make certain the workpiece rests firmly on the surface plate. If it "rocks," shim it, hold it in a vise, or clamp it to an angle plate. (A shim is a piece of very thin metal or other material. Use one or more shims to fill the space between the surface plate and the uneven bottom of a workpiece.)

13-9 Using a Template

A **template** is a pattern for marking the shape of a work piece or for marking holes or other features. It is usually made of sheet metal, and is useful when many duplicate pieces have to be laid out (Fig. 13-25). The template is laid on the work; then the lines, circles, or arcs are marked with a scriber.

REVIEW   REVIEW   REVIEW   REVIEW   REVIEW

WORDS TO KNOW

align	layout fluid	perpendicular line	scroll
bisect	parallel line	"square with"	template
intersect			

REVIEW QUESTIONS

1. Explain why accurate layout work is so important.
2. Why should the surface for a layout be colored with layout fluid?
3. After it has dried, how is layout fluid removed from a metal surface?
4. How can lines be made to last longer on a layout?
5. How should a steel rule be placed on the work when measuring?
6. Describe one method of locating the center of the end of a round rod.
7. How can you find the center of a hole in a plate?
8. What does "bisect" mean?
9. Describe the procedure for scribing parallel and perpendicular lines with a combination square on work that has only one straight edge.
10. Describe the procedure for scribing parallel and perpendicular lines with a vernier height gage.
11. What is a template? When is it used the most?

UNIT
14
Micrometers and Verniers

Micrometers, called "mikes" for short, are instruments that make very fine measurements. The full name is **micrometer caliper.** Micrometers made originally for use in the United States measure in thousandths of an inch (¹⁄₁₀₀₀″); some measure as fine as one ten-thousandth of an inch (¹⁄₁₀,₀₀₀″). Micrometers for the SI metric system measure either to one hundredth of a millimeter [¹⁄₁₀₀ mm] or to two thousandths of a millimeter [²⁄₁₀₀₀ mm]. The **vernier** devices on micrometers make these fine measurements possible.

14-1   Parts of a Micrometer

A micrometer (Fig. 14-1) has a **frame, sleeve, thimble, spindle,** and **anvil.** The opening between the anvil and the spindle is made smaller or larger by turning the thimble. The size of the opening is read on the sleeve and the thimble. The **lock nut** locks the spindle so that it will not turn.

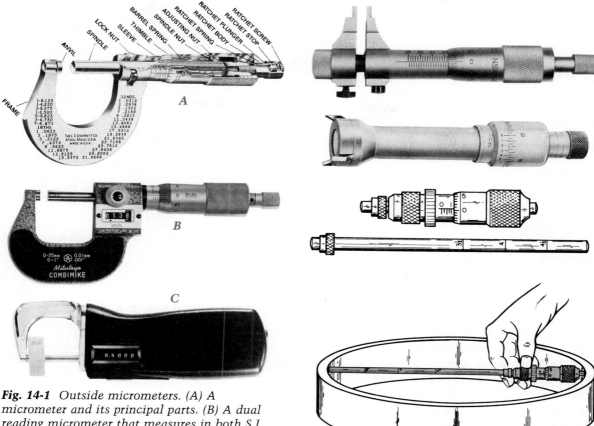

Fig. 14-1 *Outside micrometers. (A) A micrometer and its principal parts. (B) A dual reading micrometer that measures in both S.I. Metric units and U.S. Customary units. (C) An electronic direct reading micrometer. (MTI Corporation) (Quality Measurement Systems)*

Fig. 14-2 *Inside micrometers. (Yamazen USA, Inc) (Lufkin Rule Co.)*

14-2 Kinds and Sizes of Micrometers

The **outside micrometer** is used the most often. A conventional outside micrometer is shown in Figure 14-1A. **Dual reading** (metric/inch) and **direct reading** micrometers are also made (Fig. 14-1B and C). The outside micrometer is used to measure the outside diameters of round objects and the widths and thicknesses of flat pieces.

Inside micrometers are used to measure the diameters of openings (Fig. 14-2).

The **depth micrometer** is used to measure the depths of holes, grooves, and slots (Fig. 14-3).

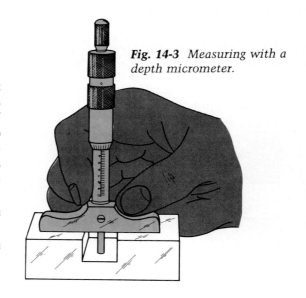

Fig. 14-3 *Measuring with a depth micrometer.*

The **screw thread micrometer** (Fig. 14-4) is used to measure the pitch diameter of screw threads.

Many other special purpose micrometers are also made.

Outside micrometers are made in many sizes (Fig. 14-5). They are identified by the maximum size they can measure; thus:

1. a 1″ [25 mm] micrometer measures from 0″ to 1″ [0–25 mm].
2. a 2″ [50 mm] micrometer measures from 1″ to 2″ [25–50 mm].

14-3 Care of Micrometers

The micrometer is a fine instrument and should be handled as carefully as an expensive watch. Dropping it on the floor or bench may damage its fine parts and make it useless. Keep it away from dust, grit, and grease. It should never be twirled. The spindle should never be left screwed tight against the anvil when not in use (Fig. 14-6). Changes in temperature cause the spindle to expand and shrink. Such changes may strain the micrometer so that it will not measure correctly.

Clean and lubricate micrometers with a light machine oil before storing them.

Precise measurements with micrometers depend on the user's sense of touch or feel. No

Fig. 14-4 Using a thread micrometer to measure the pitch diameter of a screw thread. The drawing shows the anvil and the spindle in position in respect to line AB, which corresponds to a zero reading. (L.S. Starrett Company)

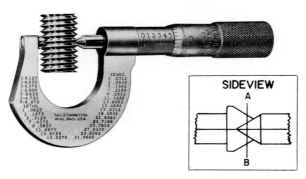

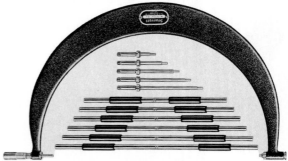

Fig. 14-5 A micrometer set that is used for measuring dimensions from 1″ to 24″ (24-600 mm). (L.S. Starrett Company)

two persons' touches are alike. If one person's touch is heavy and another person's touch is light, there will be a difference in the two measurements of the same piece.

Because of this problem, some micrometers have a **ratchet stop** or a **friction stop** (Fig. 14-1A) at the end of the thimble. This assures that metalworkers always use the same pressure in making measurements, no matter who uses the micrometer.

Fig. 14-6 Testing the accuracy of a 1″ micrometer. Never leave the spindle screwed tight against the anvil when the micrometer is not in use.

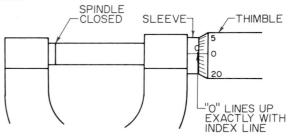

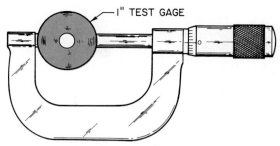

Fig. 14-7 *Testing the accuracy of a 2"
micrometer. The micrometer should read exactly
1".*

14-4 Testing the Accuracy of Micrometers

1" [25 mm] micrometers: Close the micrometer completely with the correct amount of pressure. The faces of the anvil and thimble should be in slight, firm contact. If the micrometer is set correctly, the **O** mark on the thimble will line up exactly with the **index** line running the length of the sleeve or barrel (Fig. 14-6).

Wear on the anvil or the **screw** sometimes makes it necessary to reset the micrometer. This is done by various methods, depending on the make of the micrometer. It is best to learn how to reset a micrometer from the instructions in the manufacturer's manual or catalogue. (In some cases it may be necessary to return the "mike" to the manufacturer.)

2" [50 mm] or larger micrometers: To test these micrometers, use a **gage** or **standard** of known size and set the micrometer to this size (Fig. 14-7).

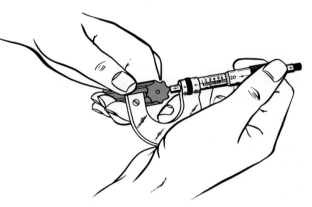

Fig. 14-8 *Holding a micrometer in one hand to
measure work held in the other hand.*

14-5 Holding a Micrometer to Measure Work Held in the Hand

Hold the work to be measured in one hand. Hold the micrometer in the other hand with the third or little finger pressing the **frame** against your palm (Fig. 14-8). This leaves the thumb and first finger free to turn the thimble.

Open the micrometer wide enough to place the work between the anvil and the spindle, then turn the thimble until a very slight pressure is felt.

Beginners need to develop a delicate sense of touch for using micrometers. A micrometer may easily be sprung .001" [.025 mm] or more by too much pressure. This gives the wrong measurement and may damage the instrument. If available, use a micrometer with a ratchet or friction stop.

14-6 How to Read Micrometers

Plain inch micrometers are designed to measure accurately to 0.001" (one-thousandth of an inch). Their spindles are made with 40 threads to the inch. Therefore, the thimble, which is locked to the spindle, must be revolved 40 times in order to move the spindle one inch. Each revolution of the thimble, then, moves the spindle 1/40th of an inch or 0.025":

$$40\overline{)1.000} \quad .025$$

The markings on the sleeve equal one revolution of the thimble, or 0.025". Every fourth line is a little longer and is marked 1, 2, 3, to 10, which stands for 0.100", 0.200", 0.300", to 1.000" (Fig. 14-9).

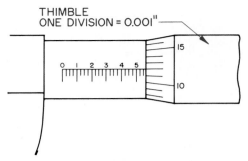

1. Five numbered graduations on the sleeve represent   0.500″
2. Two additional lines are exposed, each representing 0.025″   0.050″
3. The twelfth line on the thimble is lined up with the index line on the sleeve, each line representing 0.001″   0.012″
   Total Reading   **0.562″**

Fig. 14-9 *Graduations on the thimble and sleeve of a 1″ micrometer.*

Fig. 14-10 *Micrometer readings of basic micrometer divisions: (A) one thousandth of an inch (.001″), (B) five-thousandths of an inch (.005″), (C) twenty-five thousandths of an inch (.025″).*

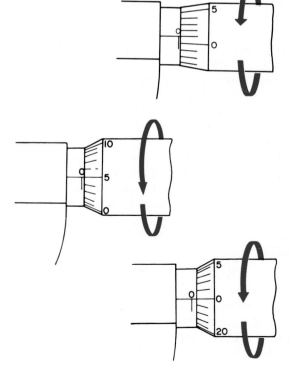

By marking the thimble with 25 equal divisions, each mark on the thimble becomes ¹⁄₂₅th of a revolution or 0.001″ (one-thousandth of an inch). A 0.001″ micrometer reading appears as in Figure 14-10A. A 0.005″ reading looks like Figure 14-10B. For each full turn of the thimble, it moves over one mark on the sleeve or 0.025″ (Fig. 14-10C).

Note the explanation of the micrometer reading in Figure 14-9. Additional inch micrometer readings are shown in Figure 14-11.

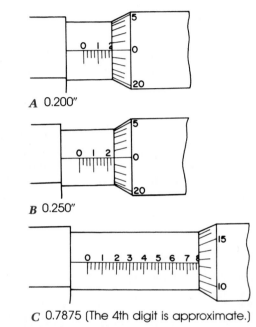

A 0.200″

B 0.250″

C 0.7875 (The 4th digit is approximate.)

Fig. 14-11 *Readings on an inch micrometer.*

Fig. 14-12 *The vernier scale of an inch micrometer.*

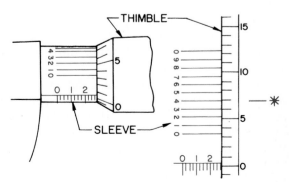

Some micrometers have a **vernier,** named after the inventor, Pierre Vernier. **Inch vernier micrometers** can be read to a ten-thousandth of an inch (1/10,000″ or .0001″). Again, each mark on the thimble is .001″. The ten divisions on the **back of the sleeve** are the vernier; the lines are numbered 0, 1, 2, 3, 4, 5, 6, 7, 8, 9, 0, as in Figure 14-12. These lines have the same space as nine divisions on the thimble.

To read the vernier micrometer, first read the thousandths as on any ordinary micrometer. Suppose that this number is between .275 and .276, as in Figure 14-12. To find the fourth decimal place, find the line on the vernier that most nearly matches a line on the thimble. In this case it is the line 4; this number 4 means 4 ten-thousandths inches (.0004″), and added to the .275″, it gives the fourth decimal place. Thus, the complete reading is .2754″ (.275 + .0004″ = .2754″).

Plain metric micrometers (Fig. 14-13) are read in much the same manner as plain inch micrometers. Their spindles have 50 threads per 25 millimeters. Therefore, two revolutions of the spindle are required to move the spindle one millimeter. Since the thimble of the metric micrometer is graduated in 50 equal divisions, and two revolutions of the thimble are required to move one millimeter, the degree of precision obtained is 0.01 mm (1/100th of a millimeter).

Note that the sleeve of the metric micrometer has both an upper and a lower set of graduations (Fig. 14-14). The upper set consists of 25 graduations, one millimeter apart, with each fifth millimeter being numbered. The lower set of graduations divides each of the upper set in two, providing 0.5 mm graduations.

Note how the metric micrometer reading of 5.78 mm is obtained in Figure 14-14.

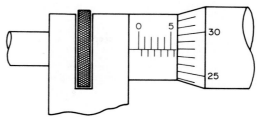

1. Upper sleeve reading (whole millimeters)   5.00 mm
2. Lower sleeve reading (half millimeters)   0.50 mm
3. Thimble reading (hundredths of a millimeter)   0.28 mm

Total Reading   **5.78 mm**

Fig. 14-14 *Graduations on a metric micrometer.*

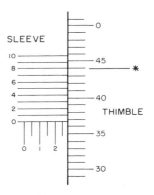

Fig. 14-15 *Graduations on a metric vernier micrometer. The reading is 2.868. The colored starred line indicates the matching line of 0.008 mm.*

The **vernier metric micrometer** is designed for measuring to 0.002 mm (two-thousandths of a millimeter). The vernier is placed on the sleeve above the usual graduations just as with vernier inch micrometers (Fig. 14-15).

14-7 Vernier Measuring Tools

Linear vernier measuring tools also make measurements accurately to one-thousandth of an inch. Unlike the micrometer, a **vernier caliper** (Fig. 14-16) can make both outside and

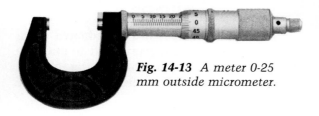

Fig. 14-13 *A meter 0-25 mm outside micrometer.*

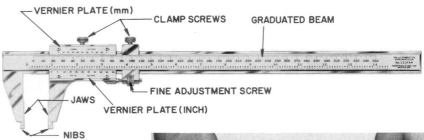

Fig. 14-16 A vernier caliper with dual inch/ metric graduations. (L.S. Starrett Company)

inside measurements (Figs. 14-17 and 14-18). Some vernier calipers also can measure depths. Inch vernier calipers are made in standard lengths of 6″, 12″, 24″, 36″, and 48″ [150, 300, 600, 900, and 1200 mm].

The **vernier height gage,** equipped with a straight or offset scriber, is often used for precision layout work (Fig. 14-19). It is also used with a dial indicator for inspecting completed work. Vernier height gages are made in standard sizes of 12″, 18″, and 24″ [300, 460, and 600 mm]. Larger sizes are also made.

A **vernier depth gage** (Fig. 14-20), like the depth micrometer, is used for measuring hole and slot depths and the distance between parallel surfaces.

The **vernier gear tooth caliper** is used for measuring the accuracy of gear teeth. It may also be used to measure some form cutters and threading tools (Fig. 14-21).

The **vernier bevel protractor** (Fig. 14-22) is a precision tool used for layout and measurement of precise angles.

Fig. 14-17 Making an outside measurement with a vernier caliper. (Manual High School, Roger Bean)

Fig. 14-18 Making an inside measurement with a vernier caliper. (L.S. Starrett Company)

14-8 Care of Vernier Tools

Vernier tools are fine instruments and deserve the finest care. Keep them free of grime and grit by wiping them after each use with a soft lint-free cloth. Never force them when making measurements. They should be periodically checked for accuracy against measurement standards of known size. When not in use, they should be stored in a suitable case.

14-9 Using the Vernier Caliper

The vernier caliper has a **graduated beam** with a **fixed measuring jaw** and a **movable jaw.** There is also a mechanism for making fine adjustments and a **vernier scale** on the movable jaw (Fig. 14-16).

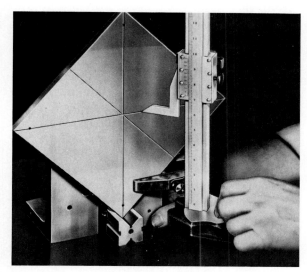

Fig. 14-19 *Precision layout with a vernier height gage.* (L.S. Starrett Company)

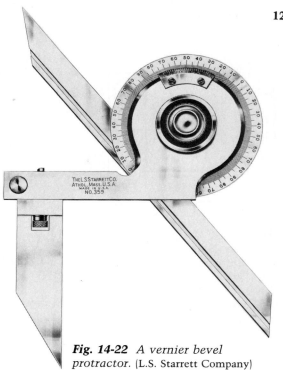

Fig. 14-22 *A vernier bevel protractor.* (L.S. Starrett Company)

Fig. 14-20 *A vernier depth gage.* (L.S. Starrett Company)

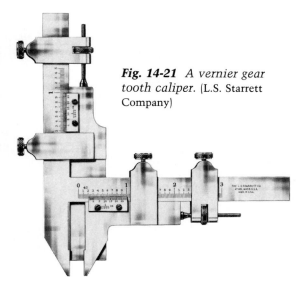

Fig. 14-21 *A vernier gear tooth caliper.* (L.S. Starrett Company)

Making accurate measurements with vernier tools requires the same care and delicate touch as when using micrometers. First, move the slide assembly along the beam until the jaws almost contact the work. Then lock the part of the slide assembly that carries the fine adjusting screw to the beam. Next, bring the jaws into contact with the workpiece by moving the **fine adjustment nut.** The jaws should make definite contact with the workpiece but should not be tight. Then, lock the main slide assembly to the beam. Finally, remove the caliper carefully from the workpiece to prevent springing the jaws, and make the reading.

14-10 How to Read Inch Vernier Calipers

The 25-division vernier: Reading this vernier is very much like reading a micrometer. Each inch of the beam is graduated into 40 equal parts just like the sleeve of a micrometer (Fig. 14-23). You will remember that the decimal equivalent of ¼₀th of an inch is .025".

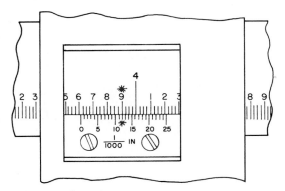

Reading explanation:

1. The zero on the vernier plate is between the 3″ and 4″ marks, thus the number of whole inches is   3.000″
2. The zero on the vernier plate has passed six 1/10th graduations, or   .600″
3. The zero on the vernier plate has not passed any 1/40th graduations, thus   .000″
4. The twelfth line on the vernier plate matches a line on the beam (see starred lines), adding   .012″

                          Total Reading   **3.612**

Fig. 14-23 *A 25 division vernier scale on an inch vernier caliper.*

Again like the micrometer, every fourth division line is a little longer than the others and is marked 1, 2, 3, through 10, which stands for tenths of an inch or .100″, .200″, .300″, through 1.000″ (Fig. 14-23). The **vernier plate** corresponds to the **micrometer thimble** and is graduated into twenty-five equal divisions, representing thousandths of an inch. Every fifth line on the vernier plate is numbered for convenience in making readings. A four- or five-power magnifying glass will aid in making accurate readings.

To read a vernier, first note how many inches, tenths (.100, .200, etc.), and 40ths (.025) the zero on the vernier plate is from the zero on the beam. Then add to this amount the number of thousandths shown by the matching lines on the vernier plate and beam.

Note the starred lines in Figure 14-23 and the explanation of the reading.

The 50-division vernier: Some vernier tools are equipped with a 50-division vernier plate (Fig. 14-24).

They are read in the same manner as the 25-division vernier plate. However, they are easier to read with the unaided eye, because

Reading explanation:

1. The zero on the vernier plate is between the 1″ and 2″ marks on the beam, making   1.000″
2. The zero on the vernier plate has passed the 6 on the beam, indicating 6/10th or   .600″
3. The zero on the vernier plate has passed the midpoint division between the sixth and seventh marks, adding 1/20th″, or   .050″
4. The 15th line on the vernier matches a line on the beam (see starred lines), adding   .015″

                          Total Reading   **1.665″**

Fig. 14-24 *A 50 division vernier scale on an inch vernier caliper. The outside reading is 1.665″*

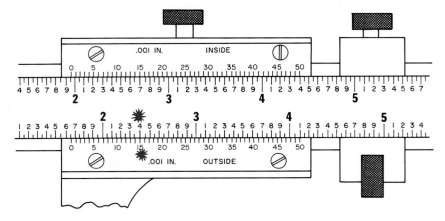

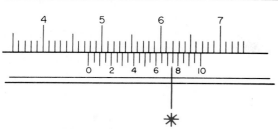

Reading explanation:

1. Main scale reading to the nearest
   millimeter   47.00 mm
2. Vernier scale reading to the
   nearest 0.05 mm   0.75 mm
           Total Reading **47.75 mm**

Fig. 14-25 *A 20 division vernier scale on a
metric vernier caliper.*

the division lines are spaced farther apart on
the vernier plate. The ¹⁄₁₀th divisions on the
beam have only two divisions representing
¹⁄₂₀th of an inch (.050) instead of the four divisions representing ¹⁄₄₀th of an inch (.025).
Note the explanation of the 1.665″ outside
reading in Figure 14-24.

14-11 How to Read Metric Vernier Calipers

20-division metric verniers: 20-divi-
sion metric vernier calipers give an accuracy
of ¹⁄₂₀th of a millimeter or 0.05 mm (Fig.
14-25). The graduations on the main scale are
one millimeter apart. If the main scale is
numbered 10, 20, 30, etc., it is read directly in
millimeters. If the main scale is numbered 1,
2, 3, etc., it is numbered in centimeters, and
the smaller divisions are millimeters.

The numbered lines on the vernier plate
indicate tenths of a millimeter. Note how the
reading is obtained in Figure 14-25.

50-division metric verniers: 50-divi-
sion metric vernier calipers give an accuracy
of 0.02 mm (Fig. 14-26). The graduations on
the main scale are one millimeter apart. The

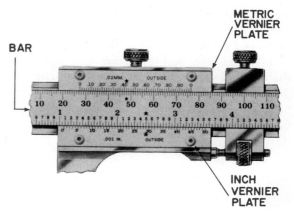

Reading explanation:

1. Main scale reading to nearest
   millimeter   27.00 mm
2. Vernier scale reading to the
   nearest 0.02 mm   0.42 mm
           Total Reading **27.42 mm**

Fig. 14-26. *This 50 division dual vernier scale
shows an inch reading of 1.079″ and a metric
reading of 27.42 mm.* (L.S. Starrett Company)

vernier plate, however, has 50 divisions instead of 20. Each numbered line on the vernier
plate indicates the number of 0.02 mm graduations at that point on the scale. Thus, 5 indicates 5 × 0.02 mm = 0.10 mm (one-tenth
of a millimeter); 10 indicates 10 × 0.02 mm
= 0.20 mm (two-tenths of a millimeter); and
15 indicates 15 × 0.02 mm = 0.30 mm.

Note the explanation of the reading in Figure 14-26.

14-12 How to Read the Vernier Protractor

The **vernier bevel protractor** (Fig. 14-22)
measures angles accurately to one-twelfth
(five minutes) of a degree. The protractor **dial**
is graduated into 360°, but it is marked
0°−90°, 90°−0°, 0°−90°, and 90°−0°. Each
five-degree line is a little longer than the one-
degree lines (Fig. 14-27). The longest lines are
the ten-degree lines, numbered 10, 20, 30,
through 90. The vernier plate is divided into
twelve equal divisions on either side of the

zero. Since there are 60 **minutes** (') in each degree, each line represents ¹⁄₁₂th of one degree (¹⁄₁₂th of 60 minutes equals five minutes).

To read the vernier protractor, first note the number of whole degrees between the zero line on the dial and the zero line on the vernier plate. Then, reading the vernier plate in the same direction (left or right of the zero) as the 90° line, add the number of minutes represented by the line past the zero that matches a line on the dial.

Note the explanation of the vernier protractor reading in Figure 14-27.

A Message on the Micrometer

Did you know that your personal safety often depends on micrometers? The exact measuring of parts used in making a car is necessary for the car's safe running. Precision measurement is a fact of life today. But where did it all begin?

The need for accurate measurement was recognized long before Jean Palmer, a Frenchman, invented the micrometer in 1848. Before his invention, others had made instruments that used the principle behind the micrometer. But no one could come up with a precision measuring tool that was convenient and easy to use.

One earlier attempt to make accurate measuring tools failed. Joseph Whitworth, an English toolmaker in the 1800s, constructed a very large micrometer screw gage for use in his shop. He built a heavy wooden base that had a backstop at one end. At the other end was a pedestal with a screw gage device. This device rotated on a large wheel that had been carefully marked with small divisions. The machine provided more precise measurements than had been possible. However, it was too large and too difficult to use to be practical.

On the other hand, the micrometer invented by Jean Palmer was a great success. Two American businessmen, Joseph R. Brown and Lucien Sharpe, saw Palmer's tool at the Paris Exposition of 1867. They liked his micrometer, and by 1869 their company was selling a similar model that could measure sheet metal accurately to 0.004 of an inch. Soon they developed other kinds of micrometers. By the 1880s, these instruments were used in machine shops all over the United States.

Micrometers based on the Palmer model are the most common and reliable measuring tools found in the toolroom. There are different kinds of micrometers for different measuring jobs. But they aren't the last word in precision measurement. Now there is an electronic gage that can be used as an inside, outside, or depth micrometer. The measurements appear on a digital readout display. With a memory function and rechargeable batteries, the electronic micrometer offers a computer-age solution to the age-old problem of precision measurement.

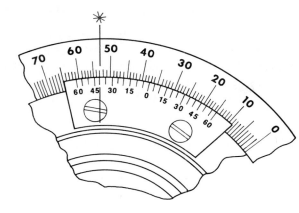

Reading explanation:

1. Number of whole degrees between the zero on the dial and the zero on the vernier plate .... 37°
2. Number of minutes indicated by the line on the vernier plate that matches a line on the dial .... 40'

       Total Reading   **37° 40'**

Fig. 14-27 *A vernier protractor scale.*
(Smithsonian Institution)

REVIEW REVIEW REVIEW REVIEW REVIEW

WORDS TO KNOW

depth micrometer
friction stop
inside micrometer
metric micrometer
metric vernier
  caliper

micrometer
anvil
frame
index line
sleeve

spindle
thimble
outside micrometer
ratchet stop
vernier

vernier caliper
vernier depth gage
vernier height gage
vernier micrometer
vernier protractor

REVIEW QUESTIONS

1. On what two parts of a micrometer are the graduations located?
2. On what two parts of a vernier caliper are the graduations located?
3. Name four kinds of micrometers.
4. Name four kinds of vernier measuring tools and tell the kinds of measurements for which they are used.
5. What is the largest size you can measure with a 1" [25 mm] micrometer?
6. What is the smallest size you can measure with a 2" [50 mm] micrometer?
7. Why should micrometers and verniers be handled with great care?
8. How is it possible that two people measuring the same object with the same micrometer or vernier may get different readings?
9. What is the use of a ratchet or friction stop on a micrometer?
10. How is the accuracy of a 1" [25 mm] outside micrometer tested?
11. How is the accuracy of a 2" [50 mm] or larger, outside micrometer tested?
12. What advantages does a vernier caliper have over a micrometer caliper?
13. How does a vernier micrometer differ from a regular micrometer?
14. Explain the difference between a 25-division and a 50-division inch vernier caliper.
15. Explain the difference between a 20-division and a 50-division metric vernier caliper.

PART 5

Benchwork

A guest checking into a large hotel in Las Vegas usually registers, takes an elevator to a room, and flips on the air-conditioner. He or she might then shower and return to the main floor for dinner. The guest seldom considers that the elevator might stick, the air-conditioner might clog, or the kitchen dishwasher might break down. But without proper maintenance, all of these things can happen.

Doug Rios is the senior engineer for maintaining and repairing all equipment of one of Las Vegas' largest hotels. At his disposal are a shop full of hand tools and small machines and a warehouse full of parts.

Doug has an excellent background for his work. He has always been interested in what makes things work. In high school he took several shop courses. Then he went on to become an apprentice and journeyman machinist. He worked in both the electrical and metal fields. By the time he was hired by the hotel, Doug had the skills of a master electrician and machinist.

Doug puts in long hours directing eight workers on the swing shift. On one shift alone, he may receive over 100 calls from the hotel management. Although Doug does bookwork and planning, much of the time he is on the job with the workers. It is important to him that a job is done competently and that his workers get along well with each other.

Over the years, Doug has seen both metals and tools become more sophisticated. He notes that MIG (metal inert gas) welding is now common, and he can carry in his hand electrical testing equipment that used to be as big as a TV set. Doug advises shop students to take some basic computer courses. He believes that is where the future of metalworking lies. Doug's future is to continue to run what he calls a "happy house."

Doug Rios
Senior Engineer

UNIT 15

Hand Sawing

The **hand hacksaw** (Fig. 15-1) is a basic tool in almost every toolbox. It is used mostly for cutting small pieces of unhardened metals that cannot be cut in a more efficient way.

15-1 Parts of a Hand Hacksaw

The parts of the hand hacksaw are the **frame, handle, prongs, tightening screw** and **wing nut,** and **blade.** Most hacksaw frames can be adjusted to hold blades of different lengths.

15-2 Blade Selection for the Hand Hacksaw

Hand hacksaw blades are made of thin high-grade steel that has been hardened and tempered. Some blades are hardened equally throughout and are therefore quite brittle. Better quality blades have hardened teeth and a softer back; these are classified as **flexible** blades. The softer back makes them springy and less likely to break.

Blade Size

Blades are made in 8″, 10″, and 12″ [200, 250, and 300 mm] lengths. The length is the distance between the centers of the holes at each end. The blades are usually ½″ [12.7 mm] wide and 0.025″ [0.64 mm] thick.

Blade Material

Blades made of several steels are available: carbon steel, molybdenum alloy steel, tungsten alloy steel, molybdenum high-speed steel, and tungsten high-speed steel. The high-speed steels are the hardest materials used for making hacksaw blades. When properly used they last longer than other blades.

Blade Pitch

The pitch of a saw blade is the distance from a point on one saw tooth to the same point on a neighboring tooth (Fig. 15-2A). In SI metrics the pitch size is indicated in millimeters. The larger the pitch number, the larger the saw teeth will be. However, tooth size of blades in the inch system of measurement is always given as the number of teeth per inch

Fig. 15-2 *The two ways of expressing hacksaw blade tooth size. (A) Tooth pitch. (B) The number of teeth per inch.*

Fig. 15-1 *A hand hacksaw.*

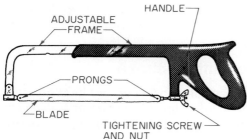

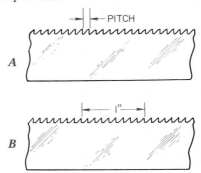

(Fig. 15-2B). Therefore, tooth size becomes smaller as the number of teeth per inch increases. The following blades are available:

(A) 14 teeth [1.8 mm pitch]: for cutting soft steel, aluminum, brass, bronze, copper alloys, and other materials 1″ [25 mm] or more in thickness.

(B) 18 teeth [1.4 mm pitch]: for cutting carbon steel, alloy tool steel, aluminum, copper alloys, and other metals ¼″ to 1″ [6 to 25 mm] in thickness.

(C) 24 teeth [1 mm pitch]: for cutting metals ¹⁄₁₆″ to ¼″ [1.6 to 6 mm] thick, such as iron pipe, metal conduits, light angle iron, etc.

(D) 32 teeth [0.8 mm pitch]: for cutting metals up to ¹⁄₁₆″ [1.6 mm] thick, such as sheet metals and thin-wall tubing.

Tooth Set

Set of saw teeth refers to the way the teeth are bent to one side or the other to provide a **kerf** (the cut made by the saw) that is wider than the thickness of the saw. The wider saw kerf prevents the saw blade from binding by providing **clearance** (Fig. 15-3A). Two kinds of set are provided, a **raker** set and a **wavy** set (Fig. 15-3B). The raker set has one tooth bent to the right, one to the left, and one straight tooth in between; this pattern is repeated the length of the blade. The wavy set has several teeth bent to the right and several teeth bent to the left, alternately. Blades with 14 and 18 teeth [1.8 and 1.4 mm pitch] have the raker set. Those with 24 or 32 teeth [1 and 0.8 mm pitch] have the wavy set.

15-3 Putting Blade in Frame

When putting a new blade in the hand hacksaw, place it so that the teeth of the blade **point away from the handle.** Fasten one end of the blade to the hook at one end of the frame and the other end of the blade to the hook at the opposite end of the frame (Fig. 15-4). Tighten the blade securely; a loose blade makes a crooked cut and is likely to bend or break.

15-4 Holding Metal for Sawing

The work should be held tightly in the vise. Put the part to be sawed near the vise jaws so that the pressure of cutting does not bend the workpiece or cause it to **chatter.** Chattering is a rattling noise made when the workpiece or cutting tool vibrates, or springs back and forth, during cutting. It makes hacksawing very inefficient.

Protect smooth workpiece surfaces from the rough vise jaws by using soft **jaw caps** made of sheet copper or aluminum (Fig. 15-5). **Whenever possible, position the workpiece so that at least two saw teeth always contact the workpiece** (Fig. 15-6). This is necessary to avoid stripping (breaking) of the saw teeth.

Sawing thin metal. If the metal to be cut is thinner than the space between two saw teeth, clamp it between two thicker pieces of metal or hard wood. Sawing through all three pieces at the same time (Fig. 15-7) is the safe way. If there is a layout on one side of the thin metal, use a C-clamp to fasten the metal so that the layout can be seen (Fig. 15-8). Then, you can see and saw near the lines on the layout.

Making long sawcuts. Sawcuts in a long workpiece can be made by turning the blade at a **right angle** (90 degrees) to the saw frame (Fig. 15-9).

15-5 Holding and Using a Hand Hacksaw

Grasp the handle firmly with your dominant hand (your right hand is dominant if you are right-handed). Use the other hand to grip the other end of the saw frame as in Figure 15-10.

The Cutting Stroke

When starting a cut, use light pressure and short strokes until the saw cut is deep enough to keep the blade from jumping out of the saw

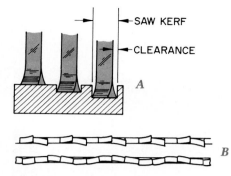

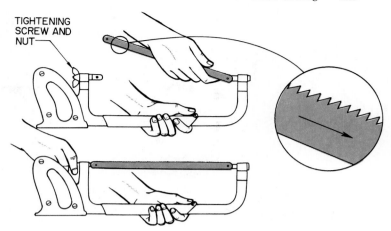

Fig. 15-3 *Hacksaw blade tooth set. (A) A cross section view of the blade. The wider saw kerf leaves clearance for the blade. (B) A cutting edge view of tooth sets: (1) raker, (2) wavy.*

Fig. 15-4 *When putting a blade in the hacksaw frame, point the teeth away from the handle.*

Fig. 15-5 *Soft jaw caps protect smooth workpiece surfaces from the rough vise jaws.*

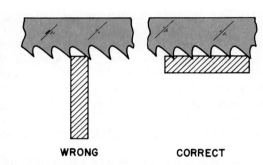

Fig. 15-6 *At least two teeth should contact the workpiece to prevent the stripping of teeth.*

Fig. 15-7 *Holding thin metal for sawing.*

Fig. 15-8 *Holding thin metal so layout lines are visible.*

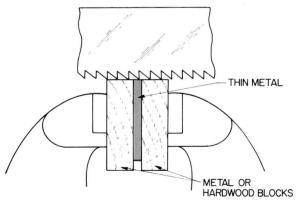

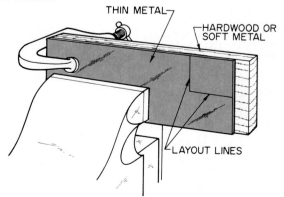

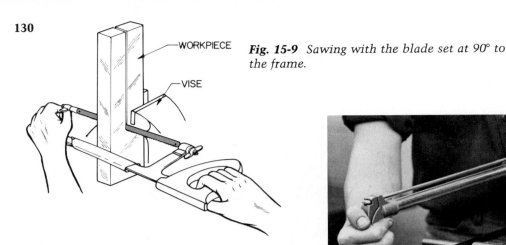

Fig. 15-9 *Sawing with the blade set at 90° to the frame.*

Fig. 15-10 *The correct way to use the hacksaw. Apply pressure on the forward, cutting stroke. Lift the blade slightly on the return stroke. Do not drag the teeth back over the metal.*

kerf. Then, increase the stroke to the full blade length and add pressure. Press down on the **forward stroke** and lift a little on the **return stroke,** because the blade cuts only on the forward stroke. Tighten the blade after a few strokes because it will stretch when it gets warm.

Make 40 to 60 **cutting strokes** per minute. Sawing faster does not appreciably speed cutting.

Wear on Sides of the Teeth

The sides of the teeth wear down by the rubbing between the blade and the metal being cut. **A worn blade makes a narrower cut than a new blade.** A new blade, if placed in an old cut, wedges and sticks and is ruined with the first stroke. If a cut cannot be finished because the blade has become too dull, start a new cut from the other side of the workpiece with a new blade.

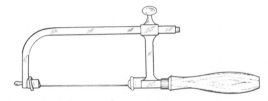

Fig. 15-11 *The jeweler's saw.*

Fig. 15-12 *Using the jeweler's saw.*

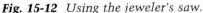

15-6 Cutting Curved Lines

Cutting curved lines is done with a **jeweler's saw** (Fig. 15-11).

Jeweler's saw blades have fine teeth and are very hard in order to cut metal. They are 5″ [127 mm] long and have from 32 to 76 teeth per inch [.08 to .03 mm pitch]. **Unlike hacksaw blades, the teeth of these blades should point toward, not away from, the handle.**

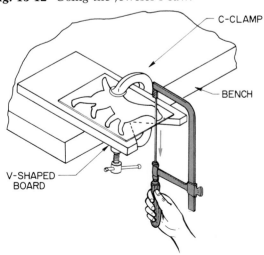

The work should be held on a board with a V-shaped notch. The board itself is held in a vise or clamped to the edge of a bench (Fig. 15-12). The saw is held with the dominant hand. **The cutting stroke is downward.** For internal cuts, the blade must first be removed from the frame. A hole must then be drilled, the blade put through the hole, and the blade fastened to the saw frame.

REVIEW   REVIEW   REVIEW   REVIEW   REVIEW

WORDS TO KNOW

adjustable frame	clearance	jeweler's saw	return stroke
backward stroke	forward stroke	kerf	tooth set
blade pitch	hand hacksaw	raker set	wavy set
chatter	jaw caps		

REVIEW QUESTIONS

1. What materials are used to make hacksaw blades? Which are hardest and will tend to last longest?
2. Which way should the teeth of a hand hacksaw blade point? Why?
3. Why should a new blade never be used in a cut made by an old blade?
4. How many cutting strokes per minute should be made when cutting with a hand hacksaw?
5. What are standard hand hacksaw blade lengths?
6. How many hacksaw teeth should be on the workpiece in order to prevent stripping the teeth?
7. How should thin sheet metal be held for sawing?
8. What kind of saw is used to cut curved lines?
9. Which way should the teeth of a jeweler's saw blade point?
10. Does the jeweler's saw blade cut on the upward or downward stroke?

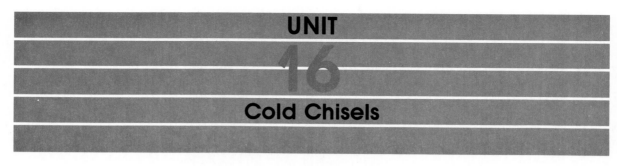

UNIT 16

Cold Chisels

Cold chisels are used to cut cold metal, hence the name. They are made of tough alloy tool steel and are made in several sizes and shapes.

16-1 Kinds of Cold Chisels

Cold chisels are known by the shapes of their **cutting edges.** Thus, we have the **flat chisel, cape chisel, diamond-point chisel,** and **round-nose chisel** (Fig. 16-1).

The flat chisel has a wide cutting edge. It may be used for cutting sheet metal, solid bars, rivets, and other cutting jobs. It is the most commonly used chisel.

Cape Chisel

The cape chisel has a narrow cutting edge and is used for cutting narrow grooves. Its cutting edge is wider than the rest of the chisel to keep the chisel from sticking in the groove.

Diamond-Point Chisel

The diamond-point chisel has a cutting edge shaped like a diamond. It is used to cut V-shaped grooves and square inside corners.

Round-Nose Chisel

The round-nose chisel has a rounded cutting edge and is used for cutting round corners and grooves.

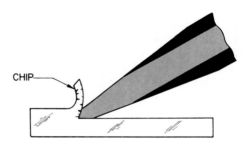

Fig. 16-2 *The wedge action of a cold chisel.*

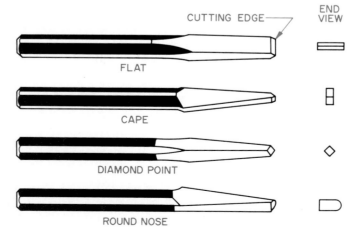

Fig. 16-1 *Kinds of cold chisels. The cutting edge of each chisel gives it its name.*

16-2 Sizes of Cold Chisels

Cold chisels range in size from ¼″ [6.35 mm] to 1″ [25 mm] in diameter. Their lengths vary from 4″ [100 mm] to 8″ [200 mm]. Always try to match the size of the chisel to the size of the job.

16-3 Angle of the Cold Chisel Cutting Edge

The **cutting edge** is a wedge that cuts into the metal as shown in Figure 16-2.

The **cutting edge angle** on most cold chisels is from 50° to 75°. The angle on a chisel should suit the kind of metal to be cut. The softer the metal, the nearer the angle should be to 50°. The harder the metal, the nearer the angle should be to 75°. For most work, it should be about 60°.

16-4 Sharpening Cold Chisels

Good work can only be done with sharp chisels. Sharpen the cutting edge on a grinding wheel as explained in Unit 45. Use a **center gage** to test the cutting edge angle (Fig. 16-3). A slightly curved cutting edge gives a better shearing action than a straight cutting edge (Fig. 16-4).

16-5 Heads of Cold Chisels

The head of the cold chisel should be **tapered** a little and rounded, as **A** in Figure 16-5. After a cold chisel has been used for some time, the head becomes flattened like a mushroom with rough, ragged edges, as **B** in

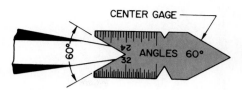

Fig. 16-3 *Testing the cutting edge of a cold chisel with a center gage.*

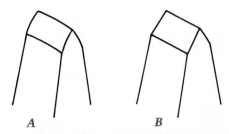

Fig. 16-4 *A slightly curved cutting edge (A) has better shearing action than a straight cutting edge (B).*

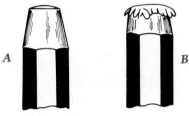

Fig. 16-5 *Keep the heads of cold chisels dressed. (A) Good. (B) Bad. The mushroom head is dangerous.*

Figure 16-5. **This mushroom head is dangerous.** One of the ragged edges may fly off and injure someone when it is struck with the hammer. The mushroom head should be removed by grinding. Shape the chisel head as shown in Figure 16-5A.

16-6 Holding the Chisel

Hold chisels loosely around the middle (Fig. 16-6), so that the shock of the hammer blows is not transferred directly to your hand.

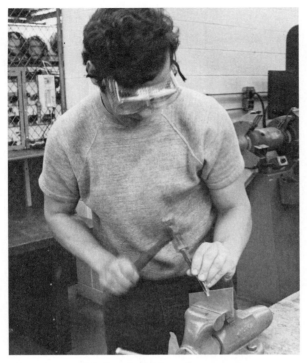

Fig. 16-6 *Hold the chisel loosely around its middle. Note the goggles the worker is wearing.*

SAFETY NOTE

When using a chisel, wear **goggles** to protect your eyes from flying chips (Fig. 16-6). Also, make sure that the chips fly against a wall, or set up a shield to protect other workers. Workers have lost eyes when they were struck by flying chips.

16-7

How to Start a Cut

Position the chisel so that its point will bite into the metal. Keep your eyes on the cutting edge of the chisel so that it can be reset after each hammer blow if needed. Use light hammer blows until the chisel point has dug into the metal. Then make the blows heavier to speed up the cutting.

16-8

Shearing

A **vise** and a **flat chisel,** used together, can be made to act like a pair of scissors or shears for cutting sheet metal (Fig. 16-7).

First, make a line to be used as a guide with a **scriber.** Then, clamp the metal tightly in a vise that has good edges so that the line will be just below the tops of the vise jaws. This leaves a little metal for filing to the line afterwards. Then proceed to cut as follows:

1. Lay the **cutting edge** of the chisel on top of the vise jaws and against the metal, as in Step 1, Figure 16-7. It is important to cut with the face of the chisel in a horizontal position. Cut as close to the top of the vise as possible, so as to make a square cut.
2. Slant the chisel in the direction of the cut and proceed to cut as in Figure 16-7, Step 2.

Fig. 16-7 *Shearing sheet metal with a flat cold chisel.*

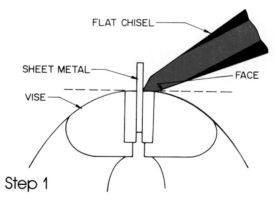

Step 1

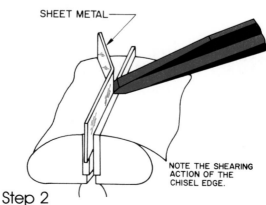

Step 2

16-9 Cutting Rods and Rivets

A small rod or bar may be roughly cut by nicking it on opposite sides with the flat chisel (Fig. 16-8A), and then bending it until it breaks. Figure 16-8B shows a **rivet head** being cut off with a flat chisel.

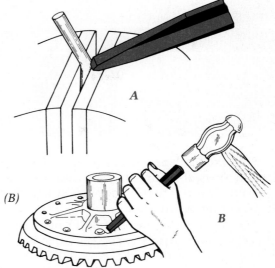

Fig. 16-8 *Cutting with a flat cold chisel. (A) Cutting a rod in a vise. (B) Cutting a rivet head.*

REVIEW   REVIEW   REVIEW   REVIEW   REVIEW

WORDS TO KNOW

cape chisel	cutting edge	flat chisel	round-nose chisel
center gage	cutting edge angle	mushroom head	tapered
cold chisel	diamond-point chisel		

REVIEW QUESTIONS

1. Name the four kinds of cold chisels and give at least one use for each.
2. What cutting edge angle is used for most work done with a flat chisel?
3. What gage may be used to test the cutting angle of a cold chisel?
4. What part of the chisel should you watch while cutting?
5. What safety precautions should you take to protect yourself and others while cutting with a chisel?

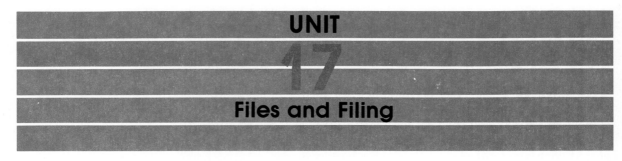

UNIT
17
Files and Filing

Files are hardened pieces of tool steel with slanting rows of teeth. They are used to shape and smooth metal parts. They can cut all metals except hardened steel.

Making surfaces smooth by filing is more difficult than might be expected. Good results depend on using the right kind of file; using sharp, clean files; and holding the file and workpiece properly.

17-1
Parts of a File

The **tang** of a file is the pointed part that fits into the handle (Fig. 17-1). The **point** is the end opposite the tang. The **heel** is the end of the file next to the handle. The face is the broad surface of the file that does the cutting. The **edge** is the narrow side of the file. If it has no teeth, it is called a **safe edge**.

For safety all files with tangs should be fitted with handles (Fig. 17-2). Tangs have sharp points and edges. If they aren't covered with handles, a worker may cut the palm of his or her hand.

Ordinary file handles are made of hardwood (Fig. 17-2A). The metal ring on the file handle is called a **ferrule**. It keeps the handle from splitting when the tang is driven in. This

kind of handle is fitted to the file shown in Figure 17-3. Higher quality handles have a metal insert that is self-threading on the soft tang of the file. Such a file can be hung by its handle (Figs. 17-2B and 17-7).

Large files should have large handles, and small files should have small handles.

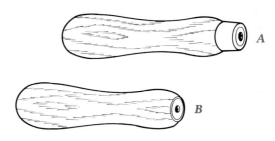

Fig. 17-2 *File handles. (A) A traditional wood handle. (B) A self-threading handle.*

Fig. 17-3 *Strike the handle on a solid surface to drive in the file tang.*

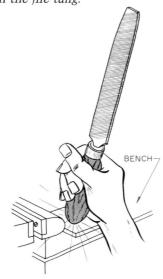

Fig. 17-1 *The parts of a file.*

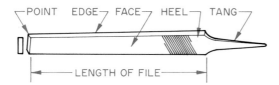

17-2

Shapes of Files

The shape of a file is its general outline or **cross section** (end view). Files are made in hundreds of shapes. A blunt file is one that has the same width and thickness from the heel to the point. A tapered file is one that is thinner or narrower at the point. Table 17-1 shows the most commonly used shapes. These are:

1. warding
2. mill
3. flat
4. hand
5. pillar
6. square
7. round or rat-tail
8. half-round
9. three-square
10. knife.

TECHNOLOGIES AND PRACTICES

A Few Points on the File

What tool appears on almost every workbench and at every machinist's work station? A simple metal file. The file has been essential to metalworkers ever since metal was discovered thousands of years ago. Over this long period of time, files have changed a lot. Different metals were used as people found out more about metal. And both the making of files and their appearance have changed, too.

Around 2500 BC, file-type tools were used by carpenters to cut, split, or scrape wood. You would hardly recognize one of these files if you saw it. They were simply small strips of bronze with no points or teeth. These files could be used to work on tin, too. But a file for use mainly on metal was not developed until iron was discovered.

The widespread use of iron gave the Iron Age (1000 BC-100 AD) its name. Files made of iron have been found in archaeological sites ("digs") all over Europe. Some of these files have slanted teeth cut into the face and are more like modern files than those simple pieces of bronze.

By the Middle Ages (500-1500 AD), steel files were being used. To make the cutting surface of a file, a toolmaker would cut raised edges across a flat piece of metal. This may have been done with a chisel, or by hitting a sharp-edged hammer with another hammer. The toolmaker would make many of these cuts very close together. The result was a row of "teeth". Next, the file was hardened by heating in a very hot fire and quenching (cooling by plunging into water).

Early files were made completely by hand. In the next stage of development, toolmakers used simple machines to speed up the process. The famous artist and inventor Leonardo da Vinci (1452-1519) designed an interesting machine to help in file-making. It was never actually built, but it was a very good idea. In da Vinci's design, the tool-maker would still make cuts in the metal, but after each cut, the file would be moved foward a short distance by turning a screw mechanism.

During the Industrial Revolution of the 18th and 19th centuries, filemaking became a completely mechanical process. Today files are made in many shapes and filing surfaces.

The file you use in the school shop may not look much like the flat strip of bronze used long ago. But the principle is the same, and the results are even better!

(Smithsonian Institution)

MACHINE FILE CUTTING ROOM

Table 17-1

Files and Their Uses

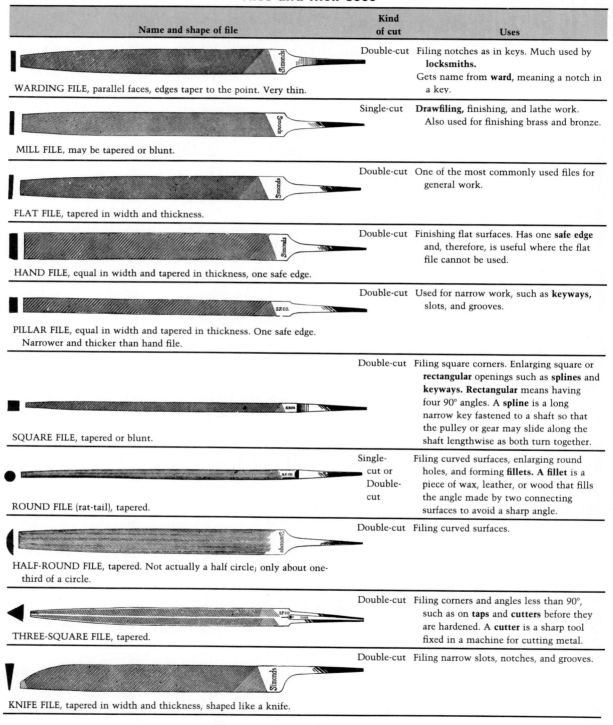

Name and shape of file	Kind of cut	Uses
WARDING FILE, parallel faces, edges taper to the point. Very thin.	Double-cut	Filing notches as in keys. Much used by **locksmiths.** Gets name from **ward**, meaning a notch in a key.
MILL FILE, may be tapered or blunt.	Single-cut	**Drawfiling,** finishing, and lathe work. Also used for finishing brass and bronze.
FLAT FILE, tapered in width and thickness.	Double-cut	One of the most commonly used files for general work.
HAND FILE, equal in width and tapered in thickness, one safe edge.	Double-cut	Finishing flat surfaces. Has one **safe edge** and, therefore, is useful where the flat file cannot be used.
PILLAR FILE, equal in width and tapered in thickness. One safe edge. Narrower and thicker than hand file.	Double-cut	Used for narrow work, such as **keyways,** slots, and grooves.
SQUARE FILE, tapered or blunt.	Double-cut	Filing square corners. Enlarging square or **rectangular** openings such as **splines** and **keyways. Rectangular** means having four 90° angles. A **spline** is a long narrow key fastened to a shaft so that the pulley or gear may slide along the shaft lengthwise as both turn together.
ROUND FILE (rat-tail), tapered.	Single-cut or Double-cut	Filing curved surfaces, enlarging round holes, and forming **fillets. A fillet** is a piece of wax, leather, or wood that fills the angle made by two connecting surfaces to avoid a sharp angle.
HALF-ROUND FILE, tapered. Not actually a half circle; only about one-third of a circle.	Double-cut	Filing curved surfaces.
THREE-SQUARE FILE, tapered.	Double-cut	Filing corners and angles less than 90°, such as on **taps** and **cutters** before they are hardened. A **cutter** is a sharp tool fixed in a machine for cutting metal.
KNIFE FILE, tapered in width and thickness, shaped like a knife.	Double-cut	Filing narrow slots, notches, and grooves.

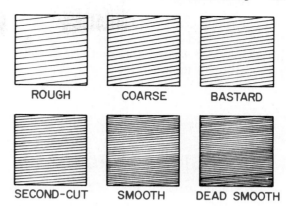

Fig. 17-5 *Six different degrees of file coarseness.*

17-3 Sizes of Files

The size (length) is given in inches or millimeters, and is the distance from the **point** to the **heel** (Fig. 17-1). The common file sizes are 6″, 8″, 10″, and 12″ [150, 200, 250, and 300 mm].

As the file length increases, width and thickness also increase.

17-4 Cuts of Files

There are four kinds of file tooth patterns, called **cuts** (Fig. 17-4). These are:

1. single cut
2. double-cut
3. rasp-cut
4. curved-cut.

A **single-cut file** has a single row of cuts across the face of the file. These **teeth** are like the edge of a chisel.

A **double-cut file** has two sets of cuts crossing each other, which give the teeth the form of sharp points. These files cut faster but not as smoothly as the single-cut file.

Fig. 17-4 *Four different cuts of files.*

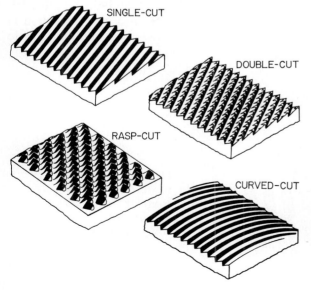

The teeth on a **rasp-cut file** are not connected and are formed by raising small parts of the surface with a punch. The rasp-cut file is used for shaping wood and other soft materials.

Curved-cut files are widely used in auto body work. Their widely-spaced, curved teeth prevent clogging when filing soft metals and plastic body fillers.

17-5 Coarseness of Files

Single-cut and double-cut files are further classified by the coarseness or spacing between the rows of teeth (Fig. 17-5). The six kinds of spacings are:

1. rough
2. coarse
3. bastard
4. second-cut
5. smooth
6. dead smooth

Files with the widest spacing between teeth are called **rough;** those with the closest spacing between teeth are known as **dead smooth.**

The files most often used are the bastard, second-cut, and smooth. The rough, coarse, and dead smooth files are used only on special jobs.

The coarseness of a file changes with its length. The larger the file, the coarser it is.

Thus, a rough cut on a small file may be as fine as a second-cut on a large file. Compare the spacings between the teeth of different sizes of files in Figure 17-6.

17-6 Storing Files

Take good care of files. They should be stored so they will not rub or hit each other. Good care will save the cutting edges of the files and make them last longer.

Hanging files as in Figure 17-7A is a good idea because a file with a loose handle cannot be hung up and should be taken out of service until repaired. Another good way to keep files is shown in Figure 17-7B.

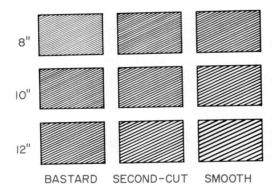

Fig. 17-6 *The longer a file is, the coarser are its teeth. These illustrations are actual sizes of teeth.*

17-7 Other Kinds of Files

Many other kinds of files are made. **Jeweler's files** are small files used for fine work. They are made in lengths of 4″ to 6″ [100 to 150 mm], and are sold in sets of various shapes (Fig. 17-8).

Rifflers are files made especially for tool, die, and mold work. They are bent in various shapes to allow filing in hard-to-reach places (Fig. 17-9).

Rotary files, or **burrs,** are made for use in electric or air-powered tools (Fig. 17-10).

17-8 Choosing the Right File

Select the size, kind, and coarseness of file according to:
1. Size of the workpiece.
2. Amount of metal to be removed.
3. Smoothness of the finish desired.

Use a small file for a small workpiece, a larger file for a larger workpiece. Start with a double-cut file for quick removal of excess metal. Then use a single-cut bastard or second-cut file to smooth the rough surface left by the double-cut file. Complete the job with a smooth single-cut file if a smooth finish is required. Table 17-1 describes the different file shapes and their uses.

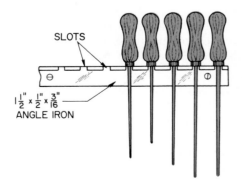

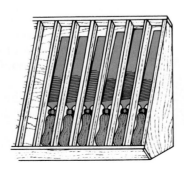

Fig. 17-7 *Proper ways to store files. (A) Hanging from their handles. (B) In a compartment-type rack.*

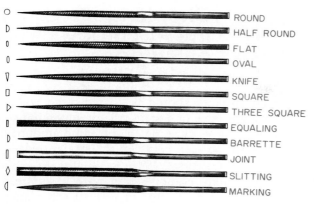

ROUND
HALF ROUND
FLAT
OVAL
KNIFE
SQUARE
THREE SQUARE
EQUALING
BARRETTE
JOINT
SLITTING
MARKING

Fig. 17-8 *Jeweler's files.*

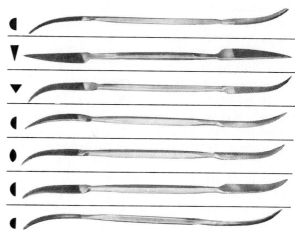

Fig. 17-9 *A set of rifflers.* (Nicholson File)

17-9 Holding Work for Filing

The workpiece should be held tightly in a vise or otherwise fastened so it cannot move. If in a vise, the part to be filed should be near the vise jaws to keep it from chattering (Fig. 17-11).

Protect polished surfaces from the rough vise jaws with soft jaw caps.

17-10 Using a File

Files will cut all kinds of metal except hardened steel. Many files are dulled because the teeth touch the hardened steel jaws of the vise during filing.

Do not use a file without a handle. Use the sharpest file available. (Sharp teeth will not have shiny cutting edges.) Hold the handle of the file with the dominant hand. For heavy filing, place the heel of the hand on the point of the file with the fingers pressing against the underside (Fig. 17-12). For light filing, the thumb should be placed on the top of the file (Fig. 17-13).

Cross-filing. In cross-filing, the file is held naturally at about a 45-degree angle to the workpiece surface (Fig. 17-14). Make the file cut by moving it back and forth in a saw-

Fig. 17-10 *Rotary files for power-driven tools.* (Nicholson File)

Fig. 17-11 *Chattering results if the workpiece surface being filed is too far from the vise.*

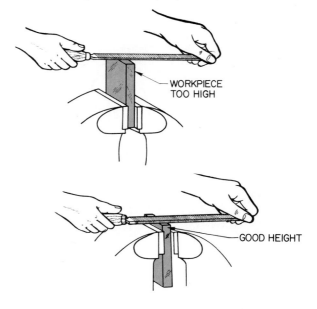

WORKPIECE TOO HIGH

GOOD HEIGHT

ing motion. Press down on the cutting (forward) stroke; lift up a little on the return stroke to prevent dulling the file. Keep the file as parallel to the surface as possible. It is almost impossible, however, to prevent rounding of the surface when cross-filing.

Draw-filing.   Draw-filing produces a smooth, flat surface (Fig. 17-15). **A mill file** or a **smooth single-cut file** is recommended for this purpose. Place the file at 90 degrees to the longest dimension of the surface to be filed. Grasp it firmly at both ends with the thumbs close to the workpiece. Keep the file at 90 degrees while pushing it back and forth across the workpiece. Press down only on the forward stroke.

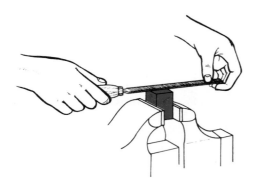

Fig. 17-12   *Holding the file for heavy filing.*

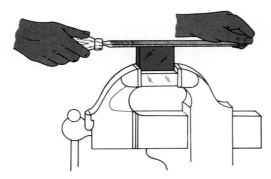

Fig. 17-13   *Holding the file for light filing.*

Checking the Accuracy of Surfaces during Filing

17-11

Flat surfaces should be tested often with the straight edge of a steel rule or square (Fig. 17-16A). The work is flat if the same amount of light can be seen between the straight-edge and all of the surface.

Test square corners often with a square. Use the bevel protractor to test all other angles (Fig. 17-16B).

17-12

Filing Cast Iron

Before filing a cast iron surface that has not been machined, remove the **scale** by tapping the workpiece surface with a large **flat cold chisel.** (Scale is a hardened layer, mostly iron oxide, that always forms on iron castings.) The file will be ruined in a few strokes if you **file** the scale. **Wear goggles when removing the scale.**

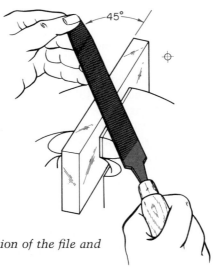

Fig. 17-14   *The correct position of the file and hands for cross filing.*

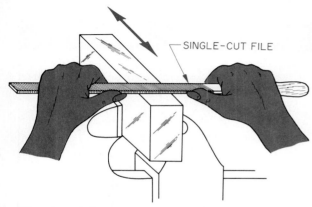

Fig. 17-15 *The correct position of the file and hands for draw-filing. This position should be maintained while the file is moved back and forth, as indicated by the arrow.*

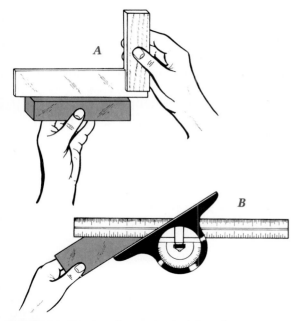

Fig. 17-16 *Testing the accuracy of surfaces being filed. (A) Using a straight edge to check the flatness of a work. (B) Using a bevel protractor to check an angle.*

Do not touch the filed part of cast iron with your fingers or hand. No matter how dry your skin may appear, there is always some oil rubbed off and left on the metal. On the next few strokes the file will slip over the oil on the part you touched. Blow away any filings that you wish to remove.

17-13

Cleaning Files

File teeth often become clogged with metal filings or chips. If not removed, these small chips stick between the teeth and scratch the work. Keep the file free from chips and filings by brushing it with a wire brush called a **file card** (Fig. 17-17).

Rub the file card over the file in the direction of the cuts. Sometimes the chips stick so tightly that the file card will not remove them. In such cases, use a thin piece of sheet metal or a pointed wire to remove them (Fig. 17-18).

A file can be cleaned more easily if chalk is rubbed on its teeth before it is used. Never try to clean a file by tapping it on the bench, vise, or workpieces. Files break easily because they are very **hard** and **brittle.** Oil may be removed from a file by rubbing chalk into the teeth and then brushing with a file brush.

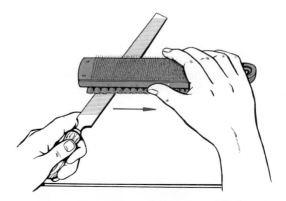

Fig. 17-17 *Cleaning a file with a file card.*

Fig. 17-18 *Remove chips with a wire to clean the file teeth.*

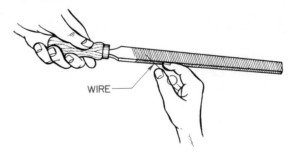

REVIEW REVIEW REVIEW REVIEW REVIEW

WORDS TO KNOW

cast iron	file cuts	mill	scale (on cast iron)
cross-filing	curved-cut	pillar	spacing between
draw-filing	double-cut	round or rat-tail	teeth
file card	rasp-cut	square	bastard
file parts	single-cut	three-square	coarse
edge	file shapes	warding	dead smooth
face	flat	jeweler's files	rough
heel	half-round	riffler	second-cut
point	hand	rotary file	smooth
tang	knife	safe edge	

REVIEW QUESTIONS

1. What is the tang of a file?
2. What is a safe edge on a file?
3. Why is it important to have a handle on a file? How is the length of a file measured?
4. Make a sketch of the cross-section shape of a flat file; a half-round file; a square file; a three-square file.
5. Make a sketch of how the teeth appear on a single-cut file; a double-cut file.
6. What is a jeweler's file?
7. How should files be stored when not in use? Why?
8. How should work be held for filing to keep it from chattering?
9. How may finished surfaces be protected from the rough jaws of a vise?
10. Explain how to choose the right file for a job.
11. How should a file be held for draw-filing?
12. Why should you not file the scale on cast iron?
13. What kind of file should be used for filing soft metals?
14. Explain how to keep files clean and free of chips.

UNIT
18
Wrought Metal Bending

Many wrought metal alloys are so ductile that they can be hammered and sharply bent without cracking or breaking. Diameters or thicknesses up to ¼″ [6.35 mm] can usually be bent cold; thicker pieces often require heating.

Wrought iron, a ductile mixture of almost pure iron and slag, was widely used by early blacksmiths for making all kinds of iron objects, both useful and decorative. Door and window hardware, harness and wagon hard-

Fig. 18-1 *Blacksmiths in the 1800's made this wrought iron gate located in Colonial Williamsburg, Virginia*

ware, fences, lamps, sign brackets, and many other items were made of wrought iron (Fig. 18-1). Present day wrought metal items are usually made of hot-rolled, low-carbon steel or ductile alloys of aluminum and copper (Fig. 18-2).

18-1 Bending and Shaping with Hand Tools

Angle Bending

A sturdy machinist's vise is very useful for bending angles. For bending angles up to 90 degrees, the workpiece may be placed upright as in Figure 18-3A, or horizontally as in Figure 18-3B. Tighten the vise securely, then use a ball-peen hammer of suitable size to drive the metal around the corner. Strike the metal close to the vise to make a sharp bend. A piece of close-fitting steel pipe 2' or 3' [600 or 900 mm] long will provide added leverage for bending rods or bars (Fig. 18-3C). According to a prominent vise manufacturer, the direction of bending may be either toward the movable jaw or the fixed jaw.

For bending angles more than 90 degrees, bend the piece 90 degrees as described above. Then, open the vise wide enough to accept the bent piece (Fig. 18-4). Closing the vise will force the metal into a sharper bend. A sturdy monkey wrench may also be used to bend the metal more sharply than 90 degrees (Fig. 18-5).

To make **offset** bends with a vise, use a pair of flat steel bars on opposite sides of the workpiece (Fig. 18-6). The thickness of the bars determines the amount of offset.

Fig. 18-2 *Modern wrought metal work.* (Roger Bean)

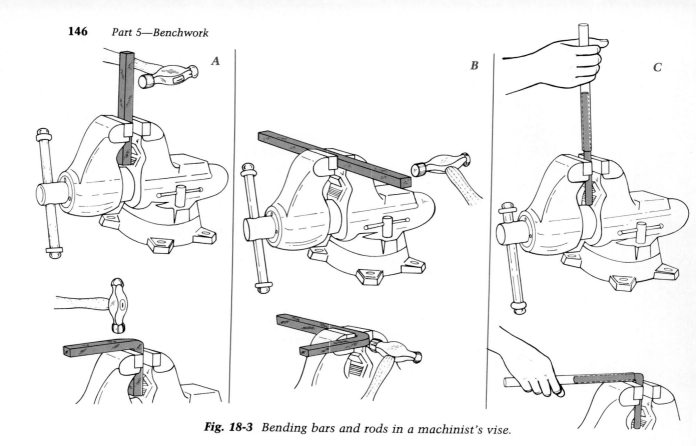

Fig. 18-3 *Bending bars and rods in a machinist's vise.*

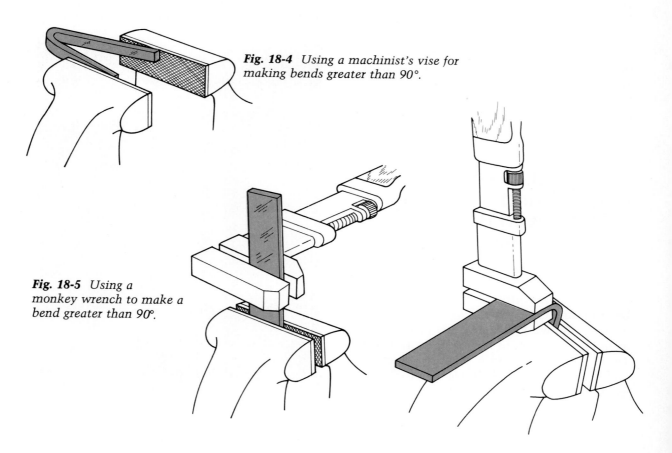

Fig. 18-4 *Using a machinist's vise for making bends greater than 90°.*

Fig. 18-5 *Using a monkey wrench to make a bend greater than 90°.*

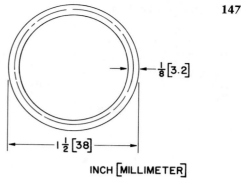

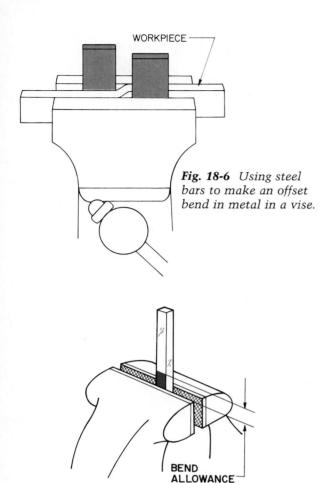

Fig. 18-6 *Using steel bars to make an offset bend in metal in a vise.*

INCH [MILLIMETER]

Fig. 18-9 *To calculate the length of a workpiece for rings and curved parts, use the length of the centerline.*

Fig. 18-7 *To figure the length of the workpiece before bending, add a bend allowance to the inside measurements. It should be 1/2 the thickness of hard metals, and 1/3 the thickness of soft metals.*

Fig. 18-8 *Include a bend allowance in the length of the metal being bent.*

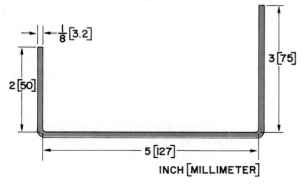

INCH [MILLIMETER]

Bend allowance. To determine the length of the straight piece needed, add to the inside dimensions of the bent piece a **bend allowance** of ⅓ to ½ the metal thickness for each bend. Allow ⅓ the metal thickness for soft metals and ½ the thickness for hard metals (Fig. 18-7). Applying the rule for hard metal, the unbent length of the shape shown in Figure 18-8 will be as follows:

2″ + 5″ + 3″ + 2(½ × ⅛″) = 10⅛″
[50 mm + 125 mm + 75 mm + 3.2 mm = 253 mm]

Place the metal in the vise so that the bend allowance is included in the length of the metal being bent (Fig. 18-8).

To figure the length of curves or circles, use the length of the centerline of the shape (Fig. 18-9). The length of the straight piece needed to make the ring in Figure 18-9 is as follows:

1⅜″ × Pi (3.14) = 4⁵⁄₁₆″
[35 mm × Pi (3.14) = 110 mm]

The formula for the circumference of a circle is Pi (3.14) × diameter. The length of a curve that is not a complete circle can be found by stepping off the centerline with dividers (Fig. 13-12).

Bending order. If a part requires many bends, plan the bending order carefully. Otherwise, it may not be possible to finish the part after making the first few bends. Generally, there will be no difficulty if bending begins at one end and proceeds across the piece (Fig. 18-10).

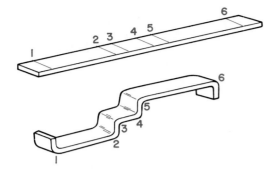

Fig. 18-10 *Plan the bending order carefully.*

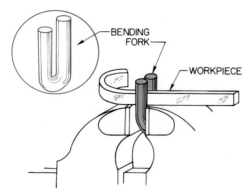

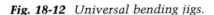

Fig. 18-11 *Bending a curved piece with a bending fork held in a vise.*

Fig. 18-12 *Universal bending jigs.*

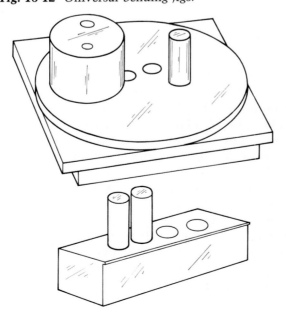

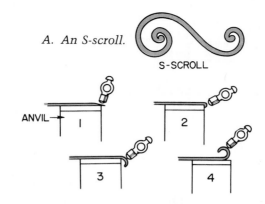

A. *An S-scroll.*

B. *Step 1: prepare the end of the strip. Flatten and flare end if desired.*

Steps 2-4: bend the strip into a scroll.

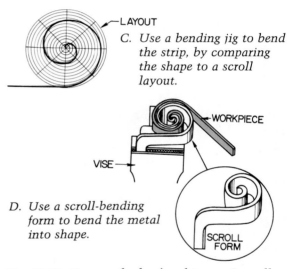

C. *Use a bending jig to bend the strip, by comparing the shape to a scroll layout.*

D. *Use a scroll-bending form to bend the metal into shape.*

Fig. 18-13 *Two methods of making an S-scroll.*

Bending Curves

Curved bends are made with the help of a **bending fork** or **universal bending jig.** A bending fork is simply a rod bent into a U shape. It must be clamped tightly in a vise when used. The curved bend is made by making a series of small bends close together (Fig. 18-11). Universal bending jigs (Fig. 18-12) are also held in a vise and are used just like a bending fork.

Scrolls may be made by bending the metal a little at a time in a bending jig and comparing the shape with a scroll layout (Fig. 18-13C). Use of a **scroll-bending form,** however, is much faster, and when several scrolls

Fig. 18-14 *Decorative treatment of scroll ends.*

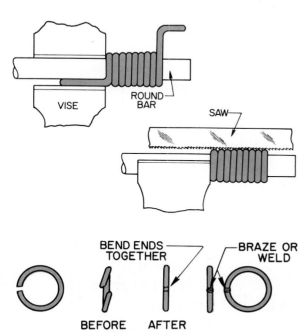

Fig. 18-15 *Making a ring from a coil.*

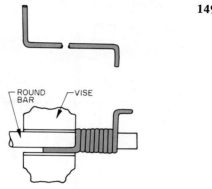

Step 1. Cut wire stock to desired length. Bend ends to "L" shape.

Step 2. Fasten one wire end and round bar in vise. Wind the wire around the bar to form coil.

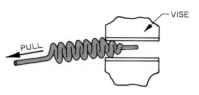

Step 3. Using pliers, stretch the coil.

Step 4. Squeeze one end of the coil in vise. Stretch the coil to form the spiral.

Fig. 18-16 *Making a spiral.*

of the same size are needed, the results are much more uniform (Fig. 18-13D). The ends of scrolls and straight pieces are often flared by hammering, then filed into decorative shapes (Fig. 18-14).

A **ring** is made quickly from a coil (Fig. 18-15).

A **spiral** is also made from a coil (Fig. 18-16).

Forming the **loop** on an eye bolt may be done around a round bar in a vise (Fig. 18-17).

Twisting Rectangular or Square Bars

Pieces are often twisted to add interest to a product design (Fig. 18-18). Twisting also strengthens the piece and may be necessary to provide convenient fastening. Twisting will shorten the piece. Determine the length needed by trial, or use a workpiece 1" or 2" [25 or 50 mm] longer, and cut it to length after twisting.

Mark the location of the two ends of the section to be twisted with chalk or a felt tip marker. Clamp one end of the section to be twisted even with the top or side of the vise jaw (Fig. 18-18A). Hold short pieces upright, long pieces horizontally. Place a sturdy monkey wrench, or other adjustable wrench, at the other end of the section to be twisted (Fig. 18-18B). Rotate the wrench clockwise for a right-hand twist, counterclockwise for a left-hand twist. Some practice is required to keep the metal from bending out of line during twisting. Twisting long sections inside a close-fitting pipe will keep them straight.

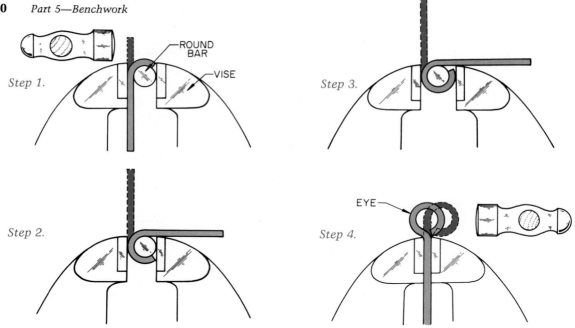

Fig. 18-17 *Bending the ring of an eye bolt in a vise.*

Fig. 18-18 *Twisting a rectangular bar in a vise.*

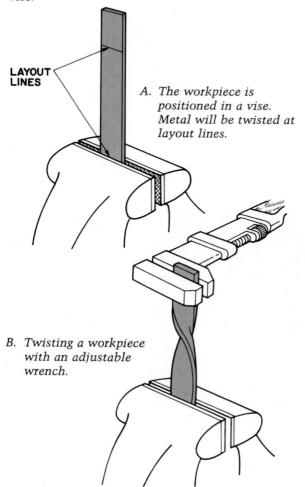

A. *The workpiece is positioned in a vise. Metal will be twisted at layout lines.*

B. *Twisting a workpiece with an adjustable wrench.*

Bending with Universal Bending Machines

18-2

Hand-operated universal bending machines are used for one-of-a-kind and short-run (small quantity) production of bent parts. They are designed for rapid bending of solid rods and bars, and tubing. A very light-duty machine intended for craft work is shown in Figure 18-19. More powerful machines (Figs.

Fig. 18-19 *A light-duty universal metal bender and some of the products made with it.* (Mark Eyelet & Stamping, Inc.)

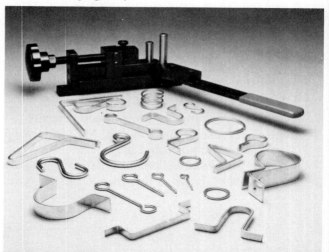

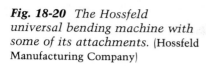

Fig. 18-20 *The Hossfeld universal bending machine with some of its attachments.* (Hossfeld Manufacturing Company)

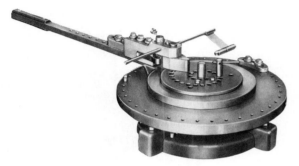

Fig. 18-21 *The DiAcro universal bending machine.* (DiAcro/Houdaille)

Fig. 18-22 *A numerically controlled bending machine can be programmed to automatically produce duplicate parts. This N/C machine is producing automotive exhaust pipes.* (MiiC, America, Inc.)

18-20 and 18-21) and power-operated bending machines of many kinds are also available (Fig 18-22). Before using any of these machines, carefully study the operating manual and make practice bends on scrap material.

The DiAcro® bender. DiAcro makes benders of several sizes, both hand- and power-operated. Use the fixtures that go with the machine to make sharp bends (Fig. 18-23), and bends of different radii (Fig. 18-24), and to bend scrolls (Fig. 18-25) and tubes (Fig. 18-26).

The Hossfeld bender. Hossfeld benders have many attachments that make them capable of bending a wide variety of shapes (Fig. 18-20). Figure 18-27 shows the setup for a sharp bend. Figure 18-28 shows how angle iron is bent. Figure 18-29 shows tubing being bent.

Fig. 18-23 *The tooling arrangement for making sharp bends.* (DiAcro/Houdaille)

Fig. 18-24 *Metal is formed around discs of different diameters to make bends of different radii.* (DiAcro/Houdaille)

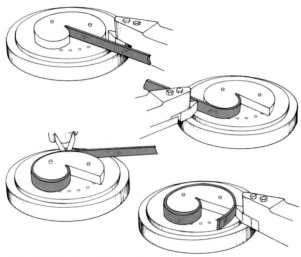

Fig. 18-25 *Scroll-bending on a DiAcro bender. Other irregular shapes may also be bent this way.* (DiAcro/Houdaille)

Fig. 18-26 *Bending tubing with a DiAcro bender.*

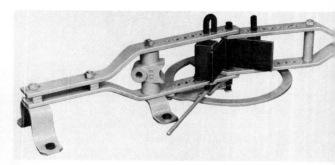

Fig. 18-27 *Making a sharp bend on a Hossfeld universal bender.* (Hossfeld Manufacturing Company)

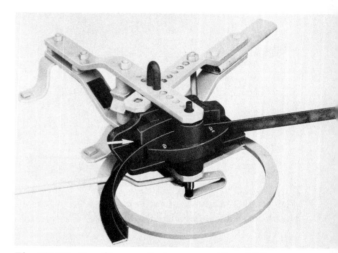

Fig. 18-28 *Bending angle iron on a Hossfeld bender.* (Hossfeld Manufacturing Company)

Fig. 18-29 *Bending tubing on a Hossfeld bender.* (Hossfeld Manufacturing Company)

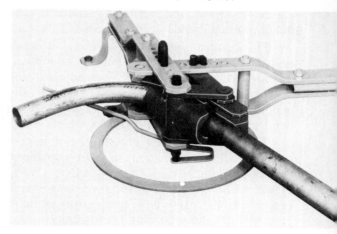

18-3 Methods for Assembling Wrought Metal Products

Mechanical fasteners. Rivets are traditionally used to fasten wrought metal parts together. With most products it is best to use rivets of the same metal. For instance, use soft iron rivets for assembling iron or steel parts, aluminum rivets for assembling aluminum parts, etc. **Blind rivets** and self-threading screws may be used for quick assembly of thin materials and tubing. Unit 25 has a discussion of these and other metal fasteners.

Welding and brazing. Electric arc and resistance welding are efficient assembly methods used for today's wrought metal products. Welding and brazing procedures are covered in Units 26 and 27.

18-4 Finishing Wrought Metal

Early wrought iron products had a hammered finish that occurred naturally as a result of shaping the product. Present-day wrought metal is made from smooth bars and rods of standard sizes and shapes. Since little or no hammering is used in shaping the metal, surfaces are often left smooth. Hammering the smooth surfaces to make a roughened texture, which is called **peening,** is sometimes done to add an interesting finish.

Wrought iron or steel is usually given a protective coating of flat or gloss black paint. Wrought aluminum is either left unpainted or is painted white. Wrought copper and brass are frequently given a coloring treatment and a coating of clear lacquer. Unit 46 describes metal coloring and finishing.

REVIEW REVIEW REVIEW REVIEW REVIEW

WORDS TO KNOW

angle bending	bending order	scroll	universal bending
bend allowance	offset bends	scroll-bending form	jig
bending fork	peening	scroll layout	universal bending machine

REVIEW QUESTIONS

1. Name several kinds of metal used for making present-day wrought metal products.
2. Give the general rule for figuring bend allowance.
3. Explain how the length of curves or circles is figured before the metal is bent.
4. When making a part with several bends, why is it important to carefully plan the bending order to be used?
5. Explain how scrolls or other curves are bent in a bending fork or a universal bending jig.
6. When long bars are twisted, how can they be kept from bending out of line?
7. Name two kinds of universal bending machines.
8. How are wrought metal products traditionally fastened together?
9. How are present-day wrought metal products often fastened together?
10. How are wrought steel products usually finished? Aluminum? Copper and brass?

PART

6

Threads and Thread Cutting

As a youngster, Larry Barton was always fixing something or making something. It was easy for him to recognize early in life that he had mechanical ability and enjoyed working with his hands. So in high school he enrolled in shop and vocational programs. He also had the opportunity to participate in a cooperative training program, in which he worked part of the day in a machine shop. Later, of course, he learned many of his skills on the job.

After 22 years in industry, Larry is supervisor of the machine division of a pattern and foundry company, with 17 workers reporting to him. His division is responsible for a wide variety of threading operations, including cutting internal threads on castings and external threads on steel shafts. Although Larry has his share of paperwork to do, he spends most of his time with the machinery and his workers. Larry most enjoys guiding the younger workers gradually up through the ranks, just as he was guided himself. He emphasizes production, but not at the expense of quality. Helping his workers become skilled threaders and machinists is the main satisfaction of his job.

Because Larry works with young people, he has many thoughts for students considering careers in metalwork. He says they will need "lots and lots of math." Electronics and computers are being applied more and more in his business. The company has eight threading machines that use Computer Numerical Control (CNC). And knowing that in business "time is money," Larry advises students to make the best use of their time in every aspect of a project, from planning to finishing. That is the way to stay competitive in industry. And that is the way Larry runs his shop—efficiently and competitively.

Larry Barton
Machine Division
Supervisor

UNIT
19
Screw Threads

A screw thread is a ridge of uniform shape that winds at a constant angle around the surface of a cylinder or a cone. Threads on bolts and screws are **external threads** (Fig. 19-1A). Threads on the inside of a hole or a nut are **internal threads** (Fig. 19-1B).

Threads may be **right-hand** or **left-hand**. A nut that is screwed **clockwise** onto a bolt has a right-hand thread (Fig. 19-2A). Most threads are right-hand. A nut that is screwed **counterclockwise** onto a bolt has left-hand threads (Fig. 19-2B).

The shaft on a grinder that has two grinding wheels (Fig. 44-1) has right-hand threads on the right side and left-hand threads on the left side. On working drawings, threads are assumed to be right-hand unless marked **LH** for left-hand.

Fig. 19-1 Screw threads. (A) External. (B) Internal.

Fig. 19-2 Threads are either right-hand or left-hand. (A) A right-hand thread advances with clockwise rotation. (B) A left-hand thread advances with counterclockwise rotation.

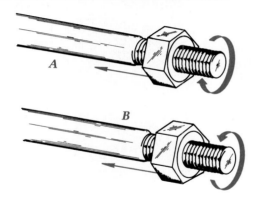

19-1 Uses of Screw Threads

Screw threads are widely used on fasteners such as bolts, nuts, and screws. They make it easy to put parts together quickly or take them apart. Screw threads are also used to change rotary (turning) motion to straight-line motion. A good example is the lead screw on a metal lathe. As it revolves, it drives the carriage and cutting tool in a straight line. Threads are often used to increase mechanical advantage because they act like a wedge. The screw in a vise provides great mechanical advantage. It multiplies the turning effort of the user to apply great clamping force between the vise jaws. Screw threads are also used to make fine adjustments on instruments, tools, and machinery. The screw in micrometers makes precision measurement possible.

19-2 How Screw Threads Are Made

Hand taps and dies are used to cut threads manually, a process Units 20 and 21 discuss in detail. However, most threads are made with machine tools. Ordinary lathes, turret lathes, automatic lathes, milling machines, drilling machines, and thread-grinding machines all can make threads routinely.

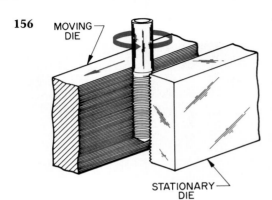

Fig. 19-3 *The technique of thread rolling used in cold heading machines.*

Most standard threaded fasteners are made from wire on automatic machines called **cold headers.** Cold headers use flat **thread-rolling dies** to form threads (Fig. 19-3). Cylindrical thread-rolling dies are available for use on lathes.

19-3 Screw Thread Terms

The following screw thread terms are adapted from American National Standards Institute (ANSI) definitions:[1]

Major diameter: The largest diameter of a straight external or internal thread (Figs. 19-4 and 19-5). The **nominal,** or **basic size** is similar to the major diameter, and is used for general identification, such as identifying the thread size as ¼″ or ½″ diameter.

Minor diameter: The smallest diameter on a straight external or internal thread (Figs. 19-4 and 19-5).

Pitch diameter: On a straight thread, the diameter of an imaginary cylinder that passes through the thread profile where the width of the thread and the width of the groove are equal (Figs. 19-4 and 19-5). The amount of clearance between mating threads is controlled by maintaining close tolerances on their pitch diameters.

[1]**Unified Screw Threads** (ANSI B1. 1-1960) Published by the American Society of Mechanical Engineers, New York, NY

Pitch: The distance from a point on one screw thread to a corresponding point on an adjacent thread, measured parallel to the thread axis (Fig. 19-4). The pitch of a thread is a measure of the **size** of the thread. For inch-based threads, pitch is equal to 1 divided by the number of threads per inch. For metric threads, pitch is expressed in millimeters.

The pitch of a thread may be determined with a steel rule or with a **screw pitch gage** (Fig. 19-6). Be sure to use customary inch tools for measuring inch-based threads, and metric tools for measuring metric threads.

Lead: The distance a thread moves along its axis in one revolution. On a single thread, the lead and pitch are the same. On a double thread, the lead is equal to twice the pitch. On a triple thread, the lead is equal to three times the pitch (Fig. 19-7).

Lead, or helix, angle: Angle made by the **helix** of a thread at the pitch diameter, measured in a plane perpendicular to the axis of the thread (Fig. 19-4).

Multiple thread: A thread having the same thread form produced with two or more helical grooves, such as a double or triple thread (Fig. 19-7).

Crest: The top surface that joins the two sides of a thread (Fig. 19-4).

Root: The bottom surface that joins the two sides of adjacent threads (Fig. 19-4).

Fig. 19-4 *The principle parts of a screw thread.*

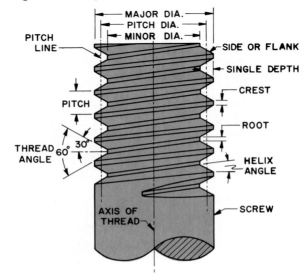

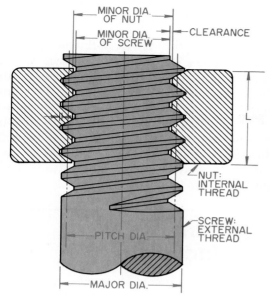

Fig. 19-5 *A comparison between the minor diameters of a screw and a nut, showing the clearance between them. External threads and internal threads of matching bolts and nuts have the same basic pitch diameters.*

Fig. 19-6 *Measuring the number of threads per inch. (A) Using a steel rule. (B) Using a screw pitch gage.*

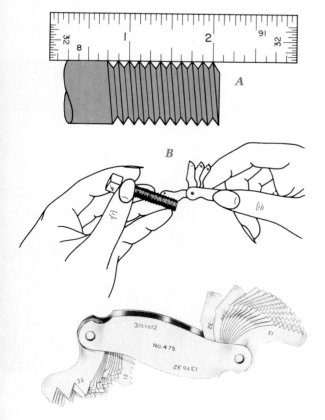

Side or flank: The surface that connects the crest with the root on either side of a thread (Fig. 19-4).

Clearance: The distance between the crest of a thread and the root of a mating thread, measured perpendicular to the thread axis (Fig. 19-5).

Height of thread: (Sometimes called the **single depth** of thread.) The distance between the major and minor diameters of the thread, measured perpendicular to the axis of the thread.

Fig. 19-7 *The pitch and leads of multiple threads are related as shown here.*

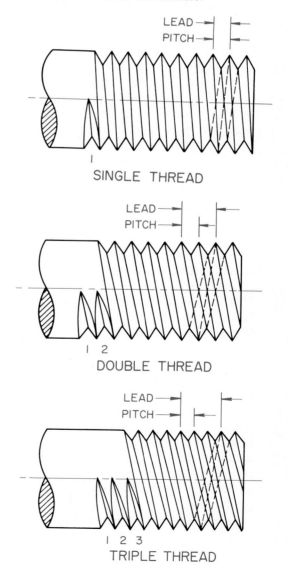

19-4 Development of Screw Threads in the United States

The cross-sectional shape of a screw thread is called its **profile** or **form**. Early threads had no flat crests. To overcome the objections to this sharp V-thread form, the United States Standard Form Thread was developed (Fig. 19-8). It was developed during the 1860s, and was first adopted by the United States Navy in 1868. This thread form was widely adopted by American industries. Some manufacturers, however, continued to make threads according to their own systems. Often, bolts made by one manufacturer would not fit nuts made by another.

TECHNOLOGIES AND PRACTICES

William Sellers: Standard Setter of American Manufacturing

Imagine that you have lost an important metal part—say, the nut that holds your bicycle tire to the frame. You go to the bicycle shop and find that none of the nuts they have will fit your bike. In fact, your lost part is one of a very limited number of parts, and it will be very difficult to get another one. Maybe you'll never be able to get your bike back together!

This imagined scene will give you some idea of what American manufacturing was like in the mid-1800s. Mass production had begun, but the industrial system had a lot of "bugs" in it. For one thing, there were no standards for screw threads, so a part made by one manufacturer often wouldn't fit a machine made by another. The lack of a standard thread greatly troubled those who were concerned about precision and quality in machine tool production.

One of these people was manufacturer William Sellers (1824-1905). Trained as a machinist and mechanical engineer, Sellers opened and operated a machine tool manufacturing plant in Philadelphia. He insisted on accuracy in all of the company's work. If a measurement was off by even a "hair's breadth," he saw that it was adjusted.

In 1864 Sellers proposed to standardize screw threads. He suggested that all screw threads be made with a sixty-degree angle. He also said that threads should be made with flat crests and roots instead of with the sharp V-shaped form then common.

Sellers' two ideas were used in designing the Standard Form Thread, which was adopted by the U.S. Navy in 1868. Within ten years, Sellers' screw thread was used all over the country. By 1894, this screw thread had become the standard for international use.

Sellers set other trends in machine tool manufacturing, including simple, practical designs and added weight for durability. Machines made by Sellers' company gained a reputation for excellent performance. His insistence on precision, standardization, and simplicity helped advance the general standard of manufacturing. And it was Sellers' influence that made shopping for replacement parts a simple task, instead of a cause for alarm.

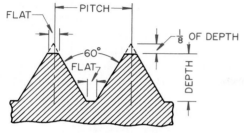

Fig. 19-8 *The American National Standards Institute (ANSI) Form for an external thread.*

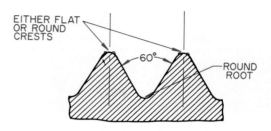

Fig. 19-9 *The Unified Screw Thread Form.*

During World War I the need arose for more standardization of screw threads. Congress established the National Screw Thread Commission to develop and adopt new screw thread standards.

This committee and other cooperating agencies produced the American National Screw Thread Standard in 1924. The thread profile was named the **American National Form Thread** and was much the same as the United States Standard Form Thread (Fig. 19-8). The Commission also established the **National Fine Thread**. This form was like a thread form the Society of Automotive Engineers (SAE) had recommended in 1911. The SAE **Extra-Fine Thread Series** was added (with modifications) to the American National Screw Thread Standard that the Commission approved in 1933.

In 1948, the United States, Canada, and Great Britain agreed to use the **Unified Screw Thread** so that threaded parts made in each of the countries would be interchangeable. American industry now uses Unified threads instead of the older American National threads.

19-5 Unified Screw Threads

The **Unified Screw Thread** generally has rounded roots and may have either rounded or flat crests (Fig. 19-9). These are the main differences from the American National thread form. American industries use flat crests, while the English prefer rounded crests. The rounded root is optional on both the external and the internal threads for most applications; however, for some applications the root must be rounded.

The calculations for an external **Unified Form** thread may be made with the following formulas (See Figs. 19-8 and 19-9):

$$\text{Pitch} = P = \frac{1}{\text{number of threads per inch}}$$
$$\text{Depth} = D = 0.61343 \times P$$
$$D = \frac{0.61343}{\text{number of threads per inch}}$$
$$\text{Flat at crest} = F = \frac{P}{8}$$

The depth of the external Unified Form Thread is slightly less than the depth for the American National Form Thread. However, these two kinds of threads are essentially the same. Production tolerances permit them to be used interchangeably in most instances.

The depth of the internal Unified Form Thread is equal to $0.51427 \times P$, or 0.51427 divided by the number of threads per inch. The following common screw thread series are included in the Unified Screw Threads[2]:

1. **Unified National Coarse Thread (UNC):** adopted from the NC thread. (See Table 19-1.)
2. **Unified National Fine Thread (UNF):** adopted from the NF thread. (See Table 19-1.)

---

[2]**Unified and American Screw Threads** (ANSI B1.1-1949) and later edition, **Unified Screw Threads** (ANSI B1.1-1960), published by the American Society of Mechanical Engineers, New York.

Table 19-1

Unified Screw Threads

Diameter			Threads per inch		
No.	Inch	Decimal Equivalent	UNC (NC) (USS)	UNF (NF) (SAE)	UNEF (NEF) (EF)
0		.0600		80	
1		.0730	64	72	
2		.0860	56	64	
3		.0990	48	56	
4		.1120	40	48	
5	⅛	.1250	40	44	
6		.1380	32	40	
8		.1640	32	36	
10		.1900	24	32	
12		.2160	24	28	32
	¼	.2500	20	28	32
	⁵⁄₁₆	.3125	18	24	32
	⅜	.3750	16	24	32
	⁷⁄₁₆	.4375	14	20	28
	½	.5000	13	20	28
	⁹⁄₁₆	.5625	12	18	24
	⅝	.6250	11	18	24
	¹¹⁄₁₆				24
	¾	.7500	10	16	20
	¹³⁄₁₆				20
	⅞	.8750	9	14	20
	¹⁵⁄₁₆				20
	1	1.0000	8	14	20

3. **Unified National Extra-Fine Thread (UN-EF):** adopted from the NEF thread. (See Table 19-1.)
4. Other less-common series, such as the **8-thread series (8UN)**, the **12-thread series (12UN)**, and the **16-thread series (16UN)** are also included.

19-6 Unified Thread Classes

Six **classes** of threads, formerly called **fits**, are used with Unified screw threads. The six classes include three external classes and three internal classes. The external thread classes are designated **1A, 2A,** and **3A.** The internal classes are designated **1B, 2B,** and **3B.** "Thread fit" means the degree of tightness between mating threads. Normally, class 2A and class 2B threads are mated. However, any Unified class of external thread may be mated with any internal class, as long as the product meets the necessary tightness requirements. The following classes of mated threads have tolerances that result in the following types of fit:

Classes 1A and 1B: loose fit
Classes 2A and 2B: free fit
Classes 3A and 3B: close fit

When classes 2A and 3B are mated, the tolerances permit an intermediate fit ranking between the free and close fits.

19-7 Other Common Thread Forms

Square Thread

A square thread is formed like a square (Fig. 19-10). The depth and width of the groove are equal. The height and width of each ridge between the grooves are also equal. Thus, the groove and ridge form two squares. The screw is very strong and is used in house jacks and similar applications.

Acme Thread

Acme threads are usually used on the **lead screw** of a lathe. They are also used on many other kinds of machine tools. The angle of the thread is 29° (Fig. 19-11). Handbooks for machinists have information about pitches, fits, tolerances, and allowances for acme threads.

Pipe Threads

American National Standard pipe threads are used for assembling pipes and pipe fittings. Plumbers and pipefitters use four types of standard pipe threads.

American National Standard Taper Pipe Threads (NPT) are used for pipe-fitting jobs that require a low-pressure seal against liquid or gas leakage. A pipe compound or sealant is normally used with this type thread. The NPT threads are tapered ¾" per foot [62.48 mm per meter] on the diameter (Fig. 19-12). The angle

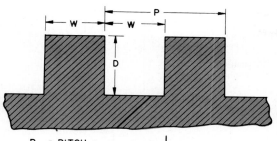

P = PITCH = $\dfrac{1}{\text{NO. THREADS PER INCH}}$

D = DEPTH = .500 X PITCH

W = .500 X PITCH

WIDTH W OF THREAD GROOVE IN NUT = (.500 X PITCH) + .001 TO .002 INCH CLEARANCE MAKE .001 TO .003 OVERSIZE TO FIT

Fig. 19-10 *The square thread.*

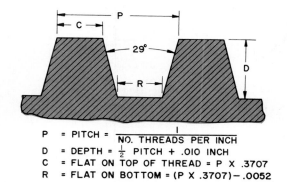

P = PITCH = $\dfrac{1}{\text{NO. THREADS PER INCH}}$

D = DEPTH = $\frac{1}{2}$ PITCH + .010 INCH

C = FLAT ON TOP OF THREAD = P X .3707

R = FLAT ON BOTTOM = (P X .3707) − .0052

Fig. 19-11 *The Acme thread.*

American National Standard Dryseal Taper Pipe Threads (NPTF) are used in applications that require a gas or liquid tight thread joint without the use of pipe compound or sealant. The four forms of Dryseal threads are listed below:

NPTF—Dryseal Standard Pipe Thread

PTF-SAE Short—Dryseal SAE Short Taper Pipe Thread

NPSF—Dryseal Standard Fuel Internal Straight Pipe Thread

NPSI—Dryseal Standard Intermediate Internal Straight Pipe Thread

Further information about the different types of pipe threads is available in handbooks for machinists.

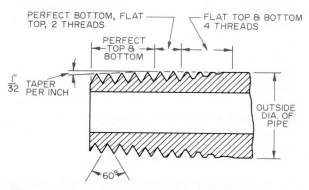

Fig. 19-12 *Taper pipe threads (NPT).*

between the sides of the thread is 60°. The farther the tapered threads are screwed together, the tighter the joint becomes. Table 19-2 provides basic data for different sizes of pipe.

American National Standard Railing Joint Taper Pipe Threads (NPTR) make a rigid, mechanical, tapered thread joint for use in railing construction.

American National Standard Straight Pipe Threads (NPS) have several types:

1. The **NPSC** thread is used in pipe couplings.
2. The **NPSM** thread is designed for use in free-fitting mechanical joints.
3. The **NPSL** is for use in loose-fitting mechanical joints with locknuts.
4. The **NPSH** is for loose-fitting mechanical joints in hose couplings.

Table 19-2

Pipe Threads, Pipe Dimensions, and Tap Drill Sizes

| Pipe diameters | | | Threads | Tap |
Nominal Size inches	Actual inside	Actual outside	Per inch	drill size
1/8	0.270	0.405	27	11/32
1/4	0.364	0.540	18	7/16
3/8	0.494	0.675	18	19/32
1/2	0.623	0.840	14	23/32
3/4	0.824	1.050	14	15/16
1	1.048	1.315	11½	15/32
1¼	1.380	1.660	11½	1½
1½	1.610	1.900	11½	123/32
2	2.067	2.375	11½	23/16
2½	2.468	2.875	8	25/8

19-8 ISO Metric Threads

In 1949, the **International Standards Organization (ISO)** recommended worldwide adoption of three series of metric threads. These threads are based on the same 60-degree thread form adopted for the **ISO Inch** (Unified) threads, (Fig. 19-9). The three series are (1) **ISO Metric coarse pitch**, (2) **ISO Metric fine pitch**, and (3) **ISO Metric constant pitch. ISO Metric and ISO Inch threads have the same thread form but are not interchangeable because of differences in diameters and pitches.**

Figure 19-13 compares the ISO Metric coarse series thread sizes with the Unified National (ISO Inch) coarse series thread sizes. Table 19-3 gives a complete listing of ISO Metric coarse and fine pitch thread sizes.

Only ISO Metric coarse pitch threads are commonly used on fasteners. ISO Metric fine pitch threads are used mostly on precision tools and instruments. The constant pitch series threads are used mainly on machine parts, but are also used on all spark plugs.

Classes of ISO Metric Threads

Basically, there are three ISO Metric classes of fit: **fine, medium,** and **coarse.** The classes of fit are more accurately identified by giving the **tolerance grade** and the **tolerance position** of the mating threads. Tolerance grades are specified by a number that can be applied to both pitch and major diameter. Tolerance position is specified with a lower case (small) letter for external threads and with a capital letter for internal threads as follows:

External Threads:

e = large allowance
g = small allowance
h = no allowance

Internal Threads:

G = small allowance
H = no allowance

Table 19-4 shows the tolerance classes for external and internal threads, and matches them with the three classes of fit.

Thread Designation

All ISO Metric thread designations begin with the capital letter "M." Next, the major diameter in millimeters is given. This is followed by the thread pitch in millimeters, separated from the first number by a "times" mark (×). The pitch may be omitted when designating coarse threads. Therefore, an ISO Metric 16 mm coarse thread with a pitch of 2 mm would simply be designated M16. The same diameter in a fine thread would be designated M16 × 1.5. Complete designations for ISO Metric threads include identification of the tolerance class.

Additional information on ISO Metric threads can be found in handbooks for engineers and machinists.

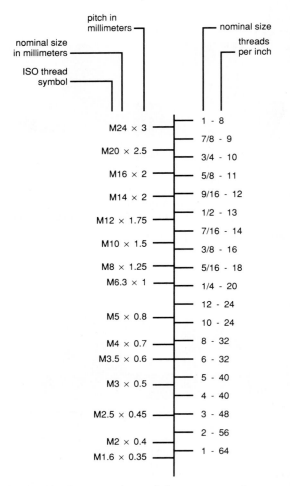

Fig. 19-13 *A comparison of the common sizes of ISO Metric Coarse threads with Unified National (ISO Inch) Coarse threads.*

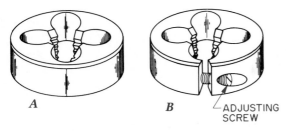

Fig. 20-1 *Threading dies. (A) Solid. (B) Adjustable.*

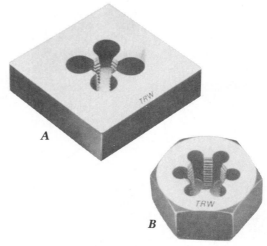

Fig. 20-3 *Rethreading dies. (A) Square. (B) Hexagonal. (Greenfield Tap & Die/Div. of TRW, Inc.)*

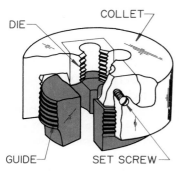

Fig. 20-2 *An adjustable die with replaceable cutters.*

A **diestock** is a tool for holding and turning a threading die (Fig. 20-5). Diestocks are made in several sizes to fit dies of different diameters.

20-2 Sizes of Threading Dies

The diameter and pitch of the thread that is produced are stamped on each die, together with the kind of thread. For example, **¼-20 UNC** means that the die will cut a Unified National Coarse thread with a major diameter of ¼" and 20 threads per inch. The sizes of inch-based threads are given in Table 19-1. A die marked M8 × 1.25 is a metric die that will cut a thread with a major diameter of 8 mm and a pitch of 1.25 mm. The sizes of metric threads are given in Table 19-3.

It should be noted that the diameter of the rod on which a thread is to be cut should be the same as the major diameter of the die.

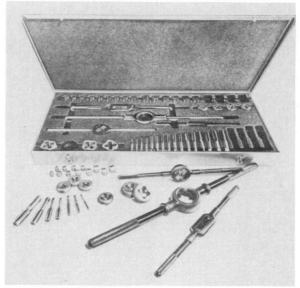

Fig. 20-4 *A screw plate (a set of taps and dies, die stock, and tap wrenches). (Greenfield Tap & Die/Div. of TRW, Inc.)*

Fig. 20-5 *A diestock.*

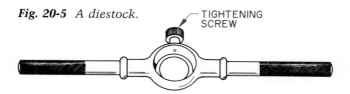

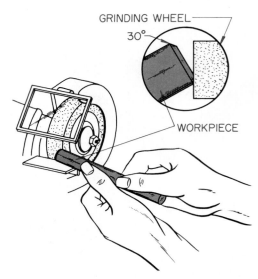

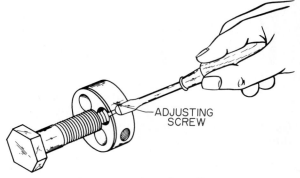

Fig. 20-6 *Beveling the end of the workpiece before threading.*

Fig. 20-7 *Adjusting a threading die to a standard bolt.*

How to Cut a Thread with a Die and Diestock

20-3

1. Bevel the end of the rod to be threaded (Fig. 20-6). ("Bevel" means to slant or taper the edge.) This makes it easier for the die to start the thread.
2. Hold the rod tightly in a machinist's vise so that it cannot turn.
3. Adjust the die to fit a **standard** bolt, that is, a bolt with threads of the same size you want to make (Fig. 20-7).
4. Mount the die in the diestock. Secure it with the **tightening screw** (Fig. 20-5).

5. Place the tapered, or **starting side,** of the die on the rod (Fig. 20-8).
6. Hold the diestock with both hands near the die (Fig. 20-9). **Keep the die as square as possible with the rod.** Press down firmly and at the same time slowly rotate the die **clockwise.** Larger die sizes require more pressure to get the die started. After two or three threads have been cut, heavy pressure on the die is no longer necessary. The die will continue to screw itself onto the rod as it is rotated.
7. Shift the position of your hands to the ends of the diestock, add a little cutting fluid, and continue to cut the thread (Fig. 20-10). Back up the die a half-turn every two or three threads to break and clean away the chips. This helps keep chips from clogging the die and roughening up the thread.

Threading to a shoulder. A shoulder is a diameter larger than the thread diameter. When full threads are needed as close to a

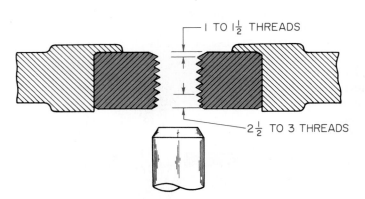

Fig. 20-8 *The starting side of the threading die has the most tapered threads.*

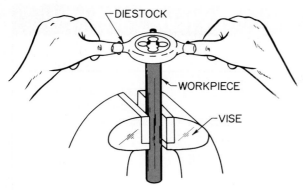

Fig. 20-9 *Placing the hands near the die on the diestock is important when starting a thread.*

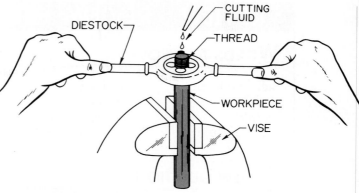

Fig. 20-10 *The hands may be moved to the ends of the diestock after cutting several threads.*

shoulder as possible, first cut the threads in the usual manner as described above. This will leave several partly cut threads near the shoulder. Then turn the die over and cut the partly finished threads up to the shoulder (Fig. 20-11). **Never cut full threads with the wrong side of the die, since the stress of cutting will usually result in broken die teeth.**

20-4 Cutting Fluids for Threading

When threading steel, use **sulfurized mineral oil** or one of the commercial cutting fluids made especially for threading steel. Special threading fluids are also available for aluminum. Cutting fluid recommendations for other metals are given in Table 50-2.

20-5 External Thread Measurements

External threads must be cut to the correct depth to produce the proper fit or class of thread. If the pitch diameter is too large, the thread fits too tightly. If it is too small, it fits too loosely.

The fit or class of external screw threads can be determined in the following ways:

1. By testing how the threaded piece fits in a standard mating nut or threaded hole.
2. By measuring the pitch diameter either with a thread micrometer (Fig. 14-4) or using the three-wire method with a plain micrometer.
3. With a thread ring gage (Fig. 93-13).
4. With a thread-roll snap gage (Fig. 93-10).

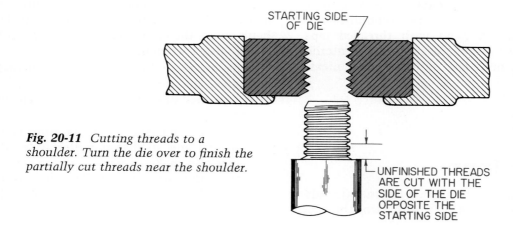

Fig. 20-11 *Cutting threads to a shoulder. Turn the die over to finish the partially cut threads near the shoulder.*

STARTING SIDE OF DIE

UNFINISHED THREADS ARE CUT WITH THE SIDE OF THE DIE OPPOSITE THE STARTING SIDE

REVIEW REVIEW REVIEW REVIEW REVIEW

WORDS TO KNOW

adjustable die	diestock	screw plate	threading die
bevel	left-hand die	solid die	thread-roll gage
collet	rethreading die	thread micrometer	starting side
cutting fluid	right-hand die	thread ring gage	

REVIEW QUESTIONS

1. What tool is used for cutting external threads?
2. Describe three kinds of dies for cutting new threads.
3. What kind of die is used for recutting damaged threads?
4. What is a screw plate?
5. What does ¼-20 UNC on a die mean?
6. What is a diestock?
7. Why should the end of a rod be beveled before threading?
8. Why is it necessary to back up the die when threading?
9. What kind of cutting fluid should be used when threading steel?
10. List several ways in which the fit or class of thread can be determined.

UNIT

21

Internal Threading with Taps

Most threaded studs, bolts, and screws have mating parts that have a hole with internal threads. Metalworkers sometimes cut these threads by hand with threaded taps. This unit describes the use of taps for internal threading, a necessary skill for most metalworkers.

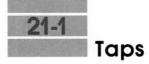

21-1 Taps

A **tap** is a tool for cutting **internal threads.** It has threads like a bolt with two, three or four **flutes** (grooves) cut across the threads (Fig. 21-1). The edges of the thread formed by the flutes are the cutting edges (Fig. 21-2). The **shank** end of the tap is square so that it can be turned with a wrench.

Taps are made from carbon steel or high-speed steel and are hardened and tempered. A set of taps includes a taper tap, a plug tap, and a bottoming tap (Fig. 21-1).

The **taper tap** has about six threads tapered at the end so that it will start easily. The taper also makes it easier to keep the tap straight as the cut is begun. The threads are cut gradually as the tap is turned into the hole.

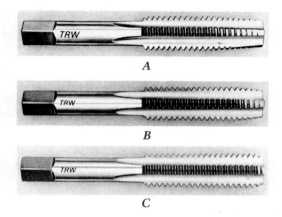

Fig. 21-1 *A set of hand taps. (A) Taper. (B) Plug. (C) Bottoming.* (Greenfield Tap & Die/Division of TRW Inc.)

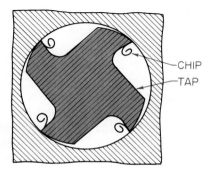

Fig. 21-2 *How the cutting edges of a tap cut.*

The **plug tap** has three or four threads tapered at the end and is used as a starting tap on easily cut metals.

The **bottoming tap** has full threads except for the first thread and is used to cut full threads as close as possible to the bottom of a hole.

Tap Styles

Taps are made in many styles to suit various hand- and machine-tapping operations.

Hand taps are straight-fluted, have three or four flutes, and have a cutting edge parallel to the center line of the tap (Fig. 21-5A). Chips tend to collect in the flutes of these taps. Unless the tap is backed out to clear it of chips, the tap may bind in the hole and break. **Gun taps** and **helical-fluted taps** are designed for efficient chip removal, thereby permitting rapid thread cutting with a minimum of tap breakage.

Gun taps are straight-fluted, with two, three, or four flutes depending on the size of the tap (Fig. 21-3). The cutting edges are ground at an angle to the centerline of the tap. The angular cutting edges cause the chips to shoot ahead of the tap. Plug-type gun taps are designed for tapping open, or **through,** holes. Bottoming-type gun taps are designed for tapping blind holes (holes that go only part-way into a workpiece), producing fine chips that can readily escape.

Helical-fluted taps, commonly known as **spiral-fluted taps** (Fig. 21-4), are designed to lift the chips out of the hole being tapped. For

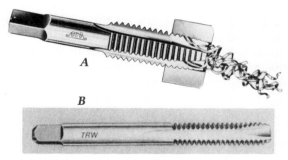

Fig. 21-3 *Gun taps. (A) Plug-type. Note the chip formation. (B) Bottoming-type* (Greenfield Tap & Die/Division of TRW Inc.

Fig. 21-4 *Spiral-fluted taps. (A) Low-angle. (B) High-angle.* (Greenfield Tap & Die/Division of TRW, Inc.)

this reason, they are well suited for tapping blind holes. **Low-angle** spiral-fluted taps are best for tapping ductile materials like aluminum, copper, or die-cast metals (Fig. 21-5B). **High-angle** spiral-fluted taps work best on tough metals, such as carbon and alloy steels. They are made with two, three, or four flutes, depending on the tap diameter, and are available in plug and bottoming types.

Serial taps are usually made in sets of three. They have one, two, or three identifying rings cut at the end of the shank (Fig. 21-6). These taps are designed for cutting threads in very tough metals. The taps are similar in appearance to the taper, plug, and bottoming taps, but they differ in **pitch diameter** and **major diameter.** Each tap is designed to remove part of the metal that must be cut away to produce the thread. The No. 1 tap is used first to make a shallow thread, then the No. 2 tap is used, and the No. 3 tap cuts the thread to final size.

Thread-forming taps (Fig. 21-7) have no cutting edges and therefore produce no chips. Threads are formed by forcing the metal to flow around the threads on the tap. This produces a strong thread, because the grain of the metal is forced to follow the thread profile and the surface is somewhat **work-hardened.** Because of the high pressures involved, thread depths are less than those produced by con-

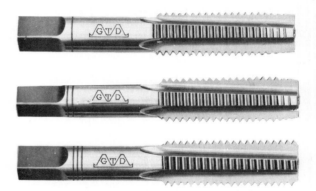

Fig. 21-6 *A set of serial taps.* (Greenfield Tap & Die/Division of TRW, Inc.)

Fig. 21-7 *A thread-forming tap.* (Greenfield Tap & Die/Division of TRW, Inc.)

ventional taps. Tap drills used with thread-forming taps (drills used to make the holes to be tapped) must be larger than those used with comparable conventional taps. The manufacturer's tap drill size recommendations should be carefully followed.

Left-hand taps cut left-hand threads. They are stamped with an "L" or an "LH." Right-hand taps are unmarked.

Fig. 21-5 *The cutting action of straight-fluted taps compared to spiral-fluted taps. (A) Straight-fluted hand tap. (B) Low-angle, spiral-fluted tap.* (Greenfield Tap & Die/Division of TRW, Inc.)

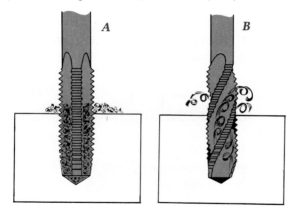

21-3

Sizes of Taps

Taps are made the same sizes as bolts and screws. The major diameter, pitch, and kind of thread are stamped on the shank of the tap. For example, **¼-20 UNC** means that the outside diameter of the tap is ¼", there are 20 threads per inch, and the thread is Unified National Coarse. Table 21-1 gives the sizes of inch-based taps.

A tap marked **M6 × 1** is a metric tap with an outside diameter of 6 mm and a pitch of 1 mm. The sizes of metric taps are given in Table 19-3.

21-4 Tap Size Limits

The size of the pitch diameter of a tap determines the **depth** and the **fit** of a tapped thread. Internal threads may be tapped for various classes of threads, such as classes 1B, 2B, and 3B. The thread may be either a loose or tight fit, depending on the pitch diameter of the tap.

Taps are available with either **cut** threads or **ground** threads. The ground threads produce tapped threads to a very accurate size. Taps with ground threads are made with **standard, oversize,** or **undersize** pitch diameters. The size limits of the pitch diameter are indicated by a **pitch diameter limit number,** such as L1, H1, H2, or H6, on the shank of ground thread taps. When purchasing taps of this type, the limits code number and the fit or class of thread to be tapped should be specified. If they are not specified, the supplier generally sends taps with pitch diameter limits for either of two sizes. One produces tapped threads for a Class 2 fit for National Form threads. The other produces threads for a Class 2B fit for Unified Form threads. These fits are used on most commercially available bolts, screws, and nuts.

The recommended taps for specific types of threads, including limits code numbers for various thread fits and classes of threads, are given in standard handbooks for machinists. For example, a ⅜-16 UNC ground thread tap for a Class 2B thread would be identified with the letter G and with the additional number H5; for a Class 3B thread, the code number would be GH3.

21-5 Internal Thread Measurement

Internal threads are checked for the correct fit or class of thread with **thread plug gages,** as shown in Unit 93.

21-6 Tap Drills

The hole to be tapped must be the right size. If the hole is too large, the thread will be too shallow; if it is too small, the tap may break. The drill that is used to make the hole before tapping is called the **tap drill.**

The tap drill should be a little larger than the diameter at the bottom, or **root,** of the thread, known as the **minor diameter** (Fig. 21-8). To save the time of figuring, tap drill sizes are put in the form of a table such as Table 21-1. The tap drill recommended for average work produces threads that are about 75% of the depth of external threads.

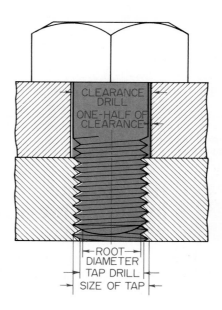

Fig. 21-8 *This drawing shows how the size of a tap, the size of a tap drill, and the minor (root) diameter of the thread compare to each other.*

Table 21-1

Tap Drills¹ and Clearance Drills² for Inch-Based Taps

| Size of tap | | Outside diameter (inches) | Root diameter (inches) | Size of tap drill (in inches) for 75% thread depth | | | Clearance drill (inches) | | |
UNC NC (USS)	UNF NF (SAE)			Number and letter drills	Fractional drills	Decimal equivalent	Size	Decimal equivalent	Clearance (inches)
	#0-80	0.0600	0.0438	. . .	3/64	0.0469	#51	0.0670	0.0070
#1-64	. . .	0.0730	0.0527	53	. . .	0.0595	#47	0.0785	0.0055
	#1-72	0.0730	0.0550	53	. . .	0.0595	#47	0.0785	0.0055
#2-56	. . .	0.0860	0.0628	50	. . .	0.0700	#42	0.0935	0.0075
	#2-64	0.0860	0.0657	50	. . .	0.0700	#42	0.0935	0.0075
#3-48	. . .	0.0990	0.0719	47	. . .	0.0785	#36	0.1065	0.0075
	#3-56	0.0990	0.0758	45	. . .	0.0820	#36	0.1065	0.0075
#4-40	. . .	0.1120	0.0795	43	. . .	0.0890	#31	0.1200	0.0080
	#4-48	0.1120	0.0849	42	. . .	0.0935	#31	0.1200	0.0080
#5-40	. . .	0.1250	0.0925	38	. . .	0.1015	#29	0.1360	0.0110
	#5-44	0.1250	0.0955	37	. . .	0.1040	#29	0.1360	0.0110
#6-32	. . .	0.1380	0.0974	36	. . .	0.1065	#25	0.1495	0.0115
	#6-40	0.1380	0.1055	33	. . .	0.1130	#25	0.1495	0.0115
#8-32	. . .	0.1640	0.1234	29	. . .	0.1360	#16	0.1770	0.0130
	#8-36	0.1640	0.1279	29	. . .	0.1360	#16	0.1770	0.0130
#10-24	. . .	0.1900	0.1359	25	. . .	0.1495	13/64	0.2031	0.0131
	#10-32	0.1900	0.1494	21	. . .	0.1590	13/64	0.2031	0.0131
#12-24	. . .	0.2160	0.1619	16	. . .	0.1770	7/32	0.2187	0.0027
	#12-28	0.2160	0.1696	14	. . .	0.1820	7/32	0.2187	0.0027
1/4"-20	. . .	0.2500	0.1850	7	. . .	0.2010	17/64	0.2656	0.0156
	1/4"-28	0.2500	0.2036	3	. . .	0.2130	17/64	0.2656	0.0156
5/16"-18	. . .	0.3125	0.2403	F	. . .	0.2570	21/64	0.3281	0.0156
	5/16"-24	0.3125	0.2584	I	. . .	0.2720	21/64	0.3281	0.0156
3/8"-16	. . .	0.3750	0.2938	. . .	5/16	0.3125	25/64	0.3906	0.0156
	3/8"-24	0.3750	0.3209	Q	. . .	0.3320	25/64	0.3906	0.0156
7/16"-14	. . .	0.4375	0.3447	U	. . .	0.3680	29/64	0.4531	0.0156
	7/16"-20	0.4375	0.3725	. . .	25/64	0.3906	29/64	0.4531	0.0156
1/2"-13	. . .	0.5000	0.4001	. . .	27/64	0.4219	33/64	0.5156	0.0156
	1/2"-20	0.5000	0.4350	. . .	29/64	0.4531	33/64	0.5156	0.0156
9/16"-12	. . .	0.5625	0.4542	. . .	31/64	0.4844	37/64	0.5781	0.0156
	9/16"-18	0.5625	0.4903	. . .	33/64	0.5156	37/64	0.5781	0.0156
5/8"-11	. . .	0.6250	0.5069	. . .	17/32	0.5312	41/64	0.6406	0.0156
	5/8"-18	0.6250	0.5528	. . .	37/64	0.5781	41/64	0.6406	0.0156
3/4"-10	. . .	0.7500	0.6201	. . .	21/32	0.6562	49/64	0.7656	0.0156
	3/4"-16	0.7500	0.6688	. . .	11/16	0.6875	49/64	0.7656	0.0156
7/8"-9	. . .	0.8750	0.7307	. . .	49/64	0.7656	57/64	0.8906	0.0156
	7/8"-14	0.8750	0.7822	. . .	13/16	0.8125	57/64	0.8906	0.0156
1"-8	. . .	1.0000	0.8376	. . .	7/8	0.8750	1-1/64	1.0156	0.0156
	1"-14	1.0000	0.9072	. . .	15/16	0.9375	1-1/64	1.0156	0.0156

¹If you cannot get the size of tap drill given here, see Table 54-2 "Drill Sizes," to find the size of drill nearest to it. Be sure to get a drill a little larger than the **root diameter** of the thread.

²The drill that makes a hole in a workpiece so that a bolt or screw may pass through is called a clearance drill.

21-7 How to Cut Internal Threads with a Tap

1. Drill the hole with the proper size tap drill.
2. Clamp the workpiece in a vise with the hole in an upright position.
3. Install a **taper tap** or a **plug tap** of the correct size in a **tap wrench** (Fig. 21-9). (The **T-handle tap wrench** is used for holding small taps.)
4. Insert the end of the tap in the hole, then grasp the tap wrench with both hands close to the tap (Fig. 21-10). Press down firmly on

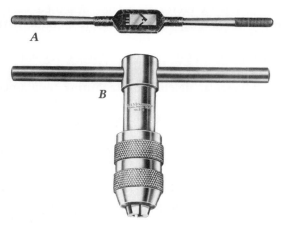

Fig. 21-9 *Tap wrenches. (A) Adjustable. (B) T-handle. (Greenfield Tap & Die/Division of TRW, Inc.) (L.S. Starrett Company)*

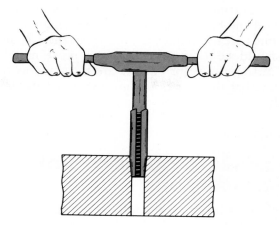

Fig. 21-10 *When starting a thread with a tap, keep your hands near the tap on the tap wrench.*

the tap while turning it clockwise. Larger taps require more pressure to get the tap started.

5. **It is very important that the tap be started parallel with the hole.** If the hole is 90 degrees to the top of the workpiece, a square or steel rule can be used to check its alignment (Fig. 21-11). A tap that is started at an angle to the hole is forced to cut a deeper and deeper thread on one side of the hole as it gets deeper. This often results in a broken tap.

6. Once several threads have been cut, it is no longer necessary to press down on the tap. Lubricate the tap with an appropriate cutting fluid. Shift your hands to the ends of the tap wrench (Fig. 21-12), and continue to turn the tap until the threads are as deep as required. If a **hand tap** is being used, back the tap up every two or three turns to break the chip. It is not necessary to back up when using a gun, helical, or thread forming tap.

   Tapping blind holes. If full threads to the bottom of a blind hole are desired, run the **plug tap** in as far as it will go. Clean out the hole now and then. In this way, the chips collecting in the bottom of the hole will not keep the tap from going to the bottom. Then change to the **bottoming tap,** and finish cutting the partially cut threads at the bottom of the hole.

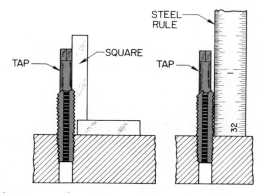

Fig. 21-11 *The tap must be parallel to the hole to minimize the chance of tap breakage.*

Fig. 21-12 *Shift your hands to the ends of the tap wrench after the thread has been started.*

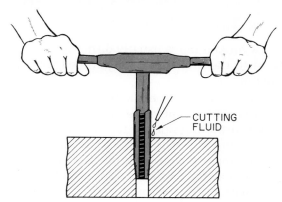

Cutting fluids for tapping. Taps are very hard and brittle and are easily broken. Cutting fluids greatly reduce the strain on the tap, and should be used when tapping most metals. Cutting fluids for tapping are the same as for external threading, and are explained in Unit 20.

21-8 Causes of Broken Taps

Taps break for the following reasons:

1. A hole that has been drilled too small forces the tap to remove more metal than it is able to; therefore, it jams and breaks.
2. A tap that is started at an angle to the hole sticks tight and then breaks.
3. The tap wrench acts like a **lever.** With it, a great twisting force can be put upon the tap. Misuse of this force breaks many taps. Applying more pressure to one side of the tap wrench than the other may also break the tap.
4. Lack of cutting fluid where required will cause a tap to stick tight and break.
5. Failure to back up the tap will cause the chips to crowd in front of the cutting edges or to pack tight in the flutes of the tap. More force is then needed to turn the tap, and this extra force is often more than the tap can stand.
6. Turning a tap after the bottom of the hole is reached will cause it to break.

21-9 Removing a Broken Tap from a Hole

A broken tap is usually difficult to remove because the broken part is jammed tightly in the hole.

A tap broken near the top of the hole may sometimes be removed by placing a dull **cape chisel** in the flute of the tap and striking light blows with the hammer, as shown in Figure 21-13. Apply **penetrating oil** first, then work the broken tap both clockwise and counterclockwise until it is loose.

A **tap extractor** is a tool designed to remove broken taps (Fig. 21-14). It is made with slender steel fingers that fit into the flutes of the tap, so that a twisting force can be applied to remove the broken tap.

Electrical discharge machining, explained in Unit 83, can be used to cut away the broken tap if the above methods fail.

21-10 Thread Inserts

Thread inserts are threaded steel **bushings.** They are used to replace worn or damaged threads. They are also used to provide strong wear-resistant threads in low tensile strength metals, such as cast aluminum and magnesium. Special tools are required for installing some types of thread inserts. However, some types of thread inserts are installed without special tooling (Fig. 21-15).

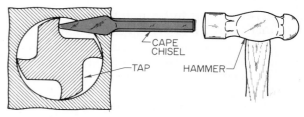

Fig. 21-13 *Removing a broken tap with a cape chisel and hammer.*

Fig. 21-14 *A tap extractor can sometimes be used to remove a broken tap.* (The Walton Company)

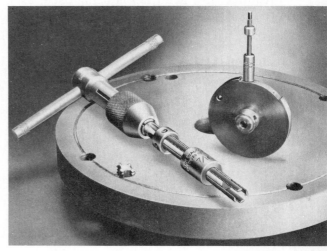

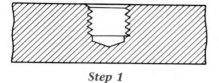

Step 1

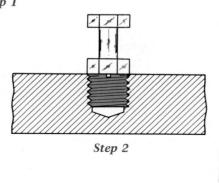

Step 2

Fig. 21-15 *The three basic steps for installing a thread insert. Step 1. Drill out worn thread and tap for thread insert. Step 2. Install thread insert. Step 3. Remove thread insertion tool.*

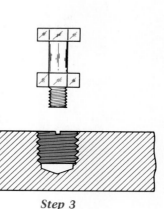

Step 3

REVIEW   REVIEW   REVIEW   REVIEW   REVIEW

WORDS TO KNOW

blind hole
bottoming tap
gun tap
hand tap

left-hand tap
plug tap
right-hand tap

serial taps
tap extractor
taper tap

T-handle tap
 wrench
thread-forming tap
thread insert

REVIEW QUESTIONS

1. What is the name of the tool used for cutting internal threads?
2. Describe a taper tap; plug tap; bottoming tap. What is each used for?
3. How does a machine tap differ from a hand tap?
4. How do thread-forming taps differ from conventional taps?
5. What does 5/16-18 UNC stamped on the shank of a tap mean?
6. What does M12 × 1.75 stamped on the shank of a tap mean?
7. What is a tap drill?
8. What size tap drill is used for a ¼"-20 UNC thread? M6 thread?
9. What is a tap wrench? Name two types.
10. When hand-tapping, why should the tap be kept square with the work?
11. What kind of lubricant should be used for tapping steel? Aluminum?
12. Why is it necessary to back up hand taps while tapping?
13. How can a broken tap be removed from a hole?
14. Name six causes of broken taps.
15. What are thread inserts? What are they used for?

PART

7

Fitting and Assembling

One of the most interesting jobs for a young welder would be to work on the wings of the XB-70 supersonic aircraft or the cone connectors for the Trident missile. Such jobs are common for those who work under Donald Clayton, manager of an electron beam welding (EBW) company. Donald, who spent his younger years on a farm, has been around machinery most of his life. He learned to weld in the Navy, but German-speaking technicians first taught him about EBW machinery.

The company Donald works for imported four EBW machines from Germany. Technical representatives and interpreters accompanied the equipment and taught Donald how to operate it. Later, his company constructed its own EBW machine. Many of the company's products are used in aerospace programs. Donald's welders work on telescopes, fuel lines, tanks, and special antennas for space shuttles. On the other hand, they also weld heart pacemakers and special tools used in brain surgery.

EBW welders are trained to use both hands and both feet to operate the controls of the machine. Sitting outside the box-like hard-vacuum chamber, he or she works levers and pedals that change the position of the workpiece and the intensity of the electron beam.

Electron beam welding is especially good for welding the latest "super-alloys," which are used extensively in spacecraft and aircraft. One potential problem with EBW is its production of X-rays. The box must have heavy shielding to protect the welders. Donald's company, however, has no trouble in meeting safety regulations.

Donald says that students should have the opportunity to learn about the latest types of nontraditional machining methods. He has invested his time and energy in this field, and it has paid off well in job satisfaction.

Donald Clayton
Manager
Electron Beam Welding

UNIT

22

Fits and Fitting

In metalworking, "fitting" means preparing parts so they go together correctly. Mating parts are assembled so that one part turns inside or slides upon another part; or, the parts are fastened tightly together so they cannot move upon each other.

Removing small amounts of material by filing, scraping, grinding, or cutting by machines may be necessary to make the parts fit properly. Most fitting is done when assembling precision machine tools and instruments. Workers must be highly skilled, therefore, to prevent ruining valuable parts.

Diemakers fit parts of dies to each other. Assemblers fit different parts of a machine together. Machinists fit parts such as wheels, pulleys, bearings, and shafts when repairing machines.

22-1 The Kinds of Standard Fits

The term **fit** is used to describe how tight two mating parts go together. The kind of fit that exists depends on the tolerances and allowances that were called for in the design of the parts. Tolerances and allowances are explained in Unit 9. When parts are produced within the maximum and minimum size limits specified on a drawing, as described in Unit 9, they may be assembled with the desired kind of fit. Some parts have to fit together tightly, while others have to fit loosely.

A system of **standard fits** has been established for the design and assembly of mating parts. It is the American National Standard Institute (ANSI) **Preferred Limits and Fits for Cylindrical Parts.**[1] It includes three general

groups of fits between plain (unthreaded) cylindrical parts. These general classifications are designated with symbols for educational purposes only. The symbols are **not** shown on drawings. Instead, the dimensional size limits for each part are specified on the drawing for the kind of fit desired. The three general groups of fits are as follows:

Running and Sliding Fits (RC)
Locational Fits (LC, LT, and LN)
   locational clearance fit (LC)
   locational interference fit (LN)
   locational transition fit (LT)
Force Fits (FN)

These letter symbols are used with additional numbers to designate specific classes of fits within each general group of fits. An example of one running or sliding fit is **RC 1,** for "free-running fit." The different fits (as indicated by two letters and a number) are included in tables in handbooks for machinists. Each symbol represents a complete fit, including minimum and maximum clearance or interference.

Fits of threads and classes of threads are explained in Unit 19.

22-2 Running and Sliding Fits (RC)

The **sliding fit** is a close fit between two parts with enough clearance so that one part can slide freely without wobbling. Examples

---

[1]Extracted and adapted from American National Standards Institute **Preferred Limits and Fits for Cylindrical Parts** (ASA B4.1-1967 R. 1974), with the permission of the publisher, The American Society of Mechanical Engineers, New York.

of sliding fits are a piston sliding up and down in a cylinder of an engine (Fig. 22-1) or the quill that must slide smoothly in the head of a drill press (Fig. 22-2).

The **running fit** is used where one part revolves inside another. A **shaft** running in a **bearing,** as in a drill press **spindle** (Fig. 22-2) must have a running fit. The fit must not be so tight that it keeps the shaft from turning, nor so loose that it wobbles from side-to-side.

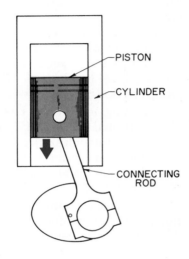

Fig. 22-1 *Engine pistons and their cylinders must have good sliding fits.*

PISTON

CYLINDER

CONNECTING ROD

Fig. 22-2 *Two examples of fits in a drill press: A. The sliding fit of the quill. B. The running fit of the spindle.*

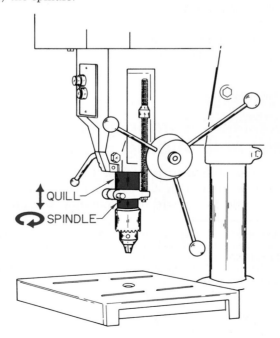

QUILL

SPINDLE

22-3 Locational Fits

Locational fits are used to accurately locate the position of mating parts (Fig. 22-3). Some mating parts must be located rigidly and accurately, while others may be located with some looseness for ease in assembling them.

Locational clearance fits (LC) are used in the assembly of stationary parts where some clearance is permissible. Fits may range from snug fits to medium amount clearance fits.

Locational interference fits (LN) are used where accuracy of location and rigidity of mating parts are most important. These fits are used where a load from one part must be transferred directly to another part without loss of motion. **Force fits** and **shrink fits** can satisfy this requirement.

Locational transitional fits (LT) are ranked between clearance fits and interference fits. They are used where accuracy of location is important and where a small amount of either clearance or interference is permissible between the mating parts.

22-4 Force and Shrink Fits (FN)

Force fits and shrink fits include several classes of fits that involve interference between mating parts. Generally, the hole size is a standard size. The shaft is slightly larger, thus causing definite interference. Parts assembled with a force fit may be assembled in three ways: (1) they may be driven together with a hammer, (2) they may be forced together with a vise or an arbor press (Fig. 22-4), or (3) they may be assembled with a **shrink fit,** which will be explained shortly.

Force fits are used where parts must be held together very tightly. With these fits, parts can be fastened together almost as tightly as though they were made from one piece. Force fits are used to assemble gears, pulleys, bearings, and similar parts on shafts.

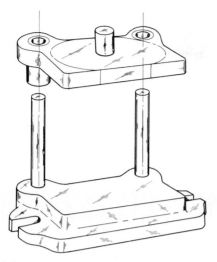

Fig. 22-3 *Die sets require an accurate locational clearance fit between the posts and their mating sockets.*

SHAFT
PULLEY

Fig. 22-4 *An arbor press is used to force-fit a shaft to a pulley.*

Shrink fits are classified under force fits, since they involve interference between mating parts. However, where heavy driving or pressing forces are not practical or possible, the parts are installed by **shrinking** one part onto the other. A pulley, gear, or collar may be fastened to a shaft with a shrink fit. The hole diameter is made slightly smaller than the shaft. The part with the hole is made larger by heating it (to cause the hole to expand). The expanded part is then placed in position on the shaft, and allowed to cool and shrink onto the shaft. If properly done, the part is held on the shaft with much greater pressure than if it were pressed on. The pulley and shaft are nearly as tight as though they were one piece.

The differences in the diameters is called the **allowance** for the fit. For example, if the shaft diameter is 0.500″ [12.70 mm] and the hole diameter is 0.501″ [12.725 mm], then the allowance is 0.001″ [0.025 mm]. The amount of allowance depends upon:
1. Size of work.
2. Kind of metal.
3. Amount of metal around hole.
4. Smoothness of hole and shaft.

Recommended allowances for different kinds and classes of fits are provided in handbooks for machinists and engineers.

22-5 Allowances for Different Fits

When a shaft is fitted to a bearing for a running or sliding fit, the diameter of the shaft should be a little smaller than the diameter of the bearing to allow space for a film of oil between the surfaces and to allow the shaft to get larger from the heat caused by rubbing.

22-6 Shims

Several layers of very thin metal are often used to separate the two halves of a plain bearing (Fig. 22-5). They are called shims. As the bearing wears down and allows the shaft to loosen, one or more layers of the shim may be removed to restore the proper fit.

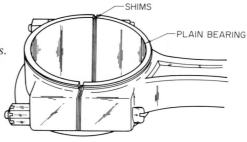

Fig. 22-5 *The use of shims allows adjustment for wear in plain bearings.*

REVIEW   REVIEW   REVIEW   REVIEW   REVIEW

WORDS TO KNOW

allowance
arbor press
force fit (FN)

locational fits
  clearance fit (LC)
  interference fit
  (LN)

transitional fit
(LT)
running fit (RC)
shim

shrink fit (FN)
sliding fit (RC)

REVIEW QUESTIONS

1. What does fitting mean?
2. List the metal-removal operations used in fitting parts together.
3. Name three kinds of standard fits that are used in the assembly of unthreaded cylindrical parts.
4. List the three kinds of locational fits.
5. Give an example of where a sliding fit is used.
6. Give an example of where a running fit is used.
7. How does a locational fit differ from a running fit?
8. Give several examples of where force fits would be used.
9. What is an arbor press used for?
10. Describe how a pulley and shaft can be assembled using a shrink fit.
11. Why are shims used in plain bearings?

UNIT

23

Scrapers and Scraping

Scraping is a process of shaving off small amounts of metal using hand-held scraping tools (Fig. 23-1). Scraping is most often done to obtain precision alignment of machine parts (Fig. 23-2). It is also done to provide shallow pockets that will hold lubricants on flat surfaces, such as machine **ways.** (Machine ways are discussed in Unit 58.)

Machined surfaces usually are not perfectly true for a number of reasons: (1) metal may be of unequal hardness, or (2) the metal may have been sprung out of true shape while being clamped for machining, or (3) the cutting tool may have worn during the machining.

If a very true surface is needed, the high spots must be located and removed by hand scraping.

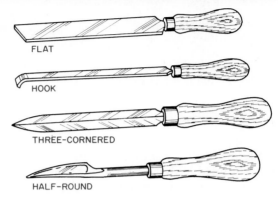

Fig. 23-1 *Scrapers. Cutting edges are of hardened steel or tungsten carbide.*

Fig. 23-2 *Precision fitting of machine parts is often accomplished by hand scraping. Here, scraping is being done on a horizontal milling machine column casting. (Cincinnati Milacron)*

23-1

Scraping Tools

Scrapers are made in several shapes and have cutting edges of **hardened steel** or **tungsten carbide** (Fig. 23-1). **Hook** and **flat scrapers** are used for scraping flat surfaces. **Half-round** and **three-cornered scrapers** are used on curved surfaces. The three-cornered scraper is also useful for removing sharp edges, or **burrs,** from around holes.

23-2

Holding a Scraper

Scrapers are held as shown in Figures 23-3 and 23-4. The handle of the scraper for

Fig. 23-3 *Scraping a flat surface.*

high spots, test again on the surface plate and again scrape off the high spots. Repeat these operations until the blue marks increase and are evenly spread over the surface of the work.

23-4 Scraping a Round Bearing

Round bearings must fit with other sliding or running parts; any **shaft bearing** is an example of this (Fig. 23-4). The same way of marking and scraping the high spots of flat surfaces is also used for round and curved surfaces. For round surfaces the Prussian blue is put on the shaft or other part that fits into the hollow surface. It is then rubbed over the round surface, leaving blue marks on the high spots (Fig. 23-5). The half-round scraper, and sometimes the three-cornered scraper, is used for scraping round and curved surfaces.

flat scraping should be held and steadied under the right (or dominant) arm while the blade is guided by both hands. All scrapers except the hook scraper cut on the pushing stroke. Lift the scraper a little on the return stroke. Experience teaches how hard one should press and at what angle the tool cuts the metal easily.

23-3 Scraping a Flat Surface

A surface plate, a flat piece of metal, is used to find the high spots on a flat surface. The surface plate should be larger than the surface to be scraped. The top of the surface plate is covered with a very thin film of **Prussian blue.** This blue paint comes in a tube, is about as thick as toothpaste, and may be applied with a small brush. The surface to be scraped is then laid on the surface plate and moved back and forth. Thus, the high spots that have to be removed will be marked with Prussian blue from the surface plate. If too thick a coat is put on the surface plate, the low spots on the work will be marked as well as the high ones.

Finding the high spots is called **spotting.** Remove the spots marked blue with a flat scraper as in Figure 23-3. After scraping off the

Fig. 23-4 *Scraping a round bearing.*

Fig. 23-5 *Prussian blue has marked the high spots to be scraped off a bearing.*

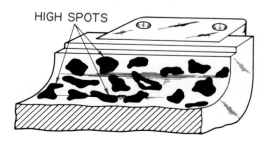

HIGH SPOTS

Fig. 23-6 *Frosting a flat surface.*

23-5 Frosting or Flowering

Frosting, or flowering, is a decorative finish that is an imitation of frost, patchwork, or a checkerboard design (Fig. 23-6). It is made by scraping off the high spots, as was explained in the scraping of flat surfaces. The strokes should be about ¼″ to ½″ [6.25 to 12.7 mm], and the direction should be changed after each stroke.

REVIEW REVIEW REVIEW REVIEW REVIEW

WORDS TO KNOW

burr	frosting	Prussian blue	surface plate
flat scraper	half-round scraper	scraping	three-cornered
flowering	hook scraper	spotting	scraper

REVIEW QUESTIONS

1. Give several reasons for scraping.
2. What is Prussian blue?
3. Why should Prussian blue be applied in a thin layer?
4. What kind of a scraper should be used when scraping a flat surface?
5. What kind of scraper should be used when scraping a curved surface?
6. Describe the procedure for scraping flat surfaces.
7. What is meant by "frosting" or "flowering"?

UNIT
24
Assembly Tools

"Assembling" means putting the parts of something together. For example, automobile parts must be put together to make complete automobiles. Machinists and many other industrial workers need tools for aligning mating parts, temporarily holding parts in place, and for installing fasteners. Many specialized assembly tools are made for workers on assembly lines in plants where products are mass-produced (Fig. 24-1).

24-1
Screwdrivers

Screwdrivers are used to turn, or **drive,** screws. They are made in many sizes and several shapes (Fig. 24-2). The size is measured by

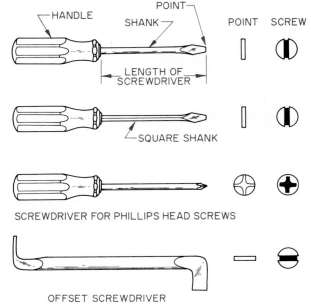

Fig. 24-2 *Common types of screwdrivers and screwheads.*

the length of the **blade,** which is made of tool steel that is **hardened** and **tempered.** The screwdriver point for driving slotted screws should be correctly shaped (Fig. 24-3). The **parallel** sides of the point must fit against the sides of the slot.

To avoid injuring the hand if the screwdriver slips, when using a screwdriver, lay small work on the bench (Fig. 24-4) instead of holding it in the hand. Burrs made by a screwdriver slipping out of a screw slot should be filed off to prevent cutting your hands.

The shafts on some larger screwdrivers are **square;** a wrench may be used to turn such a screwdriver (Fig. 24-5).

An **offset screwdriver** has a bent handle. It is used where a straight screwdriver will not reach (Fig. 24-6).

Fig. 24-1 *This mechanical wrench tightens all the lugs on this auto wheel at the same time, using the same amount of torque.* (Chevrolet Motor Division, General Motors)

Special screwdrivers are required for driving *Phillips head* and other screws that do not have standard screw slots.

24-2 Pliers

There are many kinds of pliers, some of which are shown in Figure 24-7. They are useful for cutting small wire and for holding, twisting, turning, pulling, and pushing.

Fig. 24-3 *The correct shape of a screwdriver point.*

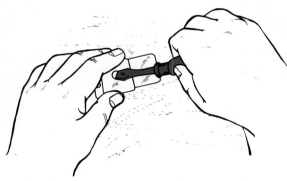

Fig. 24-4 *To use a screwdriver on small work, place the workpiece on the bench, not in your hand.*

Fig. 24-5 *Turning a screwdriver with a wrench.*

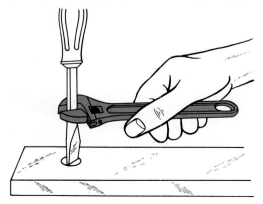

Slip-joint pliers, also known as **combination pliers,** are used for gripping; they can also cut small-size wire. The **slip-joint** makes it possible to grip large parts.

Side-cutting pliers are especially useful for cutting wire and nails. They are used by electricians for cutting electric wires. The flat square jaws are useful for bending corners on thin metal.

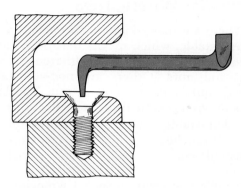

Fig. 24-6 *Using an offset screwdriver.*

Fig. 24-7 *Common types of pliers.*

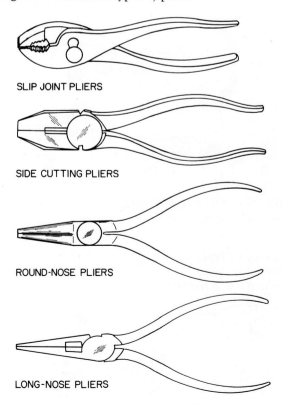

SLIP JOINT PLIERS

SIDE CUTTING PLIERS

ROUND-NOSE PLIERS

LONG-NOSE PLIERS

Round-nose pliers are used to bend small wire and thin metal, and to hold small parts.

Some pliers have long tapered jaws and are called **long-nose** pliers. They are used for handling small parts where space is limited.

24-3

Wrenches

There are many kinds of wrenches. Some are **adjustable,** which means that they can be made larger or smaller to fit different sizes of bolts and nuts. Others are **non-adjustable;** they fit only one size bolt or nut. The basic types of wrenches fit these classifications:

Adjustable Wrenches	Nonadjustable Wrenches
Adjustable-end wrench	Open-end wrench
Adjustable S-wrench	Box wrench
Monkey wrench	Socket wrench
Vise-grip® wrench	Spanner wrench
Pipe wrench	Hexagonal wrench

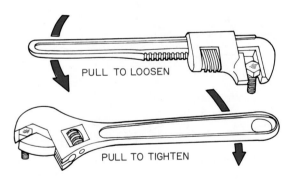

Fig. 24-8 *When using adjustable wrenches, point the jaws in the direction of pull.*

Fig. 24-9 *Types of adjustable open-end wrenches. (A) Adjustable end wrench. (B) Adjustable S-wrench.*

Adjustable Wrenches

When an adjustable wrench is used, the jaws should be tight on the nut. The wrench should also be pointed in the same direction that one intends to pull (Fig. 24-8) to avoid spreading the jaws. The **fixed** jaw is the stronger of the two and can, therefore, stand more strain.

The **adjustable-end wrench** (Fig. 24-9) is a strong tool used for general work in the shop. Its jaws are pointed at such an angle that it can be used in close corners and unhandy places.

The **adjustable S-wrench** (Fig. 24-9) is useful in many places where a straight-handled wrench cannot be used.

The **monkey wrench** (Fig. 24-10) is named after its inventor, Charles Moncky. It is used for tightening or loosening bolts and nuts, bending metal, etc.

The **Vise-grip® wrench** (Fig. 24-11), also called **Vise-grip® pliers,** works in close places and the strong steel jaws lock to the work and will not slip. It can be used as a vise, clamp, plier, pipe wrench, or open-end wrench. It can grip round, square, or other shaped objects.

The **pipe wrench** is used to hold or turn pipes or other round pieces of metal (Fig. 24-12). The teeth should be kept free of metal

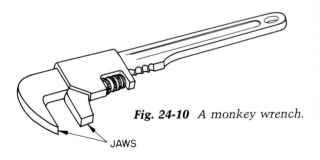

Fig. 24-10 *A monkey wrench.*

JAWS

Fig. 24-11 *A Vise-grip® wrench.*

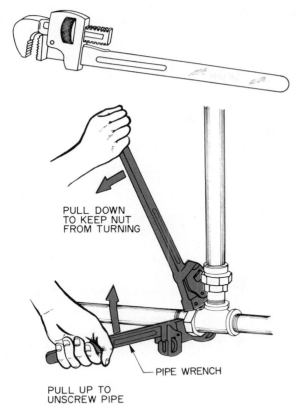

PULL DOWN
TO KEEP NUT
FROM TURNING

PIPE WRENCH

PULL UP TO
UNSCREW PIPE

Fig. 24-12 *Using two pipe wrenches.*

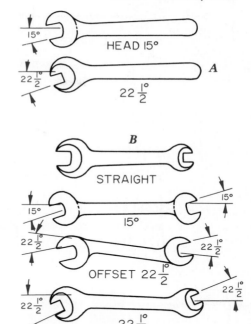

Fig. 24-13 *Open-end wrenches. (A) Single end. (B) Double end.*

Fig. 24-14 *Use of a 15 offset wrench makes it possible to turn a nut or bolt in a tight space.*

Fig. 24-15 *A box wrench. The end is closed and the handle is offset 15.*

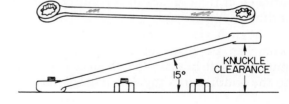

KNUCKLE
CLEARANCE

chips to keep the wrench from slipping. When using the pipe wrench, point the jaws in the direction you intend to pull, as in Figure 24-12.

Nonadjustable Wrenches

Several **open-end wrenches** are shown in Figure 24-13. Some have a **single end,** others have a **double end.** On others the **head** makes a 15° or 22½° angle with the center line of the handle.

The 15° and the 22½° wrenches are used in narrow spaces, where a straight wrench cannot make a quarter of a turn (90°) for a **square nut** or a sixth of a turn (60°) for a hexagon nut (which has six sides). Flopping the 15° wrench to the other side permits a 30° swing (Fig. 24-14). The 22½° wrench is used the same way.

Box wrenches have closed ends (Fig. 24-15); that is, the head of the wrench goes completely around the nut or bolt head. Their

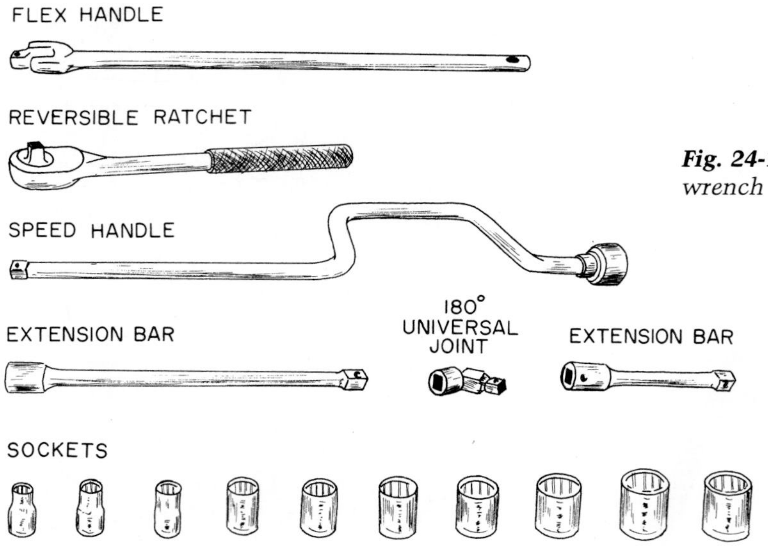

FLEX HANDLE

REVERSIBLE RATCHET

Fig. 24-16 *A socket wrench set.*

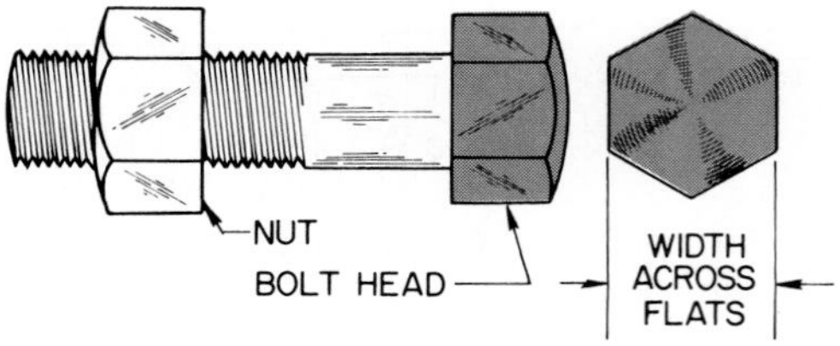

SPEED HANDLE

EXTENSION BAR

180°
UNIVERSAL
JOINT

EXTENSION BAR

SOCKETS

NUT

BOLT HEAD

WIDTH
ACROSS
FLATS

Fig. 24-17 *Wrench sizes correspond to the width of bolt heads and nuts across the flats.*

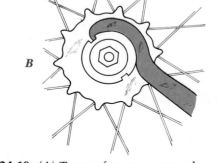

A — PINS   PIN SPANNER

FACE SPANNER

B

Fig. 24-18 *(A) Types of spanner wrenches. (B) Using a hook spanner wrench.*

handles are usually offset 15°, which provides wrench (and user's knuckles) clearance for nearby obstacles.

Socket wrenches (Fig. 24-16) are used to turn nuts and bolts that are in hard-to-reach places or below the surface of the work. A set of socket wrenches includes an assortment of **sockets** that engage the nut or the bolt head; one or more **extension bars;** a **flex handle** (commonly called a **breaker bar**) for loosening difficult nuts and bolts; a **reversible ratchet** for normal loosening and tightening; a **speed handle** for rapid assembly or disassembly of threaded parts; and a **universal joint,** which is used when the wrench handles cannot be positioned at right angles to the nut or bolt centerline.

Wrench sizes. Open end, box, and socket wrenches are made in all common sizes of nuts and bolt heads. Wrench sizes correspond to the width across the **flats** (Fig. 24-17).

They are available for use with bolts and nuts made in both U.S. Customary and S.I. metric sizes.

Spanner wrenches have a hook or one or two **pins** (Fig. 24-18). **Hook spanner wrenches** fit into a slot. **Pin spanner wrenches** fit into holes in threaded collars, and are used to loosen or tighten them.

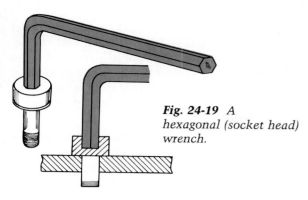

Fig. 24-19 *A hexagonal (socket head) wrench.*

Fig. 24-20 *A torque wrench.*

Hexagonal wrenches are also called **hex keys** and **Allen wrenches.** They are used with **socket cap screws** and **socket set-screws** (Fig. 24-19). They are available in a wide range of sizes, either singly or in sets. Handle length is proportional to the size of the wrench, but wrenches can be obtained with extra-long handles for reaching screws in hard-to-reach locations.

Torque Wrenches

Torque is a turning or twisting force applied to a bolt or shaft, and it is measured in pound-feet or newton-meters. The torque wrench (Fig. 24-20) is used when several bolts or nuts must all be tightened a uniform amount. It is also used to prevent overtightening a single fastener. Such overtightening produces uneven or excess stresses that may warp or pull the work out of shape. Thread stripping and bolt breakage are also avoided by intelligent use of the torque wrench.

Powered Wrenches

Electric- and air-powered wrenches (Fig. 24-21) enable workers to rapidly assemble and disassemble parts with a minimum of physical effort. These wrenches can be preset for a given amount of torque. Other powered units are available for driving screws, tapping threads, chipping and riveting.

Using Wrenches

Always use a wrench that fits the bolt or nut snugly. When using an **adjustable wrench,** set the **movable jaw** until it fits tightly on the bolt or nut. Use small wrenches for small bolts and nuts, and large wrenches on large bolts and nuts.

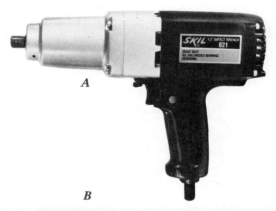

A

B

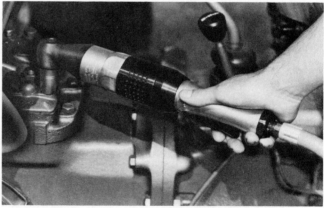

Fig. 24-21 *Power wrenches. (A) Electric. (B) Air.* (Skil Corporation)

A wrench is a **lever.** That is, the length of the handle gives the user a **mechanical advantage** in tightening or loosening a bolt or nut. The longer the handle, the greater is the multiplication of force of the wrench. **It is very important not to overtighten bolts and nuts.** Overtightening can distort and weaken threads, strip threads, or break bolts.

24-4

Punches

A **drift punch** has a long tapered end (Fig. 24-22). It is used to align holes in two parts so that bolts, rivets, or pins can be easily inserted (Fig. 24-23). It is also used for loosening **pins** or **rivets** (Fig. 24-25).

Fig. 24-22   *A drift punch.*

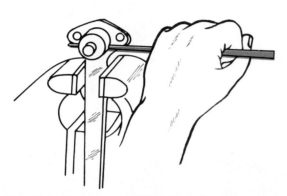

Fig. 24-23   *Aligning holes with a drift punch.*

Fig. 24-24   *A set of pin punches.* (L.S. Starrett Company)

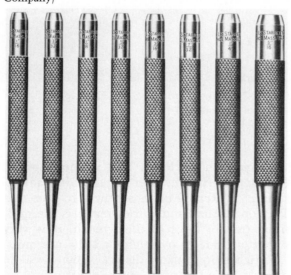

A **pin punch** (Fig. 24-24) has an end of uniform diameter and is used to drive out pins and rivets that cannot be driven out with a drift punch. The pins should first be loosened with a drift punch and then driven out with the pin punch (Fig. 24-25).

A **transfer punch** is a pin punch with a point at its end like a center punch (Fig. 24-26). It is used to transfer the location of the center of a hole on one part to another part. A matching hole can then be drilled for use in assembly.

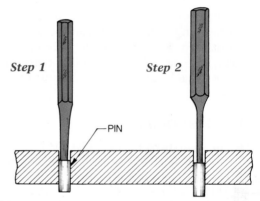

Fig. 24-25   *Using drift and pin punches correctly. (Step 1) Use drift punch to loosen pin. (Step 2) Use pin punch to drive out pin.*

Fig. 24-26   *A transfer punch is used to transfer the location of the center of a hole from one part to another. Transfer punches come in many sizes.*

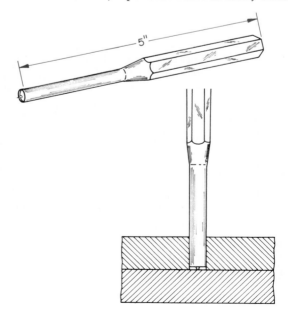

24-5 Hammers and Mallets

The **machinist's hammer,** also called the **ball-peen hammer,** has been described in Unit 12. In assembly work, it is used mostly for striking punches and driving pins used to position or assemble parts. Use a small hammer for light work and a large hammer for heavy work.

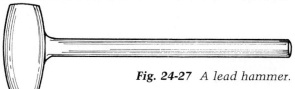

Fig. 24-27 *A lead hammer.*

Fig. 24-28 *A combination ladle and hammer mold for making a lead hammer.*

Soft hammers—with heads made of lead, copper, brass, or other soft materials—are used to strike hardened steel surfaces to avoid chipping. They are also used to strike soft metals or **finished surfaces,** which must not be damaged.

A **lead hammer** (Fig. 24-27) is used for striking finished surfaces where a harder hammer would dent or nick the surface. The head of a lead hammer is made of a lead alloy that is soft enough to be deformed when it hits a solid surface. This provides a **dead blow,** which transfers all the energy of the blow to the object struck, instead of wasting some of the energy in bouncing the hammer off the object.

Battered lead hammers can be **recast** with a **lead hammer mold** (Fig. 24-28). A lead hammer made of pure lead may be too soft and may **mushroom** too easily. It will last longer if a little **antimony** is alloyed with the lead.

Mallets are made of wood, leather, plastic, and rubber (Fig. 24-29). They are used for many of the same purposes as soft metal hammers.

Fig. 24-29 *A rubber mallet.*

24-6

Arbor Press

An arbor press is a machine for pressing parts of machinery together or forcing them apart, such as pressing a shaft in or out of a pulley or gear (Fig. 24-30).

Powerful **hydraulic** arbor presses are also made.

24-7

Machinist's Vise

The machinist's vise (Fig. 24-31) is often used to clamp parts together while they are being assembled. The size of the vise is determined by the width of the jaws. The vise jaws are made of hardened steel and have serrated faces that bite into the surface of a workpiece and mark it unless some protection is provided. Soft **jaw caps** of copper, brass, or aluminum can be made or purchased. They fit over the hardened steel jaws and protect the finished surfaces of the workpiece (Fig. 24-32).

Fig. 24-31 *A machinist's vise.* (L.S. Starrett Company)

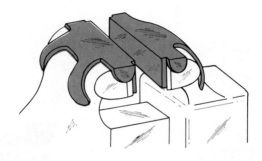

Fig. 24-32 *Soft jaw caps for a machinist's vise.*

Fig. 24-30 *Pressing a shaft into a pulley with an arbor press.*

24-8

Clamps

Clamps are often used to temporarily hold parts together while being assembled.

C-clamps are shaped like the letter C. They are made in many sizes and are very useful general purpose clamps (Fig. 24-33).

Toolmaker's parallel clamps have two parallel jaws, which are opened or closed by two screws (Fig. 24-34). They are also made in several sizes and are best suited for holding small parts together.

Toggle clamps made in many sizes and types are widely used in special workholding fixtures (Fig. 24-35). Their design provides for quick clamping and release. Clamping power can be adjusted from very light to very heavy. Air-powered toggle clamps are also available.

Spring clamps are useful where only light holding power is needed. They can be quickly applied and released because of their spring action (Fig. 24-36).

Fig. 24-33 *Two sizes of C-clamps being used to hold parts for welding.* (Adjustable Clamp Co.)

Fig. 24-34 *A toolmaker's parallel clamp.* (The Lufkin Tool Co.)

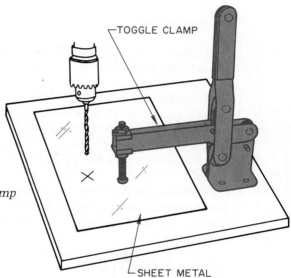

TOGGLE CLAMP

SHEET METAL

Fig. 24-35 *Using a toggle clamp fixture to hold a workpiece.*

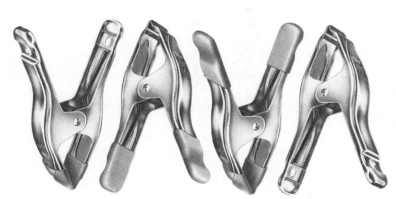

Fig. 24-36 *Spring clamps.* (Adjustable Clamp Co.)

REVIEW   REVIEW   REVIEW   REVIEW   REVIEW

WORDS TO KNOW

adjustable wrench	hexagonal wrench	pin punch	S-wrench
arbor press	long-nose pliers	pin spanner	toggle clamp
box wrench	machinist's vise	pipe wrench	toolmaker's parallel
combination	mallet	powered wrench	clamp
hammer mold	monkey wrench	round-nose pliers	torque wrench
combination pliers	offset screwdriver	side-cutting pliers	22½° wrench
dead blow hammer	open-end wrench	socket wrench	Vise-grip® wrench
drift punch	double-end	soft hammer	
face spanner	single-end	spanner wrench	
15° wrench	Phillips head screw	spring clamp	

REVIEW QUESTIONS

1. How is the size of a machinist's vise determined?
2. How may finished surfaces be protected from becoming marred when clamped in a machinist's vise?
3. Name three kinds of pliers and give several uses for each.
4. Why are soft hammers used to aid assembly of hardened steel parts instead of hard hammers?
5. How can damaged lead hammers be repaired?
6. How is a mallet different from a soft hammer?
7. What is the purpose of a square blade on a screwdriver?
8. Describe an offset screwdriver. What is it used for?
9. In what direction should the jaws point when using an adjustable wrench or a pipe wrench?
10. How does an open-end wrench differ from a box wrench?
11. Name two types of spanner wrenches.
12. What are socket wrenches? What special advantages do they have over box and open-end wrenches?
13. What are 15° and 22½° wrenches used for?
14. Describe a torque wrench and tell how it is used.
15. How are powered wrenches powered?
16. What is a drift punch used for?
17. What is a pin punch used for?
18. What is a transfer punch used for?
19. What is an arbor press used for?
20. List four kinds of clamps used in assembly work.

UNIT
25
Fasteners

Metal parts are often held together with standard metal fasteners, such as bolts, screws, pins, and rivets. Many special fasteners are also used, but this unit deals only with standard metal fasteners.

25-1
Bolts and Screws

Bolts and screws are made in many shapes and sizes. The sizes of bolts and screws are measured by the diameter and length of the **body;** the **head** is not included in the length except on flat-head bolts and screws (Fig. 25-1). The kinds most often used are shown in Figure 25-2.

Refer to Figure 25-2 as each type of bolt or screw is described in the following paragraphs.

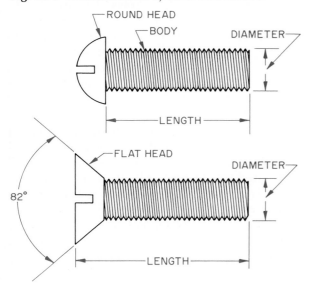

Fig. 25-1 *Measurements of bolts and screws.*

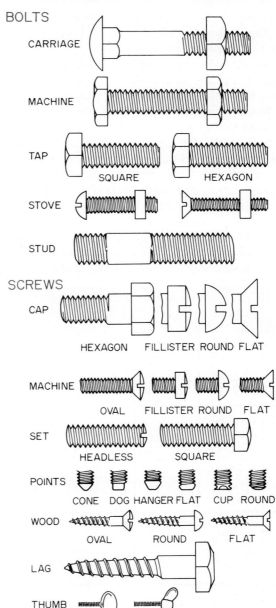

Fig. 25-2 *Common types of bolts and screws.*

A **carriage bolt** has a smooth, round head and a coarse thread: It is usually used to fasten a wooden part to metal. The square part under the head sinks into the wood and keeps the bolt from turning while the nut is being tightened.

Most **machine bolts** have hexagonal heads and are only partially threaded. They are available in several grades (Table 25-1). For additional information on bolt specifications, consult a mechanical engineering handbook.

Tap bolts are like machine bolts except that the whole body is threaded.

Stove bolts have either a round or flat head. They are made with a coarse thread. Stove bolts are used as general purpose fasteners where precision fits are unnecessary.

Stud bolts have no heads and are threaded on both ends. One end of the stud bolt has more threads than the other. They are inserted into metal parts that require projecting bolts on which to fasten other parts (Fig. 25-3).

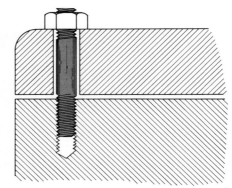

Fig. 25-3 *Use of stud bolt.*

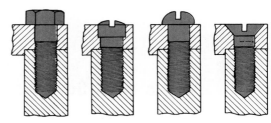

Fig. 25-4 *Cap screw heads. Note the different positions.*

Table 25-1

Selected Grades of SAE Bolts

Grade	Grade marking	Tensile strength psi (Mpa)	Material and treatment
1 2	NO MARK	55,000 (379.2) 64,000 (434.4)	Low or medium carbon steel
3		100,000 (689.5)	Medium carbon steel, cold headed
5		105,000 (723.9)	Medium carbon steel, quenched and tempered
7		133,000 (917)	Medium carbon alloy steel, quenched and tempered, roll threaded after heat treatment for improved fatigue strength.
8		150,000 (414.2)	Same as Grade 7

Cap screws are made with heads of several different shapes. They are made with either coarse or fine threads (Figure 25-4).

Machine screws are made with heads of several different shapes and are made with either coarse or fine threads. They are made of steel, **stainless steel,** or **brass.** The smaller diameters are described by gage numbers, 0-12. These sizes range from 0.060″ [1.5 mm] to 0.216″ [5.5 mm]. The gage numbers are the same for both machine screws and wood screws. Larger diameters are usually designated by their sizes: ¼″ [6.4 mm], ⁵⁄₁₆″ [7.9 mm], and ⅜″ [9.5 mm].

Setscrews are made with **square heads** or are **headless.** Both kinds are made with different **points.** Setscrews are **case-hardened** and are used to fasten pulleys and collars on shafts, as shown in Figure 25-5. (Case-hardening is explained in Unit 41.)

The headless setscrew is made for safety (Fig. 25-5). Screws with heads are dangerous on moving parts because the worker may be caught and injured.

There are two kinds of headless setscrews. One kind has a slot for a screwdriver. The other kind, known as a **socket-head setscrew,** has a hexagonal hole. A special wrench is needed to tighten this type (Fig. 25-6).

Wood screws are often used to fasten metal parts to wood. They are made with flat, round, or oval heads. The heads are slotted or recessed so they can be turned with screwdrivers. The angle of the flat head is 82°. Wood screws are made of steel, brass, and aluminum. Steel wood screws come in **bright** or **blued** finish, or they are plated with cadmium, nickel, or chromium to prevent rust or corrosion.

The diameter of wood screws and machine screws is measured on the body under the head with the **American Standard Screw Gage.** Figure 25-7 shows how a wood screw is measured by sliding it along in the opening of the screw gage until it touches on both sides; the number where it touches is the **gage number.**

Lag screws have either square or hexagonal **heads** and are threaded like wood screws. They are used for heavy work such as fastening a vise to a wooden bench top.

Thumbscrews are screws with one or two wings or with a **knurled head.** They are used where a screw must be turned by the thumb and finger.

Removing a Broken Bolt or Screw from a Hole

A broken bolt or screw that is not made of hardened steel may be removed from a hole with a **screw extractor** (Fig. 25-8). First drill a hole in the broken bolt; then put the correct size screw extractor into the hole and with a tap wrench, turn it counterclockwise. The screw extractor acts like a corkscrew. It grips into the sides of the hole in the bolt; when the right force is used, the bolt begins to turn and come out.

If a screw extractor is not handy, drive a **diamond-point chisel,** shown in Figure 16-1, into the drilled hole and remove in a manner similar to that shown in Figure 25-8.

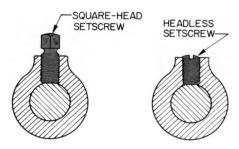

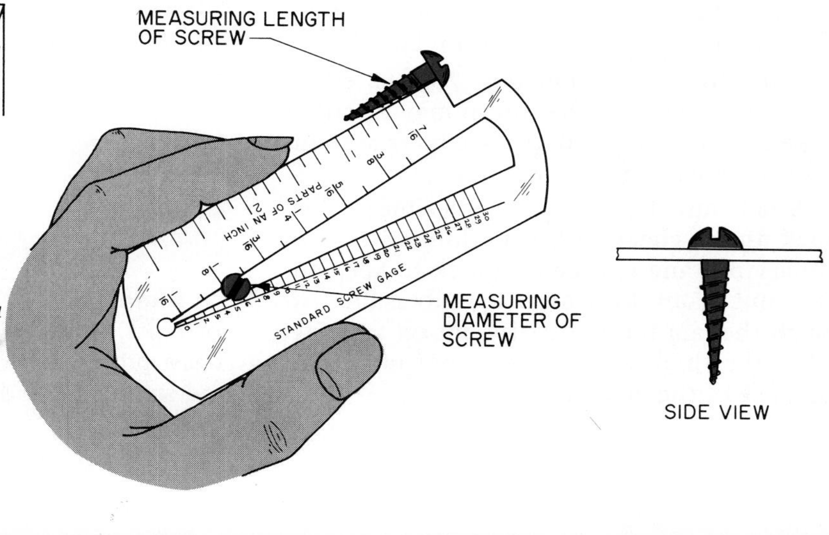

Fig. 25-5 *Headed and headless set screws.*

Fig. 25-6 *A special hex wrench is used to tighten a socket-head setscrew.*

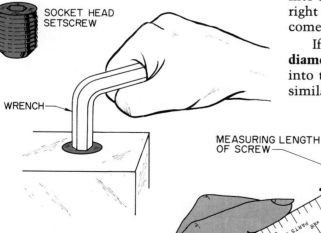

Fig. 25-7 *Gaging the diameter and length of a screw with a screw gage.*

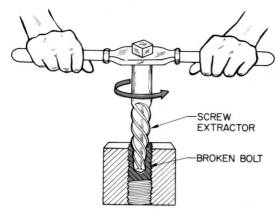

Fig. 25-8 *Removing a broken bolt with a screw extractor.*

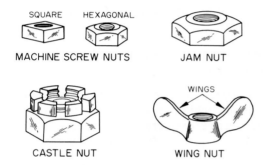

Fig. 25-9 *Types of nuts.*

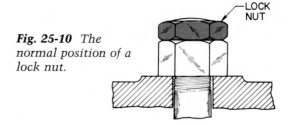

Fig. 25-10 *The normal position of a lock nut.*

Fig. 25-11 *Self-locking nuts with plastic inserts.*

25-2

Nuts

There are many different shapes and sizes of nuts; samples of these are shown in Figure 25-9. The size of a nut is measured by the diameter of the bolt it fits. For example, a ½" [12.7 mm] nut fits a ½" [12.7 mm] bolt.

A **machine screw nut** (Fig. 25-9) is either square or hexagonal. The thread may be either coarse or fine. Stove and carriage bolts are generally supplied with square nuts.

A **jam nut** (Fig. 25-9) is sometimes called a **lock nut** or **check nut**. It is thinner than an ordinary nut and is used as a lock to keep another nut from loosening by vibration. Although the jam nut is usually put on last (Fig. 25-10), the thicker nut may be put on last to make use of the greater strength.

A **castle nut** (Fig. 25-9) has slots cut into a top ring of metal. The parts that extend upward make it look like a castle, hence the name. A **cotter pin** is slipped in a slot and through a hole in the bolt to lock the nut to the bolt and thus keep the nut from jarring off. Castle nuts are usually used to hold wheel bearings and wheels in place.

Wing nuts (Fig. 25-9) have two thin, flat wings and are used where a nut has to be turned with the thumb and forefinger.

Self-locking nuts eliminate the need for lock washers, lock nuts, or cotter pins to keep the nut tightly in place. The self-locking feature is usually provided either by one or more deformed threads, or with a plastic insert (Fig. 25-11).

25-3

Washers

Plain washers are used as **bearing surfaces** for bolts, nuts, screws, and rivets (Fig. 25-12). They protect the surface under the fastener and spread the load over a greater area.

The size of a washer is measured by the diameter of the bolt that it fits; thus, a ½" [12.7 mm] washer is for a ½" [12.7 mm] bolt.

Lock washers are used to lock a nut or screw in place, thus preventing movement or loosening due to vibration. The **helical spring type lock washer** looks like a coil from a spring. Lock washers of this type are available in light, medium (regular), heavy, and extra-heavy types. They are hardened and tempered, and are used under a screw or nut as shown in Figure 25-13.

Tooth-type lock washers (Fig. 25-14) of hardened steel will wedge into bearing surfaces to prevent bolts, nuts, or screws from turning or loosening due to vibration.

Preassembled screw and washer assemblies, called **sems** (Fig. 25-15), have a lock washer fitting loosely below the screw head. The expanded rolled thread diameter prevents the washer from falling off. They are used for more rapid assembly on modern assembly lines. Preassembled **lock washer and nut units** are also available.

Pins

Pins of several types are used to hold mechanical parts together or limit the travel of moving parts.

Cotter pins, also called **cotter keys,** are made of soft steel wire. They are slipped through a hole in a bolt behind a castle nut;

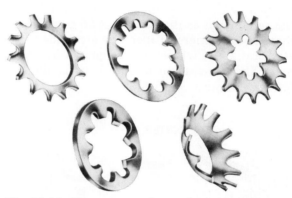

Fig. 25-14 *Common tooth-type lock washers.*

Fig. 25-12 *The shape of a plain washer.*

Fig. 25-15 *Preassembled screw and washer assemblies.*

Fig. 25-13 *The position of a helical spring type lock washer.*

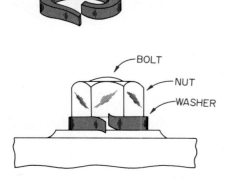

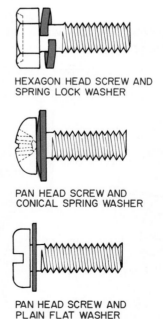

HEXAGON HEAD SCREW AND
SPRING LOCK WASHER

PAN HEAD SCREW AND
CONICAL SPRING WASHER

PAN HEAD SCREW AND
PLAIN FLAT WASHER

to keep the nut from turning. Note the right way to lock the nut (Fig. 25-16). The head of the cotter pin should fit into the slot of the nut; one leg should be bent over the end of the bolt and the other leg should be bent over the side of the nut.

A **tapered pin** is often used for such purposes as fastening a pulley or collar to a shaft (Fig. 25-17). The taper equals ¼″ per foot [20.8 mm/m]. Tapered pins are made in lengths from ³⁄₈″ [9.5 mm] to 6″ [152 mm]. The hole into which the pin fits is first drilled and then reamed with a taper-pin reamer, which has the same taper as the pin. (Unit 56 gives information on reamers.) Taper pins are made in 17 standard sizes, which are designated by numbers. These sizes are included in handbooks for machinists.

Roll pins are pins made of sheet steel rolled into a tube (Fig. 25-18). They are hardened and spring-tempered (treated by tempering so they act like a spring). They are made slightly larger than standard hole sizes so that they hold very tightly when driven into the hole.

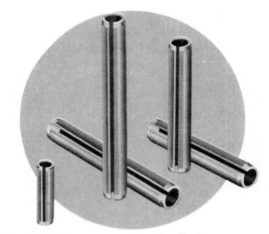

Fig. 25-18 *An assortment of roll pins.*

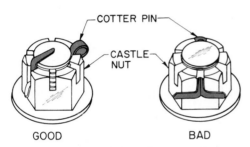

GOOD   BAD

Fig. 25-16 *The use of a castle nut and a cotter pin.*

Fig. 25-17 *Reaming a hole with a taper pin reamer for a tapered pin.*

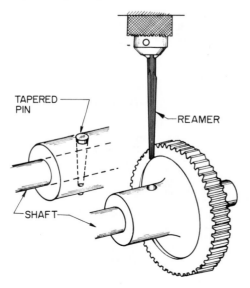

Fig. 25-19 *Types of keys.*

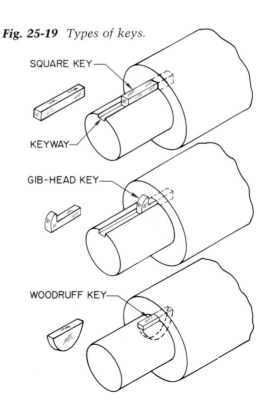

25-5
Keys

Keys are made in several shapes. They are used to keep pulleys and gears from moving on shafts (Fig. 25-19). Half of the key fits into a **keyway,** which is a slot in the shaft, and the other half fits into a slot in the pulley or gear. The plain **square key** is the one that is most used.

The **gib-head key** is useful where it is necessary to remove the key from one side of the pulley or gear. A wedge may be used to back the key out of the hole.

The **Woodruff key** is semicircular in shape and fits a matching semicircular pocket in the shaft (Fig. 25-19). The key is thus trapped in position and cannot work its way loose due to vibration.

25-6
Retaining Rings

Retaining rings (Fig. 25-20) are a relatively new type of fastener. One type is seated in either internal grooves (such as in bored holes) or in external grooves (such as on shafts or studs) with a special plier-like tool (Fig. 25-21). Self-locking types are driven into place and do not require a groove. Retaining rings provide a shoulder for holding, locking, or positioning parts of assemblies.

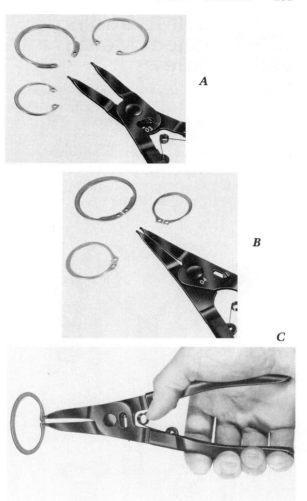

Fig. 25-21 *Special pliers are used to install retaining rings. (A) Internal rings and pliers. (B) External rings and pliers. (C) Pliers inserted into the ring.* (Waldes Kohinoor, Inc., Reprinted with permission)

Fig. 25-20 *Examples of retaining ring applications, (A) internal, (B) external.* (Waldes Kohinoor, Inc., Reprinted with permission)

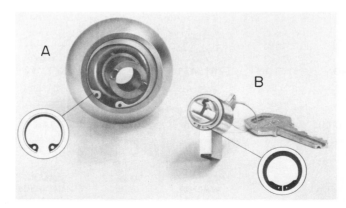

25-7 Self-Threading (Sheet Metal) Screws

Self-threading screws (Figs. 25-22, 25-23, and 25-26) cut or form their own threads when they are driven into soft metals. They are driven into holes that are slightly larger than the minor diameter of the screw body.

Self-threading screws are used for economical assembly of sheet metal and other sheet materials such as plastic, plywood, asbestos,

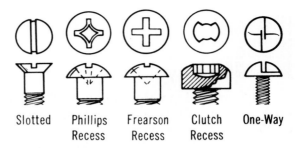

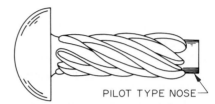

Slotted   Phillips Recess   Frearson Recess   Clutch Recess   One-Way

Fig. 25-25 *The driving recesses (slots, grooves, and holes) used on screw heads. Other styles are also available.*

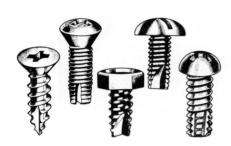

Fig. 25-22 *Thread-forming screws.*

Fig. 25-23 *Thread-cutting screws.*

PILOT TYPE NOSE

Fig. 25-26 *A drive screw (enlarged view).*

and fiber materials. Sheet-metal workers use them for installing heating, ventilation, and air-conditioning ducts and equipment. Many parts on automobile bodies, radio and television chassis, stoves, refrigerators, and other appliances are fastened or assembled with self-threading screws. They are available with most of the head styles shown in Figure 25-24. A variety of driving recesses, including clutch heads, slotted heads, Phillips recessed heads, and hexagonal heads are available (Fig. 25-25). Self-threading screws are made in diameters according to screw gage numbers, which are the same as those used for wood screws and machine screws.

Fig. 25-24 *Head styles used on threaded fasteners.*

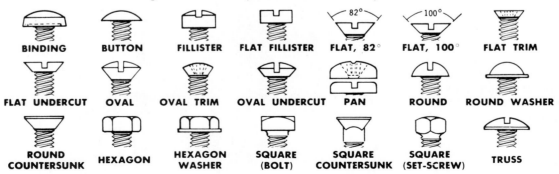

BINDING   BUTTON   FILLISTER   FLAT FILLISTER   FLAT, 82°   FLAT, 100°   FLAT TRIM

FLAT UNDERCUT   OVAL   OVAL TRIM   OVAL UNDERCUT   PAN   ROUND   ROUND WASHER

ROUND COUNTERSUNK   HEXAGON   HEXAGON WASHER   SQUARE (BOLT)   SQUARE COUNTERSUNK   SQUARE (SET-SCREW)   TRUSS

Drive screws (Fig. 25-26) are made of hardened steel and have a smooth round head, multiple threads, and a **pilot-type** (guiding) nose. These thread-forming type screws are driven into holes with a hammer. They form chip-free threads by displacing metal. The holes they are driven into should be slightly larger in diameter than the **pilot end** of the screw. They are used for permanent assembly of name plates on machines and similar applications.

25-8 Rivets and Riveting

Rivets are metal pins that look like bolts without threads. They are made of different metals, such as soft iron or steel, aluminum, copper, and brass. They are available in many different sizes and shapes of heads. The most common kinds of heads are shown in Figure 25-27. They may be either **solid** (Fig. 25-27), or they may be of **tubular** or other special forms, as shown in Figure 25-28. Blind, or "pop," rivets are another type (Fig. 25-37).

Riveting is the fastening of pieces of metal or other material together with rivets. This process is used to hold pieces together permanently. The rivet is first put through holes in the pieces to be fastened together (Fig. 25-29). The headless end of a solid rivet is than hammered into the form of a head, as shown in Figure 25-29. Hollow rivets are **clinched** at the headless end with a special riveting tool.

Many metal-fastening jobs that were formerly riveted are now welded. This is true of structural-steel products such as bridges and steel frames of large buildings.

Fig. 25-27 *Common rivet head types.*

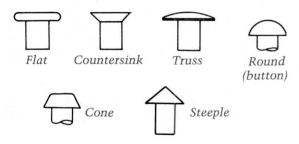

Flat   *Countersink*   *Truss*   *Round (button)*

Cone   *Steeple*

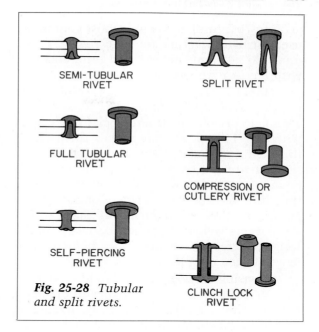

Fig. 25-28 *Tubular and split rivets.*

Fig. 25-29 *The length of a rivet needed to form a round head.*

Rivets are used for fastening metals that are not easily welded, or where welding is not practical. They are often used to fasten aluminum sheet metal in building aircraft, small boats, and other aluminum products. In modern manufacturing plants, riveting is done rapidly and economically with special riveting tools and machines.

The heads of rivets are sometimes used simply to decorate and add beauty to an object.

Rivet size. The size of a rivet is measured by the diameter and length of the body. The head is not included in the length except on those designed to be countersunk. They are available in diameters ranging from ⅛" to ⅜" [3.2 to 9.5 mm], and in lengths from ¼" to 3"

[6.35 to 76.2 mm]. The kinds most commonly used for hand riveting are solid rivets ⅛″ [3.2 mm], ⁵⁄₃₂″ [4 mm], and ³⁄₁₆″ [4.8 mm] diameter with flat or round heads.

Tinner's rivets. These are solid rivets used for riveting sheet metal (Fig. 25-30). They are made of soft steel, either plain or coated with tin. The tin coating makes them easier to solder and makes them rust-resistant. The sizes of tinner's rivets are given in ounces or pounds per 1000; a 6-oz. [170.1 g] rivet means that 1000 of this type weighs 6 ounces [170.1 g]; a 2 lb. [0.91 kg] rivet means that 1000 of these rivets weighs 2 pounds [0.91 kg]. As the weight increases, so does the diameter and length of the rivet (Fig. 25-30).

Choosing a rivet. A rivet should be .003″ to .016″ [0.08 to 0.4 mm] smaller in diameter than the holes in the pieces to be riveted. It should be long enough to extend through the pieces to be riveted and leave enough metal to form a head, which is about 1½″ times the diameter of the rivet (Fig. 25-29).

Except for decorative purposes, the rivets selected should be made of the same material as the metal being riveted.

Rivet spacing. As a rule, rivets should not be spaced closer together than three times the diameter of the rivet. For adequate strength,

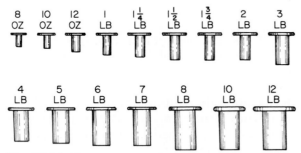

| 8 OZ | 10 OZ | 12 OZ | 1 LB | 1¼ LB | 1½ LB | 1¾ LB | 2 LB | 3 LB |

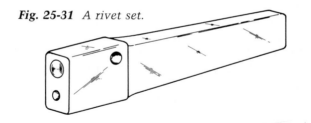

| 4 LB | 5 LB | 6 LB | 7 LB | 8 LB | 10 LB | 12 LB |

Fig. 25-30 *Tinner's rivets (actual size).*

Fig. 25-31 *A rivet set.*

they should not be spaced farther apart than 24 times the diameter. Thus, the minimum space between two ⅛″ [3.2 mm] diameter rivets is 3 × ⅛″ [3.2 mm], or ⅜″ [9.5 mm] apart. The maximum distance recommended between two ⅛″ [3.2 mm] diameter rivets is 24 × ⅛″ [3.2 mm], or 3″ [76.2 mm].

The rivet set. A rivet set is a hardened-steel tool with a **hollow** in one end (Fig. 25-31). It is used to shape the end of a rivet into a round, smooth **head**. Rivet sets are made in various sizes, designated by the following numbers: 00, 0, 1, 2, through 8. A No. 8 rivet set is used for 10- or 12-ounce [283.5 or 340.2 g] tinner's rivets. The No. 8 is the **smallest** size, and the No. 00 is the **largest**.

How to rivet.

1. Punch or drill holes through the metal pieces. The holes should provide a snug fit for the rivets. On thin sheet metals, the holes are punched (the procedure for punching holes is explained in Unit 29). Holes in thick sheet metals and metal bars are usually drilled. Countersink one of the holes if a countersunk rivet is to be used.
2. Put the rivet through the holes, and place the head of the rivet on something solid, such as a steel block. A round-headed rivet can be kept from flattening by using a riveting block. A riveting block is made of steel and has a hollow to fit the rivet head (Fig. 25-32).
3. Press the two pieces of metal together by placing the rivet set over the rivet and striking it a sharp hammer blow (Fig. 25-33, Step 1).
4. Strike blows on the end of the rivet with either the face or the peen of a ball-peen hammer or a riveting hammer until the end of the rivet is spread out a little.
5. Then strike it with the peen until it is quite round on top like a mushroom (Fig. 25-32b).
6. Next, smooth out the rivet head by placing a rivet set on the rivet and striking it sharply with the hammer (Fig. 25-33, Step 2).

If the rivet head cannot project above the surface, countersink the hole and make a countersunk rivet head as shown in Fig. 25-34.

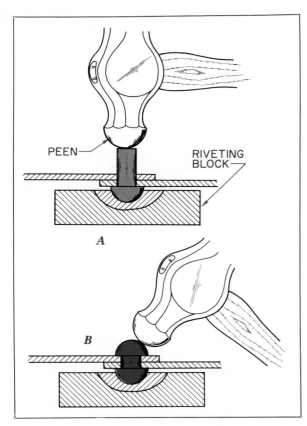

Fig. 25-32 *Forming a rivet head by peening. (A) Strike first in the center of the rivet. (B) Round the end of the rivet by peening.*

The length of rivet required for a countersunk head is about ¾ of the rivet diameter.

Hot and cold rivets. Iron and steel expand ⅛″ to ³⁄₁₆″ [3.2 to 4.8 mm] per foot [304.8 mm] when red-hot. Thus, an iron rivet gives more strength when heated before riveting because it shrinks as it cools, holding the pieces more tightly together. Large rivets, such as those used to rivet structural steel beams together, are hammered when hot. Small rivets are hammered when cold.

Removing rivets. Rivets are used to fasten pieces together permanently, but it is sometimes necessary to remove them. Figure 16-8 shows how the head of a rivet is cut off with a cold chisel and hammer. After the head is cut off, the rest of the rivet may be driven out with a drift punch and hammer.

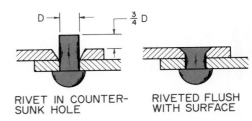

Fig. 25-34 *A countersunk rivet is hammered flush with the surface.*

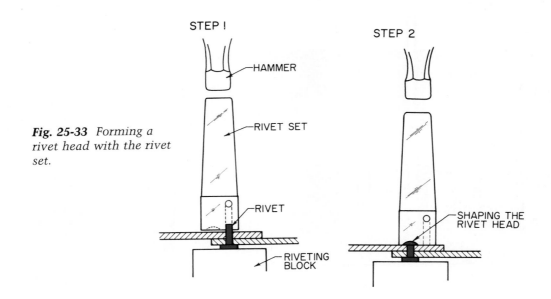

Fig. 25-33 *Forming a rivet head with the rivet set.*

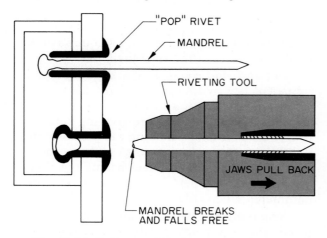

Fig. 25-35 *Pull-stem blind rivets clinch on one side with a pull by the tool from the other side.*

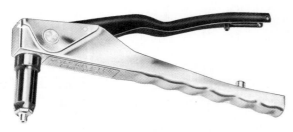

Fig. 25-36 *A hand-operated riveting tool for clinching pull-stem rivets.*

Tubular and special rivets. A wide variety of tubular rivets of standard and special design are used in producing many appliances and hardware items. Several common types are shown in Figure 25-28. In production work, these rivets are clinched with special riveting machines or tools.

Blind rivets. These rivets are so named because they can be inserted and set from the same side of the workpiece. Other types of rivets usually require access to both sides of the work being riveted.

One type of blind rivet, called the **Pop**® rivet, clinches on one side with a pull by the tool from the other side as shown in Figure 25-35. The stem, or **mandrel,** breaks off when the head is clinched. A plier-like hand tool may be used for clinching pull-stem rivets (Fig. 25-36). Power-operated clinching tools are often used in industrial plants where many rivets must be clinched. Blind rivets are used on items such as automobiles, aircraft, appliances, furniture, sheet metal duct work, and toys.

Pull-stem rivets are available in a wide variety of different designs, types, sizes, and kinds of materials. Three common pull-stem types, include the following:

1. Open-end type with hollow core and domed head. (Also available with countersunk head.) (Fig. 25-37A).

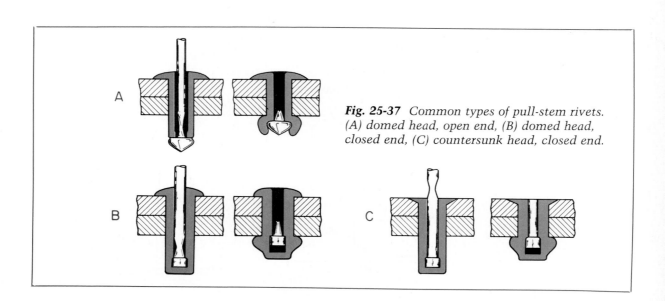

Fig. 25-37 *Common types of pull-stem rivets. (A) domed head, open end, (B) domed head, closed end, (C) countersunk head, closed end.*

2. Closed-end type with hollow core and domed head. (Also available with countersunk head.) (Fig. 25-37B).
3. Closed-end type with countersunk head and filled core. (Also available with domed head.) (Fig. 25-37C).

The closed-end type is liquid- and pressure-tight when set.

In addition to the dome-head and countersunk head types shown in Figure 25-37, pull-stem rivets are also available with larger flanged heads. They are made of aluminum, steel, copper, monel, or stainless steel. They are made in diameters ranging from ³⁄₃₂″ to ¼″ [2.38 to 6.35 mm] and in various lengths up to ¾″ [19.05 mm].

Blind rivet selection. For best results, the length of the rivet selected should be such that it will clinch with a short head (Fig. 25-37). However, with careful riveting procedures, rivets of the same length may be used for materials of various thickness (Fig. 25-38). The rivet generally should be made of metal that is similar to the metal being riveted. For added strength, the rivets may be located closer together or in double rows.

Other types of blind rivets. Other types of blind rivets include the drive-pin type and the explosive type (Fig. 25-39). The former is clinched with a drive pin that is part of the rivet assembly. The latter is clinched by expansion resulting from an explosive charge. The charge is activated by a hot iron or similar tool.

Fig. 25-38 *Pull-stem rivets in this assembly are the same length.*

25-9 How to Order Metal Fasteners

In order to assure getting the correct metal fasteners, they must be completely described on a bill of materials or order blank as follows:
1. Name of fastener
2. Quantity needed
3. Kind
  a. Kind of material (steel, brass, etc.)
  b. Kind of finish (plain, blued, etc.)
4. Size
  a. Diameter (in inches or gage number) × length
  b. Thread information, if threaded
5. Shape
  a. Shape of head
  b. Shape of point (setscrews only)

Suppliers' catalogs should be consulted for listings of sizes and types of fasteners available.

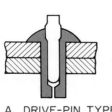
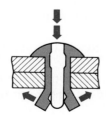

A. DRIVE-PIN TYPE

Fig. 25-39 *Other types of blind rivets.*

B. EXPLOSIVE-TYPE

REVIEW   REVIEW   REVIEW   REVIEW   REVIEW

WORDS TO KNOW

American Standard Screw Gage	explosive rivet	rivet set	tapered pin
black finish	gage number	rough finish	taper-pin reamer
blind rivet	gib-head key	screw extractor	thread-cutting screw
blued finish	jam nut	self-threading screw	thread-forming screw
bright finish	keyway	setscrew	thumbscrew
cap screw	lag screw	socket-head setscrew	tinner's rivet
carriage bolt	lock washer	spring washer	tubular rivet
castle nut	machine bolt	square key	wing nut
cotter pin	machine screw	stove bolt	Woodruff key
drive-pin rivet	Pop® rivet	stud bolt	
drive screw	pull-stem rivet	tap bolt	
	retaining ring		

REVIEW QUESTIONS

1. How is the size of bolts and screws measured?
2. What are carriage bolts used for? Stove bolts? Stud bolts?
3. Name several kinds of cap screws.
4. Name two types of setscrews and give an example of how each is used.
5. Name three kinds of heads used on setscrews.
6. Describe a lag screw. What is it used for?
7. Describe a thumbscrew. What is it used for?
8. How is the size of a nut measured?
9. What is a jam nut used for?
10. What is a castle nut used for?
11. Describe a wing nut.
12. Describe two types of lock washers.
13. How is a cotter pin used?
14. How are taper pins used?
15. What is the difference between a square key, a gib-head key, and a Woodruff key?
16. What are retaining rings, and how are they used?
17. List two types of self-threading screws. How are they used?
18. Make a bill of materials for five different kinds of screws.
19. Why are metal pieces sometimes riveted together instead of being bolted or welded?
20. List several kinds of products that use rivets in their construction.
21. What metals are rivets commonly made of?
22. Describe the shapes of rivet heads that are most commonly used.
23. How is the size of a rivet measured?
24. How much larger in diameter should the hole be than the rivet?
25. List a general rule that may be used regarding the minimum and maximum spacing between rivets.
26. What is a rivet set?
27. Why do hot rivets hold tighter than cold rivets?
28. Describe three kinds of blind rivets and explain how they are used.

UNIT
26
Welding

A weld occurs when metal from pieces being joined flows and blends together. This action may be caused by heat, pressure, or a combination of both. When heat alone is used, the weld is called a **fusion weld.**

Pressure welding usually involves heating surfaces to a pliable, or **plastic,** state and then forcing the metal together with pressure. Under certain conditions, however, welds can be made using pressure alone.

Welding is widely used as a joining technique both for manufacturing a new product and for repairs. Barges and ships, boilers and large storage tanks, pipe lines, railroad cars, and automobiles are assembled largely by welding. In many cases welded steel construction has replaced the use of iron castings in machine bases, frames, and bodies. Large frames are welded at the construction site

Fig. 26-1 This welder is arc welding the hull of a river barge.

(Fig. 26-1). Welding is widely used in constructing buildings. Appliances such as toasters, dishwashers, washing machines, and clothes driers rely heavily on **spot welding** for their assembly.

Welders are found in most manufacturing plants, foundries, construction sites, boiler and tank shops, welding shops, railroad shops, and shipyards. Welding processes are probably used in every metal industry.

26-1 Welding Processes

Figure 26-2 shows how the **American Welding Society** has classified welding processes and the related processes of thermal spraying, cutting, brazing, and soldering. Brazing and soldering, which are not welding processes but are widely used for joining metals, are covered in Unit 27.

All the welding processes listed in Fig. 26-2 have important industrial uses. However, due to space limitations, only the most widely used processes can be included in this unit.

26-2 Welding with Electric Current

There are many welding processes that use electricity. The names of some are **shielded metal arc, carbon arc, atomic hydrogen arc, tungsten inert gas arc (TIG),** and **spot welding** (Fig. 26-2). Each process has advantages over the others for a particular type of work.

Master Chart of Welding and Allied Processes

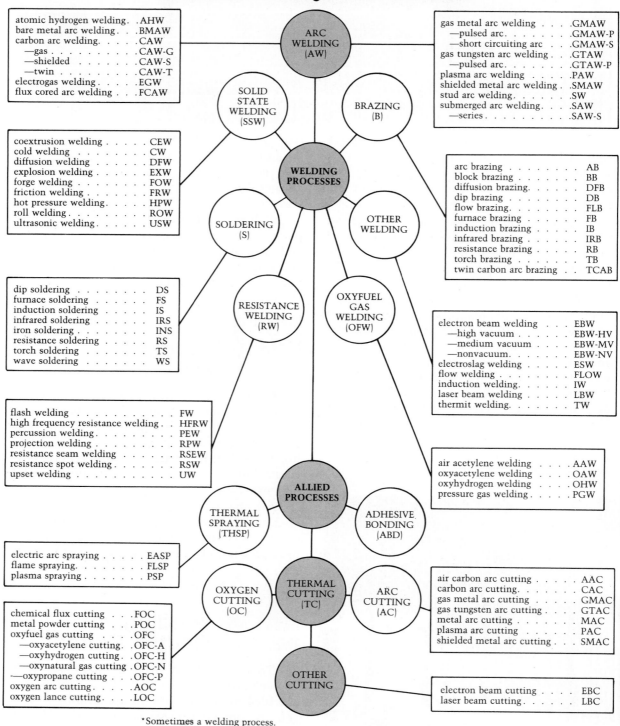

atomic hydrogen welding. . .AHW	gas metal arc welding . . . .GMAW
bare metal arc welding. . .BMAW	—pulsed arc. . . . . . . .GMAW-P
carbon arc welding. . . . .CAW	—short circuiting arc . . .GMAW-S
—gas . . . . .CAW-G	gas tungsten arc welding. . .GTAW
—shielded . . . . . . .CAW-S	—pulsed arc. . . . . . . .GTAW-P
—twin . . . . .CAW-T	plasma arc welding . . . .PAW
electrogas welding . . . . .EGW	shielded metal arc welding . .SMAW
flux cored arc welding . . .FCAW	stud arc welding. . . . . .SW
	submerged arc welding. . . .SAW
	—series. . . . . .SAW-S

coextrusion welding . . . . .CEW	arc brazing . . . . AB
cold welding . . . . CW	block brazing . . . . BB
diffusion welding . . . . .DFW	diffusion brazing. . . . . .DFB
explosion welding . . . . . .EXW	dip brazing . . . . DB
forge welding . . . . . . .FOW	flow brazing. . . . . . . .FLB
friction welding . . . . . .FRW	furnace brazing . . . . . . FB
hot pressure welding. . . .HPW	induction brazing . . . . . IB
roll welding. . . . . . . .ROW	infrared brazing . . . . . .IRB
ultrasonic welding. . . . . .USW	resistance brazing . . . . . RB
	torch brazing . . . . . . .TB
	twin carbon arc brazing . .TCAB

dip soldering . . . . . . .DS	electron beam welding . . .EBW
furnace soldering . . . . .FS	—high vacuum . . . . .EBW-HV
induction soldering . . . . .IS	—medium vacuum . . .EBW-MV
infrared soldering . . . . .IRS	—nonvacuum. . . . . .EBW-NV
iron soldering . . . . . . .INS	electroslag welding . . . .ESW
resistance soldering . . . . .RS	flow welding . . . . . . .FLOW
torch soldering . . . . . .TS	induction welding. . . . . .IW
wave soldering . . . . . .WS	laser beam welding . . . .LBW
	thermit welding. . . . . .TW

flash welding . . . . .FW	air acetylene welding . . . .AAW
high frequency resistance welding. .HFRW	oxyacetylene welding . . . .OAW
percussion welding. . . . . . . .PEW	oxyhydrogen welding . . . .OHW
projection welding . . . . . . .RPW	pressure gas welding. . . . .PGW
resistance seam welding . . . . .RSEW	
resistance spot welding. . . . . .RSW	
upset welding . . . . .UW	

electric arc spraying . . . . .EASP	air carbon arc cutting . . . . .AAC
flame spraying. . . . . . .FLSP	carbon arc cutting. . . . . .CAC
plasma spraying . . . . . .PSP	gas metal arc cutting . . . .GMAC
	gas tungsten arc cutting . . .GTAC
	metal arc cutting . . . . . .MAC
	plasma arc cutting . . . . .PAC
	shielded metal arc cutting . . .SMAC

chemical flux cutting . . .FOC	
metal powder cutting . . .POC	
oxyfuel gas cutting . . . .OFC	
—oxyacetylene cutting. .OFC-A	
—oxyhydrogen cutting. .OFC-H	
—oxynatural gas cutting .OFC-N	electron beam cutting . . . .EBC
—oxypropane cutting . . .OFC-P	laser beam cutting. . . . . .LBC
oxygen arc cutting. . . . .AOC	
oxygen lance cutting. . . .LOC	

*Sometimes a welding process.

Fig. 26-2 *A chart of welding and related processes. Welders work with at least 45 welding methods and more than 15 metal cutting techniques.*

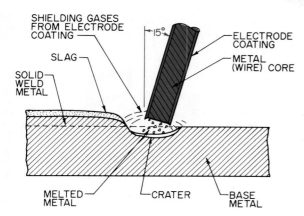

Fig. 26-3 *The welding arc.*

Only the shielded metal arc weld will be described in detail in this book. Many of the techniques, however, apply to other kinds of arc welding. Manual shielded arc welding is now used mostly for maintenance and repair welding.

Either kind of electrical current may be used for electric welding: **direct current (DC)** or **alternating current (AC)**. Direct current means that the current always flows in one direction. Alternating current means that the current rapidly reverses its direction at regularly recurring intervals of time and has alternating positive and negative values.

When electricity flows continuously through the air gap between a welding electrode and metal to be welded, it creates a **welding arc** (Fig. 26-3). Temperatures of 10,000°F [5538°C] have been measured in the welding arc.

26-3 Equipment for Shielded Metal Arc Welding

Protective clothing and shielding for your face and eyes are a "must" when you are arc welding. Your eyes, arms, legs, and feet must be protected, for in some ways the welding arc is like the sun. The arc gives off heat, a brilliant white light, infrared rays, and ultraviolet rays. If your body is not properly protected from the arc, it can be burned in much the same way as sunburn.

SAFETY NOTE

Heavy, long-sleeved, fire-resistant cotton coveralls should be worn. Pay special attention that the sleeves and legs are not turned up to form cuffs. Clothing having no front pockets, or having pockets with button cover flaps, is recommended. Pieces of hot metal from the weld often catch in cuffs and sometimes cause painful burns before they cool or can be removed. Some welders like to wear leather aprons, sleevelets, leggings, and spats. Gloves should overlap sleeves for protection from spattering metal and the arc. Gloves also help when handling hot metal (Fig. 26-4).

The helmet and face shield for arc welding are made from lightweight, pressed-fiber material (Fig. 26-5). Their black color reduces reflection. They have a window called a **lens,** made of special dark-colored glass, through which the welder looks at the welding arc. The special lens absorbs infrared and ultraviolet rays. It should be a number 10 lens for electric welding. This is much darker than the number 5 or 6 lens used in oxyacetylene goggles. To protect the more expensive, colored lens from the spatter of the weld, a clear, easily replaceable cover lens is used over the dark lens (Fig. 26-6).

Looking at the arc without a shield will burn your eyes. The severity of the burn will depend upon the length of time your eyes are exposed to the arc light. Hot spatter from the arc can also cause serious injury.

Always wear clear safety goggles underneath the welding helmet. This protects your eyes when chipping and brushing the weld **slag.**

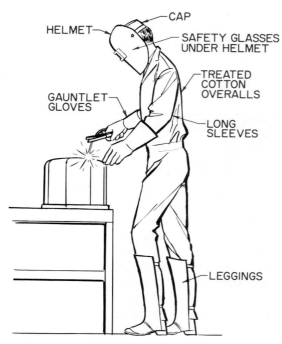

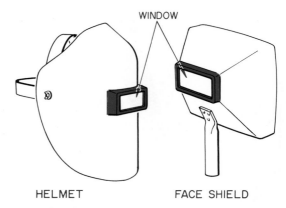

Fig. 26-5 *The helmet and face shield for arc welders.*

Fig. 26-4 *Protective clothing worn when arc welding. Safety glasses should be worn under the helmet.*

Hand tools used in shielded metal arc welding are shown in Figure 26-7 and are listed below:

1. Chipping hammer—to remove slag from the weld.
2. Wire brush—for cleaning the work and the weld.
3. Wedges and blocks—to position the work for welding.
4. Clamps—to hold the work for welding.
5. Pliers or tongs—for handling pieces of hot metal.

Four types of **arc-welding machines** are used:

1. The **direct current generator,** driven by an electric motor or gasoline engine (Figs. 26-8 and 26-9).
2. The **alternating current transformer-type welder** with a built-in transformer that operates from a power line.
3. The **direct current transformer-type welder** with a built-in transformer and rectifier that operate from a power line.

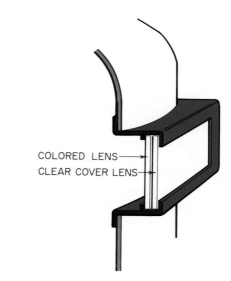

Fig. 26-6 *A cutaway drawing showing the construction of the helmet window.*

4. Other transformer-type machines that can supply either alternating or direct current (Fig. 26-10).

To produce the heat necessary to melt metal, the electric current must be changed from the 110 or 220 volts provided by power companies. The voltage must be reduced, or **stepped-down,** which increases, or **steps up,** the **amperage** (the current). A typical small arc-welding machine will produce 150-250 amperes at 20 to 40 volts.

WEDGE

BLOCK

CHIPPING HAMMER

PLIERS

WIRE BRUSH

CLAMP

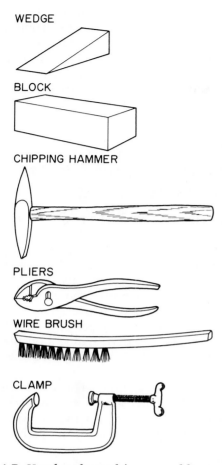

Fig. 26-7 *Hand tools used for arc welding.*

Fig. 26-8 *A motor-driven generator for arc welding.* (Hobart Brothers Company)

Fig. 26-9 *An engine-driven generator for arc welding.* (Hobart Brothers Company)

Fig. 26-10 *A transformer-type welder that supplies either alternating current (AC) or direct current (DC).* (Hobart Brothers Company)

The thickness of the metal being welded and the size of the electrode used determines the necessary amperage. Each type of welding machine has controls for adjusting the amperage. When the current setting is too high, the melted puddle is too large, the electrode melts too rapidly, and there is considerable spatter. When the current setting is too low, the puddle is too small, it is difficult to maintain the arc, and the electrode is likely to stick to the base metal.

Table 26-1

Relationship Between Decimal Inch Electrode Diameter and Welding Current
Adjust welding current to suit welding conditions

Diameter of electrode inch (mm)	Decimal equivalent in inches	Current in amperes
1/16 (1.5)	0.062	60
3/32 (2.4)	0.093	75
1/8 (3.2)	0.125	100
5/32 (4.0)	0.156	150
3/16 (4.8)	0.187	200
1/4 (6.4)	0.250	250
5/16 (7.9)	0.312	300
3/8 (9.5)	0.375	400

Table 26-1 gives amperage settings for rods of different diameters. These should be considered as **trial settings** for further adjustment.

Some welding machines have a low and high **welding range** with overlapping **current ranges.** For example, a 180-ampere machine may have a low-current range of 20 to 115 amperes, and a high-current range of 60 to 180 amperes. Welding with a ³⁄₃₂″ [2.3 mm] diameter electrode on either current range using 60

to 80 amperes is possible. The low-current range provides a higher **open-current voltage** and a more stable arc, thus making it easier to weld thin metals. The high-current range provides a lower open-circuit voltage, which produces better quality welds with larger diameter rods on thicker metals.

26-4 The Electric Circuit for Arc Welding

An **electric circuit** is a path over which an electric current can flow. If the path is interrupted or incomplete at any point, the circuit is said to be **open.** Current will not flow in an **open circuit.** Current will only flow in a **completed,** or **closed, circuit.** The diagram in Figure 26-11A is of an electric arc welding circuit. The circle with a positive sign (+) on one side and a negative sign (−) on the other is a symbol for a DC welding machine. Starting from the − side, trace the path of the current. From the machine, it leads to the **electrode holder,** the **arc,** the **material being welded,** and then back to the + side of the welder. If the arc is broken, the path is inter-

Fig. 26-11 Electric arc-welding circuits.

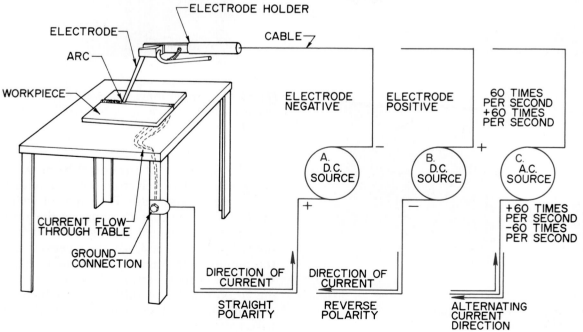

rupted and current will not flow. One cable (−) is connected to the electrode; the other (+) to the work or the metal work table. The cable connected to the work is called the ground cable.

The polarity of the electric current is important. As shown in Figure 26-11A, the path from the + side of the welder leads to the work. The path from the electrode leads to the − side of the welder. When the electrode leads to the − side of the welder, the circuit is said to have **straight polarity.** Straight polarity is also called **electrode negative.**

If the + and the − are changed around (Fig. 26-11B) the polarity is reversed and the circuit is said to have **reverse polarity.** Reverse polarity is also called **electrode positive** because the electrode leads to the positive side of the welder.

Straight polarity is normally used for DC welding. However, some types of welds can be made more easily with reverse polarity.

Straight polarity and reverse polarity refer only to DC circuits. If an AC machine is being used there is no choice of polarity (Fig. 26-11C), since the polarity reverses with each cycle of the current.

26-5 Shielded Metal Arc Welding Electrodes

The **electrode** is a metal rod that carries electric current from the electrode holder to the workpiece. Electrodes are widely used in 14″ [356 mm] lengths and in a range of diameters from ¹⁄₁₆″ to ³⁄₈″ [1.5 to 9.5 mm].

The electrode is also used to supply additional metal to the weld. Because the electrode is used up (consumed), it must be replaced frequently.

When melted metal is exposed to the air, it has a tendency to combine with nitrogen and oxygen in the air. The **nitrides** and **oxides** that are formed make the weld metal **brittle.** Most welds should be as strong or stronger than the metal being welded. **Shielded metal arc welding** is widely used because the process makes strong welds that are not brittle.

To **shield** the arc means to protect it (and the melted metal) from the surrounding air. This is done by using a **coated electrode** (Fig. 26-3). As the coating burns off in the arc, it forms gases that surround the arc and protect it from the air. The electrode coating also has a **flux.** This material quickly combines with the nitrides, oxides, and other undesirable impurities in the melted metal. These impurities are lighter than the melted metal and therefore float in the flux on top of the weld metal. When the metal cools, the impurities form a crust on top of the weld. This crust is called **slag,** and can be easily chipped away with a chipping hammer (Fig. 26-7).

26-6 The Electrode Numbering System

Examples of numbers that identify welding electrodes are E6013, E7025, and E9030. They are from a system developed by the American Welding Society **(AWS).** This system uses a letter followed by four digits.

As shown in Table 26-2 the first two digits denote the tensile strength of the electrode wire. Numbers in which the first digit is 6 (as E6013) are mild steel; other numbers (as E7025, E9030, and so on) are alloy steels.

Features and traits of welding electrodes vary from one manufacturer to the next, even though they have identical numbers under the AWS numbering system. Therefore, it is always best to follow the recommendations of the individual manufacturer concerning the use of the electrode and the proper amperage. Most dealers can supply electrode selection charts and handbooks, which list the characteristics and uses of their electrodes.

⅛″ [3.2 mm] diameter E6013 and E7024 rods are good electrodes for the beginner. Both rods can be used in all positions, and work on either AC or DC. Both rods start and restart easily, have a steady arc, make a smooth bead, and have high tensile strength. The E6013 is a mild steel rod made for welding either light or heavy gage mild steel. The E7024 rod can weld low alloy, medium, and high carbon steels as well as mild steel.

Table 26-2

American Welding Society (AWS) Numbering System for Coated Electrodes

E   .   .   .   .

Letter ——————— 1st Digit ——————— 2nd Digit ——————— 3rd Digit ——————— 4th Digit

Letter or digit	Description
E	The electrode is made for electric arc welding.
1st and 2nd Digits	These indicate the minimum tensile strength of the wire used to make the electrode. (60 means 60,000 pounds per square inch.)
3rd Digit	This shows the welding position for which the electrode can be used. If the 3rd digit is: 1—the electrode may be used for any welding position: for flat welds for vertical welds for horizontal welds for overhead welds 2—the electrode may be used for flat or horizontal welds. 3—the electrode may be used for flat welds only.
4th Digit	This indicates the kind of current and type of coating. Several examples are listed below: Electrode Number / Type of Current / Coating E6010 — DCRP only — Organic E6011 — DCRP or A.C. — Organic E6012 — DCRP or A.C. — Rutile E6013 — DCSP, DCRP, or A.C. — Rutile

(3rd Digit row: See Fig. 26-16)

The E7024 rod is the easiest to learn to use because it is a contact or "drag" rod. It is made with a heavy coating that melts slower than the steel core. This permits the rod to be dragged on the surface being welded without it shorting out and welding itself to the base metal. Successful welds with E6013 and other welding rods require the welder to maintain an arc gap of roughly the electrode diameter (Fig. 26-12).

26-7 Techniques for Starting the Arc

Select the proper electrode for the job and clamp it in the electrode holder. If you are using a DC welder, set it to the polarity desired, straight or reverse. Make an approximate cur-

rent setting—low for welding thin metal, higher for thicker metal. Check to see that you are wearing the proper protective clothing. Put on welding gloves, safety goggles, and a helmet, then turn on the welding machine.

Either of two methods can be used to start the arc. With a relaxed but firm grip on the electrode holder, put the end of the electrode near the spot where the weld will start. **Before you start the arc, protect your eyes by lowering your helmet.**

Figure 26-12 shows how to start an arc using the **tapping method.** To strike the arc, lower the electrode straight down and tap the **plate** (workpiece) lightly near the spot where the weld is to start. Quickly pull the electrode up and away—a distance about the diameter of the electrode, which is the proper arc length. The contact should be for only a fraction of a second. The action resembles a quick pecking motion.

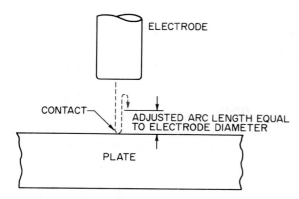

Fig. 26-12 *The tapping method for starting the arc.*

26-8 The Basic Types of Joints and Welding Positions

The **five basic welding joints** are the **butt, lap, tee, corner,** and **edge** (Fig. 26-14). These joints are welded with lines of welds that look like strings of beads. Thus, these lines of metal are called **welding beads.** Thin metals are welded with a single welding bead, or with a bead on each side of the joint. On thicker metals, the edges are **beveled** first and the weld is made with several overlapping welding beads (Fig. 26-15).

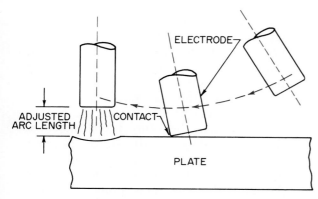

Fig. 26-13 *The scratch method for starting the arc.*

The tapping method is best. It is used by many experienced welders. At first tapping is a more difficult way to start an arc on a cold metal workpiece. With practice it becomes easy.

Figure 26-13 shows the **scratch method** of starting the arc, which is something like striking a match. Hold the tip of the electrode near the plate. With a sweeping motion, scratch the plate lightly with the electrode. Follow through by moving the electrode slightly away from the plate, stopping at the spot where the weld is to start. Adjust the length of the arc.

This method is usually a little easier to learn, particularly when striking an arc on a cold metal workpiece. It is not as good as the tapping method. With the scratch method it is harder to find the spot where the weld is to start. The scratch method also puts **arcing scars** on the plate.

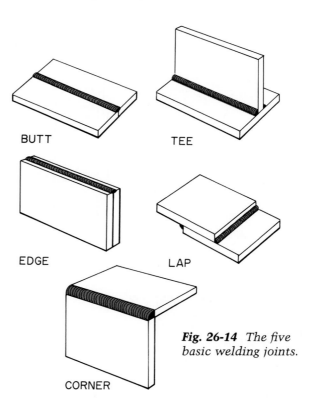

Fig. 26-14 *The five basic welding joints.*

Fig. 26-15 *To weld thick welds, bevel the edges first, and use several beads to complete the weld.*

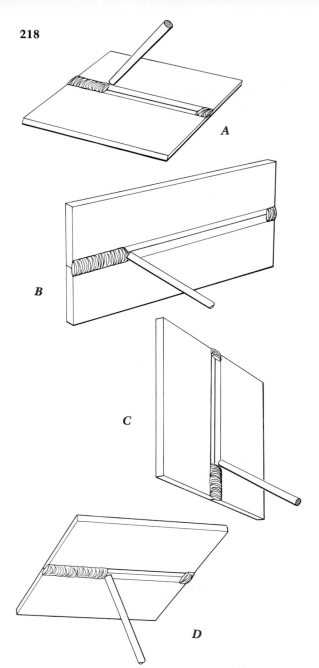

Fig. 26-16 *The four basic welding positions. (A) Flat. (B) Horizontal. (C) Vertical. (D) Overhead.*

The **four basic welding positions** are **flat, horizontal, vertical,** and **overhead.** These are illustrated in Figure 26-16. The flat position is the easiest and should be the first for beginners to practice and learn. When they have mastered the flat position, they can learn the horizontal, vertical, and overhead positions.

Steps for Making an Arc Weld in the Flat Position:

1. Place the pieces to be welded in their proper position on the welding table.
2. Put on safety goggles, a welding helmet, gloves, and other protective clothing.
3. Set the welder for the desired amperage, type of current, and **negative polarity** if direct current is to be used.
4. Put an electrode in the electrode holder.
5. Turn on the welder.
6. Position the tip of the electrode about ¼″ [6.35 mm] above one end of the joint. Hold it vertical, but slanted 10-20 degrees in the direction of travel.
7. **Flip the dark lens in place,** strike the arc and make a tack weld.
8. Make a tack weld at the other end of the joint. This is a small weld to hold the pieces temporarily together.
9. Chip the slag from the tack welds.
10. If you are right-handed, restart the weld at the left end of the joint; if left-handed, at the right end. Move the tip of the electrode back and forth across the joint an amount equal to the electrode diameter. Advance the electrode along the joint, feeding it downward as it melts, at a rate that will maintain contact with the liquid pool of metal.
11. When the weld is completed, pull the electrode away, then **turn off the welder.**
12. Allow the metal to cool for a minute. Then, with eye protection and protective clothing in place, chip off the slag with the chipping hammer and inspect the weld.

26-9 Inspecting the Arc Weld

The appearance of the arc weld tells much about its quality. A normal weld made with a weaving motion, using a ⅛″ [3.2 mm] diameter rod, will be ⅜″ to ½″ [9.5 to 12.7 mm] wide. The weld will be of uniform width, have a low profile of uniform height, and have the ripple lines uniformly close together (Fig. 26-17A). A normal weld made without a

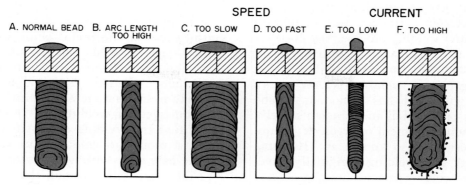

Fig. 26-17 *Shielded-metal arc welds made in the correct manner, and under several incorrect conditions.*

weaving motion will look the same but will be narrower; this kind of weld is called a **stringer bead.**

Figure 26-17 also shows the results of welds made under incorrect conditions. An arc length that is too long results in a thin deposit with poorly defined edges (Fig. 26-17B). If welding speed is too slow, more metal than necessary is deposited and there is danger of melting a hole through the metal (Fig. 26-17C). If the welding speed is too fast, a narrow bead with little penetration results (Fig. 26-17D). When the current setting is too low, there is little penetration, and most of the electrode metal is deposited on top (Fig. 26-17E). A current setting that is too high will produce excess heat and spatter (Fig. 26-17F). The bead will be ragged and uneven, and holes can be melted easily through the metal.

26-10 Advanced Arc Welding Processes

The search for more efficient methods of welding has resulted in the development of three advanced arc welding processes.

1. **Gas metal arc welding (GMAW)** has largely replaced shielded metal arc welding with stick electrodes for production welding. Also known as **MIG** (metal inert gas) welding, this process uses a consumable electrode in wire form, and an inert gas shield of carbon dioxide when welding carbon steel (Fig. 26-18).

The wire electrode provides a continuous source of filler metal so that welds of any length may be made without stopping.

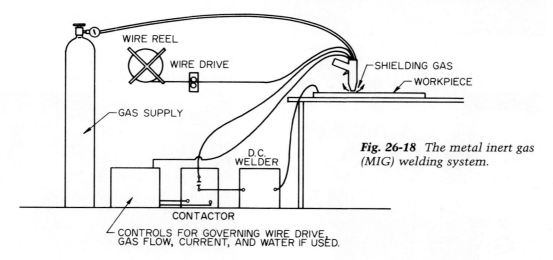

Fig. 26-18 *The metal inert gas (MIG) welding system.*

The inert gas shield eliminates slag and makes cleaner, stronger welds. Initially only a hand welding process (Fig. 26-19), it is being used increasingly with robots for automated production welding (Fig. 26-20).

2. **Gas tungsten arc welding (GTAW)** uses a welding gun that has a nonconsumable electrode of tungsten and which also delivers an inert gas shield of argon or helium. The process is also known as **TIG (tungsten inert gas)** welding. Originally developed for welding magnesium, it is now widely used for welding aluminum, copper, stainless steel, and other metals that are difficult to weld (Figs. 26-21 and 26-22).

Welds may be made either with or without consumable filler rods, depending on the thickness of the metal being welded and the type of weld. Due to the inert gas shielding, welds are very clean and strong. Welders skilled in TIG welding can often make welds that are almost invisible.

3. **Submerged arc welding (SAW)** is so named because the welding arc is submerged under a mound of granular flux (Fig. 26-23). The bare filler wire is fed automatically at a rate that will maintain the welding arc. Since the arc and the molten metal are covered with the mound of flux, there is no flash, spatter, sparks, or smoke. Welds are uniform, and have excellent physical and chemical properties. This process is widely used for welding large objects made of carbon steel and stainless steel sheets and pipes (Fig. 26-24).

Fig. 26-19 *This operation is using MIG welding to fasten a lifting eye assembly of 1/4 inch (6.35 mm) mild steel. The welding equipment shown provides semi-automatic wire electrode feed for welding guns at each work station.* (Miller Electric Manufacturing Company)

Fig. 26-20 *Robots can be programmed to automatically arc weld any contour.* (Cincinnati Milacron)

Fig. 26-21 *Tungsten inert gas (TIG) welding equipment.* (Bessler Welding, Inc., Roger Bean)

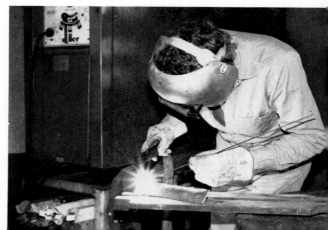

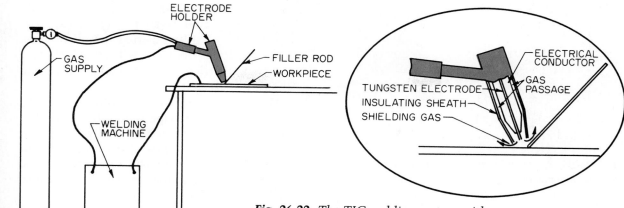

Fig. 26-22 *The TIG welding system with a cutaway drawing of a TIG welding torch.*

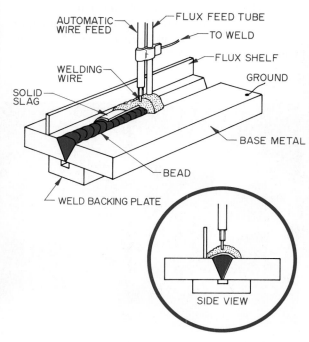

Fig. 26-23 *The submerged-arc welding process.*

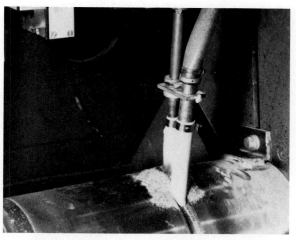

Fig. 26-24 *An example of the automatic submerged-arc welding process. Pieces of 11-1/2" (292 mm) round pipe are held in fixtures while the grooved joint is welded.* (Hobart Brothers Company)

26-11 Electric Spot Welding

Electric spot welding is a form of **resistance welding.** In spot welding, high current at a low voltage passes through a spot on two pieces of metal, usually sheet metal, for a short period of time. This is done with a **spot welder** (Figs. 26-25 and 26-26).

Resistance to the flow of current through the metal at the spot causes heat, which melts the metal and makes a **spot weld.** The pieces of metal must be held together between the welding tongs under moderate pressure, both during the weld and for a few seconds afterwards while the weld cools (Fig. 26-27).

The welding time is controlled by a timer that is built into the spot welder. Welding time commonly varies from 3 to 120 Hertz (Hz). (One Hertz equals one complete cycle per second.) With 60-Hz current, 120-Hz

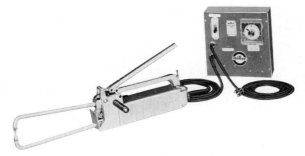

Fig. 26-25 *A portable spot welder.* (Miller Electric Manufacturing Company)

means 2 seconds of time. Two pieces of 20-gage sheet steel may be spot-welded in approximately a 15- to 20-Hz period. If the welding time is too long, the weld will be pitted from excess heat. If the time is too short, the weld will come apart.

The points on the welding tongs should be properly dressed to shape with a file, and they should be replaced when badly worn or burned. The tongs should also be adjusted for the correct pressure for the thickness of the weld desired. Too much pressure will cause pitting of the weld.

Spot welding is most frequently used to weld sheet metal joints. However, it may also be used to spot-weld sheet metal to small diameter rods or flat bars. Much production spot welding is done in automatic machines and with robots (Fig. 26-28).

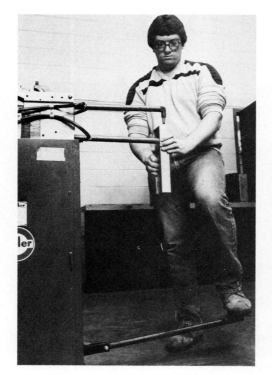

Fig. 26-26 *A heavy duty water-cooled spot welder.*

Fig. 26-28 *Robots spot welding auto body assemblies.*

Fig. 26-27 *The sequence of steps in spot welding.*

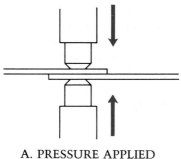

A. PRESSURE APPLIED

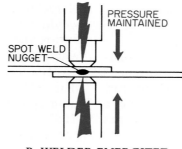

B. WELDER ENERGIZED

PRESSURE MAINTAINED

SPOT WELD NUGGET

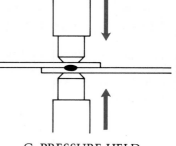

C. PRESSURE HELD MOMENTARILY

26-12 Oxyacetylene Welding

An **oxyacetylene weld** is a **gas weld.** The heat is produced by burning **acetylene gas** with **oxygen gas,** giving a temperature of about 6000°F [3,316°C]. The edges of metal to be welded are heated with the oxyacetylene flame until they melt and fuse together. When the metal cools and becomes solid, the pieces are welded together. The weld may be made so strong that the two pieces are like one piece.

Often, metal is added to the joint with a **filler rod.** This rod is usually made of the same metal as the pieces being welded. The pieces of metal to be joined are called the **base metal.** All of the melted metal from both the base metal and filler rod is called the **weld metal.**

26-13 Oxyacetylene Welding Equipment

Oxyacetylene welding requires the following special equipment:

1. A cylinder of oxygen.
2. A cylinder of acetylene.
3. Special valves called **regulators** for the cylinders.
4. Hoses to carry the gases from the cylinders to the torch.
5. A welding torch, and various sizes of torch tips.
6. A lighter that can make a spark to ignite the mixture of gases.
7. A pair of tongs or pliers to handle pieces of hot metal.

Oxygen cylinders are usually taller and smaller in diameter than acetylene cylinders (Fig. 26-29). This is because a long, slender cylinder can better withstand high pressures.

When the tank is full, oxygen tank pressures reach 2200 psi [15.2 MPa]. Because of the high pressure, the cylinder has a double-seated tank valve to prevent leakage around the valve stem. **The oxygen cylinder tank valve must be opened all the way when in use, and closed all the way when not in use. Because of the potentially explosive pressure of an oxygen cylinder, it is usually kept chained to a cart. A ruptured oxygen cylinder can smash through a concrete wall.**

Acetylene cylinders are low-pressure cylinders. When full of acetylene, the gas is contained at about 250 psi [1.7 MPa]. Acetylene is the **fuel gas** used in oxyacetylene torches. In the cylinder it is dissolved in liquid acetone.

> ⊘ **SAFETY NOTE**
> The acetylene tank valve should only be opened about ½ a turn so that the fuel supply can be shut off quickly in an emergency.

The gas pressure **regulator** (Fig. 26-30) is a device on each cylinder that delivers a constant supply of gas at a reduced pressure to the welding torch. The regulator is necessary because the welder works with only 1 to 10 psi [6.89 to 68.9 kPa] of each gas.

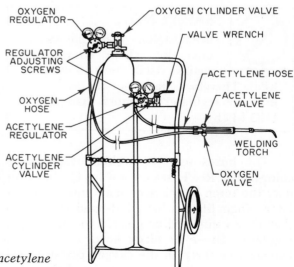

Fig. 26-29 *Equipment for oxyacetylene welding.*

CYLINDER PRESSURE GAGE

TORCH PRESSURE GAGE

REGULATOR KEY

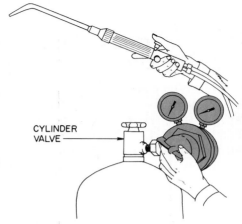

CYLINDER VALVE

Fig. 26-30 *A gas pressure regulator for an oxygen cylinder. The drawing shows the two pressure gages, the cylinder valve, and the regulator key.* (Dominion Oxygen Company, Ltd.)

The regulator attaches to the tank valve. Two pressure gages are attached to the regulator. The high-pressure gage, which is nearest the tank valve, shows the tank pressure when the tank valve is open. Gas is released from the regulator by turning a regulator key clockwise (Fig. 26-30). The amount of pressure being released through the regulator is shown on the low-pressure gage, which is farthest from the tank valve.

SAFETY NOTE

WARNING: Acetylene gas is unstable when compressed against itself above 15 psi [103 kPa]. Therefore, never set the acetylene pressure regulator for more than 15 psi [103 kPa].

The **hoses** used in welding are always color-coded. **Red hoses** are always used to **connect the torch to the acetylene pressure regulator.** Their fittings have **left-hand threads** so that they cannot be connected to the oxygen regulator. **Green or black hoses** are used to **connect the torch to the oxygen pressure regulator;** their fittings have **right-hand threads.**

The **welding torch** (Fig. 26-31) mixes the gases from the oxygen and acetylene cylinders. It controls the flow of each gas to produce the size and type of flame needed. With the welding torch, the welder can direct a maximum amount of heat to a small spot or area.

The **torch tips** used in welding come in different sizes and are attached to the welding torch with a threaded collar, (Fig. 26-31). Each tip provides the size and kind of flame needed to weld a certain thickness of metal.

Be sure to use the correct size wrench when changing tips. Some tips with rubber gaskets must be screwed only finger-tight. Table 26-3 gives information that will help in selecting tips, rods, and gas pressures. Follow the manufacturer's recommendations. Each tip has the size number marked on it.

Fig. 26-31 *A welding torch and the removable torch tip.*

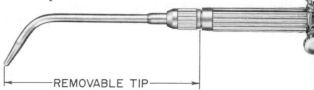

REMOVABLE TIP

Table 26-3

Tip Sizes, Regulator Pressures, and Rod Sizes for Oxyacetylene Welding

Tip size no.	Gas pressure psi (kPa)		Metal thickness inches (mm)	Filler rod diameter, inches (mm)
	Oxy-gen	Acety-lene		
1	1 (6.9)	1 (6.9)	. . . . .	. . . . .
2	2 (13.8)	2 (13.8)	1/32 (0.8)	1/16 (1.5)
3	3 (20.7)	3 (20.7)	1/16 (1.5)	1/16 (1.5)
4	4 (27.6)	4 (27.6)	3/32 (2.4)	1/16 (1.5), 3/32 (2.4), or 1/8 (3.2)
5	5 (34.5)	5 (34.5)	1/8 (3.2)	3/32 (2.4) or 1/8 (3.2)
6	6 (41.4)	6 (41.4)	3/16 (4.8)	1/8 (3.2)
7	7 (48.7)	7 (48.7)	1/4 (6.4)	3/16 (4.8)
8	8 (55.2)	8 (55.2)	5/16 (7.9)	3/16 (4.8)
9	9 (62.1)	9 (62.1)	3/8 (9.5)	3/16 (4.8)
10	10 (68.9)	10 (68.9)	7/16 (11.1)	3/16 (4.8) or 1/4 (6.4)

to open the hole, because the tip may be damaged. Some tip cleaners carry the same number as the tip. Clean the tip by inserting a tip cleaner of proper size in the hole in the torch tip.

SAFETY NOTE

Wear protective clothing when using oxyacetylene equipment (Fig. 26-33). It should include the following items:

1. A cloth or leather cap.
2. Welding goggles.
3. Coveralls of treated cotton or a full-length apron.
4. Trousers without cuffs and a shirt with full-length sleeves.
5. Leather shoes.
6. Gloves with cuffs that overlap the sleeves.

Sometimes the hole in the torch tip (called the **orifice**) becomes partly clogged with a small piece of carbon, dust, or dirt. The gases passing through the tip may make a hissing sound different from the normal sound, and the flame may have an odd shape. When this happens, it is important to use a special **tip cleaner** to clean the tip (Fig. 26-32). Do not try to use a piece of wire, wood, or a wire brush

Fig. 26-33 *Protective clothing for oxyacetylene welding.*

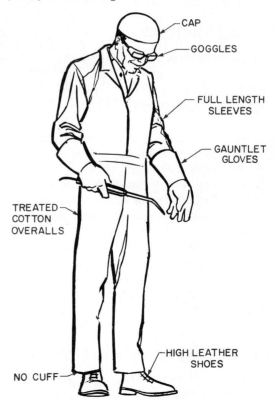

Fig. 26-32 *Tip cleaners.*

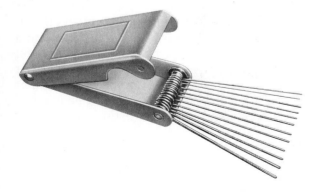

26-14 Starting-up Procedure for Oxyacetylene Welding

1. Install the correct torch tip.
2. Check to see that the regulator keys are held in place by only two or three threads. This will prevent the high pressure gas from damaging the low pressure gage when the tank valves are opened.
3. Open the **oxygen** tank valve **all the way.**
4. Open the **acetylene** tank valve **about ½ turn.** Leave the wrench on the valve stem to allow quick shut-off of fuel if necessary.
5. Open the **oxygen torch valve** about ½ turn. Then screw in the oxygen regulator key until the desired pressure is obtained. **Close the oxygen torch valve.**
6. Open the **acetylene torch valve** about ½ turn. Then screw in the acetylene regulator key until the desired pressure is obtained. **Close the acetylene torch valve.** The oxyacetylene torch is now ready for lighting.

Lighting the Torch

Before lighting the torch, be sure that the proper clothing is being worn. This includes properly fitted gas welding goggles.

1. Open the acetylene torch valve ⅛ to ¼ of a turn.
2. Point the torch tip away from your body and away from the gas cylinders.
3. Ignite the acetylene gas with a spark lighter (Fig. 26-34). **Do not use matches or a cigarette lighter because these place the hand dangerously close to the torch tip when it ignites.**
4. The acetylene burns a dark orange color and may give off a black soot. Open the acetylene valve until the flame almost separates from the torch tip.
5. Open the oxygen torch valve to obtain the desired size and kind of flame.

Types of Oxyacetylene Flames

Once the torch is lighted, the oxyacetylene flame can be adjusted to:

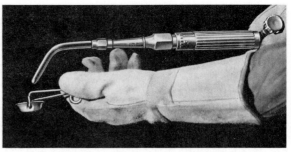

Fig. 26-34 *Using a spark lighter to light the torch.* (Linde Division of Union Carbide Corporation)

1. A **neutral flame**—the proper mixture of oxygen and acetylene for most welds (Fig. 26-35A).
2. A **carburizing flame**—a low-temperature flame for **torch brazing.** This flame has too much acetylene (or too little oxygen) for welding (Fig. 26-35B).
3. An **oxidizing flame**—this flame has an excess of oxygen (or insufficient acetylene). It will not make a strong weld. It is always harmful to the metal (Fig. 26-35C).

26-15 Welding with an Oxyacetylene Flame

1. Arrange and clamp the pieces to be welded.
2. Adjust the welding goggles over your eyes to fit comfortably, and put on welding gloves.
3. Light the torch and adjust it to produce a neutral flame.
4. **Tack weld** each end of the weld to be made. This is done by applying the flame to the seam at a 45° degree angle. The tip of the inner cone of the flame should almost touch the work. Move the flame in a small circle until a puddle of melted metal is formed on both pieces and flows together to make a weld. Put the end of the filler rod, also at a 45° angle, into the puddle and melt enough of it to fill the gap between the pieces (Fig. 26-36). On long pieces, make tack welds close enough together to keep the pieces from spreading apart while the joint is being welded.

If the torch and rod are moved too rapidly, the gap will not be filled. If the movement is too slow, the flame will melt a hole through the metal. It takes a lot of practice and experimenting to become good at this movement.

Welding from right to left or front to back as in Figure 26-37A is called the **forehand technique.** It is commonly used on **thin** metals. On thick metals the **backhand technique** is used. In this, the rod is moved from side to side and the flame held steadily, welding from the opposite end—left to right or back to front.

If the welding must be stopped for only a few minutes, it is all right to shut off the flow of gases at the torch. When the welding is to be stopped for a longer time, such as for lunch, end of the class period, or overnight, the acetylene and oxygen tank valves must be closed, the hoses drained, and the regulator keys unscrewed.

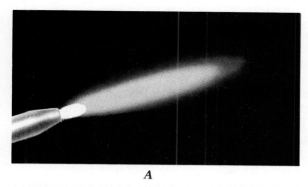
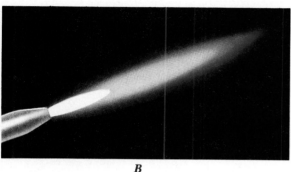
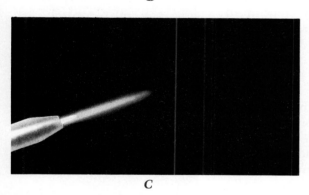

Fig. 26-35 *Adjusting the oxyacetylene flame. (A) A neutral flame. (B) A carburizing flame. (C) An oxidizing flame.*

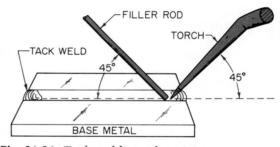

Fig. 26-36 *Tack welding a butt joint.*

Fig. 26-37 *Oxyacetylene welding with the forehand technique. The filler rod and torch move from right to left, or front to back.*

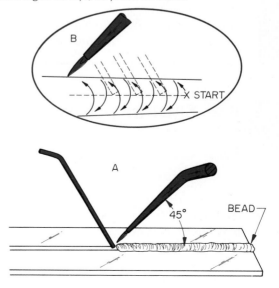

5. Begin to weld the seam by moving the torch in a small circle until each edge melts and forms a puddle. Put the end of the filler rod in the puddle. Then move the flame around three sides of the filler rod so that a half-circle is traced as shown in Fig. 26-37. After the weld has been started, move the rod and the flame along the seam at a rate that will continue to fill the gap with molten metal. Continue in this fashion until the weld is finished.

TECHNOLOGIES AND PRACTICES

To the Top of the Arch

The Gateway Arch in St. Louis, Missouri was built to honor the western pioneers and the city that was the "Gateway to the West." The steel arch is 630 feet [192 m] high and weighs 43,000 tons [39,008 t]. Designed by Eero Saarinen, it is an inverted **catenary curve.** A catenary curve is the shape made when a chain hangs freely between two points of support. Saarinen chose this shape for its simplicity and structural soundness.

This unique design presented an engineering challenge to the builders. The two sides of the arch were built at the same time to join eventually at the top. These legs were built by welding triangular sections on top of each other. Viewed from above, each of these building blocks could be seen as a triangle within a triangle. The outer triangle was 1/4-inch stainless steel. The inner triangle was 3/8-inch structural steel. Between the two layers were steel rods embedded in concrete. The mid-dle of the building block was hollow.

The triangular sections used at ground level measured 54 feet on each of the three sides and reached up 12 feet. As construction of the legs progressed, the sections used became smaller and smaller. The size of the last piece was only 17 feet on each side and six feet in length.

The first six 12-foot sections were lifted into place with cranes. Above this height of 72 feet, special movable derricks had to be used. Mounted on tracks on the outside of each leg, they crept up the sides as they raised sections above them. Workers then welded the sections in place.

As the arch neared completion, heat from the sun caused one of the legs to expand. A two-foot gap had to be jacked open an additional four feet to allow completion of the arch. The derricks then backed down the outside. Workers followed, taking up track and polishing the surface.

The hollow space within the arch legs has since been taken up by a special train system that takes visitors to the top. Visitors taking this ride have nothing to fear. The arch is so sturdy that it will sway only 18 inches (at the most) in a 150 m.p.h. wind. Completed in October, 1965, it stands as a monument to both the pioneer spirit of yesterday and the technology of today.

26-16 Shutting-down Procedure for Oxyacetylene Welding

1. To put out the torch flame, the recommended procedure is to **close the oxygen torch valve first.** When the acetylene torch valve is turned off first, the flame chases the supply of fuel back inside the torch. When this happens, it sometimes makes a loud popping sound as it burns out. This can cause carbon soot to obstruct gas passages inside the torch, and is not recommended.

2. Close the acetylene torch valve.

3. Close the oxygen tank valve.

4. Close the acetylene tank valve.
5. Drain the acetylene line by opening the acetylene torch valve. When the acetylene gas pressure gages have both dropped to zero, close the acetylene torch valve.
6. Drain the oxygen line by opening the oxygen torch valve. When the oxygen gas pressure gages have both dropped to zero, close the oxygen torch valve.
7. Unscrew the oxygen and acetylene regulator keys until they are held in place only by two or three threads.
8. Remove the torch tip if desired.
9. Coil up the hoses and store them properly.

26-17 Inspecting the Oxyacetylene Weld

When the weld is finished, remove the **scale** (the oxide that has formed on the metal) with a wire brush or tool. Look for errors that can be corrected when making the next weld. Study Figure 26-38 for examples of good and bad welds.

Fig. 26-38 *Oxyacetylene welds when finished show the skill of the welder. (A) Satisfactory. (B) The torch moved too slowly and built up too much heat. (C) The torch moved too fast, and could not deliver enough heat for the bead to form. (D) Satisfactory.*

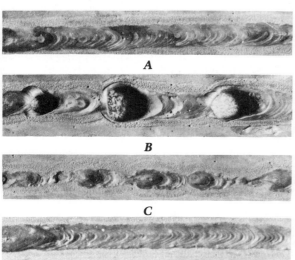

A

B

C

D

26-18 The Oxyacetylene Cutting Torch

Oxyacetylene cutting torches are widely used for the cutting of steel plate. Cutting machines use several cutting torches to speed production (Fig. 26-39). Cutting torches are also valuable tools for rescue and salvage operations.

The tip of an oxyacetylene cutting torch (Fig. 26-40) has an outer ring of small holes through which oxygen and acetylene pass to provide a **preheating** flame. The center hole in the tip passes the stream of pure oxygen necessary for efficient cutting. The cutting torch is provided with an additional valve for controlling oxygen flow to the **preheating orifices** (Fig. 26-40A). A lever-operated valve (Fig. 26-40B) controls the oxygen flow to the center hole, called the **cutting orifice.**

Fig. 26-39 *An oxyacetylene cutting machine that can cut several indentical parts at the same time. (Linde Division of Union Carbide Corporation)*

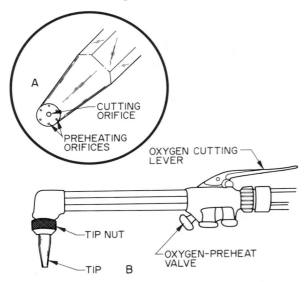

Fig. 26-40 *An oxyacetylene cutting torch attachment, with an enlarged view of the torch tip.*

Procedure for Using the Cutting Torch:

1. Place the piece to be cut on the cutting table.
2. Put on welding goggles, gloves, and other safety clothing.
3. Attach the cutting torch tip to the regular welding torch, shown in Figure 26-31. Close all valves.
4. Open the oxygen and acetylene tank valves as in "Starting-up Procedure for Oxyacetylene Welding."
5. Open the welding torch oxygen and acetylene valves as in the welding starting-up procedure, then set the oxygen and acetylene pressures according to the cutting tip size. Close the welding torch valves.
6. Open the welding torch oxygen valve all the way.
7. Open the welding torch acetylene valve about ¼ turn, and light the torch with a spark lighter.
8. Adjust the preheating flame to a neutral flame using the cutting torch oxygen valve and the welding torch acetylene valve.
9. Preheat the metal to a red heat where cutting is to begin. The torch tip should be held vertical, with the bright inner cones of the preheating flame about ¹⁄₁₆″ [1.5 mm] away from the workpiece.
10. When the metal is red-hot, press the oxygen lever to release the cutting stream of oxygen. Advance the torch as fast as the cutting action will permit.
11. Release the oxygen lever at the end of the cut. If no more cutting is to be done, turn off the torch and shut down the oxyacetylene system as described in Section 26-16.

26-19 Other Advanced Welding Processes

Three relatively new welding processes are now finding increasing use. They are electron beam welding (EBW), laser beam welding (LBW), and friction welding (FRW).

1. In **electron beam welding (EBW)**, a concentrated beam of electrons bombards the base metal, causing it to melt and fuse together (Figs. 26-41 and 26-42). The process is most efficient when done in a vacuum. There-

Fig. 26-41 *The electron beam welding system. The beam is invisible.*

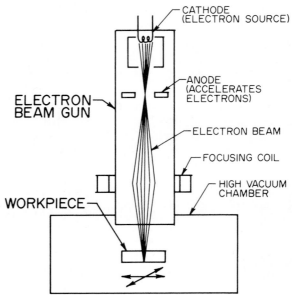

Fig. 26-42 The vacuum chamber and other equipment for electron beam welding.

fore, the size of the vacuum chamber limits the size of the workpieces that can be welded. Advantages include the ability to produce welds of extremely high purity, ability to melt any known material, ability to weld dissimilar metals, and ability to make welds with depths as great as 6 inches [152 mm].

Electron beam welding is costly for two reasons: (1) the high cost of equipment, and (2) the time lost in pumping out the vacuum chamber between welds. When the welds are not made in a vacuum, many advantages of the process are sharply reduced.

2. The energy source for **laser welding** is a concentrated beam of light (Fig. 26-43). ("Laser" comes from **L**ight **A**mplification by **S**timulated **E**mission of **R**adiation.) There are two types of lasers in use: (1) **gas lasers,** and (2) **solid lasers.** Gas lasers provide a continuous laser beam that is best suited to continuous welding and cutting operations. Solid lasers, on the other hand, release their energy in **bursts,** or **pulses,** at a rate of 6 to 10 a minute. Since each pulse lasts only a few millionths of a second, the base metal is liquid too short a time for chemical reactions to occur. Thus, flux-type protection is not required to obtain sound welds.

Laser systems (Fig. 26-44) can be precisely controlled and have sufficient power to weld and even vaporize any known material. Other advantages include the ability to make welds through transparent coverings and to make welds in locations impossible to reach with conventional welding gear. Limited depth of penetration, however, restricts the use of laser welding to relatively thin materials (Fig. 26-45).

3. **Friction welding,** also known as **inertia welding,** is a process that uses friction to generate the welding heat. The inertia welding machine rotates one of the parts being welded while applying pressure to force the two parts together (Fig. 26-46).

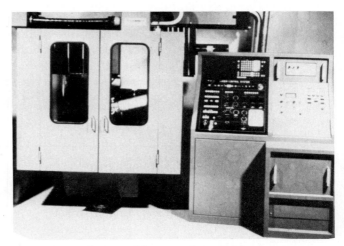

Fig. 26-44 A laser welding machine. (Coherent General, Inc.)

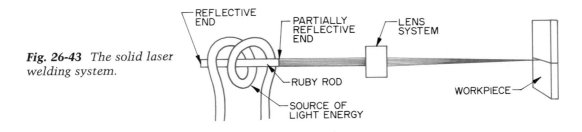

Fig. 26-43 The solid laser welding system.

REFLECTIVE END

PARTIALLY REFLECTIVE END

LENS SYSTEM

RUBY ROD

SOURCE OF LIGHT ENERGY

WORKPIECE

Fig. 26-45 *These two pieces of standing steel have been joined with a butt weld, which was done by a laser welder. The photo shows a magnified view. This steel is .125" thick.* (Coherent General, Inc.)

Fig. 26-46 *Inertia (friction) welding. (A) A weld in process. (B) The completed weld.* (MTI Corporation)

The friction thus obtained generates enough heat to soften the metal to a plastic state. Hydraulic pressure is then applied to force the softened metal together to form the weld.

Full-strength welds are made in only a few seconds. No special preparation of the surfaces being joined is required, and there is no need for fluxes or filler metals. The localized heating makes possible distortion-free welded assemblies of parts with widely different thicknesses. Metals very different from each other, such as steel and aluminum, may also be welded by this process.

REVIEW   REVIEW   REVIEW   REVIEW   REVIEW

WORDS TO KNOW

acetylene	filler rod	nitrides	spot welding
arc welding	forehand technique	oxides	spot welding tongs
argon	forge welding	oxidizing flame	straight polarity
backhand technique	fusion weld	oxyacetylene	tack weld
base metal	gas pressure	welding	tee joint
butt joint	regulator	oxygen	TIG
carbon dioxide	GTAW	plastic state	welding torch
carburizing flame	helium	pressure welding	weld metal
coated electrode	induction welding	resistance welding	weld nugget
corner joint	inertia welding	reverse polarity	
edge joint	lap joint	SAW	
electrode	laser welding	shielded metal arc	
electron beam	MIG	welding	
welding	neutral flame	slag	

(Review Continued)

REVIEW QUESTIONS

1. Describe how a fusion weld is made. How does this differ from pressure welding?
2. What temperature can the oxyacetylene flame produce? Electric arc?
3. What is the difference between base metal and weld metal?
4. Describe how a person doing oxyacetylene welding should be dressed for maximum safety.
5. What tip size, regulator settings, and filler rod diameter should be used to weld ⅛″ [3.2 mm] thick steel?
6. Why is it necessary to use a gas pressure regulator on oxygen and acetylene tanks?
7. How far should the acetylene tank valve be opened and why should the wrench be left on the valve stem?
8. Describe the correct procedure for setting up an oxyacetylene system for welding with a No. 5 tip.
9. What kind of flame should be used to make most gas welds?
10. What effect does an oxidizing flame have on the weld quality? Carburizing flame?
11. What is the purpose of a tack weld?
12. What can happen if the weld is made too slowly?
13. In what ways is the electric welding arc like the sun?
14. Why should the arc welder wear clothing without pockets and cuffs?
15. What is the purpose of the coating on arc-welding electrodes?
16. Are all E6013 electrodes the same? Why or why not?
17. Name the four basic welding positions, and make a sketch of each.
18. Name the joints commonly used in welding.
19. During the electric welding process, why should regular safety goggles be worn as well as the welding helmet?
20. What is the difference between straight polarity and reverse polarity? Which is most commonly used?
21. Describe the spot-welding process. What is it used for?
22. Describe the submerged arc welding process. What are its main advantages and uses?
23. How does TIG welding differ from MIG welding?
24. How do electron beam and laser welding differ? Name several advantages of each.
25. Describe how inertia welding is done and give several advantages.

UNIT

27

Soldering and Brazing

Soldering is a process of fastening metals together with solder, a nonferrous metal that has a lower melting point than the metals being joined. The metal being joined is heated until the solder, when brought into contact with it, melts and flows between the surfaces. The surfaces being joined must be very clean. When the liquid solder solidifies, it **adheres** (clings or sticks) tightly and forms a strong bond between the surfaces. The solder holds the parts together by the principle of adhesion.

If the solder (filler metal) melts below 800°F [427°C], the process is called **soft soldering;** if the solder melts above 800°F [427°C], it is called **hard soldering,** or **brazing.**

Soldering and brazing are different from welding. In welding, the pieces being joined are melted and fused together. The filler rod for welding is usually the same kind of metal as the pieces being joined; this is not true of soldering or brazing.

Soldering is commonly used by electronic technicians to solder wire joints for electric circuits. Sheet metal workers assemble and repair metal roofing by soldering. Plumbers solder copper plumbing pipe and pipe fittings together. Jewelers repair ornaments, rings, and other jewelry by hard soldering. Auto body repair workers often use soldering and brazing in their work.

27-1

Soft Soldering

The best **soft solder** is an alloy of **lead** and **tin.** For general work, a solder of one-half lead and one-half tin is used. It is called **half-and-half** or **fifty-fifty** solder and melts at about 400°F [204°C]. This solder works well for soldering copper, brass, bronze, steel, and tin- and zinc-coated steel. Lead/tin alloys other than 50/50 are also used for soldering.

Special solders are made for aluminum, stainless steel, and other metals. For example, a silver-tin alloy for soldering stainless steel makes joints ten times stronger than a lead-tin solder.

Solder is commonly available in coils of wire 1/16″ [1.6 mm] or 1/8″ [3.2 mm] in diameter. The wire may be solid or it may have a **rosin-** or **acid-flux core.** (Fig. 27-1). **Paste-type solders** are made of a mixture of powdered solder and paste flux. Solder is also made in ribbons, sheets, and pellets, and in pre-cut **solder forms** such as washers, rings, and other shapes.

Fig. 27-1 *Common forms of soft solders.* (Roger Bean)

Heat for Soft Soldering

Gas furnaces are often used to heat soldering coppers, the tool used for soldering (Fig. 27-2). When adjusted properly, the gas and air mix to give a blue flame. This is a hotter flame than the yellow flame obtained by burning the gas alone. A portable bottled-gas torch is a convenient and efficient heat source often used for soldering (Fig. 27-3). Electric soldering coppers are used when less heat is required (Fig. 27-4).

Fig. 27-4 *An electric soldering copper.*

Soldering Coppers

A **soldering copper** is a bar of copper, usually octagonal in cross-section. It is pointed at one end and is fastened to a steel bar that has a wooden handle on the other end (Fig. 27-5). The faces on the point of the soldering copper must be cleaned before the copper can be used for soldering. Then, the faces are coated with solder. This is called **tinning.** A properly tinned soldering copper will hold a drop of solder on the point and make soldering easier. **Heat from the soldering copper can transfer to the workpiece only through a properly tinned surface.**

The Following Steps Describe How to Tin a Soldering Copper.

1. Clean one or two adjacent faces of the soldering tip with a file. A soldering copper that has only one face or two adjacent faces tinned will hold more solder than if all faces are tinned. If the copper is too hard to file easily, soften it by heating it red hot and quenching it in water.

Fig. 27-2 *A bench-type gas furnace.* (Johnson Gas Appliance Co.)

Fig. 27-3 *A portable propane-fueled torch used for soldering.*

Fig. 27-5 *Soldering coppers, commonly called soldering irons, come in a variety of sizes and styles. The coppers are rated by weight. The weight is for a pair of soldering coppers of a given size. Thus a single 1 lb. soldering copper weighs ½ lb.*

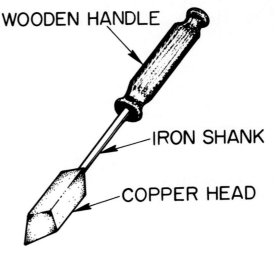

WOODEN HANDLE

IRON SHANK

COPPER HEAD

Fig. 27-6 *Tinning a soldering copper on a block of sal ammoniac.*

2. Heat the soldering copper until it is hot enough to melt solder on the point's faces. Test its heat occasionally by rubbing it on a block of sal ammoniac (a powerful flux, which is ammonium chloride, NH_4Cl) that has a drop of solder on it (Fig. 27-6). Do not overheat the soldering copper. Overheating will cause the solder to burn off and the soldering tip faces will become pitted. A badly pitted surface will hold little solder and will transfer little heat to the workpiece. Pitted surfaces should be removed by filing or by grinding on a belt grinder.

When the soldering copper is hot enough to cause the sal ammoniac to "smoke," a chemical reaction occurs that cleans the copper. This is necessary for the solder to stick to and evenly coat or "tin" the soldering tip surfaces.

⊘ SAFETY NOTE

Cleaning and tinning a soldering copper with sal ammoniac should only be done under an exhaust hood so that the sal ammoniac fumes are rapidly carried off. Avoid breathing the sal ammoniac fumes, which are corrosive.

Other fluxes such as zinc chloride ($ZnCl_2$) and rosin may be used to clean the tip of the soldering copper for tinning.

27-2 Preparing the Workpieces

Cleaning the surfaces to be soldered. The surfaces to be soldered must be **physically and chemically clean.** All visible rust, dirt, and grease must be removed. New metal usually needs no physical cleaning, but old metal may have to be polished with steel wool or abrasive cloth until bright metal appears. Any metal surface that has just been cleaned immediately begins to combine with oxygen in the air to form a layer of **oxide.** No matter how thin the oxide, it makes soldering impossible. The surfaces must be made chemically clean by applying a **flux,** which thoroughly removes the oxide film.

Table 27-1 lists the fluxes that are used for soldering different metals. Fluxes in liquid, solid, and paste forms are commercially avail-

Table 27-1

Fluxes for Soft Soldering

Metal to be soldered	Flux	Chemical name of flux
Brass Copper	Cut acid Rosin Sal ammoniac[1]	Zinc chloride Colophony Ammonium chloride
Zinc Galvanized iron (zinc coated)	Cut acid Cut acid	Zinc chloride Zinc chloride
Iron Steel	Cut acid Sal ammoniac	Zinc chloride Ammonium chloride
Tin Tin plate	Rosin Cut acid	Colophony Zinc chloride
Pewter	Rosin Tallow	Colophony
Nickel Silver	Cut acid	Zinc chloride
Aluminum	Special fluxes by different manufacturers	

[1]**Sal ammoniac** is **ammonium chloride** (NH_4Cl). It is a white solid substance that looks like rock salt or rock candy; it is used as a soldering flux. Sal ammoniac changes directly from a solid to two corrosive gases, ammonia (NH^3) and hydrogen chloride (HCl), upon heating.

able. Most of these fluxes are suitable for use on all common metals, and they produce good results. Flux is usually brushed on the surfaces to be soldered.

Rosin is an excellent flux for soldering copper, tin, and pewter. **It should always be used when soldering electrical connections because it is non-corrosive.** Rosin is a sticky, hard substance made from turpentine, which comes from pine trees. It is mixed with a solvent to form a paste.

Special fluxes are made for soldering aluminum, stainless steel, and other metals.

When **zinc chloride, sal ammoniac,** an **acid,** or any **corrosive-type** paste flux has been used as a flux for soldering, **it is necessary to wash the joint in cold, running water.** If this is not done, the joint and the metal touched by the flux will turn a black, dirty color.

A **soft-lead** (pencil) coating or a thin film of grease or shoe polish on the surface where the solder is **not wanted** will allow the solder to flow only where it is needed. This produces neater work.

LOCK JOINT   LAP JOINT

Fig. 27-7 *Joints for soft soldering.*

Fig. 27-8 *Tacking a seam keeps it from moving.*

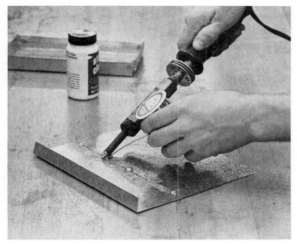

Holding the workpieces. Place the parts ready for soldering together, and fasten them so that they cannot move while being soldered. The joint to be soldered should not touch other metal because the heat will be carried away from the joint and make soldering impossible. Place the object to be soldered on a soldering block or a block of scrap wood.

27-3 Joints for Soft Soldering

Sheet metal joints to be soldered are usually various types of **lock joints** or **lap joints** (Fig. 27-7). Other joints are described in Unit 29. The parts to be joined should be close fitting; the better the fit, the stronger will be the soldered joint.

27-4 Soft Soldering Techniques

The Following Steps Are the Procedure For Soldering a Lap Seam.

1. Clean the surfaces to be soldered with steel wool or abrasive cloth if necessary.
2. Apply a small amount of flux to the surfaces to be soldered with a brush.
3. Clamp the pieces together if necessary.
4. Tack the seam together; that is, solder the seam at each end and in several places along the seam so the parts cannot move (Fig. 27-8).
5. Next, solder the whole seam. Place one of the tinned soldering copper faces on top of the seam to heat the metal. When the flux bubbles out of the joint, hold solder against the joint until it melts and runs into the joint (Fig. 27-9).
6. Move the soldering copper along the seam a short distance at a time, heating and soldering each part of the seam in the above manner.

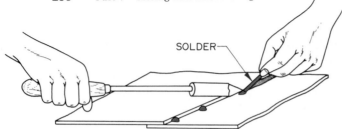

Fig. 27-9 *When soldering a seam, hold a soldering copper face flat against the top layer of metal. This provides maximum heat transfer and speeds the soldering process.*

Fig. 27-10 *Silver solders are available in many different shapes, sizes, and melting points.*

Sweat Soldering. In sweat soldering, a layer of solder is applied to each of the pieces before they are assembled. The parts are then assembled and heated until the solder already on the parts melts and fuses together.

27-5 Hard Soldering Techniques

Hard soldering (silver soldering or silver brazing) is used where a strong joint is needed or where the parts will be used in greater heat than the melting point of soft solder. Hard soldering is now commonly referred to as a brazing process.

The most widely used hard solders are the **silver-alloy solders.** Most of them melt at temperatures from 1100° to 1300°F [593° to 704°C]. Silver solders are available in ribbons, sheets, wire, and in pre-cut pieces of solder in various shapes, called pre-forms (Fig. 27-10).

Hard soldering is used in jewelry and art metal work for joining such metals as copper, silver, and gold. It can also be used on all carbon and alloy steels. It is sometimes used to join band saw blades.

Procedure for Hard Soldering

1. Carefully fit the parts together. They must be fitted much more closely than for soft soldering, because the silver solder flows out very thinly and cannot be used to fill small gaps.

2. If necessary, fasten the parts together with soft iron tying wire so they cannot move during soldering.

3. Apply flux to the joint with a small brush. For best results, use a commercial flux made for silver soldering. If a commercial flux is not available, a paste of powdered borax (sodium borate) and water can be used.

4. Place small pieces of silver solder along the joint as shown in Figure 27-11 or use a pre-form.

5. Heat the parts until the solder melts and runs into the joint (Fig. 27-12).

6. Inspect the joint to see if it is completely soldered. If necessary, add flux and solder, and reheat the parts to complete the soldering.

Heat for hard soldering is often applied directly with a flame from a torch. Natural, propane, or acetylene gas may be used. Some gas-air torches have only one hose furnishing a gas. In this type, air is drawn from the room and mixed with the gas by the torch. Some torches, however, use low-pressure air through a second hose. This raises the melting temperature above 1300°F [704°C], which is not possible without air delivered under pressure. Figure 27-13 shows a gas-air torch with an acetylene tank as commonly used by plumbers and jewelers. The oxyacetylene torch, with heat to 6000°F [3316°C], must be used with extreme care when hard soldering, in order not to melt the parts being soldered.

Fig. 27-11 *Hard soldering with silver solder. Joints must be very close fitting. Small pieces of silver solder or a preform is placed at the joint before it is heated and melted into the joint.* (Bradley University, Roger Bean)

Fig. 27-12 *Hard soldering with a torch.* (Bradley University, Roger Bean)

Fig. 27-13 *An acetylene gas-air torch system used for brazing.* (Bradley University, Roger Bean)

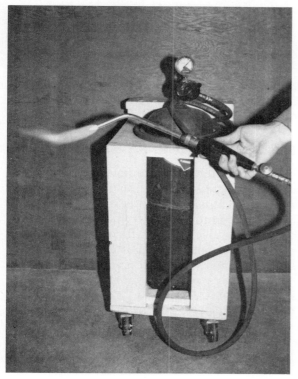

27-6 Brazing and Bronze Welding

Brazing and **bronze welding** are not welding processes. There is no melting together or fusion of the metals being joined by these processes. The filler metals used in these processes have a melting point above 800°F [427°C], but this is much lower than the melting point of the metals being joined. Hence, brazing, bronze welding, and hard soldering are really the same process because they all use nonferrous filler metals that melt above 800°F [427°C].

Bronze welding is widely used to repair gray iron and malleable iron castings (Fig. 27-14). It is preferred because the high heat of welding destroys the heat-treatment properties of malleable iron castings and also makes gray iron castings very brittle.

Fig. 27-14 *Bronze welding being done to build up a gear tooth on a cast iron gear.* (Bessler Welding, Inc., Roger Bean)

Brazing is used to assemble thousands of products. Eye glass frames, bicycle frames, carbide tipped cutting tools, welding torches, automotive fuel injector assemblies, and delicate tubing assemblies used for automatic temperature control in electric appliances are a few examples of products assembled by brazing (Fig. 27-15).

Difference between Brazing and Bronze Welding

In brazing, small amounts of filler metal are used to join the parts, just as in hard soldering. The parts to be brazed are made with close-fitting joints. When the filler metal melts, it flows into the joints by **capillary action** (the natural tendency of a liquid to be drawn between two close-fitting surfaces).

The design of joints for bronze welding, however, is the same as for fusion welding, which is described in Unit 26. Bronze welding differs from brazing in that capillary action is either not involved or plays only a small part in the strength of the joint. Bronze welding is similar to welding in that beads of filler metal are laid down to fill a joint between metal parts. However, because the base metal is not melted, and the filler metal has a lower tensile strength, the joints have less strength than can be obtained with fusion welds.

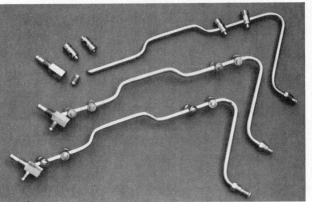

Fig. 27-15 *(A) Torch brazing an automotive fuel injector system, (B) completed fuel injector assembly.* (Handy & Harmon)

Brazing and Welding Fluxes

Many different fluxes have been scientifically developed for specific types of brazing and for welding of various metals. They are available commercially from welding supply dealers. Because of these fluxes, many metals that were formerly difficult to join may now be brazed or welded with comparative ease.

Rods for Brazing and Bronze Welding

Rods used for brazing and bronze welding are about 60% copper and 40% zinc. In addition, other elements such as iron, tin, manganese, and silicon are included in small amounts to give the rods better brazing and bronze welding characteristics. Most bronze welding rods melt at approximately 1600°F [871°C]. Some of these rods produce a bond with a tensile strength of more than 50,000 pounds per square inch [344.74 MPa] on steel and cast iron. Bronze welding rods are available with or without flux coatings. Coated rods are widely used because they speed brazing, produce good joints, and reduce costs.

How to Braze with a Torch

1. Clean the parts to be brazed and fit the parts closely together. The better the parts fit, the stronger the joint will be.
2. If necessary, clamp the parts together to hold them in place.
3. Select a flux coated brazing rod. If a bare brazing rod is used instead, heat about 1" (25 mm) of one end with the torch and dip it into the brazing flux. This will coat the end of the rod with flux.
4. Tack the parts together. Heat the joint at one end to a dark red color with an oxyacetylene torch. Then, melt enough of the brazing rod into the joint to hold it together. Repeat this at the other end of the joint.
5. Now braze the entire joint, by working the torch back and forth across the joint. The objective is to heat both pieces being joined to a dull red before melting the brazing rod into the joint. If you use a bare brazing rod, it is necessary to reheat and dip it in the flux each time after the part containing the flux has melted away.
6. Allow the parts to cool slowly to room temperature, since rapid cooling may cause the joint to crack.

Furnace Brazing

Furnace brazing is often used for mass production of brazed parts. The parts are first preassembled, then mechanically fastened together. Filler metal is pre-placed in or on the joint (Fig. 27-16). The parts are then loaded into a special furnace containing a gas that provides a **reducing atmosphere** (Fig. 27-17).

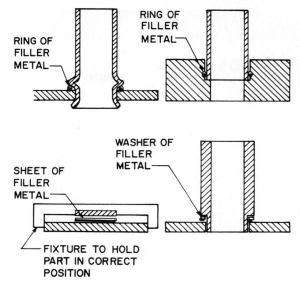

Fig. 27-16 *Parts prepared for furnace brazing. The parts are preassembled with a brazing metal preform before they enter the furnace.*

Fig. 27-17 *An inert gas brazing furnace eliminates the need for fluxes and speeds production.* (C.I. Hayes Inc.)

Fluxes are unnecessary because the reducing atmosphere removes the oxide film from the metal parts and leaves the metal bright and clean. When the parts become hot enough to melt the pre-placed filler metal, it flows into and seals the joint by capillary action.

REVIEW REVIEW REVIEW REVIEW REVIEW

WORDS TO KNOW

acid flux	flux	sal ammoniac	soldering furnace
adhesion	furnace brazing	silver-alloy solder	soldering salt
borax	hard soldering	silver soldering	sweat soldering
brazing	oxide	soft soldering	tallow
bronze welding	paste-type solder	solder forms	tinning
capillary action	reducing	soldering copper	zinc chloride
exhaust hood	atmosphere		
50-50 solder	rosin flux		

REVIEW QUESTIONS

1. How does soft soldering differ from hard soldering?
2. What tools and materials are needed for soft soldering?
3. What metals is soft solder made of? Hard solder? A brazing rod?
4. Why is flux necessary for soldering and brazing?
5. List the fluxes used for soft soldering, hard soldering, and for electrical connections.
6. Describe how a soldering copper is tinned.
7. Tell how to solder two pieces of metal together.
8. What is meant by sweat soldering?
9. Why and how should a soldered joint be cleaned after a corrosive-type flux is used?
10. Name several uses for hard soldering and brazing.
11. What kinds of filler rods are used for brazing? What is their approximate melting temperature?
12. Explain how furnace brazing is done.

UNIT
28
Adhesive Bonding

Adhesive bonding is the process of fastening parts of products together permanently with non-metallic glues or adhesives. Soldering and brazing employ **metals** as adhesives and are not generally classified as adhesive-bonding methods. They are discussed in Unit 27.

28-1 Structural and Nonstructural Bonding

Adhesives have been used to fasten materials together for thousands of years. Until recently, however, the adhesives available were only suited for use in **non-structural** metal-working applications. Adhesives were not used where failure of the adhesive would affect the structural strength of the assembly.

Nonstructural adhesive bonding is widespread. For example, in making automobiles, adhesive bonding is used (1) to attach rubber seals to auto hoods, trunks, and doors; (2) to fasten upholstery materials to metal body parts; (3) to attach metal trim to the body; and (4) to seal metal parts that are bolted or screwed together.

Structural (load-bearing) use of adhesive-bonded metals was pioneered by the aircraft industry during World War II. Since then, the advantages of adhesive bonding for many purposes have stimulated the development of new adhesives. These new bonding materials are suitable for a wide range of structural requirements.

Structural adhesive bonding is now widely used in the aerospace, automotive, appliance, instrument, and other metalworking industries (Fig. 28-1). This unit is concerned primarily with adhesive bonding of metals for structural purposes.

28-2 Advantages of Adhesive Bonding

Adhesive bonding has distinct advantages. However, they can be realized only with intelligent selection of adhesives, proper joint design, and care in surface preparation, adhesive application, and assembly. The advantages are as follows:

1. Loads are distributed more evenly in bonded joints. There are no high-stress concentrations (places that are weak) such as occur in spot-welded, riveted, or bolted joints. In some cases this allows the use of thinner metals without any loss of joint strength. Using thinner metals reduces cost and weight of the parts.
2. **Fatigue resistance** is improved because adhesives will **stretch** or **compress** under various load conditions. For example, adhe-

sive-bonded helicopter rotor blades (Fig. 28-2) have a service life of over 1,000 hours, while riveted blades have a service life of only 80-100 hours.
3. There is no loss of **part strength** and no **shape distortion** with adhesive bonding. Strong assemblies are made without the holes required for mechanical fastening, and without the distortion that results from high temperatures used during welding.

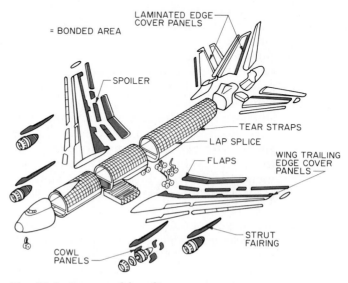

Fig. 28-1 Structural bonding.

Fig. 28-2 Adhesive bonded helicopter rotor blades have a service life ten times as long as riveted blades. (Bell Helicopter/Textron)

4. Adhesive bonding permits greater **design flexibility. Almost any combination of materials can be adhesive-bonded,** regardless of their shape, thickness, and chemical or mechanical properties. This is a great advantage in joining delicate assemblies that would be damaged when joined by conventional methods. For example, adhesive bonding has made possible the use of **honeycomb** construction in aircraft and space vehicles. Honeycomb cores of fragile aluminum foil, stainless steel, or plastic can be successfully bonded to thin sheets of aircraft metals. This results in extremely rigid but lightweight parts (Fig. 28-3).

5. Adhesive-bonded joints are automatically **sealed** against leakage of fluids and most gases, which eliminates the need and expense of separate sealing operations. The adhesive also helps reduce sound transmission. The adhesive can also insulate against **electrolytic corrosion** (corrosion caused by the electrical interaction between different metals). Adhesives, however, may be tailor-made to be electrically conductive, semiconductive, or nonconductive.

6. Adhesive bonding eliminates more expensive fastening operations such as drilling, riveting, or welding. Savings may also come from thinner or lower-cost materials and from the fewer finishing operations required with adhesive bonding.

Fig. 28-3 Honeycomb panel construction is lighter and stronger than solid metal. (Hexcel Corp.)

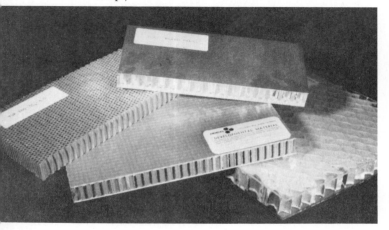

28-3 Disadvantages of Adhesive Bonding

1. *Performance limitations.* A serious disadvantage is that most adhesives fail rapidly above 500°F [260°C]. However, service temperatures are slowly being raised with the addition of heat-resistant fillers. Research with ceramic adhesives indicates that service temperatures of 1000°F [538°C] are possible.

   Some adhesives lose strength in situations where temperatures are alternately high and low. Other adhesives are subject to attack by bacteria, mold, moisture, solvents, and even small animals or insects. Adhesives must be selected carefully to meet performance requirements for a trouble-free service life.

2. *Application problems.* Surface cleanliness is very critical. In addition, parts must be closely fitted to provide a uniform gap of correct size for the application of adhesive. Adhesives must be handled with care so as to prevent contamination. Special fixtures are often needed to assure correct alignment of parts during assembly. Worker protection must be provided when toxic or flammable adhesives and solvents are used. Some adhesives require curing by heating under pressure for long periods of time.

3. *Inspection problems.* The quality of bonds is difficult to assess. Precise bond strength can only be determined by destructive testing, described in Section 28-6.

28-4 Joint Design

Adhesive-bonded joints are subject to any one or a combination of **shearing, tension, cleavage,** and **peeling** forces (Fig. 28-4). They resist shear and tension forces better than the other forces. Consequently, adhesive-bonded joints should be designed to take advantage of these characteristics.

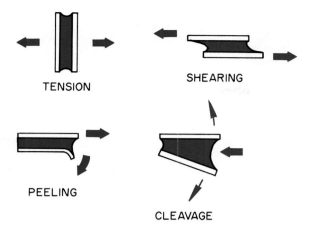

Fig. 28-4 *Forces to which adhesive bonds are subjected. They perform best under tension or shearing loads.*

Care should be taken to provide bonding areas in the joint design large enough to withstand the calculated loads. Joints with **mechanical interlocking** are stronger than plain bonded joints. Also, their assembly is faster because they are **self-aligning.** Figure 28-5 illustrates several preferred joint designs.

28-5 Types of Adhesives

Structural adhesives may be either **thermoplastic** materials, **thermosetting** materials, or a combination of both. They are all complex chemical materials.

Thermoplastic adhesives soften when heated, and harden on cooling, a cycle that can be repeated over and over. This property permits removal and replacement of parts damaged in service. Thermoplastic adhesives are preferred for assembly line operations because they are easily applied and have fast setting times. However, they are not suitable for use with parts subject to high loads over long periods of time because they are liable to **creep,** or slip. Thermoplastic adhesives are based on **acrylic, vinyl, nylon,** and **cellulosic** plastics.

Thermosetting adhesives permanently set with heat and pressure and cannot be re-softened. They are harder, less flexible, stronger, more expensive, and more difficult to use than thermoplastic adhesives. **Phenolic, epoxy, polyurethane, polyester,** and other thermosetting plastics are used in making thermosetting adhesives. **Silicones** and **rubbers** contribute flexibility to thermosetting adhesives.

To obtain the desired properties, thermoplastic materials are sometimes mixed with thermosetting materials to produce **semirigid adhesives.**

Most structural adhesives for bonding *metals* are either **phenolics** that have been modified with epoxy, vinyl, or rubber, or **epoxies,** which are either used plain or modified with phenolics, nylon, **polyamides,** or **polysulfide** rubbers.

At 75°F [23.9°C], the shear strengths of these adhesives range from a low of about 200 psi [1.38 MPa] for one rubber-modified phenolic adhesive to a high of 6,500 psi [44.8 MPa] for an unmodified epoxy adhesive. Most of these adhesives, however, have a shear strength between 2000 and 4000 psi [13.8 and 27.6 MPa].

LAP JOINTS

Fig. 28-5 *Joints that are particularly well suited for adhesive bonding.*

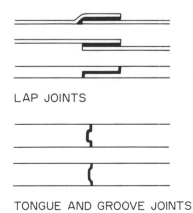

TONGUE AND GROOVE JOINTS

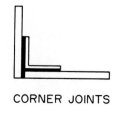

CORNER JOINTS

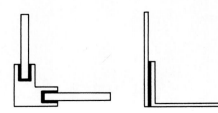

28-6 Application Methods and Techniques

Surface Preparation

Porous materials, such as wood, paper, and leather, **absorb** adhesives. Because the adhesives enter the **pores** of these materials, the contact areas between parts are increased. Thus, joint strength is improved. Porous materials are much more easily bonded with adhesives than metals.

Metals are practically **non-porous.** In bonding metals, adhesives are not absorbed but must stick to relatively smooth surfaces. **Surface preparation, therefore, is extremely important.** Every bit of joint surface must be wetted with adhesive to obtain maximum joint strength.

Dirt should be washed off with detergents or commercial alkaline cleaners. Oil or grease is removed by washing with solvents such as **acetone, carbon tetrachloride, toluene** or **xylene.** The solvent should not be allowed to dry on the metal's surface. It should be wiped off with clean rags or paper towels. Another cleaning process is **vapor degreasing,** which is done in closed tanks with such solvents as **trichloroethylene** and **perchloroethylene.**

SAFETY NOTE

Many industrial solvents, such as acetone, carbon tetrachloride, and toluene are poisonous. Use them only in a well-ventilated place.

Scale, rust, or **oxide films** that cannot be removed with solvents are removed mechanically or chemically. Abrasives are used, by hand or with power equipment, to rub or grind the scale, rust, or films off the parts to be joined. Or, the parts are prepared by **pickling** in acid solutions (a process described in Unit 5). After pickling, thorough rinsing in clean water is necessary. After drying, the parts should be bonded immediately. Otherwise, they should be wrapped in a moisture-proof barrier to prevent oxidation or other contamination until ready for bonding.

A good test of surface cleanliness is the **water-break test.** On clean surfaces water will flow out to form a continuous sheet or film, but "breaks" in the film will occur at unclean spots. Smooth surfaces are preferred for adhesive since rough surfaces require thicker layers of adhesive, which waste adhesive and weaken the bond.

Fig. 28-6 *Applying heat-resistant tiles to the body of the space shuttle. The worker on the left is checking the quality of the structure-to-tile fit before the tiles are bonded.* (NASA)

Application Methods

Adhesives are available as liquids, syrups, powders, and pastes; and in sheet, film, and tape forms. Spray systems are often used for applying liquid adhesives (Fig. 28-6). Fast and inexpensive application of liquids, syrups, and pastes is accomplished by brushing, troweling, or roller coating. An efficient way of applying powders is to first heat the parts to be joined above the melting point of the powder. Then, the powder is applied by dipping, spraying, or dusting.

Thermoplastic, or **hot-melt,** adhesives are applied with electrically heated dispensers. These dispensers melt the adhesive and use air pressure to make the adhesive stick. Sheet, film, and tape forms of adhesive are cut to size and shape, then placed on one of the surfaces to be bonded. These forms are held in place prior to bonding by tacking with a hot air or soldering gun.

Thin layers of adhesive make stronger bonds than thick layers. A thickness of .003″ to .006″ [0.08 to 0.15 mm] is recommended for most structural bonding with unreinforced adhesives. **Care should be taken, however, to apply enough adhesive to thoroughly wet both surfaces and to prevent gaps in the bond.**

Hardening or Curing of Adhesives

Adhesives become hardened, or **set,** by cooling, evaporation of solvents (drying), or by chemical reaction (**curing**). **Thermoplastic adhesives** are applied hot and only require cooling to set. **Solvent adhesives** usually require pre-drying to remove most of the solvent before assembly. Solvents trapped in the joint after assembly retard the drying process and may prevent the development of full bond strength. Drying of solvents may be speeded by drying with hot air either in or out of an oven.

Some adhesives are applied and allowed to dry completely, at which point they become inactive. Then, just before assembly, they are reactivated with a special solvent.

Thermosetting adhesives are **cured** by chemical reaction. Epoxy adhesives are made of two materials that are mixed together to form one adhesive substance. **Epoxies** require only sufficient pressure to keep the joints closed until curing (chemical reaction between the two parts of the epoxy) is complete. Some cure at room temperature while others require heating to between 250° and 350°F [121° and 177°C].

Phenolic adhesives require heating in the 325-350°F [163-177°C] temperature range while under pressure. This may be accomplished in the following ways:

1. By clamping and oven heating;
2. By using **autoclaves** (pressure vessels), which can provide both heat and pressure;
3. By using presses with heated tooling. Use of presses is preferred because of higher production capabilities.
4. By passing an electric current through heating elements placed in the **bond line** with the adhesive. The heating elements are fine wires or graphite-impregnated cloth. They remain in the joint after bonding but do not weaken the strength of the bond. With this technique large objects can be bonded without the use of costly ovens or autoclaves.

Quality Control

The best way to get high-quality adhesive bonds is to set up and follow strict controls for all steps in the bonding process. Such **in-process inspection controls** should cover the materials and equipment used and the workmanship (Fig. 28-6). They should include:

(1) Selection of the right adhesive for the job,
(2) Thorough inspection of the surfaces before adhesive application to make sure they are correctly prepared,
(3) Inspection while the adhesive is applied to make sure all the surfaces are covered, and
(4) Inspection during drying or curing.

A good quality control program also requires inspection of the completed assemblies. In such a program, quality control engineers and technicians test the product or its parts in different ways. They must determine if the product does the job for which it was designed and made.

Their tests are generally of two kinds: **destructive** and **nondestructive.** If a test uses forces so great that the product is deformed or breaks (fractures) and is destroyed, it is obviously a destructive test.

Destructive testing of standard specimens provides a reliable gage of product quality. Specimens are either prepared and processed along with the production assemblies, or are made to duplicate the same conditions of manufacturing. The properties of the production assemblies are assumed to be the same as those obtained by subjecting the specimens to standard tests. Another method of obtaining samples for testing involves cutting a small circle or "button" from the object at a location that will not affect its strength.

Visual inspection may detect gaps at the edges of joints indicating lack of adhesive or poor fit. Waviness and bulging also indicate joint separation. Tapping with the edge of a coin produces a hollow sound over unbonded areas. Small vacuum cups may be used to find any separations between thin surface panels and cores in laminated assemblies. The cups are fastened on the panel and any movement is noted when they are pulled away from the core.

Testing with ultrasonic sound waves provides a means of inspecting for unbonded areas. These are detected because they reflect or retard passage of sound waves. In contrast, bonded areas pass sound waves more freely.

Another nondestructive way to test bond strength is to measure the sound generated at the bond line while it is under a dynamic load. In this test, the stress (the load force) is increased steadily while measurements are made. A sharp increase in noise occurs at about 90% of bond strength. This enables failure strength to be closely estimated.

REVIEW   REVIEW   REVIEW   REVIEW   REVIEW

WORDS TO KNOW

acrylic	dynamic loading	nonstructural	thermosetting
adhesive bonding	electrolytic	oxide film	toluene
alkaline cleaner	corrosion	perchloroethylene	toxic
autoclave	epoxy	phenolic	trichloroethylene
bond line	fatigue resistance	pickling	ultrasonic sound
carbon tetrachloride	honeycomb core	polyamide	waves
cellulose	hot-melt adhesive	polyester	vapor degreasing
ceramic adhesives	in-process	polysulfide	vinyl
chemical reaction	inspection	polyurethane	water-break test
cleavage	mechanical	self-aligning	wetted
creep	interlocking	silicones	xylene
curing	nondestructive	structural	
destructive testing	testing	thermoplastic	

(Review Continued)

REVIEW QUESTIONS

1. How does structural bonding differ from nonstructural bonding? Give examples of each.
2. Name several industries that are leaders in the use of structural adhesive bonding.
3. List six advantages of adhesive bonding.
4. List six disadvantages of adhesive bonding.
5. Name the forces that act on adhesive bonds in such a manner as to pull them apart.
6. Which of the above forces are adhesive bonds best able to resist?
7. Why are mechanical interlocking joints preferred in adhesive bonding?
8. What materials are thermoplastic adhesives made of?
9. How are thermoplastic adhesives applied and set?
10. What materials are thermosetting adhesives made of?
11. How are thermosetting adhesives cured or set?
12. What types of adhesives are used in most structural metal bonding applications?
13. List the forms in which adhesives are available.
14. What cleaning methods and materials are used in preparing metal surfaces for adhesive bonding?
15. Why is it recommended that adhesive bonding be done immediately after parts have been cleaned and dried?
16. Describe the water-break test for surface cleanliness.
17. Describe how powdered adhesives are applied.
18. Why do solvent-type adhesives require predrying before assembly?
19. List several methods of curing thermosetting adhesives.
20. What quality control procedure is the best guarantee of obtaining consistently good adhesive bonds?
21. Name two methods used to obtain samples for destructive testing of adhesive bonds.
22. What defects in adhesive bonding can be detected visually?
23. What type of defect can be found by tapping an adhesive-bonded joint with the edge of a coin?
24. How are ultrasonic sound waves used in inspecting adhesive bonded joints?

PART

8

Sheet Metal Processing

Elmer Van Kamp, an engineer with one of the country's largest aircraft manufacturers, has worked with metals for 30 years. His specialty is designing tools and machinery for sheet metal manufacturing processes. Elmer is familiar with traditional methods of shaping metal, such as shell drawing and curvilinear bending. He also understands the newest processes, such as superplastic forming, which stretches metal more than has ever been possible.

Elmer acquired his knowledge of metals and machinery systematically. During his service in the Navy he maintained all kinds of weapons, from small arms to anti-aircraft guns. Afterwards he learned about machine tools and mechanical drawing at vocational school. Then he went on to study engineering in college.

Elmer has an I.Q. that educators label "gifted," and he most enjoys the "brainwork" of designing solutions to manufacturing problems. However, realizing that industry runs on practical application, he is soon out of his office and explaining his designs to workers. The production details are ironed out. New machinery or tools come off the assembly line. And Elmer has the satisfaction of seeing the products of his imagination working smoothly.

Elmer Van Kamp
Manufacturing Engineer

UNIT 29

Sheet Metal Pattern Development, Hand Tools, and Cutting Tools

Metal sheets less than ¼″ [6.35 mm] thick are classified as **sheet metal.** Metal sheets ¼″ [6.35 mm] and more in thickness are classified as "plate."

Sheet metalwork means making and installing objects of sheet metal. Sheet metalworkers build and install ducts for heating and air-conditioning systems, exhaust hoods and ventilator systems, metal roofs and ceilings, and structural steel buildings. They also construct sheet metal parts for boats and ships, buses, trailers, aircraft, and space vehicles (Fig. 29-1).

Objects of sheet metal are found everywhere. Street and road signs, tool parts, toys, washing and drying machine cabinets, television and file cabinets, desks, and mailboxes are common sheet metal products. The sheet metals most commonly used are steel, galvanized steel, tinplated steel, stainless steel, aluminum, copper, and brass.

Fig. 29-1 *The aircraft industry is a big user of sheet metal. This partially completed airplane body is moving to the next station on the production line.* (Boeing)

29-1 Patterns and Patternmaking

Objects to be made from any kind of sheet material require the development of a **pattern,** or **stretchout,** whether they are cloth shirts, leather wallets, plastic lampshades, or metal wastebaskets. The pattern shows the size and shape of the flat sheet needed to make the object (Fig. 29-2). Patterns are often drawn to a reduced scale on paper, then drawn full-size directly onto the metal. Units 12 and 13 describe the standard layout tools and techniques for this purpose.

Full-size paper patterns may be used to make a metal pattern in one of two ways:

1. By attaching the paper pattern to the metal with tape or rubber cement and cutting the metal to match the pattern.
2. By taping the paper pattern to the sheet metal and making small prick punch marks through the paper. Punchmarks should be made at all corners, intersections of lines, ends of lines, and centers of arcs and circles. Irregular curves are marked by placing the punch marks close together. After punching, the paper is removed and the punch marks are used as guides for scribing the lines, circles, and curves.

If two or more pieces of sheet metal are to be cut alike, the first piece can be used as the pattern, or **template,** for the others.

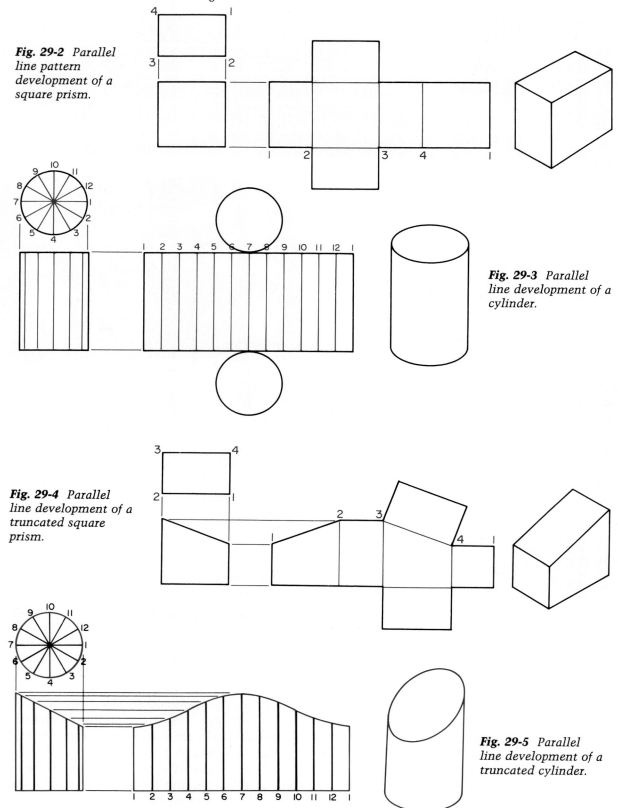

Fig. 29-2 *Parallel line pattern development of a square prism.*

Fig. 29-3 *Parallel line development of a cylinder.*

Fig. 29-4 *Parallel line development of a truncated square prism.*

Fig. 29-5 *Parallel line development of a truncated cylinder.*

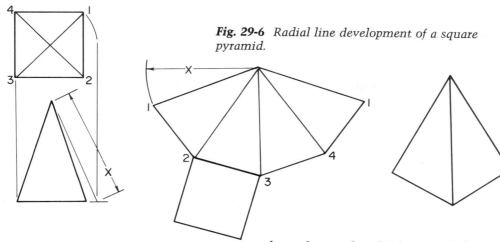

Fig. 29-6 *Radial line development of a square pyramid.*

Types of Pattern Development

There are three types of pattern development: (1) **Parallel line** development is used for developing patterns of objects that have parallel sides (Figs. 29-2 and 29-3). The development of parallel-sided, **truncated** objects, which have one side cut off at an angle, is shown in Figures 29-4 and 29-5. (2) **Radial line** development is used for objects such as cones and pyramids (Figs. 29-6 and 29-7). (3) **Triangulation** is used to develop patterns for objects with irregular shapes (Fig. 29-8).

Hem and Seam Allowances on Patterns

A **hem** is a fold along an edge that does away with the sharp edge and strengthens the resulting edge. Three types of hems are shown in Figure 29-9. A **seam** is a joint made by fastening two edges. There are many kinds of sheet metal seams, some of which are shown in Figure 29-10. The **folded corner seam** (Fig. 29-11) is used on baking pans and other pans that cannot be soldered, yet must be leakproof.

After the basic pattern for the object has been developed, hems and seams are added to complete the stretchout. The amount of metal required to make a hem or seam is the **allowance** for that part. Figure 29-12 shows a stretchout for a pan that has had hems and seams added. The width of hems and seams

depends on the thickness of the metal, the size of the object, and the method of fastening the seams. Spot-welded or riveted seams need to be wider than soldered seams. Narrow folds cannot be made on thick sheet metal.

Bending Sequence

Care must be taken to plan the bending sequence of a sheet metal layout before bending begins so as to assure that all bends can be made. For a one piece pan as shown in Fig. 29-12, always bend the hems first. Then bend the two sides that have the corner tabs attached, and finally bend the remaining two sides.

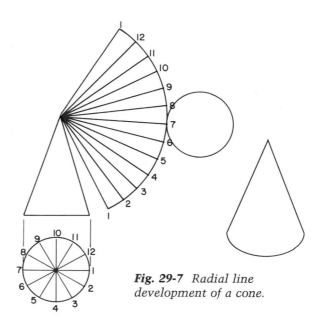

Fig. 29-7 *Radial line development of a cone.*

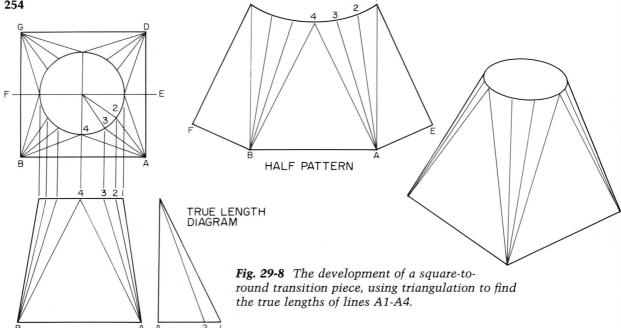

HALF PATTERN

TRUE LENGTH DIAGRAM

Fig. 29-8 *The development of a square-to-round transition piece, using triangulation to find the true lengths of lines A1-A4.*

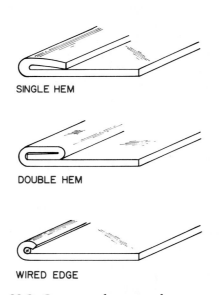

SINGLE HEM

DOUBLE HEM

WIRED EDGE

Fig. 29-9 *Common sheet metal hems.*

Fig. 29-10 *Common seams for joining sheet metal parts.*

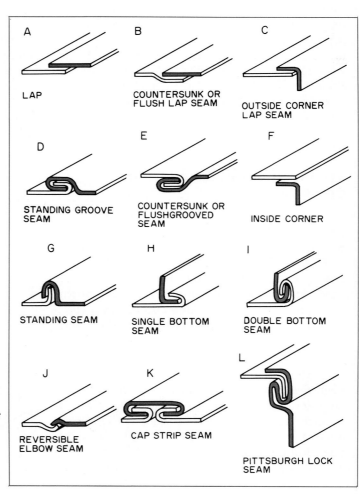

A — LAP

B — COUNTERSUNK OR FLUSH LAP SEAM

C — OUTSIDE CORNER LAP SEAM

D — STANDING GROOVE SEAM

E — COUNTERSUNK OR FLUSHGROOVED SEAM

F — INSIDE CORNER

G — STANDING SEAM

H — SINGLE BOTTOM SEAM

I — DOUBLE BOTTOM SEAM

J — REVERSIBLE ELBOW SEAM

K — CAP STRIP SEAM

L — PITTSBURGH LOCK SEAM

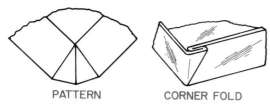

Fig. 29-11 *A folded corner seam.*

However, tables of bend allowances have been developed that are accurate enough for average use. Table 29-1 gives approximate bend allowances for 90° minimum radius bends in mild steel, and half-hard aluminum, copper, and brass. Tables of bend allowances for other materials can be found in metalworking handbooks.

Bend Allowance

To make sheet metal objects accurately to overall dimensions when they involve one or more bends, it is necessary to consider the length required for each bend. This is termed bend allowance. The bend allowance is **subtracted** from the sum of the object's outside dimensions to obtain the overall length and width of the blank needed to make the part.

Because of differences in metal hardness, whether the bend is with or across the grain, and difficulty in making an exact bend radius, exact allowances can only be obtained by trial.

Table 29-1

90° Bend Allowance for Mild Steel, and Half-Hard Aluminum, Copper, and Brass

Gage no.	Decimal inch equivalent	1 bend	2 bends	3 bends
16	.060	.093	.187	.281
18	.048	.075	.150	.225
20	.036	.056	.112	.168
22	.030	.046	.092	.138
24	.024	.037	.074	.111
26	.018	.028	.056	.084
28	.015	.023	.046	.069
30	.012	.018	.036	.054

DIMENSION TABLE

	Inches	mm
A	13	330
B	6	152
C	4	102
D	1/2	13
E	1/4	6

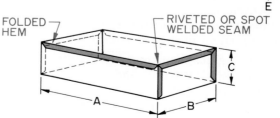

Fig. 29-12 *A pattern for a metal pan. Hems and seams are folded to the outside.*

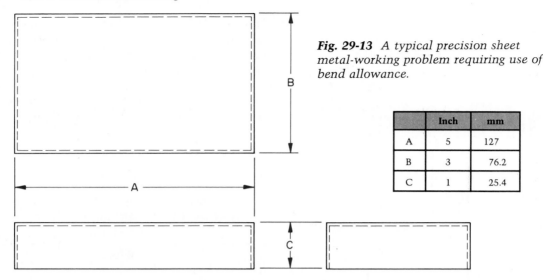

Fig. 29-13 *A typical precision sheet metal-working problem requiring use of bend allowance.*

	Inch	mm
A	5	127
B	3	76.2
C	1	25.4

Example: Find the overall length (OL) and overall width (OW) of the blank required to make the electronic chassis in Fig. 29-13.

1. OL = 2 × height + length − 2 × bend allowance.

    OL = 2(1) + 5 − 2(.046)

    OL = 2 + 5 − .092

    OL = 7 − .092

    OL = 6.908″

2. OW = 2 + 3 − .092

    OW = 5 − .092

    OW = 4.908″

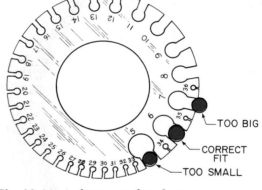

Fig. 29-14 *A sheet metal and wire gage.*

29-2 Sheet Metal and Wire Sizes

Sheet metal thicknesses and wire diameters are specified either by **gage numbers** or by their actual thickness in inches or millimeters. **Sheet metal and wire gages** have slots that correspond to the different gage sizes (Fig. 29-14). On one side of the gage is stamped the gage number; on the other side is stamped the decimal equivalent of the gage number.

Table 29-2 gives the names of the different gages, what they measure, and the decimal equivalent of the gage numbers. Note that the **Manufacturer's Standard Gage for Steel Sheets** is used to measure the thickness of iron and steel sheets. The thickness of most nonferrous metals, such as aluminum, copper, and copper alloys, is now specified in decimal parts of an inch. These were once made to the **Brown & Sharpe** or **American Standard Gage.**

Be sure you use the gage that is stamped according to the material you wish to measure, such as "U.S. Standard Gage," "American Standard Wire Gage," "American Steel & Wire Company Gage," etc.

When ordering sheet metal or wire, always specify the actual thickness wanted, and give the name of the gage and the gage number, if possible.

Table 29-2

Standard Sheet Metal and Wire Gages Used in the United States

Gage number	Manufacturers' Standard Gage[1] Iron and steel sheets	U.S. Standard[2] Gage Iron and steel sheets and plates	Galvanized Sheet Gage For galvanized steel sheets	American Standard Wire Gage or Brown & Sharpe Gage Wire & sheet metal except iron, steel & zinc[3]	U.S. Steel Wire Gage or American Steel & Wire Co. Steel wire (not music wire or drill rod)	Twist Drill and Steel Wire Gage Twist drills and drill rod	Am. Steel and Wire Co. Music (or piano) wire[4]	Birmingham or Stubs' Iron Wire Gage Iron telephone and telegraph wire & tubing walls	American (National) Standard Screw Gage Machine screws	American (National) Standard Screw Gage Wood screws
	1	2	3	4	5	6	7	8	9	10
0	. . . .	.3125	. . . .	.3249	.3065	. . . .	.009	.340	.060	.060
1	. . . .	.2813	. . . .	.2893	.2830	.2280	.010	.300	.073	.073
2	. . . .	.2656	. . . .	.2576	.2625	.2210	.011	.284	.086	.086
3	0.2391	.2500	. . . .	.2294	.2437	.2130	.012	.259	.099	.099
4	0.2242	.2344	. . . .	.2043	.2253	.2090	.013	.238	.112	.112
5	0.2092	.2188	. . . .	.1819	.2070	.2055	.014	.220	125	.125
6	0.1943	.2031	. . . .	.1620	.1920	.2040	.016	.203	.138	.138
7	0.1793	.1875	. . . .	.1443	.1770	.2010	.018	.180	. . .	.151
8	0.1644	.1719	0.1681	.1285	.1620	.1990	.020	.165	.164	.164
9	0.1495	.1563	0.1532	.1144	.1483	.1960	.022	.148	. . .	.177
10	0.1345	.1406	0.1382	.1019	.1350	.1935	.024	.134	.190	.190
11	0.1196	.1250	0.1233	.0907	.1205	.1910	.026	.120	. . .	.203
12	0.1046	.1094	0.1084	.0808	.1055	.1890	.029	.109	.216	.216
13	0.0897	.0938	0.0934	.0720	.0915	.1850	.031	.095	. . .	. . .
14	0.0747	.0781	0.0785	.0641	.0800	.1820	.033	.083	. . .	.242
15	0.0673	.0703	0.0710	.0571	.0720	.1800	.035	.072	. . .	. . .
16	0.0598	.0625	0.0635	.0508	.0625	.1770	.037	.065	. . .	.268
17	0.0538	.0563	0.0575	.0453	.0540	.1730	.039	.058	. . .	. . .
18	0.0478	.0500	0.0516	.0403	.0475	.1695	.041	.049	. . .	.294
19	0.0418	.0438	0.0456	.0359	.0410	.1660	.043	.042	. . .	. . .
20	0.0359	.0375	0.0396	.0320	.0348	.1610	.045	.035	. . .	.320
21	0.0329	.0344	0.0366	.0285	.0317	.1590	.047	.032	. . .	. . .
22	0.0299	.0313	0.0336	.0253	.0286	.1570	.049	.028	. . .	. . .
23	0.0269	.0281	0.0306	.0226	.0258	.1540	.051	.025	. . .	. . .
24	0.0239	.0250	0.0276	.0201	.0230	.1520	.055	.022	. . .	.372
25	0.0209	.0219	0.0247	.0179	.0204	.1495	.059	.020	. . .	. . .
26	0.0179	.0188	0.0217	.0159	.0181	.1470	.063	.018	. . .	. . .
27	0.0164	.0172	0.0202	.0142	.0173	.1440	.067	.016	. . .	. . .
28	0.0149	.0156	0.0187	.0126	.0162	.1405	.071	.014	. . .	. . .
29	0.0135	.0141	0.0172	.0113	.0150	.1360	.075	.013	. . .	. . .
30	0.0120	.0125	0.0157	.0100	.0140	.1285	.080	.012	. . .	. . .

[1]The **Manufacturers' Standard Gage** for steel sheets is now being used for carbon steel and alloy steel sheets.

[2]The **United States Standard Gage** was established by Congress in 1893 for measuring sheet and plate iron and steel. It was the standard gage used for many years.

[3]**Zinc sheets** are measured by a **zinc gage,** which is not given in the above table.

[4]The **Music Wire Gage** of the American Steel and Wire Company is used in the United States. It is recommended by the United States Bureau of Standards.

29-3 Hand Tools and Cutting Tools

A **scratch awl** is a steel tool with a sharp point on one end (Fig. 29-15). It is used to scratch **layout lines** on sheet metal. Some scratch awls have wooden handles. A scriber (Fig. 12-11) may be used instead.

Wing dividers are most often used by sheet metalworkers (Fig. 29-16). They are used to scribe **arcs** and **circles.**

Several kinds of hammers are used in sheet metalwork (Fig. 29-17). The **riveting hammer** is used for setting solid rivets. The **setting hammer** is used for bending or tucking in the edges of sheet metal. It is especially useful for **setting** the edges when making a single bottom seam (Fig. 29-18).

Raising hammers are used for producing curved sheet metal surfaces that cannot be made with forming machines. There are many shapes of raising hammers. The polished faces on raising hammers should be carefully protected from nicks. If you use a raising hammer with nicks, it will transfer the nicks to the workpiece and spoil the appearance.

To keep from stretching and nicking sheet metal, it should be struck with a **mallet** (Fig. 29-19). Sheet metal mallets are available in different sizes and shapes, and are made of wood, rawhide, or plastic.

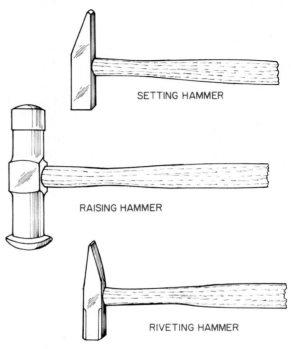

Fig. 29-17 *Hammers for sheet metalwork.*

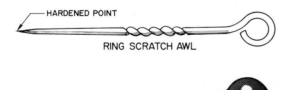

Fig. 29-15 *Scratch awls.*

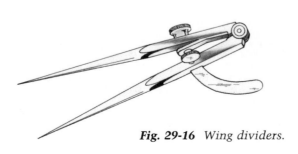

Fig. 29-16 *Wing dividers.*

Fig. 29-18 *Setting a single bottom seam with a setting hammer.*

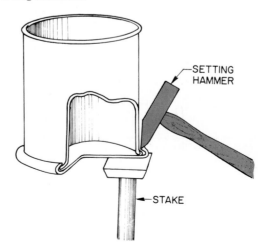

Fig. 29-19 *Forming a corner with a mallet.*

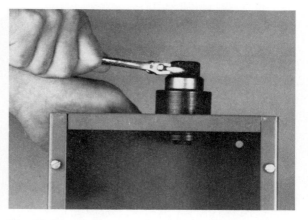

Fig. 29-21 *Chassis punches are excellent for hand punching of large holes.* (Greenlee Tool Co.)

Fig. 29-20 *Types of hand punches used for making holes in sheet metal.* (Greenlee Tool Co.)

Fig. 29-22 *A hand operated turret punch.* (Thor Tool & Die Co.)

The punches shown in Fig. 29-20 are used by hand to punch holes in sheet metal. To use a **chassis punch,** a hole must first be drilled at the center of the hole location to allow the draw bolt to pass through the metal. The bolt passes through the die and is threaded into the punch half of the chassis punch. As the bolt is tightened with a wrench, it forces the punch into the metal, eventually punching a complete hole when it has penetrated far enough (Fig. 29-21.)

The **hand punch** is used as you would use a paper punch. It can only punch holes near the edge of the metal.

A hand-operated **turret punch** (Fig. 29-22) can very efficiently punch accurate, burr-free holes of a variety of sizes and shapes.

The square jaws of **flat-nose pliers** (Fig. 29-23) are useful for bending square corners on small parts.

A. FLAT-NOSE PLIERS

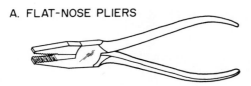

B. USING THE FLAT-NOSE PLIERS TO BEND SQUARE EDGES

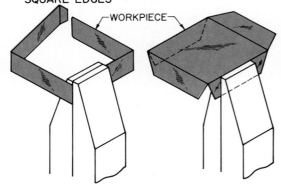
WORKPIECE

Fig. 29-23 *Using flat-nose pliers to bend square edges.*

A

B

Fig. 29-24 *Hand seamers. (A) A hand seamer. (B) A vise-grip® hand seamer.* (Roper Whitney, Inc.)

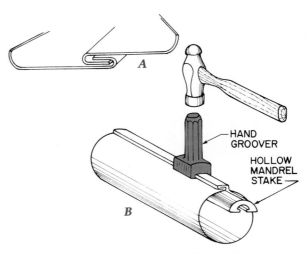

A

HAND GROOVER

HOLLOW MANDREL STAKE

B

Fig. 29-25 *Grooving a seam with a hand groover. (A) The metal is folded and hooked together. (B) Hammering the fold to close the seam.*

The **hand seamer** (Fig. 29-24A) is a tool for making hems, seams, and other straight line bends in thin sheet metal. It is used to make hems, seams, and straight line bends in places where bending machines won't go or are not available. A vise-grip version is also useful as a clamp for temporarily holding parts together (Fig. 29-24B).

The **hand groover** is a tool for finishing a standing grooved seam. The edges of the metal are first folded and hooked together (Fig. 29-25A). The hand groover is then set in place on top of the fold and hammered to close the seam (Fig. 29-25B).

Tin snips (Fig. 29-26) are used like scissors to cut thin, soft metal. They should be used to cut 20-gage or thinner metal. **To cut to a corner, the snips should be set so that the point will finish in the corner.** Keep the bolt tight; the blades must fit closely against each other.

A left-hand snip should be used by a left-handed person. Scroll, or hawk's bill, snips are used for cutting curves (Fig. 29-27).

Aviation snips are also used for cutting thin-gage metal. They are made in **left, right,** and **straight** versions (Fig. 29-28A, B, and C).

The blades of aviation snips are **serrated,** or toothed (Fig. 29-28D), which makes them grip the metal better than tin snips. In addition, aviation snips are **compound-levered.** They require less manual force than tin snips to cut metal of the same thickness.

The **double-cutting shear** has three blades and is used to cut around cans, stove and furnace pipes, and similar round sheet metal shapes (Fig. 29-29). The pointed lower blade is pushed through the metal to start the cut.

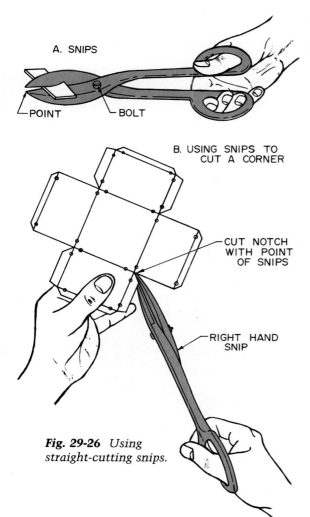

A. SNIPS

POINT

BOLT

B. USING SNIPS TO CUT A CORNER

CUT NOTCH WITH POINT OF SNIPS

RIGHT HAND SNIP

Fig. 29-26 *Using straight-cutting snips.*

Fig. 29-27 *Using hawk's bill scroll snips.*

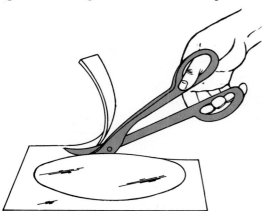

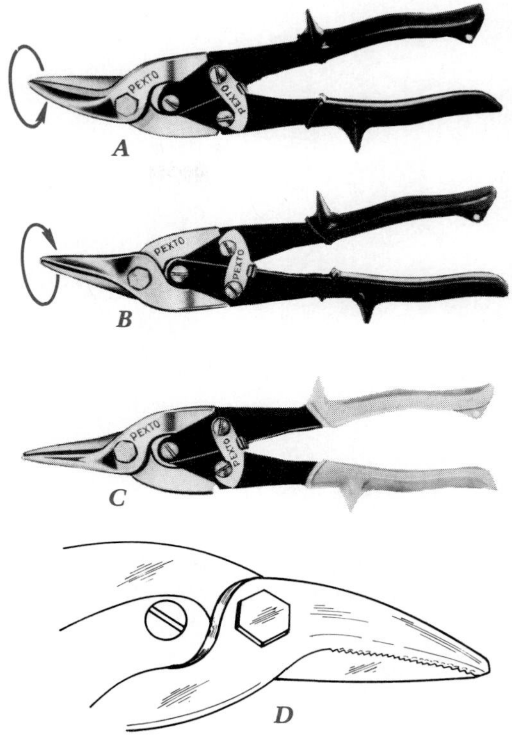

Fig. 29-28 *Aviation snips. (A) Left-cutting. (B) Right-cutting. (C) Straight-cutting. (D) A close-up view of the serrated blades.* (Roper Whitney, Inc.)

Fig. 29-29 *Using the double-cutting shear to cut a sheet metal pipe.*

STRIP REMOVED BY DOUBLE-CUTTING ACTION

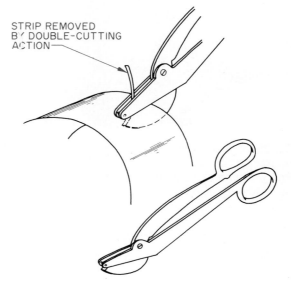

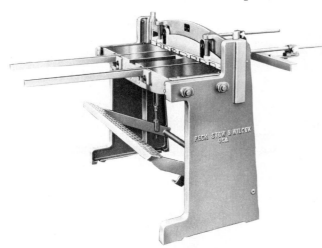

Fig. 29-30 *The manually operated squaring shear has a cutting capacity of 16 gage mild steel.* (Roper Whitney, Inc.)

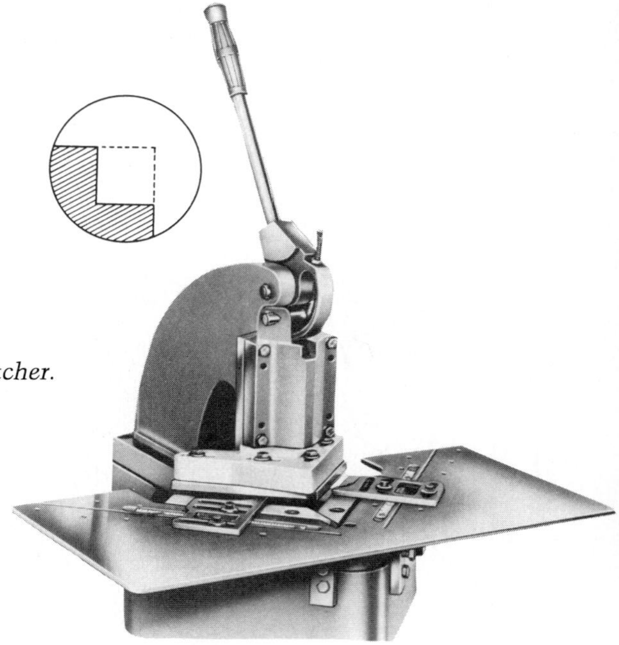

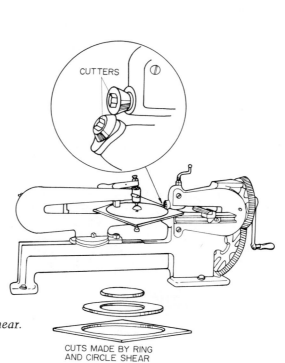

Fig. 29-31 *A plain hand operated notcher.* (Di-Acro)

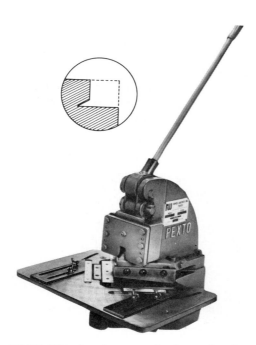

Fig. 29-32 *This hand operated tab notcher in one stroke cuts a notch up to 6" (152 mm) square with a tab up to 1" (25 mm) wide.* (Roper Whitney, Inc.)

Fig. 29-33 *A ring and circle shear.*

CUTS MADE BY RING
AND CIRCLE SHEAR

The **squaring shear** (Fig. 29-30) is used to cut metal no thicker than 16-gage mild steel. It is especially useful for cutting strips of sheet metal and for cutting and trimming the edges square to each other; hence, the name. **It should never be used for cutting wire or nails since this causes the blade to be nicked and ruins it for use with sheet metal.**

The **side guides** on the table help to keep the metal square with the cutting blades. The squaring shear is useful for cutting many pieces of the same size because the **back gage** can be locked at any desired setting.

🚫 **SAFETY NOTE**

When using the squaring shear, make sure there is a **guard** for the squaring shear blade. Keep your fingers away from the blade when using the shear. Check to see if the treadle has a **stop,** which will prevent the treadle from going all the way to the floor and injuring the operator's foot.

Fig. 29-34 *A lever shear and rod parter for cutting thick sheet metal and small diameter rods.* (Roper Whitney, Inc.)

The **notcher** is a hand- or power-operated machine that makes a 90° cut or notch in a workpiece (Fig. 29-31). It greatly speeds the work of cutting out the corners of a workpiece that will become a box, pan, or tray. The tab notcher speeds the cutting of patterns that require a tab for corner fastening (Fig. 29-32).

The **ring and circle shear** (Fig. 29-33) is used to cut circular pieces of metal such as those for the covers or bottoms of buckets.

A **lever shear** is used for cutting small rods and cutting notches and corners in heavier-gage metals (Fig. 29-34).

Electrically powered nibblers (Fig. 29-35) and **portable electric shears** (Fig. 29-36) cut thin-gage sheet metal rapidly. They are useful in production work where the quantity of cutting would make hand-operated shears tiresome and inefficient.

Fig. 29-35 *A bench-mounted nibbler for rapid cutting of thin sheet metals to any shape.* (Berkron Products, Co.)

Fig. 29-36 *A portable electric sheet metal shear.* (Robert Bosch Tool Corp.)

REVIEW   REVIEW   REVIEW   REVIEW   REVIEW

WORDS TO KNOW

aviation snips	left-hand snip	reversible elbow	standing seam
bend allowance	lever shear	seam	stretchout
cap strip seam	nibbler	ring and circle shear	template
chassis punch	notcher	riveting hammer	tin snips
double bottom seam	parallel line	scratch awl	triangulation
double-cutting shear	development	scroll snips	turret punch
flat-nose pliers	pattern	setting hammer	wing dividers
grooved seam	Pittsburgh lock	sheet metal and	wired edge
hand groover	seam	wire gage	
hand punch	radial line	single bottom seam	
hand seamer	development	single hem	
lap seam	raising hammer	squaring shear	

REVIEW QUESTIONS

1. What metal thickness represents the division between sheet metal and plate?
2. What kind of pattern development is used to develop patterns for objects with parallel sides?
3. What kinds of shapes are developed with radial line development?
4. What kinds of shapes require triangulation in their development?
5. What is meant by bend allowance? Why is it important?
6. What is the name of the gage used to measure sheet steel thickness?
7. What gage is used to measure the thickness of aluminum and copper?
8. What is a setting hammer used for? Raising hammer?
9. Why are mallets sometimes used instead of hammers?
10. Describe how to use the chassis punch.
11. What is the advantage of a turret punch?
12. What is the maximum thickness of metal that can safely be cut with tin snips?
13. Why are aviation snips able to cut metal more easily than tin snips?
14. What is a squaring shear? What thickness of metal can it safely cut?
15. What is a notcher used for? Tab notcher?
16. What cutting machine is designed for making circular cuts?
17. What is a nibbler used for?

UNIT

30

Bending Sheet Metal

This unit describes the basic operations for making sheet metal products. An article may be one-of-a-kind, for small quantity production, or for mass production in the thousands by automatic machines. In each case the sheet metal must be bent or shaped according to a design. The fundamental processes were done originally with hand tools, later with hand-powered machines. The following introduction to these basic operations should lead to a better understanding of the sheet metal manufacturing methods described in Unit 31.

30-1

Machine Bending

The **bar folder** (Fig. 30-1) is a machine for bending sheet metal edges that are used for seams and hems. Folds are limited to a width of 1″ [25 mm] or 1¼″ [32 mm] depending on the size of the bar folder.

Fig. 30-1 *A bar folder is used mainly for bending hems and seams.*

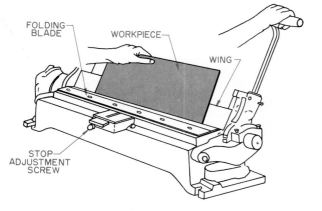

A movable **depth stop** is set to the desired width of the hem or seam (Fig. 30-2). **Angle stops** permit accurate 90- and 135-degree bends. The folding wing can be adjusted to make sharp bends or open bends needed for making wired edges (Fig. 30-3).

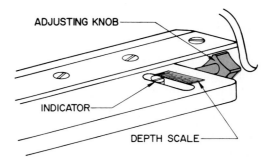

Fig. 30-2 *A depth stop details on a bar folder: the adjusting knob, depth scale, and indicator.*

Fig. 30-3 *The position of the bar-folder wing determines the bend radius.*

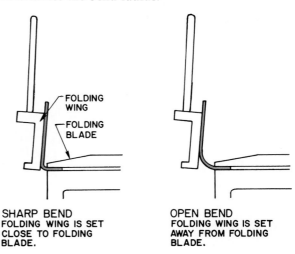

SHARP BEND
FOLDING WING IS SET CLOSE TO FOLDING BLADE.

OPEN BEND
FOLDING WING IS SET AWAY FROM FOLDING BLADE.

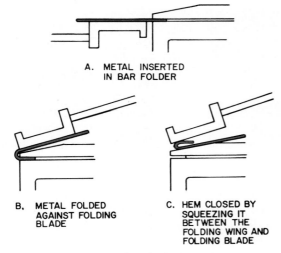

A. METAL INSERTED IN BAR FOLDER

B. METAL FOLDED AGAINST FOLDING BLADE

C. HEM CLOSED BY SQUEEZING IT BETWEEN THE FOLDING WING AND FOLDING BLADE

Fig. 30-4 *Steps in making a hem with a bar folder.*

Hemmed edges are made as follows (see Fig. 30-4):

1. Set the depth stop for the desired width of the hem.
2. Set the folding wing for a sharp bend. The metal being bent should just fit between the **folding blade** and the folding wing when the wing is held against the 90° stop.
3. Insert the metal under the folding blade and hold it firmly against the stops (Fig. 30-4A).
4. Pull the folding wing as far forward as possible (Fig. 30-4B), then return it to its normal position to release the metal.
5. Remove the metal from the folding blade, turn it over and lay the folded edge parallel and close to the edge of the folding blade.

6. Close the hem by squeezing it with the folding wing (Fig. 30-4C).

NOTE: Always make a trial bend on scrap metal of the same kind and thickness before bending the workpiece.

Brakes

A **cornice brake** (Fig. 30-5) operates on the same principle as the bar folder. Unlike the bar folder, however, the cornice brake can bend or fold the metal **any distance from the edge.** Metal of up to 24-gage can be bent on the cornice brake.

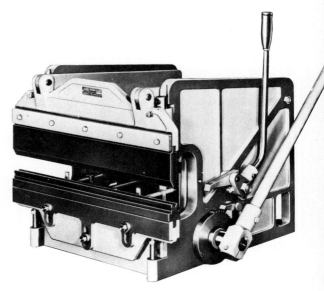

Fig. 30-6 *A hand operated press brake for bending sheet metal.*

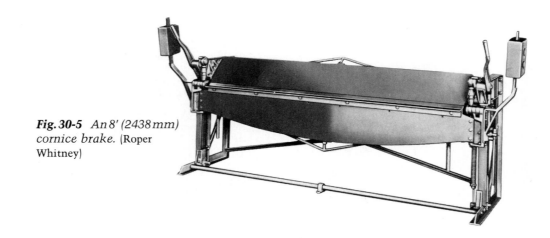

Fig. 30-5 *An 8' (2438 mm) cornice brake.* (Roper Whitney)

The hand-operated **press brake** (Fig. 30-6) is similar to the power-operated industrial press brake used for bending heavy-gage sheet metal and plate (see Fig. 31-21). The model pictured, however, has a capacity of 16-gage mild steel. **Dies** (jaws between which the metal is formed) are available to form straight line bends, offset bends, and bends of different radii (see Figure 30-7).

Curvilinear shapes can be bent in a press brake by making small bends close together either with a round-nose die or with a standard angle bending die (Fig. 30-8).

Beading, forming a tube-like bend on the edge of a sheet, can also be done on a press brake (Fig. 30-9). Beading adds great strength and improves the appearance of sheet metal objects.

The **box and pan brake** is designed to fold boxes, pans, or trays from one piece of metal. The upper jaw is made of a number of blocks of different widths. These blocks can be put together in any combination so as to make a bend of any width desired (Fig. 30-10). This feature permits sides to be bent between the opposite sides that have already been bent (Fig. 30-11).

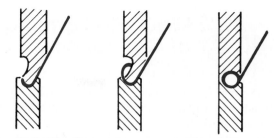

Fig. 30-9 *The dies and sequence of bends for forming a bead in a press brake.*

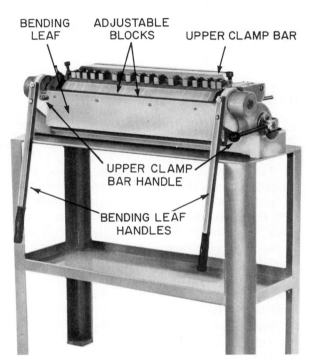

Fig. 30-10 *A hand operated box and pan brake.*

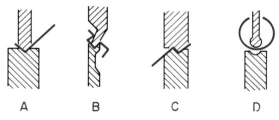

Fig. 30-7 *Different types of press brake dies for making various bends: (A) Standard angle die. (B) Offset angle die. (C) Double angle die. (D) Radius die.*

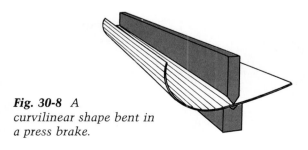

Fig. 30-8 *A curvilinear shape bent in a press brake.*

Fig. 30-11 *Folding the last two sides on a pan made from one piece of sheet metal requires use of the box and pan brake.*

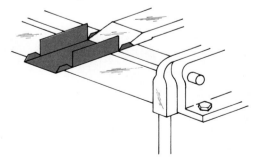

30-2 Machine Forming of Cylindrical Parts

Stove pipes, cans, and other cylindrical shapes are formed from flat sheet metal on the **slip-roll forming machine** (Fig. 30-12). It has three **rolls** that can be set different distances apart. The lower roll is adjusted to the thickness of the metal. The rear roll is adjusted to gradually roll the flat sheet into the diameter of the circle desired. If the metal to be formed has a **wired edge** (Fig. 29-9), the wired edge may be slipped into one of the **grooves** at one end of the rolls.

Turning Machine

A **turning machine** (Fig. 30-13) is used to make the rounded edge on a cylinder for a wired edge.

To make this rounded edge, set the **gage** about 2½ times the diameter of the wire away from the center of the groove in the **roll.** Be sure the rolls are set to fit each other. Then place the workpiece on the lower roll and against the gage. Screw down the top roll so that it grooves the work a little as it is revolved. For each revolution of the workpiece, screw the upper roll down a little more and raise the workpiece a little with the left hand.

When the side of the workpiece touches the side of the top roll, the rounded edge is ready for the wire and the workpiece may be taken out of the machine.

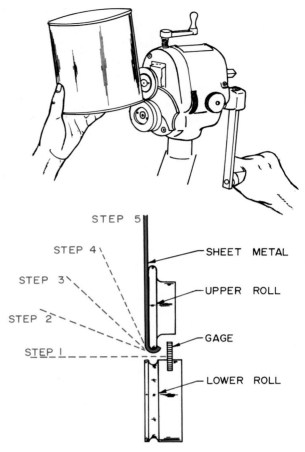

Fig. 30-13 *A turning machine prepares an edge to receive a wire reinforcement.*

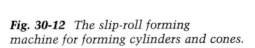

Fig. 30-12 *The slip-roll forming machine for forming cylinders and cones.*

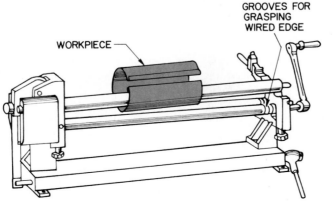

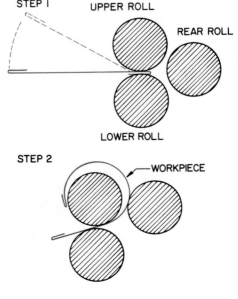

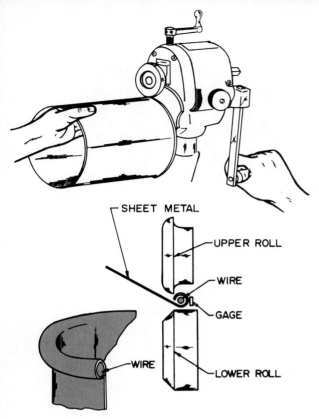

Fig. 30-14 *A wiring machine is used to close the sheet metal around a wire, completing the wired edge.*

Fig. 30-15 *A burring machine forms a burr or flange for a bottom seam on a cylinder.*

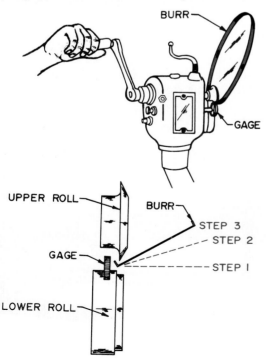

After the edge of the work has been made round in the turning machine, wire is placed into the rounded edge, which is then hammered over a little with a mallet. The edge of the metal is then formed around the wire with a **wiring machine** (Fig. 30-14).

The **burring machine** (Fig. 30-15) is used to make a **burr** or turned up edge, on the edge of the bottom for a can and on the end of a cylinder. The making of such burrs is the first step in making a single or double **bottom seam.** The handling of the metal is the same as when turning the edge on the turning machine. The beginner should practice on scraps of metal.

After the burrs on the end of a cylinder (or on the bottom piece for a can) are made with the burring machine, the pieces are brought together and the seams are closed on a **setting-down machine** (Fig. 30-16). With this machine, a seam is **set down,** or closed. If a setting-down machine is not available, seams may be set down with the use of a setting hammer and a **stake** (see Fig. 29-18).

After the burrs are set down, the seam or edge can be turned up against the sides of the can with a **double-seaming machine** (Fig. 30-17), thus making a **double seam.** If a double-seaming machine is not available, the seam or edge can be turned up against the sides of the can with a hammer and stake.

Fig. 30-16 *A setting-down machine is used to close a single bottom seam on a cylinder.*

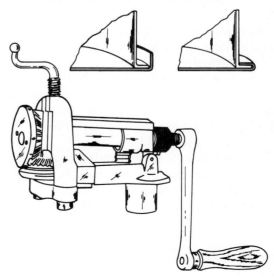

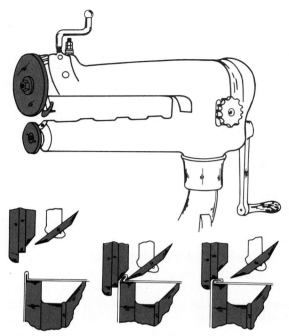

Fig. 30-17 *A double seaming machine converts a single bottom seam to a double bottom seam.*

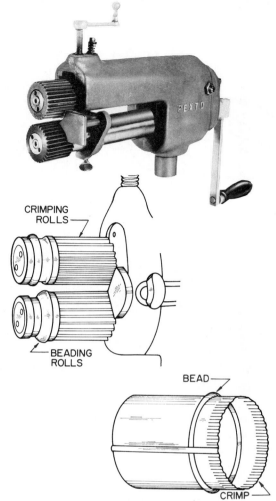

Fig. 30-18 *A crimping and beading machine is used to crimp and/or bead a pipe.* (Roper Whitney Co.)

Fig. 30-19 *A hand operated grooving machine for rapidly closing grooved seams.* (Roper Whitney Co.)

The making of the wavy end on a stove or furnace pipe is called **crimping.** It makes the end of the pipe smaller so that it will fit into another pipe of the same size.

A **bead,** a raised ring of metal, is made as an ornament and to stiffen the object. Stove and furnace pipes are beaded on one end.

Crimping and beading are done on a **crimping and beading machine** (Fig. 30-18). Crimping may also be done in a **crimping machine,** which does only the crimping. Beading may be done on a **beading machine,** which only does beading.

The **grooving machine** (Fig. 30-19) is a machine that makes either **standing** or **countersunk grooved seams.** It **grooves** and flattens the seams that have been started on the bar folder.

The **Pittsburgh lock forming machine** is designed to rapidly form the **pocket part** of a **Pittsburgh lock seam** (Fig. 30-20). Attachments can be used to form **cap strips** and other kinds of seams (Fig. 29-10).

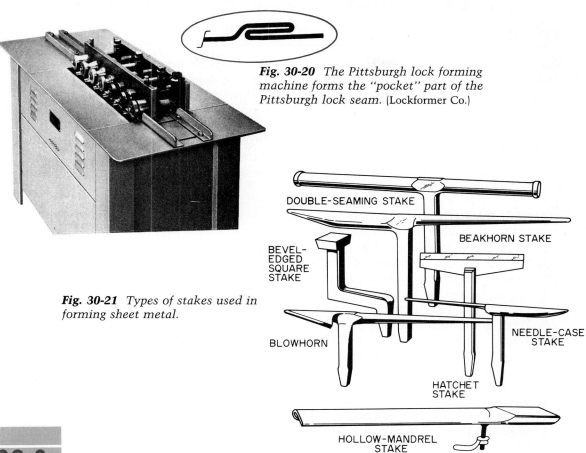

Fig. 30-20 *The Pittsburgh lock forming machine forms the "pocket" part of the Pittsburgh lock seam.* (Lockformer Co.)

Fig. 30-21 *Types of stakes used in forming sheet metal.*

30-3

Hand Bending

Sheet metal stakes (Fig. 30-21) are used along with hammers to do the forming and bending operations that cannot be done on machines. The stake is supported by inserting the tapered square end in a matching hole in a **bench plate** (Fig. 30-22). It is then used as a support or form for metal bending.

The **double-seaming stake** is used to support a cylinder when closing a double seam with a hammer.

The **beakhorn stake** is used for riveting, forming round and square surfaces, bending straight edges, and making corners.

The **bevel-edged square stake** is used to form corners and edges.

The **hatchet stake** is used to make straight, sharp bends.

Fig. 30-22 *A bench plate for holding sheet metal stakes.*

Small tubes and pipes may be formed on the **needle-case stake.**

Cone-shaped articles may be formed on the **blowhorn stake.** The use of the **hollow-mandrel stake** is shown in Figure 29-25.

REVIEW   REVIEW   REVIEW   REVIEW   REVIEW

WORDS TO KNOW

bar folder	crimping and	grooving machine	setting-down
beading	beading machine	hatchet stake	machine
beakhorn stake	curvilinear bending	hollow-mandrel	slip-roll forming
bench plate	dies	stake	machine
blowhorn stake	double-seaming	needle-case stake	turning machine
box and pan brake	machine	Pittsburgh lock	wiring machine
burring machine	double-seaming	forming machine	
cornice brake	stake	press brake	

REVIEW QUESTIONS

1. What is the difference between a bar folder and a cornice brake?
2. What is the unique feature of the box and pan brake?
3. Describe how a press brake differs from a cornice brake.
4. Name 5 kinds of dies used in press brakes.
5. What is the slip-roll forming machine used for?
6. What is the turning machine used for?
7. What is the wiring machine used for?
8. What is the burring machine used for?
9. What is the setting-down machine used for?
10. What is the double-seaming machine used for?
11. What is the crimping and beading machine used for?
12. What is the grooving machine used for?
13. Make a sketch of the seam made by the Pittsburgh lock former.
14. What is a bench plate used for?
15. What are stakes used for?

UNIT
31
Sheet Metal Manufacturing Methods

Millions of sheet metal parts are produced daily by the thousands of metal stamping and forming presses in our factories. **Punch presses** (Fig. 31-1), numerically controlled turret punch presses (Fig. 31-2), and **press brakes** produce the greatest portion of sheet metal parts.

Other important sheet manufacturing processes include roll forming, metal spinning, shear spinning, and chemical milling. High-energy-rate processes for forming sheet metal include explosive, electro-hydraulic, and electromagnetic forming.

Fig. 31-1 At an aluminum auto bumper production line, a piece of straight, extruded aluminum is stamped into an almost finished shape. Five more press operations will put it into final form. (Reynolds Metals Company)

31-1 Pressworking Processes

Sheet metal pressworking operations may be classified under four types: drawing, shearing, bending, and squeezing.

Drawing operations include the following:
1. shell drawing
2. embossing
3. stretch forming.

Shearing operations include the following:
1. blanking
2. punching
3. perforating
4. lancing
5. shaving.

Bending operations include the following:
1. angle bending
2. curvilinear bending
3. beading.

Squeezing operations include the following:
1. coining
2. burnishing.

31-2 Drawing Operations

Shell drawing, also known as **cup drawing**, is a forming process that produces one piece cylindrical or rectangular containers from sheet metal (Fig. 31-3). Most shell drawing is performed in a punch press, using matched metal dies (Fig. 31-4). The metal dies are mounted in a **die set** (Fig. 31-5), which assures accurate alignment of the upper and lower tooling. The upper half of the die is usually the punch half; the lower half of the die is usually the die half.

Fig. 31-2 A numerically controlled turret punch press. These machines are used for prototype and short-run production of flat panels. Lasers or plasma arc cutting torches are sometimes built into these machines for rapid cutting of large irregular contours. (Strippit/IDEX Corp.)

Fig. 31-3 *Some panels in this fabricated metal unit were made by shell drawing.*
(White Consolidated Industries)

Fig. 31-4 *The shell or cup drawing process. (A) Initial contact of punch with metal blank. (B) Drawing partially completed. (C) First draw completed.*

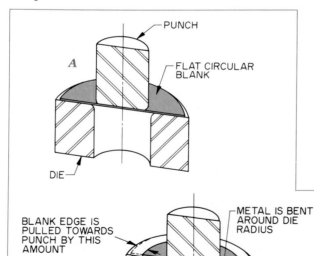

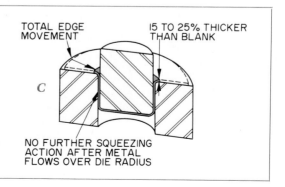

The maximum depth of draw possible in a single operation is expressed as a percentage of reduction (Fig. 31-6). For the first draw, the maximum percentage of reduction is in the vicinity of 50%; for example, a 6″ [152 mm] diameter blank being reduced to a 3″ [76 mm] diameter cup. The exact reduction permissible depends on the kind and thickness of metal being drawn, the die radius, the condition of the die tooling, and the lubrication used.

Additional drawing operations after the first draw are called **redraws.** Each successive redraw must be made at a smaller percentage of reduction. The redraw at less reduction helps to control wrinkling and prevents punching out the bottom of the cup (Fig. 31-7).

In several other shell-drawing processes a metal die half is not used. The Guerin process, Fig. 31-8, and the Marform process in Fig. 31-9, both use a rubber pad. The Marform process is capable of deeper draws than the Guerin process because it uses a pressure pad to hold the edges of the sheet metal against the rubber pad.

A newer process, called **flexforming,** replaces the metal die with a polyurethane bag that is inflated with hydraulic fluid (Fig. 31-10). The process is relatively slow but is capable of forming very accurate parts. It is being used by several auto manufacturers for making prototype parts and for production runs of up to 12,000 parts.

Embossing is a very shallow drawing operation usually done for decorating, such as raised lettering or other designs (Fig. 31-11).

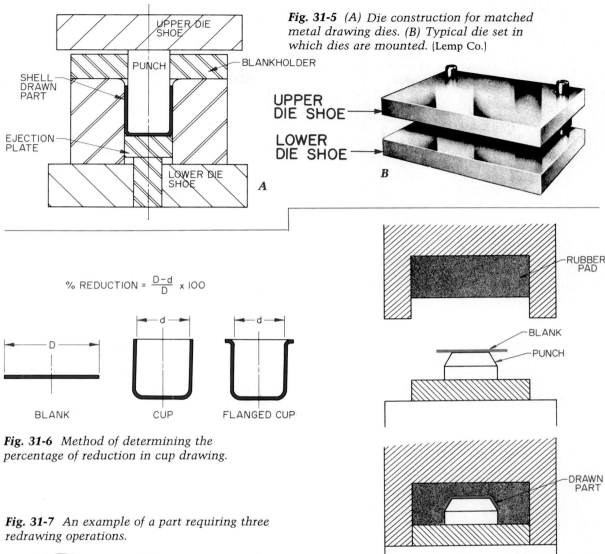

Fig. 31-5 *(A) Die construction for matched metal drawing dies. (B) Typical die set in which dies are mounted.* (Lemp Co.)

$$\% \text{ REDUCTION} = \frac{D-d}{D} \times 100$$

Fig. 31-6 *Method of determining the percentage of reduction in cup drawing.*

Fig. 31-7 *An example of a part requiring three redrawing operations.*

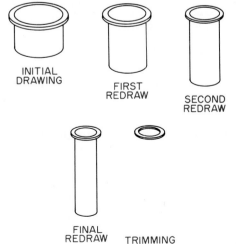

Fig. 31-8 *The Guerin process for sheet metal forming.*

Fig. 31-9 *The Marform process for sheet metal forming.*

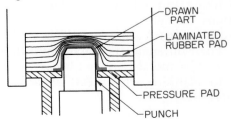

THE FLEXFORMING PROCESS

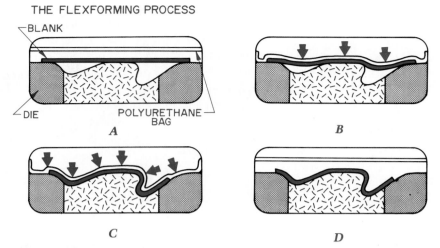

Fig. 31-10. *The flexforming process for forming sheet metal parts. (A) The metal blank placed over the die. (B) Hydraulic pressure is applied to the polyurethane bag. (C) Uniform pressure is applied over the entire blank, providing great accuracy. (D) Hydraulic pressure is removed after forming the part.*

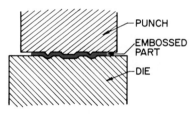

Fig. 31-11 *Embossing with matched metal dies.*

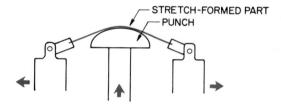

Fig. 31-12 *The stretch-forming process.*

Stretch forming was developed for the air craft industry. Metal is first stretched tight, then formed over a single punch (Fig. 31-12). The process is a low-cost method for drawing large metal sheets into shallow shapes.

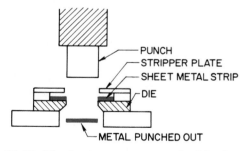

Fig. 31-13 *The basic arrangement for blanking or punching.*

31-3 Shearing Operations

Blanking and punching are both shearing operations that are done with a punch press using a punch and a die, as shown in Figure 31-13. Their difference is one of definition. In punching, the metal **removed** becomes scrap, while in blanking, the metal **remaining** is scrap (Fig. 31-14).

Perforating is simply punching a large number of holes close together. It is often done to form decorative patterns (Fig. 31-15).

Lancing is a piercing operation that can vary from providing a simple slit to creating expanded metal. No metal is lost in this process (Fig. 31-16).

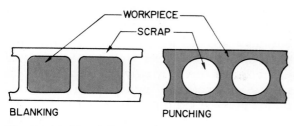

Fig. 31-14 *The difference between punching and blanking.*

Fig. 31-15 *Decorative patterns in sheet metal made by perforating.*

Fig. 31-16 *This slip-resistant safety grating is made by lancing heavy gage steel or aluminum sheets.* (United States Gypsum Company)

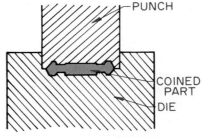

Fig. 31-17 *The process of coining requires great pressure to force the metal into the die contours.*

Shaving, as the name implies, removes only a very small amount of metal. It is a punch and die-cutting operation that is done on parts already punched. It produces smoother edges, edges of more accurate shape, or a more accurately sized piece than can usually be obtained by punching.

31-4 Squeezing Operations

Coining is a pressworking process used to make coins, medals, and parts requiring fine detail or exact size. Coining requires close-fit-ting closed dies and high pressures. They must be high enough to make the metal flow throughout the die, thereby taking on the shape of the die (Fig. 31-17). Pressures as high as 100 tons per square inch [54.25 MPa per square millimeter] are sometimes required.

Burnishing is done to improve the finish on drawn parts. The part is forced through a slightly tapered die that has its small end slightly smaller than the workpiece. The rubbing against the highly polished sides of the die smooths the workpiece.

31-5 Punch Press Production Methods

Large sheet metal stampings are processed in several punch presses, each press containing a forming or punching die to process one or two parts (Fig. 31-18). For example, to make an automobile dashboard, sheets are first cut to the proper rectangular blank size. These are automatically fed into a press that forms the dashboard to its proper contour. The formed dashboard is then partially trimmed of excess metal and partially punched in a second punch press. A third punch press performs additional trimming and punching to complete the dashboard stamping. The processing is rel-

---

TECHNOLOGIES AND PRACTICES

Behind the Battle-lines in World War II

Rosie the Riveter, the main character in a 1940s movie, became the symbol of millions of women who worked in defense plants during World War II. Women had been working in manufacturing since Samuel Slater's first American factory opened in 1789. But it was not until World War II that many more women took over the heavier, dirtier, and more dangerous jobs in metalworking factories.

Most men went into the armed forces. The critical labor shortage opened up new jobs for women in defense-related industries such as steelmaking, ship building, and ammunition production. The most dramatic increase in female employees was in the aircraft industry.

Before Pearl Harbor was bombed in 1941, only 4,000 women were employed in aircraft plants. By 1943, more than 300,000 women were at work in every phase of airplane production, from the cutting of metal to the final assembly.

In fact, women seemed better suited than men for some jobs. During assembly of the tail end of the airplane, for example, small women were especially good at riveting inside the cramped work space. Women also excelled in operating small drills, which demanded a light touch.

Other jobs that required a great deal of muscular strength had to be adjusted. Several improvements were made on airplane assembly lines to increase productivity. Heavy steel jigs were replaced with lighter Masonite® ones. Large machines were changed so they could be operated with push buttons, pedals, and levers. Easier-to-handle air-powered drill presses and the now-common aviation snips were especially developed to serve the needs of women employees.

After the crisis of World War II, these benefits carried over into post-war industrial practice. The changes made initially for women improved conditions for all workers. In addition, employers and employees alike realized that old ideas about the abilities of men and women were not always true. They saw that productivity increased when workers, both women and men, were treated as individuals with special capabilities and talents.

(The Bettmann Archive, Inc.)

atively slow because it involves several punch presses and movement of the workpieces from press to press. In some cases, the parts are automatically carried by conveyor from press to press in order to minimize hand labor.

Smaller workpieces, however, are produced much more efficiently by using a progressive die, or a transfer die.

Progressive dies are used for small parts. A progressive die has all the cutting and forming dies required to make a complete part lined up in proper order in one die (Fig. 31-19). A strip of sheet metal wider than that required to make the part is fed into the starting end of the die. With each stroke of the press, the metal strip is advanced one station in the die, and another operation is performed on the part. The last die station cuts the finished part from the strip, leaving a metal skeleton as scrap. A completed part is made with each stroke of the press, and production rates of 10,000 parts per hour are not unusual with this process.

Transfer dies are used for medium size parts. A transfer die is similar to a progressive die in that a completed part is made with each stroke of the press. Instead of metal strip, however, parts are made from pre-cut blanks (Fig. 31-20). A bar feed mechanism provides sets of gripper fingers at each die station that automatically transfer the workpiece from die station to die station until the part is completed. The fingers release the workpiece during the stamping operation so the metal is free to move as required by the die. The completed part is removed from the press with the last set of grippers and dropped in a bin or on a conveyor.

Fig. 31-18 *A metal-stamping press.* (General Motors Corporation)

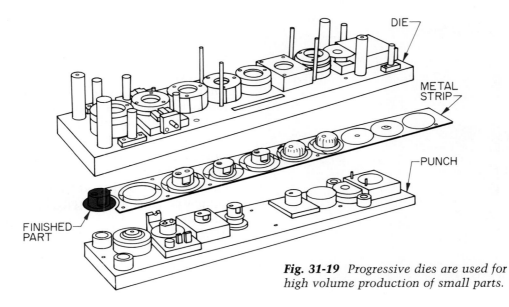

Fig. 31-19 *Progressive dies are used for high volume production of small parts.*

OPERATIONS PERFORMED

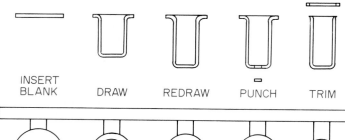

| INSERT BLANK | DRAW | REDRAW | PUNCH | TRIM |

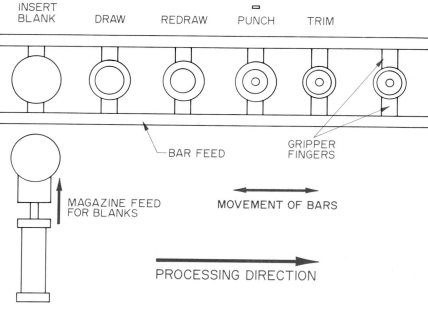

Fig. 31-20 *The transfer die feed mechanism moves each workpiece separately from die station to die station.*

BAR FEED

GRIPPER FINGERS

MAGAZINE FEED FOR BLANKS

MOVEMENT OF BARS

PROCESSING DIRECTION

31-6 Bending Operations

Bending of large parts made of thick sheet metal and metal plate is done chiefly on industrial press brakes (Fig. 31-21). These are large power-operated machines, the largest of which can bend steel plate up to 1″ [25.4 mm] thick. They are used mostly for low volume production of parts used in the construction and ship building industries.

When equipped with the proper dies, they can perform angle, curvilinear, and radius bends (see Figs. 30-7, 30-8, and 30-9). Some industrial press brakes are now available with computer numerical controls (see Units 91 and 92).

Fig. 31-21 *An industrial press brake.*

31-7

Roll-Forming

A **roll-forming machine** rapidly bends and forms sheet metal into complex shapes (Fig. 31-22). Metal moldings, downspouts and gutters for buildings, and welded tubes and pipes are some of the typical products (Fig. 31-23). A roll-forming machine has several sets of rollers. Each set makes a different bend or form in the sheet metal as it passes through the rollers.

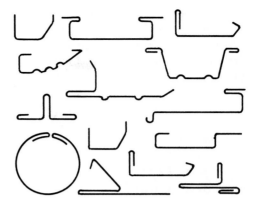

Fig. 31-23 *Complex sheet metal shapes are quickly and economically made by roll forming.*

31-8

Metal Spinning

Metal spinning is a process by which a rotating disc of thin sheet metal (a **blank**) is formed into a hollow shape. The metal is shaped by gradually forcing it around a form called a **spinning chuck** (Fig. 31-24). Spinning

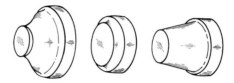

Fig. 31-24 *Chucks for metal spinning.*

Fig. 31-22 *A roll-forming machine.*

FORMED STRIP

chucks for short production runs are usually made of close-grained hardwoods, such as maple or birch. Steel chucks are used when the quantity of pieces to be produced is high enough to pay for the cost of their construction.

Hand-held spinning tools are made of hardened and polished steel (Fig. 31-25). Soft metals, however, such as pewter and the softer aluminum alloys, may be spun with a tool made from a hardwood dowel (Fig. 31-26).

Figure 31-27 shows hand-controlled metal spinning as it is done in a production shop.

Steps for spinning a metal disc:

1) Mount the spinning chuck on the **headstock spindle** of the spinning lathe (Fig. 31-28) between the faceplate and the tailstock spindle.

2) Center the disc on the end of the chuck, and secure it in place with a **follow block** on the tailstock. Note the ball bearing **back center** that holds the follow block in the tailstock (Fig. 31-28A).

Fig. 31-27 This worker is spinning a 20″ (508 mm) aluminum blank. (Williamsburg Metal Spinning & Stamping Corp.)

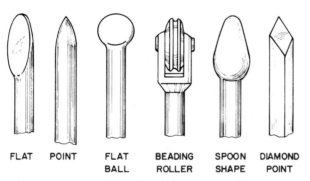

FLAT   POINT   FLAT BALL   BEADING ROLLER   SPOON SHAPE   DIAMOND POINT

Fig. 31-25 Several kinds of spinning tools are used in spinning operations.

Fig. 31-26 Spinning soft metal with a tool made from a hardwood dowel.

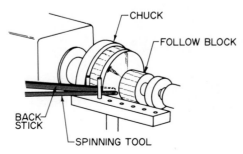

CHUCK
FOLLOW BLOCK
BACK STICK
SPINNING TOOL

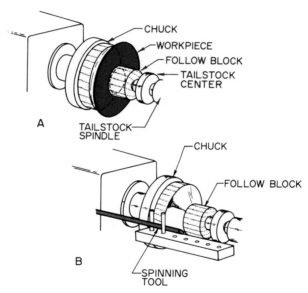

CHUCK
WORKPIECE
FOLLOW BLOCK
TAILSTOCK CENTER
A
TAILSTOCK SPINDLE

CHUCK
FOLLOW BLOCK
B
SPINNING TOOL

Fig. 31-28 (A) The lathe setup for metal spinning. (B) The spinning tool should contact the metal below the follow block, then sweep outwards and back inwards. Make more strokes towards than away from the chuck.

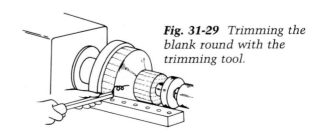

Fig. 31-29 Trimming the blank round with the trimming tool.

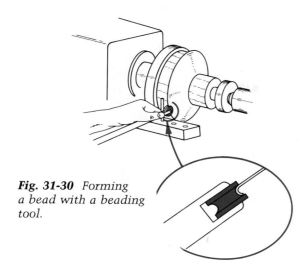

Fig. 31-30 *Forming a bead with a beading tool.*

3) Lubricate the metal disc with grease, tallow, or paraffin. The lubricant allows the spinning tool to slide easily over the metal, and helps to produce a smooth, polished surface.

4) Rotate the disc slowly at first, and quickly form the metal around the base of the chuck. The disc can then be brought to the desired **rpm, revolutions per minute** without danger of throwing the disc from the lathe.

5) Beginning as close to the center of the metal disc as possible, move the spinning tool slowly across its face. Make more strokes toward, rather than away from, the chuck (Fig. 31-28B). This is necessary to shrink the metal down to the diameter of the chuck.

6) Avoid working the tool too much in one direction. Doing so causes thinning of the metal until it ruptures.

7) Trim the disc periodically to keep it round (Fig. 31-29).

8) If any wrinkles develop, remove them immediately with the spinning tool. Press a **back stick** against the back of the disc while pressing the front of the disc with the spinning tool at the same time (Fig. 31-26). This makes the forming pressure equal on both sides of the workpiece.

Discs up to 7″ [178 mm] in diameter may be turned as fast as 1800 rpm. Larger discs should be turned at slower rpm's. Thinner metal should also rotate slowly, sometimes as

slow as 300 rpm. Parts spun of thin metal are often strengthened by rolling a bead on their edge (Fig. 31-30).

Metals such as copper and brass **work-harden** quickly during spinning and must be removed and **annealed** (softened) often to allow the metal to be spun down to the chuck. To anneal copper or brass, heat it to a uniform dull red, (1000°F [538°C]), then quench it in clean water. The black oxide left on the surface may be removed by dipping in a **pickling solution** of five parts water to one part sulfuric acid.

> 🚫 **SAFETY NOTE**
> Caution: Wear a face shield and rubber gloves to protect against possible acid burns.

Rinse the part thoroughly in clean, cold water after pickling.

Manually operated production metal spinning lathes are equipped with hydraulically powered spinning tools (Fig. 31-31). Automatic metal spinning lathes using numerical control are now being used also.

Fig. 31-31 *Production spinning lathes use hardened steel rollers activated by hydraulic power to form the metal.*

Shear Spinning

In ordinary metal spinning, thin sheet metal blanks must be shrunk down to the chuck diameter. For shear spinning, however, the blanks are much thicker, and only slightly larger in diameter than the largest diameter of the chuck (Fig. 31-32). Extremely high tool forces are required to cause the metal to become plastic and flow ahead of the spinning tool, thus taking on the shape of the chuck.

Because of the high tool forces required to make the metal flow ahead of the tool, shear spinning can only be done in special machines made for this purpose. Power spinning, flo-turning, and hydrospinning are other names for shear spinning.

Parts made by this process benefit from the cold working of the metal. Improved tensile strength, resistance to fatigue, and good surface finish result. Spinning is not limited to relatively soft metals, such as aluminum, copper, brass, and mild steel. Shear spinning makes possible the spinning of difficult metals such as high-strength copper alloys, tool steels, stainless steels, and titanium.

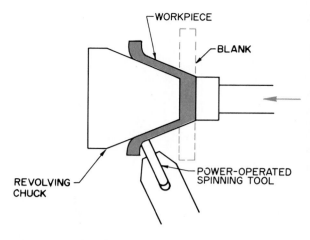

Fig. 31-32 *The shear-spinning process.*

High-Energy-Rate-Forming (HERF) Processes

Powerful explosives, when detonated, release the energy for **explosive forming,** a HERF process. The aircraft and aerospace industries use this method to make low-volume quantities of large, complex shapes from sheet metal. Explosive forming easily shapes high-strength materials that are difficult to form by usual methods.

There are two types of explosive forming. **Pressure forming** uses the gas pressure produced by slow-burning explosives such as gunpowders. It must be done in a closed container. **Shock forming** is done in open or partially open containers. The energy from rapidly burning explosives is transmitted to the workpiece through plastic, water, oil, or other liquid (Fig. 31-33).

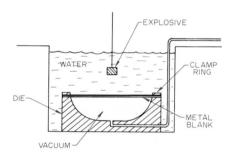

Fig. 31-33 *A diagram of the explosive forming process.*

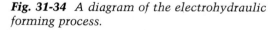

Fig. 31-34 *A diagram of the electrohydraulic forming process.*

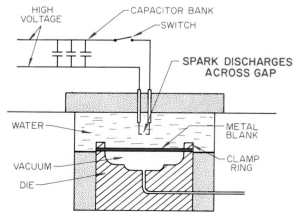

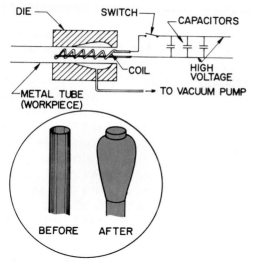

Fig. 31-35 *A diagram of the electromagnetic forming process.*

Electrohydraulic forming, sometimes called **spark forming,** is similar to shock forming with explosives. The energy rates, however, are lower. The shock waves are created by one or more **spark discharges** in a liquid as shown in Figure 31-34. The process has most of the advantages of explosive forming but is used for smaller workpieces.

Electromagnetic forming uses the force of a sudden, intense magnetic field. An electric coil placed inside, around, or next to the workpiece generates this magnetism. The workpiece is strongly repelled by the magnetic field, which forces it into shape in a non-magnetic die (Fig. 31-35). This process is widely used for sizing, bulging, and assembling tubing, but flat pieces can also be formed. It works best with metals that are good conductors of electricity.

REVIEW REVIEW REVIEW REVIEW REVIEW

WORDS TO KNOW

acid solution	die set	headstock spindle	redraw
alkaline solution	electrohydraulic	HERF	roll forming
angle bending	forming	lancing	shaving
annealing	electromagnetic	Marform process	shear spinning
back stick	forming	metal spinning	shell drawing
blank	embossing	perforating	spinning chuck
blanking	explosive forming	pickling solution	stretch forming
burnishing	flexforming	progressive dies	sulfuric acid
coining	follow block	punching	transfer dies
cup drawing	Guerin process	punch press	work-harden

REVIEW QUESTIONS

1. List the four basic types of pressworking operations.
2. Name three kinds of drawing operations.
3. Describe the flexforming process for forming sheet metal parts.
4. How does embossing differ from coining?
5. Name five kinds of shearing operations.
6. Explain the difference between punching and blanking.
7. Explain how a progressive die works.
8. How does a press brake differ from a punch press?
9. Explain the roll-forming process and name several products made that way.
10. How are copper and brass annealed?
11. Name several advantages shear spinning has over metal spinning.
12. How do explosive forming and electrohydraulic forming differ?
13. How is electromagnetic forming done? What are its main uses?

PART

9

Metal Casting and Forming

The ability to become absorbed in a work assignment has been a big factor in Pat Kramer's career in a large midwest foundry. Although he had general vocational courses in sand casting, metalwork, welding, and sheet metal, his present skills were developed on the job. Pat came to his job with a plan. It seemed logical to him to observe everything possible, to learn as much as he could, and to put it to work as quickly as he learned it. Pat has followed his own program most successfully.

For six years he poured castings of many different sizes. As he became more skillful, Pat advanced and felt more and more involved each day. He began to help others with their molds. He learned how to control the scrap rate and work out other pouring problems. Of prime importance to Pat was, and still is, developing a good casting process.

Not only has Pat been promoted, he has also been asked to represent his company as a sales representative and in furthering its customers' education. He has traveled to other cities to give seminars and lab sessions on the processes of pouring molds. He has also become a troubleshooter for other firms that want to draw on his casting knowledge.

Pat advises students to try to "learn something all the time." Find out what this part is made to do. Take an extra course—possibly drafting or special metals courses. Be ready for change always. His own company has introduced robots, for example. Through all changes Pat has remained totally committed to his work and looks forward to continuing to help others. Although he is greatly pleased when asked to represent his company, Pat's widest smile appears when a casting is perfect.

Pat Kramer
Foundry Process Technician

Charles Zilch

UNIT
32
Sand Casting

Metal casting takes place when liquid metal is poured or otherwise forced into a mold. The metal cools and solidifies in the mold, taking on its shape in every detail. Casting processes make it possible to produce metal parts rapidly and economically. They can be of almost any complexity, of almost any size, and of any metal that can be melted.

Parts made by casting are called **castings.** Because of its many advantages, casting is one of the most important methods of manufacturing metal parts. Castings are most commonly made of alloys of iron, steel, aluminum, brass and bronze, magnesium, and zinc. A factory that specializes in making castings is called **a foundry.**

Table 32-1

Comparison of Molds Used to Make Metal Castings

	Sand molds			Metal molds		Special molds	
	Green sand mold	Dry sand mold	Shell mold	Die casting	Permanent mold	Investment mold	Plaster mold
Chief Materials for Mold	Sand + Clay Binder + Moisture	Sand + Oil Binder + (Oven Bake)	Sand + Resin Binder + (Oven Cure)	Hardened Steel	Usually Steel	Silica Sand + Special Binder + (Air & Oven Cure)	Gypsum + Water
Usual Metals Cast	Most Metals	Most Metals	Most Metals	Alloys of Aluminum, Zinc, Magnesium	Aluminum, Brass, Bronze Some Iron	Special Alloys	Aluminum Brass Bronze Zinc (Metals that melt under 2000°F.)
Surface Finish of Casting	Rough	Rough	Smooth	Very Smooth	Smooth	Very Smooth	Very Smooth
Accuracy of Casting	Not Very Accurate	Not Very Accurate	Fairly Accurate	Very Accurate	Fairly Accurate	Very Accurate	Fairly Accurate
Usual Weight of Castings	Less than 1 Lb. to Several Tons	Less than 1 Lb. to Several Tons	½ Lb. to 30 Lb.	Less than 1 Lb. to 100 Lb.	Less than 1 Lb. to 200 Lb.	Less than 1 Ounce to 5 Lb.	Less than 1 Lb. to 20 Lb.
Cost of Mold	Low	Low	Medium	High	High	High	Medium

There are six main types of casting processes: (1) **sand casting,** (2) **die casting,** (3) **permanent mold casting,** (4) **investment casting,** (5) **plaster mold casting,** and (6) **centrifugal casting.** Table 32-1 (p. 287) compares the main features of most of these processes. This unit discusses sand casting processes. The other casting processes are presented in Units 33, 34, and 35.

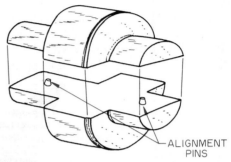

32-1 Patterns

A metal casting begins with the making of a **pattern,** which has the shape of the part to be made, but is slightly larger. Patterns for sand casting are usually made of fine grained wood, or metals such as aluminum. A person who makes patterns is called a **patternmaker.**

The simplest patterns are one-piece patterns (Fig. 32-1). Their use is limited to parts of simple shape. **Split patterns** are used for parts that cannot be molded easily from a one-piece pattern (Fig. 32-2). A split pattern is made in two parts that are "split" along the **parting line** that separates the two halves of the mold. One half of the pattern forms the mold cavity in the drag, or lower part of the mold. The other half of the pattern forms the mold cavity in the cope, or upper part of the mold.

When large quantities of castings are needed, the patterns are attached to wood or metal plates. When each half of a split pattern is mounted on opposite sides of a plate, it is known as a **match plate pattern** (Fig. 32-3). Match plate patterns eliminate the handling of loose patterns, thereby speeding production.

The gate and runner system needed to pour the casting are also attached to the match plate patterns, eliminating the need to cut these into the mold by hand.

Cope and **drag patterns** work like match plate patterns except that the cope part of the pattern is attached to one plate, and the drag part of the pattern is attached to another plate. With two plates, two workers can make the different parts of the mold at the same time, thereby speeding production.

Fig. 32-2 A part that requires a split pattern.

ALIGNMENT PINS

Fig. 32-3 (A) A diagram of a match plate pattern. The sprue base, runner, riser base, and the gates provide paths into the mold cavity for the molten metal. (B) The casting made from the pattern, after the gates and runners are removed.

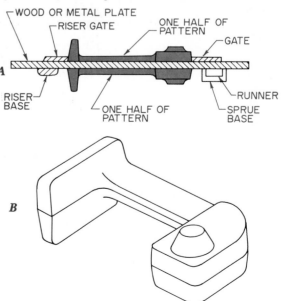

WOOD OR METAL PLATE
RISER GATE
ONE HALF OF PATTERN
GATE
A
RISER BASE
ONE HALF OF PATTERN
RUNNER
SPRUE BASE

B

Fig. 32-1 A one-piece pattern for a bookend.

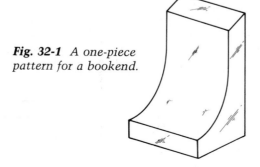

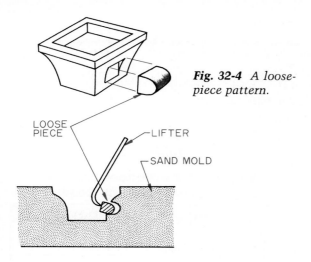

Fig. 32-4 *A loose-piece pattern.*

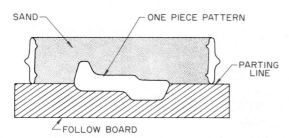

Fig. 32-5 *A follow-board, one-piece pattern, and the follow-board molding arrangement.*

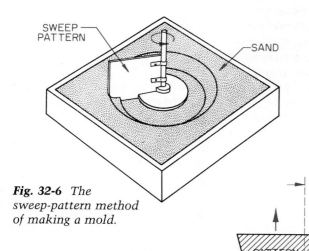

Fig. 32-6 *The sweep-pattern method of making a mold.*

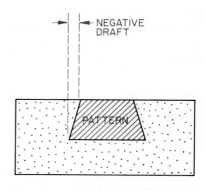

Fig. 32-7 *Positive draft and negative draft.*

PATTERN CAN BE EASILY WITHDRAWN FROM MOLD.

PATTERN CANNOT BE WITHDRAWN FROM MOLD WITHOUT BREAKING THE MOLD.

Loose-piece patterns are required when the shape of a pattern would make it impossible for it to be removed without damaging the mold (Fig. 32-4). The pattern is constructed so the main part of the pattern can be removed first, after which the loose piece can be safely withdrawn.

One-piece patterns of irregular shape that cannot be cast by using normal procedures can be successfully cast by using a **follow board** (Fig. 32-5). A cavity is cut in the follow board to hold it in position for molding. If necessary, the follow board is built up or cut down so that its surface follows the parting line of the pattern.

A **sweep pattern** may be used for making molds having a cylindrical cross-section (Fig. 32-6). This method eliminates the need to construct expensive patterns for making large castings of this type.

Draft

Draft refers to the degree that the sides of a pattern are **tapered.** When the pattern is tapered so that it can be removed easily from a mold, it has **positive draft** (Fig. 32-7). If the pattern is tapered so that it cannot be withdrawn from the mold without breaking it, it has **negative draft.** When the sides of the pattern are straight, the pattern has **zero draft.**

Shrinkage Allowance

Metal shrinks as it cools. Thus, a casting is larger when it is hot than after it has cooled.

Fig. 32-8 *Shrink rules used in patternmaking.*

To allow for this **shrinkage,** the pattern is made larger than the desired size of the finished casting. For convenience in measuring, a shrink rule (Fig. 32-8) is used when making the pattern. Shrink rules are larger than standard rules and are made to allow for different rates of shrinkage.

The amount of allowance for shrinkage depends on the kind of metal being cast and how large the casting is. The shrinkage allowance for small castings is given in Table 32-2.

Fillets

Whenever two surfaces come together on a pattern, they should be connected with a **radius,** or curve, instead of a sharp edge or corner. External corners can easily be rounded to provide a radius. For internal corners, a **fillet** is attached to provide the desired radius. Fillets help prevent cracks at surface intersections. The size of the fillet should be as large as is compatible with the pattern. Commonly used fillet sizes are ⅛" [3.2 mm], ³⁄₁₆" [4.8 mm], and ¼" [6.35 mm].

Fillets are made of pre-shaped strips of wax, leather, or wood. Putty-like plastic filler materials are also used. Leather and wood fillets are glued to the pattern, while wax fillets are set in place with a warm fillet tool (Fig. 32-9). A plastic filler is prepared by mixing it with a catalyst to proper consistency. It is applied with any convenient tool and is smoothed to shape with a fillet tool. The material hardens in 5-15 minutes, depending on the amount of the catalyst used.

32-2   Cores

In molding, a **core** is used to form a hole or a deep cavity in a casting (Fig. 32-10). A core may be formed as a part of a sand mold

Table 32-2

Shrinkage Allowances Used in Patternmaking for Small Castings

Kind of metal	Shrinkage allowance
Aluminum and Zinc-aluminum alloys	5/32"/ft. (13 mm/M)
Brass	3/16"/ft. (15.6 mm/M)
Iron	1/8"/ft. (10.4 mm/M)
Steel	1/4"/ft. (20.8 mm/M)

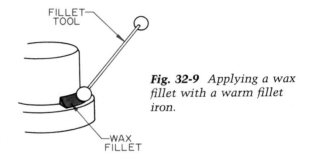

Fig. 32-9 *Applying a wax fillet with a warm fillet iron.*

by simply lifting a hollow pattern out of the mold (Fig. 32-10A). Most cores, however, must be placed horizontally in the mold, and cannot be made as a part of the mold. Most cores are sand mixtures that have been made hard and strong by various methods described below.

Patterns for parts that require cored holes are made with **core prints** (Fig. 32-10B). The core prints provide one or more seats in the mold for supporting the core. After the pattern is removed from the mold, the core is set in place (Fig. 32-10C). When metal is poured into the mold, it flows around the core. After the casting has been removed from the mold, the core is removed, leaving a hole in the casting. Under ideal conditions, the heat of the casting will cause the binder in the core to decompose. This reduces the core to loose grains of sand that are easily removed from the casting.

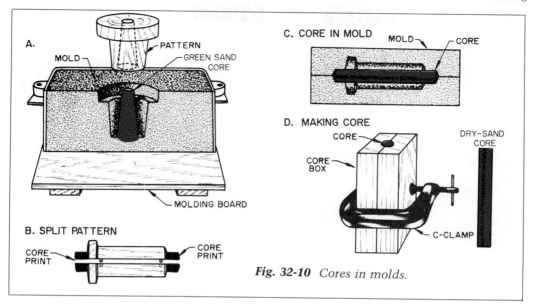

Fig. 32-10 *Cores in molds.*

Cores are made in wood or metal molds called **core boxes.** If only a few cores are needed, the core boxes are made of wood (Fig. 32-10D). For volume production, core boxes are made of metal for durability. Multiple cavity core boxes and core blowing machines make volume production of cores highly efficient.

Rigid cores are made by dry sand molding (Section 32-11), air-set molding (Section 32-12), and shell molding (Section 32-13).

32-3 Hand Molding Equipment

The container in which the mold is made is called a **flask** (Fig. 32-11A). It is made in two halves of either wood or metal. The top is called the **cope,** and the bottom is called the **drag.** When assembled, pins attached to the drag fit snugly into holes in the cope, accurately aligning the two halves. The plane that separates the cope from the drag is called a parting plane or, more commonly, a **parting line.**

The board on which a loose pattern is laid for molding is called a **molding board** (Fig. 32-11B). It should be slightly larger than the flask and strong enough that it will not bend under pressure of ramming the sand. In making many hand molds, the drag half of the mold is made first, with its parting plane down against the molding board. To complete the mold, it must be turned over so that the cope can be attached. When this is done, another molding board called a **bottom board** is placed on the bottom of the drag before it is turned over. It is used along with the molding board to prevent the sand in the drag from falling out when it is turned over. It should be noted that some patterns are better suited for casting in the cope.

A **riddle** is a large sieve used to sift sand (Fig. 32-11C). It is used to sift out foreign materials and break up lumps of sand. This provides clean sand that will pack uniformly around the pattern, which is important for making castings that are free of surface defects. A riddle with a fine mesh is used for facing sand (sand that comes in contact with the pattern). A riddle of coarser mesh may be used for the rest of the sand needed to fill the mold.

A **rammer** (Fig. 32-11D) is a tool used to ram or pack sand around the pattern. This is done so that the sand will become strong enough to hold the shape of the pattern while the liquid metal is poured into it.

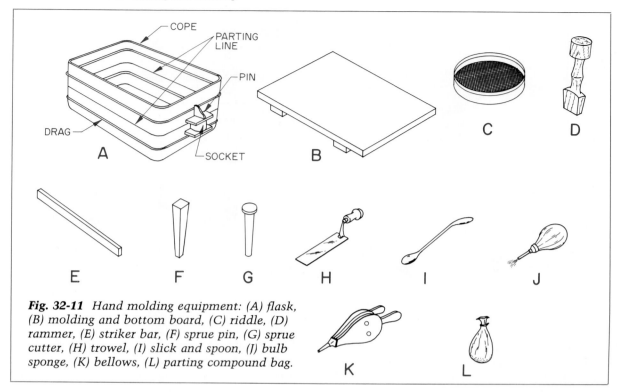

Fig. 32-11 *Hand molding equipment: (A) flask, (B) molding and bottom board, (C) riddle, (D) rammer, (E) striker bar, (F) sprue pin, (G) sprue cutter, (H) trowel, (I) slick and spoon, (J) bulb sponge, (K) bellows, (L) parting compound bag.*

A **striker bar** is a straight steel bar used to strike off or remove excess sand from the mold halves (Fig. 32-11E).

A **sprue pin** (Fig. 32-11F) is a tapered wooden pin of square or round cross section that is placed in the cope when it is rammed. When it is withdrawn, it forms the sprue hole in the mold, the hole into which the molten metal is poured. A **sprue cutter** (Fig. 32-11G) may be used to make a sprue hole instead of using a sprue pin.

Trowels (Fig. 32-11H) and **slick-and-spoons** (Fig. 32-11I) are used for sand work such as mold repair, and cutting pouring basins, runners and gates.

A **bulb sponge** is a rubber bulb with a brush attached (Fig. 32-11J). It is used to apply a small amount of water around the pattern before it is removed from a water-moistened green sand mold.

A **bellows** (Fig. 32-11K) is used to blow loose sand off the pattern or elsewhere from the mold as needed. Care should be taken with its use. If used too vigorously, it can destroy delicate mold details.

Parting compound is a fine powder used to keep the molding sand from sticking to the pattern. It is sprinkled on the pattern and also on the sand at the parting line before the cope is rammed. This keeps the mold halves from sticking together. It is applied by shaking a small cloth bag of the powder over the area to be treated (Fig. 32-11L).

32-4 Mold Vents

Air, steam, and gas trapped in the mold cavity will cause defects in the casting. Molds that are packed too hard will not allow gases to escape and need venting. **Vent holes** are made by pushing a wire into the cope over the pattern. The vent holes need not penetrate into the mold cavity to be effective (Fig. 32-30). Oil-bonded sands seldom need venting.

32-5 Gating of Sand Molds

The molten metal reaches the **mold cavity** (the hollow space left in the mold after removing the pattern) through a hollow **gating system** (Fig. 32-12). This system has four parts:

1. A **pouring basin** into which the molten metal is poured.
2. A **sprue** through which the metal flows down to the **sprue base.**
3. A **runner** which delivers the metal close to the mold cavity.
4. One or more **gates** through which the metal flows into the mold cavity.

The sprue base, runner, and gate are formed in the mold as parts of a match plate pattern or by cutting away the sand after the mold is opened. The sprue is formed by packing sand around a sprue pin (Fig. 32-28), then removing the pin. A sprue hole may also be made by cutting through the rammed sand with a piece of tubing called a sprue cutter.

The pouring basin (Fig. 32-13) helps to reduce turbulence and deliver clean metal into the sprue. When the rate of pouring is fast enough to keep the sprue full, the lighter dross (oxidized metal) floats to the top and is prevented from entering the mold. Pouring into the pouring basin also reduces the amount of loose sand that is washed into the gating system.

Ideally, the sprue should be square in cross-section and tapered to help reduce turbulence. This helps prevent air from being drawn into the mold with the liquid metal. The small end of the sprue should have a cross-sectional area of about ¼ square inch [½″ × ½″] or 161 sq. mm [12.7 × 12.7 mm] (Fig. 32-14). The sprue base should be about 2½ times the width of the runner and twice as deep as the runner. The sprue base helps reduce the turbulence of the metal as it flows into the runner.

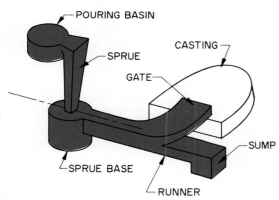

Fig. 32-12 *The gating system for a sand mold.*

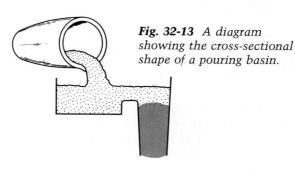

Fig. 32-13 *A diagram showing the cross-sectional shape of a pouring basin.*

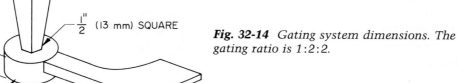

Fig. 32-14 *Gating system dimensions. The gating ratio is 1:2:2.*

The runner and gate dimensions are determined according to the gating ratio used. The **gating ratio** is the ratio of the cross-sectional areas of the small end of the sprue, the runner, and the total cross-sectional area of the gates. A gating ratio often used is 1:2:2. In such a case, a cross-sectional area of the small end of the sprue of ¼ square inch (161 sq. mm) will result in a cross sectional area for both the runner and the gates of 2″ × ¼″ or ½ square inch [51 × 6 mm or 306 sq. mm].

The runner and the gates should be designed to provide for smooth flow of the metal. Gates should be located in the cope also to provide smooth metal flow. The runner should extend beyond the last gate so that the metal first entering the mold (which may contain sand or slag) will not be carried into the mold cavity. Deepen the end of the runner to make a sump to receive the damaged metal.

A gating system may also have a riser, a structure similar to a sprue. Metal flows to the riser from the cavity through another gate. Risers are used to help reduce shrinkage in thicker parts of castings.

32-6 Water-moistened Green Sand Molding

About 85% of the castings made in the United States are made in **green sand molds.** Water-moistened green-sand molds are made chiefly from a mixture of sand, clay, and water. Enough water is added to make the mixture of sand and clay moist. The damp, sticky clay coats the grains of sand and makes them stick together. The mixture is called "green" because the mold is not dried, baked, or cured before it is used. Other ingredients may be mixed with the sand to make the sand easier to work with, or to make it more suitable for casting metals with high melting points.

In water-moistened green-sand molding, **tempering** means mixing water with the sand-clay mixture to obtain a certain dampness. When the proper amount of moisture has been added, the sand will pack somewhat like snow when squeezed in the hand. It will break with

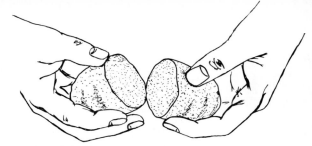

Fig. 32-15 Testing the temper of green sand.

Fig. 32-16 An instrument used to test the moisture content of green sand mixtures. (Harry W. Dietert Co.)

even, sharp edges (Fig. 32-15). Also, the sand will not be so wet that it will stick to the hand. It will fall away, leaving the hand almost clean.

If the sand is too dry before casting, some of the sand will be washed loose by the force of the liquid metal. The loose sand is then carried by the molten metal into the mold. If it is deposited in the mold cavity, it could spoil the casting.

 SAFETY NOTE
If the sand is too wet, the hot metal changes the excess moisture into steam. This steam may cause holes, called **blowholes,** in the casting, or it may cause the entire mold to explode.

Fig. 32-18 *An instrument for testing the hardness of green sand molds. (Harry W. Dietert Co.)*

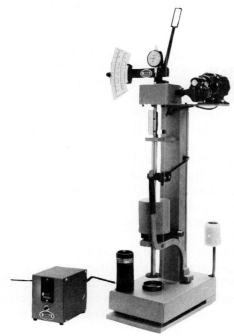

Fig. 32-17 *A sand rammer for making standard test samples of green sand. (Harry W. Dietert Co.)*

Foundries use a special instrument to test water-moistened green sand for proper moisture content (Fig. 32-16). Other instruments used for testing sand include a **standard sand rammer** (Fig. 32-17), and a **green sand hardness tester** (Fig. 32-18). The standard sand rammer prepares a standard sample of green sand for testing the various properties of the sand. The green sand hardness tester is used to measure the surface hardness of molds. Instruments for measuring shear, tensile, and compression strength are also used.

32-7 Oil-bonded Green Sand Molding

Oil-bonded sand is used to make molds in the same manner as the water-moistened green sand. It is made up of pure silica sand that is mixed with a formulated bonding material and a special oil.

Oil-bonded sand has many advantages and few disadvantages when used in schools. It may be used for making aluminum, magnesium, bronze, brass, and zinc castings. Its advantages include greater precision, less **gassing** (formation of gasses in the mold), and finer finishes. Oil-bonded sand molds may be left for several days before pouring without deterioration of the mold. Lower ramming pressures can be used than for water-moistened green sand. Gates may be made smaller, and vent holes are not generally needed.

Oil-bonded sand must be conditioned and thoroughly mixed in a **mulling** (mixing) **machine** before its initial use (Fig. 32-19). If the sand is riddled and turned over frequently with a shovel, it will need to be reconditioned only about once a year for school use. The manufacturer's recommendations should be followed carefully when mixing the ingredients and mulling oil-bonded sand. This service may be performed by a nearby foundry or by a foundry supplier.

 SAFETY NOTE

Casting in oil-bonded sand molds requires good ventilation to carry away fumes and odors.

Fig. 32-19 *A portable mulling machine for mixing foundry sands.* (McEnglevan)

3. Now shovel enough sand into the drag to overfill it. Then pack the sand into the drag with the rammer (Fig. 32-22), first with the peen end, then with the butt end. Be careful not to strike the pattern or the sides of the drag. Add more sand as needed and ram the drag full.

4. Remove the excess sand from the drag with the striker (Fig. 32-23), using a sawing motion.

5. Place the bottom board on top of the drag. Then, holding the drag, molding board, and bottom board tightly together at the sides, roll over the drag so the bottom board rests on the molding bench (Fig. 32-24).

6. Remove the molding board from the drag. The flat side of the pattern is now up (Fig. 32-25). Make sure that the sand is packed firmly around the edges of the pattern. Add sand if necessary and smooth it with a trowel.

32-8 Making a Green-sand Mold with Hand Molding Equipment

Suppose that a mold for a bookend is to be made. A one-piece pattern is to be used and the flat back of the pattern will be at the parting line between the cope and the drag. The surfaces of the pattern must be smooth, clean, and dry; otherwise sand will stick to them. The steps for making the mold are as follows:

1. Put the flat side of the pattern on the molding board (Fig. 32-20). Put the drag around the pattern with the pins pointing down. Dust a light coating of parting compound over the pattern.

2. Set the riddle on top of the drag, fill it with sand, and sift the sand over the pattern (Fig. 32-21) until it is at least 2" [50 mm] thick. Press the sand around the pattern with the fingers, or very lightly with the rammer. Repeat this operation if necessary.

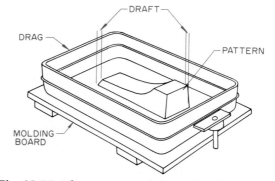

Fig. 32-20 *The pattern and drag placed on a molding board.*

Fig. 32-21 *Riddling sand over the pattern.*

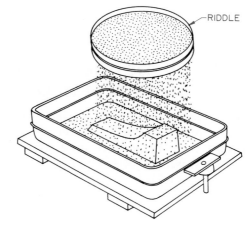

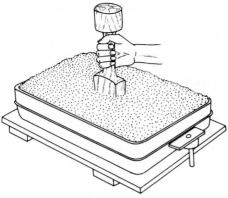

Fig. 32-22 *Ramming the drag half of the flask.*

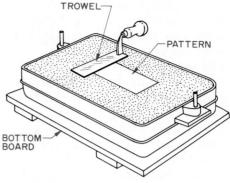

Fig. 32-25 *Smoothing the surface of a mold with a trowel.*

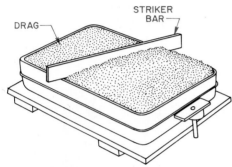

Fig. 32-23 *Striking off the excess sand with a striker bar.*

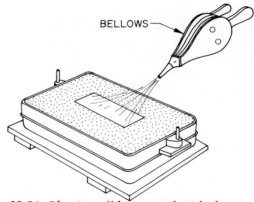

Fig. 32-26 *Blowing off loose sand with the bellows.*

Fig. 32-24 *Turning the drag over after putting on the bottom board.*

7. Blow off loose sand with a bellows (Fig. 32-26). Dust parting compound over the pattern and the mold to keep the cope and the drag from sticking together (Fig. 32-27).
8. Set the cope part of the flask on the drag and put the sprue pin in place (Fig. 32-28).
9. Riddle sand into the cope and ram as in steps 2 and 3.
10. Strike off the top with the striker bar. Cut the sprue hole with a sprue cutter if a sprue pin was not used. Use a slick-and-spoon to cut a pouring basin next to the sprue hole (Fig. 32-29). Remove the sprue pin or sprue cutter, then compress the loose sand around the top of the sprue hole and pouring basin with a finger.

Make vents if needed (ask your instructor for guidance) by pushing a small diameter wire into the cope to about 1" (25 mm) from the pattern (Fig. 32-30).

11. Lift the cope half of the mold off and lay it on its side on the molding bench. Dampen the edges of the mold next to the pattern with a bulb sponge (Fig. 32-31). Dampening makes the sand around the pattern firmer so that the pattern can be removed without breaking out the edges of the mold. (Do not dampen oil-bonded sands.)

12. Cut the sprue basin and runner in the drag, if necessary, with a slick-and-spoon (Fig. 32-32).

13. Lift the pattern out with a draw pin, which is a rod of steel with threads on one end (Fig. 32–32). The pin is screwed into a hole in the pattern. The draw pin should be rapped lightly on all sides to loosen the pattern so it can be lifted out easily.

Blow off any loose sand with the bellows, then patch up any defects in the mold. Cut a gate in the cope part of the mold connecting the mold cavity with the runner (Fig. 32–14).

14. Carefully put the cope back on the drag. Then put the flask on the floor where the mold will be poured. For castings with a large surface, the mold should be weighted or clamped shut to keep the molten metal from lifting up the cope when it is poured. This would cause molten metal to run out between the cope and drag onto the floor, and would ruin the casting.

After the mold is poured and cooled, the casting is removed from the mold. It will look as shown in Fig. 32-33.

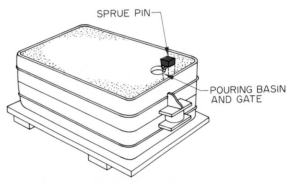

Fig. 32-29 *Before removing the sprue pin or sprue cutter, the pouring basin and gate should be made.*

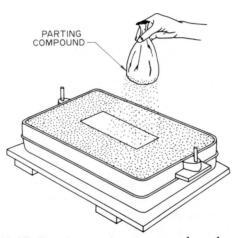

Fig. 23-27 *Dusting parting compound on the mold.*

Fig. 32-28 *The cope set on the drag with the sprue pin in place.*

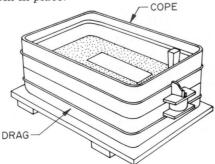

Fig. 32-30 *Making vents in the mold. Vents are not necessary for most molds if the mold is rammed correctly.*

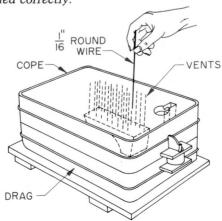

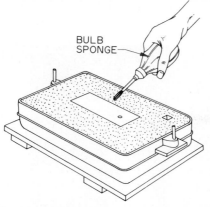

Fig. 32-31 *Wetting the edges of the mold with the bulb sponge. This step is omitted when using oil bonded sand.*

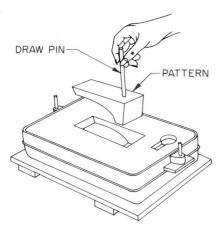

Fig. 32-32 *Lifting the pattern out of the mold. Note that the sprue base and runner were made before the pattern was removed.*

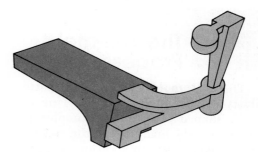

Fig. 32-33 *A casting as taken from a mold.*

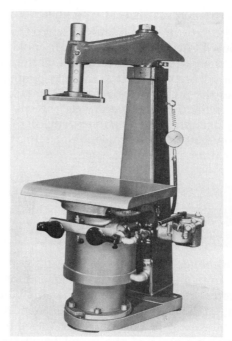

Fig. 32-34 *A jolt-squeeze machine.* (Beardsley and Piper)

32-9 Production Molding Equipment for Green Sanding Molding

For low volume production, molds are made in **jolt-squeeze machines** (Fig. 32-34). The prepared sand is delivered to the molding machine by a chute connected to an overhead conveyor. The jolt-squeeze machine is air powered, eliminating the need for most hand ramming. If hand ramming is needed, portable air-powered rammers are usually used. On larger jolt-squeeze machines, the operator uses a small crane to lift the heavy flasks and molds.

Special machines are made for high volume green sand molding that eliminate the need for loose flasks. The molds are automatically made and delivered back-to-back on a conveyor to the point where they are poured. The castings cool while moving on the conveyor to a **shakeout machine.** They are automatically removed from the conveyor onto a shakeout table that removes the sand from the casting by vibration. The castings are sent by conveyor to the warehouse for storage or to the machine shop for further processing, and the sand is sent by conveyor for recycling.

The Full-mold Process

The **full mold process** uses patterns of polystyrene foam (Fig. 32-35). This material can be shaped very easily. Complex patterns can be quickly made by gluing together several simple shapes. In addition, a sprue, riser, and gating system made of polystyrene are glued to the pattern. Sand must be gently packed around the polystyrene pattern because the material is easily crushed.

The pattern is not removed when the mold is poured; hence the name "full mold". Because the pattern is not removed, pattern draft can be ignored. When the mold is poured, the heat of the metal vaporizes the polystyrene almost instantly. The metal fills the space formerly occupied by the polystyrene. Because of the low pattern cost, full-mold casting is economical for even one casting.

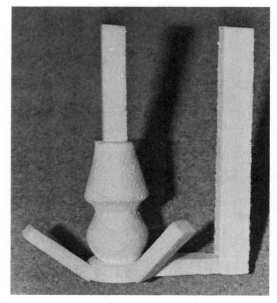

Fig. 32-35 *A polystyrene pattern with the sprue, gate and runner, and riser system attached.*

Dry Sand Molding

Oil-bonded dry sand molds and cores are made from a mixture of sands, special foundry oil, cereal flour, water, and other ingredients. There are several formulas for oil-bonded dry sand mixtures. The formulas are varied to suit the melting point of the metal being poured, the size of the core or mold being made, and the method of packing the sand. A recommended general purpose mixture for aluminum is as follows:

Washed silica sand:	80 lbs (36.3 kg)
Bank sand:	20 lbs (9.1 kg)
Cereal flour:	0.8%
Water:	4.2%
Core oil:	0.4 to 1.0%
Kerosene:	0.33%

The purpose of the water and cereal flour is to give the mixture **green strength.** Green strength enables the mixture to hold its shape during handling after molding. The molded parts are baked in an oven at 300-600°F (149-316°C), during which time the water evaporates and the volatile elements in the kerosene and oil are vaporized. Upon removal from the oven, the sand mixture is dry, hard, and brittle, and must be carefully handled.

Before use, oil-bonded dry sand cores and mold surfaces are usually given a brush coating of a mixture of graphite and water. The coating provides a smoother finish and prevents sand from sticking to the metal casting.

Carbon dioxide (CO_2) **dry sand molding.** For this process, the sand is thoroughly mixed with a solution of **sodium silicate.** After the sand is pressed or blown into the mold or core box, CO_2 gas is blown through the sand mixture for several seconds. The CO_2 gas reacts chemically with the sodium silicate to form a silica gel, which binds the sand grains together into a rigid mass. CO_2 molds and cores can be used immediately after gassing. However, surface hardness and strength of the sand mixture will increase slowly in still air at room temperature.

Because there is no moisture in a dry sand mold or core, the casting cannot be spoiled by pockets of steam, which can form in water-moistened green-sand molds.

32-12

Air-set Molding

Air-set molding, sometimes called no-bake molding, uses a special binder that hardens in air. The binder is usually a mixture of **urea, formaldehyde,** and **furfuryl alcohol.** Addition of a catalyst, usually **phosphoric acid,** increases the speed at which the molds or cores harden. (A catalyst is a liquid or solid that causes or helps a chemical process.) Increasing the temperature of the sand also shortens the setting time.

A common air-set sand mixture consists of clean silica sand, 2% binder, and a catalyst amounting to 30 to 40% of the weight of the binder. The sand mixture begins to set or cure as soon as the catalyst and binder are mixed together. The working life of the mixture is usually less than 30 minutes. However, this can be increased to several hours by reducing the amount of the catalyst.

A special mold release must be used to prevent air-set sand mixtures from sticking to core boxes and patterns.

32-13

Shell Molding

Another type of sand mold is called a **shell mold.** A fine-powdered **resin** is mixed with dry molding sand. The sand-resin mixture is poured around a metal pattern that is already heated to 400° to 600°F [204° to 316°C]. The heat melts the resin. It coats the grains of sand, causing the grains of sand to stick to each other. At the proper time, the pattern is turned upside down and excess sand mixture falls off. Only ¼″ to ½″ [6.35 to 12.7 mm] of the sand-resin mix sticks to the hot pattern.

The pattern is turned upright again and put into an oven to cure (allow the resin to harden). When the pattern is removed from the oven, the mold is hard and thin. Because of these qualities, it is called a "**shell** mold" (Fig. 32-36).

The shell mold is made in two halves (Fig. 32-37). When they are supported in a bed of sand as a complete shell, melted metal can be poured into the mold. Castings made in a shell mold are smooth. Hence, they require less machining than castings made from a green-sand mold. Shell molds are being used more and more where accuracy and good finish on castings are important. This process is also widely used for making shell cores. The sand from shell molds, however, cannot be easily reused.

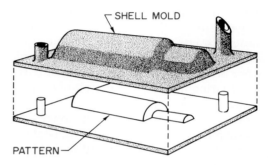

Fig. 32-36 *Making a shell mold.*

Fig. 32-37 *Industrial shell molding. (A) Forming one half of the shell mold. (B) Assembling both halves of the shell mold.*

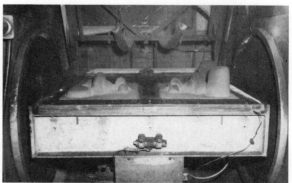

A

B

REVIEW   REVIEW   REVIEW   REVIEW   REVIEW

WORDS TO KNOW

air-set molding
bellows
blowholes
bottom board
bulb sponge
centrifugal casting
CO_2 process
cope
cope-and-drag
   patterns
core box
core oil
core prints
die casting
draft
drag
draw pin
dross
dry-sand mold

fillet
flask
follow board
follow-board pattern
formaldehyde
foundry
full-mold process
gate
gating ratio
gating system
green-sand molding
investment mold
loose-piece pattern
match-plate pattern
mold
mold cavity
molding bench
molding board

mulling machine
negative draft
oil-bonded sand
one-piece pattern
parting compound
parting line
pattern
permanent mold
phosphoric acid
polystyrene foam
positive draft
pouring basin
rammer
ramming
resin
riddle
riser
runner

sand casting
shell molding
shrinkage
silica gel
slag
slick and spoon
sodium silicate
split pattern
sprue
sprue base
sprue pin
striker bar
sweep pattern
taper
temper
turbulence
vent holes
zero draft

REVIEW QUESTIONS

1. What is metal casting?
2. What is a foundry?
3. Why is green sand called "green"?
4. Name the materials used to make green sand.
5. What does sand temper mean? How is it tested?
6. What are the advantages of oil-bonded sand when compared to water-bonded green sand?
7. Name some materials that are used to make patterns.
8. List the different kinds of patterns and give the main advantage of each kind.
9. What is meant by positive draft? Negative draft?
10. What is shrinkage? How does the pattern-maker allow for shrinkage?
11. What is a fillet?
12. What materials are fillets made of and how are they applied?
13. What is a flask? Name its two major parts.
14. Why is parting compound used?
15. What is a riddle? What is it used for?
16. Why are molds vented?
17. Name the four main parts of a gating system.
18. What hazard is associated with using green sand that is too wet?
19. Describe the full-mold casting process.
20. Explain the CO_2 molding process.
21. How does air-set molding differ from dry-sand molding?
22. Explain the shell molding process.

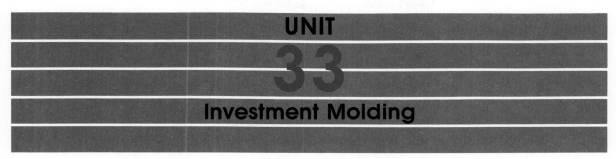

UNIT
33
Investment Molding

Most molds are made using a pattern that has a **positive draft.** Such patterns can be withdrawn from the mold and used over and over. **Investment molding,** however, uses patterns made from wax, plastic, or frozen mercury. These patterns are removed from the mold by melting. Therefore, the patterns do not need to have positive draft. For this reason, almost any shape of casting can be made by investment molding, including those with zero or negative draft. Whether the pattern is wax, plastic, or mercury, the procedures are similar.

33-1 Patternmaking for Investment Molding

Single patterns are carved of wax or plastic (Fig. 33-1). When many identical castings are needed, a **mold** is made. The patterns are produced by injecting liquid wax into the mold, where it solidifies (Fig. 33-2). To speed production and reduce costs, small patterns are attached to a central sprue to make a **pattern tree** (Fig. 33-3).

Fig. 33-1 *Investment casting. (A) The wax pattern attached to mold base. (B) The finished casting.* (Sybron/Kerr)

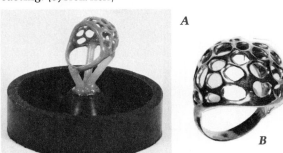

33-2 Investment Flask Molding

For **investment flask molding,** the pattern or pattern tree is attached to a flat surface, and a round steel flask is set in place (Fig. 33-4A).

Fig. 33-2 *The pressure in this injector forces liquid wax into a mold for making identical patterns.* (Sybron/Kerr)

Fig. 33-3 *A "tree" of wax patterns for turbine blades attached to a common sprue for efficiency in mold making and pouring.* (Arwood Corporation)

Fig. 33-4 *Investment flask molding.*

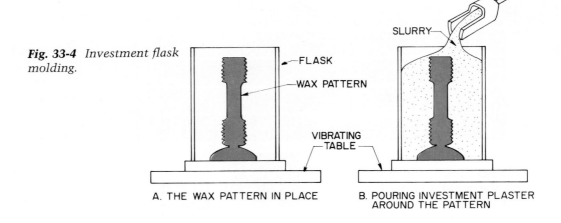

A. THE WAX PATTERN IN PLACE

B. POURING INVESTMENT PLASTER AROUND THE PATTERN

The steel flask is sealed to the flat surface with wax. Then it is filled with a special **investment plaster** and shaken on a vibrating table. The vibration settles the plaster against the pattern(s) and shakes out air bubbles (Fig. 33-4B). The mold is then left to harden and air-dry for at least 8 hours.

Fig. 33-5 *Investment shell mold making. (A) Dipping a pattern into ceramic slurry. (B) Coating with sand.* (Arwood Corporation)

33-3 Investment Shell Molding

For **investment shell molding,** also called **ceramic shell molding,** no flask is used. An investment shell mold is made by alternately coating the patterns with a thin ceramic slurry and then adding a layer of ceramic sand (Fig. 33-5). A coating of suitable thickness, usually about ¼" [6.35 mm], is gradually built up this way.

Fig. 33-6 *Investment mold making and casting.*

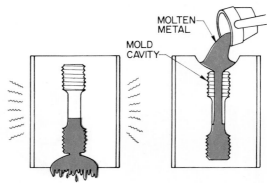

33-4 Preparing the Molds

The air-dried investment or ceramic shell molds are placed upside-down in an oven and heated to about 300°F [149°C]. The wax melts out, leaving the shape of the wax pattern in the mold (Fig. 33-6). Because the wax pattern is lost in making the mold, investment molding is commonly called the **lost wax process.** Before pouring, the molds are gradually heated to about 1200°F [649°C] for aluminum alloys, 1600°F [871°C] for copper alloys, and 1900°F [1038°C] for ferrous alloys (Fig. 33-6). After the molds have been poured and have cooled, the molds are broken to remove the castings.

Investment molding can produce complex castings with great precision and with very smooth surfaces. This reduces or eliminates the need for machining and finishing operations on many castings. Investment molding is used for jet engine parts, dental castings, jewelry, and other castings that require high quality.

REVIEW REVIEW REVIEW REVIEW REVIEW

WORDS TO KNOW

ceramic shell molding
investment flask molding

investment plaster
investment shell molding

lost wax process

pattern tree

REVIEW QUESTIONS

1. Name three materials used for making investment molding patterns.
2. Explain how large quantities of patterns are made for investment molding.
3. What is a pattern tree and why is it used?
4. How is investment flask molding different from investment shell molding?
5. How thick are the walls of an investment shell mold made?
6. Why is investment-mold casting also called the lost wax process?
7. How long should investment flask molds be air-dried before melting out the wax?
8. Name several advantages of investment castings.

UNIT
34

Permanent-Mold Casting and Die Casting

For most casting processes, the mold must be destroyed in order to release the casting. **Permanent mold casting** and **die casting,** however, use molds that are reusable for making thousands of castings.

34-1 Permanent-Mold Casting

Most non-ferrous alloys, steel, and some gray iron alloys can be cast in **permanent molds.** This process is also known as **gravity die casting,** because **gravity** forces the liquid metal into the mold. It is used for making large quantities of identical castings. Permanent molds are usually made from iron or steel. Up to 200,000 low melting-point alloy castings can be made in some molds before the molds wear out.

Gravity alone will not provide enough pressure to force molten metal into openings much smaller than ¼″ [6.35 mm]. Therefore, permanent molding is not suitable for thin-walled castings.

Permanent mold castings can be made to tolerances of ±0.010″ [0.25 mm]. They have good surface finish and higher tensile strength than sand castings.

Molds made of **graphite** are becoming increasingly popular. The molds are easy to machine, have good surface finish, do not warp when heated, and can withstand higher temperatures than metal molds. Railroad car wheels can be cast so accurately in graphite molds that no machining is required.

34-2 Die Casting

When liquid metal is forced, or **injected,** into a die under high pressure, the process is called **die casting.** Except for this feature, the process is like permanent mold casting. Die-casting machines are capable of applying pressures from 1000 psi [6.89 MPa] to 100,000 psi [6894.75 MPa] (Fig. 34-1). As a result, die castings have greater strength and better surface finish than permanent mold castings. Casting accuracy of ±0.006″ [0.15 mm] can be maintained, and walls as thin as 0.031″ [0.8 mm]

Fig. 34-1 A large cold chamber die casting machine. Note the robot at left for automatically removing the castings from the machine. (Doehler-Jarvis Castings)

are possible. Most die castings are made so accurately that only the removal of gates and **flash** (the metal edge that forms at the **parting line** between the halves of the die) are required to make them finished castings.

Two types of die casting machines are made: **cold-chamber** and **hot-chamber.** In cold-chamber machines, the liquid metal must be ladled into a **shot cylinder.** The operating cycle of a cold chamber machine is shown in Figure 34-2. Cold-chamber machines are used for the higher melting point alloys of aluminum, magnesium, and copper. In hot-chamber machines, the liquid metal is forced into the die from a cylinder that is kept submerged in a **melting pot** (Fig. 34-3). Hot-chamber machines are used for low-melting-point metals, such as zinc alloys.

Die castings range in size from less than one ounce [28.35 grams] to as much as 100 lbs. [45.5 kg] (Fig. 34-4). Much hardware and many auto, appliance, machine, and instrument parts are made by die casting.

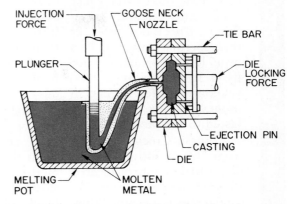

Fig. 34-3 *A diagram of the hot chamber die casting system.*

Fig. 34-2 *The cold chamber die casting machine process. (A) Metal being ladled into the shot cylinder. (B) Plunger forces metal into the mold. (C) Mold opens after cooling cycle. (D) Casting is pushed from the mold by ejector pins.*

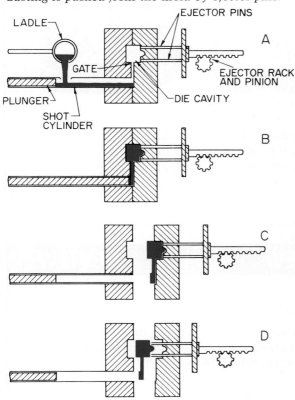

Fig. 34-4 *A die casting for a large complex automotive transmission case, with a built-in hydraulic control section. (Doehler-Jarvis Castings)*

TECHNOLOGIES AND PRACTICES

King Croesus and his Coins

How would it be if nickels, dimes, and quarters had to be weighed to determine their value every time you bought something? Check-out lines at the supermarket would be a mile long! Fortunately for us, a king who lived 2500 years ago started a trend in money-making that has lasted to the present day.

King Croesus ruled from 560 to 546 BC in Lydia, a little country located in what is now Turkey. Before Croesus became king, gold and silver (as well as animals and produce) were used in trade. But there were no standard gold or silver pieces, only a set value per ounce. The merchants used scales to weigh the precious metals.

Croesus thought that he could make buying easier for his subjects. He had his men mine a quantity of electrum, a natural alloy (mixture) of gold and silver. Then he directed his craft workers to make coins in a two-part process.

First, they cast the electrum in molds. These molds were made of stone or baked clay. Each one had a series of little holes dug into it. The melted electrum was poured into the mold, and when the metal hardened, it was chipped out of the holes.

Then these small pellets, or blanks, were turned into coins by stamping them flat and imprinting a picture on them. To do this, the craft workers took blocks of iron or bronze and cut a mirror-image of a lion's head into the metal. Then they placed the electrum blanks on the metal dies and hammered them into the cut surface. When the piece of electrum was removed, it had a lion's head on one side.

Because the workers could not make blanks or dies of exactly the same size, the coins were not identical. But King Croesus had the clever idea to stamp a sign on the coins that certified they were all the same size, and therefore all worth the same amount.

The Lydian people found that equal-value coins made buying and selling much more convenient. The custom soon spread to other lands.

So today, when you go shopping at the supermarket, thank old Croesus for not having to weigh your money along with your produce!

REVIEW   REVIEW   REVIEW   REVIEW   REVIEW

WORDS TO KNOW

cold chamber	graphite	inject	plunger
die casting	gravity die casting	melting pot	shot cylinder
flash	hot chamber	permanent mold	

(Review Continued)

REVIEW QUESTIONS

1. Why is permanent mold casting also called gravity die casting?
2. What materials are permanent molds made of?
3. Why can't thin-walled castings be made by permanent molding?
4. How accurate can permanent mold castings be made?
5. Explain the die-casting process.
6. Explain the difference between hot-chamber and cold-chamber die-casting machines. What kinds of metal is each used for?
7. How much pressure is used in making die castings?
8. How accurate can die castings be made?
9. What is the minimum wall thickness possible in die castings?
10. Name several items made by die casting.

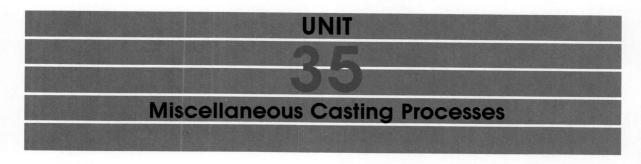

UNIT 35
Miscellaneous Casting Processes

Many different methods of making castings have been developed for special purposes. The most frequently used processes are described in this unit.

35-1 Plaster-mold Casting

Plaster molds are sometimes used to make castings from alloys of copper, aluminum, and other metals that melt at temperatures from 400° to 1700°F [204 to 927°C]. Since they are easy to make, plaster molds are especially useful when only a few castings are to be made (Fig. 35-1).

The plaster for the molds is made by mixing water with **foundry plaster.** The plaster should be added to the water (rather than the other way around) to minimize **air entrapment.** After mixing, air is removed from the plaster in a vacuum chamber. The wet plaster is then poured over the pattern.

After the plaster has hardened, the pattern is removed, and the mold is air-dried. The mold is then heated to 400°F [204°C] to drive off all remaining moisture before it is poured.

Wood patterns can be used to make plaster molds, but they are not as good as patterns made from metal or plastic. Wood patterns will absorb moisture and swell.

Castings made from plaster molds have a very smooth surface. Sculptors use plaster molds to cast bronze into statues and fine ornamental work. Special foundries also use plaster molds. The procedure for making a plaster mold is shown in Figure 35-2.

Fig. 35-1 *Plaster mold making.*

35-2 Centrifugal Casting

In **centrifugal casting**, the mold is rotated on its **longitudinal axis** at speeds from 300 to 3000 rpm while the metal is being poured. **Centrifugal force** causes the molten metal to flow against the mold, where it takes the same shape. This process makes possible the rapid production of cast-iron pipe, large-diameter gun barrels, brake drums, and similar hollow objects.

Semi-centrifugal casting may be used for casting wheels and gear blanks (Fig. 35-3). To speed production, molds are stacked and poured through a connecting central sprue.

35-3 Centrifuge Casting

This process differs from centrifugal casting in that the molds do not rotate about their own centers. Instead, small molds are placed in a circle around a central sprue (Fig. 35-4). The molds are rotated, or centrifuged, while being poured. Centrifuged castings have higher density and finer detail than gravity-poured castings.

35-4 Slush Casting

This is a method of making hollow castings without the use of cores. The liquid metal is poured into a preheated metal mold. Then the mold is quickly emptied, and a hardened shell of metal clings to the inside of the mold (Fig. 35-5). Decorative castings are made by slush casting. **Dip casting** is a form of slush casting that produces a hollow casting by dipping a highly polished metal pattern into a pot of molten metal. The pattern is immediately withdrawn, and the metal coating is allowed to cool. The pattern is then removed, thus creating the hollow casting.

35-5 Silicone Rubber Molding

Silicone rubber molds are used for **prototypes** (original models of new products) and small quantities of castings made of metals with low melting points. Castings with excellent surface finish and fine detail are possible. Jewelry, toys, nameplates, and similar objects are easily made by this method (Fig. 35-6).

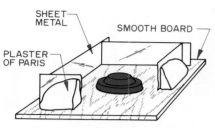

Step 1. *Lay Part B on board and form a box. Note that hardened pieces of foundry plaster hold the box in place.*

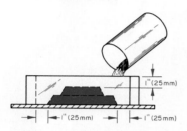

Step 2. *Pour foundry plaster into mold.*

Step 3. *Remove sides and slide mold off board.*

Step 4. *Turn mold upside down, lift out Part B, and repair mold.*

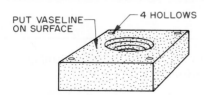

Step 5. *Make four hollows with penny.*

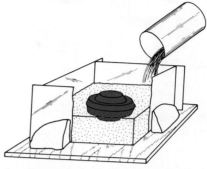

Step 6. *Place whole pattern (A and B) in mold, build a higher box, and fill with foundry plaster.*

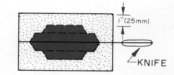

Step 7. *Remove box and separate halves.*

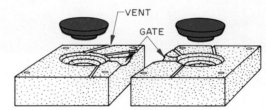

Step 8. *Remove pattern, repair mold, cut gate, and make vents.*

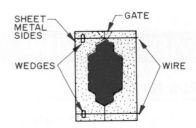

Step 9 *The mold is ready for melted metal. Be sure the plaster is dry before pouring in the metal.*

Fig. 35-2 *The procedure for making a plaster mold.*

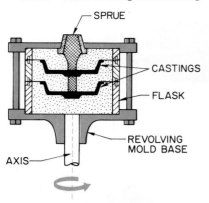

Fig. 35-3 *A diagram showing the arrangement for semi-centrifugal casting.*

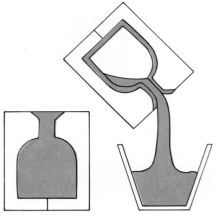

Fig. 35-5 *The slush casting process.*

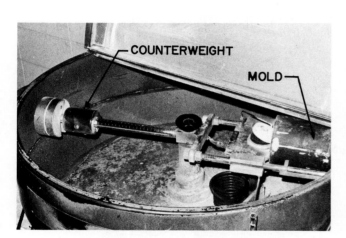

Fig. 35-4 *In this casting arrangement, a single mold is balanced by a counterweight.*

Fig. 35-6 *Silicone rubber molds.* (Tekcast Industries Inc.)

REVIEW   REVIEW   REVIEW   REVIEW   REVIEW

WORDS TO KNOW

axis	dip casting	plaster mold casting	silicone rubber
centrifugal casting	foundry plaster	semi-centrifugal	casting
centrifuge casting		casting	slush casting

(Review Continued)

REVIEW QUESTIONS

1. Describe how plaster molds are made.
2. What kinds of objects are made by plaster-mold casting?
3. Explain how centrifugal castings are made.
4. What kinds of objects are made by centrifugal casting?
5. How is semi-centrifugal casting different from centrifugal casting?
6. Describe how centrifuged castings are made.
7. How are centrifuged castings better than gravity castings?
8. Describe how slush casting is done.
9. How is dip casting different from slush casting?
10. Molds of silicone rubber are useful for making what kinds of castings?

UNIT
36
Melting and Pouring Metal

Metal casting requires heating the metal until it becomes liquid. Sound metal castings can only be obtained by pouring clean metal at the correct pouring temperature into the mold. This unit describes the tools and equipment, safety precautions, and procedures for melting and pouring metals.

36-1 Furnaces for Melting Metal

Small quantities of low-melting-point metals can be melted in some bench-type, **soldering furnaces** (Fig. 36-1). For melting larger quantities of metal in the school shop, a gas-fired **crucible furnace,** like the one shown in Figure 36-2 is used. With this type of furnace, natural or manufactured gas and air are mixed and burned inside the furnace. A gas furnace of this type is good for melting such metals as aluminum, and zinc. These metals melt at relatively low temperatures.

Fig. 36-1 A soldering furnace with provision for a small melting pot.

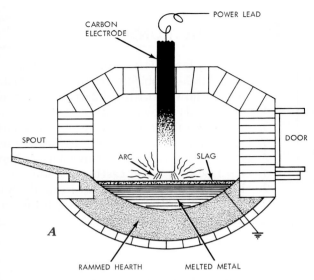

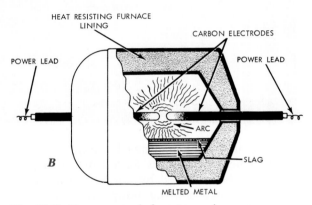

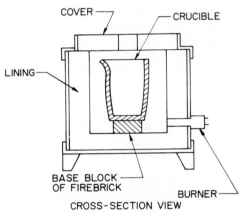

COVER — CRUCIBLE

LINING

BASE BLOCK
OF FIREBRICK

BURNER

CROSS-SECTION VIEW

Fig. 36-2 *A gas fired crucible furnace with automatic spark ignition.*

Fig. 36-3 *Two types of electric arc furnaces used for melting metals. (A) Direct arc. (B) Indirect arc.*

Fig. 36-4 *Schematic of an induction furnace for melting metal.*

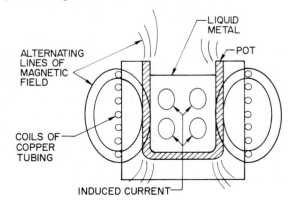

Where higher temperatures are needed to melt metal, electric furnaces are sometimes used. One type of electric furnace is called an **electric arc furnace** (Fig. 36-3). It operates, in principle, like a giant electric arc welding machine. Inside the furnace, electricity jumps from a rod made of carbon, called an "electrode," through an air space, called "the gap." The electricity creates an arc in the gap that gives off a brilliant white light and large amounts of heat.

Electric induction furnaces of several kinds are also used (Fig. 36-4). Alternating current is passed through coils of copper tubing that surround the crucible or **melting pot.** It produces a rapidly expanding and collapsing magnetic field that induces (causes) (or creates) an alternating current on the surface of the metal inside the furnace. The heat generated by this induced current quickly melts the metal.

Some iron foundries use a **cupola furnace,** which acts like a small blast furnace (Figs. 4-3 and 4-4).

Protective Clothing for Melting and Pouring Metal

Without the proper protective clothing, melting and pouring metal can be dangerous. Metal may be spilled from the **ladle.** Also, gas pockets in the mold and moisture in the ladle or mold can cause explosions. These explosions can spray melted metal and cause body burns and injury to the eyes.

To guard against burns and properly protect the eyes, wear the following: a cap, safety glasses and a face shield, a heavy leather apron, heat-proof leggings that also cover leather shoes, and heavy, heat-proof gloves (Fig. 36-5).

36-3 Melting of Metals

Some **furnace linings** and new crucibles should be carefully and slowly **preheated** to minimize the danger of their cracking. Others do not require this treatment. (Be sure to read the manufacturer's instructions for using the furnace.) Furnaces and crucibles that have already been used can be **charged** without preheating. (The **charge** is the metal that is to be melted. It consists usually of ingots, or in some cases a mixture of ingots and scrap.) **Crucibles should not be packed tightly** because expansion of the charge may cause the crucible to crack.

The crucible should be placed in the center of a pot-type furnace so that it will be uniformly heated. It should be supported on a **firebrick** so that the bottom will heat more quickly. A piece of corrugated cardboard placed between the crucible and the firebrick will prevent their sticking together. Before lighting the furnace, if melting copper-based alloys, add a **coverall flux** to the charge. This protects the metal from absorbing oxygen and combustion gases as it melts.

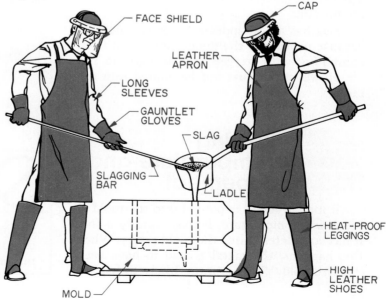

Fig. 36-5 *Protective clothing for melting and pouring metal.*

FACE SHIELD

CAP

LEATHER APRON

LONG SLEEVES

GAUNTLET GLOVES

SLAG

SLAGGING BAR

LADLE

HEAT-PROOF LEGGINGS

HIGH LEATHER SHOES

MOLD

SAFETY NOTE

In the case of magnesium, a coverall flux is **required** to keep the metal from burning. Because of this danger, use of magnesium is not recommended for school shops.

Aluminum, zinc, and lead alloys do not require a coverall flux.

Light the furnace and allow it to preheat with a low flame. Then bring the flame up to full heat. After the initial charge of metal has melted, add as much clean, dry metal as is needed for the pour.

SAFETY NOTE

Never allow moisture to enter a pot of liquid metal. The moisture rapidly turns to steam and can cause the molten metal to **explode.**

When the desired amount of metal has melted, check its temperature often to guard against overheating.

Just before pouring, use a slagging bar to skim the **slag** or **dross** from the top of the molten metal (Fig. 36-5). Slag or dross is the waste material that floats on the melted metal. It contains impurities such as sand, scale, and dirt, and metal that has combined with oxygen and nitrogen from the surrounding air during melting.

Slag has a dull appearance. It is beneficial because it protects the underlying metal from combining with oxygen and nitrogen in the air. However, **it must not be poured into the mold.**

 Pouring Temperature and Superheat

If melted metal is poured into the mold at too low a temperature, it may solidify before it has completely filled the mold cavity. When this happens, the metal is said to have been "poured cold." This is more likely to happen with molds that have thin sections through which melted metal must flow to fill the mold.

On the other hand, there are several disadvantages if the metal is poured too hot:

1. The castings are coarse-grained and weak. This condition occurs because the molten metal absorbs hydrogen gas from the air in the furnace. When the metal cools and hardens, it is filled with many small holes.
2. Time, fuel, and heat are wasted.
3. The mold is more likely to be damaged when the metal is poured.
4. The metal becomes more dangerous to handle.

The proper temperature to pour metal is called the **pouring temperature.** The pouring temperature depends on the kind of metal being used, the shape of the mold, and the number of molds to be poured. If several molds are to be poured, the melted metal may be hot enough for the first molds, but too cold for the last mold.

The pouring temperature of a metal is often given in terms of its **superheat.** Superheat is the number of degrees above the melting temperature. For example, aluminum melts at 1218°F [659°C]. If it is poured into the mold when it reaches 1418°F [770°C], it is said to have 200°F [93°C] of superheat. In general, low pouring temperatures produce better castings. Table 7-2 gives the melting points of various metals.

 The Ladle

A ladle is used to transfer melted metal from a pot-type furnace to the mold (Fig. 36-5).

SAFETY NOTE

Keep the ladle free from moisture. If there is moisture in the ladle, it will suddenly turn to steam when melted metal touches it. An explosion may result, causing bits of molten metal to spatter over a wide area.

Safe practice requires preheating of the ladle. This dries out the ladle and reduces the amount of heat absorbed by the ladle when molten metal is taken from the furnace.

36-6 Preparation for Pouring

The mold should be placed near the melting furnace so that the melted metal will not have to be carried far. Molds should be placed on a bed of dry sand at least an inch [25 mm] thick, the bed extending some distance beyond the molds on all sides. If there are several molds to be poured, place them in a row for convenience and safety of pouring. Place a **pig mold** after the last mold to accept the excess liquid metal (Fig. 36-6).

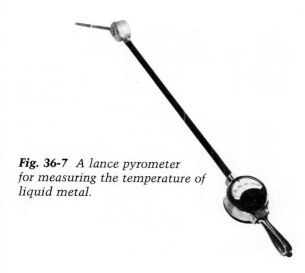

Fig. 36-6 *A pig mold made from channel iron with end plates welded on.*

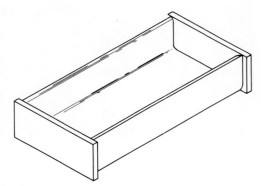

Fig. 36-7 *A lance pyrometer for measuring the temperature of liquid metal.*

SAFETY NOTE

All persons directly involved in the pouring should be dressed with the proper safety clothing. Set up a barrier to keep observers a safe distance away from the pouring area. See that there is a clear path from the furnace to the mold area. There should be nothing to stumble over or bump into while carrying the hot metal.

Before the melted metal reaches the pouring temperature, it should be decided who will handle and read the **pyrometer,** or temperature meter (Fig. 36-7); who will operate the furnace; who will handle the ladle; and who will direct the pourer. **It is desirable to make one or more practice runs to be sure that everyone knows his or her job and is able to carry it out safely.**

36-7 Pouring the Mold

When the melted metal reaches the pouring temperature, the furnace is shut off. The crucible is then removed from the furnace with crucible tongs and placed in the crucible pouring tool (Fig. 36-8). The slag is skimmed off, and the person directing the pouring should direct the pourer to the mold that is to be poured first. This is done by giving clear, exact directions. The pourer should then pour the melted metal into the mold smoothly and steadily, keeping the **pouring basin** of the mold **full.** The stream of metal should be continuous until the mold is full.

Figure 36-9 shows the pouring of aluminum from a large crucible handled by two workers. Figure 36-10 shows molds on a conveyor line. A single worker, operating a ladle supported by an overhead crane, is pouring metal into the molds. The operator controls the crane mechanism. Thus, he can easily raise or lower the ladle, position the pouring spout over the mold, and tilt the ladle to control the rate of pouring.

Fig. 36-8 *Crucible lifting and pouring tools.*
(McEnglevan Heat Treating and Manufacturing Co.)

Fig. 36-9 *Pouring aluminum by hand into a sand mold.*

Fig. 36-10 *A single worker, operating a crane-supported ladle, can pour a continuous series of molds on a conveyor.* (John Deere)

36-8 Cleaning and Finishing the Casting

After the mold has cooled so that it can be handled safely, it can be broken apart and the casting removed. This is called the **shakeout operation.** In large foundries, the mold is put on a vibrating conveyor or table. The sand falls through the conveyor or table, leaving the casting (Fig. 36-11).

Fig. 36-11 *Molds being automatically dumped from tilting conveyor trucks onto the shakeout table.*

Fig. 36-12 *Cleaned castings emerging from a tumbling barrel onto a conveyor.*

Fig. 36-13 *This ductile iron casting for two crankshafts shows how it comes from the mold with the gating and riser systems attached.*

When the casting has been shaken out of the mold, it may still have much sand clinging to it. Before the casting can be machined, the sand must be removed. Several methods are used to clean castings. Among them are sand blasting, shot blasting, and tumbling.

In **sand blasting,** abrasive grains or glass beads are blown at high speed against the casting. The sand and scale on the casting are rubbed and blown away.

In **shot blasting,** small pellets of metal about the size of air rifle BBs called shot, are thrown against the casting.

In **tumbling,** small castings are put into large metal barrels and the barrel is revolved. The knocking and rubbing of the castings against each other removes the sand and scale (Fig. 36-12).

Before the casting becomes a **finished casting,** the sprues, gates, and risers (Fig. 36-13) must be sawed or broken off. Also, the **flash** and sharp edges that occur at the parting line must be removed with a grinder or file. The casting is then a finished casting.

REVIEW REVIEW REVIEW REVIEW REVIEW

Words to know

coverall flux	electric induction	pig mold	shot blasting
crucible	furnace	preheating	slag
crucible furnace	firebrick	pyrometer	slagging bar
crucible pouring	flash	sand blasting	soldering furnace
tool	flux	scale	superheat
crucible tongs	ladle	shakeout	tumbling
cupola furnace	oxides		
electric arc furnace			

Review questions

1. Describe how metal is melted in a crucible furnace.
2. Describe the operation of an electric arc furnace.
3. How is metal heated in an electric induction furnace?
4. Describe a cupola furnace.
5. List the special clothing that should be worn when melting and pouring metal.
6. Why is it important to pour metal at the proper temperature?
7. What is a ladle? Why should it be dry when used for pouring metal?
8. What is a pyrometer used for?
9. How should the metal be poured into the mold?
10. Describe what must be done to make a finished casting.

UNIT

37

Powder Metallurgy

Powder metallurgy (P/M) is the technology of producing metal parts by compressing metal powders in precision dies or molds. This process is usually done at room temperature, and produces a fragile **green compact**. "Green" means that the compacts are not yet hardened or **cured.** The compacts are then heated in a **sintering furnace** that has an **oxygen-free,** or **controlled,** atmosphere.

Sintering. Sintering (heating metals to elevated temperatures but not to their melting points) strengthens green compacts through bonding of the metal particles. Parts requiring high strength may be further compressed after sintering and may also be heat-treated. When so treated, the strength and density of the parts approach that of solid metal parts.

Density control. The quality of P/M parts depends largely on compacting the powders to a **uniform density.** Compacting pressures from 5 to 50 tons per square inch [68.95 to 689.48 MPa] may be used. In industry, however, most parts are compressed with between 10 and 30 tons per square inch [137.9 to 413.69 MPa]. Metal powders do not flow readily or uniformly when compressed even when mixed with lubricants. Therefore, a die with a single punch (Fig. 37-1A) is satisfactory only for parts with the simplest of shapes. To obtain uniform density, most parts require dies with one or more **upper** and **lower** punches (Fig. 37-1B).

Due to their complexity, P/M dies are expensive, and the process is generally not economical for less than 20,000 parts. P/M is therefore almost always a mass production process.

Powder-metal materials. Most powder-metal parts are made of iron-base or copper-base materials. The four main types of iron-base powders used are **straight iron, iron/carbon, iron/carbon/copper,** and **iron/copper.** Copper-base powders most widely used are **straight copper, copper/zinc, copper/tin,** and **copper/nickel/zinc.** P/M parts are also made of many other metals.

Advantages of the P/M process. Two unusual features make the P/M process especially important: 1) it enables materials to be combined that previously could not be combined, and 2) it permits parts of controlled **density** or **porosity** to be made. (Porosity is a measure of the amount of small holes, or **pores,** in a material.)

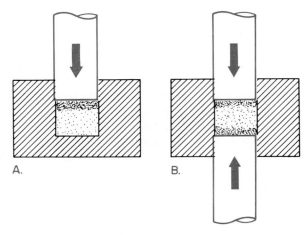

Fig. 37-1 *Compaction with a single punch (A) produces less uniform density than when both upper and lower punches are used (B).*

A.   B.

Fig. 37-2 *Typical parts made by powder metallurgy. (American Powder Industries Federation)*

Control of porosity is of particular advantage in making self-lubricating bearings and in the manufacture of filters. Porosity of P/M bearings is controlled so that they may be filled, or **impregnated,** with from 10 to 40 percent of oil by volume, an amount usually calculated to lubricate the bearing for life. Filters can be made to trap particles of selected size or to separate liquids of different densities.

The porosity of P/M parts may be eliminated by filling the pores with a metal of lower melting point, a process known as **infiltration.** Infiltration may be needed to effectively seal a part from leaking fluids or gases or to improve the mechanical properties of the part.

Uses of P/M parts. Typical examples of P/M parts include bearings, gears, cams, and levers; other drive mechanisms and mechanical parts; filters of various types; and magnets and magnetic cores for electrical and electronic uses (Fig. 37-2). P/M parts generally weigh less than a pound [0.45 kg], but parts up to four pounds [1.8 kg] are commonly made, and 100-pound [45.5 kg] parts are possible.

The largest user of P/M parts in the United States is the automotive industry, which uses over half of all P/M products.

REVIEW   REVIEW   REVIEW   REVIEW   REVIEW

WORDS TO KNOW

green compact	infiltration	P/M	sintering
impregnation	porosity	powder metallurgy	sintering furnace

REVIEW QUESTIONS

1. Explain how parts are made by powder metallurgy.
2. What are two special advantages of powder metallurgy? List several products that are made possible by these advantages.
3. What is the meaning of porosity in powder metallurgy?
4. What does impregnation of powder-metal parts mean?
5. Explain what infiltration of powder-metal parts means.

Anyone interested in chemistry has one of the basic requirements for a career in the heat treating of metals. Troy Carson attended an industrial high school, where he concentrated on chemisty, shop math, and drafting. When searching for a financially rewarding job, he found work as a trainee at a forging and heat-treating plant.

Troy progressed from trainee to heat-treating operator, then to technician trainee, then to heat-treating technician. It was a long, hard process, with each step requiring one or two years. Now, after 15 years at the plant, Troy is superintendent of all heat treating.

Noting that heat treating is based on the ancient skill of blacksmithing, Troy points out that enormous changes have taken place in the process. Time and temperature, mere guesswork in early days, are now controlled precisely.

On a particular project, Troy may bring oven temperature up to 1600°F. The metal remains in the oven for a precise period of time. Then it is quenched—immersed in water, oil, or molten salt—or air-cooled. Next it goes back into the oven, and the temperature is brought up to 500°F. This process gives the metal its initial hardness before tempering.

Troy is familiar with both the general properties of metals and the heat-treating requirements of specific products. Razor blades must be flexible, not brittle, while industrial files must be tough and hard. With his many years of experience, Troy matches treatment to product and makes sure it turns out the way it should.

Troy Carson
*Superintendent of Heat
Treating*

UNIT 38

Industrial Forging

Forging is the oldest of the metalworking processes. It consists of hammering or pressing metal into the desired shape, with or without the use of dies. Many small parts made of **ductile** metals are forged at room temperature. Large parts and metals of low ductility must be forged while hot to prevent cracking. Quantity production of forged parts is now done entirely with machines. **Hand forging** is limited largely to repair work and making custom parts.

38-1 Advantages and Disadvantages of Forging

When metal is hot, it is in a soft, **plastic** (pliable) state and forms easily under pressure without breaking. Other advantages include the following:

1. Forged parts are stronger than machined parts of the same material. Machining cuts through the **grain** of the metal (similar to the grain in wood). But forging causes the grain to follow the shape of the workpiece (Fig. 38-1). Metal is strongest in the direction of grain flow.
2. Strong parts of complex shape can be produced much more economically than by machining.
3. Since shape is produced by hammering or squeezing, not cutting, much less metal is lost in the process.

Forming does have disadvantages, however. These include:

1. The high forging temperatures cause rapid oxidation. This produces a surface scale that has a poor finish.
2. Because of scaling, close tolerances cannot be obtained.

38-2 Industrial Forging Processes

Several methods of forging have been developed, making it economical to forge one piece or thousands of interchangeable parts. They are:

1. drop forging
2. press forging
3. hammer or smith forging
4. upset forging
5. roll forging
6. swaging.

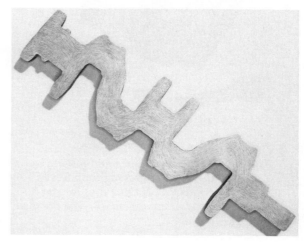

Fig. 38-1 *In a forged part, the grain of the metal follows the shape of the workpiece.* (National Machinery Company)

Drop forging. Drop forging is a mass production technique that hammers the metal between closed dies (Figs. 38-2 and 38-3). **Steam hammers** and **board hammers** are used for drop forging.

Half of the die is attached to the hammer and half to the anvil. The hot metal is placed in the lower half of the die and struck one or more times with the upper die. This forces the metal to flow in all directions, filling the die cavity.

Excess metal squeezed out between the die faces is called **flash.** After the forging is completed, the flash is cut off in another press with a **trimming die.**

Drop forging can produce parts ranging from a few ounces to hundreds of pounds in weight. Examples are such items as hand tools, fasteners, gear blanks, machine parts, chain hardware, and military hardware. Steel, aluminum, titanium and several other metals can be forged.

Fig. 38-2 *A gravity drop hammer. This type of hammer is widely used to produce drop forgings.*

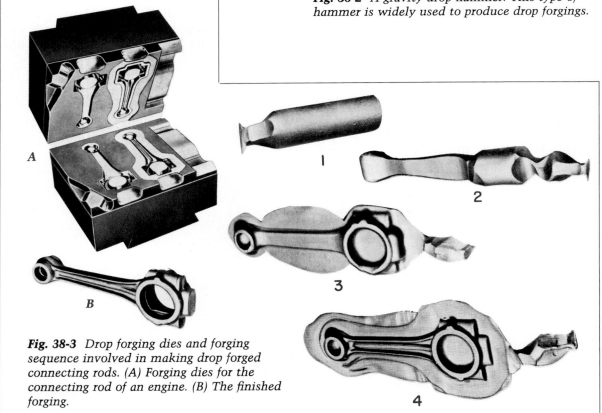

Fig. 38-3 *Drop forging dies and forging sequence involved in making drop forged connecting rods. (A) Forging dies for the connecting rod of an engine. (B) The finished forging.*

Press forging. In press forging, a slow squeezing action is used to form the metal. The slow squeezing action penetrates the entire workpiece, making possible the forging of large objects (Fig. 38-4). Press forges are made in sizes exceeding 50,000 tons [45,360 t] capacity. Those up to 16,000 tons [14,443 t] capacity may be either mechanically or hydraulically operated, but the larger presses are hydraulically powered.

Press forging may use either open or closed dies. **Open dies** are often simply flat surfaces between which the metal is squeezed, but they may also be V-shaped or slightly **convex** (rounded outward). Small parts are often forged in closed dies in one stroke. Larger parts may require one or more additional strokes.

Large objects such as train wheels, main spars for aircraft wings and aircraft landing gear parts are press-forged.

Hammer or smith forging. This type of forging is the same as is done by the **blacksmith,** except that the forging power comes from a steam or air hammer instead of a hammer swung by hand (Fig. 38-5). Open-frame steam hammers with capacities up to 5,000 pounds [2273 kg] or double-frame steam hammers with capacities up to 25,000 pounds [11,364 kg] are used.

In hammer forging both the anvil and hammer are flat, and the desired shape is obtained by turning the workpiece between hammer blows. Accessories may be used for punching holes, cutting off, and producing cylindrical shapes. Close accuracy cannot be obtained with hammer forging. Only parts of relatively simple shape can be made. Forgings of up to 100 tons [90.9t] can be made in this manner.

Fig. 38-5 *A double frame steam hammer.* (Chambersburg Engineering Co.)

Fig. 38-4 *A large hydraulic press forge in operation shaping a huge shaft.* (American Iron and Steel Institute)

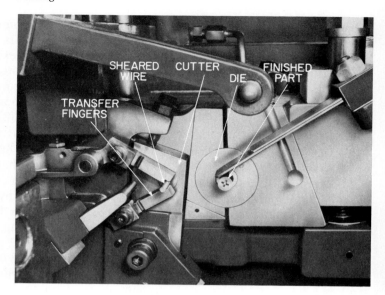

Fig. **38-6** *This cold heading machine produces recessed head screw blanks from wire.*

Upset forging. Upset forging, also called **hot heading,** is a process by which the cross-sectional size of a bar is increased, either at an end or at some point along its length. It is done on specially designed **upsetting** machines, using closed dies to control size and shape.

Typically, dies have several stations, and the part is formed by moving it from one die station or cavity to another until forging is complete.

Upset forging machines are made in several sizes: the largest is capable of handling bars ten inches [254 mm] in diameter. Heads of bolts, valves, single and cluster gear blanks, and artillery shells are examples of parts made by upset forging.

This same process, when done cold, is called **cold heading** (Fig. 38-6). Cold heading makes possible the economical mass production of fasteners such as nails, machine and wood screws, bolts, rivets, hinge pins, and other small parts (Fig. 38-7).

Roll forging. The purpose of roll forging is to reduce or taper the diameter or thickness of a bar, thereby increasing its length (Fig. 38-8). It is done on a machine that uses cylindrical dies with grooves of various shapes and sizes. This process is used for making such parts as leaf springs, axles, shafts, levers, tapered tubing, and aircraft propeller blade blanks.

Swaging. Swaging is a forging method used for sizing, pointing, tapering, and otherwise shaping the ends of rod or tubing (Fig. 38-9). Swaging is done in machines like the one shown in Figure 38-10.

Fig. **38-7** *Parts formed by cold heading.* (National Machinery Corp.)

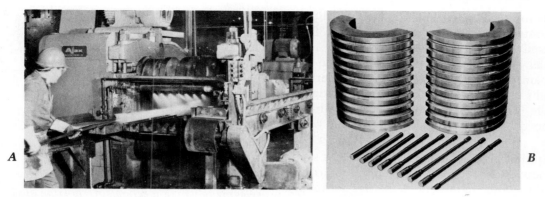

Fig. 38-8 *Roll forging. (A) This roll-forging machine produces I-beam axles for trucks. (B) These half-round forging dies produced the axles shown below the dies.*

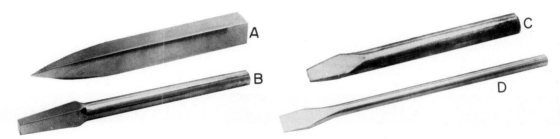

Fig. 38-9 *Some different shapes produced by swaging. (A) Harrow spike. (B) Auger bit shank. (C) Soldering iron tip. (D) Screwdrive blade.* (Fenn Manufacturing Co.)

Fig. 38-10 *A swaging machine.* (Fenn Manufacturing Co.)

In **rotary die swaging,** the forming dies in the center of the machine spindle (Fig. 38-11) are held between blocks of metal that function as hammers. A **spindle** carries the dies and hammers. As it revolves, the hammers are brought into action by rollers surrounding the spindle. This results in a series of rapid blows to the dies, which quickly shape the workpiece.

Stationary die swaging operates in a similar manner, except that the spindle carrying the dies and hammers remains stationary while the rollers are rotated. This allows the shaping of parts that do not have round cross-sections.

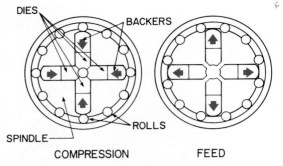

Fig. 38-11 *A diagram of a stationary die swaging machine mechanism, showing dies, hammer blocks, and rolls.*

REVIEW REVIEW REVIEW REVIEW REVIEW

WORDS TO KNOW

board hammer
closed dies
cold heading
drop forging

flash
grain
hammer or smith
   forging
hot heading

open dies
press forging
roll forging
rotary die swaging

stationary die
   swaging
steam hammer
swaging
upset forging

REVIEW QUESTIONS

1. What is forging?
2. List three advantages and three disadvantages of forging.
3. Describe the drop-forging process. Name some familiar objects that are made by drop forging.
4. How does press forging differ from drop forging? What kinds of parts are made by press forging?
5. What is meant by hammer or smith forging? How accurate is this forging process?
6. Describe how upset forging is done. Name some objects that are made by upset forging.
7. What kind of shaping is done by roll-forging machines?
8. What is meant by swaging and how is it done?
9. Name several common objects made by swaging.

UNIT
39
Hand Forging

Hand forging is now done chiefly by service workers who maintain production equipment, tools, and machines. It is also done occasionally in the construction of **pilot models** of products, or **prototypes.**

39-1 Equipment for Hand Forging

Heat sources. Metal to be forged is usually heated either in a gas furnace (Fig. 39-1) or in a gas forge (Fig. 39-2). **Care must be taken when lighting this equipment.** Automatic lighting systems with electrical ignition are safest. The lighting procedure generally calls for the following steps:

1. Switch on the **blower motor** (but keep the **air valve** closed).
2. Open the **gas valve** partially.
3. Immediately ignite the gas either electrically or with a torch made of a rolled-up paper towel placed in the **combustion chamber.**

SAFETY NOTE
Under no circumstances should gas be allowed to accumulate in a furnace chamber before it is ignited, since an explosion will result.

4. Open the air and gas valves as far as necessary to obtain a clean-burning flame of the desired size.
5. When turning the forge or furnace off, **always shut off the gas first,** then the air.

Fig. 39-1 *A gas furnace.* (Johnson Gas Appliance Company)

Fig. 39-2 *A gas-fired forge.* (Johnson Gas Appliance Company)

The anvil. In hand forging, metal is hammered to shape on an anvil (Fig. 39-3). The anvil **body** is made of soft steel, but the **face** is made of hardened steel and is welded to the body.

The **horn** is shaped like a cone and is tough and unhardened. Rings, hooks, and other curved parts are formed on it.

The **cutting block** is between the face and the horn. Its surface is not hardened. Metal may be cut upon it with a cold chisel; the face should not be used for cutting.

The **hardy hole** is a square hole in the face of the anvil. Various tools can be mounted in the hole for different kinds of work.

The **pritchel hole** is the small, round hole in the face of the anvil. It is used for bending small rods.

Anvils weigh from a few pounds or kilograms to as much as 300 pounds [139 kg]. An anvil weighing between 100 and 200 pounds [45 and 90 kg] is suitable for school use. It should be fastened securely to a stable wood or metal base that will position the face of the anvil about 30" [760 mm] from the floor.

Hand-forging tools. **Tongs** are used to hold and handle hot metal (Fig. 39-4). Two of the most commonly used types of tongs are listed in the next column.

1. **Straight-lip tongs,** also called **flat-jawed tongs**—used to hold flat work.
2. **Curved-lip tongs,** sometimes called **bolt tongs**—used to hold round work, such as bolts or rivets. The opening behind the jaws allows space for the head of a bolt.

These are made in several sizes for holding work of different diameters.

Always use tongs that grip the work firmly (Fig. 39-5). A ring, or link, may be slipped over the handles to hold them together, relieving this stress from the worker. The job will be made more difficult if the tongs do not fit the work. There is also the danger of the hot workpiece slipping from the tongs and injuring the worker. The tongs should never be left in the fire with the work; they are ruined by repeated heated and cooling.

For light forging work, ball peen and cross peen hammers are used. For heavier work, a blacksmith's hand hammer is used (Fig. 39-6).

Fig. 39-4 *Forging tongs.*

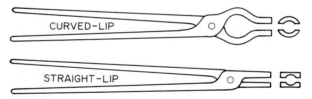

Fig. 39-3 *An anvil for hand forging.*

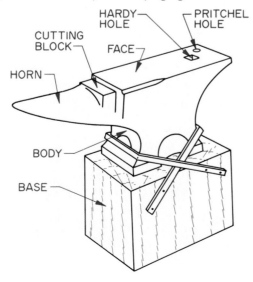

Fig. 39-5 *Holding a workpiece with tongs.*

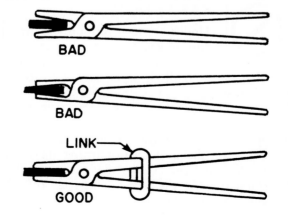

39-2 Forging Temperature

Forging calls for heating the workpiece well above the **upper critical temperature** but short of a temperature that would produce extreme **grain coarsening**—which, in turn, would weaken the metal. (Unit 41 gives de-tailed information on the effect of temperature on metal grain.) An experienced worker can tell the approximate temperature of steel by its color. As steel is heated, the first **incandescent** color (color produced by heat) to appear in daylight is a **dark red** at about 1,050°F [565.5°C]. This is followed by **cherry,** or **bright red,** then **orange, yellow,** and finally **white** at about 2,200°F [1204.4°C]. At this point it begins to throw off sparks—which indicates **forge welding heat.** Table 39-1 gives the incandescent colors of steel and their corresponding temperatures.

Forging should be done when the metal is heated between bright red and yellow. If hammered at a lower temperature, **work hardening** can occur and the metal may crack or split. The metal should be heated no longer than necessary so as to minimize the production of surface scale and loss of surface carbon. (Section 41-13 contains a discussion of surface carbon.)

Fig. 39-6 Hammers used in forging.

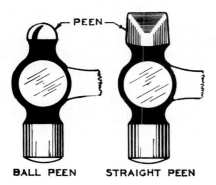

BALL PEEN   STRAIGHT PEEN

CROSS PEEN

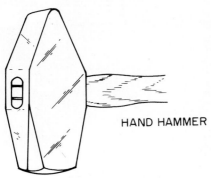

HAND HAMMER

39-3 Hand-forging Techniques

Forge welding is the joining of two pieces of metal by (1) making them soft and pasty with heat and (2) pressing, hammering, or melting them together. Wrought iron and steel containing up to .50% carbon can easily be welded.

Table 39-1

Incandescent Colors and Corresponding Temperatures of Steel

Color	Temp. F. (Celsius)
Faint Red	900 (482)
Blood Red	1,050 (566)
Dark Cherry Red	1,175 (635)
Medium Cherry Red	1,250 (677)
Cherry or Full Red	1,375 (746)
Bright Red	1,550 (843)
Salmon	1,650 (899)
Orange	1,725 (941)
Lemon Yellow	1,825 (996)
Light Yellow	1,975 (1079)
White	2,200 (1204)

Scale must be kept from forming if a good weld is to be made. **Flux** is used for this purpose. There are many kinds of fluxes. Clean **sharp sand** is a good flux for wrought iron; powdered **borax** is good for steel. (Borax is a white crystalline chemical, hydrated sodium borate, $Na_2B_4O_7 \cdot 10H_2O$, that has several industrial and home uses.) The flux may be sprinkled with a long-handled spoon on the hot metal where the weld is to be made. It melts and keeps air away from the hot workpiece. Otherwise, oxygen in the air would combine with the metal surface to form scale.

There are different kinds of forged welds. Only the **fagot weld** is described here. **Fagot** means to make a bundle; to tie together in a

The Blacksmith and the Magic Anvil

Metal, particularly iron, has played an important part in the superstitions of the past. The village blacksmith was a central figure in many of these beliefs.

The traditional use of horseshoes to bring good luck dates back to tenth-century England. It was said that Dunstan, the patron saint of blacksmiths, was visited one night by the devil, who needed a new shoe on one of his split hooves. The smith recognized his customer, grabbed the devil by the nose with a pair of hot tongs, and tied him to the wall. Then Dunstan put new shoes on the devil, hurting him so much that the evil one promised to never again enter a building that displayed a horseshoe.

Villagers believed that the sound of the blacksmith's anvil would keep away demons and witches. The steel face on a good anvil rang like a bell when the blacksmith struck it. Every Saturday night at closing time, the smith hit the anvil three times to keep evil away from the shop. Extra-careful blacksmiths kept the spell in force during the week by striking the anvil an extra blow every fourth stroke when shaping horseshoes.

But the blacksmith's "magic" went beyond keeping away "evil spirits." The smith's shop was thought to have healing powers as well. For example, people believed that they would be cured of warts if they dipped their hands in the blacksmith's water trough.

Other "magic" was performed on sick children. The first step was to place the child on the anvil. Then the blacksmith pounded the horn of the anvil sharply to drive out the sickness. In a more elaborate cure, the child was laid on the anvil after being bathed in the smith's trough. Then three blacksmiths with the same name passed iron tools over the child.

Variations of these and other superstitions existed in all parts of the world. Of course, blacksmiths did much more ordinary and routine work. But the "magic" of iron and the anvil made the smith a respected, "mystical" member of the community.

TECHNOLOGIES AND PRACTICES

bundle, as a bundle of sticks. A fagot weld is made as follows:

1. Heat two pieces of iron to a bright red and put on the flux.
2. Heat to forge **welding heat.** The pieces must be heated evenly so that the inside will be as hot as the outside.
3. Lay them on top of each other on the anvil and quickly strike a few light blows in the center to make them stick. Continue hammering until they are welded together (Fig. 39-7A).

SAFETY NOTE

Contact with the hot metal causes burns, and the scale flies off when a workpiece is hammered. During the forging process, do not touch the metal; wear goggles, gloves, and protective clothing.

The more often the metal is heated, the harder it is to weld. More pieces may be welded on, one at a time. Another way to make a fagot weld is to bend or fold the end of a piece of metal once or twice and weld it into a solid lump (Fig. 39-7B).

Upsetting means to thicken or bulge. A bar may be **upset** by heating the end to a **welding heat** then placing it, hot end down, on the top of the anvil and striking the other end with a hammer (Fig. 39-8). If the bar is long, it may be grasped with both hands (if cool enough), and the end can be **rammed** upon the anvil.

Heading means to form a **head** as on a rivet or bolt. It is done with a **heading tool** and a hammer (Fig. 39-9). The heading tool has a hole that is slightly **tapered.** There should be a heading tool for each size of rod. The hole should be about 1/32" [0.8 mm] larger than the rod for rods up to 1/2" [12.7 mm] in diameter and a little larger as the diameter is increased.

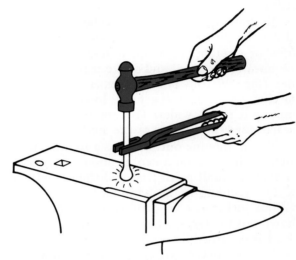

Fig. 39-8 Upsetting by hammering.

Fig. 39-9 Heading using a heading tool and hammer.

Fig. 39-7 Forged (fagot) welds.

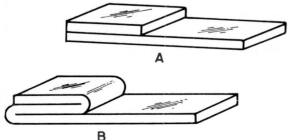

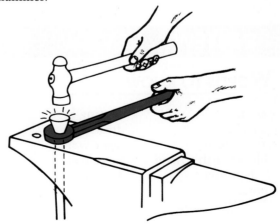

The steps for heading are listed below:

1. **Upset** the end of the bar.
2. Slip the bar into the small end of the hole in the heading tool and into the **hardy hole.**
3. Strike heavy blows with the hammer until the head is the right thickness.
4. Finish the sides of the head on the face of the anvil with a hammer. Heads of different shapes may be formed this way.

Drawing out metal means to stretch or lengthen it by hammering. The tapered part of a flat cold chisel is an example of metal that is drawn out.

In drawing, the metal must be heated until it is bright red; otherwise, it will crack. To draw or stretch the metal quickly, lay it on the **horn** of the anvil and strike it with a hammer (Fig. 39-10). This makes a number of **notches** and makes the piece longer without making it much wider. The notches can then be **flattened** on the face of the anvil.

When drawing out metal to a round point, such as the type on a center punch, it is best to make a small point first and then lengthen it. The point must be hammered only while red-hot; otherwise, it will tear. It should be drawn out in stages, as shown in Figure 39-11. The bar is turned for each blow of the hammer so that the metal will be uniformly drawn to a point.

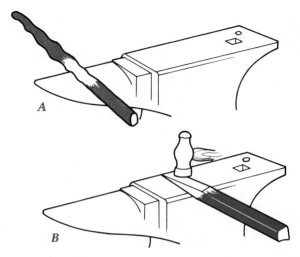

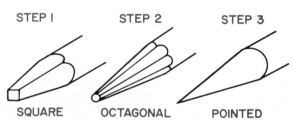

Fig. 39-10 *Drawing out metal. (A) Stretching the metal. (B) Flattening the metal.*

STEP 1   STEP 2   STEP 3

SQUARE   OCTAGONAL   POINTED

Fig. 39-11 *Steps in drawing a round bar to a point.*

REVIEW   REVIEW   REVIEW   REVIEW   REVIEW

WORDS TO KNOW

anvil	cutting block	hardy	pritchel hole
anvil face	drawing out	hardy hole	tongs
anvil horn	fagot weld	heading	upsetting
blacksmith's hand hammer	forge weld	incandescent	work hardening
borax	gas forge		

(Review Continued)

REVIEW QUESTIONS

1. How is metal usually heated for forging?
2. Describe a safe lighting and shutoff procedure for a gas furnace or forge.
3. What part of an anvil is made of hardened steel? Why?
4. On what part of an anvil is cutting done?
5. Name the two holes in an anvil and tell how they are used.
6. Which tongs are made especially for holding flat stock? Round stock?
7. What is the safe temperature range for forging steel?
8. What may happen to metal that is forged too cold?
9. Tell how forge welding is done.
10. Describe how to upset and make a square head on the end of a round bar.
11. What is meant by drawing out metal? How is it done?

UNIT
40
Extrusion

Extrusion is the process of shaping solid metal by forcing it under high pressure through an opening in a die. Extrusion may be **forward** or **reverse** (Fig. 40-1). Extruded shapes may be **solid** or **hollow,** and the process may be done **hot** or **cold.**

In **hot extrusion,** the metal **blank** (the unformed shape) is softened by preheating. This lowers the pressure required for forming. It also makes possible extrusions of complex shapes. Most hot extrusions are made in hydraulically powered horizontal presses (Fig. 40-2). Extrusion lengths of 20 feet [6 m] are common, and some machines are capable of

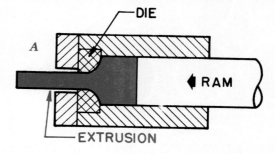

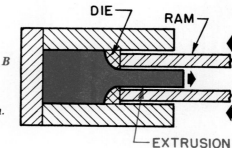

Fig. 40-1 *The two basic methods of extrusion. (A) Forward extrusion. (B) Reverse extrusion.*

Fig. 40-2 *Extruded metal stock emerging from an extruding machine.*

making 50-foot [15-m] lengths. Typical hot-extruded products are moldings of brass and aluminum, rods, bars, tubes, and structural shapes of aluminum and steel (Fig. 40-3). Aluminum extrusions may be as large as 2 feet [610 mm] in diameter, but steel extrusions are limited to about 6 inches [152 mm] in diameter.

Cold extrusion is usually done with the metal at room temperature, although some metals, such as magnesium, are heated a few hundred degrees Fahrenheit [about 150°C]. The pressures required for cold extrusion are several times higher than those for hot extrusion, which limits its use to making small and medium-size parts. Cold extrusions must also have a **uniform wall thickness** throughout and be of **balanced** or **symmetrical cross-section.**

Parts may be cold-extruded from aluminum, steel, brass, copper, tin, magnesium, lead, zinc, and titanium. Examples include tubular aluminum cans for food, beverages, and photographic film; and steel ammunition projectile casings, hydraulic cylinders, and wrist pins.

Impact extrusion is a form of cold extrusion. It is used mainly for the manufacture of metal tubes for packaging toothpaste and similar products and for beverage containers (Fig. 40-4). The tube begins as a solid disc of metal at the bottom of a closed die cavity. A punch strikes the disc a sharp blow. This causes the metal to squirt backwards up the sides of the punch, thus forming the **tube.** The **blank thickness** determines the length of the tube. After the punch is withdrawn from the die cavity, the tube is blown off the punch by air pressure. The process is very fast, with production rates reaching as high as 80 tubes per minute. Many aluminum, brass, and steel containers are made this way.

Fig. 40-3 *These shapes for electric motor housings made through the aluminum extrusion process save both labor and energy.* (Reynolds Metals Co.)

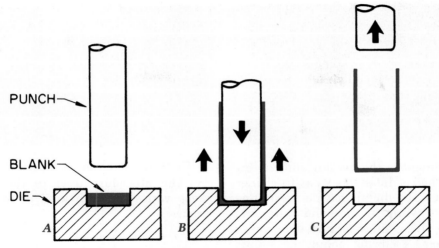

Fig. 40-4 *The impact extrusion sequence. (A) The blank inserted in a die. (B) Extrusion. (C) Separation of the tube from the punch.*

REVIEW   REVIEW   REVIEW   REVIEW   REVIEW

WORDS TO KNOW

balanced cross- section	blank cold extrusion	forward extrusion hot extrusion	impact extrusion reverse extrusion

REVIEW QUESTIONS

1. Explain the process of extrusion.
2. Explain the difference between forward and reverse extrusion.
3. List three advantages of hot extrusion over cold extrusion.
4. List several products familiar to you that are made by extrusion.
5. What is a common length extrusions are made to?
6. What are the largest diameter extrusions possible with aluminum and steel?
7. Explain the impact-extrusion process.
8. What kinds of products are made by impact extrusion?

UNIT 41

Heat Treatment of Steel

Heat treatment is the heating and cooling of metals in their solid states so as to change their properties. All metals have a crystalline grain structure while in the solid state, and the nature of the grain structure determines their properties. To bring about the proper grain structure, and thus produce the desired properties, the metals are heated and cooled in different ways. The common properties of metals are described in Unit 2.

The grain structure of steel may be changed in several ways by heat treatment. The properties of steel that can be changed by heat treatment include hardness, brittleness, toughness, tensile strength, ductility, malleability, machinability, and elasticity.

41-1 Heat-treatment Processes

Following are the principal kinds of heat treatment processes:

1. hardening
2. tempering
3. annealing
4. normalizing
5. spheroidizing
6. case-hardening
7. flame hardening
8. induction hardening.

All heat-treatment processes involve heating and cooling metal according to a time-temperature cycle that includes the following three steps:

1. Heating the metal to a certain temperature.
2. Holding the metal at this elevated temperature for a certain period of time. (This is called **soaking.**)
3. Cooling the metal at a certain rate.

The procedure used in the above three steps varies for each kind of heat-treatment process.

41-2 Furnaces and Temperature Control

The various heat-treatment processes require that steel parts be heated to precise temperatures. The parts are usually heated in temperature-controlled furnaces. However, the parts may also be heated with an open flame from a portable gas torch or an oxyacetylene welding torch.

Kinds of Furnaces

Electric heat-treatment furnaces are capable of providing heats to temperatures within a range from 300° to 2300°F [149° to 1260°C]. Figure 41-1 shows a pair of electric furnaces: a high-temperature furnace for hardening and a low-temperature furnace for tempering.

A **gas-fired heat-treatment furnace,** which heats to temperatures up to 2300°F [1260°C], is shown in Figure 41-2. A **gas-fired pot-type liquid-hardening furnace** is shown in Figure 41-20. This kind of furnace heats salt, lead, and cyanide baths for liquid case-hardening processes and for other special heat-treating processes. An ordinary **bench-type** gas furnace, such as the kind that is often used for heating soldering coppers (Fig. 27-2) also may be used to heat small parts for heat treating.

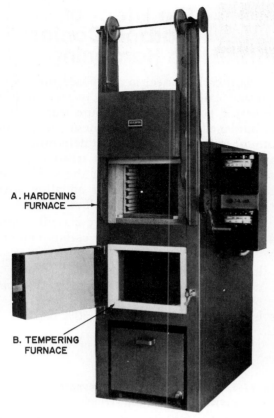

A. HARDENING
FURNACE

B. TEMPERING
FURNACE

Fig. 41-1 *An electric heat treating furnace with separate chambers for hardening and tempering. The furnace is equipped with automatic temperature controllers.*

Fig. 41-2 *A gas-fired heat treatment furnace equipped with an automatic temperature controller.* (Johnson Gas Appliance)

Fig. 41-3 *A temperature-indicating furnace controller.* (Honeywell)

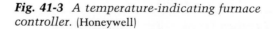

Temperature Control

For best results, heat-treatment furnaces should be equipped with temperature-indicating control devices (Fig. 41-3). With controls of this type the desired temperature is set with a control knob. The furnace then heats to the desired temperature and maintains this temperature within a few degrees. It turns the gas or electric current on and off as necessary to hold a steady temperature. The furnaces in Figures 41-1 and 41-2 are equipped with temperature-indicating controls.

Temperature Colors

When clean, bright steel is heated, various colors appear at different temperatures, as shown in Table 41-1. These colors are helpful if the furnace used for heat treating is not equipped with a temperature-indicating and control device. The temperature can be estimated by observing the color of the steel as it is heated. This is the way old-time blacksmiths determined the temperature of steel for heat-treatment purposes. **This method, however, is not very accurate.** Without skill and experience, the temperature-reader can easily be off 20 to 30°F [10 to 15°C] in the range from 375° to 600°F [191 to 312°C].

Temperature-indicating Material

An inexpensive way to determine temperatures of heated steel is through the use of temperature-indicating pellets, crayons, or paints (Fig. 41-4). These materials are made to melt at various temperatures from 100 to 2500°F [38 to 1371°C]. Simply select the crayon or other material that is designed to melt at the desired temperature. Rub the crayon or other identifying material on the workpiece. When it is heated to the desired temperature, the identifying materal will melt, thus indicating the temperature of the workpiece.

Table 41-1

Typical Tempering Temperatures for Various Tools

Degrees °F (°C)	Temper color	Tools
380 (193)	Very light yellow	Tools that require maximum hardness: lathe centers and cutting tools for lathes and shapers
425 (218)	Light straw	Milling cutters, drills and reamers
465 (241)	Dark straw	Taps, threading dies, punches, dies, and hacksaw blades
490 (254)	Yellowish-brown	Hammer faces, shear blades, rivet sets, and wood chisels
525 (274)	Purple	Center punches and scratch awls
545 (285)	Violet	Cold chisels, knives, and axes
590 (310)	Pale blue	Screwdrivers, wrenches, and hammers

41-3 The Effect of Carbon Content on Hardening

Plain carbon steel is composed mainly of iron and carbon. The carbon in steel makes hardening possible because pure iron cannot be hardened by heat treatment. **It is the amount of carbon content that determines the maximum hardness that heat treatment will produce.** This is true whether the steel is an alloy mainly with carbon or an alloy with other metallic elements as well as carbon.

The plain carbon steels are classified into three groups according to the carbon content by weight:

1. low-carbon steel, 0.05 to 0.30% carbon;
2. medium-carbon steel, 0.30 to 0.60% carbon;
3. high-carbon steel, 0.60 to 1.50% carbon.

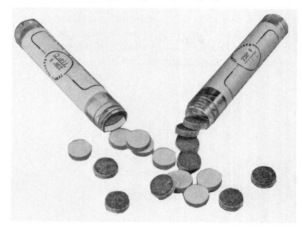

Fig. 41-4 *Temperature-indicating materials: pellets, crayons, and liquid.* (Tempil°)

The **high-carbon steels** can be made very hard, brittle, or tough by heat treatment. Some metal-cutting tools, such as drills, milling cutters, taps, and dies, are made of high-carbon steel with carbon content ranging from approximately 0.90 to 1.10%. See Table 6-1.

The **medium-carbon steels** can be made relatively hard by heat treatment. However, they cannot be hardened sufficiently to make drills, taps, threading dies, or similar metal-cutting tools. Some uses of medium-carbon steels are also shown in Table 6-1. The hardness of metals can be measured with instruments, as explained in Unit 94.

Figure 41-5 compares the maximum hardness obtainable for 1045 steel (a medium-carbon steel) and 1095 steel (a high-carbon steel) according to the commonly used Rockwell hardness scale. Before tempering, the 1095 steel was hardened to a Rockwell hardness of C-66. The 1045 steel was hardened to Rockwell C-59. A hardness of Rockwell C-60 or higher, **after tempering,** is generally required for metal-cutting tools such as drills and files. Rockwell hardness is explained in Unit 94.

Low-carbon steels can be hardened only a small amount by direct hardening. However, a thin outside case on these steels can be hardened by **case-hardening.** Uses for low-carbon steels are shown in Table 6-1.

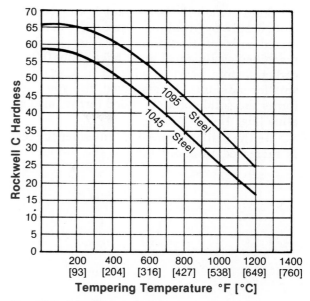

Fig. 41-5 *The effect of various tempering temperatures on the hardness of carbon steel. The surface hardnesses of carbon steel bars, SAE 1045 steel 3/4" (19.05 mm) square and SAE 1095 steel 1/2" (12.7 mm) diameter, after tempering at various temperatures are shown by the curves. Both steels were hardened in water quench, the 1045 steel at 1500° F (816° C) and the 1095 steel at 1450° F (788° C).*

Fig. 41-6 *A microscopic view of pearlite magnified 2500 times. Dark areas are cementite (iron carbide) and light areas are ferrite (nearly pure iron).* (USX Corporation)

41-4

Form of Carbon

Knowledge about the form of carbon helps to understand hardening and other heat treatment processes. At temperatures below 1330°F [721°C], the carbon in unhardened steel combines chemically with iron to form iron carbide (FeC), also called **cementite.** In unhardened steel, the cementite is normally a mechanical mixture with **ferrite** (nearly pure iron). This mixture of tiny, platelike layers of ferrite and cementite is called **pearlite** (Fig. 41-6).

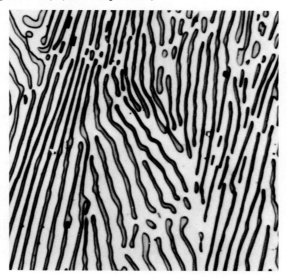

Solid cementite is so hard it can be machined only by grinding. However, when it is mixed with soft ferrite, as in pearlite, it can be machined easily. Steel must have about 0.03% carbon before pearlite will form. Carbon in smaller amounts is dissolved in iron, and forms the solid solution called ferrite, also an alloy (Fig. 41-7).

As the carbon content in unhardened steel is increased to about 0.80%, the amount of pearlite also increases. The strength of unhardened steel also increases as the amount of pearlite increases. When hardened by heat treatment, hardness increases with the amount of pearlite, up to about 0.80%. **Higher carbon contents contribute greater wear resistance to the steel, but not hardness.** Steel with 0.80% carbon is called **eutectoid steel.** In the unhardened condition, its grain structure is all pearlite.

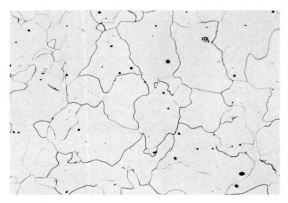

Fig. 41-7 *Ferrite (alpha iron) magnified 100 times. The dark spots are impurities that are not chemically combined with the iron. Such foreign matter is said to be in the form of inclusions.* (USX Corporation)

41-5 Iron-Carbon Phase Diagram

The relationship between the amount of carbon and the grain structure of steel can be seen in the iron-carbon phase diagram in Fig. 41-8. When steel is heated to certain temperatures, the form and distribution of the carbon changes. At the same time, the grain structure also undergoes transformations called **phase changes.** The diagram shows the temperatures at which these changes occur.

Fig. 41-8 *The phase diagram for carbon steels.*

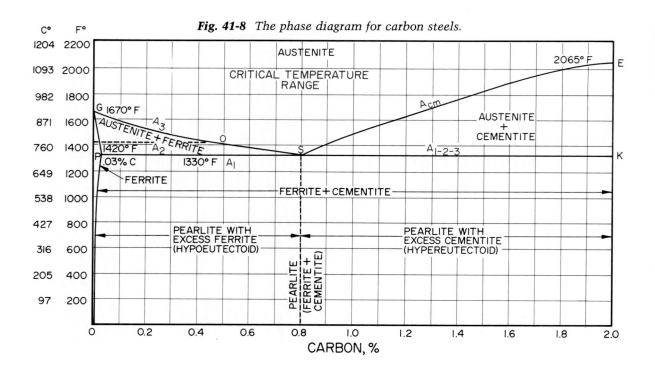

Eutectoid steel, which is all pearlite at temperatures below 1330°F [721°C], is represented by the dotted line extending downward from the letter S. The term "eutectoid" is given to the steel with such a composition that it has the lowest upper and lower transformation temperature. The line A_1, labeled PSK, represents the **lower transformation temperature** of 1330°F [721°C]. This temperature is also known as the **lower critical temperature.** The line A_3, labeled GOSK, represents the **upper transformation temperature,** also known as the **upper critical temperature. Note that the upper critical temperature decreases as the carbon content of the steel increases toward 0.80%.** The temperature range between lines A_1 and A_3 is called the **transformation or critical temperature range.** It is so named because of the structural change that takes place in the steel within this range.

The dotted line designated A_2 indicates the **magnetic point,** 1420°F [771°C]. Above this temperature, steel is no longer magnetic. The magnetic point also continues along line OSK. The hardening temperature of medium and high carbon steel, therefore, may be estimated with a magnet if more accurate temperature measuring equipment is not available.

Note also that for steels with carbon contents above 0.80%, lines A_1, A_2, and A_3 are the same (line SK).

At temperatures below line A_1, the iron in steel has the body-centered cubic lattice structure called **alpha iron** (Fig. 41-9). When steel is heated to temperatures above line A_1, the grain structure begins to change to the face-centered cubic lattice structure called **gamma iron** (Fig. 41-10). This form of iron is called **austenite** (Fig. 41-11). Transformation to austenite continues as the temperature of the steel is increased from line A_1 to line A_3. At line A_3, transformation to austenite is complete.

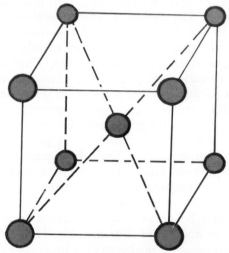

Fig. 41-9 *Alpha iron (ferrite) has eight atoms arranged in the form of a cube around a ninth atom in the center. This is called a bodycentered, cubic unit arrangement of atoms.*

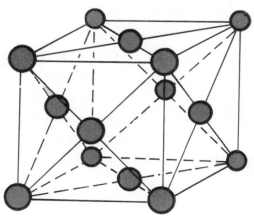

Fig. 41-10 *Gamma iron (austenite) has atoms arranged like the corners of a cube, with six of the atoms at the center of each side. This is called a facecentered, cubic unit arrangement of atoms.*

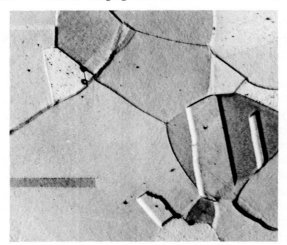

Fig. 41-11 *Austenite magnified 500 times.* (USX Corporation)

Austenite is a solid solution of carbon in face-centered cubic iron. When steel transforms to austenite, the carbon which was in a combined state breaks down into pure carbon and iron. The carbon is then absorbed in the iron in the form of a solid solution. In this form, the carbon is distributed evenly, just as sugar is when dissolved in water. This condition usually is necessary for obtaining maximum hardness when the steel is quenched.

When steel is heated to the proper temperature for hardening, the internal structure not only should be transformed to austenite; it must also possess a fine grain structure. In stress-relieved steel, the grain size is usually coarse at temperatures below line A_1. As the temperature is increased toward line A_3, the grain size becomes finer. The finest grain size exists at line A_3, as shown in Fig. 41-12. When the temperature of the steel is increased above line A_3, the grain size again starts to increase. Note that at temperatures more than 100°F [38°C] above line A_3, the grain size rapidly becomes coarse.

41-6 Martensite Formation

When high carbon steel is quenched at the critical temperature and cooled rapidly to a temperature below about 400°F [204°C], the

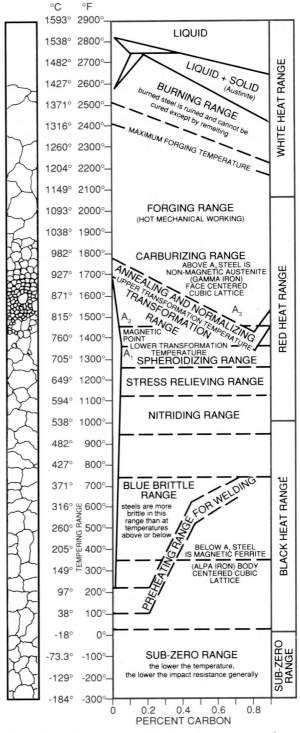

Fig. 41-12 *Ferrous metallurgy temperature and grain size chart.*

austenite transforms to a structure called **martensite** (Fig. 41-13). Martensite is the hardest and most brittle form of steel. It is a supersaturated solid solution of carbon in iron which has a body-centered tetragonal lattice arrangement (Fig. 41-14). Under high magnification, martensite has an extremely fine needle-like appearance. Pure martensite does not contain cementite. For maximum hardness after quenching, the grain structure of steel usually must be completely martensitic.

When steels are cooled slowly from the hardening temperature, austenite begins to transform to pearlite at temperatures below 1330°F [721°C]. The rate of transformation depends on the temperature. In carbon steels, austenite decomposes rapidly to pearlite after one second in the temperature range from 1000 to 1100°F [538 to 593°C]. After three seconds in this temperature range, transformation to pearlite is almost complete. Consequently, when carbon steels are quenched at the hardening temperature, they must be cooled below the 1000°F [538°C] temperature range in one second or less. So long as cooling through this range takes place in less than one second, several additional seconds may be allowed to cool the steel below 250°F [121°C].

Therefore, it is evident that the hardening process in steel is essentially the avoidance of pearlite grain formation while it is being quenched.

Hardening

Medium-carbon, high-carbon and most alloy steels are hardened by heating slowly to the proper **hardening temperature** (Fig. 41-15) and then cooling them rapidly. They are cooled rapidly by **quenching** in water, brine (salt water), or oil. Some alloy steels are quenched in air.

Fig. 41-14 *Martensite has a body-centered tetragonal unit arrangement of atoms. A tetragonal crystal system has three axes mutually at right angles with equal edges only on two lateral axes.*

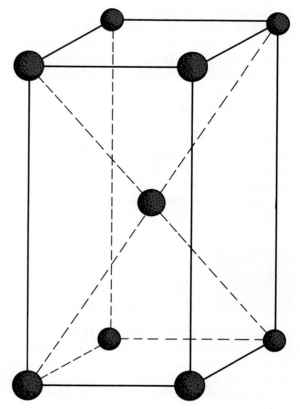

Fig. 41-13 *Martensite magnified 2500 times.* (USX Corporation)

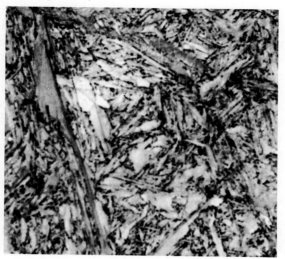

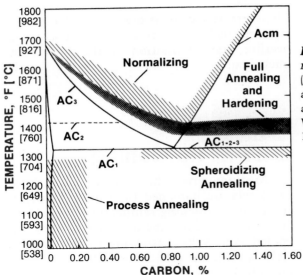

Fig. 41-15 *The recommended temperature ranges for heat treating plain carbon steels.* (Adapted from Thomas G. Digges, Samuel J. Rosenberg, and Glenn W. Geil, Heat Treatment Properties of Iron and Steel, National Bureau of Standards Monograph 88, Washington, D.C.: U.S. Government Printing Office, 1966.)

The hardness obtainable by heat treatment depends upon these factors:

1. The amount of carbon in the steel.
2. The temperature at which the steel is quenched (the hardening temperature).
3. The speed of cooling.

When high-carbon steel has been hardened, it becomes very brittle due to internal stresses that result from rapid cooling. In fact, it is frequently so brittle that if struck by a hammer it will crack or shatter. Therefore, a hardened piece of high-carbon steel requires an additional heat-treatment process, called *tempering*, before it can be used. **Hardened steel should be tempered immediately or as soon as possible after hardening.** Occasionally, hardened steel will crack if cooled improperly or if allowed to remain hardened but not tempered for a period of time.

41-8 Hardening Temperature

The **hardening temperature** is the temperature to which a piece of steel should be heated before quenching. The hardening temperatures for plain carbon steels are shown in the shaded area on the chart in Fig. 41-15. The

hardening temperature is 50 to 100°F [10 to 38°C] above line A₃, the upper critical temperature. Note that the proper hardening temperature depends on the carbon content of the steel. The more carbon the steel contains, up to 0.80%, the lower its hardening temperature.

At temperatures greater than 100°F [38°C] above the upper critical temperature, the grain rapidly becomes coarser. If the steel is cooled rapidly in this condition, it will be very hard and brittle and may crack. It will also lack the desired toughness after tempering. Hence, it is important that the hardening temperature be within the hardening temperature range.

41-9 Quenching Solutions

Steel is quenched in water, brine, oil, or air. Air, however, is only effective for quenching certain alloy steels. The rate of cooling is most rapid with brine, less rapid with water, slow with oil, and slowest in air. If steel is quenched and cooled too rapidly, it will crack. Brine or water should be at a temperature of about 60°F [16°C] for quenching purposes. Oil, unlike water, cools best when it is at a temperature of about 100 to 140°F [38 to 60°C]. Several kinds of oils are used as quenching solutions. A light grade of straight mineral oil is often recommended.

Plain-carbon steels are usually quenched in water or brine. Brine cools about twice as rapidly as water and tends to remove the scale from the steel. This causes the steel to cool more uniformly. **If small carbon steel parts vary in thickness, such as screw-driver blades or cold chisels, they often crack when quenched in water.** This is due to the uneven rate of cooling for thick and thin sections. Parts of this type may be quenched in oil. However, the parts will not be as hard after quenching in oil, which cools more slowly than water.

It is best to follow the steel manufacturers' recommendations when selecting quenching solutions for alloy steels or expensive tool steels. Most alloy steels are quenched in oil or air to prevent cracking.

Gas bubbles will form on the surface of hot metal when it is immersed in the quenching solution. These bubbles form a temporary insulation on the surface of the metal. As a result, the metal cools more slowly in that area. When steel is quenched, the parts should be **agitated** (moved about) in the solution. Either an **up-and-down** or a **figure-eight** movement should be used. The agitation causes the steel to cool evenly. This prevents cracks because the gas bubbles cannot stick to the metal's surface. **Very rapid agitation can double the cooling speed. Excessive agitation of small parts in a water or brine quench may cause cracking.**

41-10
Tempering

Tempering is often called **drawing** or **drawing the temper.** It is a heat-treatment process that relieves internal strain in hardened steel and thus increases its toughness. Properly tempered steel will not crack or break under heavy stress, vibration, or impact.

The hardness and toughness of steel are related to each other, but in **inverse proportion.** That is, the harder the steel, the more brittle it is; the softer the steel, the tougher it is. Thus, the toughness of **hardened** and **tempered** steel parts may be estimated, indirectly, by determining the hardness of the steel. Hardness testing is explained in Unit 94.

The problem in tempering is to determine the correct **tempering temperature.** The temperature to which steel is heated for tempering depends on the following factors:
1. the type of steel (carbon steel or special alloy steel)
2. the carbon content
3. the hardness required
4. the toughness required.

Recommended tempering temperatures and the color of polished steel at these temperatures are shown in Table 41-1. Tempering temperatures range from about 300 to 1100°F [145 to 593°C]. Most carbon-steel tools, however, are tempered in the range from 380 to 600°F [193 to 316°C]. Temperatures above 800°F [427°C] are used for tempering items that require extreme toughness and little hardness, such as medium-carbon steel parts for the steering mechanisms on automobiles.

Tempering procedure. Tempering should follow as soon as possible after hardening. The steel should be heated slowly and uniformly to the correct tempering temperature (see Table 41-1). The parts should be held at the tempering temperature (this is called **soaking**) for one hour per inch of part thickness. This provides time for necessary atomic rearrangement (internal changes) within the grain structure of the steel. **Parts ¼" [6.35 mm] or less in thickness do not require soaking.** After the required soaking period, the parts may be cooled in air, or they may be quenched in water.

41-11
Annealing

Annealing is a heat-treatment process that is used to soften steel. It relieves internal stress and strain that may have been caused by machining or previous heat treatment, or by cold-working operations such as rolling, stamping, and spinning. **Annealing, therefore, is the opposite of hardening.** Three kinds of annealing may be done:
1. full annealing
2. process annealing
3. spheroidizing annealing.

Full annealing. This process produces **maximum softness** in steel. The following procedure is used for full annealing:

1. Heat the steel uniformly to the **full-annealing temperature.** This temperature is 50 to 100°F [10 to 38°C] above the upper-transformation temperature represented by line A$_3$ in Figure 41-15. The full-annealing temperature range is within the same range of temperature as the hardening temperature range. It varies according to the carbon content of the steel.

2. Allow the steel to **soak** at the full-annealing temperature for about one hour per inch of part thickness.

3. Allow the steel to cool **very slowly.** It may be removed from the furnace and packed in ashes or lime for slow cooling, or the furnace may be shut off and the part allowed to cool in the slowly cooling furnace.

Process annealing. This process is often called **stress-relief annealing.** It is used for relieving stresses in steel due to cold-working processes such as machining, bending, or rolling. Process annealing is more frequently used with **low-carbon steels.** The following procedure is used for process annealing:

1. Heat the steel uniformly to a temperature ranging from 1000 to 1300°F [538 to 704°C] (Fig. 41-15).

2. Allow the part to soak at the desired temperature for a period of about one hour per inch of part thickness.

3. Remove the part from the furnace and allow it to cool in air.

Spheroidizing annealing. This process involves heating steel to relatively high temperatures, usually from 1300 to 1330°F [704 to 721°C] (Fig. 41-15). The steel is soaked at this temperature for several hours so that it will develop a grain structure in which almost all of the carbon is in tiny globules, or **spheres,** of iron carbide (Fe$_3$C) (Fig. 41-16). The grain thus formed is very soft and machinable. This process generally is applied to **high-carbon steels.** Steel annealed by this process should cool slowly to about 1000°F [538°C]. Below that temperature it may cool at any rate of speed.

41-12

Normalizing

Normalizing is a heat-treatment process in which steel is heated to the **normalizing temperature,** soaked at this temperature for a period of time, and allowed to cool in air. Normalizing relieves internal stresses in steel due to forging, machining, or cold working. It also removes the effects of other heat-treatment processes. It softens hardened steel and improves its machinability. It is somewhat similar to **annealing,** except that steel that is normalized is not as soft as when fully annealed. The following procedure is used for normalizing:

1. Heat the steel uniformly to the normalizing temperature. This temperature varies for steels of different carbon content and is shown in Figure 41-15.

2. Allow the steel to soak at the normalizing temperature for a period of about one hour per inch of thickness.

3. Remove the steel from the furnace and allow it to cool in air.

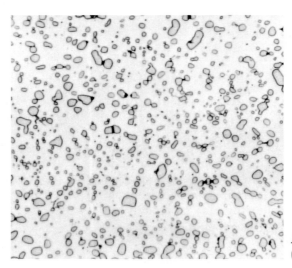

Fig. 41-16 *Spheroidite magnified 100 times.* (USX Corporation)

41-13

Case-hardening

Case-hardening is a **surface-hardening** process. A thin surface layer on the steel is hardened while the inner core remains quite soft (Fig. 41-17). This process generally is applied to **low-carbon steels.**

The case-hardening process involves two important steps: first **carburizing, carbonitriding,** or **nitriding,** then **hardening.** The first step puts carbon, nitrogen, or a combination of both into the surface of the steel. Iron carbide or iron nitride is thus formed in enough quantity for hardening to occur. Most case-hardening involves carburizing or carbonitriding. **Nitriding** produces extremely hard surfaces, but is restricted to use with special alloy steels.

Carburizing is a relatively slow process. Steel must be soaked at the **carburizing temperature** for about 8 hours to carburize to a depth of $\frac{1}{16}$" [1.57 mm] and about 24 hours for a depth of $\frac{1}{8}$" [3.2 mm]. Case-hardened products generally are carburized to a surface depth of from 0.020" to 0.030" [0.5 to 0.75 mm] during a period of about 2 to 4 hours. The length of time required for penetration of carbon during the carburizing process varies with (1) the **carburizing temperature,** (2) the **carburizing substance used,** and (3) the **depth of penetration desired.**

Several kinds of **carbonaceous** substances may be used to introduce carbon into steel at the carburizing temperature. These materials include solid materials, liquids, and gases. Thus carburizing processes are named according to the kind of carburizing material used. Solid materials are used for **pack carburizing** (Fig. 41-18). Pack carburizing is an older process that can be done easily without specialized equipment. Industry, however, uses mostly gases for carburizing, and liquids to a lesser extent. Liquid or natural gas is used for **gas carburizing** in special furnaces (Fig. 41-19). Special kinds of salt are heated to form a molten salt bath for **liquid carburizing.** A liquid heat-treatment furnace for this process is shown in Figure 41-20.

During the second step in the case-hardening process, the steel is **hardened.** The same procedure is used as that for hardening high-carbon steel. Thus, the case-hardening process produces a hardened **case,** or layer of steel, over a softer inner core. The surface hardness value, before tempering, is usually from Rockwell C-60 to C-66. The core hardness for case-hardened low-carbon steels usually ranges from about Rockwell C-20 to C-30. Since the core of the steel has less carbon content, it does not harden to the same degree as the outer surface.

Fig. 41-18 *Packing parts for case hardening in a carburizing compound.*

Fig. 41-17 *Cross-sections of case hardened steel bars. Note the fine grain of the hardened case and coarse grain of the unhardened core.*

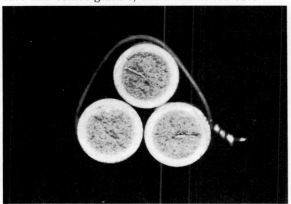

Fig. 41-19 *Gas carburized roller bearing races ready to be discharged from the carburizing furnace.*

Fig. 41-20 *The liquid carburizing of gears in a salt bath.*

Carburized parts may be hardened by quenching directly from the carburizing temperature, or they may be allowed to cool first. If they are allowed to cool first, the parts are reheated to the hardening temperature and then quenched. This allows for partial refinement of the coarse grain that often develops during carburizing. When quenched directly from the carburizing furnace, less oxidation scale builds up on the parts. Thus, there is less difficulty in cleaning the parts.

Case-hardened parts may be tempered or not, as desired. Since the inner core is relatively soft, and the hardened surface layer is very thin, there is little danger of cracking or fracturing. Deeply case-hardened parts should be tempered. Low tempering temperatures of 300 to 400°F [145 to 204°C] are generally used.

Tools and parts that need high strength or a hard-wearing surface are case-hardened. Pliers, wrenches, and hammers are often case-hardened. Gears, screws, bolts, and other parts that wear only on the surface are case-hardened.

 41-14

How to Case-harden Steel

Using a commercial carburizing compound is one of the safest methods for case-hardening. A nonpoisonous, noncombustible carbonaceous substance, such as Kasenit®, is recommended. Pack carburizing with this type of material is done in an open or well-vented container. The container may be made of heavy-gage sheet steel. The following procedures are generally used.

Pack Method

For case depths up to 0.015″ [0.38 mm]:
1. Place the steel part in an open, well-vented, shallow container. Cover the part with Kasenit or a similar carburizing compound. A vented cover may be placed on the container, if desired.
2. Place the container in a heat-treatment furnace and heat to 1650°F [899°C]. Soak the part at this temperature for 15 to 60 minutes, depending on the depth of case desired. With this procedure, a case depth of 0.005″ to 0.020″ [0.13 to 0.5 mm] can be obtained.
3. Remove the part from the molten compound with dry tongs and quench in clean water immediately.

4. Temper the part, if desired. A tempering temperature of 300 to 400°F [145 to 204°C] is satisfactory for most applications.

Dip Method

For a shallow case, several thousandths of an inch (hundredths of a millimeter) in depth:

1. Heat the part uniformly to 1650°F [899°C]. This will be a bright red color.
2. Dip or roll the part in Kasenit or a similar case-hardening compound, and continue to heat the part for several minutes. The coating of compound will bubble and form a crust on the steel as it is heated.
3. With the part heated to 1650°F [899°C], quench in clean cold water.
4. To increase the depth of the carburizing, repeat Step 2 one or more times, as desired.
5. Temper, if desired.

41-15 Other Methods of Heat Treatment

Flame hardening is a surface-hardening process that is used on steels that have hardening properties. It hardens the surface to depths ranging from $\frac{1}{32}$" to $\frac{1}{4}$" [0.8 to 6.35 mm] deep. It is done by heating the surface layer of steel very rapidly to the hardening temperature with an oxyacetylene flame (Fig. 41-21). The surface is immediately quenched

Fig. 41-21 *Flame-hardening the ways of a lathe bed.*

with a spray of water or other coolant. It is then tempered. Flame hardening is used on gear teeth, lathe parts, and other surfaces that must resist wear. Because of their softer tough cores they have the advantage of exterior hardness without being brittle.

Induction hardening also is a surface-hardening process that is used on steels with hardening properties. It hardens to depths ranging up to $\frac{1}{4}$" [6.35 mm]. It is similar to flame hardening except that high-frequency electric current is used as a source of heat for hardening.

Fig. 41-22 *The hardening of four track rollers simultaneously, using high frequency induction heating. (A) Assembly setup. (B) Parts being heated. (C) Parts being water quenched.*

The current passes through a coil surrounding the object being treated. The high-frequency current rapidly heats the steel to the hardening temperature. Then, the object is immediately quenched with water or another coolant (Fig. 41-22, p. 351).

Laser and **electron beam hardening** are used mostly for surface hardening of parts that need only certain areas hardened (Fig. 41-23). Heating is so rapid with these methods that metal next to the heated area remains cold. This enables heat to be conducted away so quickly that hardening occurs without quenching in a liquid.

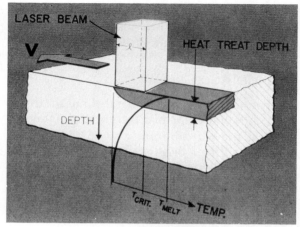

Fig. 41-23 *The way in which a laser beam is used in the heat treating of metal. The inset photo shows a splined shaft that has been heat treated in this way.* (Coherent General, Inc.)

REVIEW   REVIEW   REVIEW   REVIEW   REVIEW

WORDS TO KNOW

alpha iron	electron beam	induction-hardening	pearlite
annealing	hardening	Kasenit	phase change
austenite	eutectoid	laser-hardening	process annealing
carbonitriding	ferrite	liquid carburizing	quenching
carburizing	flame-hardening	lower-critical	Rockwell hardness
case-hardening	full annealing	temperature	scale
cementite	gamma iron	magnetic point	spheroidizing
crystalline grain	gas carburizing	martensite	annealing
drawing	grain structure	nitriding	tempering
temperature	hardening	normalizing	upper-critical
	heat treatment	pack carburizing	temperature

REVIEW QUESTIONS

1. What is meant by heat treatment?
2. List the principal properties of steel that can be changed by heat treatment.

(Review Continued)

3. List the principal kinds of heat treatment.
4. Explain how medium- or high-carbon tool steel is hardened.
5. What is meant by soaking during heat treatment?
6. Why is it desirable to have a temperature-indicating and controlling device on a heat-treatment furnace?
7. Name three ways the hardening temperature of steel can be determined when a temperature-controlled furnace is not available.
8. How does the carbon content of steel affect its ability to harden?
9. List the three groups of plain carbon steels.
10. To what extent can medium-carbon steels be hardened?
11. List four factors that affect the hardness.
12. What phase change occurs in the structure of steel when it is heated through the critical range?
13. What is the carbon content and structure of eutectoid steel?
14. How is the hardening temperature of steel determined?
15. Is the hardening temperature the same for all steels? Why or why not?
16. What kind of grain structure must steel have before it is quenched for hardening?
17. Why is steel weaker if it is heated more than 100°F [38°C] above the upper critical temperature before it is quenched?
18. What kind of grain structure does steel have after it is quenched at the proper hardening temperature?
19. List four kinds of quenching solutions. Which cools most rapidly? Which cools most slowly?
20. Why should steel parts be agitated during quenching?
21. What is the purpose of tempering? How is it done?
22. What factors must be considered in deciding what tempering temperature to use on a steel part?
23. In what range of temperatures are most carbon-steel tools tempered?
24. Why is it important that hardened steel be tempered as soon as possible?
25. List three kinds of annealing processes and explain the purpose of each kind.
26. Explain how full annealing is done.
27. Explain how normalizing is done.
28. What is meant by case-hardening? What is it used for?
29. List three kinds of case-hardening methods.
30. What two important steps are involved in case-hardening?
31. What is meant by carburizing? How is it done?
32. What kind of steel is case-hardening generally used on?
33. What is the Rockwell hardness range for case-hardened surfaces and for the cores of case-hardened parts?
34. What factor determines whether case-hardened parts should be tempered?
35. Explain how to case-harden parts with Kasenit or a similar carburizing compound, using the pack method.
36. Explain how to case-harden parts with Kasenit or a similar carburizing compound using the dip method.
37. Explain the flame-hardening process and its use.
38. Explain the induction-hardening process and its use.
39. Laser and electron beam hardening are used mostly for what kind of hardening?

PART

11

Abrasives and Utility Grinding

Shortly after completing basic Air Force training four years ago, LaPonte Graham chose a career in metalworking. He had always been fascinated by machinery and was naturally skilled with his hands. He spent only three months as a "3-level" apprentice machinist, and progressed quickly through the stages of Air Force career development. Now a 5-level journeyman and a Career Airman, LaPonte manufactures and repairs aircraft parts in the machine shop of a large southwestern air base.

As a member of a Component Repair Squadron, LaPonte operates a variety of machines, including a lathe, milling machine, radial drill press, and surface grinder. Among other maintenance tasks, he sharpens and trues grinding wheels with a diamond dresser. He works frequently with stainless steel, aluminum, brass, and titanium. His two years of high school mechanical drawing have been particularly helpful in reading blueprints.

LaPonte realizes that products are only as good as the people who make them and the material they are made from. He takes pride in his work, and his main satisfaction comes from finishing a part correctly.

In his several years in the service, LaPonte has already seen improvements in the quality and versatility of Air Force machinery. He expects to see even more in the next few years. With his ability to learn quickly and the thorough training he has received, LaPonte should have little difficulty keeping in touch with whatever metalworking developments the future may bring.

E4 Sgt. LaPonte Graham, USAF

Journeyman Machinist

UNIT
42
Abrasives

Abrasive comes from the word **abrade,** which means to rub off. An abrasive substance is a very hard, tough material. When crushed and ground into grains like sand, it has many sharp cutting edges and points. Several common forms in which abrasives are used in metal working include the following:

1. abrasive cloth (also called coated abrasive)
2. loose grain and powder abrasive
3. abrasive compounds (in the form of paste, sticks, or cakes)
4. grinding wheels
5. sharpening stones.

42-1 Properties of Abrasives

Abrasives must possess three common properties: (1) hardness, (2) fracture resistance, and (3) wear resistance.

Hardness means the ability of the abrasive to cut the surface of the material being polished, or ground.

The **fracture resistance** of an abrasive is its toughness; that is, how well it resists breaking or crumbling during polishing or grinding when pressed hard against the work. The fracture resistance should be neither too high nor too low. It should be such that when the abrasive grains become dull they will break away. When so broken, new sharp cutting edges are exposed. The fracture resistance of grinding wheels is related to the kind of bonding material that binds the grains together.

The **wear resistance** of an abrasive is its ability to resist wear and stay sharp. This is related to the hardness of the abrasive mate-rial. Thus, harder abrasive materials generally are more wear-resistant.

42-2 Kinds of Abrasives

Abrasives are classified as either **natural** or **artificial.** Natural abrasives are minerals that occur in nature. Artificial abrasives, also known as synthetic or manufactured abra-sives, are man made. With the exception of diamond, artificial abrasives are harder than the natural abrasives. Artificial abrasives have largely replaced natural abrasives in metal-working because of their greater hardness and wear resistance.

Natural Abrasives

Emery is one of the oldest kinds of natural abrasives used for metalworking. It is black and is composed of a combination of corun-dum and iron oxide. **Corundum** is aluminum oxide. Gemstones such as emerald and ruby are the purest form of corundum. Emery is about 60% corundum. Emery grains are not as sharp as artificial abrasives. The cutting ac-tion of emery is slight; therefore, it is used largely for hand polishing.

Crocus is a fine, soft, red abrasive of iron oxide, or rust. It is produced artificially or found naturally and is used to polish steel sur-faces to a high gloss. It is available in the form of **crocus cloth** or as a polishing compound known as **rouge.**

Diamond is the hardest substance known. **Industrial diamonds** are known as **black** or **bort** diamonds. They are much less expensive than the clear diamonds used for jewelry.

Most industrial diamonds are crushed into grains or powder, then used to make grinding wheels. Diamond grinding wheels are used to grind very hard materials such as carbide cutting tools, glass, ceramics, and stone.

Diamond chips are brazed to the tips of steel rods to make **dressing** and **truing** tools for grinding wheels. Fine diamond dust is used to make polishing compounds for finishing hardened steel and other very hard materials.

Artificial Abrasives

Pure **aluminum oxide** is produced by heating bauxite ore in electric furnaces at extremely high temperatures. With the addition of small amounts of **titanium,** greater toughness can be given to the aluminum oxide. It is broken up and crushed into fine grains for making grinding wheels, abrasive stones, and coated abrasives.

Aluminum oxide abrasives are recommended for grinding and polishing materials of high tensile strength. These include carbon steels both while soft and after hardening; malleable iron; wrought iron; and tough bronze. Approximately 75% of all grinding wheels in use today are made with aluminum oxide.

Silicon carbide is made by heating a mixture of powdered sand, coke, sawdust, and common salt in an electric furnace. It comes from the furnace in masses of beautiful, bluish crystals. The crystals are crushed into fine abrasive grains. Then, the grains are used in making grinding wheels, abrasive stones, and coated abrasives.

Silicon carbide is more brittle than aluminum oxide. However, it is hard enough to cut aluminum oxide. Silicon carbide is used for polishing or grinding materials of low tensile strength. These include cast iron, aluminum, bronze, tungsten carbide, copper, rubber, marble, glass, ceramics, magnesium, and plastics.

Boron carbide is produced from coke and boric acid in an electric furnace. It is harder than either aluminum oxide or silicon carbide, and can cut either of them. However, it is not as hard as diamond. It is used in stick form to dress or true grinding wheels 10″ [254 mm] or

less in diameter. It is also used in powder form, instead of diamond dust, for polishing hardened steel or other very hard materials.

Cubic boron nitride (CBN) is made from hexagonal boron nitride. When hexagonal boron nitride, along with a catalyst, is compressed at temperatures up to 1,000,000 lbs/sq. inch (689475.7 MPa) while being heated to 3000°F [1645°C], it is converted to CBN. CBN is twice as hard as aluminum oxide, and ranks in hardness between silicon carbide and diamond. Two forms of CBN are made, uncoated or Type I, and nickel coated or Type II. Both types are superior to diamond for grinding space-age alloys and hardened high speed steels. Both forms are used chiefly in the manufacture of grinding wheels.

Artificial diamonds were first made by the General Electric Company in 1955. They are not of gem quality but are suitable for industrial use. Most are so small that they are used as manufactured. They are used mostly for making diamond grinding wheels and polycrystalline diamond metal-cutting tools. (Polycrystalline means many crystals with their axes in various different directions.)

42-3 Grain Size of Abrasives

Grain size refers to the size of the abrasive grains used in the manufacture of abrasive materials.

The grain refers to the number of holes per lineal inch [25.4 mm] in a **sieve,** or screen (Fig. 42-1). Thus, a 10-grain abrasive is one that will just pass through a 10-mesh screen (a screen that has 10 meshes per inch, or 100 meshes per square inch [25.4 mm²].

In Figure 42-2:
(A) is a 60-grain screen;
(B) is the 60-grain screen magnified 16 times;
(C) is the actual size of the grain that passes through the 60-grain screen; and
(D) is the grain magnified 16 times.

The abrasive grain sizes used for coated abrasives are given in Table 42-1.

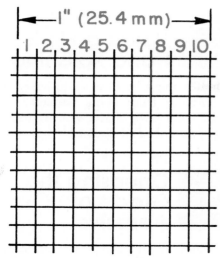

Fig. 42-1 *A 10 grain screen, actual size.*

Table 42-1

Abrasive Grain Sizes for Coated Abrasives

Extra coarse	Coarse	Medium	Fine	Extra fine
12	40	60	120	220
16	50	80	150	240
20		100	180	280
24				320
30				360
36				400
				500
				600

Fig. 42-2 *A 60-grain screen and the size of the abrasive grains that pass through it. (A) 60-grain screen. (B) 60-grain screen enlarged 16 times. (C) 60-grain abrasive. (D) Abrasive grains enlarged 16 times.* (Norton Abrasive Company)

The relative coarseness or fineness of abrasive grains is rated by size according to industry standards. However, the grain size standards for coated abrasives, described below, are somewhat different than the grain sizes for grinding wheels, described in Unit 43. Grain sizes for grinding wheels are shown in Table 43-1.

42-4

Coated Abrasives

A coated abrasive is composed of a flexible backing material to which abrasive grains are bonded with an adhesive. Coated abrasives used in the metalworking industry include emery, aluminum oxide, silicon carbide, and crocus. Coated abrasives are made in many forms for both hand and machine polishing or grinding. They are available in the form of belts, rolls, sheets, discs, spiral points, and cones (Fig. 42-3).

The backing materials used in making coated abrasives are listed below:

1. **Paper.** Used for hand applications for woodworking and fine-finishing abrasives.
2. **Cloth.** Two weights of cloth are used as backing. The lightweight cloth is called **jean** and is flexible for hand polishing. The heavyweight cloth is called **drill.** It is more stretch-resistant, and is used for machine applications.
3. **Fiber.** This type of backing is extra strong and durable, and is used for tough machine polishing and grinding applications.

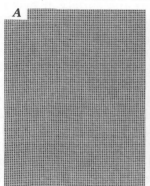

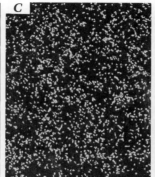

Fig. 42-3 *Coated abrasives are made in many sizes and shapes.* (Norton Company)

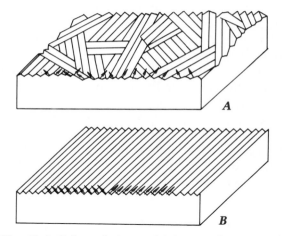

Fig. 42-4 *Enlarged views of (A) a rough, uneven surface, and (B) a surface with uniform and parallel grooves.*

Fig. 42-5 *Hand polishing a flat surface.*

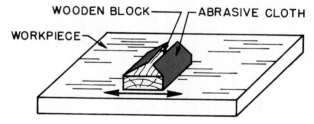

42-5 Holding Work for Hand Polishing

When using a metalworking vise, protect the workpiece from being damaged by the hardened steel jaws of the vise by using **soft jaw caps,** described in Unit 24.

42-6 Choosing the Grade of Abrasive

To hand polish a rough surface, start with a medium grade of abrasive, such as No. 80 or 100 abrasive cloth; then continue with finer grades until the desired finish is obtained. For polishing a smooth surface, start with No. 120 or 150 abrasive cloth and finish with No. 180 or a finer grade.

42-7 How to Polish

A rough surface (Fig. 42-4A) contains many irregular grooves of various depths and widths that run in different directions. Such a surface has a dull appearance because the light is reflected in many directions. To have a **bright finish,** the cuts and grooves must be changed so that they will be parallel and equal in depth (Fig. 42-4B). The shallower the cuts or grooves, the smoother and brighter the finish will become.

Begin by **draw-filing** the surface if necessary (see Unit 17). Then follow with No. 120 or 150 abrasive cloth, and finer grades if desired. Wrap the abrasive around the file or a block of wood so that pressure can be applied evenly across the surface (Fig. 42-5). Polishing in the direction of the **longest surface dimension** will make the finish appear smoother and brighter than polishing in the direction of the short dimension.

Polishing of round work should be done by rotating the workpiece in a lathe or drill press.

When polishing steel, finish with a piece of worn-out abrasive cloth moistened with a drop of oil. The oil-polished surface will not rust as quickly as it would if polished dry.

42-8 Lapping

Lapping is the removal of small amounts of metal from a **hardened steel** surface. It is done when ordinary grinding would remove too much metal, especially on measuring tools where smooth surfaces and exact sizes are needed. The tool used for this purpose is called a **lap;** it is made of copper, brass, soft cast iron, or lead; it must be of a material softer than the metal to be lapped.

A fine **powder abrasive,** known as **lapping powder,** is used for lapping. The lapping powder is made into a paste by mixing it with Vaseline® or **lard oil;** it is then called **lapping compound.** The lap is coated with the paste and then rubbed against the surface of the part that is to be slightly ground to size. Lapping can be a hand or machine operation (Fig. 42-6).

Fig. 42-6 *A machine for lapping flat surfaces.* (Speed Fam Corporation)

42-9 Polishing with Steel Wool

Polishing or cleaning metal by hand may be done with fine **steel wool,** which is made of **steel shavings.** The fine, sharp edges of the steel shavings scratch the metal and thus polish it. Steel wool is made in seven grades ranging from fine to coarse as follows: 0000, 000, 00, 0, 1, 2, and 3. The fine grades, 0000 and 000, will provide a low-luster finish on copper, aluminum, and other non-ferrous metals.

42-10 Working with Abrasives

 SAFETY NOTE
Eye protection should always be worn when working with abrasives, especially when using any kind of grinding machine.

Whenever possible, grinding should be done wet so as to prevent abrasive dust from getting into the air. Long exposure to abrasive dust particles can cause a lung disorder known as **silicosis.** In situations that produce high concentrations of abrasive dust, the lungs can be protected by wearing an effective respirator (Fig. 42-7).

Fig. 42-7 *Respirators should be worn in a work environment that contains abrasive dust.*

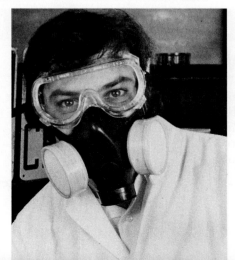

TECHNOLOGIES AND PRACTICES

Spheres in Space

Houston: "Ground Control to Bearing Factory One, Come in."

BF One: "Roger, Ground Control. We copy."

Houston: "BF One, we have a rush order for one million 15-millimeter 8220 bearings. When can you ship? Over."

BF One: "Roger, Ground Control. Tomorrow on the shuttle, leaving 0900 your time."

The idea of ball bearings made in space factories is not as far-fetched as it may sound. NASA (the National Aeronautics and Space Administration) is already considering the future industrialization of space. Advances in space technology are bringing the dream of space factories one step closer to reality.

But why make ball bearings in space? Let's consider the current method of making the round metal balls used in bearings. First, high quality alloy steel is pressed between dies into rough spheres. Next, the balls are heat-treated and put through a series of roughing and finish-grinding operations. Polishing with a fine abrasive completes the process. After all this, the ball bearings are still not flawless or perfectly round.

Completely accurate metal balls can be produced only in the weightlessness of space. Scientists know that molten metal will immediately form into precise spheres when it is melted at zero-gravity. Therefore, making bearings out of free-floating metal should require no molds or grinding operations. The resulting metal balls should be much closer to perfect than any similar products made on Earth.

A space station where zero-gravity exists naturally would be the ideal place to make high-quality ball bearings.

Ball bearings made in space would help machines back on Earth last longer than they do now. Considering the present rate of progress in space technology, we may not have long to wait for this benefit from space.

REVIEW   REVIEW   REVIEW   REVIEW   REVIEW

WORDS TO KNOW

abrasive	coated abrasive	fracture resistance	mesh
abrasive cloth	corundum	grain size	natural abrasive
aluminum oxide	crocus	grinding compound	silicon carbide
artificial abrasive	diamond	lapping	steel wool
boron carbide	emery	lapping compound	wear resistance

(Review Continued)

REVIEW QUESTIONS

1. Name five forms in which abrasives are used in metalworking.
2. List three properties that abrasives must possess.
3. Explain the main difference between natural and artificial abrasives.
4. List four natural abrasive materials.
5. List five artificial abrasives.
6. List several kinds of materials that are ground or polished with aluminum oxide abrasives.
7. List several kinds of materials that are ground or polished with silicon carbide materials.
8. What is boron carbide used for?
9. What is cubic boron nitride used for?
10. How are diamonds used in metalworking?
11. Explain how abrasive grain size is determined.
12. What is the meaning of the term "coated abrasive"?
13. What kinds of coated abrasives are used for metalworking?
14. In what forms are coated abrasives available?
15. What is lapping? What is it used for?
16. What is steel wool? What is it used for?

UNIT

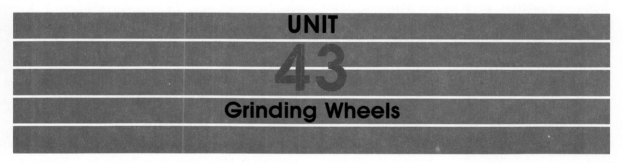

43

Grinding Wheels

Grinding wheels are abrasive tools used for shaping and finishing metals. Conventional grinding wheels are made by mixing abrasive grains with a **bonding material** and pressing this mixture into grinding wheel shapes. Then, they are baked until **cured** (hardened). **Mounted wheels** are small grinding wheels that are made with a steel shaft permanently attached. Figure 43-1 indicates the wide range of grinding wheel sizes and shapes that are available.

Fig. 43-1 *Common types of conventional grinding wheels.* (Norton Company)

43-1 The Reasons for Grinding

Grinding is used primarily for the following:

1. To sharpen cutting edges on drills, milling cutters, taps, and other cutting tools made from hardened steel and other hard metals.
2. As a machining process to cut metal to its desired shape and size.
3. To make smooth, polished surfaces such as those required for bearings and on rolls for processing various materials (such as on roll-forming machines).

43-2 The Cutting Action of Grinding Wheels

Grinding wheels are made of thousands of abrasive grains that are held together by a bonding material. Each of the abrasive grains has sharp cutting edges that cut off tiny chips from the metal being ground (Fig. 43-2). Because grinding speeds are very high, many small chips are made for the total amount of metal removed.

Fig. 43-2 *A magnified view of metal chips produced by grinding.* (Norton Company)

Table 43-1

Abrasive Grain Sizes for Grinding Wheels			
Coarse	Medium	Fine	Very fine
10	30	70	220
12	36	80	240
14	46	90	280
16	54	100	320
20	60	120	400
24		150	500
		180	600

43-3 Abrasives

Most grinding wheels are manufactured from two kinds of artificial abrasive materials: **aluminum oxide** and **silicon carbide.** The properties and kinds of abrasives used in manufacturing grinding wheels, and the materials that may be ground with each kind of abrasive, are explained in Unit 42.

43-4 Grinding Wheel Abrasive Grain Sizes

Grinding wheels are made with the abrasive grain sizes shown in Table 43-1. Grinding wheels with coarser grain sizes are used for fast cutting and where quality of finish is not important. Wheels with finer grain sizes are used when only a small amount of metal is to be removed and when a fine finish is required.

43-5 Grinding Wheel Bonding Materials

The **bond** is the adhesive that binds or holds the abrasive grains together in the grinding wheel. Some of the bonding materials used in manufacturing grinding wheels are:

vitrified clay (a glassy substance)

sodium silicate (sticky compounds of silicon and oxygen)

rubber (natural from the tree, or artificial)

resinoid (a plastic substance)

shellac (a resinous adhesive secreted by the lac bug)

A number of additional bonding materials that are modifications or combinations of the above bonding materials are also used. The type of bonding material used in a grinding wheel is identified by a code letter or letters (Fig. 43-6).

The best bond is one that is not softened by heat during grinding, and that holds the cutting points of the abrasive until they are dull. The dull grains are then pulled away from the bond because more pressure is used in trying to make them cut. New, sharp grains are then uncovered, which help the wheel to continue cutting.

43-6 Vitrified Bond Wheels

To **vitrify** means to make hard and glasslike by heating. The bond used in vitrified wheels is a kind of clay. The wheels are baked in an electric furnace at about 3000°F [1649°C] for about 100 hours. Most grinding wheels are made this way. Vitrified bond wheels have large pores, cut easily, and do not glaze (dull) easily. Heat, cold, water, oil, or acids do not hurt them.

About 75% of all grinding wheels produced are vitrified or modified-vitrified types. These wheels, however, are not **elastic** (flexible); thin wheels made this way break very easily.

43-7 Silicate Bond Wheels (Semivitrified)

Silicate bond, also known as **water-glass bond,** is made by melting sand, charcoal, and soda. Silicate bond wheels require less manu-

facturing time, and can be made thinner than with the vitrified process. Hard silicate wheels are used for grinding fine edges on tools and knives. They are not recommended for rough grinding.

43-8 Shellac Bond Wheels

Shellac bond wheels produce very smooth and bright finishes. They are used for grinding mill rolls, bearings, and other surfaces requiring fine finishes.

43-9 Elastic Wheels

The bond of elastic wheels is usually reinforced **rubber, shellac,** or **resinoid** (plastic). Very thin, strong wheels are made this way. They can be run faster than vitrified wheels. Elastic wheels can be made as thin as 1/64" [0.4 mm] and are used for sharpening saws, grinding in narrow spaces, making narrow cuts, and cutting off metal (Fig. 43-3).

Fig. 43-3 *Cutting off the end of a drill with an elastic bond abrasive cutoff wheel.* (Norton Company)

43-10 Grades of Wheels

Grinding wheels are made in several **grades** ranging from **soft** to **hard**. On a soft wheel, the dull grains are easily released or torn off the wheel during grinding. On a hard wheel, the grains are held tightly and do not tear off easily. Thus, the grade of a grinding wheel refers to the **looseness** or **tightness** with which the abrasive grains are held together.

Softer grades of grinding wheels are used for grinding very **hard** materials, such as hardened tool steel. The abrasive grains dull more easily on hard materials, and they must, therefore, be torn away more easily. When they tear away, new sharp grains are exposed. The sharp points can then cut into the hard material. Harder grades are used for grinding **softer** materials. **Thus, the terms hard or soft, as related to the grade of grinding wheels, have no relationship to the abrasive grain itself.** One kind of abrasive grain, such as aluminum oxide, may be used in hard-, medium-, or soft-grade grinding wheels. **With any given bonding material, the amount of bonding material determines the grade.** The grade of a grinding wheel is identified by a letter of the alphabet, as shown in Figure 43-6.

43-11 The Structure of Wheels

The structure of a grinding wheel refers to the **spacing** between the abrasive grains. Some wheels have abrasive grains that are more **dense,** or closely spaced. **Open-grain** wheels have grains spaced farther apart. Open-grain wheels grind more rapidly than close-grain wheels. Manufacturers identify the structure of grinding wheels by numbers from 1 to 15. Number 1 is the most dense, while Number 15 is the least dense (Fig. 43-6).

43-12 Shapes, Faces, and Holes of Grinding Wheels

Grinding wheels are made in a wide variety of shapes chosen by the Grinding Wheel Manufacturers Association of the United

Fig. 43-4 Some common shapes of conventional grinding wheels.

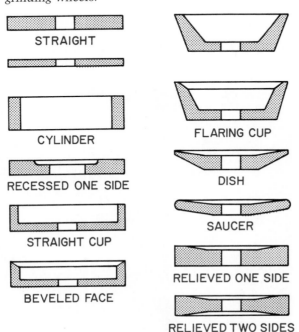

STRAIGHT

CYLINDER

RECESSED ONE SIDE

STRAIGHT CUP

BEVELED FACE

FLARING CUP

DISH

SAUCER

RELIEVED ONE SIDE

RELIEVED TWO SIDES

Fig. 43-5 Grinding wheel faces are known by different letters.

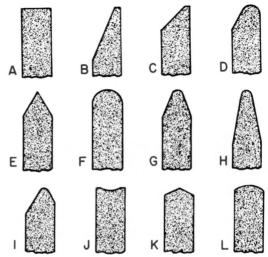

States and Canada. Their names describe their shapes. Some common shapes are shown in Figure 43-4.

The shapes of grinding wheel faces are indicated by letters (Fig. 43-5).

The hole in a grinding wheel should be about .002″ [.05 mm] larger than the diameter of the shaft on which it is mounted. This allows the wheel to slide freely, but not too loosely, on the shaft. If the wheel is so small that the wheel has to be forced onto the shaft, there is danger of the wheel cracking.

43-13	# Wheels for Different Kinds of Work

All materials cannot be ground equally well with the same wheel. The following factors should be considered in selecting a grinding wheel for a specific job:

1. Type of grinding operation: hand grinding, surface grinding, tool grinding, cylindrical grinding, or other types.
2. Material to be ground: steel, cast iron, carbide tools, or other metals.
3. Amount of stock to be ground: heavy or light stock removal.
4. Quality of finish desired: rough or smooth finish.
5. Area of wheel contact: a wheel with a wide face may require a softer grade.
6. Wheel speed: the wheel must be rated at or above the maximum rpm of the grinding machine.
7. Whether grinding is done dry or with a cutting fluid.

It is best to refer to manufacturers' catalogs for the kind of wheel to use. Recommended grinding wheels for various kinds of grinding operations on various types of materials are also listed in handbooks for machinists.

Fig. 43-6 *The standard marking system for indentifying aluminum oxide and silicon carbide grinding wheels.*

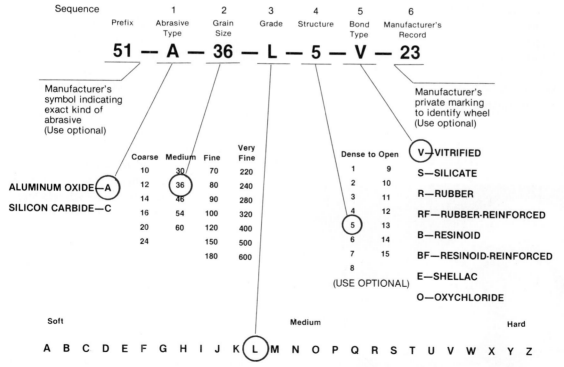

*Extracted from American National Standards Institute, ANSI B74.13-1970 with permission of the publisher, the American Society of Mechanical Engineers, 29 West 39th Street, New York 18, New York

43-14 The Grinding Wheel Marking System

Grinding wheel manufacturers use a standard marking system for identifying the following characteristics of grinding wheels:

1. abrasive type
2. grain size
3. grade
4. structure
5. bond type.

The characteristics of a grinding wheel identified with the code number 51A36-L5V23 are shown in Figure 43-6. The **prefix** in the code number is the manufacturer's symbol to indicate the exact kind of abrasive. (This is optional and may not be given.) The **suffix** is the manufacturer's private code to identify the wheel (optional).

43-15 Ordering Grinding Wheels

When ordering a grinding wheel, always provide the following information:

1. **Shape** of wheel.
2. **Type** of wheel face.
3. **Diameter** of wheel.
4. **Width** (or thickness) of wheel.
5. **Diameter** of hole.
6. **Speed** (rpm) of machine.

7. The standard marking system information (Fig. 43-6):
   a. Abrasive type: use a prefix number, if known.
   b. Grain size.
   c. Grade.
   d. Structure.
   e. Bond type.
   f. May specify the manufacturer's record number if desired.

43-16 Superabrasive Grinding Wheels

Diamond grinding wheels have a thin layer of natural or artificial diamond grains bonded to the operating face of a metal or hard plastic wheel core (Fig. 43-7). Diamond wheels are used for cutting and grinding materials that are very hard or abrasive. They are used for sharpening carbide cutting tools, and for cutting and grinding concrete, glass, and ceramic materials.

Cubic boron nitride can tolerate temperatures up to 2500°F (1321°C), whereas diamond decomposes to carbon dioxide and carbon monoxide at 1500°F (816°C). For this reason, CBN grinding wheels are superior to diamond for grinding space-age alloys and hardened high speed steels. Because of the high hardness and toughness of CBN, grinding wheels made from it have very low wear, seldom require dressing, and are therefore capable of holding very close tolerances.

Most CBN grinding wheels are made like diamond grinding wheels (Fig. 43-7). However, some small diameter CBN wheels are made with vitrified and resin bonds like conventional grinding wheels.

For more information on diamond and CBN grinding wheel shapes, composition, sizes, and wheel markings, consult a manufacturer's catalog or a handbook for machinists.

Fig. 43-7 *Commonly used shapes of diamond and cubic boron nitride grinding wheels.* (Norton Company)

REVIEW   REVIEW   REVIEW   REVIEW   REVIEW

WORDS TO KNOW

bond	grade	resinoid bond	structure
cured	grinding wheel	rubber bond	vitrified bond
elastic wheel	mounted grinding	shellac bond	wheel core
glaze	wheel	silicate bond	wheel face
	semivitrified wheel		

REVIEW QUESTIONS

1. How are conventional grinding wheels made?
2. Name several reasons for grinding.
3. Name the two abrasives most used for making grinding wheels.
4. How is the grain size of an abrasive measured?
5. What is meant by the bond of a grinding wheel?
6. Name the kind of bonding materials used in grinding wheels.
7. What does vitrify mean?
8. What is meant by the grade of a grinding wheel?
9. What is meant by the structure of a grinding wheel?
10. Name several common shapes of grinding wheels.
11. Where can you find a list of kinds of grinding wheels recommended for different jobs?
12. Explain the makeup of a grinding wheel with a label marking of 23A60G9V16.
13. List the information needed to order a grinding wheel for your shop.
14. What kinds of work are diamond grinding wheels used for?
15. How does the construction of a diamond grinding wheel differ from the construction of a conventional grinding wheel?
16. Name two types of metals that CBN grinding wheels work best on.

UNIT

44

Utility Grinders

Utility grinders are used for nonprecision grinding operations done by hand. Either the grinder or the work being ground is hand-held. Examples of work done with utility grinders include removal of burrs and other sharp edges; removal of flash and other casting imperfections (called **snagging**); preparation of joints for welding; smoothing of welds; and sharpening of cutting tools.

44-1 Types of Utility Grinders

A **bench grinder** (Fig. 44-1) is a small grinder that can be bolted to the top of a bench. This grinder is used for sharpening small tools and for other light grinding. Bench grinders are made for use with grinding wheels up to about 1″ [25.4 mm] in width and 8″ [203.2 mm] in diameter.

A **pedestal grinder** is a utility grinder mounted on a free-standing base, or **pedestal** (Fig. 44-2). Various sizes of pedestal grinders are made, the heavy-duty ones using wheels 3″ [76.2 mm] or more in width and 20″ [508 mm] or more in diameter. The smaller pedestal grinders are used for the same kind of work as bench grinders. The larger machines are generally used for a rougher class of work, such as snagging of castings.

The **wet grinder** (Fig. 44-3) has a pump to supply a flow of **coolant** to the wheel. The coolant runs back into a tank and is used over and over again. It carries off the heat caused by grinding and washes away bits of metal and abrasive.

Portable grinders are powered by electricity (Fig. 44-4) or compressed air (Fig. 44-5). Some portable grinders are equipped with a **flexible shaft** for versatility and ease of handling. These are often used for delicate work such as the grinding of dies (Fig. 44-6).

Fig. 44-1 A bench grinder. (Rockwell)

Fig. 44-2 A pedestal grinder. (Baldor Electric Company)

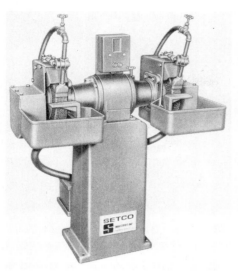

Fig. 44-3 *A pedestal grinder with a built-in coolant system is called a wet grinder.* (Setco Industries, Inc.)

Fig. 44-5 *An air-powered portable grinder.*

Fig. 44-4 *Using a portable electric grinder.* (Rockwell International/Power Tool Division)

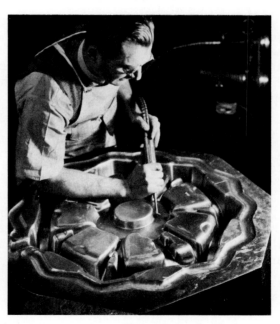

Fig. 44-6 *Using a small grinding wheel on a flexible shaft grinder.*

44-2 Threads on the Grinder Shaft

The ends of the grinder shaft hold the grinding wheels. The ends are always threaded so that the nuts that fasten the wheels to the shaft will tighten as the shaft turns. For this reason, the left sides of bench and pedestal grinders have **left-hand threads** on the shaft and nut, while the right side has **right-hand threads** on the shaft and nut.

Be careful to turn the nuts in the right direction when removing or replacing them. **To remove the nuts, turn them in the direction that the wheels turn when grinding.**

The Tool Rest

Every grinder should have a tool rest, upon which the work is rested while grinding (Fig. 44-7). **The tool rest should be set as close to the wheel as possible without touching it.** This is done to keep the work from being pulled between the wheel and the tool rest. Should this happen, the jammed tool can cause the wheel to break (Fig. 44-8).

The Water Pot

Some grinders have a **water pot** (Fig. 44-2). It is filled with water and is used to keep the work cool (by dipping it into water often). If the grinder has no water pot, a small container filled with water should be kept near the grinder.

Wheel Guards

The grinding wheel should be enclosed by a **wheel guard** that nearly surrounds the wheel (Figs. 44-2 and 44-3). Just enough of an opening is left to do the grinding.

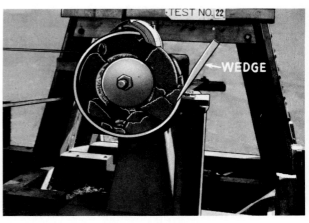

Fig. 44-8 *This view shows how the wheel guard protects against danger from a broken grinding wheel.*

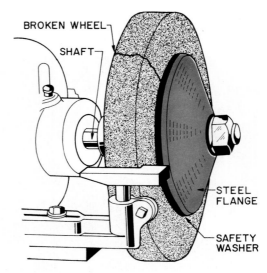

Fig. 44-9 *Flanges hold broken parts of the grinding wheel together.*

Proper wheel guards give complete protection against broken grinding wheels. In a series of tests, not once did a piece of the wheel leave the guard in a manner that could have caused injury to the operator (Fig. 44-8). The wheels in the tests were broken by dropping a steel wedge between the tool rest and the wheel. This is one of the most common causes of grinding wheel breakage.

Fig. 44-7 *Use of the tool rest makes grinding safer.*

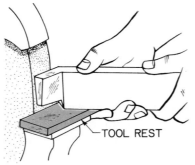
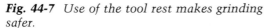

Safety Flanges

Safety flanges are large metal washers placed on each side of the grinding wheel (Fig. 44-9). They clamp the wheel in place on the shaft and also hold the parts of the wheel together if it breaks. The **outside flange** is secured by the same nut that attaches the wheel to the grinder shaft. The **inside flange** is **keyed** or **pressed** onto the shaft.

Safety Washers

Soft washers made of **blotting paper, leather,** or **rubber** should be placed between the wheel and the flanges. These washers should be a little larger than the flanges. The soft material is forced into the pores of the wheel, thus locking the wheel in place between the flanges.

Fig. 44-10 *A reinforced glass eye shield for a grinder.* (U.S. Electrical Manufacturing Co.)

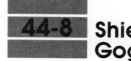

Shields and Goggles

Some grinders have **glass shields** for eye protection during grinding (Fig. 44-10).

🚫 **SAFETY NOTE**
The shield, however, does not alone provide adequate eye protection. For complete protection, always wear safety goggles when using any grinding machine.

If a grain of **abrasive**, which has rough, sharp edges and points, gets into the eye, it often has to be removed by a doctor. The eye may be swollen and very sore after the grain is removed, and the worker may not be able to work for several days.

Inspecting Grinding Wheels for Cracks

Before a new wheel is used, it should be carefully inspected for cracks. While supporting the wheel on a wood dowel through its hole, strike the wheel gently with a light object. Use the handle of a screwdriver for light wheels and a mallet for heavy ones. A good wheel will ring clearly when struck. Wheels must be clean and dry when they are being tested this way.

Mounting the Grinding Wheel

Grinding wheels may break because of incorrect **mounting.** The wheel should not be forced onto the shaft, since this may cause it to crack. **Safety washers** a little larger than the diameter of the **flanges** should be placed between the sides of the wheel and the flanges. The nut should be tightened only enough to hold the wheel firmly.

After mounting a wheel, **stand to one side** and turn on the grinder. The wheel should then be **trued** with a **grinding wheel dresser** before being used (see Unit 45).

44-11 Speeds of Grinding Wheels

Grinding wheels are usually run at a **surface speed** of 4000 to 6500 **feet per minute** **(fpm)** [1219 to 1981 meters per minute, mpm]. Surface speed is the speed of the rim of the wheel and the distance it would travel if rolled on the floor for one minute. At the same rpm, the surface speed of the wheel gets slower as the diameter gets smaller. **Make sure that the grinder does not exceed the safe rpm marked on the wheel.**

REVIEW   REVIEW   REVIEW   REVIEW   REVIEW

WORDS TO KNOW

bench grinder	pedestal grinder	safety washer	utility grinder
coolant	portable grinder	snagging	water pot
eye shield	revolutions per	surface speed	wet grinder
feet per minute	minute	tool rest	wheel guard
flexible shaft grinder	safety flange		

REVIEW QUESTIONS

1. What are utility grinders? What are they used for?
2. How does a wet grinder differ from other pedestal grinders? Name three advantages of wet grinding.
3. Name two ways portable grinding machines are powered.
4. What is the advantage of a grinder with a flexible shaft?
5. What is a tool rest used for? How close should it be set to the wheel?
6. What is a grinding wheel flange? What is its purpose?
7. What is a safety washer's purpose? What is it made of?
8. How should a grinding wheel be inspected for cracks?
9. What is meant by the surface speed of a grinding wheel?

UNIT

45

Sharpening Tools by Hand Grinding

Grinding wheels, oilstones, and slipstones are used to sharpen tools by hand. Properly shaped and sharpened tools are essential to high quality metalwork. Sharp tools require less force to do the work for which they were designed. They produce higher quality finishes, and they are safer to use because they perform in an expected way. Grinding wheels themselves must be sharp and as near perfectly round as possible to do their best work.

45-1 The Causes of Loaded and Glazed Wheels

A **loaded** grinding wheel is one that has become clogged with bits of metal or other material (Fig. 45-1). This clogging occurs during the grinding of soft materials, such as lead, copper, brass, and aluminum. For this reason, **soft materials should not be ground on a**

Fig. 45-1 *(A) A loaded grinding wheel; (B) after dressing.* (Norton Company)

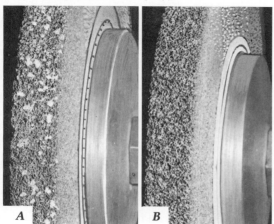

A   B

grinding wheel. A loaded wheel cuts very poorly, if at all, so the clogged surface of the wheel must be removed with a **grinding wheel dresser.**

A **glazed** wheel is one that has become dull through normal use or because the wheel is not suited to the work. If a wheel glazes quickly, it is probably too hard for that particular task. Use of loaded or glazed wheels causes rapid heat buildup in the workpiece, which may cause a tool to lose some of its hardness.

45-2 Dressing and Truing Grinding Wheels

When the grinding wheel becomes glazed, loaded, or out of shape, it must be **dressed** and **trued. Dressing** means sharpening a wheel. **Truing** means cutting the wheel so that there will be no high spots when the wheel is running. Every new wheel should be trued after mounting.

A **grinding wheel dresser** is a tool used for sharpening and shaping grinding wheels (Fig. 45-2). There are four kinds of grinding wheel dressers commonly used:

1. diamond   3. abrasive stick
2. Huntington   4. abrasive wheel.

The **diamond dresser** has one or more diamonds set in the end of a holder (Fig. 45-2). It is the best of all dressers. It lasts much longer than the others if it is properly cared for.

The **Huntington dresser** uses hardened steel cutters (Fig. 45-2). The cutters consist of alternate star- and disc-shaped wheels, which are free to rotate on a shaft. When the dresser is pressed against the face of a revolving grind-

ABRASIVE WHEEL DRESSER

HUNTINGTON DRESSER

DIAMOND DRESSER

ABRASIVE STICK DRESSER

Fig. 45-2 *Grinding wheel dressers.* (Desmond Stephan Manufacturing Company)

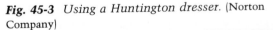

ing wheel, the cutters turn with the grinding wheel and break off the dull abrasive grains. Replacement cutters are inexpensive and are easy to install.

The **abrasive stick dresser** (Fig. 45-2) uses a replaceable cutting element of silicon carbide or boron carbide held in a steel tube.

The **abrasive wheel dresser** uses an abrasive wheel mounted at a slight angle in a hooded holder (Fig. 45-2). It works in a manner similar to the Huntington dresser.

To use a dresser, grasp it firmly with both hands. Then set it against the tool rest. Bring it into light contact with the wheel, and move it slowly and steadily across the wheel face (Fig. 45-3). Repeat this process until the face of the wheel is straight or at its proper angle, the wheel runs true (no high spots), and it is no longer loaded.

SAFETY NOTE

Close-fitting goggles should be worn when dressing or truing grinding wheels. This operation produces a cloud of sharp abrasive particles that can be very painful and difficult to remove if they enter the eye.

45-3 Tool Sharpening on the Grinding Wheel

Grind only on the face of the wheel, and move the workpiece across the whole width of the wheel to prevent wearing grooves into the wheel face. Grinding on the side of the wheel spoils its shape. Because the side is not properly trued or dressed, it tends to burn the tool quickly, as described in Section 45-4. Special wheels are made for side grinding.

Grinding a tool should require only light pressure on the wheel. Avoid applying sudden, heavy pressure which will cause the wheel to wear rapidly and become out-of-round.

Fig. 45-3 *Using a Huntington dresser.* (Norton Company)

Unit 45—Sharpening Tools by Hand Grinding

SAFETY NOTE

1. Always wear close-fitting goggles when grinding.
2. Use only a grinder that has a sharp grinding wheel.
3. Make sure the grinding wheel is properly enclosed with a wheel guard.
4. Keep the tool rest as close as possible to the wheel without touching it.

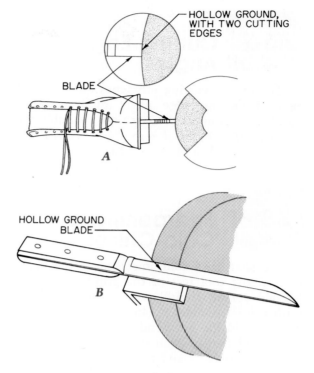

45-4 What Does "Burning the Temper" Mean?

When grinding such tools as chisels and punches, be careful not to burn the thin edges or points. The tool is being burnt when it turns to a purple or blue color. This causes the steel to lose its **temper;** that is, it loses some of its hardness. Merely grinding off the blue color does not bring back the hardness.

Keep the tool cool by dipping it in water often.

Fig. 45-5 *Hollow-ground blades are produced by grinding on the curved wheel face. (A) Ice skate blade. (B) Paring knife.*

45-5 Grinding Tools of High-speed Steel

Tools made of high-speed steel need special care in grinding. If such a tool is overheated by grinding and then dipped in cold water, it may crack. Figure 45-4 shows a drill that was over heated during grinding and then cooled in water that was too cold. Most of the cracks could not be seen until the drill was dipped in an acid that ate into the cracks and made them more visible. Cracking can be avoided by grinding only on sharp wheels and by keeping the tool cool by frequently dipping it in water.

Fig. 45-4 *Cracks in a high speed steel drill resulting from improper cooling during grinding.*

45-6 Hollow Grinding

A tool sharpened on the curved face of a grinding wheel has a **hollow-ground** surface behind its cutting edge. The curved sides of a carving knife are an excellent example of hollow grinding (Fig. 45-5). Sharp edge tools such as chisels, plane irons, and knives do their best work when they are hollow-ground.

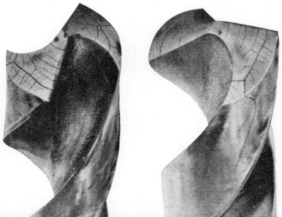

45-7 Cutting Edge Angles

For proper cutting efficiency, the recommended **cutting edge angle** for each tool should be maintained. Gages are available for checking the angles of some tools. A protractor can be used in place of a gage.

45-8 Sharpening a Cold Chisel

To sharpen a cold chisel, place the blade end on the tool rest of the grinder. A right-handed person should steady the blade end with the left hand (Fig. 45-6). The right hand should hold the head end of the chisel. Press the chisel lightly against the rotating wheel and move it back and forth across the wheel face.

Keep the chisel cool by frequently dipping it in water. Examine the chisel often to make sure the same amount of metal is ground off both sides and that the same angle is ground on both sides. Check the cutting edge angle with a center gage (Fig. 16-3).

45-9 Drill Sharpening

Drills are sharpened manually on utility grinders or on special purpose drill grinders. Because drill grinding is complex, it is treated separately in Unit 57.

45-10 Grinding Screwdrivers

Screwdrivers often have flat-tapered blade faces that tend to climb out of the screw slot during use. Hollow grinding of screwdrivers provides parallel faces which make the screwdriver a safer tool to use (Fig. 24-3). The parallel faces help the screwdriver stay in the screw slot much better.

45-11 Oilstones

Small abrasive **oilstones**, also called hones, are smooth abrasive stones made in many sizes and shapes (Fig. 45-7). They are used for putting the final touches on cutting tools, and for deburring and fitting in tool and die work. They work best when kept clean and lightly oiled.

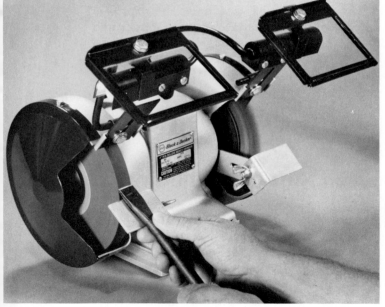

Fig. 45-6 *Sharpening a cold chisel.* (Black & Decker)

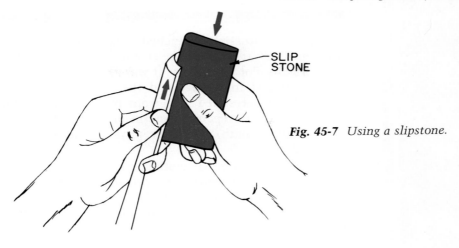

SLIP
STONE

Fig. 45-7 *Using a slipstone.*

REVIEW   REVIEW   REVIEW   REVIEW   REVIEW

WORDS TO KNOW

abrasive stick	diamond dresser	hone	slipstone
dresser	dressing	Huntington dresser	truing
burning the temper	glazed wheel	loaded wheel	wheel dressing
cutting edge angle	hollow grinding	oilstone	

REVIEW QUESTIONS

1. Why is tool sharpening important?
2. What is a loaded wheel?
3. What is a glazed wheel?
4. Describe the four kinds of grinding wheel dressers.
5. Why should goggles be worn during grinding?
6. What is meant by dressing a wheel?
7. What is meant by truing a wheel?
8. What is meant by "burning the temper"? How can it be avoided?
9. Why should only the face of the grinding wheel be used for grinding?
10. Why should wood and soft metals such as lead, copper, brass and aluminum not be ground on a grinding wheel?
11. What is meant by hollow grinding?
12. What are oilstones used for?
13. Describe the kind of care an oilstone should have.

When the Russians launched project Sputnik into space in 1957 and 1958, it changed the scientific thinking and education of Americans. For Tom Barry, it was also the beginning of a continuing interest in science and the mechanics of how things work. That interest led him from building small things as a young teenager to repairing cars in high school. It took him on to the study of math, chemistry, physics, and finally to an engineering degree.

For 20 years Tom has worked for a large appliance manufacturing company. Presently, his special concern is the application of the finish to a required appliance or machine. Tom began work as a new engineer, then advanced to process engineer, and is now a senior process engineer with nine people under his direction.

The process design specifications are of great importance in getting the correct finishing coat on a product such as a washing machine. Among Tom's responsibilities are: evaluation of raw material, control of the chemical bath, weight checking, and testing the final finish.

Tom's advancement in the firm has been due to his self-motivation and overall high standard of performance. For students interested in a metalworking career, Tom suggests that they make their education as broad as possible. With things moving fast in scientific circles, it is hard to tell from which area information will be drawn. He thinks it is smart to experience as many different procedures and ideas as possible. Tom himself has drawn from many experiences and study. He now finds great satisfaction in producing a gleaming, smooth, and durable finish on products that consumers will enjoy.

Tom Barry
Supervisor Process Engineering

Charles Zilch

UNIT

46

Metal Finishing

Metal finishing is the final treatment given to the metal surface of a product to improve its appearance and make it more salable, and, make it wear longer or protect it from corroding. It is also done to improve electrical conduction and to neutralize the reaction of a metal to certain chemicals. Also, objects finished by electroplating with precious metals are improved in value.

Some metal finishes are described in other units. **Buffing** is described in Unit 47; **filing** and **draw-filing** in Unit 17; **scraped, frosted, spotted,** and **flaked** finishes in Unit 23; **abrasive polishing** in Unit 42; and **grinding** in Unit 82.

46-1 Surface Preparation for Coated Metal Finishes

Coated metal finishes will not stick to the metal properly unless the metal has been properly cleaned. **Scale** and **rust** should be removed from old metal by **wire brushing, polishing with abrasive cloth,** or **sand blasting.** All dirt and dust should be removed by brushing or wiping. This step is usually followed by washing or wiping with a solvent to remove all traces of oil or grease (Fig. 46-1). (A **solvent** is a liquid that dissolves other materials.)

For surfaces to be **painted** or **enameled, mineral spirits** is a recommended solvent.

Lacquer thinner should be used to degrease surfaces to be **lacquered.** Solvents such as **benzene** and **carbon tetrachloride** are **toxic** (hazardous to health) and should be avoided.

🚫 **SAFETY NOTE**
Gasoline should never be used as a solvent because it is so highly flammable.

Surfaces that have been degreased should not be handled with bare hands, because body oil from fingerprints will contaminate the surface. Clean surfaces should have the finishing material applied as soon as possible. **Any dust, dirt, or grease that collects between coats must be removed before applying the next coat.**

Pickling is a metal-cleaning process that dissolves metal oxidation with acid solutions. Pickling solutions consist of water with 10 to 50% sulfuric, hydrochloric, nitric or other acids, depending on the kind of metal to be cleaned. The metal is usually pickled by dipping in the solution for several minutes. After pickling, the acid must be completely neutralized in an alkaline solution. The metal is then rinsed with clean water.

Fig. 46-1 Parts gather grease, oil, and dirt on their surfaces during manufacturing operations. Before painting, it is necessary to clean the parts with the proper solvent.

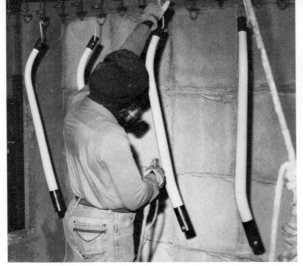

Fig. 46-2 *Steel aircraft tubing is chromated to provide good corrosion resistance and paint adhesion.* (Cessna Aircraft)

46-2 Metal Coatings

Chemical conversion coatings are very thin protective films formed on metal surfaces by chemical reaction with certain chemical solutions. **Chromate coatings** result when acid solutions of chromium compounds react with steel, aluminum, zinc, copper, and other metals (Fig. 46-2). **Phosphate coatings** are formed with acid solutions of metal phosphates. Chromate and phosphate coatings are used mostly as a corrosion-resistant base for paints.

Black oxide coatings may be applied to steel, aluminum, and other metals with either hot or cold chemical solutions. They are used either as a base for painting or as a final finish when sealed with oil or wax.

46-3 Painted, Enameled, Lacquered, and Bronzed Finishes

Paint is often used to decorate and protect metal finishes (Fig. 46-3). It is available in many colors that dry with a **flat,** or dull, finish. **Flat black paint** is a popular interior finish

for wrought iron products. **Aluminum paint** provides good protection for iron and steel fences, signposts, flagpoles, and other metal products exposed to the weather.

A **primer** is a paint that will **adhere,** or stick, well to a metal surface. It is therefore used as a first coat. Some metals require a special primer. Galvanized steel, for example, should be primecoated with a **zinc chromate primer.** A good primer for iron and steel surfaces exposed to the weather is **red lead.**

> ⊘ **SAFETY NOTE**
> Leaded primers and paints should never be used indoors. There are many cases of infant poisoning due to teething or chewing objects painted with leaded paints.

Enamel is a type of paint that is available in a wide range of colors. It dries hard and provides either a **high gloss** (shiny) or **semigloss** finish. **Quick-drying** enamels will dry in about four hours. Some enamels are baked onto the metal, as with many appliances, machines, and tools.

Fig. 46-3 *Painting auto wheels by dipping. When properly applied, painted finishes provide good protection for metals.* (Norris Industries)

Lacquer is a very quick-drying finishing material widely used as a metal finish. **Clear lacquer** is colorless; it allows the color of the metal to show while protecting it from tarnishing or rusting. **Flat lacquer** has no gloss. Lacquers are made of synthetic materials and require special solvents for thinning and cleaning. Some lacquers are applied by brushing, others by spraying. Lacquers are also available in many colors.

🚫 **SAFETY NOTE**

Lacquer is flammable and must be kept away from open flames. Containers should be closed immediately after use, and, to protect against noxious and explosive fumes, lacquer should be applied only in a well-ventilated room.

Chemical technology has provided a long list of new paints made of synthetic materials. For example, acrylic finishes are noted for their brilliant colors and smooth finishes. Polyurethane finishes have superior scratch and chemical resistance. Phenol-formaldehyde paints provide maximum protection against moisture. For more information on synthetic paints, consult a metal finishing handbook.

Most synthetic finishes harden by air drying like oil-base paints. However, some require radiation or use a catalyst to cause the paint to harden.

Bronzing is giving an article a metallic bronze color. Powdered brass or bronze is often used for bronzing. If the entire surface is to be a bronze color, **bronze paint** is used. If the article is to be only partly bronzed, it is first coated with paint, enamel, or lacquer.

Then, before the finish dries, bronzing powder is dusted on with a pepper shaker or blown on with a **powder blower** (Fig. 46-4). Colored bronzing powders are also available.

46-4 Methods of Applying Paint, Enamel, and Lacquer

Finishes are applied by brushing, dipping, spraying, or powder coating. Automated finishing systems in factories use dipping, (Fig. 46-3), spraying (Fig. 46-5), and powder coating (Fig. 46-6) methods.

Fig. 46-5 *Robots are used for many paint spraying operations.* (General Motors Corp.)

Fig. 46-6 *In powder coating, heated parts are dipped or sprayed with thermoplastic powders. The heat causes the powders to melt and flow together into a smooth finish.* (DeVilbiss)

Fig. 46-4 *A powder blower for applying bronzing powders.*

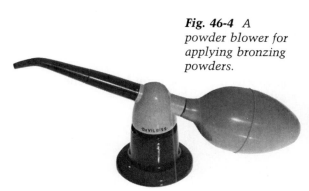

Brushing is convenient for finishing relatively small objects and for touch-up. For brushing, finishing materials can usually be used directly from the can without thinning. A brush is also simpler to use and can be cleaned more quickly than a spray gun. Good brushing technique calls for working the finishing material onto the surface by moving the brush evenly in any convenient direction. Finish by wiping the excess material from the brush, then lightly stroke the surface. Make sure all the brush marks flow in the direction of the longest dimension of each surface.

Hand spraying. Custom finishing and touch-up is often done with a hand-held spray gun (Fig. 46-7). Excellent finishes can be obtained by hand spraying.

Before spraying the workpiece, practice adjusting and manipulating the spray gun, and thin the finishing material to a proper consistency. If possible, set the surface to be sprayed in a **vertical position.** Hold the nozzle of the spray gun a constant distance from the surface to be sprayed, usually 8-12" [200-300 mm]. Spraying strokes should run the length of the surface, and strokes should overlap each other by about 2" [50 mm]. Remove runs immediately by wiping. **A rule in applying finishes is that several thin coats always produce a better finish than one thick coat.** This is especially true for spraying.

Fig. 46-7 *Hand spraying is used for custom finishing and repair.*

46-5 Cleaning Spray Guns and Brushes

Clean spray guns and brushes immediately after use. Spray guns should be emptied, wiped, and rinsed with the proper solvent. Clean solvent should be sprayed through the gun until all the passages are clean. The gun nozzle is usually taken apart for cleaning.

Reusable brushes should first be wiped on the edge of the container. Then, as much of the remaining finishing material as possible is removed by brushing on newspaper or paper towels. The brush is then rinsed in a suitable solvent two or three times. It is important that the heel of the brush (where the bristles join the handle) be flushed out. This is best done by holding the solvent-laden brush handle-down and squeezing the bristles to aid the flow of the solvent through the heel.

After most of the finishing material has been washed out with solvent, the brush is washed with a liquid detergent. Rinse the brush very thoroughly to remove all the detergent. Squeeze as much water as possible from the brush. Reshape the brush by brushing on paper towels, then carefully wrap it in one or two layers of paper towelling to help it hold its shape (Fig. 46-8). Inexpensive disposable paintbrushes made of plastic foam are sometimes a satisfactory substitute for conventional brushes (Fig. 46-9).

Fig. 46-8 *After cleaning, wrapping the brush with a paper towel helps it to hold its shape.*

Fig. 46-9 *A disposable paint brush made of plastic foam.*

T E C H N O L O G I E S   A N D   P R A C T I C E S

The Rust You Can Trust

Leave a new car or bicycle outside in the rain and air. In time the once shiny steel and chrome will be spotted and pitted with ugly, flaky rust. Rust is one example of corrosion. Through contact with the oxygen in air, the iron in steel changes to iron oxide. Rainwater washes off the outer layer of rust and exposes underlying metal to the weather. The process continues, leaving gaping holes in your most valued possessions. Most people get very upset about rust.

Yet there are ways to fight back. One way is to apply protective paints and coatings. Another is to develop new types of metal that resist corrosion. A third defense is to follow the philosophy, "If you can't beat 'em, join 'em."

U.S. Steel chose this third battle plan when developing COR-TEN® steel. Two to three percent of this "weathering steel" is made up of elements other than iron and carbon, such as copper, chromium, and phosphorus. Buildings made with this alloy do not need protective coatings. After five or six years, COR-TEN steel weathers evenly to a deep rust-like color. While resisting the destructive pitting of rust, COR-TEN works with the environment to create a maintenance-free surface.

First developed in 1933, COR-TEN has been put to a wide variety of uses in architecture. In addition to decorative use in roof decks and crosses atop churches, the alloy has been the primary material used in entire buildings. The 64-story Pittsburgh office of U.S. Steel was built using COR-TEN for all of its 841 feet with 18 massive columns.

It is hard to believe that weather can actually **improve** the finish on steel, instead of harming it. If COR-TEN becomes more widely used, we may have to "un-learn" our traditional reactions to something that looks like rust!

46-6
Coloring Metal by Treating with Chemicals or Heat

Many attractive oxide colors can be obtained on some metals by treating them with chemical solutions or by heating them. This treatment causes oxygen to combine with the metal, forming a thin layer of colored **metallic oxide.** Oxide finishes should always be protected with a coat of lacquer. There are dozens of formulas for chemical coloring solutions, but only a few can be given here.

Copper is easier to color than any other metal. It can be colored yellow, brown, red, blue, purple, or black. The beginner can get good results with the following solution:

Ammonium sulfide . . 1 ounce [28.35 grams]
Cold water . . . . 1 gallon [3.79 liters]

The work is dipped into this solution. The color produced depends on the length of time the work is left in the solution. When the desired color has been obtained, dry the work in sawdust and give it a coat of lacquer.

Ammonium sulfide must be handled with great care because it stains the fingers and has a bad odor. It should be kept in a dark bottle. Ammonium sulfide is only good for coloring copper. **Potassium sulfide** may be used instead of ammonium sulfide.

Brass can be given an antique green finish that will make it look as if it were very old. Make a solution of:

Household ammonia . . . . 4 ounces [113.4 grams]
Sal ammoniac . . . . 2 ounces [56.7 grams]
Common salt . . . . 2 ounces [56.7 grams]
Water . . . . 1 gallon [3.79 liters]

Large work can be brushed with the solution. Small work may be dipped into the solution. The work may have to be brushed or dipped several times to get the desired color. It should then be rinsed with clear water, dried, and lacquered.

One of the many formulas for chemically **coloring steel blue** follows:

Lead nitrate . . . . . 1 ounce [28.35 grams]
Ferric nitrate . . . . . ½ ounce [14.2 grams]
Sodium thiosulfate . . 4 ounces [113.4 grams]
Water . . . . 1 gallon [3.79 liters]

The solution should be mixed and stored in a glass, earthenware, or enameled container. The solution is used hot, at 190-210°F [88-99°C]. Soak the clean steel workpiece in the solution until the desired color has been obtained. After careful drying, protect the finish with oil or lacquer.

Oxide colors can be obtained on **polished steel** by heating to between 380° and 590°F [193° and 310°C]. See Table 41-1. The colors in order of appearance are yellow, brown, purple, violet, blue, and gray. Brighter colors are obtained on highly polished surfaces than on dull surfaces. Surfaces freshly polished with abrasive cloth are clean enough for heat-coloring; however, buffed surfaces must first be degreased.

Since as little as 10°F [4.7°C] can cause a change in color, the piece must be heated evenly if a uniform color is desired. Heating in a furnace with thermostatic controls gives best results. Colored surfaces should be protected with a coat of oil or lacquer.

46-7 Electrochemical Finishing

Electroplating is coating an object with a thin layer of metal by **electro-deposition.** Metals that are commonly deposited by electroplating are copper, nickel, chromium, tin, zinc, brass, gold, and silver. Figure 46-10 shows a typical electroplating arrangement for electroplating an object with copper. A **direct current** is passed from a pure copper plate (the **anode,** or **positive electrode**) to the workpiece (the **cathode,** or **negative electrode**) through a **copper sulphate** solution (the **electrolyte**).

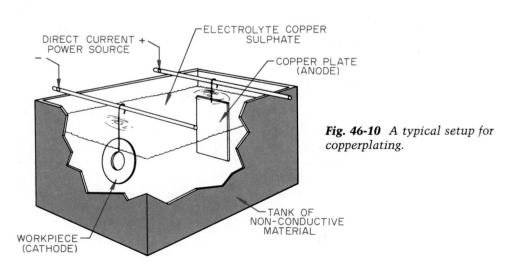

DIRECT CURRENT +
POWER SOURCE
−

ELECTROLYTE COPPER SULPHATE

COPPER PLATE (ANODE)

TANK OF NON-CONDUCTIVE MATERIAL

WORKPIECE (CATHODE)

Fig. 46-10 *A typical setup for copperplating.*

This removes copper from the anode and deposits copper on the cathode. The thickness of the plating depends on how strong a current is used and how long the workpiece is left in the plating bath.

Equipment and materials needed for electroplating copper are inexpensive and readily available. The following is a list of equipment needed:

1 earthenware or polyethylene container of 2-5 gallon [7.5-19 liter] capacity
2 dry cells or one auto battery, battery charger, or transformer
1 small sheet of copper
1 gallon [3.79 liter] copper sulphate solution
1 **ammeter**
1 **rheostat**

The sheet of copper should be about one-and-a-half times the surface area of the article to be plated. The **positive** (+) side of the dry cells or battery should be connected to the sheet of copper. The **negative** (−) side of the dry cells or battery should be connected to the object to be plated. Connect an ammeter and a rheostat in the circuit to measure and control the current.

The plating **current** should be approximately 15 amperes per square foot [161 amperes per square m] of area being plated. Thus, a test strip 1″ × 6″ [0.0254 × 0.1524 m] having 6 square inches [0.00387 square m] per side or a total of 12 square inches [0.00774 square m] of surface, would have 12/144ths or 1/12th of 15 amperes [0.00774 × 161 amperes] or 1¼ amperes as the correct plating current. The voltage may vary from ¼ to 2 volts, depending on the resistance of the plating circuit, but in this example it would not exceed 2 volts.

Electroforming is the process of making an object entirely by electroplating (Fig. 46-11).

Anodizing is an electrochemical finishing process commonly applied to aluminum and magnesium. Anodizing provides improved corrosion resistance and surface hardness, and is electrically insulating. Some anodized finishes are **porous** and can be dyed any color.

Fig. 46-11 *Electroforming can be used to make entire parts with many different shapes.* (GAR Electroforming)

Colored finishes are used on containers such as pitchers and tumblers, and on sports equipment, appliance trim, hardware, and novelties.

46-8 Surface Preparation for Electroplating

Electroplating will exaggerate defects in the surface finish. Therefore, if a smooth, bright plating is desired, surfaces must first be polished to a mirror finish by **buffing.** This process is described in Unit 47. This is followed by solvent cleaning to remove grease, wax, buffing compound, and other **organic contamination.** A thin film of organic soil always remains after solvent degreasing and is removed by soaking in a **hot alkaline cleaner.** After a clean water rinse, all traces of oxidation are removed by dipping in an acid solution **(pickling).** After another clean water rinse, the metal should be ready for plating. (Parts should not be allowed to dry between steps in the cleaning cycle.) Plating defects such as blisters, pitting, discoloration, peeling, and spotting can result from careless and improper cleaning.

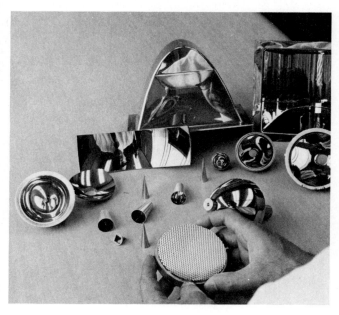

46-9 Other Metal-plating Methods

Liquid metal-plating. Parts are plated by dipping in molten zinc, aluminum, tin, or lead. This process is used commonly with steel sheet, pipe, and wire. Dipping is an inexpensive method of applying thick metal coatings.

Electroless plating. Metal from a chemical solution is deposited directly on plastic or metal surfaces without the aid of electricity. This method is becoming increasingly popular because of its energy savings.

Mechanical plating. Parts are placed in a closed container along with a metal powder and glass beads. The container is rotated and vibrated so that the parts, powdered metal, and glass beads collide, forcing some of the powdered metal to cling to the metal parts. Thin coatings of zinc, lead, tin, and cadmium can be applied in this way.

Vacuum metallizing. Very thin metal coatings are deposited on metal, or plastic parts. Aluminum is most commonly used. The aluminum is vaporized electrically in a vacuum chamber containing the parts. The aluminum vapor then condenses evenly on the parts, providing a very thin, bright coating (Fig. 46-12).

Cladding. A thin layer of corrosion-resistant metal is laminated to another metal, thus forming a kind of metal sandwich. Most cladding is done by rolling sheets together. Common examples are nickel-clad copper used for coins, and tough aluminum alloys clad with corrosion-resistant pure aluminum.

46-10 Porcelain and Ceramic Enameling

Porcelain and ceramic enamels are hard, glass-like coatings 0.003″ to 0.010″ [0.08-0.25 mm] thick bonded to metal. The enameling materials are first mixed with water and clay, then applied by brushing or spraying. After drying, the object is **fired** in a kiln at temperatures high enough to fuse the particles together (Fig. 46-13).

These coatings are bright, smooth, hard, and heat-resistant. They are commonly used on bathtubs, pots and pans, and appliances because they are attractive, durable, and easy to clean. They are also used in many industrial applications where surfaces resistant to chemical attack, wear, or high temperatures are required.

Fig. 46-12 *A rack of several hundred glass reflectors that have been metallized in the vacuum chamber.* (Mueller Corporation)

Fig. 46-13 *Hot water tanks that have received porcelain enamel coatings are moving into a furnace for firing.*

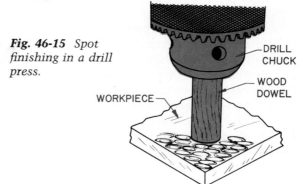

Fig. 46-14 Microroller® burnishing has been used on these parts. Note the difference between the burnished and unburnished areas. (Madison, a Sandvik Company)

Fig. 46-15 Spot finishing in a drill press.

DRILL CHUCK
WOOD DOWEL
WORKPIECE

46-11 Burnishing

Burnishing means to make smooth and bright by rubbing with something hard and smooth. No metal is lost in this process. Instead, the pressure **flattens** the points or roughness on the surface of the object being burnished. **Roller burnishing** is sometimes used for final sizing and finishing of machined cylindrical and conical parts (Fig. 46-14). **Barrel burnishing** is a finishing process in which parts are tumbled in a barrel along with balls, shot, or pins with rounded ends. The peening and rubbing action thus created can produce a finish almost as good as buffing.

46-12 Spot Finishing

An ornamental finish called **spot finishing** can be made on flat metal surfaces as follows: cut a piece of wood dowel about 2″ [50 mm] long and of the same diameter as the desired spots. (A ⅜″ [9.5 mm] diameter is probably the most commonly used dowel size.) Insert the dowel in a drill press chuck. Put oil and **abrasive flour** on the surface to be spotted. Run the drill press at highest speed and press lightly and repeatedly on the surface. Round, polished spots are thus formed (Fig. 46-15).

REVIEW   REVIEW   REVIEW   REVIEW   REVIEW

Words to know

acetic acid	chromate coating	liquid metal plating	potassium sulphate
anode	cladding	mechanical plating	powder coating
anodizing	electroforming	mineral spirits	primer
black oxide coating	electroless plating	nitric acid	red lead paint
bronzing	electroplating	oxide colors	solvent
burnishing	enamel	phosphate coating	spot finishing
cathode	flat lacquer	phosphoric acid	sulfuric acid
chemical	flat paint	pickling	thinner
conversion	hydrochloric acid	porcelain and	vacuum metallizing
coating	lacquer	ceramic coating	zinc chromate

(Review Continued)

REVIEW QUESTIONS

1. Name at least four benefits of metal finishing.
2. Describe how metal surfaces should be cleaned before being painted.
3. Name three kinds of chemical conversion coatings, and give a use for each.
4. What is a primer?
5. Why are leaded paints hazardous?
6. How do enamels differ from paints?
7. Name two advantages lacquers have over paints and enamels.
8. What is bronzing? How is it done?
9. Name three methods of applying paints.
10. Describe how to clean a conventional paintbrush.
11. Name two ways that oxide colors are produced on metals.
12. What is meant by electroplating? How does it differ from electroforming?
13. What is meant by anodizing?
14. Tell how electroplating is done.
15. Name five ways of plating metals other than electroplating.
16. Explain how porcelain enamels are different from enamel paints.
17. Name several advantages of porcelain enamels.
18. What does burnishing mean? How is it done?
19. Tell how spot finishing is done.

UNIT
47
Buffing

Buffing means to polish to a smooth, bright finish. It is done by rubbing the metal surface with a **buffing wheel** to which a **buffing compound** has been applied (Fig. 47-1). On most metals, this process can produce a mirror finish, which is often the finishing treatment desired. Buffing is also done to smooth a metal surface in preparation for electroplating.

Buffing wheels are made of cloth, felt, or leather (Fig. 47-2). Leather and felt make hard wheels. They are used with coarse buffing compounds for fast initial buffing of rough surfaces. Cloth wheels of **cotton muslin** are used for intermediate buffing. Soft **cotton flan-** nel wheels and fine buffing compounds are used to obtain smooth, bright finishes.

Goblet buffing wheels are ball-shaped so they can buff the inside of bowls and goblets (Fig. 47-3).

Some polishing wheels are set with fiber or wire bristles (Fig. 47-4). Fiber bristle and **wire wheels** are used mostly for cleaning and burnishing. A **satin finish** can be obtained on aluminum by wire brushing. Light scratch brushing is recommended just before a chemical coloring treatment as an aid in obtaining uniform coloring.

Fig. 47-1 *This worker is loading a metal sheet into a buffing machine. The entire surface of the sheet will be buffed automatically as it is drawn through the machine.* (Apollo Metal Inc.)

Fig. 47-4 *Polishing wheels: (A) wire wheel; (B) abrasive flap wheel; (C) abrasive impregnated nylon wheel.* (DoAll) (Merit Abrasives)

Fig. 47-2 *A cloth buffing wheel.*

Fig. 47-3 *A goblet buffing wheel can polish the inside of bowls and goblets.*

Abrasive flap and **abrasive impregnated nylon wheels** are used for deburring and fast smoothing of rough surfaces prior to buffing (Fig. 47-4).

Buffing machines, also called **buffers** and **buffing heads,** look very much like ordinary grinding machines (Fig. 47-5). Some buffing wheels have **arbor holes.** The spindle, or **arbor,** of the buffing machine goes through this hole. The wheel is attached to the end of the arbor with a washer and nut (Fig. 47-2). Jewelers' buffing wheels have only a pinhole at center and are screwed directly on a tapered buffing spindle (Fig. 47-6).

Fig. 47-5 *A small buffing machine.*

Fig. 47-6 *A tapered spindle is used to hold jeweler's buffing wheels.*

Fig. 47-7 *Bars of various buffing compounds.*

47-1 Buffing Compounds

Buffing compounds are abrasive materials. When applied to buffing wheels, they do the actual work of cutting and polishing the metal. Some of the abrasives used are **lime, tripoli, crocus** and **rouge, emery,** and **aluminum oxide.** Tripoli is a weathered, decomposed limestone also called **rottenstone.** Rouge is a soft iron oxide. It comes in different shades of red; the darker the color, the harder the rouge. The lighter product is called "rouge" and the darker "crocus." **Emery** and **aluminum oxide** are described in Unit 42. These materials are mixed with **tallow** or some other heavy grease, and pressed into bars or cakes (Fig. 47-7). Coarse compounds are used for the first, or **rough,** buffing while fine compounds are used for the final buffing. Table 47-1 lists some buffing compounds and the metals they are used for.

Table 47-1

Buffing Compounds and Uses

Metal	Compound	
	Roughing	Finishing
Aluminum	Tripoli	Rouge
Brass	Tripoli	Lime
Copper	Tripoli	Lime
Pewter	Tripoli	Rouge
Steel	400 Silicon Carbide	Rouge

47-2 How To Buff

Choose a buffing compound according to the kind of metal to be buffed. Put it on the buffing wheel by holding it against the edge of the revolving wheel. **It is best to put only a little buffing compound on the wheel at a time.** When the surface of the wheel is coated with the compound, it is then ready for buffing.

Fig. 47-8 *The workpiece is held against the buffing wheel so that if it is pulled out of the hands it will fly from you. A respirator should be worn to protect against dust inhalation.* (Manual High School, Roger Bean)

Hold the work on the underside of the front of the wheel. If it is then pulled out of your hands, it will fly **away from you,** not toward you (see Fig. 47-8). When the work is held on the underside of the wheel, the **dust** produced will also fly away from you. If considerable buffing is to be done, a **respirator** should be worn. It will filter out the dust and grit created by the buffing operations (Fig. 47-8).

The work should be moved and turned as it is held lightly against the wheel. In this way, the wheel rubs every corner and curve of the work. **Let the buffing compound do the work of polishing.** Pushing the workpiece hard against the wheel only creates friction and makes the workpiece hot. If the buffing proceeds too slowly, use a coarser compound first.

Change from a wheel with a coarse buffing compound to a wheel with a finer compound when all scratches and blemishes have been removed. Buff with the fine compound until you are satisfied with the finish. If the work comes from the wheel looking greasy and dirty, too much buffing compound has been put on the wheel. The grease can be removed by washing with hot water and mild soap or **washing soda.**

When thousands of identical parts require buffing, automatic buffing machines are used (Fig. 47-9).

Fig. 47-9 *Automatic buffing machines are used when thousands of identical parts need buffing.* (Divine Finishing Machinery/Munson)

REVIEW REVIEW REVIEW REVIEW REVIEW

WORDS TO KNOW

arbor	cotton flannel	lime	tallow
buffing compound	cotton muslin	respirator	tripoli
buffing head	crocus	rouge	washing soda
buffing machine	goblet buffing wheel	satin finish	wire brush
buffing wheel			

REVIEW QUESTIONS

1. What is meant by buffing?
2. Name the different kinds of buffing wheels, and tell when each is used.
3. What kind of finishing operations are wire wheels used for?
4. Name two ways of fastening buffing wheels to buffing machine spindles.
5. What buffing compounds are used for polishing aluminum? Brass? Steel?
6. What is the cause of dirty, greasy-looking work that has been buffed? How should the work be cleaned?
7. Why should a respirator be worn if buffing is done for a long period of time?
8. Tell how the workpiece should be held for safe buffing.

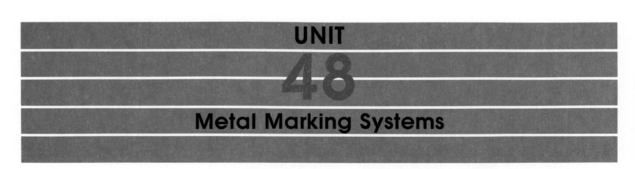

UNIT
48
Metal Marking Systems

The **marking** of industrial products and materials is essential to many businesses. Machines, cars, appliances, watches, and other products are marked with **serial numbers.** Many of the individual parts of these products are marked with a **part number** and sometimes a **trademark.** Tools such as **drills, reamers, taps, dies, wrenches,** and **gages** require size and other markings for correct identification and use (Fig. 48-1). Metal **materials** are often marked to tell what kind, grade, or size they are (Fig. 48-2).

Fig. 48-1 Typical tool marking showing tool size and type, and manufacturer's trademark.

GR-AN-REYNOLDS – 6061-T6511-QQ-A-200/8 .

Fig. 48-2 *Markings on aluminum bar stock show its size, alloy number, and manufacturer.*

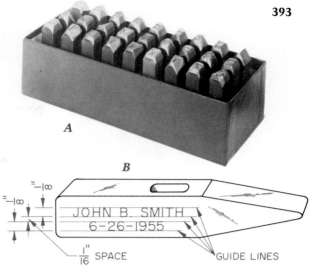

A

B

Stamping

Stamping is a fast and inexpensive method of marking metal labels and parts. Equipment for stamping may be fully automatic, such as when punch presses are used.

Many manually operated machines are also used for stamping. **Rolltype** marking machines use a **cylindrical die** for marking, and are capable of very high production rates (Fig. 48-3).

Steel letter and **number stamps** are made in sets in sizes from ¹⁄₆₄″ to 1″ [0.4 to 25 mm]. They may be used individually, by striking with a **ball-peen hammer** (Fig. 48-4). They may also be used several at a time in holders. The holders are either hand-held or used with a press.

When using letters and numbers by hand, use penciled guidelines to help do a neat job. Try out the stamp on a piece of metal scrap before stamping the product; unless this is done, the letter or figure is often stamped upside down. A center punch may be used for making periods.

Fig. 48-4 *(A) A set of steel letter stamps; (B) use guidelines when hand stamping.* (Numberall Stamp & Tool Company)

Stamping tools are made of hardened and tempered steel. They will be damaged or ruined if used on other hardened and tempered steel parts. Therefore, any stamping of steel parts that are to be hardened should be done while the steel is soft.

48-2 Etching and Engraving

Chemical etching is a way of marking or decorating by using acid to eat into the metal. This process, also known as **chemical milling**, is described in Unit 88. It is one of the few ways of marking **hardened steel**.

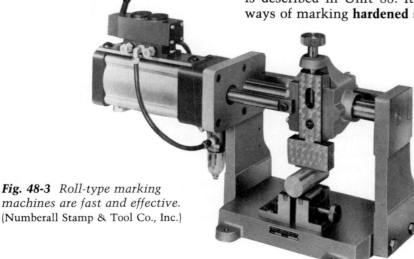

Fig. 48-3 *Roll-type marking machines are fast and effective.* (Numberall Stamp & Tool Co., Inc.)

Fig. 48-5 *An electrically powered engraving tool.* (Duane Zehr)

Fig. 48-7 *Laser-engraved part.* (Coherent General Inc.)

Fig. 48-6 *Precision engraving machines use revolving cutters to engrave machine dials, signs, panel markings, and mold details.* (Lars Machine Inc.)

Electrochemical etching is similar to electrochemical machining, which is described in Unit 84. In this process, the desired design or message is first drawn or typed on a stencil. The stencil is then attached to the electrochemical tool, in contact with a felt pad that is soaked with an electrolyte. The lines typed or drawn on the stencil permit the electrolyte to pass through and contact the workpiece.

When electricity is passed through the tool, the electrolyte, and the workpiece, metal is dissolved from the workpiece in the shape of the lines typed or drawn on the stencil.

Electrical etching is done with an electric pencil that has a carbon point. The electric pencil is powered either by a battery or by alternating current. In this process, a small electric arc does the actual cutting.

Conventional **engraving** uses mechanical tools to cut into the surface of the metal. Hand-held electrically powered engraving tools have a pointed carbide tip that can cut the hardest of metals (Fig. 48-5). Precision engraving is done with engraving machines that use revolving cutters (Fig. 48-6). Laser engraving is one of the most efficient ways of marking metal parts of any hardness (Fig. 48-7). Laser machining, a similar but more complex process, is discussed in Unit 86.

48-3
Printing

Temporary, removable markings are made on metal by printing with rubber plates or type, or by stenciling. **Rubber plates** are made to customer order for use either as hand stamps or on printing presses. **Rubber type** is assembled into strips and is also used in hand stamping or on printing presses.

Stenciling calls for cutting the design or message through a thin piece of metal or stiff cardboard. The stencil is laid over the surface to be marked. Then, a **stencil brush** containing ink is rubbed over the stencil, and the ink transfers the message through the stencil to the workpiece.

Stenciling is also done with hand stamps. As pressure is applied to the **hand imprinter,** ink is forced through the stencil from a pad mounted behind it, and the message is printed.

REVIEW   REVIEW   REVIEW   REVIEW   REVIEW

WORDS TO KNOW

carbide tip	electrochemical	rubber plate	stencil
carbon point	etching	rubber type	stencil brush
chemical etching	engraving	stamping	
electric pencil	roll-type marking	steel letters and	
electrical etching	machine	numbers	

REVIEW QUESTIONS

1. Why are metal marking systems necessary?
2. How is metal marked with metal dies or stamps?
3. Why can't hardened steel be marked with metal dies or stamps?
4. To assure a neat job, what should be done before hand stamping with steel letters and numbers?
5. Describe how chemical etching is done.
6. How does electrochemical etching differ from chemical etching? What other electrochemical process is similar to electrochemical etching?
7. How is electrical etching done?
8. Describe two ways conventional engraving is done.
9. What high technology machining method is also very efficient for engraving?
10. How are rubber plates and rubber type used in marking metal?
11. What is stenciling? Name two methods of using stencils for marking.

PART

13

Introduction to Machining

Connie Douglas' introduction to machining began in the shop of a large milling machine company. She says that a basic math background and a knowledge of tooling would be of great help to such a beginner. However, Connie learned her skills on the job. She is a steady, willing worker and has the keen eyesight required to read the small numerical measurements and changes connected with the work. Connie also learned how to read blueprints—another plus.

Five years later, Connie advanced to the position of internal grinder operator. This gave her the opportunity to specialize in one procedure. At the same time, there is such variety in her work that it is always challenging. The more specialized the workpiece, the more creativity Connie must bring to it. She considers the many possibilities and then determines the best way to fasten a certain piece to the grinding machine.

Not only is Connie happy with the variety in her work, she is also very pleased with the wages. She is satisfied that a woman with her background is a well-paid employee. Connie feels that women make especially good operators because they try very hard and usually have a lot of patience.

Charles Zilch

To others who may wish to enter her field, Connie says, ''Grinding applications are expanding and procedures are becoming more intricate. More operators, especially women, will be needed in the field as it continues to grow.''

Connie Douglas
Internal Grinder Operator

UNIT
49
Holding Workpieces for Machining

To keep a workpiece from moving or turning under the pressure of cutting, always clamp it securely in a vise or to the machine table. If the workpiece **springs** or moves while it is being machined, the cutting tool may break. In addition, the workpiece may be thrown from the machine, and injury may result to the operator, workpiece, or machine. Figure 49-1 shows the results of **workpiece spring** during drilling.

SAFETY NOTE
Even when work seems well clamped, it often pulls loose. When this happens, shut off the machine and step away from it.

Fig. 49-1 *A broken drill, the result of workpiece springing during drill breakthrough.*

49-1 Setting Up Work

Properly positioning and clamping a workpiece in a machine vise or holding fixture, or directly attaching it to a machine tool table, is known as **setting up.** The setup tools and the procedures used are similar for setting up workpieces on **drill presses, milling machines, shapers,** and **planers.** Most of these machines have tables with **T-slots** through which bolts may be slipped for clamping vises and workpieces (Figs. 49-2 and 49-3).

49-2 Holding Devices and Accessories

A variety of devices are used alone or together to hold workpieces.

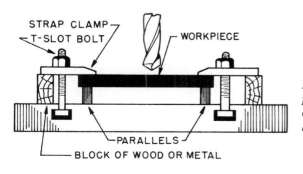

STRAP CLAMP
T-SLOT BOLT
WORKPIECE
PARALLELS
BLOCK OF WOOD OR METAL

Fig. 49-2 *Holding a flat workpiece on parallels. With this setup, use light pressure on tools to minimize workpiece springing and danger of tool breakage.*

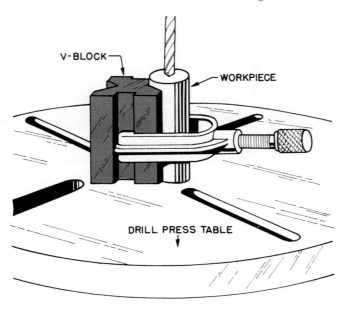

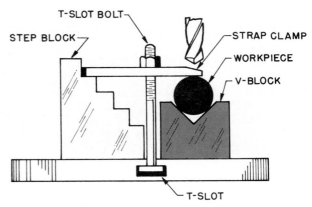

Fig. 49-3 *Two methods of holding a round workpiece with V-blocks.*

Strap Clamps

Six kinds of **strap clamps** are shown in Figure 49-4. They are the **plain clamp,** or **strap;** the **U-clamp;** the **gooseneck clamp;** the **screw-heel clamp;** the **finger clamp;** and the **double-finger clamp.** They are used to hold down the workpiece (Figs. 49-2, 49-3). The U-clamp can be removed without removing the nut from the bolt. The gooseneck clamp can be used with a shorter bolt than the other clamps.

Sometimes the workpiece is too high to be clamped in the ordinary way. In such cases, one or more holes are sometimes drilled in the sides of the workpiece, and finger clamps are placed in these holes to clamp the work to the table.

Parallel Clamps

Parallel clamps, also called **toolmakers'** or **machinists' clamps,** are used for light workpiece clamping (Figs. 49-4 and 49-5).

C-Clamps

C-clamps, shaped like the letter C, are useful for general purpose clamping. See Figures 49-4 and 49-6.

Fig. 49-4 *Setup tools for holding workpieces.*

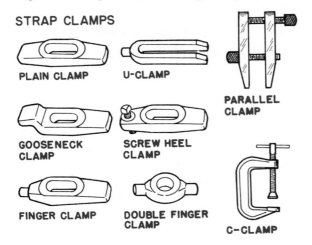

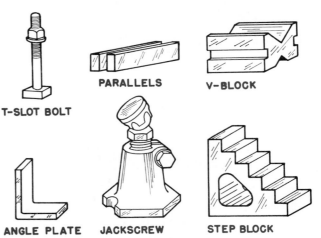

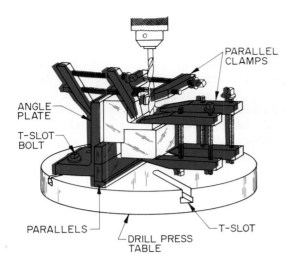

Fig. 49-7 *A complete clamping set.* (DoAll)

Fig. 49-5 *Using an angle plate, parallels, and parallel clamps to hold a workpiece.*

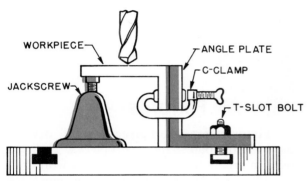

Fig. 49-6 *Using a C-clamp, angle plate, and jackscrew to hold a workpiece.*

Fig. 49-8 *Studs can be combined in different lengths to provide the length needed for large workpieces.* (Manual High School, Roger Bean)

T-Slot Bolts

T-slot bolts are usually used with the strap clamps. They also are used to bolt the vise to the machine table. The head of the bolt is made to fit the **T-slot** in the table (Figs. 49-2, 49-3, 49-4, and 49-9).

T-Nuts and Studs

T-nuts and studs serve the same purpose as T-bolts but can be used in more ways. A complete clamping system including T-nuts and studs is shown in Figure 49-7. If necessary, studs of several lengths can be combined to get the required length as in Figure 49-8.

The Angle Plate

Work is sometimes clamped to an angle plate that is clamped to the machine table. See Figures 49-4, 49-5, and 49-6.

Parallels

Parallels are strips of cast iron or hardened steel with opposite sides ground parallel. They come in pairs exactly alike in size. Parallels are used in leveling and supporting the work. A parallel is placed under each end of the work. They are expensive precision tools and deserve the best of care. See Figures 49-2, 49-4, and 49-9.

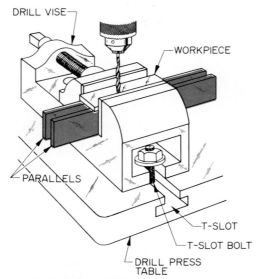

Fig. 49-9 *Using a drill press vise and parallels to hold a workpiece.*

The Jackscrew

The jackscrew, also known as a **planer jack,** ranges in height from two inches [50 mm] upward. It may be used for leveling or supporting odd-shaped work (Figs. 49-4 and 49-6).

V-blocks

The V-block gets its name from its V-shaped angles (Fig. 49-4). The angle of the V is usually 90°. V-blocks are used to hold round work (Fig. 49-3). They should be made or purchased in pairs so that one can be placed under each end of long work. They are made with or without matching clamps.

The Step Block

The step block is used to support and **block up** one end of a strap clamp. This levels the clamp so that both ends are the same height from the table (Figs. 49-3 and 49-4). If a level on the step block does not match the height of the workpiece, pick the nearest step higher than the workpiece.

Step blocks may be purchased in sets, with or without matching strap clamps.

Vises

Vises are made in many sizes and shapes. For light drilling, reaming, tapping, and similar operations, vises are not usually fastened to the drill press table. Most vises, however, can be and should be fastened to the machine table when accurate or heavy machining is involved (Fig. 49-9).

Holding Flat Work

Flat work, such as a plate, may be clamped to the table as shown in Fig. 49-2. The workpiece may also be clamped to the table with a piece of plywood, Masonite®, or particle board under it to keep the tools from cutting into the table.

49-4 Fixtures

Fixtures are workpiece-holding devices used to hold odd-shaped workpieces. They are used in production work to enable a worker to quickly support and clamp a workpiece for machining. **Fixtures have no provision for guiding the cutting tools.** They are usually custom-made to hold a specific part. Figure 49-10 shows a typical fixture.

Fig. 49-10 *Fixtures provide quick and accurate alignment and clamping of irregularly shaped parts for machining.* (John Deere)

TECHNOLOGIES AND PRACTICES

Three-Dimensional History

The history of the American system of manufacturing cannot be exactly traced through documents and precise historic dates. Many people contributed to the overall progress. But records of their contributions often no longer exist, if they ever did. What does remain, in many cases, are the machines that people developed and used. By viewing the changes made in these machines through time we can learn the story of American industry.

The directors of the American Precision Museum are dedicated to preserving the memory of the people and machines that laid the foundation for modern metalworking. The museum is located in a building that was once the Robbins & Lawrence Armory in Windsor, Vermont. This historic shop was in operation from 1838 to 1855. In 1851, Robbins & Lawrence displayed guns with interchangeable parts at the Crystal Palace Industrial Exhibition in London. They immediately gained world recognition.

Now the museum is gaining international fame with its growing collection of historic machinery. More than 150 restored machines, many over 100 years old, are a part of museum property. Fifty or so are displayed at a time, and the exhibits are changed periodically.

Visitors can see early measuring tools, typewriters, and steam engines, as well as get a close-up look at the metalworking machines that produced them.

Among the exhibits are a lathe from the late 18th century and the original Brown and Sharpe universal grinder built in 1876.

History comes alive in three dimensions as the machines, many of which are still operable, show the story of the American way of work. The American Precision Museum is well on its way to reaching its goal of having the best collection of significant machine tools in the world.

Drill Jigs

If many pieces of the same kind have to be drilled, time and money can be saved by designing and making a **drill jig** (Fig. 49-11), which is a tool for holding the work while it is being drilled. There are many forms of drill jigs. The time that would be necessary to lay out the holes to be drilled in every piece is saved by using a drill jig.

Drill jigs are fitted with hardened steel bushings, called **drill bushings.** Figure 49-12 shows three kinds of drill bushings, namely, **flush, flanged,** and **slip bushings.** The drill bushing guides the drill.

Fig. 49-11 An example of a box drill jig.

Slip bushings are used at locations where reaming, tapping, or counterboring must take place. The hole is drilled with the slip bushing in place. Then the slip bushing is removed, providing clearance for tools of larger diameter to be used at the same location.

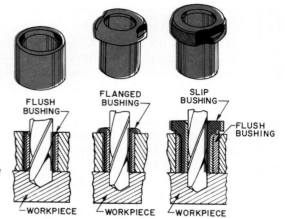

Fig. 49-12 Types of standard drill bushings.

REVIEW   REVIEW   REVIEW   REVIEW   REVIEW

WORDS TO KNOW

angle plate	flanged bushing	screw-heel clamp	T-bolts
double-finger clamp	flush bushing	setting up	T-nuts
drill bushing	gooseneck clamp	slip bushing	T-slots
drill jig	jackscrew	step block	U-clamps
finger clamp	parallel clamps	strap clamp	V-blocks
fixture	parallels	studs	

REVIEW QUESTIONS

1. What is meant by setting up a workpiece for machining?
2. Why is it important for workpieces to be accurately positioned, solidly supported, and clamped?
3. What are T-slots? What is their purpose?
4. Describe how the different strap clamps are used.
5. How do T-bolts differ from T-nuts and studs?
6. Name two types of general purpose clamps that can aid workpiece setup.
7. What are step blocks and how are they used?
8. Describe how V-blocks are used in setup work.
9. What are fixtures? In what way do they differ from jigs?
10. How are drill jigs used?

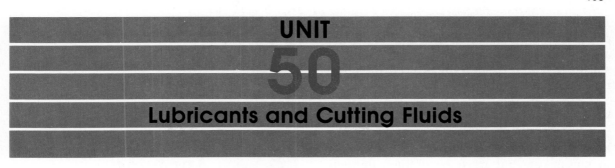

UNIT 50

Lubricants and Cutting Fluids

Lubricants are materials that are used to reduce friction, heat, wear, and vibration between moving surfaces. The materials used as lubricants include petroleum oils, animal oils, vegetable oils, greases, metallic films, mineral films, plastics, synthetic fluids, and gases.

Cutting fluids are specially compounded liquids that are applied to metal-cutting tools to make them cut easier.

50-1 Lubricating Oils

There are three main kinds of lubricating oils:
1. mineral oils
2. animal oils
3. vegetable oils.

Mineral oils. These oils are by far the most versatile and best-known lubricants. Petroleum is the leading source of mineral oils.

Lubricating oil is obtained from petroleum. It is used to oil the **bearing** surfaces of machinery. Its stiffness or thickness is called its **viscosity.** This is measured by the length of time in seconds that a standard amount of oil at a certain temperature can flow through a hole.

A medium-heavy oil is used for general machine oiling. It has a **Saybolt universal viscosity rating** of 250 to 500 seconds at 100°F [37.8°C] and may be called **Type C.** A thinner oil (70 to 100 second rating) is used in reservoirs such as at lathe spindles and may be called **spindle oil** or **Type A.**

Bed way lubricant is a heavy oil (300 to 500 seconds) for sliding surfaces such as cams and lathe beds. **Gear lubricant** is used to reduce noise from gears that do not run in oil. (Table 50-1 lists typical brands.)

Cylinder oil, or **motor oil,** is also obtained from petroleum. It is used for oiling **hot** parts, such as the pistons that slide in the cylinders of an engine. **It is not recommended for machine tool lubrication.**

Animal oils. These oils are obtained from the fats of animals. Fish oils are obtained from such fish as herring, salmon, sardine, and cod. Sperm oil from the sperm whale is rare and expensive. It is thinner than the other animal oils and is used to oil fine, delicate instruments and machinery.

Table 50-1

Typical Lubricating Oils for Machines

| Company name | Saybolt Universal Viscosity Rating in seconds at 100° F. | | |
	100 second: type A LIGHT (SPINDLE OIL)	150-240 sec.: type B MEDIUM LIGHT	250-500 sec.: type C MEDIUM HEAVY
Mobile	Velocite Oil 10	Gg. Vactra Oil Light	Gg. Vactra Hvy. Med.
Pure	Spindle Oil D	Puropale Medium	Puropale Hvy. Med.
Shell	Vitrea Oil 923	Vitrea Oil 27	Vitrea Oil 33
Sinclair	Cadet Oil A	Warrior Oil	Commander Oil B
South Bend Lathe	CE 2017	CE 2018	CE 2019
Standard (Ind)	Spindle Oil C	Indoil #15	Indoil #31

Note: This partial listing of typical brands is given as an aid in procuring comparative grades from the company of your preference.

Glycerin is a thick, oily, syrupy, colorless, odorless liquid obtained from animal fats. It is also produced synthetically from petroleum or sugar. Glycerin is sometimes used for oiling machines, especially engines.

Vegetable oils. These oils are obtained from plants and vegetables, especially from their seeds. **Castor oil,** made from the castor bean, is a very good lubricant. It is often used in racing cars but must be drained immediately after the engine is stopped, since it solidifies on cooling.

50-2 Greases

Greases are obtained from animal fats and petroleum. Most lubricating greases are petroleum oils that are thickened with soaps, clays, carbon, graphite, lead, zinc oxide, and other materials having lubricating properties.

Greases are often used in place of oils because (1) they can be sealed better against loss, (2) they protect against entrance of dirt and moisture, and (3) they tend to cling better to some surfaces.

Greases are classified from 0, **softest,** to 6, **stiffest,** by the **National Lubricating Grease Institute.** Grease selection should follow the machine manufacturer's recommendations.

50-3 Other Lubricants

Graphite, a form of carbon, is black, very soft, and slippery. It is used for lubricating some machine parts, especially where there is low speed and moderate heat. Graphite lasts longer than oil, does not get gummy, and does not attract dust.

White lead, a compound of lead, is a white powder. When mixed with **linseed oil,** it is a good high-pressure lubricant. When work is turned between centers in a metal lathe, the **tailstock,** or **dead-center,** is often lubricated with white lead.

SAFETY NOTE
White lead is poisonous and should be handled with due care.

50-4 Methods of Applying Lubricants

Oil is supplied to **lubrication points** in a variety of ways.

An **oil hole** is a small hole through which oil flows to a surface that must be oiled. An **oil groove,** which is usually connected to an oil hole, is a small groove through which oil is spread evenly over a surface that needs oil.

An **oil cup** is a small covered glass or metal cup attached near a surface that must be oiled. The oil which is put into the cup flows through a hole to the surface to be oiled.

An **oil tube,** or **oil pipe,** is often used to deliver oil to moving parts of machinery that cannot be reached directly.

Oil tube systems that provide lubrication to an entire machine from one central reservoir are called **"one-shot" lubrication systems.** These systems are either fully automatic or are manually operated.

Grease is often packed directly into **bearings** and **grease cups** by hand. A **grease cup** is a small covered cup installed near a surface that must be greased. The grease is forced out of the cup by screwing down its cap. Grease is also forced through **grease fittings** with a **grease gun** to lubrication points (Fig. 50-1).

50-5 Cutting Fluids

Cutting fluids function in the following ways to improve the cutting or machining of metals:
1. Cool the cutting tool and the work.
2. Lubricate the face of the cutting tool and the chip.

Fig. 50-1 *Using a grease gun to grease a fitting on a drill press.*

3. Prevent the **adhesion,** or **pressure welding,** of a **built-up edge** on the cutting tool. A built-up edge is caused by a small metal chip sticking to the cutting edge of a cutting tool.
4. Aid in flushing away chips.
5. Improve the quality of the machined surface.
6. Increase tool life by reducing tool wear.
7. Permit higher cutting speeds than those used for dry machining.

Cutting fluids can be classified under three groups: **cutting oils, emulsifiable oils,** and **chemical cutting fluids.** However, based on their origin and composition, there are six types of cutting fluids:

1. lard oil
2. mineral oil
3. mineral and lard oil combinations
4. sulfurized and chlorinated mineral oils
5. emulsifiable (soluble) oils
6. chemical cutting fluids.

Lard oil is an animal oil obtained from lard, or hog fat. It is an excellent cutting oil, but is so expensive that it is usually mixed with mineral oils. Pure lard oil also tends to develop a bad odor. Bacteria that breed in lard oil can also cause **dermatitis** and skin irritation among machine operators. Lard oil is useful for machining metals that would otherwise be stained by using mineral oils containing sulfur.

Mineral oils are used in light-duty cutting operations, especially with nonferrous metals and **free-cutting** (easily cut) steel. **Mineral-lard** oil, a mixture, provides better lubricating properties, and is used in medium-duty cutting operations. **Sulfurized and chlorinated** mineral oils are recommended for cutting tough metals and for severe machining operations, such as **broaching** and **tapping,** that put a heavy strain on the tool.

Emulsifiable oil is often called **soluble oil** or **water-soluble oil.** A soluble oil cutting fluid is made by adding **the oil to the water** (never water to oil), which forms a milky-white solution. The proportions of water and oil vary according to the severity (difficulty) of the machining operation. The more severe the machining operation, the more oil is added to the water. For best results, follow the manufacturer's recommendations for specific ratios of water and oil to be used for the different machining operations.

Soluble oil solutions have excellent lubricant and coolant qualities. They are also relatively inexpensive.

Chemical cutting fluids are solutions of various chemical compounds in water. They generally do not contain petroleum products. Two types are made. Those with lubricants and wetting agents added are used for a wide range of machining operations, including severe machining. Plain fluids (having no lubricants or wetting agents added) are used mainly for surface grinding operations.

Kerosene, a thin oil obtained from petroleum is sometimes used as a lubricant in cutting metals (see Table 50-2). **Because it is flammable, it must be used carefully.**

SAFETY NOTE

When using kerosene as a cutting fluid, store it in approved containers because it is flammable.

Never use kerosene near an open flame or other heat source that is hot enough to ignite it.

50-6 Cutting Fluid Selection

For efficient cutting or machining of most metals, a cutting fluid should be used. Metals such as cast iron and magnesium, however, are often cut dry. Cast iron contains graphite, which lubricates the tool as it cuts. Table 50-2 contains further information on cutting fluid selection.

SAFETY NOTE

Water-based cutting fluids should never be used on magnesium because of the fire hazard. When water reacts to hot magnesium, hydrogen gas is released, which catches fire and explodes or burns vigorously.

50-7 Methods of Applying Cutting Fluids

Cutting fluids may be applied to taps, dies, and drills with an oil can or a brush. Production machine tools and many general purpose machines have built-in **coolant systems,** which pump cutting fluid to the points of cutting through systems of pipes (Fig. 51-3).

Table 50-2

Cutting Fluids for Cutting Common Metals

Metals	Power sawing	Drilling	Reaming	Threading	Turning	Milling	Grinding
Carbon Steels Malleable Iron	EO, MO, ML	EO, Sul, ML	ML, Sul, EO	Sul, ML, EO	EO, Sul, ML	EO, Sul, ML	EO
Wrought Iron Stainless Steels Tool Steels High-Speed Steels	EO, ML, MO	EO, Sul, ML	ML, Sul	Sul, ML, EO	EO, Sul, ML	EO, Sul, ML	EO
Gray Cast Iron	Dry, EO	Dry, EO	Dry, EO	Dry, EO, ML	Dry, EO	Dry, EO	EO, MO
Aluminum Alloys	Dry, EO, MO	EO, MO, ML	ML, MO, EO	ML, MO, EO, K	EO, MO, ML, K	EO, MO, ML	EO, MO
Copper-base Alloys Brass Bronze	Dry, MO, ML, EO	EO, MO, ML	ML, MO, EO	ML, MO, EO	EO, MO, ML	EO, MO, ML	EO
Magnesium Alloys	Dry, MO	Dry, MO	Dry, MO	Dry, MO	Dry, MO	Dry, MO	Dry, MO

Key:
  K—Kerosene
  L—Lard Oil
  MO—Mineral Oils
  ML—Mineral-Lard Oils
  Sul—Sulfurized Oils, with or without chlorine
  EO—Emulsifiable (soluble) Oils and Compounds
  Dry—No cutting fluid

In factories with many machines using the same cutting fluid, it is often pumped from one large tank to the several machines. It is then pumped back to the tank, where it is strained and used over and over again.

Spray-mist coolant systems use a water-base fluid that is delivered to the cutting tool under pressure of compressed air. The compressed air **atomizes** (breaks into tiny particles) the cutting fluid. This atomized mist provides considerable cooling but little lubrication. The fluid is lost in the process.

REVIEW   REVIEW   REVIEW   REVIEW   REVIEW

WORDS TO KNOW

animal oil	cylinder oil	lard oil	sperm oil
atomize	dermatitis	lubricant	spindle oil
bed way lubricant	emulsifiable oil	machine oil	spray-mist coolant
built-up edge	gear lubricant	mineral oil	system
castor oil	glycerin	mineral-lard oil	sulfurized and
chemical cutting	graphite	oil cup	chlorinated
fluid	grease cup	one-shot lubrication	mineral oil
coolant	grease fitting	system	viscosity
cutting oil	grease gun	soluble oil	white lead

REVIEW QUESTIONS

1. Name the three main kinds of lubricating oils.
2. What types of oils are the most versatile and best known?
3. What kind of oil should be used for lubricating machines?
4. What is meant by the viscosity of oil? How is it measured?
5. What materials are lubricating greases made from?
6. Why are greases used instead of oils in some cases?
7. How are greases classified according to stiffness?
8. What is graphite? What kind of lubrication is it used for?
9. What kind of lubrication is white lead used for?
10. Why should care be taken in handling white lead?
11. Explain how a one-shot lubrication system works.
12. List two ways of getting grease to the point of lubrication.
13. List the ways in which cutting fluids improve the machining of metals.
14. Name the three groups of cutting fluids.
15. List the six types of cutting fluids.
16. How is emulsifiable cutting fluid prepared?
17. What are chemical cutting fluids?
18. How are cutting fluids applied on production machines?
19. How does a spray-mist coolant system work?
20. Why are cast iron and magnesium often machined dry?
21. Why should water-based fluids never be used for machining magnesium?

PART

14

Power Sawing

Donald Wright has worked with metals for over 30 years. In high school, he took several shop courses and worked in a factory during summer vacations. In college, he was trained in industrial tooling. And through the years, he has worked with metal specialists and technology engineers. Now Donald is Vice President of Sales for a company that makes industrial saw blades. He uses his accumulated knowledge to serve the company's potential customers.

Donald's job is to help his customer, often a machine shop owner, choose the right blade for a particular saw. First he evaluates the type of metal the blade must cut. Then he determines the kind of cutting and the speed and feed required for the job. If the cut is to be on expensive steel, Donald wants to supply the customer with a blade that will remove the least amount of metal. Good clean cuts, as burr-free as possible, are important of course in cutting any metal, whether it is steel, brass, or copper.

After Donald has discovered just what his customer needs, he works out the production details with his company's toolmakers. Some of his real work, however, involves salesmanship. He must know saw blades thoroughly. In addition, he must apply his well-developed communication skills. In many sales situations, Donald must explain to a customer the benefits of using his company's products.

Donald is friendly and out-going. He says that he thoroughly "enjoys people." With his extensive metal-working knowledge and his ability to communicate easily with prospective clients, Donald is able to make sure that both his blade and his customer are "always right."

Donald Wright
Vice President of Sales

UNIT
51

Stock Cutoff Machines

Stock is a general term used for the metal sheets, plates, rods, bars, and other shapes that come from the rolling mill. Four types of power machines are used for cutting off stock: (1) power hacksaws, (2) horizontal band saws, (3) cold saws, and (4) abrasive cutoff saws.

51-1

Power Hacksaws

Power hacksaws (Fig. 51-1) operate similar to hand hacksaws. On the cutting stroke, the blade teeth are forced into the metal either by gravity or by hydraulic pressure. The pressure is automatically removed on the return stroke to reduce wear on the blade. Most power hacksaws have a **chip tray** and a cabinet base that holds the **cutting fluid** and its pump.

Fig. 51-1 *A power hacksaw.* (Racine Hydraulics & Machinery Inc.)

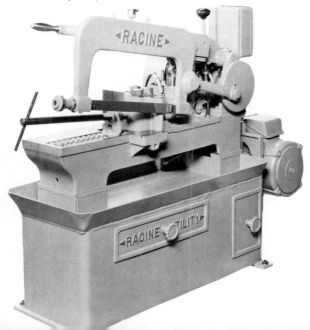

Power hacksaw vises may be **plain** or a special **swivel** type, which allows cutting at different angles. The movable jaw can be positioned quickly along a toothed rack (Fig. 51-2). Most machines are also equipped with a **cutoff gage.** Once set, the operator can then cut several pieces the same length without having to measure each piece.

Power hacksaws are of two basic types, **dry-cutting** and **wet-cutting.** With the wet-cutting machines a **cutting fluid** is used (Fig. 51-3). With cutting fluid the saw may be operated at higher cutting speeds and the blade lasts longer.

The **cutting speed** for power hacksaws ranges from about 35 to 150 **cutting strokes** per minute, depending on the make and type of machine.

With cutting tools, the **feed** is the movement of the tool into the workpiece with each stroke or revolution. The **feeding pressure** is the amount of pressure exerted on the blade during the cutting stroke. Large work needs more feeding pressure than small work. A worn blade needs more feeding pressure to make it cut than a new blade. Most power hacksaws are equipped with a control device for adjusting the feeding pressure during the cutting stroke.

Fig. 51-2 *A toothed rack provides quick adjustment of the power hacksaw vise jaw.*

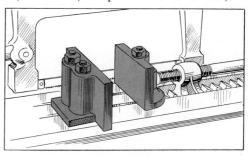

Fig. 51-3 *Cutting fluid being used on a power hacksaw. Cutting fluids prolong blade life, allow higher cutting speeds and feeds, and provide smoother workpiece finishes.* (Joseph T. Ryerson & Son, Inc.)

Power hacksaws may be **single-speed, 2-speed, 3-speed,** or **4-speed.** Each different speed is expressed as the number of strokes per minute. Hard and tough metals, such as high-carbon steel or tool steel, should be cut at lower cutting speeds than ordinary low-carbon steels. Table 51-1 gives recommended cutting speeds for power hacksaws.

Blades and Their Selection

Length. Blades are made in lengths ranging from 12″ [305 mm] for small machines to 30″ [762 mm] for very large machines.

Thickness. Blades are made in thicknesses of:

0.032″ [0.8 mm]	0.075″ [1.9 mm]
0.050″ [1.27 mm]	0.088″ [2.24 mm]
0.062″ [1.57 mm]	0.100″ [2.54 mm].

Width. Blades are made in widths of:

⅝″ [15.86 mm]	1¾″ [44.45 mm]
1″ [25.4 mm]	2″ [50.8 mm]
1¼″ [31.75 mm]	2½″ [63.5 mm].
1½″ [38.1 mm]	

Table 51-1

Cutting Speeds Recommended for Power Hacksaws

Material	Strokes per minute dry	Strokes per minute wet
Low-carbon Steel	70-100	100-140
Medium-carbon steel	70	100-140
High-carbon steel	70	100
High-speed steel	70	100
Drill rod	70	100
Alloy steel	70	100
Cast iron	70-100	(cut dry)
Aluminum	100	140
Brass	70	100-140
Bronze	70	100

Tooth pitch. Pitch refers to the spacing between the blade teeth (see Fig. 15-2). Blades are available with 3, 4, 6, 10, 14, and 18 teeth per inch [8.5, 6, 4, 2.5, 1.8, and 1.4 mm pitch].

Blade selection. For most applications in the school shop, blades with 6, 10, or 14 teeth per inch [4, 2.5, and 1.8 mm pitch] are used. Blades with 14 or 10 teeth [1.8 or 2.5 mm pitch] are used for the majority of light-duty sawing operations in school shops. The 14-tooth [1.8 mm pitch] blades are used for cutting thin-wall tubing, thin angles, and other metals of less than about ¼″ [6.35 mm] thickness. The 10-tooth [2.5 mm pitch] blades are used for general-purpose sawing applications on metals from ¼″ [6.35 mm] to about ¾″ [19 mm] thickness. A 6-tooth [4 mm pitch] blade should be selected for efficient cuts on workpieces from about 1″ to 2″ [25.4 to 50.8 mm] thickness and a 4-tooth [6 mm pitch] blade for workpieces greater than 2″ [50.8 mm] in thickness.

The following principles apply to the selection of power hacksaw blades:

1. A minimum of **two** teeth should contact the workpiece at all times.
2. Soft, easily machined materials and large workpieces require **coarse-toothed** blades for adequate **chip clearance,** so that chips do not clog the blade.
3. Small workpieces and thin-walled tubing require **fine** teeth.
4. **Harder** materials require **finer** teeth.

51-2 Horizontal Band Saws

Most stock cutoff **band saws** are horizontal machines designed especially for cutting stock. Figure 51-4 shows a machine of medium size. Band saws have several advantages over other stock cutoff machines:

1. Their saw blades make a kerf (saw cut) of only $\frac{1}{16}$" [1.5 mm] width, compared to $\frac{1}{8}$" [3 mm] for power hacksaws and abrasive disc saws, and $\frac{1}{4}$" [6 mm] for cold saws. This provides considerable savings when cutting large stock or expensive material.

2. Cutting rates are faster because their endless blades cut continuously instead of intermittently (on and off) like power hacksaws.

3. Because the blades are thinner, they require less power for cutting.

Portable band saw. Some metal that must be sawed cannot be easily moved to a saw, so a portable band saw (Fig. 51-5) may be carried to the job.

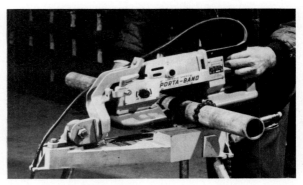

Fig. 51-5 *A portable band saw.* (Rockwell International-Power Tool Division)

Fig. 51-4 *A horizontal band saw is an efficient cutoff tool.* (DoAll)

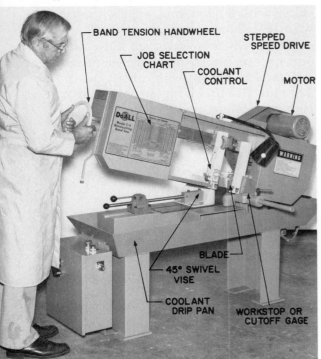

BAND TENSION HANDWHEEL
STEPPED SPEED DRIVE
JOB SELECTION CHART
COOLANT CONTROL
MOTOR
WARNING
BLADE
45° SWIVEL VISE
COOLANT DRIP PAN
WORKSTOP OR CUTOFF GAGE

Table 51-2

Band-Saw Blade Widths and Pitches for Stock Cutoff

Workpiece thickness	Blade width	Pitch
up to 5/8" (16 mm)	1" (25 mm)	10* (2.5 mm)
5/8" (16 mm) to 1" (25 mm)	1" (25 mm)	8 (3 mm)
1" (25 mm) to 4" (100 mm)	1" (25 mm)	6 (4 mm)
4" (100 mm) to 10" (250 mm)	1" (25 mm) to 1-1/4" (32 mm)	4 (6 mm)
10" (250 mm) to 20" (500 mm)	1-1/4" (32 mm) to 2" (50 mm)	3 (8 mm)

*Teeth per inch

Blade selection. Band-saw blades of carbon tool steel, alloy tool steel, and high-speed steel are available. Composite blades with high-speed steel or tungsten carbide teeth welded to a carbon steel back are also available. High-speed steel blades are preferred for cutoff work because they give long service life at high cutting speeds. Blades 1" [25.4 mm] or wider are usually used because their high strength can withstand heavy cutting pressures.

Blades with **regular tooth form** are used for cutting material up to 1" [25 mm] thick. **Hook tooth blades** are recommended for cutting thicker material. Tooth form profiles are shown in Figure 52-8. Table 51-2 gives blade width and pitch recommendations for cutting different material thicknesses. Unit 52 gives further information on band-saw blade selection.

Speeds and feeds. Recommended cutting speeds and feeds vary with (A) the kind of blade material, (B) the size and condition of the blade, (C) the kind and thickness of material to be cut, and (D) whether or not a cutting fluid is used. Most horizontal band saws have a provision for setting the **feed rate**. Table 52-1 gives the cutting speeds for use with various materials.

51-3 Cold Saws

Cold saws are low-speed (low rpm) circular saws made especially for cutting metals. They range in size from hand-operated models with 8″ [200 mm] blades to automatic machines with blades of 3′ [900 mm] or more. Light-duty machines usually have a swivel head that allows cuts to be made at any angle (Fig. 51-6). Cold saws are most efficient for cutting I-beams, angles, and channels because the circular blades can complete their cuts with less travel than straight blades. Heavy-duty machines with automatic feed are efficient for cutting solid bars up to 10″ [250 mm] thick.

Fig. 51-6 *A manually operated cold saw with a swivel head.* (Kasto-Racine)

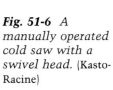

Cold-saw blades. Blade widths for cold saws refer to the width of the kerf they make. The blade width increases with blade diameter, and ranges from ⁵⁄₆₄″ [2 mm] to ⁵⁄₁₆″ [8 mm]. Blades 14″ [350 mm] and over have inserted teeth of high-speed steel. Solid high-speed steel blades may be resharpened up to 20 times. Tooth pitches range from very fine at ⅛″ [3 mm] to very coarse at ⅝″ [16 mm]. Fine-pitch blades are used for cutting tubing and solid bars up to ½″ [12.7 mm], medium-pitch blades for cutting solid bars from ½″ [12.7 mm] to 1½″ [37.5 mm], and coarse-pitch blades for cutting solid bars above 1½″ [37.5 mm].

51-4 Abrasive Cutoff Saws

Abrasive cutoff saws (Fig. 51-7) use **abrasive discs** for stock cutoff. They are made either for manual operation or with power feeds, and with either **fixed** or **oscillating** wheel heads. Oscillating wheel head machines are best for cutting thick pieces of tough metals such as titanium and high-alloy steels. Machine sizes range from small bench-top machines with 8″ [200 mm] wheels, to machines with 20″ [500 mm] and larger wheels.

Abrasive cutoff saws are most useful for cutting very tough or hardened metals that cannot be easily cut with other types of saws. They are also useful for cutting small sizes of bar stock, tubing, and structural shapes.

51-5 Stock Cutoff Machine Operation

The following procedures apply to the operation of all types of stock cutoff machines:
1. Wear safety glasses or goggles.
2. On machines with swivel vises, check that the vise is set at the desired angle and is securely fastened.

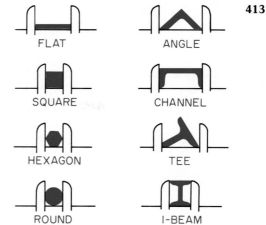

Fig. 51-7 *A manually operated abrasive cutoff machine.* (Everett Industries)

Fig. 51-8 *Correct method of holding different shapes of metal in a power saw vise.*

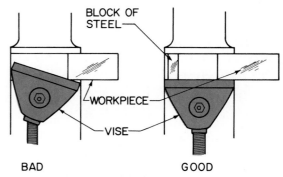

Fig. 51-9 *Holding a short piece of metal in a power saw vise.*

3. Position the stock properly in the vise (Fig. 51-8). Several pieces may be cut at the same time if they can be held securely.
4. If the piece of stock to be cut is short, place another piece of the same size on the opposite side of the vise. Then the vise jaws stay parallel (Fig. 51-9). If the stock is long, support the over-hanging end(s) with a **stock support** (Fig. 51-10).
5. Change the blade if it is in poor condition, or if it is the wrong kind of blade for the metal being cut.
6. Lower the saw blade and rest it lightly on the stock so that the length of the piece can be measured. If several pieces of the same size are to be cut, set the **stock stop,** or cutoff gage, to eliminate the need for measuring each piece (Fig. 51-11).
7. Set the machine for the correct cutting speed and feed.
8A. On machines with power feed systems, start the machine, turn on the coolant, and engage the feed system. **Be prepared to slow down the feed rate or reduce the feeding pressure if the machine starts to labor (strain), or to shut off the machine in case the blade breaks or the workpiece shifts.** The feed rate or feeding pressure

should be set so that the blade enters the work steadily and produces a steady flow of chips.
8B. On machines with manual feed, start the machine and turn on the coolant, if any. Grasp the feed handle firmly and feed the blade into the workpiece at a rate that allows it to cut freely and steadily.
9. When the cut has been completed, raise the saw frame and shut the machine off. Some hydraulically powered machines will automatically stop the blade and raise the saw frame in preparation for the next cut.
10. Measure the cut piece to determine whether it is the correct length. If it is not, adjust the stock stop accordingly.
11. Loosen the vise, position the stock for the next cut, if there is to be one, then proceed as in steps 6, 7, and 8.

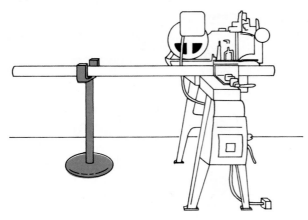

Fig. 51-10 *A stock support must be used to support long bar stock being cut in a power saw.*

Fig. 51-11 *Measuring metal to be cut in a power saw. (A) Holding the rule against the saw blade when measuring. (B) Using the cutoff gage.*

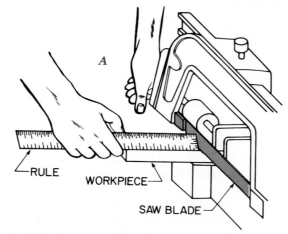

RULE

WORKPIECE

SAW BLADE

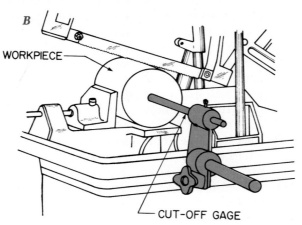

WORKPIECE

CUT-OFF GAGE

⊘ **SAFETY NOTE**

Using Cutoff Saws

1. Mount or remove workpieces **only when** the saw **is stopped** and is raised **well above** the vise.
2. Clamp the workpiece tightly in the vise. If a vise is provided on both sides of the blade, and the workpiece is long enough, clamp it in both vises. Injury can result when brittle blades break because of rolling or shifting of the workpiece under the pressure of cutting.
3. Use only blades that are in good condition, and are the correct kind for the material being cut.
4. Operate the machine at a cutting speed and feed rate that does not strain the machine or the blade.
5. Keep your hands away from the saw blade when it is cutting.
6. Stand out of line with the blade when starting an abrasive cutoff saw to avoid abrasive particles that spin off.
7. Do not bend over close to the front of a power hacksaw when it is running.
8. Support long pieces of stock so that they will not fall and cause injury. Hang a cloth on the protruding ends to warn others of the potential danger.
9. Broken blades can result on power hacksaws with hydraulic feeds if at the start of the cut blades are brought closer to the workpiece than ¼″ [6 mm].
10. Take care when handling freshly cut pieces. They have sharp edges and can be hot enough to burn.
11. Always wear approved eye protection.

REVIEW REVIEW REVIEW REVIEW REVIEW

WORDS TO KNOW

abrasive cutoff saw	cutoff gage	feed rate	power hacksaw
abrasive disc	cutting fluid	hook tooth form	regular tooth form
chip clearance	cutting speed	horizontal band saw	stock support
cold saw	feed	portable band saw	tooth pitch

REVIEW QUESTIONS

1. What is meant by the cutting speed of a saw?
2. What is meant by the feed rate of a saw?
3. Of what advantage is using a cutting fluid on a power hacksaw?
4. What is meant by blade tooth pitch and why is it important?
5. List three advantages of band-saw cutoff machines.
6. What kind of material is used to make band-saw blades preferred for cutoff work?
7. Describe the shape of cold-saw blades and name the kind of materials they cut most efficiently.
8. What kind of blades are used on abrasive cutoff saws?
9. Abrasive cutoff saws are best for cutting off what kind of materials?
10. What is a cutoff gage used for?
11. What is a stock support used for?
12. Describe how short pieces can be safely held in the vise for cutoff.

UNIT
52
Band Sawing and Machining

Unit 51, "Stock Cutoff Machines," introduced the horizontal band saw and told how it is used in stock cutoff operations. This unit discusses another type of band saw, the **vertical band saw,** and describes how the vertical band-sawing machine is used for both sawing and machining. This unit also presents further details on band-saw cutting speeds, blade tension, and blade selection.

52-1 Vertical Band Saws

Vertical band saws (Fig. 52-1) are not limited to making straight-line cuts, as horizontal band saws are. They also are used for band filing and band polishing. This flexibility makes it possible to make some parts completely by band machining.

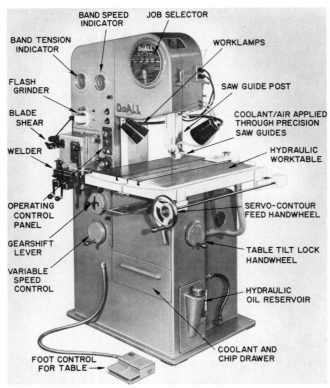

Fig. 52-1 *A vertical band saw.* (DoALL)

Band sawing. Vertical band saws may be used for making **straight-line cuts, angular cuts** (Fig. 52-2), or **curved line cuts** (Fig. 52-3). Curved line cuts are also called contour cuts. Thus, vertical band saws are also called **contouring machines.** The saw table may be tilted at any desired angle up to 45° for making angular cuts (Fig. 52-2).

When **internal contour cuts** are to be made, a hole must be drilled in the workpiece first (Fig. 52-3). The blade is then cut with the **blade shear,** inserted through the drilled hole in the workpiece, and rewelded with the **blade welder** (Fig. 52-1). Next, the blade is installed on the machine and properly tensioned. The contour cut may then be made. Of course, the blade must again be removed from the machine and sheared to remove the finished workpiece.

Band filing. A **band file** is made up of short segments of file blade that are riveted to steel tape and hooked together (Figs. 52-4 and 52-5). Band filing is much faster than hand filing. A workpiece may be band-filed by simply holding it against the moving file band until the desired surface finish and shape are obtained.

Fig. 52-2 *The table of a vertical band saw tilted for an angular cut.* (DoALL)

Fig. 52-3 *A band saw inserted through a drilled hole for internal contour sawing.* (DoALL)

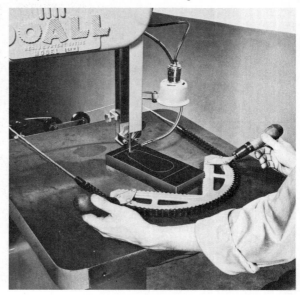

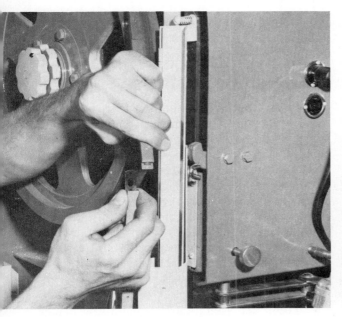

Fig. 52-4 *Coupling the band file.* (DoALL)

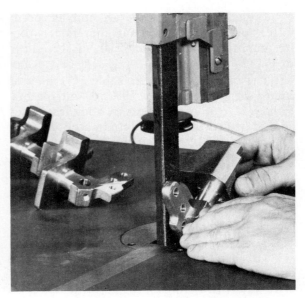

Fig. 52-6 *Band-polishing with an abrasive belt on the band saw.* (DoALL)

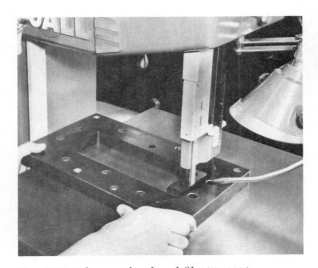

Fig. 52-5 *Filing with a band file.* (DoALL)

Band polishing. An abrasive belt is installed on a vertical band sawing machine for band polishing. For this purpose, a special guide is mounted on the **saw guide post** (Fig. 52-1). The abrasive belt is installed on the machine and is held in position by the guide provided. Polishing is done by holding the workpiece against the moving abrasive band (Fig. 52-6).

52-2 Band-saw Cutting Speeds

The cutting speed for band saws may be varied in several ways, depending on the type of motor drive system on the machine. On many band saws the speed is changed by changing the position of the V-belt on the motor and machine drive pulleys. In contrast, many band saws have a **variable-speed drive** mechanism.

Caution With the variable-speed drive mechanism, the speed of the machine should be changed only while the machine is running.

Recommended cutting speeds vary because of the following:
1. The kind of material being cut.
2. The hardness of the material.
3. The thickness of the material.
4. Whether the cutting is **wet** or **dry.**

Slower cutting speeds are used when harder metals are cut, and also for cutting thick materials. Higher cutting speeds are used for wet cutting than for dry cutting.

Table 52-1 suggests average cutting speeds in feet per minute (fpm) and meters per minute (mpm) for cutting material ½″ [12.7 mm] to 1″ [25.4 mm] thick.

The cutting speeds in Table 52-1 may be **increased** approximately 25% for cutting materials ¼″ [6.35 mm] or less in thickness. They should be **decreased** by approximately 25% for materials 2″ [50.8 mm] or more in thickness.

52-3 Blade Tension on the Band Saw

The band-saw blades on both horizontal and vertical-type machines should be installed with the teeth pointing in the same direction the blade travels. The blade should be tightened with the proper tension, as recommended by the manufacturer of the machine. Some band saws are equipped with a **blade tension indicator** which shows when the proper tension is applied for the width of the blade installed.

52-4 Band Saw Blade Selection

Blade material. Metal-cutting band-saw blades are made of high-carbon steel, special alloy steel, and high-speed steel. **Composite blades** are made of carbon steel with high-speed steel teeth. Tungsten carbide tipped blades are also made. The alloy steel blades, high-speed steel blades, composite blades, and tungsten carbide tipped blades are designed for heavy-duty production work. High-carbon steel blades have hardened teeth and a softer flexible back. They are the least expensive to purchase, and are probably the most widely used.

Tooth set. Metal-cutting band-saw blades have two kinds of **set, raker** set and **wavy** set (Fig. 52-7). Both types may be used in either horizontal or vertical machines. The raker set is recommended for most contouring cuts in vertical machines. The wavy set is recommended for most operations on horizontal machines and for cutting thin metals or thin-wall tubing.

Table 52-1

Cutting Speeds for Band Saws*

Material	Cutting speed fpm (mpm)	
	Dry	Wet
Alloy Steel (tough)	125 (38.1)	175 (53.3)
Aluminum	250 (76.2)	800 (243.8)
Bakelite®	300 (91.4)	
Brass (soft)	500 (152.4)	800 (243.8)
Brass (hard)	200 (61.0)	300 (91.4)
Bronze	200 (61.0)	300 (91.4)
Copper	250 (76.2)	400 (122)
Drill Rod (annealed)	75 (22.9)	125 (38.1)
Gray Cast Iron (soft)	125 (38.1)	
Hard Rubber	200 (61.0)	
High-Speed Steel	50 (15.2)	75 (22.9)
Low-Carbon Steel	125 (38.1)	175 (53.3)
Malleable Iron	125 (38.1)	175 (53.3)
Medium-Carbon Steel	100 (30.5)	150 (45.7)

*Speeds are for cutting materials 1/2″ (12.7 mm) to 1″ (25.4 mm) thick. *Increase* speeds 25% for cutting materials less than 1/2″ (12.7 mm) thick. *Decrease* speeds 25% for cutting materials over 1″ (25.4 mm) thick.

Fig. 52-7 *Tooth-set patterns used for metal cutting band saw blades.*

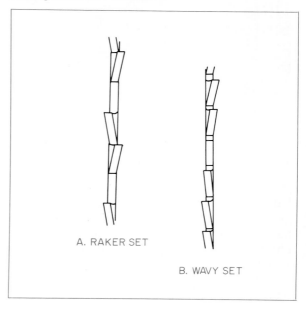

A. RAKER SET

B. WAVY SET

Tooth form. Figure 52-8 shows the tooth forms of band-saw blades. The **regular tooth form** is used for blades of 6 teeth per inch [4 mm] pitch and finer. The **hook tooth form** is used for blades of 6 teeth per inch [4 mm] pitch and coarser. Most cutting is done with regular tooth form blades. They have good chip clearance for making fast cuts with good finishes. **Skip-tooth form** blades use the same rake and clearance angles as regular tooth form blades. That is, they form the same type of kerf. However, the teeth are shorter and spaced farther apart. The wider spacing gives more chip clearance for making fast cuts through thick pieces of soft metals. Table 52-2 gives cutting speed recommendations for skip-tooth blades. The **tungsten carbide tooth form** has deep notches and wide tooth spacing. These provide generous chip clearance for making fast cuts on thick pieces.

Blade widths and thicknesses. Contour sawing blades are made in the widths and thicknesses shown in Table 52-3. A narrow width blade cuts a smaller radius, or curve, than a wider blade. However, narrow width blades break more easily when the **feed rate** is too great. The following shows the minimum radius that can usually be sawed with blades of various widths:

Blade Width	Radius
½″ [12.7 mm]	2½″ [63.5 mm]
⅜″ [9.5 mm]	1¼″ [31.8 mm]
¼″ [6.35 mm]	⅝″ [15.9 mm]
3⁄16″ [4.8 mm]	⅜″ [9.5 mm]
⅛″ [3.2 mm]	7⁄32″ [5.6 mm]
3⁄32″ [2.4 mm]	⅛″ [3.2 mm]

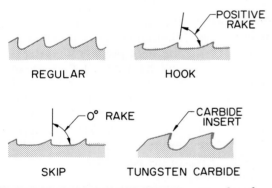

Fig. 52-8 *Tooth forms for metal cutting band saw blades.*

Table 52-2

Cutting Speeds for Skip-Tooth Band-Saw Blades

Material	Speed in feet per minute fpm (mpm)
Aluminum	2000 to 3000 (609.6 to 914.4)
Aluminum Alloys	300 to 2000 (91.4 to 609.6)
Asbestos	800 to 1500 (243.8 to 457.2)
Bakelite®	2500 to 3500 (762 to 1066.8)
Brass	400 to 1000 (122 to 304.8)
Copper	1000 to 1500 (304.8 to 457.2)
Formica®	800 to 2000 (243.8 to 609.6)
Lucite-Plexiglass®	2000 to 3000 (609.6 to 914.4)
Magnesium	3000 to 5000 (914.4 to 1524)
Wood	2000 to 3000 (609.6 to 914.4)

Table 52-3

Metal-Cutting Band-Saw Blade Sizes

Width inch (mm)	Thickness inch (mm)	Pitch	
		Teeth per inch	Millimeters
3/32 (2.4)	0.025 (0.64)	18	1.4
1/8 (3.2)	0.025 (0.64)	14-18-24	1.8-1.4-1.1
3/16 (4.8)	0.025 (0.64)	10-14-18	2.5-1.8-1.4
1/4 (6.4)	0.025 (0.64	10-14-18-24	2.5-1.8-1.4-1.1
3/8 (9.5)	0.025 (0.64)	8-10-14-18	3.2-2.5-1.8-1.4
1/2 (12.7)	0.025 (0.64)	6-8-10-14-18-24	4.2-3.2-2.5-1.8-1.4-1.1
5/8 (15.9)	0.032 (0.81)	8-10-14-18	3.2-2.5-1.8-1.4
3/4 (19.1)	0.032 (0.81)	6-8-10-14-18	4.2-3.2-2.5-1.8-1.4
1 (25.4)	0.035 (0.89)	6-8-10-14	4.2-3.2-2.5-1.8

Blade pitch. Pitch refers to the coarseness of the teeth. Blades are made with various pitches, as shown in Table 52-3. A coarse pitch should be selected for sawing large thicknesses or soft metals. A finer pitch should be selected for sawing thinner or harder metals. There should be a minimum of **two teeth** in contact with the work at all times, except for very thin sheet metal, which is cut at higher speeds. For general-purpose metal-cutting operations, band-saw blades of the following pitches produce good results:

Pitch	Metal Thickness
18* [1.4 mm]	up to ¼" [6.35 mm]
14 [1.8 mm]	¼" to ½" [6.35 mm] to 12.7 mm]
10 [2.5 mm]	½" to 2" [12.7 mm] to 50.8 mm]
8 [3.2 mm]	2" [50.8 mm] and larger

*Teeth per inch

"Band" Aid for Metal Cutting

TECHNOLOGIES AND PRACTICES

Imagine that you're a hungry camper faced with a can of beans and no opener. You may have to resort to desperate measures. Begin by placing the point of a knife against the rim of the can and hitting its handle with a hammer. Repeat this process around the rim until you can insert the blade to pry off the lid. Although it is time-consuming, this last resort method will eventually have supper bubbling over the fire.

This crude metal-cutting procedure is similar to that used by diemakers in the early 1900's. The only way manufacturers could cut out shapes in steel was to drill a number of holes very close together along the pattern line. The excess metal was hammered and chiseled away. Then the workpiece was filed to its final shape. Even the simplest die required many hours of difficult handwork.

A Minneapolis tool-and-die maker, Leighton A. Wilkie, changed all this in 1933 by inventing the metal-cutting contour band saw. Wood-cutting band saws had been in existence since the 1850's. However, the blades on these saws could not stand up to the extreme friction produced in metal cutting. At the time Wilkie began experimenting with blades, the best ones wore out after cutting through only six inches of one-inch-thick steel plate. After much experimentation, he succeeded in producing long-lasting blades of hardened and tempered steel.

In addition to the improved blade, Wilkie designed a rigid frame for the machine to give the band saw greater support. Other additions, such as a guide that gripped the band close to the cut and a butt welder to use when making internal cuts, helped make Wilkie's band saw a success.

The contour band saw filled a definite need in the metal-cutting industry. Diemakers were relieved of the long process of drilling and hammering to remove metal. Many hours of costly handwork was eliminated forever. No wonder that Mr. Wilkie can look proudly at a recent model of his band saw.

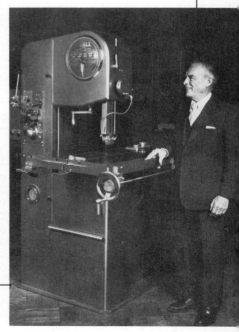

REVIEW   REVIEW   REVIEW   REVIEW   REVIEW

WORDS TO KNOW

band filing	blade welder	internal contour	tooth pitch
band polishing	composite blades	cuts	tungsten carbide
blade shears	contour sawing	raker set	tipped blades
blade tension	cutting speed	regular tooth form	vertical band saw
blade tension	hook tooth form	skip-tooth form	wavy set
indicator			

REVIEW QUESTIONS

1. What kinds of cuts or other operations can be performed on a vertical band saw?
2. Why are vertical band saws often equipped with a blade shear and welder?
3. How can the cutting speed be changed on your vertical band saw?
4. What precaution should be taken when changing the speed on a machine with a variable-speed drive mechanism?
5. Recommended cutting speeds for band sawing vary according to four important factors. Name them.
6. What is the recommended band-saw cutting speed for low-carbon steel ¾″ [19 mm] thick without cutting fluid? With cutting fluid?
7. What recommendation should be followed concerning blade tension?
8. What factors should be considered in the selection of a band-saw blade for a vertical band saw?
9. Name the two kinds of band-saw blade tooth set, and give the recommended use for each.
10. Name the four kinds of band-saw tooth forms and give the main use for each.

PART

15

Drilling Machines and Drilling Operations

Sometimes a trainee or apprentice on a new job is reluctant to ask too many questions. Gene Wilson, drill press operator in a Michigan job shop, has never been afraid to ask questions. The job shop makes parts for many different kinds of machinery, and Gene must visualize from a blueprint what his end product will be. If even a small detail is not clear to him, he will ask either his employer or the customer for direction.

Gene operates both a horizontal boring mill and a radial arm drill, which can drill holes in most metals except those with high Diamond Pyramid Hardness ratings. His interest in machinery drew him to metal processing courses in high school. Later he served an apprenticeship at the job shop under an extremely competent owner. He has worked there for nearly seven years.

Gene finds most of his satisfaction in seeing his work, such as a series of small holes on a die-casting machine, "come together" and work in a complete unit. The job shop also repairs almost any kind of machinery, so Gene works with a variety of metal parts from many industries.

On the job, Gene wears safety glasses and safety shoes. His work requires strong, steady hands, but he feels that even more important are "a clear head and good concentration." In addition, Gene says that a solid background in mathematics is essential. There is much exact measurement to be done before precise holes can be drilled. With the knowledge he has acquired over the years, Gene is now giving trainees the answers to many of the questions he once asked as an apprentice.

Gene Wilson
Drill Press Operator

UNIT
53
Drilling Machines

A drilling machine or *drill press* is a machine that holds and turns a drill to cut holes in metal.

Among the kinds of drilling machines are:

1. the handfeed drill press
2. the back-geared upright drill
3. the gang drill
4. the multiple-spindle drill
5. the radial drill press
6. the turret drill press.

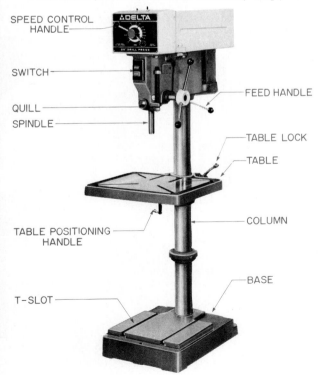

Fig. 53-1 *This handfeed floor model drill press has a drilling capacity of 1/2" [13 mm] diameter in mild steel.* (Delta International Machinery Corp.)

SPEED CONTROL HANDLE

SWITCH

QUILL

SPINDLE

FEED HANDLE

TABLE LOCK

TABLE

TABLE POSITIONING HANDLE

COLUMN

BASE

T–SLOT

53-1 The Handfeed Drill Press

Small, light work may be drilled on the **handfeed drill press.** This is a small press in which only the smaller drills are used. It may be one that sets on the bench, called a bench drill, or it may be a floor model (Fig. 53-1). It is the simplest drill press, and may be called **sensitive** because you can feel all the strains on the drill in the **feed handle.**

53-2 The Back-Geared Upright Drill Press

This machine is like the handfeed drill press except that it is larger and more powerful (Fig. 53-2). It has a gear box with several levers for changing the speeds. Also, besides feeding by hand as on the sensitive drill press, this machine has an **automatic feed;** that is, it uses power to force the drill into the metal. Larger drills can be used than in the handfeed drill.

53-2 The Gang Drill

The gang drill (Fig. 53-3) is a drilling machine in which two or more drill presses are **ganged,** or made into one machine. Each **spindle** may be run alone. This machine is used mainly in **mass production** where different drill press operations are done, one after another. Some work may be done by one spindle and then passed to the next spindle for the next operation, and so on. One spindle may hold a small drill, a second may hold a large drill, a third may hold a **countersink** (Fig. 56-6) or another special tool. The work is thus passed along the table from one spindle to the next.

53-4 The Multiple-Spindle Drill Press

This drilling machine has a number of spindles fastened to the main spindle with **universal joints** (Fig. 53-4). Each holds a drill, and all the drills run at once, thus drilling at one time as many holes as there are drills. This method is a great timesaver when many pieces, each having a number of holes, have to be drilled.

Fig. 53-3 *A gang drill press used to rapidly perform drilling operations in sequence.* (Atlas Press Co., Clausing Div.)

Fig. 53-4 *A multiple-spindle drill press speeds production by drilling all holes at the same time.* (Precision Tool)

Fig. 53-2 *A heavy-duty upright drill press with gear drive and power feed for drilling large holes.* (Kelly Powell Studio)

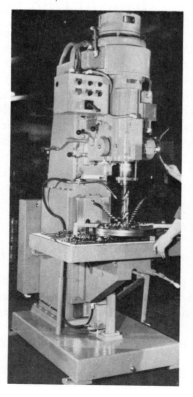

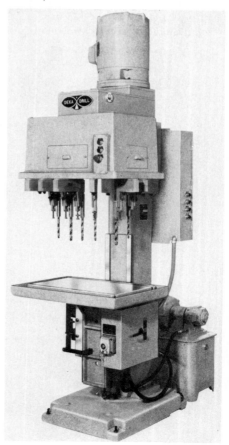

Fig. 53-5 *This two-station radial drill press is equipped with indexing jigs to hold a large workpiece. (Carlton Machine Tool Co.)*

Fig. 53-6 *A numerically controlled turret drill press eliminates the need for expensive drill jigs.*

53-5 The Radial Drill Press

This machine has a **movable arm** on which the spindle is mounted (Fig. 53-5). The spindle may be moved and set at different distances from the **post** or column. The arm can be swung around to the left or right. It can also be raised or lowered so that work of different heights can be drilled. The radial drill press is used for large, heavy work, such as machine frames, which cannot be moved easily. It is necessary, therefore, to shift the position of the **drill** instead. The radial drill makes this possible.

53-6 The Turret Drill Press

The **turret drill press** (Fig. 53-6) has a **multiple-spindle turret** with 6, 8, or 10 spindles. A tool is placed in each spindle. The desired tool is brought into operating position by **indexing,** or revolving the turret. Like the gang drill, the turret drill press is a production machine. It is designed for performing several drill press operations in quick order. The turret drill press shown in Figure 53-6 can perform up to 6 different drilling operations automatically. Small hand-operated turret drill presses are also made.

53-7 Parts of the Drill Press

The names of drill press parts are the same for all drill presses (Fig. 53-1). The **base** of the drill press is the support for the machine; it is bolted to the floor and may have **T-slots** so that large work can be bolted to it for drilling. The **column** is the post to which the **table** is fastened. The table holds the work in place while it is being drilled. It may also have **T-slots.** By turning the **table positioning handle,** which causes the **table elevating screw** to turn, the table can be raised or lowered. It can then be clamped in place by tightening the **table lock.**

The **spindle** holds and turns the drill. It is upright on most machines, and is held by an arm that is fastened to the column. To keep the spindle from dropping, it is balanced by a **spindle return spring.** This also supports the **quill,** the housing around the rotating spindle. The quill is moved up and down by the **feed handle.** Some spindles may be balanced by a weight that moves up and down inside the column.

Spindle speeds are changed according to the drill press **drive system.** On **cone-pulley systems,** one **cone pulley** is fastened to the spindle and another is connected to the **motor.** The **steps** of the cone pulley give as many speeds as there are steps. On upright drilling machines, the **back gears,** located inside the front pulley, give additional speeds. **With this drive system, you must stop the motor before shifting gears.** A **variable-speed drive** gives a continuous range of speeds shown on a dial (Fig. 53-7). **It is adjusted only while the drill is running.**

A **feed stop,** or **depth scale,** may be set so the drill will stop cutting when the desired depth is reached. This is useful for drilling several holes of the same depth.

Fig. 53-7 *A variable-speed pulley drive system allows quick setting of correct drill speeds.* (Atlas Press Co., Clausing Div.)

53-8 Sizes of Drilling Machines

Drilling machines range widely in sizes. The size of an **upright drill press** is measured by the distance from the center of the spindle to the column multiplied by two. Thus, a 20-inch [508 mm] drill press can drill to the center of a 20-inch [508 mm] circle.

The size of a **radial drill press** is also measured from the drill to the column. Thus, a 6-foot [1.83 m] radial drill press can drill the center of a 6-foot [1.83 m] circle.

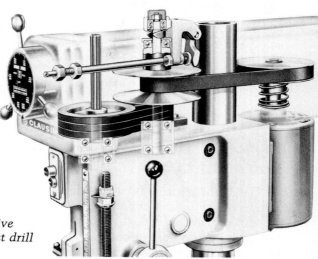

REVIEW REVIEW REVIEW REVIEW REVIEW

WORDS TO KNOW

automatic feed	back gears	quill	multiple-spindle
back-geared upright	base	spindle	drill press
drill press	column	table clamp	radial drill press
bench drill press	cone pulley	table elevating	sensitive drill press
cone-pulley drive	depth scale	screw	turret drill press
drill press	feed handle	table positioning	variable-speed drive
automatic feed		handle	
stop		gang drill press	

(Review Continued)

REVIEW QUESTIONS

1. Name and briefly describe the six kinds of drill presses.
2. Name the main parts of a drill press.
3. Why is a hand-feed drill press called "sensitive"?
4. What is meant by automatic feed?
5. What is the purpose of back gears?
6. How is the size of an upright drill press measured? A radial drill press?
7. What do gang drill presses and turret drill presses have in common?
8. How is the speed of a drill press changed if it has a cone pulley drive system? Variable-speed drive system?

UNIT
54
Drills, Sleeves, Sockets, and Chucks

The common kinds of drills are the twist drill, the straight-fluted drill, and the spade drill. This unit discusses the twist drill in detail. It also describes various sleeves, sockets, and chucks used to hold drills.

54-1 The Twist Drill

The twist drill is the type of drill most often used in metalwork. Twist drills are made with two, three, or four **cutting lips** (Fig. 54-1).

The **two-lip drill** is used to drill holes into solid metal. Three- and four-lipped drills, called **core drills,** are used for drilling out **cored holes** in castings.

An **oil-hole twist drill** feeds cutting fluid to the cutting edges through holes in the drill (Fig. 54-1).

Fig. 54-1 *Kinds of twist drills. (A) Two-flute. (B) Three flute. (C) Four flute. (D) Two flute with oil hole.* (Cleveland Twist and Drill Company)

54-2 The Straight-Fluted Drill

The straight-fluted drill, or **farmer drill,** named after its inventor, is used for drilling brass, copper, and other soft metals (Fig. 54-2A). It may also be used to drill thin metal.

A variation of the straight-fluted drill, called a **gun drill,** is used for drilling very deep holes.

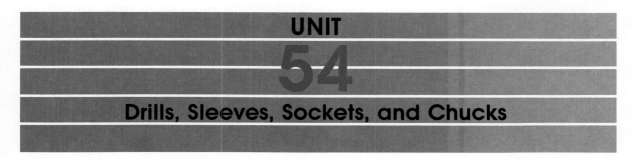

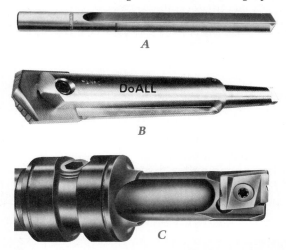

Fig. 54-2 *(A) A farmer drill. (B) spade drill. (C) and insert drill.* (Cleveland Twist and Drill Company) (GTE Valenite Corp, Troy, MI)

The Spade Drill

Spade drills with replaceable blades are used for drilling large holes. They are available in sizes from 1″ to 5″ [25.4 to 127 mm] and are much cheaper than twist drills (Fig. 54-2B).

Insert Drills

Insert drills use one or more replaceable carbide inserts, depending on the drill size, to do the cutting (Fig. 54-2C). They are available in sizes from ⅝″ (16 mm) to 2½″ (64 mm) or more. They excel in drilling large holes in tough materials, and for production drilling of softer materials.

Carbon Steel, High-Speed Steel, and Carbide Drills

Twist drills are made of **carbon steel, high-speed steel,** and **tungsten carbide.** If the drill shank is not stamped **HS,** meaning **high-speed,** it is made of carbon steel. High-speed steel drills cost two or three times as much as carbon-steel drills. Note in Table 54-1 that high-speed drills may be run twice as fast as carbon-steel drills.

For drilling very hard or very abrasive materials, either tungsten carbide tipped or solid tungsten carbide drills are available.

Table 54-1

Drilling Speeds and Feeds (For Use with High-Speed Steel Drills)

| Diameter of drill inch (mm) | Speed in revolutions per minute (rpm) for high-speed steel drills (Reduce rpm one-half for carbon-steel drills) | | | | Feed per revolution inches inch (mm) |
	Low-carbon steel Cast iron (soft) Malleable iron 80-100 (24.4-30.5)	Medium-carbon steel Cast iron (hard) 70-80 (21.3-24.4)	High-carbon steel High-speed alloy steel 50-60 (15.2-18.3)	Aluminum and its alloys Ordinary brass Ordinary bronze 200-300 (61.0-91.4)	
1/8″ (3.2)	2445-3056	2139-2445	1528-1833	6112-9168	0.002 (0.05)
1/4″ (6.35)	1222-1528	1070-1222	764-917	3056-4584	0.004 (0.10)
3/8″ (4.5)	815-1019	713-815	509-611	2038-3057	0.006 (0.15)
1/2″ (12.7)	611-764	534-611	382-458	1528-2292	0.007 (0.18)
3/4″ (19.1)	407-509	357-407	255-306	1018-1527	0.010 (0.25)
1″ (25.4)	306-382	267-306	191-229	764-846	0.015 (0.38)

*FPM (MPM)

54-6 Parts of a Twist Drill

The parts of a twist drill are shown in Figure 54-3. The **body** is the part in which the **grooves** are cut. The grooves that run along the side of the drill are called **flutes.** During drilling, the drill is held by the **shank.** The **neck** is a short part between the shank and the body. The cone-shaped cutting end is the **point.** The **margin** is the narrow edge alongside the flute. **Body clearance** is the amount of metal that has been cut away between the margin and the flute. It reduces the rubbing between the drill and the walls of the hole so that less power is needed to turn the drill.

The **web** is the metal in the center running lengthwise between the **flutes.** It is the backbone of the drill; it gets thicker near the shank and makes the drill stronger. Section **A** in Figure 54-3 was cut from a drill near the shank. Section **B** was cut near the point.

The **tang** is the flattened end of the shank. It fits into the slot in a **drill sleeve** (Fig. 54-7) or into the **drill-press spindle.** It drives the drill and keeps the shank from slipping, especially on large drills. The **lips** are the **cutting edges** of the drill. The **dead center** is the end at the point of the drill; it should always be in the exact center of the point. The **heel** is the part of the point behind the cutting edges.

The flutes are shaped to:
1. Help form the cutting edges at the point.
2. Form passages for the chips to come out of the hole.
3. Allow the **cutting fluid** to travel to the cutting edges of the drill.

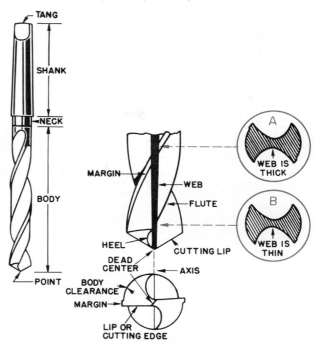

Fig. 54-3 *Parts of a twist drill.*

Fig. 54-4 *Drill shanks: (A) Straight shank. (B) Taper shank.* (Cleveland Twist and Drill Company)

54-7 Kinds of Drill Shanks

Drill shanks are either **straight** or **tapered** (Fig. 54-4). Tapered-shank drilling tools use the **American Standard (Morse) Taper.** There are No. 1, No. 2, No. 3, and larger Morse tapers, with No. 1 being the smallest.

54-8 Sizes of Drills

Small drills are usually purchased in sets. The size of a drill is known by its diameter, which may be a **numbered gage,** a **letter,** or a **fractional inch size,** or a size in **millimeters.** Table 54-2 shows sizes from the smallest twist drill, which is No. 80 [0.34 mm] up to 1" [25.4 mm] in diameter. Table 54-3 shows sizes of metric drills up to 12.5 mm.

Number drills. Number drills are made in sizes from No. 80 to No. 1 (0.0135″ [0.34 mm] to 0.228″ [5.79 mm] diameters). Note that the larger the number, the smaller the drill.

Letter drills. Letter drills are labeled from A to Z (0.234″ [5.94 mm] to 0.413″ [10.49 mm] diameters). Note that the letter drills begin where the number drills end.

Table 54-2

Inch-Based Drill Sizes

Number and letter drills	Fractional drills	Decimal equivalents	Number and letter drills	Fractional drills	Decimal equivalents	Number and letter drills	Fractional drills	Decimal equivalents	Number and letter drills	Fractional drills	Decimal equivalents
80	. . .	.0135	42	. . .	.0935		13/64	.2031		13/32	.4062
79	. . .	.0145		3/32	.0937	6	. . .	.2040	Z	. . .	.4130
	1/64	.0156	41	. . .	.0960	5	. . .	.2055		27/64	.4219
78	. . .	.0160	40	. . .	.0980	4	. . .	.2090		7/16	.4375
77	. . .	.0180	39	. . .	.0995	3	. . .	.2130		29/64	.4531
76	. . .	.0200	38	. . .	.1015		7/32	.2187		15/32	.4687
75	. . .	.0210	37	. . .	.1040	2	. . .	.2210		31/64	.4844
74	. . .	.0225	36	. . .	.1065	1	. . .	.2280		1/2	.5000
73	. . .	.0240		7/64	.1094	A	. . .	.2340			
72	. . .	.0250	35	. . .	.1100		15/64	.2344		33/64	.5156
71	. . .	.0260	34	. . .	.1110	B	. . .	.2380		17/32	.5312
70	. . .	0.280	33	. . .	.1130	C	. . .	.2420		35/64	.5469
69	. . .	.0292	32	. . .	.1160	D	. . .	.2460		9/16	.5625
68	. . .	.0310	31	. . .	.1200	E	1/4	.2500		37/64	.5781
	1/32	.0312		1/8	.1250	F	. . .	.2570		19/32	.5937
67	. . .	0.320	30	. . .	.1285	G	. . .	.2610		39/64	.6094
66	. . .	.0330	29	. . .	.1360		17/64	.2656		5/8	.6250
65	. . .	.0350	28	. . .	.1405	H	. . .	.2660			
64	. . .	.0360		9/64	.1406	I	. . .	.2720		41/64	.6406
63	. . .	.0370	27	. . .	.1440	J	. . .	.2770		21/32	.6562
62	. . .	.0380	26	. . .	.1470	K	. . .	.2810		43/64	.6719
61	. . .	.0390	25	. . .	.1495		9/32	.2812		11/16	.6875
60	. . .	.0400	24	. . .	.1520	L	. . .	.2900		45/64	.7031
59	. . .	.0410	23	. . .	.1540	M	. . .	.2950		23/32	.7187
58	. . .	.0420		5/32	.1562		19/64	.2969		47/64	.7344
57	. . .	.0430	22	. . .	.1570	N	. . .	.3020		3/4	.7500
56	. . .	.0465	21	. . .	.1590		5/16	.3125			
	3/64	.0469	20	. . .	.1610	O	. . .	.3160		49/64	.7656
55	. . .	.0520	19	. . .	.1660	P	. . .	.3230		25/32	.7812
54	. . .	.0550	18	. . .	.1695		21/64	.3281		51/64	.7969
53	. . .	.0595		11/64	.1719	Q	. . .	.3320		13/16	8125
	1/16	.0625	17	. . .	.1720	R	. . .	.3390		53/64	.8281
52	. . .	.0635	16	. . .	.1770		11/32	.3437		27/32	.8437
51	. . .	.0670	15	. . .	.1800	S	. . .	.3480		55/64	.8594
50	. . .	.0700	14	. . .	.1820	T	. . .	.3580		7/8	.8750
49	. . .	.0730	13	. . .	.1850		23/64	.3594		57/64	.8906
48	. . .	.0760		3/16	.1875	U	. . .	.3680		29/32	.9062
	5/64	.0781	12	. . .	.1890		3/8	.3750		59/64	.9219
47	. . .	.0785	11	. . .	.1910	V	. . .	.3770		15/16	.9375
46	. . .	.0810	10	. . .	.1935	W	. . .	.3860		61/64	.9531
45	. . .	.0820	9	. . .	.1960		25/64	.3906		31/32	.9687
44	. . .	.0860	8	. . .	.1990	X	. . .	.3970		63/64	.9844
43	. . .	.0890	7	. . .	.2010	Y	. . .	.4040		1	1.0000

Fractional drills. Fractional drills range from 1/64″ [0.40 mm] to 4″ [102 mm] in diameter or larger. The sizes increase by 64ths of an inch [0.40 mm] in the smaller sizes and by 32nds [0.79 mm] and 16ths [1.59 mm] in the larger sizes. Note that the number and letter drill sizes fall between the fractional drill sizes.

Metric drills. Metric drill sizes range from 0.15 mm [0.006″] to 100 mm [3.94″]. The smallest sizes differ by only 0.01 mm [0.0004″]. As the sizes increase, the difference between drill sizes increases to 0.02 mm, then 0.05 mm, 0.1 mm, and 0.5 mm (Table 54-3).

Table 54-3

Metric Drill Sizes

Dia. mm	Dec. equiv. inch	Dia. mm	Dec. equiv. inch	Dia. mm	Dec. equiv. inch	Dia. mm	Dec. equiv. inch
0.15	0.0059	1.20	0.0472	3.75	0.1476	7.20	0.2835
0.16	0.0063	1.25	0.0492	3.80	0.1496	7.25	0.2854
0.17	0.0067	1.30	0.0512	3.90	0.1535	7.30	0.2874
0.18	0.0071	1.35	0.0531	4.00	0.1575	7.40	0.2913
0.19	0.0075	1.40	0.0551	4.10	0.1614	7.50	0.2953
0.20	0.0079	1.45	0.0571	4.20	0.1654	7.60	0.2992
0.21	0.0083	1.50	0.0591	4.25	0.1673	7.70	0.3031
0.22	0.0087	1.55	0.0610	4.30	0.1693	7.75	0.3051
0.23	0.0091	1.60	0.0630	4.40	0.1732	7.80	0.3071
0.24	0.0094	1.65	0.0650	4.50	0.1772	7.90	0.3110
0.25	0.0098	1.70	0.0669	4.60	0.1811	8.00	0.3150
0.26	0.0102	1.75	0.0689	4.70	0.1850	8.10	0.3189
0.27	0.0106	1.80	0.0709	4.75	0.1870	8.20	0.3228
0.28	0.0110	1.85	0.0728	4.80	0.1890	8.25	0.3248
0.29	0.0114	1.90	0.0748	4.90	0.1929	8.30	0.3268
0.30	0.0118	1.95	0.0768	5.00	0.1969	8.40	0.3307
0.32	0.0126	2.00	0.0787	5.10	0.2008	8.50	0.3346
0.34	0.0134	2.05	0.0807	5.20	0.2047	8.60	0.3386
0.35	0.0138	2.10	0.0827	5.25	0.2067	8.70	0.3425
0.36	0.0142	2.15	0.0846	5.30	0.2087	8.75	0.3445
0.38	0.0150	2.20	0.0866	5.40	0.2126	8.80	0.3465
0.40	0.0157	2.25	0.0886	5.50	0.2165	8.90	0.3504
0.42	0.0165	2.30	0.0906	5.60	0.2205	9.00	0.3543
0.44	0.0173	2.35	0.0925	5.70	0.2244	9.10	0.3583
0.45	0.0178	2.40	0.0945	5.75	0.2264	9.20	0.3622
0.46	0.0181	2.45	0.0965	5.80	0.2283	9.25	0.3642
0.48	0.0189	2.50	0.0984	5.90	0.2323	9.30	0.3661
0.50	0.0197	2.60	0.1024	6.00	0.2362	9.40	0.3701
0.55	0.0217	2.70	0.1063	6.10	0.2402	9.50	0.3740
0.60	0.0236	2.75	0.1083	6.20	0.2441	9.60	0.3780
0.65	0.0256	2.80	0.1102	6.25	0.2461	9.70	0.3819
0.70	0.0276	2.90	0.1142	6.30	0.2480	9.75	0.3839
0.75	0.0295	3.00	0.1181	6.40	0.2520	9.80	0.3858
0.80	0.0315	3.10	0.1220	6.50	0.2559	9.90	0.3898
0.85	0.0350	3.20	0.1260	6.60	0.2598	10.00	0.3937
0.90	0.0354	3.25	0.1280	6.70	0.2638	10.50	0.4134
0.95	0.0374	3.30	0.1299	6.75	0.2657	11.00	0.4331
1.00	0.0394	3.40	0.1339	6.80	0.2677	11.50	0.4528
1.05	0.0413	3.50	0.1378	6.90	0.2717	12.00	0.4724
1.10	0.0433	3.60	0.1417	7.00	0.2756	12.50	0.4921
1.15	0.0453	3.70	0.1457	7.10	0.2795		

54-9 How to Measure a Drill

The diameter of a drill is stamped on the drill near the shank. Very small drills are not stamped and must be measured with **drill gages** (Fig. 54-5) or with a **micrometer** (Fig. 54-6). A new drill is measured across the **margins** at the **point;** a worn drill must be measured at the **ends of the flutes** near the **neck.**

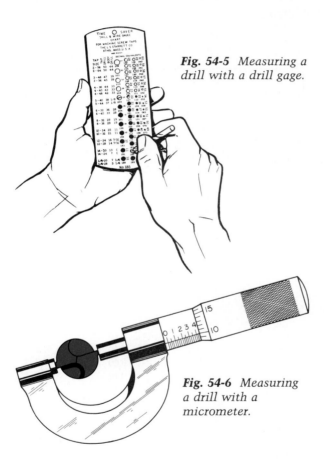

Fig. 54-5 *Measuring a drill with a drill gage.*

Fig. 54-6 *Measuring a drill with a micrometer.*

Fig. 54-7 *Drill sleeves allow use of a smaller taper shank size than would otherwise be possible.* (Cleveland Twist and Drill Co.)

54-10 Drill Sleeves

Tapered shanks on drills come in several sizes, such as No. 1, 2, 3, or 4 **Morse tapers.** The **drill-press spindle** has a hole with a No. 2 or a No. 3 Morse taper.

A drill with a No. 1 taper will not fit into a spindle with a No. 2 or No. 3 taper. Therefore, to make the drill fit, a **sleeve** like the one shown in Figure 54-7, with a No. 1 **tapered hole,** is placed on the drill shank. The outside of this sleeve has a No. 2 taper. If this taper is

Fig. 54-8 *A drill socket allows use of a larger taper shank size than would otherwise be possible.* (Cleveland Twist and Drill Co.)

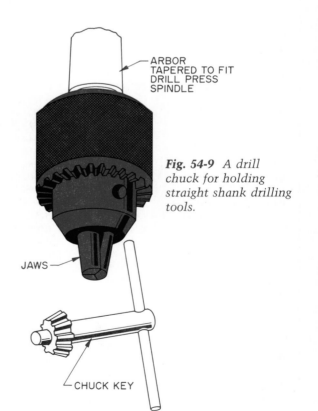

ARBOR
TAPERED TO FIT
DRILL PRESS
SPINDLE

Fig. 54-9 *A drill chuck for holding straight shank drilling tools.*

JAWS

CHUCK KEY

still too small to fit into the drill-press spindle, a sleeve with a No. 2 tapered hole and a No. 3 outside taper is also used. This enlarges the drill shank until it fits into the drill-press spindle. The first sleeve is known as a **No. 1 to No. 2 Morse-taper sleeve,** while the second is a **No. 2 to No. 3 Morse-taper sleeve.**

Drill Sockets

Sometimes it is necessary to use a drill with a No. 3 taper shank in a drill-press spindle with a No. 2 tapered hole. The **drill socket** (Fig. 54-8) makes this possible. It has a large hole and a small Morse-tapered shank.

The Drill Chuck

Straight shank drills must be held in a **drill chuck** (Fig. 54-9). This is fitted with a **Morse-taper shank,** called an **arbor,** which fits into the drill-press spindle. The drill chuck has three **jaws,** which are self-centering. The chuck is adjusted by turning the toothed outside ring with a **chuck key.**

🚫 **SAFETY NOTE**

Chuck keys should be removed from the chuck immediately after installing or removing a drill.

REVIEW REVIEW REVIEW REVIEW REVIEW

WORDS TO KNOW

arbor	drill-press spindle	gun drill	spade drill
body	drill shank	high-speed steel	straight-fluted drill
body clearance	drill sleeve	drill	straight-shank drill
carbide drill	drill socket	insert drill	tang
carbon steel drill	drill stand	letter drill	tapered-shank drill
chuck key	farmer drill	margin	three-lip drill
cutting lip	flutes	Morse taper	twist drill
drill chuck	four-lip drill	number drill	two-lip drill
drill gage	fractional drill	oil-hole drill	web

REVIEW QUESTIONS

1. Name the three kinds of drills. Which one is used most for metalwork?
2. Name three kinds of materials used for making drills.
3. How can you tell whether a drill is made of carbon steel or high-speed steel?
4. Describe an oil-hole drill.
5. What advantage do insert and spade drills have over other drills?
6. What is a gun drill used for? What kind of a drill is it?
7. What is the tang on a drill? What is its purpose?
8. What purpose do the flutes of a drill serve?
9. What is the name of the taper used on tapered-shank tools?
10. Drills are made according to four different size systems. Name them.
11. What part of the drill should be measured with a micrometer to find its size?
12. What is a drill gage?
13. What is a drill sleeve used for?

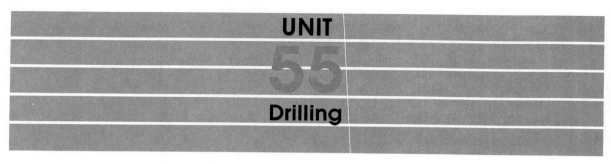

UNIT 55

Drilling

Drilling means to make a hole with a drill. It is one of the basic methods of machining solid materials. This unit describes how to calculate drill cutting speeds, how to insert and remove drills from spindles and chucks, how to lay out holes for drilling, and other drilling procedures.

55-1 Cutting Speeds and Feeds for Drilling

Cutting speed is the distance a drill would travel in 1 minute if it were laid on its side and rolled. The circumference of a circle = diameter × 3.1416. Thus, a 1″ drill, turning 100 revolutions per minute, would roll 1″ × 3.1416 × 100 ÷ 12″ = 26.18′. [If a metric solution is desired, the calculation is 25.4 mm × 3.1416 × 100 ÷ 1000 mm = 7.98 m per minute.]

The speed at which a drill may be turned depends upon:
1. Its diameter.
2. Whether it is made of **carbon steel, high-speed steel,** or **tungsten carbide.**
3. The hardness of the metal that is being drilled.

The smaller the diameter of the drill, the greater should be the speed; the larger the diameter, the slower should be the speed. Too slow a speed in drilling small holes is inefficient and can cause the drill to break. Table 54-1 shows that high-speed drills can be run twice as fast as carbon-steel drills. It also shows the speeds at which different metals should be drilled. Use a slow speed to drill hard metal, and a fast speed to drill soft metal. If the corners of the cutting edges wear away

quickly (Fig. 55-1), the speed should be reduced. Because drilling conditions vary so much, the operator, relying on experience and common sense, will decide what is the best speed at which to run a drill.

Calculating correct drill rpm: The rpm for a given cutting speed may be calculated with the following formulas:

A. **U.S. Customary (Inch) System**
$$\text{rpm} = \frac{\text{CS}' \times 12}{\text{D}'' \times \pi}$$
where: CS = Cutting speed in feet per minute
     D = Diameter in inches
     π = Pi or 3.1416

A shortcut formula that gives the **approximate** rpm follows:
$$\text{rpm} = \frac{4 \times \text{CS}'}{\text{D}''}$$

B. **S.I. Metric System**
$$\text{rpm} = \frac{\text{CS (mpm)} \times 1000}{\text{D (mm)} \times \pi}$$
where: CS (mpm) = Cutting speed in meters per minute
     D (mm) = Diameter in millimeters
     π = Pi or 3.1416

Fig. 55-1 *The drill corners are worn off when the cutting speed of the drill is too high. This prevents further drilling until the drill is resharpened.*

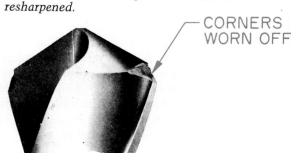

CORNERS WORN OFF

Example: Calculate the correct rpm for a ⅜″ [9.5 mm] diameter drill to cut at a cutting speed of 100 fpm [30.48 mpm].

Inch Solution:

$$\text{rpm} = \frac{100 \times 12}{.375 \times 3.1416}$$
$$= \frac{1200}{1.178}$$
$$= 1019$$

Using the shortcut formula:

$$\text{rpm} = \frac{4 \times 100}{.375}$$
$$= \frac{400}{.375}$$
$$= 1067$$

Metric Solution:

$$\text{rpm} = \frac{30.48 \times 1000}{9.5 \times 3.1416}$$
$$= \frac{30480}{29.845}$$
$$= 1021$$

Differences in the above answers are due to rounding off and are not enough to harm the drill in most cases.

The **feed** of a drill is the distance it cuts into the metal in one revolution. It differs for each size of drill and the kind of material to be drilled.

As with speed, rules about feed cannot be strictly followed. Experience and judgment must again help to decide how fast the drill should be fed into the metal. Drill sizes and general feeds are given in Table 54-1.

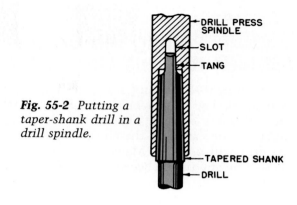

Fig. 55-2 *Putting a taper-shank drill in a drill spindle.*

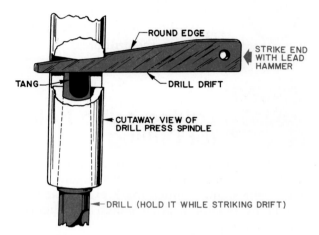

Fig. 55-3 *Removing a taper shank drill from the drill press spindle with a drill drift.*

55-2 Putting the Drill in the Drill-Press Spindle

A **tapered-shank** drill must be cleaned well before putting it in the drill-press spindle. Examine the shank of the drill to make sure that it is not scratched or nicked. A scratched or nicked shank will not fit perfectly in the spindle and will cause the drill to wobble.

The **tang** of the drill should be in the same position as the **slot** in the spindle; a quick upward push fastens the drill in the spindle (Fig. 55-2).

55-3 Removing the Drill from the Drill-Press Spindle

The drill or drill chuck should be removed from the drill-press spindle with a **drill drift** (Fig. 55-3). Note that one edge of the drill drift is rounded, while the other edge is flat.

Put the end of the drill drift into the slot of the spindle with the rounded edge of the drill drift against the upper, rounded part of the slot (Fig. 55-2). Hold the drill with one hand so that it will not drop and nick the drill press table. Strike the wide end of the drill drift lightly with a **lead hammer.**

55-4 Putting the Drill in the Drill Chuck

A **straight-shank drill** must be held in a drill chuck (Fig. 54-9), which is held in turn in the drill press spindle. Tighten the chuck as much as you can with the chuck key so that the drill will not slip. Many drill shanks get chewed up and ruined because they slip in the chuck.

> **SAFETY NOTE**
> Be sure to remove the chuck key from the drill chuck before turning on the drill press.

55-5 Laying out a Hole for Drilling

The first step in laying out a hole to be drilled is to mark its center with layout lines. Next, put a small punch mark exactly at this center by tapping a **prick punch** very lightly with a hammer.

If the punch mark is to one side (Fig. 55-4A), slant the prick punch to move the mark exactly to the center (Fig. 55-5). Finish up with a light blow on the prick punch held upright. When completed, the punch mark should be exactly in the center (Fig. 55-4B). After enlarging the prick punch mark with a center punch, the workpiece is ready for center drilling.

55-6 Center Drilling

Center drilling is done with a tool called a **center drill,** or **combination drill and countersink** (Fig. 55-6). Center drills are made in several sizes, and are used to establish hole centers for guiding drills (Fig. 55-7). They are also used to provide properly shaped bearing surfaces for metal lathe centers.

Fig. 55-4 *A punch mark before and after correction.*

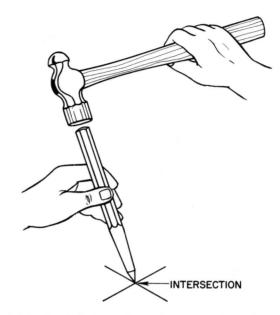

Fig. 55-5 *Technique of moving a punch mark.*

55-7 Drilling Large Holes

The larger the drill, the thicker is the **web** between the **flutes** and the wider is the **dead center** (Fig. 54-3). The dead center does not cut; it interferes with the drill cutting into the metal. To overcome this when drilling a large hole, a small hole (a little larger than the thickness of the web of the large drill) is first drilled through the metal. This small hole is called a **pilot hole** (Fig. 55-8). The large drill may then be used to enlarge the hole. The pilot hole must be drilled exactly to the layout because the large drill will follow the pilot hole exactly.

Fig. 55-6 *Center drills: (A) plain, (B) bell.* (Cleveland Twist and Drill)

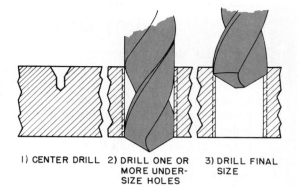

1) CENTER DRILL 2) DRILL ONE OR MORE UNDER-SIZE HOLES 3) DRILL FINAL SIZE

Fig. 55-9 *Step-drilling procedure for drilling holes of accurate size.*

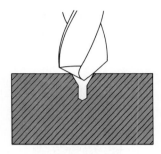

Fig. 55-7 *A center-drilled hole helps provide an accurate location for the drill.*

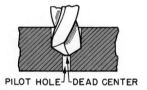

PILOT HOLE — DEAD CENTER

Fig. 55-8 *Using a pilot hole makes it easier to use a large drill.*

55-8 Drilling Accurately Sized Holes

All drills cut **oversize,** that is, the holes they make are slightly larger in diameter than the drills themselves. Larger drills and poorly sharpened drills tend to cut more oversize than small drills or correctly sharpened drills.

The amount a drill will drill oversize can be minimized by a procedure known as **step drilling.** Step drilling simply involves using one or more smaller drills first to remove the bulk of the material, leaving only a small amount of material for the final drill to remove (Fig. 55-9). For drill sizes ⅜″ [9.5 mm] and smaller, the diameter of the next-to-last drill should be about ¹⁄₆₄″ [0.40 mm] smaller than the final drill diameter. Above ⅜″ [9.5 mm], allow a ¹⁄₃₂″ [0.79 mm] size difference.

55-9 Drilling Holes to the Proper Depth

Most drilling machine quills are marked in inches or millimeters and have a **feed stop.** This stop may be set to a certain depth on the **depth scale,** so that cutting will stop when the desired depth is reached. This is especially useful when many holes of the same depth have to be drilled.

SAFETY NOTE

A twist drill that is just breaking through the bottom of the hole acts just like a corkscrew. This can cause a dangerous situation. The drill may grab and break off or the work may be torn loose from its holdings. To prevent this, feed the drill very slowly until the entire drill point has broken through the underside of the work. Larger drills are more dangerous than smaller drills in this respect. **Straight-fluted drills** do not act this way.

TECHNOLOGIES AND PRACTICES

Tiny Drills and Beams of Light

What do a brain surgeon, a jeweler, and a baby bottle manufacturer have in common? They all use products that have small holes. In industry, the demand for precise small hole drilling has been increasing. This has come about as parts for surgical instruments, computers, and a variety of other products have decreased in size.

Just how "small" is a small hole? Definitions vary, but the following terms are widely used. **Miniature** holes have a maximum diameter of 0.062″ [1.57 mm]. **Subminiature** applies to holes up to 0.015″ [0.38 mm] in diameter. Holes smaller than 0.005″ [0.13 mm] are termed **ultraminiature.** The photograph at the right is an enlarged view of a 0.0002″ [0.005 mm] drill compared with a human hair.

Laser drilling is growing in importance in small hole drilling. One use of the laser's concentrated beam of light is the drilling of industrial diamonds. Diamond dies with laser-drilled holes as small as .001″ [.0254 mm] are used in drawing fine wire. Laser drills have also been used to drill holes in medical needles, jet turbine components, and baby bottle nipples.

While the technology of laser drilling is still being perfected, a variety of small-scale mechanical drilling machines are widely used. These include small pivot drills, hand-operated sensitive drill presses, and microdrilling presses. Whatever the machine used, special care must be taken in order to drill tiny holes successfully. The setup is critical. The workpiece-holding device must be completely rigid. Any vibration can cause the fragile drill to break. And the drills themselves must be handled with extreme care, usually with tweezers. Mechanically produced small holes are used in watches and jewelry, fuel injection nozzles, and aerospace components.

Miniaturization is a major trend in many fields. Whether done with beams of light or tiny drills, small hole drilling will become even more important in the future.

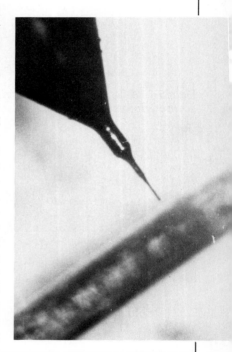

55-10

Chips

Figure 55-10 shows the difference between **cast iron chips** and **steel chips** or **shavings.** When the drill is correctly sharpened, cast iron chips are small, broken pieces of metal, while steel shavings are long curls of metal.

SAFETY NOTE

Long steel chips are dangerously sharp. They should be broken up by interrupting the feed when drilling. Chips and shavings may cause bad cuts if picked up with the fingers. They should be removed from the work with a blunt tool or a brush.

During the drilling, be sure that the flutes of the drill are kept open. Clogged flutes may cause the drill to break. To prevent this, the drill may have to be pulled out of the hole a number of times and the chips cleared away.

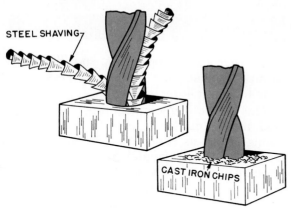

Fig. 55-10 *The difference between steel shavings and cast iron chips.*

55-11 Drilling with Cutting Fluids

During the drilling process, so much heat is generated that it can soften the cutting edges of the drill if care is not taken. A **cutting fluid** may therefore be used to take the heat away from the drill and wash away the chips. The drill will last longer, and the hole will be smoother.

Cast iron and copper do not require a cutting fluid. A soluble oil solution is often used for cooling purposes when drilling metals. See Table 50-2 for cutting fluids to be used with other metals.

REVIEW   REVIEW   REVIEW   REVIEW   REVIEW

Words to Know

center drill	cutting speed	pilot hole	step drilling
combination drill and countersink	drill drift		

Review Questions

1. What is meant by cutting speed? Why is it important?
2. What is meant by the feed of a drill? Why is it important?
3. Should a small drill run slower than a large drill if they are drilling the same material?
4. How can you tell when a drill is running too fast?
5. Calculate the correct rpm for a ½″ [12.7 mm] drill to cut at 200 fpm [61 mpm].
6. Why must the hole in the drill-press spindle be clean before putting a drill, sleeve, or chuck into it?
7. How should a drill chuck or drill sleeve be removed from the drill-press spindle?
8. What is involved in making a layout for drilling a hole?
9. What is a center drill? What is it used for?
10. Why are twist drills somewhat dangerous to use when drilling holes that go completely through a workpiece?
11. Tell what step drilling is and why it is done.
12. How can you prevent chips from clogging the drill when drilling a deep hole?

UNIT
56
Other Drill-Press Operations

Other work than drilling may be done on the drill press. Six basic kinds of **hole machining operations** (Fig. 56-1) are commonly performed on a drill press:

1. drilling
2. reaming
3. countersinking
4. counterboring and spot facing
5. tapping
5. boring.

Fig. 56-1 Six common machining operations that can be done on a drill press.

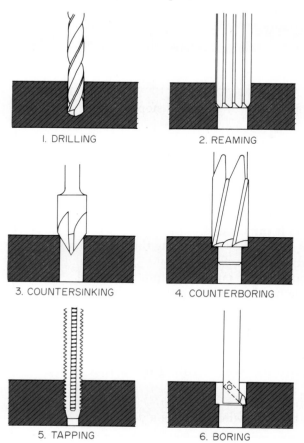

1. DRILLING   2. REAMING

3. COUNTERSINKING   4. COUNTERBORING

5. TAPPING   6. BORING

Another kind of operation, **spot finishing,** can also be done on a drill press. This is explained in Unit 46.

The basic hole-machining operations listed above can also be performed on metal-turning lathes, as is described in Unit 62 and on vertical and horizontal milling machines, as is explained in Unit 75.

56-1 Reamers and Their Uses

Reaming is done with a multiple-tooth cutting tool called a **reamer** (Fig. 56-2). The reamer is a **finishing tool** that can machine holes rounder, straighter, and more accurately to size than drills.

Fig. 56-2 Types of machine reamers. (A) Helical flute, straight shank. (B) Straight flute, taper shank. (C) Shell. (D) Arbor for shell reamer. (E) Adjustable, taper shank. (DoAll Company; Cleveland Twist Drill)

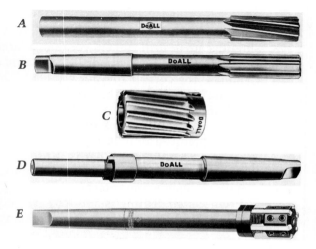

A

B

C

D

E

Reamers are available in a wide variety of types and sizes. They are made of carbon-tool steel or high-speed steel. They are also available with carbide-tipped cutting edges. Carbon-tool steel reamers generally are satisfactory for hand-reaming applications. For machine-reaming applications, high-speed steel reamers and reamers with carbide-tipped cutting edges stay sharp longer.

Principal Kinds of Reamers

The many types of reamers can be classified in two ways: those used on machines, called **machine reamers** (Fig. 56-2), and those turned by hand, called **hand reamers,** (Fig. 56-3). Some machine reamers have a straight shank for use in chucks and are called **chucking reamers** (Fig. 56-2A). Others have a tapered shank for use in tapered spindles (Fig. 56-2B). Hand reamers have a straight shank with a square end. They are turned with a tap wrench that fits over the square end (Fig. 56-4).

Fig. 56-3 *Types of hand reamers. (A) Straight flute. (B) Taper pin. (C) Morse taper roughing. (D) Morse taper finishing. (E) Expansion, straight flute. (F) Adjustable.* (DoAll Company; Cleveland Twist Drill)

Solid reamers. Most hand and machine reamers are made from one solid piece of steel (Fig. 56-2A & B, and Fig. 56-3A). They are made to produce holes of one size.

Taper reamers are also solid reamers. **Taper pin reamers** (Fig. 56-3B) are used to ream tapered holes for taper pins (see Unit 25). **Taper socket reamers** are made for reaming Morse, Brown and Sharpe, and other standard tapered sockets. Fig. 56-3C shows a Morse taper roughing reamer; Fig. 56-3D shows a Morse taper finishing reamer.

Shell reamers (Fig. 56-2C) are designed for economical reaming of large holes. The reamer is made for use with a special holder called an **arbor** (Fig. 56-2D). Several sizes of shell reamers will fit the same arbor. When the reamer is worn out, it is discarded and a new reamer is placed on the arbor.

Expansion reamers (Fig. 56-3E) are hand reamers that can be expanded slightly to produce a slightly oversize hole. This is often necessary in assembly and maintenance work. The maximum amount of expansion varies with the diameter of the reamer. It ranges from 0.006″ [0.15 mm] for a ¼″ [6.35 mm] reamer to 0.012″ [0.30 mm] for a 1½″ [38 mm] reamer. The size of the reamer is changed by turning an adjusting screw at the end of the reamer. An undersize **pilot** is provided on the end of some expansion reamers to help align the reamer with the hole.

Fig. 56-4 *Steadying a hand reamer with a lathe center in the drill press spindle when hand reaming.*

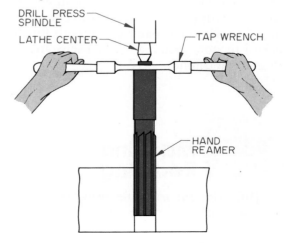

Adjustable reamers (Figs. 56-2E and 56-3F) are adjustable through a range of about 1⁄32" [1 mm]. The cutting blades slide in precise tapered slots. The diameter of the reamer is changed by loosening the nut on one end of the blades, then tightening the nut on the other end of the blades. This forces the blades to slide in the slots, thus changing the diameter.

Flutes

Both hand and machine reamers may have either straight or helical flutes. Straight-fluted reamers work well for reaming materials that are easy to machine. Helical-fluted reamers are better for reaming materials that are hard to machine. The helical flutes aid in producing smoother and more accurate holes.

Cutting Action

Machine reamers are end-cutting tools like drills. Their cutting edges are on a 45° bevel at the end of the reamer.

Hand reamers, however, cut on their **periphery** (outside). The flutes on solid hand reamers are straight for the entire length except for a starting taper at the end. The length of the taper is about equal to the diameter of the reamer. This taper permits the reamer to easily enter the hole, and also does most of the cutting.

Care of Reamers

Reamers are very fine tools and should be handled with great care. Take particular care to protect the cutting edges, because even a small nick or burr may cause it to cut oversize or prevent it from making a smooth finish. It is best to store each reamer in a separate space in the tool cabinet.

56-2 Machine Reaming

Hole size for machine reaming. Reamers are used only to make light finishing cuts.

The usual allowance for machine reaming is 1⁄64" [0.4 mm] for holes under 1⁄2" [12.7 mm], and 1⁄32" [0.8 mm] for holes 1⁄2" [12.7 mm] and over.

Machine reamers are held in the drill press just like a drill (Fig. 56-5). The drill press spindle centerline should always be in a straight line with the center of the hole being made. For this reason, **it is best to fasten the workpiece in place, so that it cannot move during the drilling and reaming operations.**

Procedure for machine reaming.

1. Drill the hole using the drilling procedures described in Unit 55. The final drill size should provide a reaming allowance as recommended above.
2. If the hole must be accurately located, bore the hole to make it concentric with the machine spindle. (Concentric means to have the same center.) Boring is described in Section 56-8.
3. Ream the hole, using a cutting speed that is 1⁄2 to 2⁄3 of the speed that would be used for a drill of the same size. The feed rate (rate of advance) of the reamer should be two to three times as fast as for a drill of the same size. An appropriate cutting fluid should always be used when reaming.

56-3 Hand Reaming

Hand reaming is done when extreme accuracy is required. A cut of 0.002" [0.05 mm] is usually recommended. **Never take cuts greater than 0.005" [0.13 mm] with a hand reamer.** Holes that are to be hand-reamed are drilled about 1⁄64" [0.40 mm] to 1⁄32" [0.79 mm] undersize first. They are then bored about 0.002" [0.05 mm] to 0.005" [0.13 mm] under the desired size of the reamed hole before hand-reaming.

Another method involves drilling and rough machine-reaming to about 0.002" [0.05 mm] undersize, followed by hand reaming. **Rough reaming** is done with a reamer intentionally ground about 0.002" [0.05 mm] undersize.

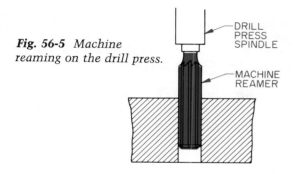

Fig. 56-5 *Machine reaming on the drill press.*

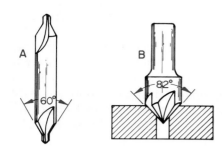

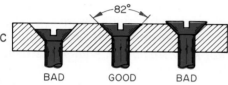

Fig. 56-6 *(A) Combination drill and countersink, (B) countersink for flat-head screws, (C) countersunk holes.*

It helps, when hand-reaming, to put a **lathe center** (Fig. 56-4; also Fig. 59-18) into the drill-press spindle. The lathe center is held tightly against the small hole in the end of the reamer while the reamer is turned with a tap wrench. The lathe center steadies the reamer and keeps it in line with the hole until it is started. A slow, steady, screwlike motion by the reamer with heavy pressure gives the best results. The reamer should never be forced or strained, **and should always be turned clockwise even when removing it from the hole.**

56-4
Countersinking

Countersinking is done with a **countersink** (Fig. 56-6). There are several kinds of countersinks. The difference in them is the angle of the cutting edges. One kind has an angle of 82° for flat-head screws. A **combination drill and countersink,** or **center drill,** has an angle of 60°.

56-5
Counterboring

Counterboring is done with a cutting tool known as a **counterbore** (Figs. 56-1 and 56-7). It has a pilot to guide the tool into the hole and keep it centered.

Counterboring is done after the hole is drilled. The pilot should be oiled before entering the hole to keep it from roughening the hole. Use cutting oil when counterboring steel.

Counterboring is done to recess the heads of **cap screws** below the workpiece surface.

Fig. 56-7 *Counterboring for a cap screw.* (The Foote-Burt Co.)

56-6 Spot Facing

Spot facing is somewhat like counterboring, except that in spot facing only a little metal is removed around the top of the hole. Only the surface is made smooth and square to form a flat **bearing surface** for the head of a cap screw or for a nut (Fig. 56-8). Spot facing is done with a **spot-facing tool** after the hole is drilled (Fig. 56-9).

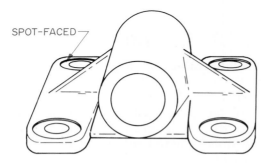
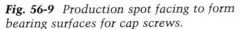

Fig. 56-8 *Spot faced holes on a casting.*

Fig. 56-9 *Production spot facing to form bearing surfaces for cap screws.*

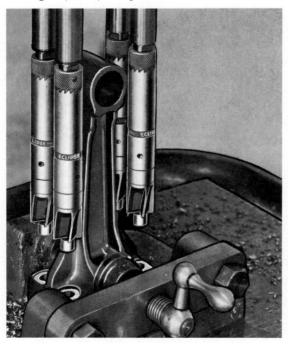

56-7 Tapping with the Drill Press

The forming of **screw threads** on the inside of a hole, such as the threads in a nut, is called **tapping.** Tapping is explained in Unit 21.

Tapping with the drill press may be done by hand or with a **tapping attachment.**

Hand tapping. Drill the required hole for the size tap to be used. Refer to Table 21-1 on tap drill sizes for this information. Without moving the workpiece, remove the tap drill from the drill chuck and replace it with the tap (Fig. 56-10). Be sure the tap is either a **starting tap** or a **plug tap.** Apply a suitable cutting fluid and rotate the drill chuck **by hand** while applying pressure with the drill press feed lever.

After three or four threads have been cut, release the tap from the drill chuck, attach a tap wrench, and finish tapping the hole. This method of hand tapping assures good alignment of the tapped threads with the hole.

Tapping with power. A **tapping attachment** may be mounted on a drill press as shown in Figure 56-11. The tap is mounted in a **collet chuck,** which is provided in the tapping attachment. **The workpiece to be tapped must be mounted securely in a vise. The vise should be clamped or bolted down to the drill press table.**

The tapping attachment in Figure 56-11 is **nonreversing.** This means that **the drill-press spindle does not have to be reversed to back out the tap** after tapping the hole. With this type of attachment, the tap enters the hole with clockwise rotation as pressure is applied downward on the drill-press feed handle. When the hole is tapped to depth, pressure on the feed handle is released and the tap stops rotating, even though the drill press spindle continues to rotate. The tap is backed out of the hole by applying upward pressure on the spindle with the drill-press feed handle. The upward pressure engages a reversing mechanism in the tapping attachment. This causes the tap to rotate counterclockwise, which backs it out of the hole.

Some tapping attachments used on drill presses are **reversing.** With this type, the drill press spindle must be reversed to extract the tap after tapping to the desired depth.

Spiral ground and helical-fluted taps work best with tapping attachments.

Fig. 56-10 *Hand tapping with the drill press. This is an accurate method for getting the tap started straight.*

Fig. 56-11 *A tapping attachment mounted on a drill press.*

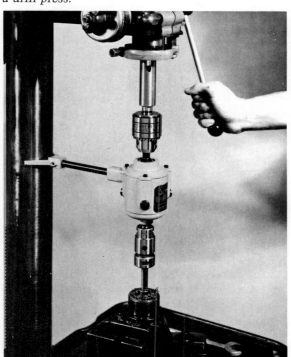

56-8 Boring

Boring is done to straighten out drilled holes and to produce holes of accurate size when a drill or reamer of the desired size is not available. For boring, a hole is drilled $\frac{1}{16}''$ to $\frac{1}{8}''$ [1.6 to 3.2 mm] undersize, and is then bored to the correct size.

Boring is done with a single-point cutting tool, as shown in Figures 56-1 and 56-12. For boring small holes, solid boring bars are used that have a built-in cutting edge. Larger boring bars use a replaceable high speed steel tool bit or a carbide insert. In Figure 56-12, the boring bar is inserted in a boring head, which is inserted in the tapered spindle of a drill press or milling machine. The boring head can be adjusted to bore holes accurately to 0.001'' [0.025 mm] or less.

 SAFETY NOTE

To be done safely, boring must be done at low rpm with automatic feed, and the workpiece must be clamped solidly to the machine table.

Holes may also be bored on a metalworking lathe, as shown in Figure 63-9.

Fig. 56-12 *A boring head and boring bars.*

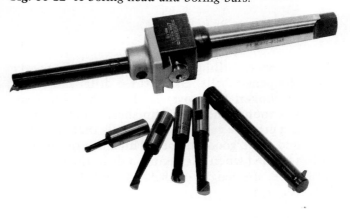

REVIEW   REVIEW   REVIEW   REVIEW   REVIEW

WORDS TO KNOW

adjustable reamer	chucking reamer	finishing cut	shell reamer
boring	counterbore	hand reamer	solid reamer
boring bar	counterbore pilot	machine reamer	spot facing
boring head	countersink	reaming	tap drill
center drill	expansion reamer	reaming allowance	tapping attachment

REVIEW QUESTIONS

1. What is the main reason why reamed holes are sometimes more desirable than drilled holes?
2. Name several kinds of hand reamers.
3. Name several kinds of machine reamers.
4. What is the difference in construction between a machine reamer and a hand reamer?
5. How much metal should be left for a hand reamer to cut away? Machine reamer?
6. Explain how a machine reamer cuts. Does a hand reamer cut the same way?
7. In what way is an expansion reamer different from an adjustable reamer?
8. What is meant by countersinking?
9. What are the angles of countersinks?
10. What is the difference between countersinking and counterboring?
11. What is the difference between counterboring and spot facing?
12. Explain how the drill press is used in hand tapping.
13. How can you find out what size tap drill to use?
14. Explain what boring is and how it is done on a drill press.

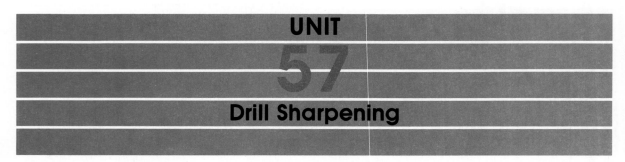

UNIT
57
Drill Sharpening

Most drilling troubles are caused by poorly sharpened drills. Using these drills can result in: broken drills, oversize holes, holes that are not round, and rough finishes. Good machining practice calls for using drills that are sharp and leave good finishes. Three things must be watched when sharpening a drill: the lip clearance, the length of the lips, and the angle of the lips.

57-1

Lip Clearance

The **heel** of a drill is the part of the point behind each cutting edge. This surface must be ground back from the level of the lips to provide room, or **lip clearance,** for the edges to cut into the metal (Fig. 57-1).

If there were no lip clearance, as on **A** in Figure 57-1, the end of the drill would rub, but not cut. The metal behind the cutting edges must be ground away as on **B** and **C**. Note in **B** and **C** how much farther ahead the **cutting lip** is than the **heel**.

If the angle of lip clearance is much less than 8°, it acts the same as when there is no clearance. As a result, the drill cannot cut into the metal. It may then break in the center along the **web**.

57-2 The Angle of Lip Clearance

The correct lip clearance for a regular point for drilling most steels should be from 8° to 12°. For drilling soft materials under heavy feeds the angle of lip clearance may be increased to 15°. If it is more than 15°, the corners of the cutting edges are too thin and may break off.

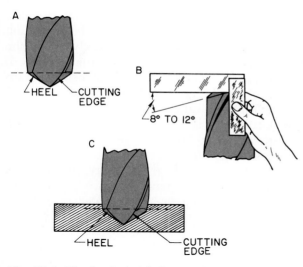

Fig. 57-1 *The heel of a drill must be ground back from the level of the cutting edge to provide clearance.*

Fig. 57-2 *On a correctly sharpened drill, both cutting edges have the same angle and same length.*

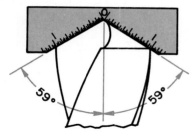

57-3 The Length and Angle of the Lips

The two lips on a drill must be the same length, and their angles must be equal (Fig. 57-2). For ordinary work, a point angle of 118° (the sum of two 59° angles) is recommended. 135° is recommended for hard materials, and 90° for soft materials. If the two lips are the same length and at equal angles, the dead center will also be centrally located (Fig. 57-3). The line across the **dead center** should be between 120° and 135° with the cutting edge.

Only one lip will cut if the dead center is in the center but the angles are different as in Figure 57-4A. One cutting edge will wear quickly, and the hole will be oversize.

If the angles on the cutting edges are equal, but the lips are of different lengths (Fig. 57-4B) the dead center will not be in the center. The hole will then be larger than the drill.

The worst condition occurs when the lips are of unequal lengths and the angles of the cutting edges are also unequal (Fig. 57-4C). The hole is then larger than the drill, and the drill and drill press are strained.

Fig. 57-3 *The angle of the dead center with the cutting edge on correctly sharpened drills.*

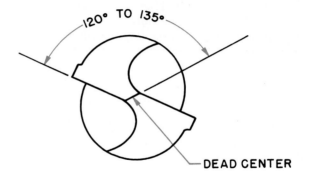

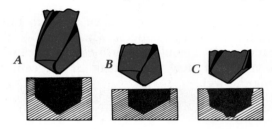

Fig. 57-4 *The results of incorrect cutting edge angles and lengths. (A) The angles of the cutting edges are unequal. (B) The length of the cutting edges are unequal. (C) The angles and lengths of the cutting edges are unequal.*

57-4   Rake Angle

The **rake angle** of the drill is the angle between the flute and the workpiece (Fig. 57-5). If the rake angle is less than 90°, the drill will have a **positive rake** (Fig. 57-5A). If the rake angle is more than 90°, the drill will have a **negative rake** (Fig. 57-5B).

The rake angle helps to curl the chips; a large rake angle rolls the chips tightly, while a small rake angle rolls them loosely. Rake angle is made negative by grinding the cutting edge so that it projects an angle greater than 90° (Fig. 57-5B). **The rake angle should not be changed for ordinary drilling.**

SAFETY NOTE

When drilling **free-machining** brass and some types of plastics, drills with standard rakes tend to screw themselves into the material, sometimes breaking the drill, the material, or both. This can be avoided if the drills are reground to provide a slightly negative rake (Fig. 57-5B).

57-5   Grinding Drills by Hand

With practice, drills can be successfully sharpened by hand. The following procedure is recommended:

1. Hold the drill shank in the dominant hand and support the front of the drill about 1" [25 mm] back from the point with the other hand.
2. Holding the drill with one of its cutting edges horizontal, position it close to the face of the grinding wheel at an angle of 59° as in Figure 57-6A.
3. While holding the drill as above, position the body of the drill so it is horizontal as in Figure 57-6B.
4.. Grind the first cutting edge, using light pressure on the drill while moving it slightly back and forth on the wheel face.
5. When a small amount has been ground from the cutting edge, slowly raise the front of the drill while pushing forward to keep the heel of the drill in contact with the wheel (Fig. 57-6C). This is necessary to grind the clearance on the cutting edge.
6. Grind the second cutting edge as above, then check the drill point with a drill-grinding gage.
7. Regrind the drill, if necessary, to make the angles, lengths, and clearance of both cutting edges as equal as possible.

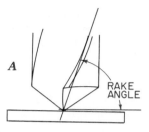

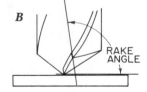

Fig. 57-5 *Rake angles on twist drills.*

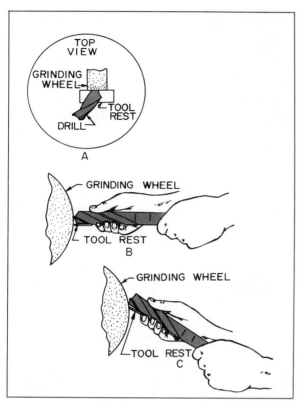

57-6 Grinding Drills by Machine

Drills can be ground better and faster with a **drill-grinding attachment**, or on a special purpose **drill-grinding machine.**

Drills sharpened by machine are **precision-ground** to correct angles and clearances. If your shop has a drill-grinding machine, do not attempt to operate it until obtaining instructions from your instructor.

Fig. 57-6 *Grinding a drill by hand. (A) Top view of correct drill position. (B) Side view of correct drill position. (C) Lifting the drill to grind the clearance.*

REVIEW REVIEW REVIEW REVIEW REVIEW

WORDS TO KNOW

cutting lip
drill-grinding
   attachment

drill-grinding gage
drill-grinding
   machine
lip angle

lip clearance
lip length
negative rake

positive rake
rake angle

REVIEW QUESTIONS

1. What three things should be watched when sharpening a twist drill by hand?
2. What is lip clearance?
3. What is the result of too much lip clearance?
4. What is the result of too little lip clearance?
5. How does a drill behave when the angles of the cutting edges are unequal?
6. How does a drill behave when the lips of a drill are of unequal lengths?
7. Explain the difference between positive and negative rake.
8. Drills with negative rake are recommended for drilling what materials?
9. How does a drill-grinding gage aid hand sharpening of drills?
10. Is it better to grind a drill by machine than by hand? Why or why not?

The average shopper who selects a jar of pickles from the grocery shelf may notice that it is round, does not topple over when set down, and has a convenient wide mouth for extracting pickles. It probably seldom occurs to the shopper that metalworking plays a central part in the forming of a perfect glass jar. For veteran lathe operator Sam Campbell, however, the connection is obvious.

Sam has worked at a bottle-making factory for 42 years. One of his responsibilities is making the metal cores used in the glass-forming process. These "plungers" drop down into molten glass "blanks," shape the inside of the jars, and are then withdrawn. The blanks are then transferred by a mechanical arm to metal molds, which shape the outside.

Sam runs a manually operated lathe and does much of his work on the hardest grade of stainless steel. Using his keen eyesight and knowledge of math, he prepares an individual template for each type of jar. The template must be exact. Sam says there are "no ups, downs, or in-betweens. It has to be right on." He then secures the template onto a bracket on the lathe. As he follows the pattern with a tracer, the shape is reproduced on metal stock.

Like everyone else at the factory, Sam wears safety glasses. But he seldom uses gloves. In his case, they are a hazard because they could catch in the lathe.

Sam finds the wages good and the work steady. There is enough variety to make each job interesting. And, even after all his years in the trade, he says that he "learns a little bit more each day."

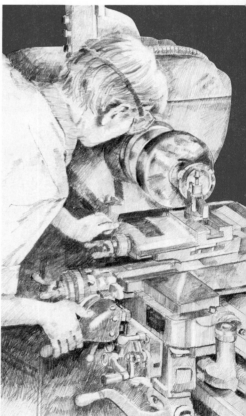

Sam Campbell
Lathe Operator

UNIT
58
The Metalworking Lathe

The metalworking lathe is the most basic of all the metalworking machine tools (Fig. 58-1). It operates on the principle of a single-point cutting tool removing metal as it is fed into a revolving workpiece (Fig. 58-2). Lathes are used to make cylindrical and conical parts such as axles, pistons, pulleys, gear blanks, pins, and threaded fittings.

58-1
Kinds of Lathes

The basic **manually operated lathe** shown in Figure 58-1 is like those found in schools and in maintenance, tool-and-die, and job shops. It is used for making single parts and small quantities of identical parts, or for repairing worn parts.

Many other kinds of lathes are made, only a few of which can be shown here. Most of them are made either for mass production of identical parts or for making very large parts. Manually operated **screw machines** (Fig. 58-3) and **turret lathes** (Fig. 58-4) are used for production runs of a few hundred parts. **Numerically controlled** turret lathes (Fig. 58-5) are rapidly replacing manually operated turret lathes because they are much more efficient. **Automatic lathes** (Fig. 58-6) are used for production runs of thousands of identical parts. **Vertical turret lathes** are made for machining parts of very large diameters.

No matter how large or complicated a lathe may appear, the basic principles of lathe operation are the same as for smaller and simpler lathes.

Fig. 58–1 A modern manually operated lathe. (Emco Maier Corp.)

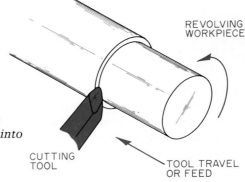

Fig. 58–2 Lathes operate on the principle of a cutting tool removing metal as it is being fed into a revolving work piece.

REVOLVING WORKPIECE

CUTTING TOOL

TOOL TRAVEL OR FEED

Fig. 58–3 *A hand screw machine is a small manually operated turret lathe used for short production runs of small parts.* (Hardinge-Bros., Inc.)

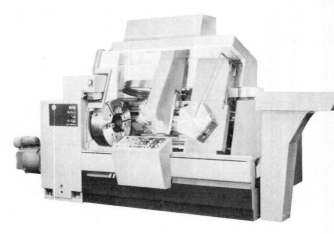

Fig. 58–5 *A numerically controlled turret lathe equipped for chucking work. These automatic machines are replacing manually operated turret lathes for short production runs.* (Warner & Swasey Company)

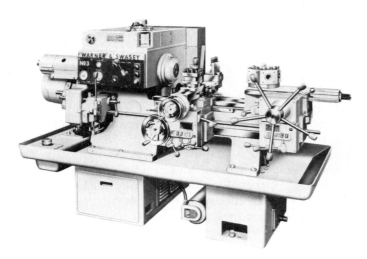

Fig. 58–4 *A manually operated turret lathe used for producing small quantities of medium-sized parts.* (Warner & Swasey Company)

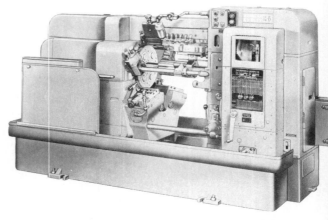

Fig. 58–6 *A six-spindle automatic lathe used for very high production volume.* (Warner & Swasey Company)

58-2 Lathe Sizes

Lathes range in size from tiny jeweler's lathes that are used to repair watches (Fig. 58-7), to huge machines used to machine steel mill rolls and hydroelectric generator shafts (Fig. 58-8).

Figure 58-9 shows that the size of a lathe is measured by its **swing** and length of bed.

The swing is measured by the largest diameter of work that can be turned in the lathe. For example, a piece 10″ [254 mm] in diameter is the largest work that can be turned in a 10″ [254 mm] lathe. A **10″ × 5′ lathe** has a 10″ [254 mm] swing and a bed 5′ [1524 mm] long.

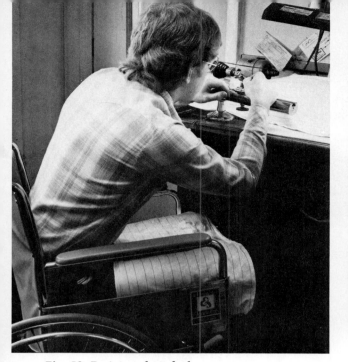

Fig. 58–7 *A jeweler's lathe.*

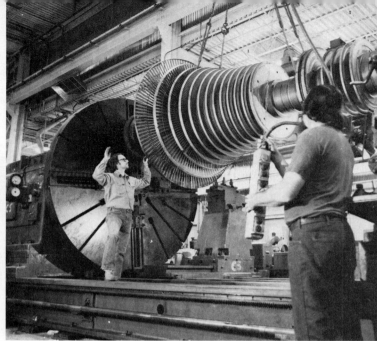

Fig. 58–8 *This huge lathe is used to machine steam turbine generator shafts for electric power stations.*

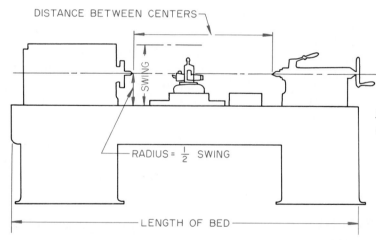

Fig. 58–9 *Dimensions that describe the size of a lathe.*

The Main Parts of a Lathe

Before attempting to operate a lathe, you should become familiar with its main parts, controls, and accessories. By studying Figure 58-10 carefully and reading the text, you will begin to learn the purpose of each lathe part and how it works with other parts of the lathe.

The operating controls on different lathes are often designed somewhat differently. However, all lathes are equipped with controls that perform similar functions.

The **lathe bed** is the main frame upon which the machine is built. The **headstock** is permanently fastened to the left end of the bed, and the **tailstock** can be clamped at any point along the bed to the right of the headstock. Both the headstock and the tailstock have **spindles.** The headstock spindle is driven by a motor in a cabinet beneath the head-

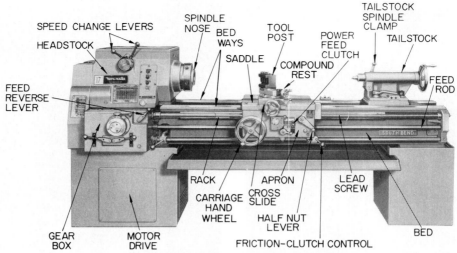

SPEED CHANGE LEVERS SPINDLE NOSE BED WAYS TOOL POST POWER FEED CLUTCH TAILSTOCK SPINDLE CLAMP TAILSTOCK
HEADSTOCK SADDLE COMPOUND REST FEED ROD
FEED REVERSE LEVER
RACK APRON LEAD SCREW
CARRIAGE HAND WHEEL CROSS SLIDE HALF NUT LEVER BED
GEAR BOX MOTOR DRIVE FRICTION-CLUTCH CONTROL

Fig. 58—10 Parts of a modern lathe.

stock. The tailstock spindle does not turn; however, it can be moved in and out of the tailstock with the **tailstock handwheel.** Both spindles can hold **lathe centers** that support long workpieces between them (Fig. 59-21). The tapered hole of the tailstock spindle also accepts drill chucks and tapered-shank drills and reamers for drilling operations.

The **carriage** is the part that slides back and forth on the bed between the headstock and the tailstock, and which carries the cutting tool. The precision V-shaped and flat surfaces of the bed, on which the carriage and tailstock slide, are called **bed ways.**

58-4 Lathe Headstock Drive Systems

Several different kinds of headstock drive systems are found on lathes. With **flat-belt drives** (Fig. 58-11), which use a **cone-pulley drive system,** spindle speeds are changed by first loosening the belt with a **belt tension** lever. The belt is then moved by hand to the desired step on the **cone pulley.**

SAFETY NOTE

🚫 Most lathes must be stopped while changing speeds or any of the controls on the headstock end of the machine.

Cone-pulley drive systems have either three or four steps on each pulley. They also have a **back-gear** system (Fig. 58-12) which provides an additional three or four slower speeds. For **direct drive** (high speeds), the **bull-gear pin** is pushed in and the back gear lever is pushed back to disengage the back gears. For **back-geared drive** (slow speeds), the bull-gear pin is pulled out and the back-gear lever is pulled forward.

Fig. 58—11 A lathe with a flat belt-drive system.

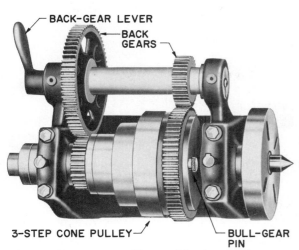

Fig. 58–12 A cone-pulley and back-gear drive system for a lathe.

Fig. 58–14 A lever-shift V-belt drive system. (Sheldon Machine Co., Inc.)

Fig. 58–13 A manual-shift V-belt drive.

Several types of **V-belt drive** systems are made. With the **manual-shift** system shown in Figure 58-13, belt tension is first released with a belt tension lever. The V-belt is then moved manually to the desired pulleys. With the **lever-shift** system shown in Figure 58-14, speed changes are made by shifting the two levers to any of four different positions. This system provides four direct-drive and four back-geared speeds.

Some lathes have a **variable-speed V-belt drive** system, which can provide any desired rpm within the **speed range** of the lathe (Fig. 58-15).

Fig. 58–15 A variable-speed drive system. (Clausing Machine Tools)

SAFETY NOTE

Variable-speed V-belt drives often provide two or three speed ranges. **Shifting from one speed range to another must be done with the machine stopped.** However, speed changes within each range must be done with the spindle running.

Large lathes usually have a **geared-head drive** (Fig. 58-16). Speed changes with this type of drive are made by shifting speed change levers on the front of the headstock.

SAFETY NOTE

As with most other drive systems, speed changes on geared-head lathes must be made only when the headstock spindle is stopped. **Attempting to shift gears while the spindle is running could cause serious damage to the gears.**

Fig. 58–16 An interior view of the headstock of a lathe with an all-gear drive system. (South Bend Lathe, Inc.)

Fig. 58–17 Power feed directions. (1) Longitudinal feed for turning (A) and boring (B). (2) Cross feed for facing (C).

Carriage Feed and Threading Mechanisms

58-5

The lathe is designed so that the cutting tool may be fed manually or automatically along the work while machining. The feed is called **longitudinal feed** when the tool is fed **along** the work, parallel to the lathe bed. The longitudinal feed is used for operations such as turning (Fig. 58-17A) and boring (Fig. 58-17B). The feed is called **cross feed** when the tool is fed **across** the end of the workpiece as in facing operations (Fig. 58-17C). "Feed" also refers to **feed rate,** the distance that the tool moves along the workpiece during one revolution of the workpiece.

The **power feed,** both longitudinal and cross feed, is controlled through the **feeding** and **threading** mechanisms on the lathe. These mechanisms include the **end gears** (Fig. 58-18); the **quick-change gear box** (Fig. 58-19); and the **carriage and apron assembly,** shown in Figure 58-20.

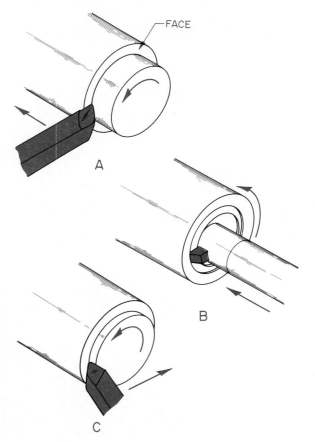

Fig. 58–18 *The end-gear train of a lathe.*

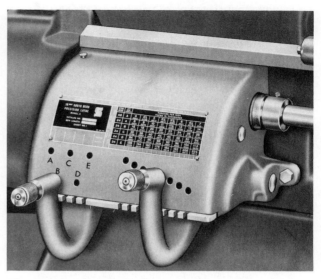

Fig. 58–19 *The quick-change gear box of a lathe, with feed rate index chart.* (South Bend Lathe, Inc.)

The end gears transmit power from the headstock spindle to the **lead screw** (Fig. 58-10) through the gear box. The position of the levers on the gear box determines how fast the lead screw revolves in relation to the head-stock spindle. The lead screw transmits power to the carriage and apron assembly.

The controls on the carriage and apron (Fig. 58-20) control all tool and carriage movements. The **apron handwheel** is used for manual longitudinal movement of the carriage. The **cross-feed knob** is used to move the **cross slide** in and out manually. The **compound rest,** which holds the toolholder and cutting tool, is mounted on the cross-slide. It is fed manually with the **compound-rest knob.** The **carriage-lock screw** may be tightened to lock the carriage. This prevents longitudinal movement during operations such as facing. (Unit 63 describes facing and other operations.)

The compound rest is normally set at an angle of about 29° from the crosswise position (Fig. 58-20). This is the angle at which it is set for cutting 60° screw threads. This angle also is convenient for performing many other lathe operations. The compound rest may be set at any angle required for turning or boring short tapers as explained in detail in Unit 64.

The **apron feed-change lever** is used to select longitudinal feed or cross feed. For longitudinal feeding the lever is moved to the upper position. For cross feeding the lever is moved to the lower position. For thread-cutting the feed change lever is moved to the center position, as shown in Figure 58-20.

COMPOUND-REST KNOB

COMPOUND REST

CROSS SLIDE

CROSS-FEED KNOB

APRON HANDWHEEL

TOOLPOST

CARRIAGE-LOCK SCREW

APRON FEED-CHANGE LEVER

THREAD DIAL

HALF-NUT LEVER

AUTOMATIC-FEED FRICTION CLUTCH

Fig. 58–20 *The parts of a lathe carriage and apron assembly.* (South Bend Lathe, Inc.)

The **clutch-knob,** also called the **automatic-feed friction clutch** (Fig. 58-20), is used to start and stop automatic longitudinal or cross feed. The **half-nut lever** is used to engage the feed for thread-cutting operations only. The **feed-reverse lever,** located on the headstock (Fig. 58-10), is used to reverse the direction of the lead screw. This reverses the direction of both the longitudinal and cross feeds.

The levers on the quick-change gear box (Fig. 58-19) are used to set feed rates. An **index chart** is located on the front of the gear box. There are two numbers for each box in the "Threads per Inch" section of the index chart. On machines having inch measurements, the **larger** of the two numbers indicates the number of threads per inch for threading operations only. This means that if the number 16

The Slide Rest: "Turning" Point in Machining Metals

T E C H N O L O G I E S   A N D   P R A C T I C E S

No one person can be given credit for the invention of the lathe. Like many tools, the modern lathe was developed gradually over many years. The principle of shaping wooden objects, such as poles, by turning them mechanically and holding a cutting tool against them dates back to 1000 A.D. But efficient metalworking lathes were not developed until the late 18th century.

While woodworkers at that time had good lathes available to them, metalworkers had a real problem in cutting, or "turning," metal. Machinists found it very difficult to hold a scraping tool against a rapidly turning piece of iron for more than a few minutes. Until this problem could be solved, development of metalwork technology would remain at a standstill.

The solution was to replace the hand-held cutting tool with a mechanical device—the slide rest (a part of the present carriage and apron assembly). This revolutionary idea was developed by two men at about the same time, but in different parts of the world. David Wilkinson of Rhode Island designed a slide-rest lathe in 1798. Englishman Henry Maudslay produced a similar machine a short time later. Although Wilkinson patented the idea first, Maudslay's machine was more expertly designed. This fact, plus Maudslay's already-established reputation, brought the major credit to the Englishman.

The slide rest was a metal carriage that held a rigidly clamped cutting tool. It moved on tracks set in the lathe bed. The cutting tool could be placed anywhere along the length of the workpiece or at right angles to it. This gave the machinist much greater control over the metal-cutting process. Many types of lathe operations became easier to accomplish.

Whether the creation of the slide rest is attributed to Wilkinson or Maudslay, it is seen as a true turning point in machine tool technology. The lathe could now be used in the mass production of other machine tools, such as milling machines and planers. These tools were key factors in the development of modern industry.

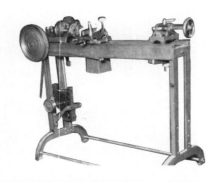

were selected, the carriage would travel longitudinally ¹⁄₁₆″ for each revolution of the workpiece, or 1″ for 16 revolutions of the workpiece.

On metric machines, the larger number indicates the thread pitch in millimeters.

The **smaller decimal numbers** on the index chart indicate the amount of feed per revolution for longitudinal and cross feeds. In inch measurement this is given in thousandths of an inch; in metric measurement it is given in hundredths of a millimeter. **It should be noted that the amount of cross feed is not always the same as the amount of longitudinal feed.** The ratio of cross feed to longitudinal feed varies for different lathes and is usually indicated on the index chart. For the lathe shown in Figure 58-18, the cross feed is equal to 0.375 times the longitudinal feed. Thus, if a longitudinal feed of 0.0105″ [0.27 mm] were set, the cross feed would equal 0.375 × 0.0105″ [0.27 mm], or 0.004″ [0.10 mm] per revolution of the workpiece.

58-6 Lathe Accessories

Many lathe accessories are available for doing different machining operations on the lathe. They include various devices for holding workpieces and for machining different shapes. These are described in the units that follow.

REVIEW REVIEW REVIEW REVIEW REVIEW

Words to Know

apron	compound rest	geared-head drive	power feed
apron handwheel	cone pulley	headstock	tailstock
automatic-feed	cone-pulley step	headstock spindle	tailstock handwheel
friction clutch	cross feed	index chart	tailstock spindle
automatic lathes	cross slide	lathe bed	turret lathe
back gear	feed change lever	lathe swing	variable-speed drive
bed ways	feed rate	lead screw	V-belt drive
bull-gear pin	feed-reverse lever	longitudinal feed	vertical turret lathe
carriage	flat-belt drive		

Review Questions

1. What kinds of parts are made on metal-working lathes? Give several examples.
2. How is the size of a lathe measured?
3. Name the four main parts of a lathe.
4. Name two main uses for the lathe tailstock.
5. Name three kinds of headstock drive systems.
6. What danger is there in trying to change speeds on a geared-head lathe while the headstock spindle is running?
7. What is meant by longitudinal feed on a lathe?
8. What is meant by cross feed on a lathe?
9. What is meant by feed rate on a lathe?
10. At what angle should the compound rest be set for most lathe operations?
11. What is the name of the lever that selects longitudinal or cross feed?
12. What is the name of the control that reverses the direction of the power feed?

UNIT
59

Methods of Holding Workpieces in a Lathe

Lathe operations require secure methods of holding workpieces. This unit describes the parts of the lathe and the lathe accessories that apply directly to workpiece holding.

59-1 Spindle Noses

Workpiece-holding devices on lathes are attached to and driven by the **headstock spindle.** There are three types of spindle ends, called **spindle noses,** in common use:
1. the threaded spindle nose
2. the cam-lock spindle nose
3. the long-taper key-drive spindle nose.

With the **threaded spindle nose** (Fig. 59-1), a chuck or **faceplate** is screwed onto the spindle. Chucks (Section 59-2) are workpiece-holding accessories. The faceplate (Fig. 59-21) is another accessory that is used to drive the **lathe dog** (Fig. 59-20). Workpieces or other holding devices are also sometimes bolted directly to the faceplate.

With the **cam-lock spindle nose** (Fig. 59-2), notched rods attached to the back of the chuck are inserted in holes in the spindle **face.** The chuck is then locked in place by turning the **cam-locks** with a T-handle wrench.

With the **long-taper key-drive spindle nose** (Fig. 59-3), the chuck is placed so that the key on the spindle nose lines up with the **keyway** in the chuck. The threaded ring of the spindle nose is then threaded onto the chuck threads to pull it tightly in place.

Fig. 59–1 A threaded spindle nose. (South Bend Lathe, Inc.)

When mounting or removing chucks or faceplates, take care to avoid damage to the threads of the chuck or on the nose of the spindle. With the tapered key drive and cam-lock spindle noses, take care to avoid nicking the mating surfaces of the chuck and spindle nose. A small chip, nick, or burr will keep the chuck from running true.

59-2 Lathe Chucks

There are five kinds of lathe chucks:
1. the four-jaw independent chuck
2. the three-jaw universal chuck
3. collet chucks
4. spindle chucks
5. step chucks.

Fig. 59–2 *A cam-lock spindle nose.* (South Bend Lathe, Inc.)

Fig. 59–3 *A spindle nose with a long taper key drive.* (South Bend Lathe, Inc.)

Fig. 59–4 *A 4-jaw independent chuck with its chuck key. Jaws are shown reversed for holding large workpiece diameters.* (South Bend Lathe Works)

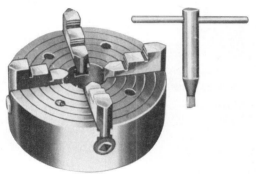

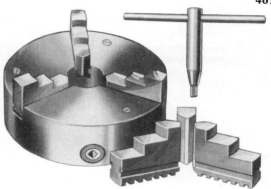

Fig. 59–5 *Three-jaw universal chucks are self-centering. The jaws are numbered and must be installed in 1-2-3 order.* (South Bend Lathe Works)

Each jaw of the **four-jaw independent chuck** (Fig. 59-4) must be moved separately with a **chuck key,** also called a **chuck wrench.** This chuck may be used to hold work that is round, square, rectangular, or irregular in shape. The jaws on this kind of chuck are **reversible;** that is, they can be taken off and put on again in the opposite direction. The **steps** of the jaws allow different sizes of work to be held.

The **three-jaw universal chuck** (Fig. 59-5) automatically centers the workpiece like a drill chuck. This kind of chuck usually has two sets of jaws; one set holds larger workpieces, while the other set holds small workpieces. Three-jaw universal chucks in good condition center work accurately to within 0.002″ to 0.003 ″ [0.05 to 0.08 mm].

Collet chucks of the **spring-collet** type (Fig. 59-6) are made to hold work that is close to a specific diameter. A spring collet should be used only for holding work that is within about 0.005″ [0.13 mm] of the size marked on the collet.

There are several types of collet chucks available. A common one is the **draw-in** type, which fits into the nose of the lathe spindle and is tightened with a **hand-wheel draw bar.** This bar extends through the entire length of the headstock (Fig. 59-7). Collets are made in standard bar stock sizes. Different collets are made to hold round, square, and hexagonal shapes. Collet chucks are very accurate, save time in mounting work, and speed up production.

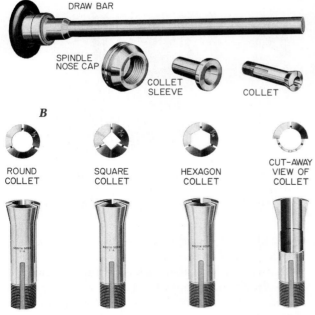

Fig. 59–6 *A draw-in type collet chuck (A), and different spring collets (B).*

Fig. 59–8 *A spindle chuck.* (South Bend Lathe Works)

The **step chuck** (Fig. 59-9) is made for holding small round discs. It is held in the spindle and works the same way as a draw-in collet chuck. Small diameter step chucks do not require a separate step-chuck closer.

Care of Chucks

Chucks should be handled carefully. They should be oiled regularly, kept clean, and not abused. The threads should be kept clean with a **thread-cleaning tool** shown in Figure 59-10.

59-3 Installing and Removing Threaded Chucks

To install a threaded chuck:
1. Lock the headstock spindle so it cannot rotate.
2. Clean the spindle nose threads with a shop rag.
3. Clean the chuck threads with a thread-cleaning tool.

Before installing a collet chuck, clean the **spindle hole,** the **collet sleeve,** and the collet itself. Grit or chips left between the mating surfaces spoil the accuracy of the chuck and the parts held in it.

The **spindle chuck** (Fig. 59-8) is a drill chuck that is designed to screw onto the nose of the lathe spindle. It is used for holding small round workpieces for light machining or polishing operations.

Fig. 59–7 *A cross-section diagram of a collet chuck installed in a lathe spindle.* (South Bend Lathe Works)

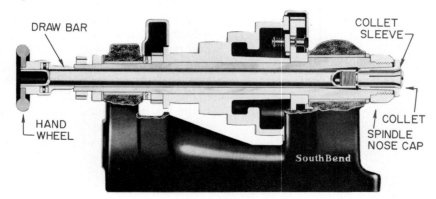

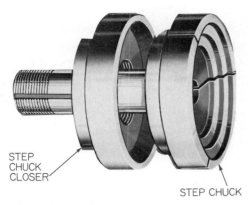

Fig. 59–9 *A step chuck and closer.* (South Bend Lathe Works)

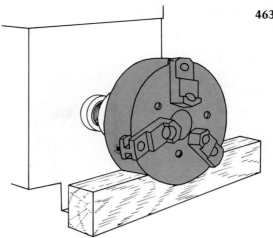

Fig. 59–11 *A lathe chuck supported with a chuck cradle.*

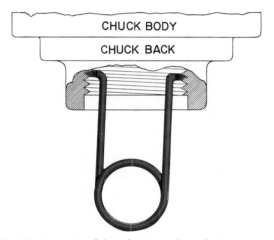

CHUCK BODY

CHUCK BACK

Fig. 59–10 *A tool for cleaning threads in a chuck.*

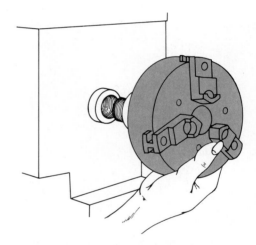

Fig. 59–12 *Mounting a lathe chuck on a threaded spindle nose.*

4. Protect the bed ways of the lathe with a board or **chuck cradle** (Fig. 59-11).
5. Hold the chuck squarely against the spindle nose (Fig. 59-12). Thread the chuck clockwise until its hub gently contacts the shoulder of the spindle.

SAFETY NOTE

Large chucks are very heavy and should not be mounted without help. Do not risk injury to yourself or damage to the chuck or machine by trying to lift a chuck that is too heavy.

To remove a threaded chuck:

1. Lock the headstock spindle.
2. Place a board or chuck cradle under the chuck.
3. Use a large adjustable wrench (Fig. 59-13) or a bar placed between the opened chuck jaws to loosen the chuck.
4. If the chuck will not loosen as above, place a block of wood between a chuck jaw and the rear bed ways (Fig. 59-14). Set the lathe speed for its slowest back-gear speed. Rotating the spindle backwards (by hand if possible) will usually loosen the chuck.
5. Carefully unscrew the lathe chuck and place it in its storage rack.

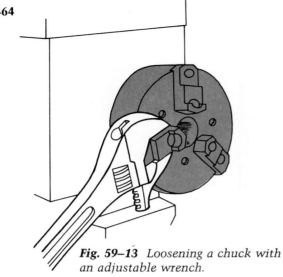

Fig. 59–13 *Loosening a chuck with an adjustable wrench.*

Fig. 59–14 *Loosening a chuck with the aid of a block of wood.* (South Bend Lathe, Inc.)

Fig. 59–15 *Circles machined into the chuck face aid in centering the workpiece in a four-jaw chuck.*

59-4 Centering Workpieces in 4-Jaw Independent Chucks

Centering without Mechanical Aids

1. Place the workpiece in the center of the chuck between the four jaws and tighten them. Use the machined circles on the chuck face (Fig. 59-15) to help center the workpiece.

2. Mount a **toolholder** and **tool bit** (Figs. 60-1 and 60-7) in the **tool post** (Fig. 58-10) and set the tool bit on the approximate center of the workpiece. (Unit 60 provides additional information about toolholders and tool bits.)

3. Rotate the workpiece slowly **by hand,** and advance the tool until it almost touches the part of the workpiece **farthest off center.** Then rotate the chuck until the chuck jaw nearest to the tool is horizontal. Note the gap between the tool and the workpiece.

4. Now rotate the workpiece 180 degrees and note the gap between the tool and workpiece. If the two gaps are not the same, adjust these opposite jaws until the gaps are equal.

5. Repeating this process for the other two jaws will center the workpiece.

Centering with a Dial Indicator

1. After centering the workpiece as described above, mount a **dial indicator** on the toolpost.

2. Contact the workpiece with the dial indicator in line with the chuck jaw that is farthest off center. Then advance the cross slide by turning the cross feed knob until the dial pointer has moved almost one revolution. Note the dial reading.

3. Rotate the chuck 180 degrees to the opposite jaw and note this dial reading. If the dial readings are different, adjust this pair of jaws until the dial readings are the same.
4. Repeat this process with the other pair of jaws. Minor adjustments may be needed with each opposite pair of jaws until the same dial reading is obtained at each of the four jaws.
5. Check short parts for wobble by using the dial indicator on the end of the workpiece.

Centering with a Wiggler

A **wiggler,** or **center finder** (Fig. 59-16), is an aid in centering from a prick-punch mark or small hole. Wigglers are most useful for centering holes or workpieces that must be held off-center in the lathe.

1. Prick-punch the center location on the part of the workpiece to be cut.
2. Mount the workpiece in the lathe and center the punch mark approximately.
3. Install a wiggler in a drill chuck in the tailstock and insert its point in the prick-punch mark (Fig. 59-17).

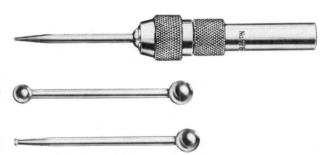

Fig. 59–16 *A wiggler with interchangeable points.* (L.S. Sarrett)

Fig. 59–17 *Centering an offset boss on a workpiece with a wiggler.*

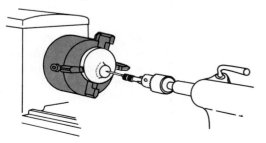

4. Rotate the workpiece **by hand** and note the circular path made by the point of the wiggler.
5. Adjust the workpiece in the chuck until the point of the wiggler no longer moves in a circle when the workpiece is rotated.

59-5 Mounting Workpieces between Centers

Two **lathe centers** are used to support the workpiece for turning between the headstock and tailstock spindles (Figs. 59-18 and 59-21). The **headstock center** is also called the **live center** because it turns with the headstock spindle. The **tailstock center** is usually called the dead center because the tailstock spindle does not turn. A dead center must be lubricated. A special **live** tailstock center (Fig. 59-18E), however, turns on ball bearings and does not have to be lubricated.

Fig. 59–18 *Types of lathe centers: (A) Soft center for use in headstock only. (B) Hardened tailstock center. (C) Carbide-tipped tailstock center. (D) Reducing sleeve. (E) Ball bearing or live tailstock center.*

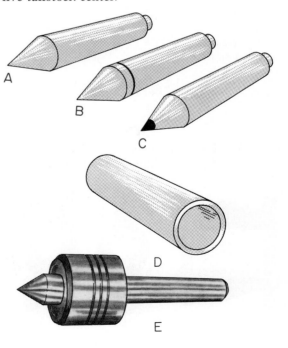

Mounting workpieces between centers is a common way of holding workpieces for machining. The procedure is as follows:

1. **Center-drill** both ends of the workpiece. (Unit 62 describes the use of the center drill in the lathe.)
2. Install a **faceplate** on the lathe headstock spindle (Fig. 59-19).
3. Install centers in the headstock and tailstock spindles. Use a ball-bearing tailstock center if available. Otherwise, be sure to put a small amount of **center lubricant** into the center-drilled hole for the dead center.
4. Attach a **lathe dog** to the workpiece (Figs. 59-20 and 59-21). The lathe dog keeps the workpiece from slipping during lathe operation. When attaching a lathe dog to a finished surface, place a small piece of soft metal under the clamp screw to prevent damage to the finished surface.

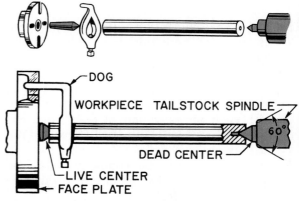

Fig. 59–21 *A workpiece held between lathe centers.*

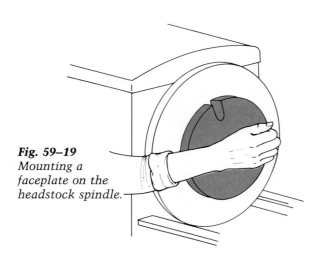

Fig. 59–19 *Mounting a faceplate on the headstock spindle.*

Fig. 59–22 *A lathe mandrel. Standard taper is 0.006"/ft. (0.5 mm/M). (South Bend Lathe, Inc.)*

5. Place the workpiece between the headstock and tailstock centers (Fig. 59-21). The tail of the lathe dog slips into a slot in the faceplate. Adjust the tailstock spindle so that it presses lightly against the workpiece.
6. Adjust the lathe dog if necessary. Rotate the headstock spindle by hand to be sure that the tail of the lathe dog clears the headstock.

59-6 Mounting a Workpiece on a Mandrel

A **mandrel** (Fig. 59-22) is a solid steel bar with a slight taper. Sometimes it is necessary to machine cylindrical parts accurately in relation to a drilled or bored hole that is in the part. Gear blanks and pulleys are parts of this type. When these kinds of parts are machined, the mandrel is pressed into the hole in the part. A lathe dog is then clamped on the mandrel, and it is mounted between centers in the lathe, as shown in Figure 59-23. The outside diameter and the faces of the part are then machined accurately in relation to the hole.

Fig. 59–20 *Types of lathe dogs: (A) Clamp dog. (B) Bent tail dog. (C) Safety bent tail dog with recessed clamp screw.*

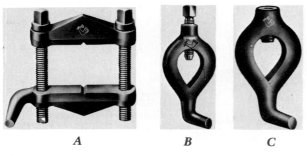

A   *B*   *C*

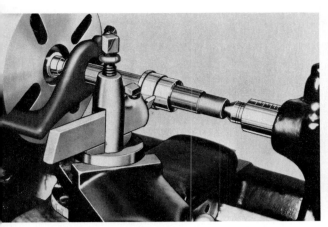

Fig. 59–23 *A workpiece being turned on a mandrel.* (South Bend Lathe, Inc.)

Fig. 59–24 *A workpiece fastened to a lathe faceplate with bolts and straps.* (South Bend Lathe Works)

59-7 Mounting Workpieces on the Faceplate

Because of their size or shape, some workpieces can be held only by fastening them to the lathe faceplate. Some parts can be fastened directly to the faceplate using bolts or straps (Fig. 59-24). Other parts require the use of an angle plate or other special fixture (Fig. 59-25).

Fig. 59–25 *A workpiece bolted to an angle plate that is attached to a faceplate with bolts.* (South Bend Lathe Works)

59-8 Using a Steady Rest and a Follower Rest

Fig. 59–26 *Using a steady rest for boring or internal threading.* (South Bend Lathe, Inc.)

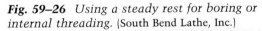

A **steady rest** is a device that is clamped to the lathe bed and used to support workpieces for machining. The steady rest can be used to support work mounted in the chuck as in Figure 59-26. It also can be used to support workpieces mounted between centers, as shown in Figure 59-27. The jaws in the steady rest are adjusted so that they rub the work lightly.

A **follower rest** is a supporting device that is attached to the **saddle** of the lathe (Fig. 59-27). The follower rest moves along with the cutting tool, thus holding the workpiece steady while it is being machined. The follower rest can be used alone, or it can be used along with the steady rest.

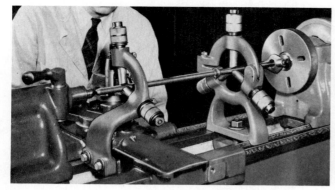

Fig. 59–27 *Using both a steady rest and a follower rest for cutting threads on a long bar.* (South Bend Lathe, Inc.)

REVIEW   REVIEW   REVIEW   REVIEW   REVIEW

WORDS TO KNOW

angle plate	dial indicator	live headstock	steady rest
cam-lock spindle	faceplate	center	step chuck
center finder	follower rest	live tailstock center	threaded spindle
center lubricant	four-jaw	long-taper key-drive	three-jaw universal
chuck cradle	independent	spindle	chuck
collet chuck	chuck	spindle chuck	wiggler
dead center	lathe dog	spindle nose	

REVIEW QUESTIONS

1. Name the three kinds of lathe spindle noses.
2. Why is cleanliness so important when attaching lathe chucks to the lathe spindle nose?
3. Name the five kinds of lathe chucks.
4. Which lathe chuck can hold the most different workpiece shapes?
5. What is a chuck cradle used for?
6. Describe how to remove a lathe chuck that is stuck on a threaded lathe spindle.
7. Explain how to center a workpiece with the use of a dial indicator.
8. Explain how to center a workpiece with the use of a wiggler.
9. How is a live tailstock center different from a dead tailstock center?
10. What is a lathe dog used for?
11. Name two ways of holding workpieces to faceplates.
12. What is a steady rest used for?
13. What part of the lathe is a steady rest fastened to?
14. How is a follower rest different from a steady rest?

UNIT
60

Lathe Cutting Tools, Toolholders, Cutting Speeds, and Feed Selection

This unit introduces the main types of lathe cutting tools and **toolholders.** It also explains how to determine the correct rpm for a workpiece, and discusses feed selection.

Cutting in the lathe is done with cutting tools, or **tool bits.** The cutting edges are shaped differently depending on the type of toolholder in which they will be mounted, the type of metal to be machined, and the type of cut to be made. Figure 60-1 shows a variety of tool bit shapes for different machining operations.

60-1 Cutting Tool Materials

Lathe cutting tools are made of the following materials:
1. high-speed steel
2. cast alloys
3. cemented carbide
4. ceramics
5. diamond.

Fig. 60-1 Lathe tool bit shapes for various lathe operations.

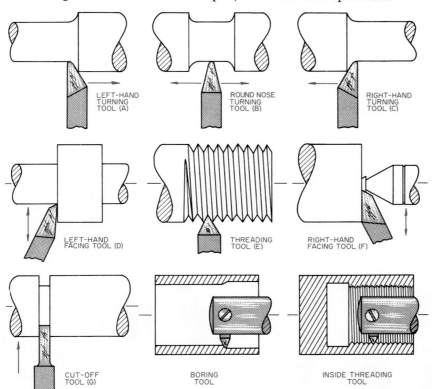

LEFT-HAND TURNING TOOL (A)

ROUND NOSE TURNING TOOL (B)

RIGHT-HAND TURNING TOOL (C)

LEFT-HAND FACING TOOL (D)

THREADING TOOL (E)

RIGHT-HAND FACING TOOL (F)

CUT-OFF TOOL (G)

BORING TOOL

INSIDE THREADING TOOL

High-speed steels. High-speed steel tools are most commonly used in schools. They rank higher in toughness, but are less wear-resistant than other tools. They hold their hardness up to a temperature of about 1000° F [538° C], and are easily sharpened on aluminum oxide grinding wheels.

Cast alloys. The cast alloys are made of various nonferrous metals in a cobalt base. Cast alloy tools can withstand cutting temperatures up to 1400° F [760° C]. They are capable of cutting speeds 50 to 70 percent higher than high-speed steel tools.

Cemented carbide. Cemented carbide tools are made of powdered tungsten or tantalum carbide cemented with a cobalt binder. They are used either as **brazed tips** on tool blanks (Fig. 60-2) or as **throw-away inserts** (Fig. 60-3). Cemented carbides can withstand cutting temperatures up to 1700° F [927° C]. Cutting speeds two to four times faster than for high-speed steel can be used. To obtain good results, carefully select the correct grades of carbide and use the correct cutting speeds.

Following are the basic carbide grades and their recommended uses according to the Carbide Industry Classification System:

Cast iron and nonferrous metals:
C-1: Finishing to medium roughing cuts
C-2: Roughing cuts
C-3: High impact dies

Steel and steel alloys:
C-4: Light high speed finishing cuts
C-5: Medium cuts at medium speeds
C-6: Roughing cuts
C-7: Light finishing cuts
C-8: General purpose and heavy rough cuts

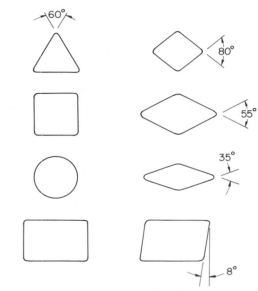

Fig. 60–3 *Standard shapes for throw-away insert cutting tools.*

Fig. 60–2 *(A) Standard shapes for carbide-tipped lathe tool bits. Other shapes are also available. (B) Photo of Style AR carbide tipped tool.* (DoALL)

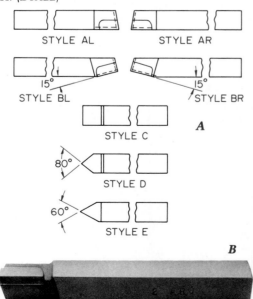

STYLE AL   STYLE AR

15° STYLE BL   15° STYLE BR

STYLE C   **A**

80° STYLE D

60° STYLE E

B

Fig. 60–4 *Cold-pressed ceramic, silicon nitride, and whisker reinforced ceramic throwaway inserts.* (Greenleaf Corporation)

In production work most of the cutting tools used are carbides.

Coated carbides have a very thin layer of one or more vary hard materials on the surface. The coatings most often used are titanium nitride, titanium carbide, aluminum oxide, or combinations of these. Coated carbides are capable of longer tool life or higher cutting speeds than uncoated carbides of the same grade.

Ceramics. Most ceramic cutting tools are made of aluminum oxide or silicon nitride, (Fig. 60-4). They are so hard and brittle that small percentages of metallic binders are added to improve their strength. Ceramic tools can be used only as throw-away inserts, since they cannot be brazed. These tools can be operated at speeds two to four times faster than cemented carbide tools. Furthermore, they are capable of cutting hardened steels without the use of cutting fluids.

Diamond. Both natural and artificial diamonds are used for metal cutting. The diamond tool may be a single crystal, a cluster of crystals, or sintered **polycrystalline diamond** (Fig. 60-5). Polycrystalline diamond tools are made of fine crystals of diamond bonded together to form a solid tool shape. These shapes may be brazed to steel shanks or clamped in special toolholders like throw-away inserts.

Fig. 60–5 *A polycrystalline diamond cutting tool in operation.* (GTE Valenite Division)

Diamond tools are used mostly for light cuts on abrasive materials at very high cutting speeds. They last from 10 to 450 times as long as carbide tools.

60-2 Cutting Tool Shapes

High speed-steel and cast-alloy cutting tool materials are supplied in unsharpened small square bars known as **tool blanks.** Carbide-tipped tool bits with ready-to-use cutting edges are also supplied as small square bars (Fig. 60-2).

Cemented carbide, ceramic, and some diamond tools are supplied as ready-to-use throw-away inserts of various shapes (Fig. 60-3). Instead of being resharpened after all their cutting edges have been dulled, they are thrown away. This is not as wasteful a practice as it may seem. The inserts have cutting edges on both the top and bottom surfaces. When one cutting edge becomes dull, the tool is unclamped and **indexed,** or rotated, to the next cutting edge. When all the cutting edges on the top surface are dull, the insert is turned over, exposing a fresh set of cutting edges. Some of the used carbide material is now being recycled. It is mixed with new material to make new inserts.

60-3 Cutting Tool Terms

Following are some of the terms that apply to cutting tools used on lathes, shapers, and planers. See Figure 60-6 for an illustration of each term.

The **cutting edge** is the part of the tool bit that does the actual cutting. It has two parts: the **side cutting-edge** and the **end cutting-edge.** However, the cutting edge is continuous around the nose, or rounded point of the cutting end.

The **face** is the top surface of the tool.

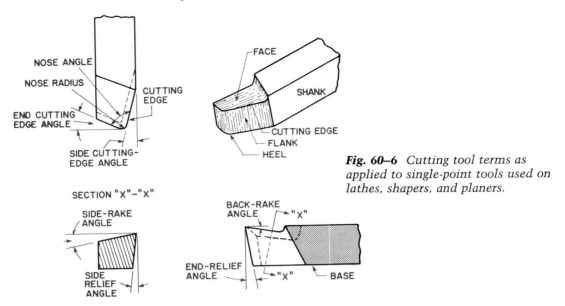

Fig. 60–6 *Cutting tool terms as applied to single-point tools used on lathes, shapers, and planers.*

The **flank** is the side of the tool below the side cutting edge.

The **nose** is the point of the tool.

The **nose angle** is the angle formed by the side cutting-edge and the end cutting-edge.

The **nose radius** is the dimension of the arc that forms a round-nose tool. For heavy roughing cuts, a small nose radius, about 1/64″ [0.4 mm], is used. For light finishing cuts, a nose radius of 1/64″ to 1/16″ [0.4 to 1.6 mm] is used.

The **shank** is the body of the tool.

The **side cutting-edge angle** is the angle formed by the side cutting-edge and a line drawn from the side of the shank.

The **end cutting-edge angle** is the angle formed by the end cutting-edge and a line drawn 90° to the side of the shank.

Side-relief, or **side clearance,** is the angle between the tool flank and the original side of the tool. It allows the side cutting-edge to penetrate the workpiece.

End-relief, or **front clearance,** is the angle between the end of the tool and a line drawn 90° to the base of the toolholder in which the tool is normally held. It allows the end cutting-edge to penetrate the workpiece.

Side-rake is the angle formed between the tool face and a horizontal plane.

Back-rake is the angle formed between a horizontal plane and a line sloping back from the tip of the tool across the tool face.

Both side-rake and back-rake promote smooth cutting of ductile metals because they cause the chip leaving the cutting tool nose to break off easily. They also reduce the power required for cutting.

Lathe tool bits are **left-hand** or **right-hand.** A **right-hand tool** has its cutting edge on the left, and it cuts from right to left. A **left-hand tool** has its cutting edge on the right, and it cuts from left to right (Fig. 60-1).

60-4 Toolholders

Tool bit holders. There are two types of tool bit holders: **16½° toolholders** and **zero-degree toolholders** (Fig. 60-7). When the tool bit is mounted in a 16½° toolholder, it is tilted upward 16½°, increasing the back rake angle. The 16½° toolholders are used with tools of high-speed steel and cast alloys. When a tool bit is mounted in a zero-degree toolholder, no back rake is provided by the holder. Any necessary back rake must be ground into the tool bit.

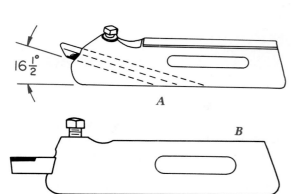

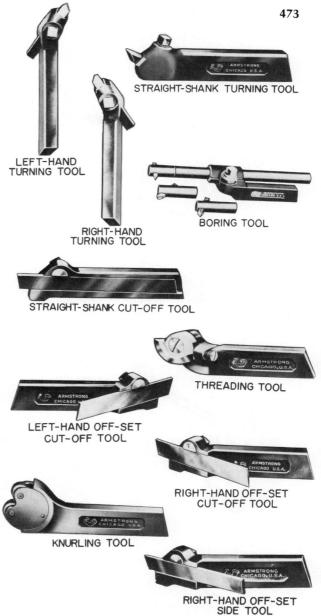

Fig. 60–7 *Toolholders: (A) 16-½ toolholder for high speed steel and cast alloy tools, (B) zero-degree toolholder for carbide tools.*

STRAIGHT-SHANK TURNING TOOL

LEFT-HAND TURNING TOOL

RIGHT-HAND TURNING TOOL

BORING TOOL

STRAIGHT-SHANK CUT-OFF TOOL

THREADING TOOL

LEFT-HAND OFF-SET CUT-OFF TOOL

RIGHT-HAND OFF-SET CUT-OFF TOOL

KNURLING TOOL

RIGHT-HAND OFF-SET SIDE TOOL

Fig. 60–8 *Commonly used lathe toolholders and cutting tools.*

The zero-degree toolholder is used for holding carbide-tipped tools. Since the carbide tip is brittle, it must have minimum relief angles and be rigidly supported to prevent chipping of the cutting edge.

There are three styles of tool bit holders: **left-hand, straight,** and **right-hand** (Fig. 60-8). The **left-hand toolholder** is bent so that cutting can be done close to the chuck without the chuck striking the carriage or compound rest. The **right-hand toolholder** is used for cutting from left to right, and for making heavy facing cuts.

The **straight toolholder** is used for straight turning on long workpieces, and as a general purpose toolholder.

Other kinds of toolholders. **Cutoff toolholders** (Fig. 60-8) are used for holding **cutoff blades.** These are used for cutting grooves and for cutting off stock (Fig. 60-1). **Boring toolholders** (Fig. 60-8) are used for holding **boring bars.** These are used for machining precision holes and making holes larger than can be made by drilling (Fig. 60-1). **Threading toolholders** (Fig. 60-8) are used for cutting external threads with the lathe (Fig. 60-1). Ordinary tool bits may also be ground for thread cutting.

Knurling tools (Fig. 60-8) are used to form a roughened surface on a workpiece to provide a nonslip hand grip.

Throw-away insert toolholders. Special toolholders must be used to hold each different type and shape of throw-away insert. One type of throw-away insert toolholder is shown in Figure 60-9. Some boring bars are also made for holding throw-away inserts.

Quick-change toolholding systems (Fig. 60-10) use a specially designed toolpost that provides for quick clamping and release of toolholders. With a full assortment of toolholders, any turning operation can be quickly set up.

LOCK PIN DESIGN

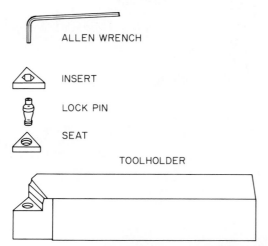

ALLEN WRENCH

INSERT

LOCK PIN

SEAT

TOOLHOLDER

Fig. 60–9 *A toolholder system for holding one type of throwaway insert cutting tool.*

Cutting speed on a lathe is the speed at which the circumference of the work passes the tool bit. It is expressed in feet per minute (fpm) or meters per minute (mpm).

Cutting speed is related to **rpm.** On a lathe, rpm means the number of revolutions of the work in one minute. **For a given cutting speed, work of large diameter must run at a slower rpm than work of small diameter.**

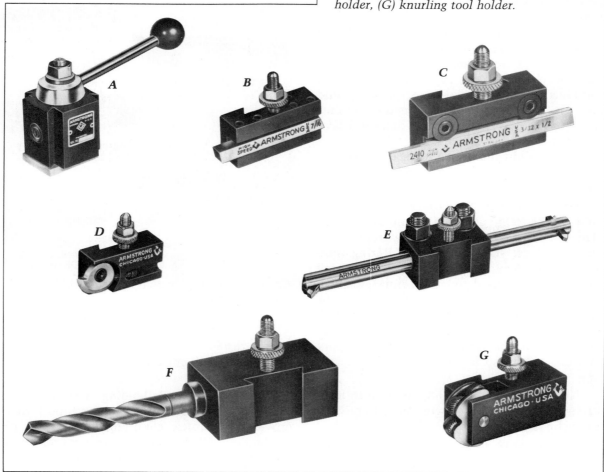

Fig. 60–10 *A quick-change toolholder system. (A) Tool post, (B) plain cutting tool holder, (C) cutoff tool holder, (D) threading tool holder, (E) boring bar tool holder, (F) drill holder, (G) knurling tool holder.*

The rpm at which a workpiece should be turned in the lathe depends upon:

1. The cutting speed of the metal being machined. Suggested cutting speeds are given in Table 60-1.
2. The workpiece diameter.
3. The kind of material the cutting tool is made of.
4. The kind of machining operation. A heavy rough cut is made at a slower cutting speed than a light finishing cut.

Calculating Correct Workpiece rpm

The rpm for a given cutting speed may be calculated with the following formulas:

A. U.S. Customary (Inch) System

$$rpm = \frac{CS' \times 12}{D'' \times \pi}$$

where: CS = Cutting speed in feet per minute

D = Diameter in inches

π = Pi or 3.1416

The following shortcut formula gives the approximate rpm:

$$rpm = \frac{4 \times CS'}{D'}$$

B. S.I. Metric System

$$rpm = \frac{CS \ (mpm) \times 1000}{D \ (mm) \times \pi}$$

where: CS (mpm) = Cutting speed in meters per minute

D (mm) = Diameter in millimeters

π = Pi or 3.1416

Example: Calculate the correct rpm for a workpiece ½" [12.7 mm] in diameter to be cut at a cutting speed of 100 fpm [30.5 mpm].

Inch Solutions:

$$rpm = \frac{100 \times 12}{.5 \times 3.1416}$$

$$= \frac{1200}{1.57}$$

$$= 764$$

Table 60-1

Cutting Speeds for Metals and Plastics*

Material	Cutting tool material	Heavy cut fpm[1]	Heavy cut [mpm[2]]	Finishing cut fpm	Finishing cut [mpm]
Free machining steels	H.S.S.	115	[35.0]	300	[91.4]
	cast alloy	250	[76.2]	475	[144.8]
	carbide	400	[122.0]	675	[205.7]
Low-carbon steels	H.S.S.	100	[30.5]	260	[79.2]
	cast alloy	215	[65.5]	425	[129.5]
	carbide	350	[106.7]	625	[190.5]
Medium-carbon steels	H.S.S.	95	[29.0]	225	[68.6]
	cast alloy	190	[58.0]	350	[106.7]
	carbide	300	[91.4]	500	[152.4]
High-carbon steels	H.S.S.	80	[24.2]	200	[61.0]
	cast alloy	175	[53.3]	300	[91.4]
	carbide	250	[76.2]	450	[137.2]
Cast iron, soft gray	H.S.S.	80	[24.4]	135	[41.1]
	cast alloy	140	[42.7]	250	[76.2]
	carbide	225	[68.6]	400	[122]
Brass and bronze free machining	H.S.S.	175	[53.3]	350	[106.7]
	cast alloy	350	[106.7]	550	[167.6]
	carbide	575	[175.3]	900	[274.3]
Aluminum	H.S.S.	125	[38.1]	300	[91.4]
	cast alloy	175	[53.3]	375	[114.3]
	carbide	250	[76.2]	600	[182.9]
Plastics	H.S.S.	100	[30.5]	250	[76.2]
	cast alloy	150	[45.7]	375	[114.3]
	carbide	200	[61.0]	500	[152.4]

*Speeds should be adjusted ± 10-20% to suit cutting conditions.

1. Feet per minute
2. Meters per minute

Using the shortcut formula:

$$rpm = \frac{4 \times 100}{.5}$$

$$= \frac{400}{.5}$$

$$= 800$$

Metric Solution:

$$rpm = \frac{30.5 \times 1000}{12.7 \times 3.1416}$$

$$= \frac{30500}{39.898}$$

$$= 764$$

60-6 Feed Selection and Depth of Cut

Feed, or **feed rate,** is the distance the cutting tool moves in one revolution of the workpiece. The amount of feed varies with the type of metal, the **depth of cut,** and the power of the machine tool that is making the cut. Fin-ishing cuts are made with finer feeds than roughing cuts. Suggested feeds for machining steel are .005" [0.13 mm] for a rough cut and .002" [0.05 mm] for a finish cut.

Depth of cut means the distance the tool is advanced into the work at a right angle to the work (Fig. 60-11). A deeper cut may be taken on soft metals than on hard metals. The depth of a finishing cut is less than the depth of a roughing cut. On small lathes a common rough cut depth in steel would be .060" to .125" [1.52 to 3.18 mm]. Finishing cuts are usually .010" to .020" [0.25 to 0.5 mm] on any lathe. A .010" [0.25 mm] cut removes .020" [0.5 mm] from the diameter. A 1/16" or .063" [1.59 mm] cut removes 1/8" or .125" [3.18 mm] from the diameter (Fig. 61-11).

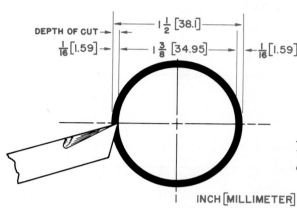

Fig. 60–11 *The diameter of the workpiece is reduced twice the depth of the cut when it is turned.*

REVIEW REVIEW REVIEW REVIEW REVIEW

WORDS TO KNOW

coated carbide
cutting speed
cutting tool terms:
  back-rake
  cutting edge
  end cutting-edge
    angle
  end-relief
  face
  flank

nose
nose angle
nose radius
shank
side cutting-edge
  angle
side-rake
side-relief
feed rate

Tool bits:
  cast alloy
  cemented carbide
  ceramic
  diamond
  high-speed steel
Tool holders:
  boring
  cutoff
  knurling

left-hand
quick-change
right-hand
16½ degree
straight
threading
throw-away insert
zero-degree

REVIEW QUESTIONS

1. What are lathe cutting tools commonly called?
2. Name five kinds of materials lathe cutting tools are made of.
3. Which kind of lathe cutting tool material is used mostly in school shops? Why?
4. Which kind of lathe cutting tool material is used most for production work? What are its advantages?

(Review Continued)

5. What is a throw-away insert?
6. Which side does a right-hand cutting tool have its cutting edge on?
7. Name the two relief angles on a cutting tool. Why are they needed?
8. Name the two rake angles on a cutting tool. How do they promote better cutting?
9. What kind of cutting is a left-hand toolholder used for? Right-hand?
10. Why must zero-degree toolholders be used for carbide-tipped tools?
11. What is a knurling tool used for?
12. Should the nose radius for roughing cuts be smaller or larger than for finishing cuts?
13. Name four factors that determine the correct rpm for a workpiece.
14. Calculate the correct rpm for a workpiece 2″ [50.8 mm] in diameter that is to be cut at 300 fpm [91.4 mpm].
15. What is meant by the feed rate of a tool?
16. What feed is best for making a finishing cut?
17. How much would a workpiece diameter be reduced with a depth of cut of .040″ [1.02 mm]?

UNIT
61
Sharpening Lathe Cutting Tools

Accurate work and good finishes cannot be done without sharp cutting tools. A medium-soft aluminum oxide grinding wheel of about 60 grit is recommended for sharpening high-speed steel and cast-alloy tool bits. The grinder may be an ordinary pedestal grinder (Fig. 44-2) or a tool grinder with a tilting table. Carbide-tipped tools must be ground with special silicon carbide or diamond grinding wheels.

61-1 Turning and Facing Tools

The two tool bit shapes most used for lathe work are the **right-hand turning tool** and the **right-hand facing tool** (Fig. 61-1). The suggested shapes and grinding angles for these two tools are shown in Figures 61-1 and 61-2.

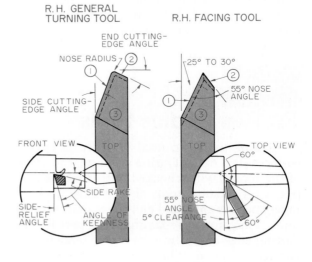

Fig. 61–1 *Shapes of the two most-used lathe tool bits.*

NOSE RADIUS:
$\frac{1}{64}''$ ROUGH TURNING
$\frac{1}{32}''$ GENERAL TURNING
$\frac{1}{16}''$ FINISH TURNING

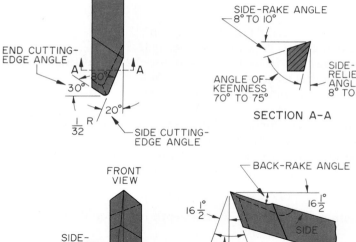

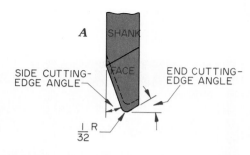

Fig. 61–2 *Rake and relief angles for a general purpose right-hand lathe tool bit for mounting in a 16-½° toolholder.*

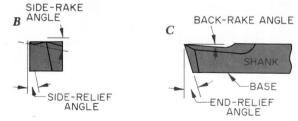

Fig. 61–3 *A left-hand cutting tool ground correctly for use in a zero degree toolholder. (A) Top view. (B) Front view. (C) Side view.*

A **left-hand tool** ground for use in a zero-degree toolholder, as it should be for use in a shaper, is shown in Figure 61-3. The angles should be changed for machining different metals, as shown in Table 61-1.

Radius Tools

Radius tools are used for cutting curved surfaces (Fig. 61-4). During grinding, the shape of the tool may be checked with a **radius gage** (Fig. 61-4). Radius tools should have no back rake, and less side- and end-relief than turning tools. This provides maximum support for the cutting edge and minimizes their tendency to **chatter** (a rapid vibration that produces a rough cut). Both the radius tool and the workpiece must be rigidly supported. Low cutting speed, low feed rate, and lubrication are necessary for good results.

Cutoff Tool

The **cutoff tool** (Fig. 61-5) should be ground only on the top and front, never on the side. An end-relief angle of about 5° is adequate. No back-rake is required, but an angle up to 5° is sometimes used. There should be no side-rake.

An angle of 10° to 15° ground across the end of the cutoff tool will provide a cleaner cutoff than a blade with a square end (Fig. 61-6).

Table 61-1

Relief and Rake Angles for High-Speed Steel Lathe and Shaper Cutting Tools*

Material	Side relief	End relief	True back rake	Side rake
Aluminum	10°	10°	35°	15°
Brass	10°	8°	0°	0°
Bronze	10°	8°	0°	0°
Cast Iron, Hard	8°	8°	5°	8°
Cast Iron, Malleable	8°	8°	8°	10°
Cast Iron, Soft	8°	8°	8°	10°
Fiber	15°	15°	0°	0°
Free-Machining Steel	10°	10°	16°	10°
High-Carbon Steel	8°	8°	8°	8°
Low-Carbon Steel	10°	10°	16°	10°
Medium-Carbon Steel	10°	10°	12°	10°
Plastics, Acrylics	15°	15°	0°	0°
Plastics, Molded	10°	12°	0°	0°

*All angles are true working angles measured from horizontal and vertical planes.

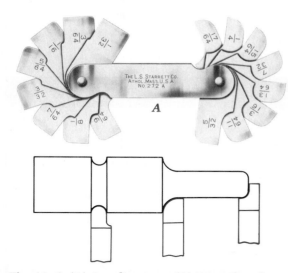

Fig. 61–4 *(A) A radius gage. (B) Examples of how radius tools are used to shape a workpiece.* (L.S. Starrett Company)

Fig. 61–5 *The grinding angles for a cutoff blade.*

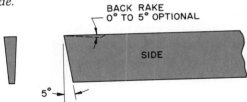

BACK RAKE
0° TO 5° OPTIONAL
SIDE
5°

61-4

Threading Tools

Threading tools for 60° threads are given end- and side-relief angles of 8° to 10° (Fig. 60-8). The tool should have no back-rake, but a side-rake of about 5° helps produce a smooth finish. A small flat surface ground on the point of the tool will help prevent the sharp point from chipping off.

A **formed threading tool** and toolholder are shown in Figure 61-7. This type of threading tool comes already shaped to 60°, and should only be sharpened across the top. After re-sharpening, the tool is repositioned on the holder by adjusting its setscrew.

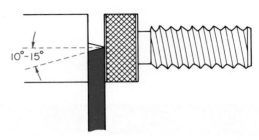

10°-15°

Fig. 61–6 *A small angle ground on the end of a cutoff tool provides a clean cutoff.*

Fig. 61–7 *Threading tool angles.*

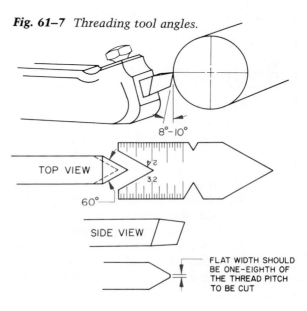

8°–10°

TOP VIEW

60°

SIDE VIEW

FLAT WIDTH SHOULD BE ONE-EIGHTH OF THE THREAD PITCH TO BE CUT

61-5 Procedure for Grinding Lathe and Shaper Tool Bits

1. Grind the side cutting-edge angle first (Fig. 61-2). Hold the tool blank so that more is ground off the bottom than the top. In this way, the side-relief angle is ground at the same time as the side cutting-edge angle.

2. Grind the end cutting-edge angle and end-relief angle.
3. Check the accuracy of the relief angles with a **tool grinding gage** (Fig. 61-8). **If the tool is to be used in a 16½° holder, the end-relief angle must be checked with the tool in the holder.**
4. Grind the side-rake angle across the top of the tool.
5. Grind the nose radius.

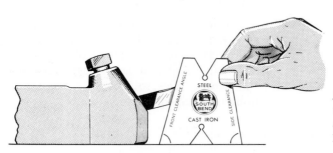

Fig. 61–8 *A tool grinding gage is used to check the relief (clearance) angles on a tool bit.* (South Bend Lathe, Inc.)

REVIEW REVIEW REVIEW REVIEW REVIEW

WORDS TO KNOW

chatter	formed threading	radius tool	right-hand turning
cutoff tool	tool	right-hand facing	tool
	radius gage	tool	tool grinding gage

REVIEW QUESTIONS

1. What kind of grinding wheel should be used for sharpening high-speed steel and cast alloy tool bits?
2. What two kinds of grinding wheels may be used for sharpening carbide tools?
3. What two tool bit shapes are used most for lathework?
4. Compare the cutting tool relief and rake angles recommended for machining low-carbon steel with those recommended for machining brass.
5. What kind of cutting are radius tools used for?
6. How can the accuracy of radius tools be checked?
7. What is meant by tool "chatter"?
8. How should cutoff tools be sharpened to provide a clean cutoff?
9. What back-rake and side-relief angles should be used for threading tools?
10. List the procedure for sharpening a right-hand turning tool.

UNIT

62

Drilling, Reaming, Countersinking, and Counterboring in a Lathe

Drilling and other drill-press operations (see Part 15) are readily done in the lathe. The workpiece is usually mounted in a lathe chuck or attached to a faceplate. The drilling tools are mounted in the tailstock.

Center-drilling with a **combination drill and countersink** should always be the first step in drilling a hole in solid metal held in a lathe. The center-drilled hole acts as a guide for the drill that follows (Fig. 62-1). Center drilling is also required to provide holes with proper bearing surfaces for using lathe centers (Fig. 62-2).

SAFETY NOTE

Before center-drilling can be done in a lathe, the tailstock must be in accurate alignment with the headstock. If the tailstock is not aligned with the headstock, the point of the center drill will likely be broken off.

Check the tailstock position with the **alignment marks** on the rear of the tailstock (Fig. 62-3). If adjustment is necessary, unclamp the tailstock from the lathe bed and align the marks with the **setover screws.** Ask your instructor how to do this properly, or follow the lathe manufacturer's operating manual.

All straight-shank drilling tools are held in a drill chuck mounted in the tailstock (Fig. 62-4). Taper-shank tools are held directly in the tailstock spindle (Fig. 62-5). The workpieces should be rotated by the lathe so that drills are "run" at normal drilling speeds, as discussed in Unit 55. Reamers, countersinks, and counterbores should be "run" at ½ to ⅔ of the cutting speed for drills of the same size.

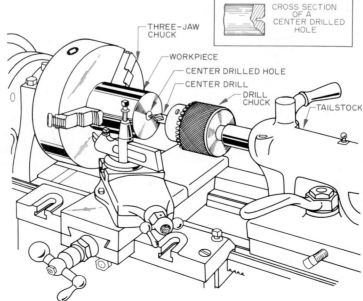

Fig. 62–1 Center drilling in the lathe.

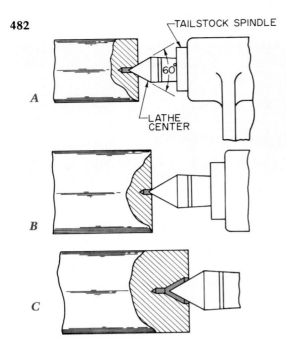

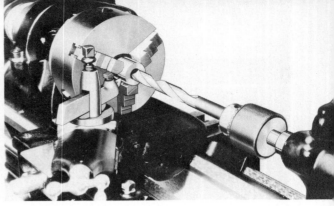

Fig. 62–4 *Straight-shank drilling tools are held in a drill chuck mounted in the tailstock.* (South Bend Lathe, Inc.)

Fig. 62–2 *Center drilled holes: (A) A correctly drilled center hole. (B) The center hole is too shallow. (C) The center hole is too deep.*

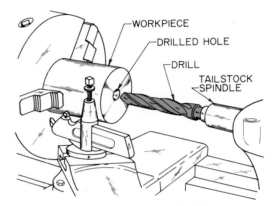

Fig. 62–5 *Taper shank tools are held in the tailstock spindle.*

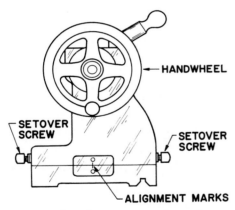

Fig. 62–3 *The alignment marks and setover screws on the tailstock of a lathe.*

Procedure for Drilling Operations

1. Check the tailstock alignment. Adjust it if necessary.
2. Mount the workpiece and center it accurately.
3. Install a drill chuck in the tailstock.
4. Install a center drill in the drill chuck.
5. Set the lathe for a suitable rpm.

6. Advance the tailstock until the tool is about ¼" [6.35 mm] from the workpiece, then clamp the tailstock to the lathe bed.
7. Start the lathe. Slowly advance the center drill by turning the tailstock handwheel until the hole is the correct depth. Stop the lathe. Note: When drilling steel, keep the center drill lubricated with cutting oil.
8. Remove the center drill and install a straight-shank drill.
9. Adjust the rpm if necessary, then start the lathe and drill the hole. When drilling deep holes, withdraw the drill as necessary to clear the flutes of chips. Stop the lathe when the drilling operation is finished.
10. For a larger hole, install the next size drill, adjust the rpm, and drill the hole.
11. For reaming, countersinking, and counterboring holes, reduce the rpm as recommended above before proceeding.

REVIEW REVIEW REVIEW REVIEW REVIEW

WORDS TO KNOW

alignment marks   center drill   combination drill   setover screws
                                    and countersink

REVIEW QUESTIONS

1. Give two reasons for using center drills.
2. Make a sketch of a center hole that has been correctly drilled to provide a bearing surface for a lathe center.
3. Why must the tailstock center be aligned with the headstock center before center drilling?
4. What are tailstock alignment marks used for?
5. How can the tailstock alignment be changed?
6. How are center drills and other straight-shank tools held in the lathe?
7. How are tapered-shank tools held in the lathe?
8. At what rpm should reamers and other drilling tools be run as compared to drills of the same size?

UNIT

63

Straight Turning, Facing, and Boring

Straight turning, facing, and boring are basic lathe machining operations. They are used in making a high percentage of cylindrical parts, ranging from simple discs to precision gear blanks, shafts, and cylinders.

63-1

Straight Turning

Straight turning means to cut along the outside diameter of the workpiece so as to produce a true cylinder (Fig. 63-1). For turning, the tip of the cutting tool may be set between 0° and 5° above the **center of the workpiece** (Fig. 63-2). A right-hand tool bit should be mounted in a left-hand toolholder, and the toolholder should be positioned so that the cutting edge is about 80° from the side of the workpiece (Fig. 63-3). To cut as close as possible to a lathe dog or chuck, position the toolholder on the left side of the compound rest and set the cutting edge at 90° to the workpiece (Fig. 63-4).

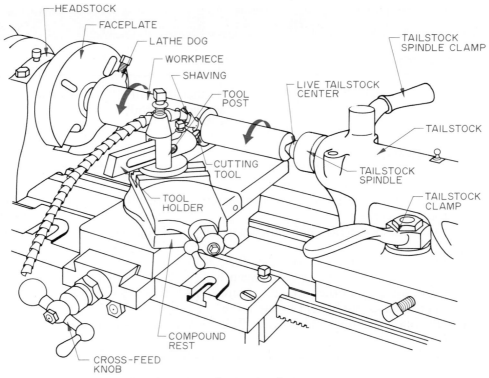

Fig. 63–1 *Straight turning between centers.*

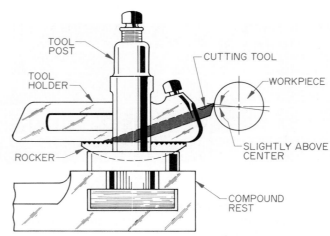

Fig. 63–2 *A correctly positioned cutting tool for turning. The cutting tool is rigidly supported since it projects no more than necessary from the toolholder, which projects no more than necessary from the toolpost.*

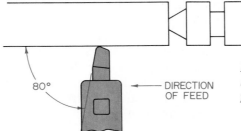

Fig. 63–3 *The cutting edge positioned at 80° to the workpiece, the best angle for turning.*

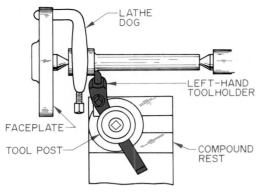

Fig. 63–4 *Setting the cutting edge at 90° to the workpiece, and the toolholder on the left side of the compound rest, to enable cutting close to the lathe dog.*

SAFETY NOTE

Never set the cutting edge at an angle greater than 90° to the workpiece. An angle greater than 90° can cause the tool to cut more deeply than desired, which may ruin the workpiece.

The cutting should be from the tailstock toward the headstock whenever possible. The pressure of cutting then will be on the headstock bearings, which are designed to withstand these pressures.

Procedure for Turning a Precision Diameter

1. Mount the workpiece accurately and securely.
2. Mount the toolholder and cutting tool and position them properly.
3. Set the lathe for the correct rpm, and the gearbox for the desired feed rate.
4. The **reference cut** is the first cut, from which other cutting measurements start. To start this cut turn the lathe on and advance the cutting tool until it touches the workpiece. Then move the tool off to the right end of the workpiece. Next, advance it toward the center of the workpiece for an additional amount that leaves the workpiece larger in diameter than the desired finished size. Be sure to leave 0.010 to

0.030" [0.25 to 0.76 mm] on the diameter for a finish cut. Turn a cylinder about 1/8" (3.2 mm) long at this setting.

5. Stop the lathe and measure the diameter obtained (Fig. 63-5). Reposition the tool if necessary before completing the rough cut.
6. Stop the lathe. Move the tool off the right end of the workpiece, and advance it far enough to make the cylinder the correct diameter.
7. Start the lathe and allow the cut to proceed about 1/8" [3.2 mm].
8. Stop the lathe and measure the diameter.
9. Adjust the tool position if necessary and make the finish cut.

63-2 Facing

Facing means to cut across the end of a workpiece (Fig. 63-6). The tip of the cutting tool should be set exactly in line with the center of the workpiece (0°), and the cutting edge should be set at an angle of 80° to the face. A right-hand tool bit is used for facing cuts that start at the center and proceed outward. A right-hand tool is limited to shallow facing cuts unless the workpiece has a sizeable hole in the center. Facing cuts as deep as the length of the cutting edge may be made using a left-hand tool and facing from the outside towards the center.

Fig. 63–5 *Measuring the diameter of a workpiece with a micrometer.*

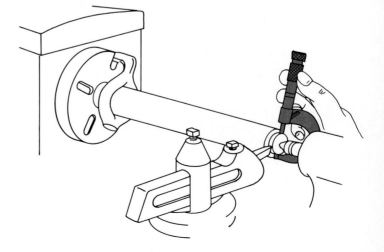

A right-hand facing tool and its setting for facing a workpiece supported between the centers of a lathe are shown in Figure 63-7.

63-3 Boring

Boring is the name given to internal machining using a **single-point cutting tool.** Boring is done with a **boring tool.** Some boring tools consist of a **boring bar** made to hold a tool bit (Fig. 63-8A). **Forged boring tools** are one piece (Fig. 63-8B).

Boring enables a hole to be made larger, rounder, more concentric with its axis, and more accurately sized than can be obtained by drilling and reaming.

Boring is used for making straight holes, tapered holes, internal grooves, and internal threads (Fig. 63-8C). The boring tool is held in the lathe tool post, and cutting is done as shown in Figure 63-9.

Boring can also be done with **boring heads** on drill presses, milling machines, and on specially built boring machines. In these machines, the workpiece is held stationary and the boring tool revolves.

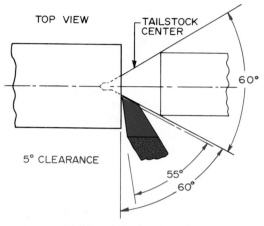

Fig. 63–7 *A right-hand facing tool facing the end of a workpiece supported with a lathe center.*

Fig. 63–8 *Tools for boring in a lathe. (A) A boring bar that uses tool bits. (B) A forged boring bar and its holder. (C) Types of boring operations include turning, grooving, and threading.*

Fig. 63–6 *Facing a workpiece mounted in the chuck with a left hand tool. Heavy facing cuts can be made this way.*

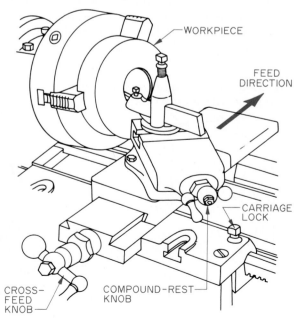

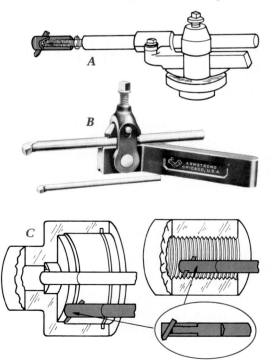

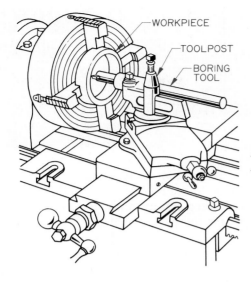

Fig. 63–9 *Boring a workpiece in the lathe.*

Labels in figure: WORKPIECE, TOOLPOST, BORING TOOL

REVIEW   REVIEW   REVIEW   REVIEW   REVIEW

WORDS TO KNOW

boring	boring tool	forged boring tool	straight turning
boring bar	facing	reference cut	workpiece center
boring head	finish cut	single-point cutting tool	

REVIEW QUESTIONS

1. What is meant by straight turning?
2. For turning, where should the tip of the cutting tool be set in relation to the workpiece center?
3. At what angle should the cutting edge of the tool bit be set in relation to the workpiece?
4. Why should the cutting edge never be set at an angle greater than 90° to the workpiece?
5. Why should the direction of cutting be towards the headstock whenever possible?
6. How much material should be left for a finish cut?
7. Why is a reference cut made first?
8. What is meant by facing?
9. Name the kind of tool and direction of cut to use for making heavy facing cuts.
10. Name the two kinds of lathe boring tools.
11. Name four reasons why boring is done.
12. Name three other machines on which boring can be done.

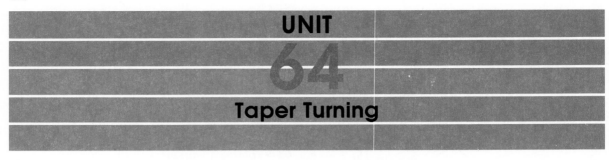

UNIT 64

Taper Turning

The machining of tapers is an important operation on the lathe. There are three methods of turning tapers. The method used depends on:

1. the angle of the taper
2. the length of the taper
3. the number of pieces to be turned.

The compound rest method is best suited to turning short, steep tapers. The **tailstock offset method** and the **taper attachment method** are used for long, shallow tapers.

64-1 Compound Rest Method

To use the **compound rest method,** set the compound rest for the angle, and turn the **compound rest feed screw** by hand. Both internal and external tapers can be turned by this method. An internal taper can be bored as shown in Figure 64-1.

Fig. 64–1 *Boring an internal taper with the compound rest set at the desired angle.*

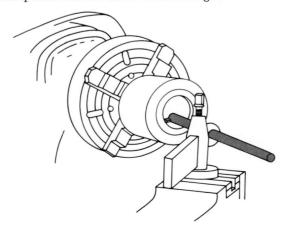

When the angle of taper is not given, it can be found by using the mathematics of **trigonometry.** For example, to find the angle of taper for the part shown in Figure 64-2:

1. Construct the line A-B parallel to the center line so that it intersects the corner of the workpiece and forms the right triangle A-B-C.
2. The length, or **base,** of the right triangle A-B-C is ½" [12.7 mm] as read from the drawing.
3. By subtraction we find that the height of the triangle A-B-C is ¼" [6.35 mm].
4. Using the **tangent function** of trigonometry,

$$\text{Tangent} \angle x = \frac{\text{side opposite}}{\text{side adjacent}}$$
$$= \frac{\frac{1}{4}" \ [6.35 \text{ mm}]}{\frac{1}{2}" \ [12.7 \text{ mm}]}$$
$$= \frac{.250 \ [6.35 \text{ mm}]}{.500 \ [12.7 \text{ mm}]}$$
$$= .500$$

Fig. 64–2 *A problem in calculating the taper angle.*

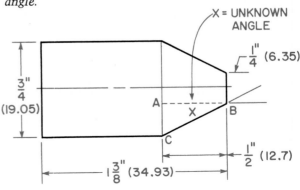

Consulting a table of **trigonometric functions,** we find that .500 in the tangent column corresponds to an angle of approximately 26° 35′. Since the compound rest is marked in whole degrees only, the fractional part of degrees can only be estimated.

64-2 Tailstock Offset Method

In the tailstock offset method, the taper is produced by moving the tailstock out of alignment with the headstock. Moving the tailstock **toward** the operator will produce a smaller right end on the workpiece being tapered. Moving it **away** from the operator will result in a smaller left end on the piece. The amount of tailstock **setover** needed for a certain taper may be calculated with the formula:

$$\text{Setover} = \frac{T \times L}{2}$$

where T = rate of taper
  L = **total length** of the workpiece − **expressed in feet or meters**

Example: Calculate the setover required to machine the taper on the workpiece shown in Figure 64-3.

Solution:

$$\text{Setover} = \frac{T \times L}{2}$$

U.S. Customary Calculation	S.I. Metric Calculation
$= \dfrac{.600''/ft \times .67'}{2}$	$= \dfrac{50 \text{ mm/m} \times .203 \text{ m}}{2}$
$= \dfrac{.402''}{2}$	$= \dfrac{10.15 \text{ mm}}{2}$
$= .201''$	$= 5.08 \text{ mm}$

Fig. 64–3 *A problem in calculating tailstock setover.*

Inch	mm
.625	15.88
.875	22.23
5	127
8	203.2

When the rate of taper is not given, it may be calculated by subtracting the small diameter (d) from the large diameter (D), and dividing by the length of the **tapered section** (L_t) measured in feet or meters.

Example: Find the rate of taper of the workpiece in Figure 64-3.

Solution:

$$\text{Rate of taper} = \frac{D - d}{L_t}$$

U.S. Customary Calculation	S.I. Metric Calculation
$= \dfrac{.875'' - .625''}{.417'}$	$= \dfrac{22.225 \text{ mm} - 15.875 \text{ mm}}{.127 \text{ m}}$
$= \dfrac{.250''}{.417'}$	$= \dfrac{6.35 \text{ mm}}{.127 \text{ m}}$
$= .600''/ft$	$= 50 \text{ mm/m}$

Adjusting the tailstock. The tailstock is offset by turning the **setover screws.** The amount of offset may be measured between the **alignment marks** or between the lathe centers (Fig. 64-4). For more precise measurement, mount a dial indicator in the toolpost, and place it in contact with the tailstock spindle while turning the setover screws. Use of the dial indicator is introduced in Section 59-4 and further discussed in Section 93-10.

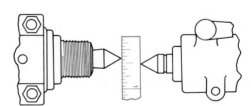

Fig. 64–4 *Using a steel scale to measure the amount of tailstock setover.*

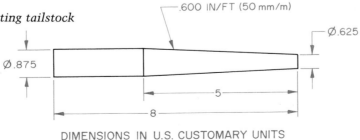

RATE OF TAPER
.600 IN/FT (50 mm/m)

Ø.875   Ø.625

5

8

DIMENSIONS IN U.S. CUSTOMARY UNITS

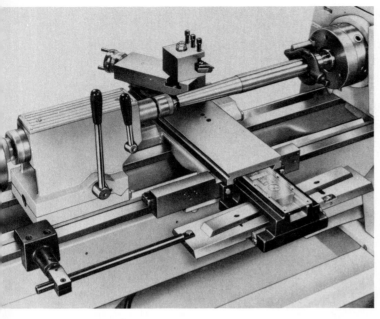

64-3 Taper Attachment Method

The **taper attachment** (Fig. 64-5) eliminates the need to offset the tailstock. In use, the **taper bar** at the rear of the lathe is set to the desired angle of taper and fastened to the lathe bed so it cannot move. The cross-slide on which the tool is mounted is then clamped to a block that slides along the taper bar. As the carriage is moved along the lathe bed, the cross-slide is moved to duplicate the angle of the taper bar.

Fig. 64–5 *Taper turning with a telescopic taper attachment.* (Weld Communications)

REVIEW REVIEW REVIEW REVIEW REVIEW

WORDS TO KNOW

alignment marks   rate of taper   tailstock setover   taper bar
compound rest   tailstock offset   taper attachment
  taper turning   taper turning

REVIEW QUESTIONS

1. Name the three methods of turning tapers.
2. Which method of turning tapers is used for short, steep tapers?
3. How can the amount of tailstock offset be measured?
4. What advantage does the taper attachment method have?
5. What angle should the compound rest be set at to machine a center punch with a 90° point?

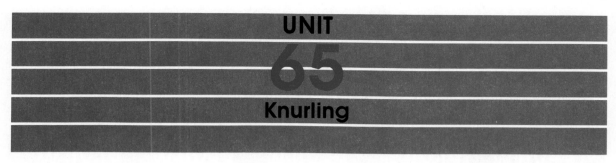

UNIT
65
Knurling

Knurling is a lathe operation that forms raised diamond-shaped or straight-line projections on a workpiece (Fig. 65-1). It is used on some types of screws, tools, and machine handles to provide a non-slip gripping surface, or simply to improve appearance. It is also used to increase the diameter of a workpiece in order to make an interference fit (see Section 22-4).

Knurling is done by pressing the two hardened steel wheels, called **knurls,** of the **knurling tool** into the revolving workpiece (Fig. 65-2). Knurling tools have removable knurls so that one toolholder can be used for making fine, medium, and coarse knurls of either diamond or straight-line pattern (Fig. 65-3).

Procedure for Knurling

1. Set the knurling tool in the toolpost so that the faces of the knurls are as parallel as possible to the surface of the workpiece.
2. Adjust the height of the knurling tool so that the knurling wheels are centered on the workpiece (Fig. 65-2). **Both the knurling tool and the workpiece should be tightened very tightly.**

Fig. 65–1 Knurling a diamond pattern. (South Bend Lathe, Inc.)

3. Set the lathe rpm at between one-third and one-half of the rpm used for a turning operation.
4. Set the lathe for a feed of about 0.020″ to 0.035″ [0.50 to 0.89 mm].
5. Start the lathe, force the tool slowly and firmly into the workpiece, and apply cutting fluid.

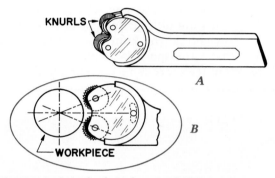

Fig. 65–2 (A) The knurling tool, (B) correct knurling tool position in relation to workpiece.

Fig. 65–3 (A) Removeable knurling wheels, (B) coarse, medium, and fine diamond knurling, (C) coarse, medium, and fine straight-line knurling.

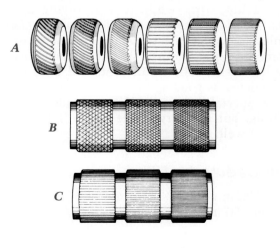

6. Engage the longitudinal feed, and let the tool feed across the workpiece to the desired length.
7. When the tool reaches the end of the workpiece, disengage the longitudinal feed. Release the pressure on the knurling tool without disengaging it completely, and handcrank the knurling tool to the starting end of the knurled surface.
8. Re-apply pressure to the knurling tool. Engage the longitudinal feed, and allow the tool to make a second pass. Repeat this procedure until the knurl is formed to the desired depth.

REVIEW   REVIEW   REVIEW   REVIEW   REVIEW

WORDS TO KNOW

diamond pattern knurl

knurling tool

straight-line pattern knurl

REVIEW QUESTIONS

1. What is knurling, and why is it done?
2. What kind of knurling patterns are available?
3. How should the knurling tool be positioned in relation to the workpiece?
4. What lathe speed is recommended for knurling?
5. What feed rate is recommended for knurling?

UNIT 66

Filing and Polishing

Filing work while it is revolving in the lathe is done to remove sharp edges. Using files to reduce the workpiece diameter or to smooth a rough finish should be done only as a last resort. The results obtained from filing are never as good as the results from machining. Special long-angle files are made for lathe filing, but ordinary single-cut mill files also work well.

Procedure for Filing

1. Obtain a clean, sharp file of 8″ or 10″ [200 or 250 mm] length.
2. Set the rpm of the lathe for filing at the speed for turning a workpiece of the same diameter.
3. For lathe filing, hold the file handle in the left hand and grasp the file tip with the right (Fig. 66-1). This keeps the hands and arm as far away from the revolving face plate or chuck as possible.
4. Press lightly on the file and at the same time move it forward and across the workpiece. At the end of each stroke, raise the file and pull it back for the next stroke. Clean the file every few strokes by tapping its edge lightly on the toolpost or using a

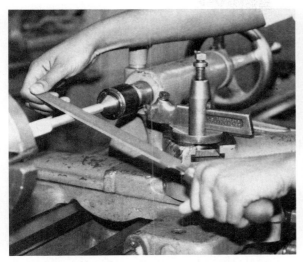

Fig. 66–1 The safest way to file a workpiece in a lathe is to hold the file handle in the left hand, and the file tip in the right hand. (Manual High School, Roger Bean)

Fig. 66–2 Polishing a workpiece in the lathe using a file to apply pressure to the abrasive strip. (Manual High School, Roger Bean)

file card. Continue in this manner until finished.

Polishing in the lathe is done with abrasive cloth. Hard metals like steel can be polished to a **mirror finish** this way. On soft metals like aluminum, a **satin finish** results.

Procedure for Polishing

1. Obtain a strip of abrasive cloth, usually aluminum oxide. A piece about 1″ [25 mm] wide and 6″ [150 mm] long is a convenient size. The kind of abrasive and grit size depend on the kind of metal being polished and the roughness of its surface.

2. Set the rpm for polishing at two to three times faster than the speed used for turning the workpiece.

3. Use a flat file to back up the abrasive cloth. Move the abrasive slowly forward while moving it across the workpiece surface (Fig. 66-2). Make as many strokes across the workpiece as needed to make it uniformly smooth. Change to a fresh piece of abrasive of the same grit if necessary.

4. If a smoother finish is needed, use a finer grade of abrasive. When polishing steels, add a few drops of oil to the abrasive.

REVIEW REVIEW REVIEW REVIEW REVIEW

WORDS TO KNOW

long-angle lathe file   mirror finish   single-cut mill file   satin finish

REVIEW QUESTIONS

1. What kind of files are recommended for filing in the lathe?
2. How fast should the workpiece turn for filing?
3. What kind of finish can be obtained on hard metals by polishing with abrasive cloth?
4. What kind of finish will result when polishing soft metals with abrasive cloth?
5. How fast should the workpiece turn for polishing with abrasive cloth?

UNIT

67

Cutting Threads on the Lathe

Screw threads are often cut on work mounted in a lathe (Fig. 67-1). The threads may be **right-hand** or **left-hand** and **internal** or **external.**

Thread-cutting Tools

Two kinds of thread-cutting tools are used for cutting threads on a lathe. An ordinary lathe tool bit may be ground as shown in Figure 67-2 for cutting 60° threads. A **formed threading tool** is shown in Figure 67-3.

The threading tool should be set on the workpiece centerline (Fig. 67-4). It is set square with the work with the aid of a **center gage** (Fig. 67-5).

Fig. 67–1 *Cutting a right-hand external thread on a lathe.* (GTE Valenite Division)

Setting the Compound Rest

When right-hand 60° threads are cut, the compound rest should be set at a 29° angle to the right, as in Figure 67-6. The tool travels from the right toward the left for right-hand external threads. Several cuts are required. The tool is fed into the work with the compound rest for each additional cut until the thread is cut to the desired pitch diameter (Fig. 67-6).

When left-hand external threads are cut, the compound rest is swung 29° to the left. The feed is then reversed, and the carriage and the tool travel from the left toward the right.

Procedure for Cutting a 60° Right-Hand External Thread

1. Determine the number of threads per inch to be cut. Set the gearbox levers to this number (Fig. 58-19).
2. Mount the stock in the lathe.

Fig. 67–2 *A threading tool bit sharpened for use in a 16-½° toolholder.*

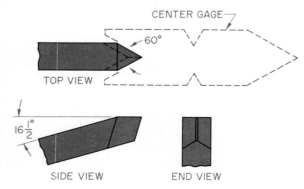

Fig. 67–3 *A formed threading tool.* (Armstrong Bros. Tool Co.)

Fig. 67–4 *The top of the tool bit is set on the center line of the lathe for cutting screw threads. Note that the cutting tool has no back rake.*

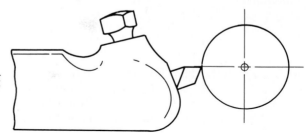

WORKPIECE

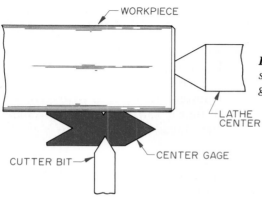

LATHE CENTER

Fig. 67–5 *Setting the threading tool square with the workpiece using a center gage.*

CUTTER BIT

CENTER GAGE

Fig. 67–6 *The action of the threading tool with the compound rest set at 29°.*

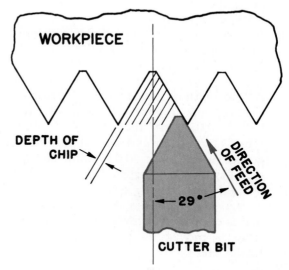

WORKPIECE

DEPTH OF CHIP

DIRECTION OF FEED

29°

CUTTER BIT

3. Lay out the length to be threaded, and mark it with a lead pencil or with the point of a tool bit. A groove, or undercut, should be cut at the left end of the thread as shown in Figure 67-7. The depth of the groove should be equal to the depth of the thread. The groove makes it easier to avoid breaking off the point of the cutting tool when the tool is withdrawn after each cut. Then **chamfer** the end of the workpiece (Fig. 67-7).

4. Set the compound rest at a 29° angle to the right.

5. Set the point of the tool bit on the centerline of the work (Fig. 67-4) and square with the work, as in Figure 67-5.

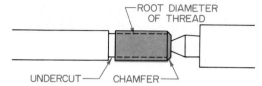

Fig. 67–7 *The workpiece should be chamfered and undercut before threading.*

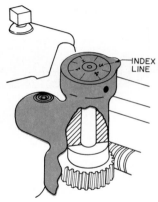

Fig. 67–8 *The lathe thread dial. (Figure 58–21 shows where the dial is located on the apron assembly.)*

6. Set the lathe at a low rpm when cutting your first threads. The speed should be slower than for turning operations. With experience, you can cut threads at higher speeds.

7. Set the **feed-change lever** (Fig. 58-20) to the **threading** position. On most lathes this is located in the center position. (Fig. 58-20 illustrates carriage and apron controls.)

8. Advance the tool until it just touches the work. If possible, set the **micrometer collar** on the **cross-feed knob** to zero. Also set the micrometer collar on the **compound-rest feed knob** to **zero.**

9. Bring the carriage to the right end of the work, clear of the work.

10. Advance the tool 0.003″ [0.076 mm] with the **compound-rest feed knob.**
   NOTE: The depth for each additional cut is set with the compound-rest feed knob. As the depth of thread increases with succeeding cuts, reduce the depth of cut to 0.002″ [0.05 mm] then to 0.001″ [0.025 mm]. The last several cuts should not be deeper than 0.001″ [0.025 mm] so as to guard against cutting the thread too deep.

11. If the **thread dial** (Fig. 67-8) is not engaged, engage it and tighten it in position. (The dial is engaged if it revolves when the carriage is moved by turning the carriage handwheel.)

12. Start the lathe. When a line on the number circle of the thread dial is in line with the **index line** on the body of the dial, engage the **half-nut lever.** *Any line* may be used for cutting an *even number of threads per inch.* Use any *numbered line* for cutting an *odd number of threads per inch.*

13. At the end of the thread, disengage the half-nut lever, and at the same time, turn the cross-feed knob one complete turn counterclockwise, to withdraw the tool.

14. Bring the carriage back to the right end of the thread in position to start the next cut.

15. Turn the cross-feed knob one revolution to the right to the original zero starting position.

16. If the workpiece is steel, add a few drops of cutting oil to the threaded area.

17. Make additional cuts until the thread is cut to the desired depth. As the depth of thread increases, the pitch diameter should be measured with a **thread micrometer** or **thread gage** to avoid cutting the thread too deeply. If these are not available, use a standard nut of the correct thread diameter and pitch as a gage. The nut should turn freely but without excess looseness.

Other Thread-cutting Procedures

An internal thread is cut with a threading tool bit inserted in a boring tool holder as shown in Figure 63-8. If you wish to cut internal threads, acme threads, or any other kind of special thread on a lathe, ask your instructor to show you the correct procedure.

REVIEW   REVIEW   REVIEW   REVIEW   REVIEW

WORDS TO KNOW

center gage	cross-feed knob	half-nut lever	right-hand thread
chamfer	external threads	internal threads	thread dial
compound rest	formed threading	left-hand thread	undercut
compound-rest feed	tool		
knob			

REVIEW QUESTIONS

1. Name two kinds of single-point cutting tools that can be used for cutting threads in a lathe.
2. At what angle and direction should the compound rest be set for cutting 60° right-hand external threads?
3. Before cutting the thread, why should a groove be cut where the thread will end?
4. How high should the threading tool be set in relation to the workpiece center?
5. What tool is used to help set the threading tool square with the workpiece?
6. At what general rpm should the lathe be set for cutting the first threads?
7. Which feed knob is used to advance the threading tool for each cut?
8. How far should the threading tool be advanced for each cut?
9. Which lines on the thread dial are used for cutting an even number of threads per inch? Which lines are used for cutting an odd number of threads per inch?
10. List three ways of checking the thread for correct depth.

PART

17

Milling Machines and Milling Operations

Bob Drake understands metalworking from the point of view of both the tradesman and the executive. He began his career 16 years ago as an apprentice machinist. As a journeyman, he took every opportunity to assume responsibility. Gradually he worked into a management position. Now the president of a medium-sized milling company, Bob is the busiest person in the plant.

Although he spends some time at his desk, Bob is most often "on the move." He must oversee the movement of raw materials through the plant, check the work being done by machine operators, and examine the end products. He also calculates most of the cost estimates and sets prices on work to be done for the plant's customers.

Tons of steel, bronze, copper, brass, and titanium are moved through the plant by huge overhead cranes. The metals are deposited near several different milling machines: vertical machines, horizontal machines, and boring mills. Workers produce shafts, machine tool fixtures, and even machinery itself, such as roll-forming equipment for steel mills. Bob's particular job satisfaction is seeing the raw materials progress smoothly through various machining steps to become perfectly formed products.

When Bob was working as a machinist, he also earned an associate degree in data processing. His knowledge of computers is proving beneficial now that his company is experimenting with the use of numerically controlled machines.

Bob agrees with many others that a person must be mechanically inclined to work in the metalworking industries. But training is equally important. Students should be given every opportunity to learn about the working world before deciding on a particular career.

Bob Drake
Milling Company President

UNIT

68

Milling Machines

A **milling machine** is a machine tool that cuts metal with a multiple-tooth cutting tool called a **milling cutter** (Fig. 68-1). The workpiece is mounted on the milling machine table and is fed against the revolving milling cutter.

On heavy-duty milling machines, several milling cutters may be mounted on the machine arbor. With this arrangement more than one surface can be machined at the same time (Fig. 68-2). A wide variety of milling cutters are made for machining many kinds of surfaces. These cutters and their uses are described in Unit 70.

Milling machines, particularly vertical milling machines (Fig. 68-3), can also perform all the hole-machining operations commonly performed on drill presses.

Accessories that expand the variety of operations that can be performed on milling machines are described in Unit 69.

Fig. 68-2 *Milling a casting with several milling cutters on a heavy-duty horizontal milling machine. This is known as gang milling.* (Cincinnati Milacron)

Fig. 68-3 *Overall view of a vertical milling machine.* (Clausing)

Fig. 68-1 *An end-milling cutter after completing a cut on a vertical milling machine.* (Manual High School, Roger Bean)

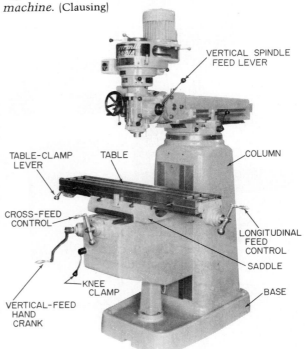

VERTICAL SPINDLE
FEED LEVER

TABLE-CLAMP
LEVER

TABLE

COLUMN

CROSS-FEED
CONTROL

LONGITUDINAL
FEED
CONTROL

SADDLE

KNEE
CLAMP

BASE

VERTICAL-FEED
HAND
CRANK

68-1 Types of Milling Machines

Most milling machines can be classified under two basic types. These include **bed-type** and **column-and-knee** milling machines. Bed-type milling machines are manufacturing milling machines that are used for mass-production purposes. The table does not move transversely (crosswise) toward the column. However, the spindle, on which the cutter is mounted, may be adjusted vertically as well as horizontally. Many milling machines are numerically controlled (Fig. 68-4).

Bed-type machines may be equipped with one, two, three, or more spindles and cutters. Such a machine may have three spindles and three heavy-duty **face-milling cutters**. Parts are mounted on both sides of the table, and three surfaces are **face-milled** at the same time.

Planer milling machines (Fig. 68-5) are so called because they are constructed and operated in much the same manner as the older conventional single-point cutting tool planers (Figs. 77-9 and 77-10). They are used for milling operations on very large workpieces.

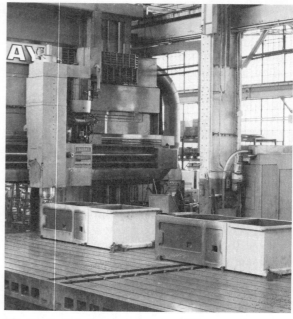

Fig. 68-5 *A large planer-type milling machine.* (G.A. Gray Co.)

Fig. 68-6 *A small thread milling machine.*

Fig. 68–4 *A numerically controlled vertical milling machine.*

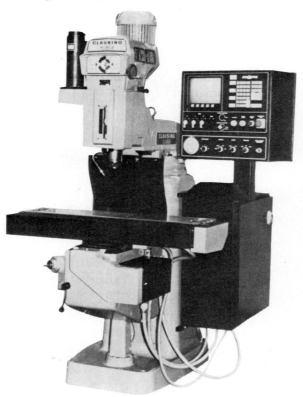

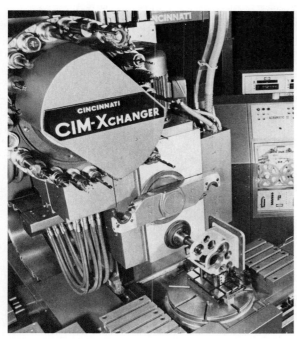

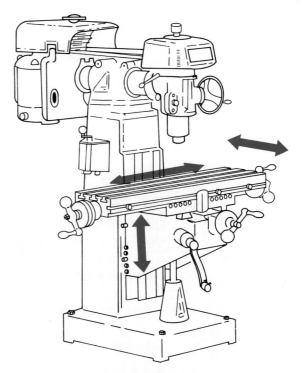

Fig. 68-7 *A small horizontal boring mill.* (Cincinnati Milacron)

Fig. 68-8 *The column-and-knee design provides table movement in three directions.*

Special purpose milling machines include **thread-milling machines** and **gear-hobbing machines.** The thread-milling machine shown in Figure 68-6 rapidly machines precision threads on a production basis. It can cut several threads simultaneously with only slightly more than one revolution of the workpiece.

Gear-hobbing machines cut gear teeth on gear blanks with a milling cutter called a gear hob. Horizontal gear hobbers are used for cutting gears of small diameter. Vertical gear hobbers are used for cutting large diameter gears.

Milling operations are also performed on **horizontal boring mills** (Fig. 68-7). These versatile machines are also built for machining large workpieces such as machine bases. They are capable of performing all of the precision hole-machining operations as well as milling.

68-2 Column-and-knee Milling Machines

The body, or frame, of a **column-and-knee** milling machine is a large casting that includes the **base** and the upright portion called the **column** (Fig. 68-3). The front of the column has accurately machined dovetail ways on which the **knee** is mounted.

The knee can be raised and lowered **vertically** to the desired elevation. The **saddle** and **table** are mounted on top of the knee. The table can feed **longitudinally** (horizontally to the right or to the left), and it can feed **transversely** (crosswise, or in and out from the column). Thus the table on column-and-knee milling machines can be fed or adjusted in three directions (Fig. 68-8).

The table can be fed manually or with power feed if so equipped.

Column-and-knee milling machines can be further classified into the following types:
1. horizontal milling machines
   a. plain (Fig. 68-9)
   b. universal (Fig. 68-10)

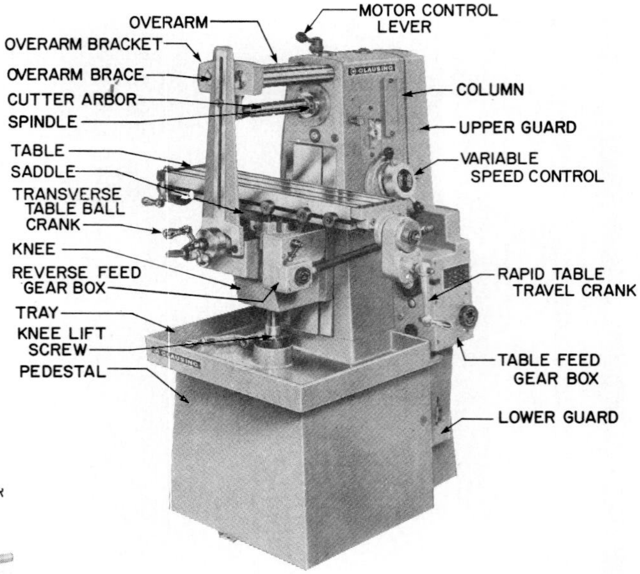

Fig. 68-9 *A small plain horizontal milling machine.*

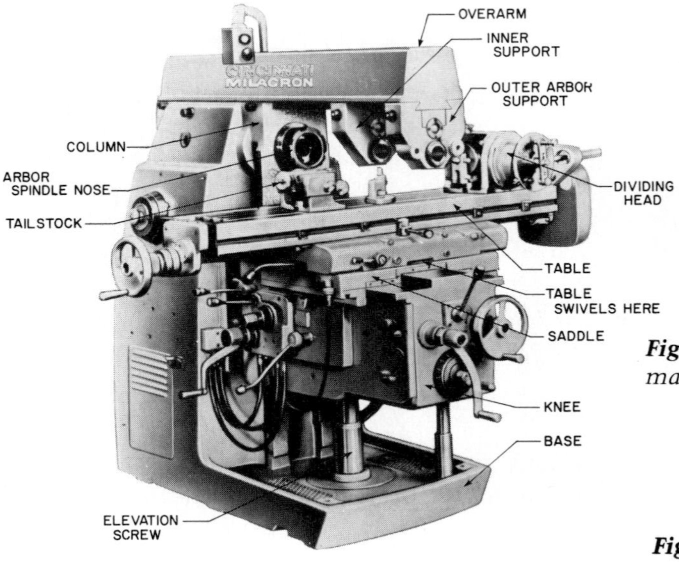

OVERARM
OVERARM BRACKET
OVERARM BRACE
CUTTER ARBOR
SPINDLE
TABLE
SADDLE
TRANSVERSE TABLE BALL CRANK
KNEE
REVERSE FEED GEAR BOX
TRAY
KNEE LIFT SCREW
PEDESTAL

MOTOR CONTROL LEVER
COLUMN
UPPER GUARD
VARIABLE SPEED CONTROL
RAPID TABLE TRAVEL CRANK
TABLE FEED GEAR BOX
LOWER GUARD

OVERARM
INNER SUPPORT
OUTER ARBOR SUPPORT
COLUMN
ARBOR SPINDLE NOSE
TAILSTOCK
DIVIDING HEAD
TABLE
TABLE SWIVELS HERE
SADDLE
KNEE
BASE
ELEVATION SCREW

Fig. 68-10 *A small universal milling machine with its principal parts labeled.*

Fig. 68-12 *A small lathe equipped with a vertical milling attachment.*

Fig. 68-11 *Vertical milling with a combination horizontal and vertical milling machine.*

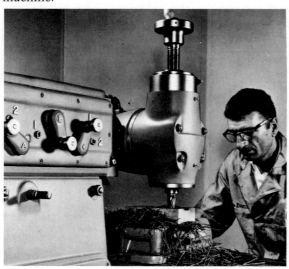

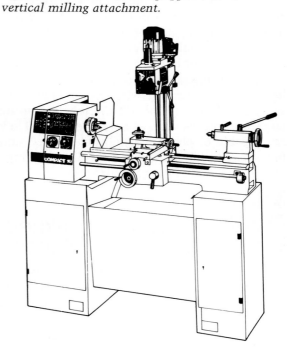

2. vertical milling machines
3. combination horizontal and vertical milling machines (Fig. 68-11).

Column-and-knee milling machines are manufactured in a wide range of sizes and weights. Many schools have smaller, lightweight machines such as the one shown in Figure 68-9. Some school shops have standard heavy-duty milling machines as shown in Figure 68-10. Regardless of the size of the machine, the principles involved in milling operations are the same. Heavy cuts on a milling machine require a heavy-duty, sturdy machine. Hence, lighter cuts and lighter feeds must be taken when using smaller, lightweight machines.

68-3 Horizontal Milling Machines

Horizontal milling machines may be either the column-and-knee or bed type. They have the milling cutter mounted on a horizontal arbor as shown in Figure 68-2. The arbor fits into the spindle nose, which is located on the machined face of the vertical column. The arbor is supported rigidly with an **arbor** support or **overarm support.**

End-milling cutters, called **end mills,** can also be mounted horizontally in the spindle nose of horizontal milling machines. End-milling operations, however, are more commonly performed on vertical milling machines (Fig. 68-3).

Plain Horizontal Milling Machine

A plain horizontal milling machine (Fig. 68-9) is used for milling flat horizontal surfaces, vertical surfaces, angular surfaces, curved surfaces, irregular surfaces, grooves, and keyways. These surfaces and the cutters used to machine them are described in Unit 70.

The table on plain milling machines cannot be swiveled for helical (spiral) milling operations. However, with the use of a dividing head and a **universal spiral milling attachment,** such operations can be performed. This attachment is shown in Figure 69-6. A **vertical milling attachment,** as in Figure 68-11, may be used to perform vertical milling operations on a plain milling machine.

The plain milling machine in Figure 68-9 is equipped with power longitudinal table feed. Handfeed is used for transverse (cross) table feed or for raising and lowering the table.

Universal Horizontal Milling Machine

A universal horizontal milling machine is shown with its principal parts labeled in Figure 68-10. The main difference between plain and universal machines is that the table can be swiveled in a horizontal plane on the universal machine. Universal machines usually are equipped with a dividing head, tailstock, and a dividing-head lead driving mechanism. These accessories make it possible to perform helical milling operations, as in Figure 69-7. Helical milling is required for cutting helical gears or for making helical cutting tools, such as drills, reamers, or milling cutters.

68-4 Vertical Milling Machines

Vertical milling machines are also manufactured as column-and-knee or bed-type machines. The spindle on vertical milling machines normally is in a vertical position, like the spindle on a drill press. However, the head may be swiveled on some machines for angular milling or hole-machining operations.

Vertical milling machines use end-milling cutters. The end mills are mounted in the nose of the vertical spindle with collets or with end mill adapters (Fig. 69-14).

Operations

Vertical milling machines can machine horizontal surfaces, angular surfaces, shoulders, grooves, keyways, dovetails, and T-slots. In addition, vertical milling machines can perform hole-machining operations such as drilling, countersinking, boring, counterboring, and reaming.

Heavy-Duty Machines

Heavy-duty vertical milling machines are capable of taking very heavy cuts. They are equipped with power longitudinal feed, power cross feed, and power vertical feed for table elevation. The spindle in the head is also provided with power vertical feed.

Light-Duty Machines

Light-duty and medium-duty vertical milling machines are widely used in tool rooms, small industrial machine shops, and school shops. They may be purchased with manual feed only, or with one or more of the following kinds of power feed:

North Shoots for the Best

TECHNOLOGIES AND PRACTICES

A collector of antique firearms may prize a one-of-a-kind, handmade pistol. But a nation's army needs thousands of guns made so well that its soldiers can make repairs with parts from another gun. The United States faced this situation during the War of 1812 when the army needed mass-produced guns with interchangeable parts. At that time such guns were rare and difficult to make. Arms manufacturer Simeon North was given the task of successfully mass-producing them.

The government's contract with North ordered 20,000 pistols at $7 apiece with parts so alike that "any limb or part of one Pistol of the Twenty Thousand" would fit into another one. To fill this request, North had to open a new factory in Middletown, Connecticut, at a cost of $100,000.

The investment paid off. The guns made in his new plant met the requirements for interchangeable parts. War Department officials were so impressed by the results that they asked North to reorganize production at the government's armory at Harper's Ferry, Virginia.

To machine interchangeable parts more efficiently, North made important changes in production techniques both at Harper's Ferry and in his own armories. At the government facility, he installed a Wilkinson lathe with the latest turning capabilities. It machined musket barrels very efficiently and eliminated hand grinding. In his own factories, the newly developed milling machine was in operation by 1818. It replaced the expensive and time-consuming job of hand filing. In addition, pieces machined this new way were consistently accurate and thus interchangeable. With this equipment, North produced about 50,000 pistols and 33,000 rifles for the United States. All were highly dependable.

North continued to contribute to machining and quality arms production throughout his life. The production techniques he introduced were major steps in the development of modern American manufacturing.

1. power longitudinal table feed
2. power transverse feed (cross feed)
3. power vertical spindle feed
4. power table elevation.

Light-duty machines produce good results when used for cuts that are within their capacity.

Light-duty vertical milling operations can also be done on lathes equipped with vertical milling attachments (Fig. 68-12).

68-5 Principal Parts of Milling Machines

Before attempting to operate a milling machine, you should know the names of the principal parts and the controls on the machine.

The names of the principal parts and controls of horizontal milling machines can be found in Figures 68-9 and 68-10. The names of the principal parts and controls on vertical machines can be found in Figure 68-3.

68-6 Milling Machine Controls and Adjustments

Before operating a milling machine, you must know how to make several kinds of adjustments on the machine. These include knee elevation, table adjustments, speed, and feed.

Knee Elevation

The knee must be raised or lowered to establish the proper elevation of the workpiece under the cutting tool. For **horizontal** milling operations the knee must be raised to establish the **depth of cut.** For **vertical** milling operations, the depth of cut may be established either by raising the knee or by feeding the tool to the desired depth with the **vertical spindle handwheel** or **feed lever** (Fig. 68-3). Generally, it is best to set the depth of cut by raising the knee.

A **knee clamp** (a lever or a locking nut) locks the knee securely to the column during milling operations. The knee clamp must be loosened before raising or lowering the knee. The knee is then raised or lowered with the **vertical-feed hand crank.** Notice that there is a **micrometer collar** with 0.001″ [0.025 mm] graduations on the vertical-feed hand crank, the **longitudinal-feed control,** and the **cross-feed control.** These permit precise location of the workpiece in each direction of movement.

Transverse Table Movement

Transverse table movement is movement of the **saddle** and **table** toward or away from the column. During most milling operations, the saddle is clamped securely to the knee with one or more **saddle-clamp levers.** This clamping reduces table vibration. Therefore, before making transverse table adjustments, loosen the saddle clamp. Then the table can be moved toward or away from the column with the **cross-feed handwheel** or **handcrank.** After table adjustment, the saddle clamp again must be tightened.

Saddle clamps must also be loosened when performing operations that involve tansverse table feeding.

Longitudinal Table Movement

Longitudinal table movement is table travel from side to side, toward either the right or the left. The table may be fed manually with the **table traverse handwheel,** also called the **longitudinal feed.** Many machines are equipped with power longitudinal table feed, which is engaged with the **power table-feed lever.**

Most milling machine tables are provided with a **table-clamp lever,** which should be tightened during hole-machining operations.

Rapid Traverse

Larger milling machines are equipped with a **rapid-traverse control.** This control enables the operator to move the knee or table rapidly in any direction with power.

SAFETY NOTE

Beginners should be very careful in using this control. Serious damage can result if the workpiece strikes the cutter or arbor when the knee is raised rapidly or when the table is traversed rapidly. It is best to ask your instructor to show you how to use the rapid-traverse control before attempting to use it yourself. Skilled operators are able to speed up production by using this control.

Spindle Speed Adjustment

The spindle speed is designated in rpm (revolutions per minute). On some machines the rpm is selected and set by turning a **speed-change dial** to the desired rpm. Other machines may be equipped with levers that shift gears for the desired rpm. Machines of the type shown in Figure 68-9 are equipped with a **variable-speed drive. This type of drive must be adjusted while the machine is running.** On machines with a step pulley and V-belt drive, the rpm is changed by shifting the belt to a different step on the pulley **while the drive motor is off.**

The direction of spindle revolution may be changed on most milling machines. This may be done with a spindle-reversing switch, button, or lever.

Feed Adjustment

The rate of feed and the method for determining the rate of feed are explained in Unit 71. On most machines, the feed rate is changed through a series of change gears in a **feed-change gear box.** On some machines, the feed rate is changed by turning a **feed dial** directly to the desired rate.

The table is fed manually on small machines not equipped with power feeds. The operator then must use his or her best judgment in feeding the table at the proper rate of feed. Feeding too rapidly can cause cutter breakage. Feeding too slowly causes more rapid tool wear.

68-7 Direction of Feed

The direction of feed in relation to the direction of cutter rotation is an important factor in all milling operations. Two methods of feed are possible.

In **up milling** (also known as conventional milling), the workpiece is fed **against** the direction of cutter rotation (Fig. 68-13). In **down milling** (also called climb milling), the workpiece is fed **with** the direction of cutter rotation (Fig. 68-14).

SAFETY NOTE

Down milling is done only on machines equipped with anti-backlash devices; check your operator's manual.

Smaller milling machines, and many older machines, are not equipped with anti-backlash devices. **Therefore, they should not be used for down milling.**

Up (Conventional) Milling

In up milling, the cutter tooth starts into the work with a chip of zero thickness and ends with a thick chip (Fig. 68-13). The cutter starts into clean metal and ends by lifting off the rough surface scale. Thus the cutter stays sharp longer. However, the workpiece must be clamped very tightly in the vise or to the table. The cutting forces tend to lift or pull the work out of the vise. The direction of feed forces the work against the cutter, thus compensating for wear, or **backlash,** in the table lead-screw and feeding mechanism.

Down (Climb) Milling

In down milling, the cutter tooth starts into the work with a thick chip and ends with a thin chip (Fig. 68-14). The scraping action of the cutter tooth at the end of the chip tends to produce a smoother surface. **The cutting forces tend to pull the workpiece under the cutter. Thus, any backlash in the leadscrew or**

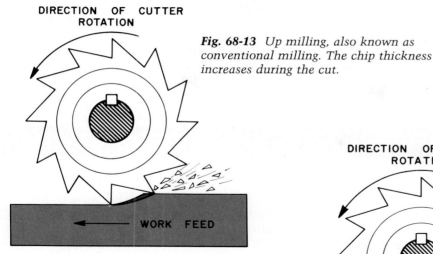

DIRECTION OF CUTTER ROTATION

WORK FEED

Fig. 68-13 *Up milling, also known as conventional milling. The chip thickness increases during the cut.*

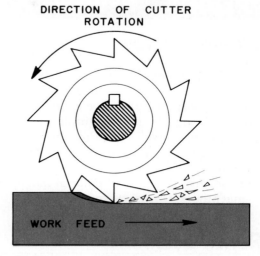

DIRECTION OF CUTTER ROTATION

WORK FEED

Fig. 68-14 *Down milling, also known as climb milling. The chip size decreases during the cut.*

feeding mechanism can cause vibration, chatter, and possible cutter breakage. A hard surface scale on the workpiece will dull the cutter more rapidly.

Down milling is gaining wider use today on certain production milling operations. It generally produces a better surface finish on the harder steels. Small thin parts and parts that are otherwise difficult to hold can be machined more easily by this method. **But remember that to be used with this method, the machine must be equipped with an antibacklash device.**

The principles involved in these methods of milling also apply to vertical end-milling and face-milling operations.

68-8

Safety for Milling

1. Wear approved safety goggles.
2. Wipe up any oil on the floor around the machine.
3. Be certain that the table is clean and dry before making a setup.
4. Always be certain that work-holding devices such as a vise, angle plate, dividing head, or tailstock are fastened tightly to the table.

5. Select the right kind of cutter for the job, as described in Unit 70.
6. Always be sure that the arbor, cutter, and collars are clean before mounting them in the spindle. Use a rag for handling sharp cutters.
7. Use a lead hammer to seat the workpiece securely in the vise.
8. Be certain that the vise or other holding devices clear the arbor and overarm supports.
9. Select the proper cutting speed, rpm, and rate of feed for the job.
10. Disengage the control handles when using automatic feeds.
11. Be certain that the column clamps, saddle clamps, and table clamps are loosened when making setup adjustments. Be certain to tighten them after the setup.

12. **Keep your hands away from the revolving cutter at all times.**
13. Clear chips away from the cutter with a brush, such as a paint brush.
14. Release any automatic feeds after completing the job.
15. Do not allow unauthorized persons within the safety zone of the machine.
16. Clean and wipe the machine when you are finished. Remove chips with a small shovel or scoop. Never touch them with your fingers.

REVIEW   REVIEW   REVIEW   REVIEW   REVIEW

WORDS TO KNOW

anti-backlash device	horizontal boring	horizontal	rapid traverse
arbor	mill	plain	saddle
arbor support	knee clamp	universal	saddle clamp
down milling	longitude feed	vertical	speed-change dial
end-milling cutter	milling cutter	milling table	thread-milling
face-milling cutter	milling machine	milling table clamp	machine
feed dial	bed-type	planer milling	transverse feed
gear-hobbing	column-and-knee	machine	up milling
machine	combination	power feed	vertical feed

REVIEW QUESTIONS

1. Describe the machining process known as milling.
2. Why are milling machines considered to be more efficient than machines such as shapers and planers?
3. List three kinds of flat surfaces that can be machined with a milling machine.
4. What other kinds of surface-machining operations can be done with a milling machine?
5. What kinds of hole-machining operations can be performed with a milling machine?
6. List the three directions in which the table can be adjusted on column-and-knee milling machines.
7. List three types of knee-and-column milling machines.
8. What is the main difference between plain and universal horizontal milling machines?
9. What kinds of operations can be performed on a universal milling machine that cannot be performed without special accessories on a plain milling machine?
10. How can vertical milling operations be performed on either plain or universal milling machines?
11. List the kinds of operations that can be performed with vertical milling machines or with vertical milling attachments on horizontal machines.
12. Why should the knee clamps and saddle clamps be tightened when milling?
13. What is the purpose of a rapid-traverse control on a milling machine?
14. Explain how the spindle rpm must be adjusted or changed on a milling machine with a variable-speed drive system.
15. Explain how the power feed rate can be changed on one kind of milling machine.
16. Explain the difference between up milling and down milling. Why must up milling be used on machines without anti-backlash devices?

UNIT
69

Workpiece-Holding Devices and Accessories

Many attachments or accessories are available for use on milling machines. Some make it possible to hold the workpiece more effectively. Others make it possible to do many more, different cutting operations on the milling machine.

69-1

Vises

Vises used on milling machines must be strong enough to hold the workpiece tightly under the pressure and vibration of milling. Three types of vises are commonly used: (1) plain, (2) swivel, and (3) universal.

Plain vise. The plain vise (Fig. 69-1A) is normally bolted to the milling machine table with the jaw faces either parallel or at a right angle to the direction of table travel (69-1B). The vise may be fastened to the table at any angle, but swivel vises are more convenient for this purpose.

Swivel vise. The swivel vise (Fig. 69-2) can be turned to any desired angle. The angle is indicated by the degree graduations on the swivel base. Alignment of the vise is explained in Unit 72.

Universal vise. The universal vise (Fig. 69-3) is used for machining compound angles on workpieces. The vise can be swiveled at any desired angle on its swivel base. The vise jaws can be tilted at any desired angle in any direction from 0° to the 90° vertical position.

Fig. 69-2 *A swivel vise permits it to be mounted at any angle to the table travel.* (Cincinnati Milacron)

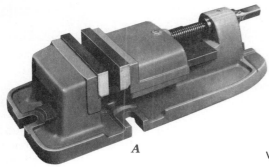

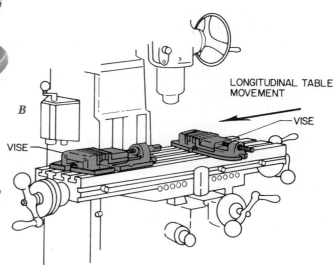

LONGITUDINAL TABLE MOVEMENT

VISE

B

VISE

A

Fig. 69-1 *(A) A plain vise, (B) the slots in the base of the vise permit mounting it in two different ways on the milling table.* (Cincinnati Milacron)

Fig. 69-3 *A universal vise can be swivelled and also tilted in both vertical axes.* (Cincinnati Milacron)

Fig. 69-4 *Using the dividing head and its tailstock to cut a spur gear.* (Cincinnati Milling Machine Co.)

69-2

Dividing Head

A **dividing head,** or **index head,** (Figs. 69-4 and 69-5) is used for holding a workpiece and for dividing or indexing it into a number of equally spaced angular divisions. Indexing is explained in Unit 76.

A **tailstock** is bolted to the table and is used with the dividing head for holding a workpiece between centers (Fig. 69-4). Both the tailstock and the dividing head are equipped with 60° centers, the same as lathe centers. The tailstock center can be raised above the center point of the dividing head. This is done when tapered grooves or tapered surfaces are to be machined on a workpiece.

In a typical dividing head operation, a workpiece, such as the gear blank in Figure 69-4, is pressed on a **lathe mandrel.** The mandrel has a driving dog clamped on the driving end. The mandrel is mounted between the centers of the dividing head and the tailstock.

A universal 3-jaw chuck may be mounted on the spindle nose of the dividing head for holding short workpieces (Fig. 69-5). This makes many kinds of horizontal or vertical milling operations possible. The dividing head may be swiveled vertically to any desired an-

Fig. 69-5 *A workpiece held in a universal chuck that is mounted on a dividing head.* (Cincinnati Milling Machine Co.)

gular position, from 0° to 90°. With a round workpiece mounted in the chuck in a vertical position, any number of equally spaced flat surfaces on its circumference can be milled. This procedure can be used for machining a square or hexagonal head on a bolt or on the end of a shaft.

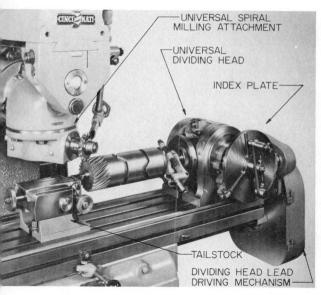

Fig. 69-6 *Milling helical gear teeth with the aid of a universal spiral milling attachment.* (Cincinnati Milling Machine Co.)

Fig. 69-7 *Cutting a left-hand helix with the table swiveled on a universal milling machine.* (Cincinnati Milling Machine Co.)

69-3 Universal Spiral Attachment

This attachment makes it possible to machine helical (spiral) surfaces or grooves with a plain horizontal milling machine (Fig. 69-6). The attachment is mounted on the column and is driven by the machine spindle.

On universal milling machines, a spiral attachment is not necessary. Helical milling is done by swinging the milling machine table on its swivel base (Fig. 69-7). Three actions take place at the same time: (1) the lead driving mechanism of the dividing head causes the work to revolve, (2) the table travels longitudinally, and (3) the milling cutter machines a groove in the workpiece. As a result the groove is helical.

69-4 Vertical Milling Attachment

This attachment can be mounted to the column and the spindle of horizontal milling machines (Fig. 69-8). The vertical milling at-

Fig. 69-8 *A vertical milling attachment and a circular milling attachment of the hand feed type mounted on a horizontal milling machine.* (Cincinnati Lathe and Tool Co.)

tachment makes it possible to perform a wide variety of vertical milling operations on horizontal machines. The attachment may be used in a vertical position or at an angle for milling angular surfaces.

69-5 Circular Milling Attachment

Several kinds of circular milling attachments are available for use with milling machines. Such attachments consist basically of a circular or square table that can be swiveled in a horizontal plane. Hand feeds and power feeds are available. The hand feed attachment shown in Figure 69-8 is widely used in many shops. A workpiece can be bolted directly to the attachment table, or it may be mounted in a vise that is bolted to the attachment table.

The circular milling attachment on vertical-type machines makes it possible to machine circular edges, shoulders, or grooves. The swivel base of the attachment table is marked with degree graduations. This attachment can be used to mill grooves at any angle across the top of a workpiece.

69-6 Arbors, Collets, Adapters, and Holders

A wide variety of milling machine arbors, collets, adapters, and holders is available for holding milling cutters.

Arbor Shanks

Most manufacturers of standard and heavy-duty milling machines use the **national milling machine taper** for the tapered hole in the machine spindle. The shanks of the arbors used with these machines have the same kind of taper. Standard milling machine arbor tapers are steep tapers with 3½″ taper per foot [291.7 mm per M]. Because of the steep taper, they are the **self-releasing** type. Hence they must be held in place with a locking device or collar or a **draw bar** (Fig. 69-9).

Standard milling arbor tapers are made in several sizes, designated by the numbers 30, 40, 50, and 60. The No. 50 is the most common and is used on machines of the type shown in Figures 68-5 and 68-7. Smaller machines use either the No. 40 or No. 30 taper.

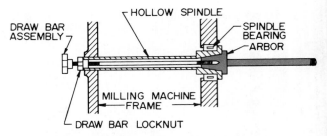

Fig. 69-9 *Typical drawbar arrangement for holding milling arbors with self-releasing tapers.*

Some milling machine spindles have a standard shallow taper, such as the **Brown & Sharpe taper** or the **Morse taper**. A few manufacturers use a special taper for the spindle hole on their milling machines.

Arbors

Style-A arbor. This arbor (Fig. 69-10A) has a small pilot at the outer end. The pilot fits in a small bearing in a style-A arbor support (Fig. 69-11). The style-A arbor support permits the use of small diameter cutters. This arbor support easily passes over the vise when using small cutters close to the vise jaws. Style-A arbors generally are used for light-duty milling operations. An additional outer arbor support can also be used with the style-A arbor for more rigid support (see Fig. 68-12). The single **bearing sleeve** of the style-A arbor runs in the outer arbor support.

Style-B arbor. This arbor (Fig. 69-10B) does not have a pilot at its outer end. It has one or more bearing sleeves, which run in the large bearings in the style-B arbor supports (Fig. 69-12). Style-B arbors are used for heavy-duty milling operations.

Spacing collars are provided on both style-A and style-B arbors. They hold the arbor rigid and permit spacing the milling cutter at any location along the arbor. The ends of the collars are precision-ground to extreme accuracy. Thus, the collars hold the arbor straight when the cutter is installed and the arbor nut is tightened. **A tiny nick or chip between the collars can cause the arbor to bend and the cutter to run untrue. The arbor, cutter, and**

collars must be wiped clean before the cutter is installed on the arbor. The cutter may be **keyed** to the arbor. The key should be long enough so that it extends into one collar on each side of the cutter.

Style-C arbor. This arbor is shown in Figure 69-10. It is used for holding shell end mills (Fig. 70-15). Thus, style-C arbors are often called **shell end mill arbors.**

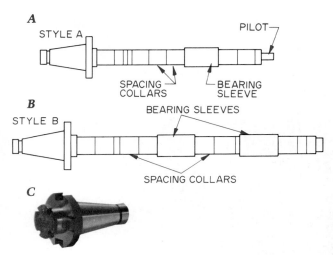

Fig. 69-10 *Milling arbors. (A) Style A for light-duty milling. (B) Style B for heavy-duty milling. (C) Style C for holding shell end mills.* (DoALL)

Fig. 69-11 *A style A arbor with cutters in place for a straddle milling operation.* (Cincinnati Milling Machine Co.)

Adapters

Adapters are devices that are used to mount cutters of various kinds on the milling machine spindle. An **arbor adapter** (Fig. 69-13A) is used for mounting large face mills directly to the machine spindle. The **collet adapter** (Fig. 69-13B) is used for mounting taper shank end mills (Fig. 70-12) on the spindle. The tapered hole in the adapter is the **self-holding** type, usually either a Morse taper or a Brown & Sharpe taper. A **reducing sleeve** (Fig. 69-13C) is inserted into the adapter if the tapered hole is larger than the shank on the end mill. The collet adapter may also be used with collets (Fig. 69-13D and E) for holding straight-shank end mills.

Fig. 69-12 *Milling a crankshaft in a special fixture. The style B arbor is used in this heavy-duty milling operation.* (Cincinnati Milling Machine Co.)

Fig. 69-13 *A group of devices for holding milling cutters. (A) an arbor adapter. (B) A collet adapter. (C) A reducing sleeve. (D) A solid collet. (E) A split collet.* (Cincinnati Milling Machine Co.)

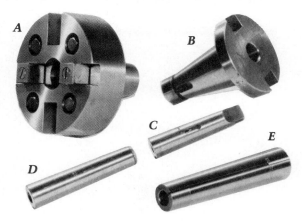

Holders

Holders of the types shown in Figure 69-14 are used for holding straight-shank end mills. The holders are available with holes of various sizes for end mill shanks of different diameters. The setscrew holds the end mill securely in place. A variety of end-mill holders is available. Some are designed to fit directly into the machine spindle. Others are inserted into a collet adapter that is installed in the machine spindle.

Quick-change Toolholding Systems

Quick-change toolholding systems shorten tool-changing time and increase productivity (Fig. 69-15). Adapters are available for holding drill chucks, shell-end mills, and all straight- and taper-shank cutting tools, such as end mills, drills, and reamers.

Boring heads (Fig. 69-16) provide the best way to machine accurately sized straight holes with fine finishes. The end of the boring head that holds the boring tool is adjustable so that holes of different sizes may be bored. A micrometer dial provides precision adjustment of the tool. Some boring heads are also capable of limited facing.

*Fig. 69-14 Holders for straight-shank end mills use a setscrew to fasten the end mill.
(A) Self-holding taper style for use with a drawbar.
(B) Self-holding type for use without a drawbar.
(C) Self-releasing type for use with a drawbar.*

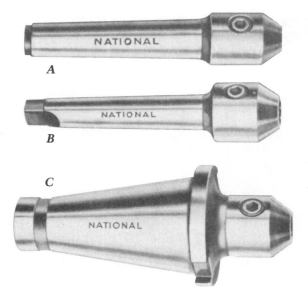

A

B

C

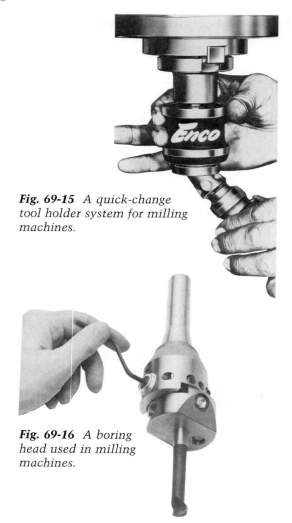

Fig. 69-15 A quick-change tool holder system for milling machines.

Fig. 69-16 A boring head used in milling machines.

69-7 Removing Standard Arbors

Most milling machines use arbors and collet adapters that have standard national milling machine taper shanks. These are held in the machine spindle with either a locking collar or a draw bar (Fig. 69-9). Arbors or adapters that are held with a draw bar are removed in the following manner:

1. Turn the power to the machine OFF.
2. Loosen the draw bar two or three turns. **Do not unscrew the draw bar all the way.**
3. Strike the end of the draw bar with a lead hammer.

4. While holding the arbor with one hand, unscrew the draw bar with the other hand.
5. Remove the arbor from the machine spindle.

69-8 Removing Self-Holding Arbors

Some older milling machines and many smaller vertical milling machines have arbors or adapters with a Brown & Sharpe taper, Morse taper, or special taper. These usually are self-holding tapers, which also are held in the machine spindle with a draw bar. The draw bar should not be turned up too tightly, or it will be very difficult to remove the arbor or adapter.

Some draw bars have right-hand threads, while others have left-hand threads. Before removing an arbor or adapter, check to see whether the threads are right- or left-hand. Self-holding arbors or adapters are removed in the following manner:

1. Turn the power to the machine OFF.
2. While holding the arbor with one hand, loosen the draw bar by turning it in the proper direction.
3. As the draw bar is loosened, it presses against a **retaining collar,** which forces the arbor or adapter out of the spindle at the opposite end.

If the arbor does not release when reasonable force is applied to the draw bar with a wrench, request assistance from your instructor.

REVIEW REVIEW REVIEW REVIEW REVIEW

Words to know

arbor adapter	collet adapter	quick-change	swivel vise
arbor, Style A	dividing head	toolholder	universal spiral
arbor, Style B	draw bar	retaining collar	attachment
arbor, Style C	index head	self-holding taper	universal vise
bearing sleeves	national milling	self-releasing taper	vertical milling
boring head	machine taper	spacing collars	attachment
circular milling	plain vise		
attachment			

Review questions

1. Name three kinds of vises used on milling machines.
2. What is a dividing head used for?
3. What is a vertical milling attachment used for?
4. What is a universal spiral milling attachment used for?
5. What is a circular milling attachment used for?
6. Explain the characteristics of the national milling machine taper.
7. Briefly describe the uses for style-A, style-B, and style-C arbors.
8. How will nicks on the face of spacing collars affect the straightness of style-A or B arbors?
9. What are the advantages of quick-change toolholding systems?
10. What are boring heads used for?
11. Explain how to remove an arbor that has a national milling machine taper and is held in the machine spindle with a draw bar.

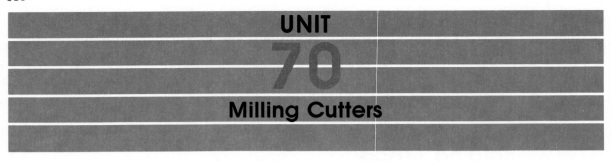

UNIT
70
Milling Cutters

Milling cutters are made in many standard shapes and sizes. They can be used for machining flat surfaces, grooves, angular surfaces, and irregular surfaces. Also available are milling cutters of special design for machining surfaces of special shapes.

have fewer teeth and a steeper helix angle. For instance, a 2½" [63.5] diameter cutter generally has 8 teeth, and the helix angle is 45°. Heavy-duty cutters are best for heavy cuts but they also work well for light and moderate cuts.

70-1 Plain Milling Cutters

Plain milling cutters have cutting teeth only on their outer part, the circumference, or **periphery** (Figure 70-1). They have precisely ground holes in their centers. Plain milling cutters are used on horizontal milling machines for machining plain, flat surfaces. Sometimes they are used in combination with other kinds of cutters for gang milling.

Light-duty plain milling cutters (Fig. 70-1) have relatively fine teeth. For example a 2½" [63.5 mm] diameter cutter generally has 14 to 18 teeth. Cutters of this type that are less than ¾" wide have straight teeth parallel to the axis of the cutter. Cutters ¾" [19 mm] and wider have helical teeth with an 18° helix angle. These cutters are available in many widths and diameters.

Heavy-duty plain milling cutters are like the light-duty plain cutters except that they

70-2 Side-Milling Cutters

Side-milling cutters are similar to plain milling cutters; however, they also have cutting edges on the sides.

Side milling cutters are used for milling the sides of a workpiece or for cutting slots or grooves. They also can be used for **straddle milling.** This involves cutting two parallel sides at the same time (Fig. 69-11). The width between the two cutters is established with spacing collars and shims.

The cutting edges on the periphery of side-milling cutters do most of the cutting. The teeth may be either **straight** (Fig. 70-2), **staggered** (Fig. 70-3), or **helical** (Fig. 70-4).

Plain side-milling cutters (Fig. 70-2) have straight teeth on the periphery and both sides. They are used for moderate-duty side-milling, slotting, and straddle-milling operations.

  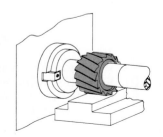

Fig. 70-1 *Light-duty plain milling cutters.* (National Twist Drill and Tool Co.)

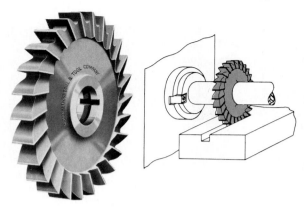

Fig. 70-2 *A plain side-milling cutter.* (National Twist Drill and Tool Co.)

Fig. 70-3 *A staggered-tooth side-milling cutter.* (National Twist Drill and Tool Co.)

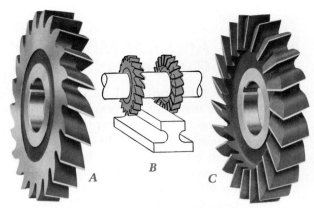

Fig. 70-4 *A pair of helical, half side-milling cutters (A and C), with teeth on opposite sides, that are used in straddle milling.* (National Twist Drill and Tool Co.)

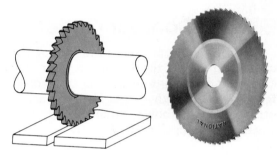

Fig. 70-5 *A plain metal-slitting saw.* (National Twist Drill and Tool Co.)

Staggered-tooth side-milling cutters (Fig. 70-3) are cutters with teeth that alternate to either side. This tooth arrangement provides more chip clearance and reduces **scoring** (grooved marks) on the side surfaces being machined. Cutters of this type are recommended for heavy-duty machining of grooves or keyways.

Half side-milling cutters (Fig. 70-4) have teeth on the periphery and only one side. They are recommended for heavy-duty side-milling and straddle-milling operations.

70-3 Metal-slitting Saws

Metal-slitting saws (Fig. 70-5) are used for ordinary cutoff operations and for cutting narrow slots. They are available with several kinds of teeth.

Plain metal-slitting saws (Fig. 70-5) have teeth on the periphery only. They are available in widths from 1/32" to 3/16" [0.8 to 4.8 mm] and in diameters from 2½" to 8" [63.5 to 203 mm]. They have fine teeth, and the sides of the teeth taper toward the hole. The taper prevents the blade from binding in the slot or saw kerf as it rotates. The feed rate used for these saws should be low, usually about 1/4 to 1/8 that used for plain milling cutters. See Table 71-3.

Staggered-tooth metal-slitting saws are recommended for cuts of 3/16" [4.8 mm] and wider.

Screw-slotting cutters are special fine-tooth plain slitting saws. They are available in widths from 0.020" to 0.182" [0.5 to 4.6 mm].

70-4 Angular Milling Cutters

Angular milling cutters (Figs. 70-6 and 70-7) are used for machining V-notches, grooves, serrations, dovetails, and reamer teeth.

Single-angle cutters (Fig. 70-6) have a single angle with cutting edges on both sides of the angle. Generally they are available with either 45° or 60° angles.

Double-angle cutters (Fig. 70-7) have V-shaped teeth. They usually are available with 45°, 60°, or 90° angles.

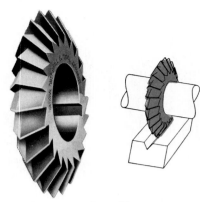

Fig. 70-7 *A double-angle milling cutter.* (National Twist Drill and Tool Co.)

70-5 Contour Cutters

Contour cutters are used for cutting curved surfaces of regular or irregular shape. Several kinds of contour cutters are shown in Figures 70-8 through 70-11. They are used for cutting curved grooves, rounded corners, or flutes in reamers, milling cutters, or gear teeth.

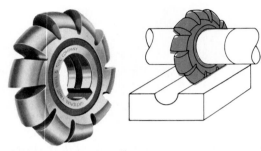

Fig. 70-8 *A convex milling cutter.* (National Twist Drill and Tool Co.)

70-6 The "Hand" of Milling Cutters

The term **hand** is used to describe the following factors involved in milling:
1. hand of the cutter
2. hand of the helix

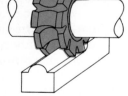

Fig. 70-9 *A concave milling cutter.* (National Twist Drill and Tool Co.)

Fig. 70-6 *A single-angle milling cutter.* (National Twist Drill and Tool Co.)

Fig. 70-10 *Corner-rounding milling cutters.*

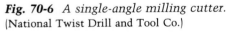

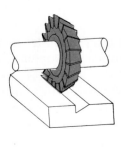

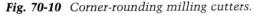

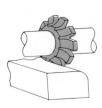

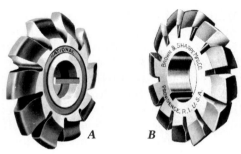

Fig. 70-11 *(A) A gear-tooth milling cutter. (B) A fluting cutter.*

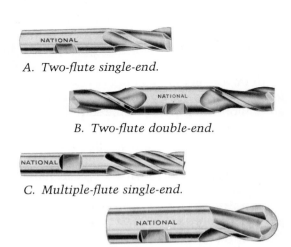

A. *Two-flute single-end.*

B. *Two-flute double-end.*

C. *Multiple-flute single-end.*

D. *Two flute ball-end.*

E. *Carbide-tipped straight flutes.*

F. *Carbide-tipped with taper shank and helical flutes.*

Fig. 70-12 *Different types of end mills.*
(National Twist Drill and Tool Co.)

Hand of the cutter refers to the direction in which the cutter must rotate to cut. A cutter may be a right-hand cutter or a left-hand cutter. The hand is determined by looking at the front end of the cutter (looking toward the spindle nose or column) while the cutter is mounted in the machine spindle. A **right-hand** cutter must rotate **counterclockwise** to cut. A **left-hand** cutter must rotate **clockwise** to cut.

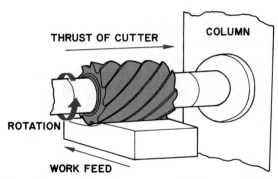

Fig. 70-13 *A helical cutter should be installed so that the cutting thrust forces the cutter toward the column.*

Thus, end mills, reamers, drills and similar cutting tools are designated right-hand (RH) or left-hand (LH). All of the end mills in Figure 70-12 are right-hand.

Hand of the helix describes the direction of the helical flutes on the milling cutter or on other cutting tools such as drills and reamers. The hand of the helix is determined by looking at either end of the cutting tool and noting the direction in which the helical flutes twist. If they twist away and toward the right, they have **right-hand** helical flutes (Fig. 70-1). If they twist away and toward the left, they have **left-hand** helical flutes.

Helical cutters should always be installed so that the **end thrust** on the cutter tends to force the cutter toward the column (Fig. 70-13). That is, the helix should point in the same direction as the spindle rotation.

70-7 End-Milling Cutters

End-milling cutters are commonly called **end mills.** They are designed for milling slots, shoulders, curved edges, keyways, and pockets where ordinary arbor-type cutters cannot be used. However, end mills can also be used for performing many of the same operations performed by arbor-type cutters.

End mills are of two basic types, **solid** and **shell.** In solid mills, the teeth and the shank are all one piece. A variety of solid end mills is shown in Figure 70-12.

Shell end mills have a body with the cutting edges, but no shank (Fig. 70-14). Shell end mills are mounted on stylc-C arbors (Fig. 69-10C).

All end-milling cutters have teeth on the circumference and some have teeth on the end. On **square-nose end mills,** most of the cutting is done by the teeth on the circumference. On ball end mills (Fig. 70-12D), a large portion of the cutting is done at the **end.** The teeth on the circumference may be straight or helical.

The shanks of solid end mills are either **straight** or **tapered.** The flat surface on the straight shank provides a means for holding the end mill securely in the end-mill holder with a setscrew (Fig. 69-14). The tapered-shank end mills have a flat drive-tang that prevents them from turning. They are mounted in the machine spindle with adapters (Fig. 69-13).

Two-flute end mills (Fig. 70-12A and B) are designed with **end-cutting teeth** for **plunge** and **traverse** milling. This kind of end mill can be fed into the work piece like a drill. After penetrating the workpiece, it then can be fed longitudinally.

Multiple-flute end mills have three, four, six, or eight flutes depending on their diameter (Fig. 70-12C). Only those with end-cutting teeth may be used for plunge milling to depth as well as for longitudinal milling.

Ball-end mills (Fig. 70-12D) are used for milling pockets in dies. They are also used for milling fillets or slots. **Four-fluted ball-end mills** are also available and are used for similar operations.

Shell end mills (Fig. 70-14) are made in larger sizes than shank-type end mills. They are made in diameters from 1¼″ to 6″ [31.75 to 152.4 mm] and may have either helical or straight teeth. Cutters of this type are used for machining larger shoulders or surfaces. The teeth on all types of milling cutters stay sharp longer if they have a chamfer or a radius ground on the corner of the teeth (Fig. 70-14).

T-slot milling cutters (Fig. 70-15) are used for milling T-slots such as those on milling machine tables. The narrow portion of the T-slot is machined first with a side-milling cutter or an end mill. The wide portion then is cut with the T-slot cutter. **Dovetail cutters** are also available for cutting dovetail grooves. Milling grooves and keyways is discussed in Unit 74.

Fig. 70-15 *A staggered-tooth T-slot cutter.*

Fig. 70-14 *Shell end mills are available with square, chamfered, or rounded corners.*

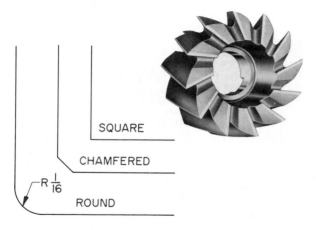

SQUARE

CHAMFERED

R 1/16

ROUND

Fig. 70-16 *Woodruff key-seat cutters.*

Key-seat cutters (Fig. 70-16) are used for cutting seats for woodruff keys. They are available in sizes for all standard woodruff keys. The end-mill type is made in sizes from ¼" to 1½" [6.35 to 38 mm] diameter. The arbor-mill type is made in diameters from 2⅛" to 3½" [54 to 90 mm].

Depth of cut is an important factor in preventing end-mill breakage. As a general rule, **the maximum depth of cut should not be greater than one-half the diameter of the end mill.** On hard, tough steel, the maximum depth should not exceed ¼ the diameter of the end mill. Suggested feeds for end mills are indicated in Table 71-3.

70-8 Cutter Materials

Milling cutters may be made of the same material throughout, such as carbon tool-steel, high-speed steel, or tungsten carbide. The majority of milling cutters used in school shops are of the **solid** type and are made of high-speed steel.

Milling cutters are also available with **tungsten-carbide teeth.** The carbide teeth are brazed on the tips of the cutter, as shown in E and F in Figure 70-12. Large cutters have **inserted teeth,** as in Figure 70-17. Inserted teeth may be made of high-speed steel, tungsten carbide, or **cast alloy.** The body of insert cutters is made of a lower cost alloy steel.

High-speed steel cutting tools rank high in impact resistance, wear resistance, and general toughness. They withstand the abuse and vibration that often occur on lightweight milling machines used in school shops.

Carbide-tipped cutters should be used on rigid setups and on heavy machines. Vibration or chatter causes them to fracture quite easily. However, they can be used with cutting speeds two to four times greater than those used for high-speed steel cutters.

Fig. 70-17 *Large milling cutters used for production work are of the throwaway insert type.* (GTE Valenite Corp, Troy, MI)

70-9 Importance of Using Sharp Milling Cutters

Milling cutters must be sharp to produce a good surface finish and to cut efficiently. When the cutter becomes dull, extreme forces are exerted on the cutter, the arbor and the machine spindle. Dull cutters cause poor finishes and possible cutter breakage. On horizontal machines, the extreme forces can bend the arbor, and it will no longer run true.

Only experienced persons should sharpen milling cutters. Cutters are expensive and can be damaged if sharpened improperly. This kind of instruction normally is included in advanced machine shop classes. It is not within the scope of this book.

70-10 Using Cutting Fluids

Cutting fluids are used for all production milling operations on steel, aluminum, and copper alloys. Gray cast iron may be machined dry, or with an emulsifiable (soluble) oil solution. Cutting fluids and their selection are explained in Unit 50. Table 50-2 shows the cutting fluids recommended for common metals.

REVIEW   REVIEW   REVIEW   REVIEW   REVIEW

WORDS TO KNOW

angular milling
   cutters
ball-end mill
double-angle
   milling cutter
end-milling cutters
form-relieved
   milling cutter
half side-milling
   cutter
hand of cutter

hand of helix
heavy-duty plain
   milling cutter
key-seat milling
   cutter
light-duty plain
   milling cutter
metal-slitting saw
plain side-milling
   cutter

screw-slotting
   cutter
shell end-milling
   cutter
single-angle milling
   cutter
solid end-milling
   cutter

staggered-tooth
   side-milling
   cutter
staggered tooth
   metal-slitting
   saws
straddle milling
T-slot milling
   cutter

REVIEW QUESTIONS

1. List three kinds of cutting tool materials from which milling cutters may be made.
2. What kinds of operations are plain milling cutters used for?
3. What kinds of operations are side-milling cutters used for?
4. List several kinds of side-milling cutters and explain their uses.
5. What operations are metal-slitting saws used for?
6. List two types of angular milling cutters.
7. What are form-relieved cutters used for?
8. What are the two kinds of hand in milling cutters and how are they determined?
9. What kinds of operations are end mills used for?
10. List two types of shanks on end mills.
11. What type of end mills can be used for plunge and traverse milling?
12. What kinds of cutting operations are ball-end mills used for?
13. Explain how a T-slot is machined.
14. List the general rule for determining the maximum depth of cut for end mills.
15. Cutting fluids should be used when cutting which metals?

UNIT

71

Cutting Speeds and Feeds for Milling

Cutting speed in milling refers to the distance a point on the circumference of the milling cutter travels in one minute. This is expressed in **feet per minute** (fpm) or **meters per minute** (mpm).

You can visualize the cutting speed of a milling cutter by imagining it as the distance the cutter rolls across the floor during one minute.

Different cutting speeds should be used when machining different metals. If the cutting speed is too fast, the cutter overheats and dulls rapidly. If the speed is too slow, time is wasted and production costs will increase.

Table 71-1

Cutting Speeds for Milling Roughing Cuts with High-Speed Steel Cutters

| Material | Cutting speed range | |
	FPM	MPM
Low-carbon steel	80-100	24.4-30.5
Medium-carbon steel, annealed	75-95	22.9-29.0
High-carbon steel, annealed	60-80	18.3-24.4
Tool steel, annealed	60-80	18.3-24.4
Stainless steel	60-80	18.3-24.4
Gray cast iron, soft	60-80	18.3-24.4
Malleable iron	80-100	24.4-30.5
Aluminum and its alloys	400-1000	122-305
Brass	200-300	61.0-91.4
Bronze	100-200	30.5-61.0

These suggested speeds may be varied as follows:
For finishing cuts . . . . Increase 25-50%
For carbon-steel cutters . . . . Decrease about 50%
For cutters with cast-alloy tips. . . . . . Increase 50-75%
For cutters with cemented-carbide
  tips . . . . Increase 200-400%
Feeds should be as much as the cutter, the setup, and the equipment will safely stand. Recommended cutting fluids should be used, see Table 50-2.

71-1 Factors Affecting Cutting Speeds

One of the most important factors affecting cutting speed is the **machinability rating** of the metal. Metals with high machinability ratings can be machined at higher cutting speeds than those with lower ratings. For example, brass has a much higher machinability rating than stainless steel. Thus, it can be machined much faster (see Table 71-1). Sections 2-3 and 6-3 also discuss machinability.

When the machinability rating is doubled, the cutting speed may be doubled, provided that proper cutting fluids are used. For example, steel with a rating of 100 may be machined at twice the cutting speed of steel with a rating of 50. The machinability ratings for various metals are included in handbooks for machinists.

The following factors affect cutting speeds for milling operations:
1. Kind of metal being machined.
2. Machinability rating of the metal.
3. Hardness of the metal (if heat-treated).
4. Kind of cutting tool material (high-speed steel, cast alloy, or cemented carbide).
5. Whether proper cutting fluids are used.
6. Depth of cut and rate of feed (roughing or finishing cut).

Suggested cutting speeds for roughing cuts with high-speed steel milling cutters are given in Table 71-1. There is no one correct cutting speed for milling one kind of metal. A certain **range** of speeds generally will produce good results. It is common practice to select an average cutting speed or a speed that is somewhat less than average. With satisfactory results, the cutting speed may be increased.

Revolutions per Minute (rpm)

After the cutting speed to be used has been determined, the machine spindle must be set at the proper rpm. Cutting speed and rpm have different meanings, and they should not be confused. **A small diameter milling cutter must turn at a higher rpm than a larger diameter cutter for both to cut at the same cutting speed.** An example shows this more clearly: A 1″ [25.4 mm] diameter end mill and a 2½″ [63.5 mm] diameter arbor cutter are to cut at the same cutting speed. For both to cut at 70 fpm [21.3 mpm], the 1″ [25.4 mm] diameter cutter must turn at 267 rpm, while the 2½″ [63.5 mm] diameter cutter must turn at 107 rpm. See Table 71-2.

Table 71-2 can be used for determining the rpm for milling, drilling, turning, and boring operations up to diameters of 3″ [76.2 mm]. The machine spindle speed should be adjusted to the rpm indicated on the machine dial or chart that is nearest the desired rpm.

Calculating rpm

The rpm of a given cutting speed for milling and hole-machining operations can be calculated with the following formulas:

Inch Formula:
$$rpm = \frac{CS(fpm) \times 12}{D'' \times \pi}$$

or the following shortcut formula:
$$rpm = \frac{4 \times CS(fpm)}{D''}$$

Table 71-2

Rpm for Tool or Workpiece Diameters up to 3″ (76.2 mm) at Different Cutting Speeds

	Cutting speeds												
fpm mpm	30 (9.1)	40 (12.2)	50 (15.2)	60 (18.3)	70 (21.3)	80 (24.4)	90 (27.4)	100 (30.5)	110 (33.5)	120 (36.6)	130 (39.6)	140 (42.8)	150 (45.7)
Diameter						Revolutions per minute							
¹⁄₁₆ (1.6)*	1833	2445	3056	3667	4278	4889	5500	6111	6722	7334	7945	8556	9167
⅛ (3.2)	917	1222	1528	1833	2139	2445	2750	3056	3361	3667	3973	4278	4584
³⁄₁₆ (4.8)	611	815	1019	1222	1426	1630	1833	2037	2241	2445	2648	2852	3056
¼ (6.35)	458	611	764	917	1070	1222	1375	1528	1681	1833	1986	2139	2292
⁵⁄₁₆ (7.9)	367	489	611	733	856	978	1100	1222	1345	1467	1589	1711	1833
⅜ (9.5)	306	407	509	611	713	815	917	1019	1120	1222	1324	1426	1528
⁷⁄₁₆ (11.1)	262	349	437	524	611	698	786	873	960	1048	1135	1222	1310
½ (12.7)	229	306	382	458	535	611	688	764	840	917	993	1070	1146
⅝ (15.9)	183	244	306	367	428	489	550	611	672	733	794	856	917
¾ (19.1)	153	203	255	306	357	407	458	509	560	611	662	713	764
⅞ (22.2)	131	175	218	262	306	349	393	436	480	524	568	611	655
1 (25.4)	115	153	191	229	267	306	344	382	420	458	497	535	573
1⅛ (28.6)	102	136	170	204	238	272	306	340	373	407	441	475	509
1¼ (31.8)	92	122	153	183	214	244	275	306	336	367	397	428	458
1⅜ (34.9)	83	111	139	167	194	222	250	278	306	333	361	389	417
1½ (38.1)	76	102	127	153	178	204	229	255	280	306	331	357	382
1⅝ (41.3)	70	94	117	141	165	188	212	235	259	282	306	329	353
1¾ (44.5)	65	87	109	131	153	175	196	218	240	262	284	306	327
1⅞ (47.6)	61	81	102	122	143	163	183	204	224	244	265	285	306
2 (50.8)	57	76	95	115	134	153	172	191	210	229	248	267	287
2¼ (57.2)	51	68	85	102	119	136	153	170	187	204	221	238	255
2½ (63.5)	46	61	76	92	107	122	137	153	168	183	199	214	229
2¾ (69.9)	42	56	69	83	97	111	125	139	153	167	181	194	208
3 (76.2)	38	51	64	76	89	102	115	127	140	153	166	178	191

*inches (mm)

This table also gives the cutting speeds produced by various rpm with the diameters given.

Metric Formula:

$$rpm = \frac{CS(mpm) \times 1000}{D(mm) \times \pi}$$

Where:

CS = Cutting speed
D = Diameter of cutter
π = Pi or 3.1416

Example: Calculate the rpm for a 3″ [76.2 mm] diameter cutter that is to mill steel at 90 fpm [27.43 mpm].

Inch Solutions:

A.

$$rpm = \frac{CS(fpm) \times 12}{D'' \times \pi}$$

$$rpm = \frac{90 \times 12}{3 \times 3.1416}$$

$$rpm = \frac{1080}{9.4248}$$

$$rpm = 114.6$$

(Compare this to Table 72-2.)

B.

$$rpm = \frac{4 \times CS(fpm)}{D''}$$

$$rpm = \frac{4 \times 90}{3}$$

$$rpm = \frac{360}{3}$$

$$rpm = 120$$

Metric Solution:

$$rpm = \frac{CS(mpm) \times 1000}{D(mm) \times \pi}$$

$$rpm = \frac{27.43 \times 1000}{76.2 \times 3.1416}$$

$$rpm = \frac{27430}{239.39}$$

$$rpm = 114.6$$

71-2 Feed Rate

The **feed rate** for milling is the rate at which the workpiece advances into the milling cutter. The feed rate, together with the width and depth of cut, determines the rate of metal removal.

The tendency for beginners is to use too light a feed and a cutting speed that is too high. This dulls the cutter rapidly and shortens tool life. In general, the feed rate should be as great as the cutting tool, the machine, and the work setup can stand without excessive vibration.

Table 71-3

Feeds in Inches (mm) per Tooth for Milling Roughing Cuts with High-Speed Steel Cutters

Material	Plain mills (heavy-duty)	Plain mills (light-duty)	Face mills	Side mills	End mills	Form-relieved mills	Slitting saws
Low-carbon steel, free-machining	.010 (.25)	.006 (.15)	.012 (.30)	.006 (.15)	.006 (.15)	.004 (.10)	.003 (.08)
Low-carbon steel	.008 (.20)	.005 (.13)	.010 (.25)	.005 (.13)	.005 (.13)	.003 (.08)	.003 (.08)
Medium-carbon steel	.008 (.20)	.005 (.13)	.009 (.23)	.005 (.13)	.004 (.10)	.003 (.08)	.002 (.05)
High-carbon steel, annealed	.004 (.10)	.003 (.08)	.006 (.15)	.003 (.08)	.002 (.05)	.002 (.05)	.002 (.05)
Stainless steel, free-machining	.008 (.20)	.005 (.13)	.010 (.25)	.005 (.13)	.004 (.10)	.003 (.08)	.002 (.05)
Stainless steel	.004 (.10)	.003 (.08)	.006 (.15)	.004 (.10)	.002 (.05)	.002 (.05)	.002 (.05)
Cast iron, soft	.012 (.30)	.008 (.20)	.014 (.36)	.008 (.20)	.008 (.20)	.004 (.10)	.004 (.10)
Cast iron, medium	.010 (.25)	.006 (.15)	.012 (.30)	.006 (.15)	.006 (.15)	.004 (.10)	.003 (.08)
Malleable iron	.010 (.25)	.006 (.15)	.012 (.30)	.006 (.15)	.006 (.15)	.004 (.10)	.003 (.08)
Brass and bronze, medium hardness	.010 (.25)	.008 (.20)	.013 (.33)	.008 (.20)	.006 (.15)	.004 (.10)	.003 (.08)
Aluminum and its alloys	.016 (.41)	.010 (.25)	.020 (.51)	.012 (.30)	.010 (.25)	.007 (.18)	.004 (.10)

These feeds are suggested for roughing cuts on heavy-duty machines, and they may be increased or decreased depending on machining conditions.

Feed

Each tooth on the milling cutter should cut a chip of proper size. On cutters with small, fine teeth, the chip should be small. The feed for each tooth on a milling cutter is indicated in **inches** (or mm) **per tooth** for each revolution of the cutter. Suggested average feeds, in inches and millimeters per tooth, for milling roughing cuts with high-speed steel cutters are listed in Table 71-3 (p. 525). On light-duty milling machines, these feeds should be reduced. For finishing cuts, the feeds should be reduced by 50%.

Inches per Minute

The feed rate on most milling machines is set in terms of **inches** [mm] **per minute.** The feed rates may be set from about ¼" to 30" [6.35 to 762 mm] per minute with feed-selector dials or levers on the machine.

Calculating the Rate of Feed

The following procedure is used for calculating the rate of feed:

1. Determine the desired cutting speed (see Table 71-1). For example, 100 fpm [30.5 mpm] for low-carbon steel.
2. Determine the rpm of the cutter (see Table 71-2).
3. Count the number of teeth on the cutter.
4. Determine the feed in inches (or mm) per tooth (see Table 71-3).
5. Calculate the feed rate with the following formula:

$$F = R \times T \times rpm$$

Where:

F = Feed rate in inches [or mm] per minute
R = Feed per tooth per revolution
T = Number of teeth on cutter
rpm = Revolutions per minute of the cutter

Example: Determine the feed rate for milling low-carbon steel at 100 fpm [30.5 mpm] and 127 rpm, using a heavy-duty plain milling cutter 3" [76.2 mm] in diameter with 10 teeth and a feed of 0.008" [0.20 mm] per tooth.

F = 0.008" [0.20 mm] × 10 × 127
F = 10.16 inches [254 mm] per minute

With the feed-selector dial or levers, adjust the feed rate to the feed closest to 10.16 inches [254 mm] per minute.

REVIEW REVIEW REVIEW REVIEW REVIEW

WORDS TO KNOW

cutting speed   feed rate

REVIEW QUESTIONS

1. What is meant by the cutting speed of a milling cutter?
2. Why is it important to know about cutting speed?
3. List the six factors that affect cutting speeds for milling.
4. Calculate the correct rpm for a ½" [12.7 mm] diameter end mill to cut aluminum at 400 fpm [122 mpm].
5. What is meant by the feed rate of a milling cutter?
6. Calculate the correct feed rate for a 6" [152.4 mm] diameter slitting saw to cut low-carbon steel at 100 fpm [30.5 mpm] with a feed per tooth of 0.003" [0.08 mm]. The cutter has 60 teeth.

UNIT

72

Milling Flat Surfaces, Bevels, and Chamfers

Broad flat surfaces are usually milled by **plain milling** or **face milling.**

Plain milling means to machine a flat surface with a plain milling cutter mounted on a horizontal milling machine arbor (see Fig. 70-1).

Face milling means to machine a flat surface parallel to the face (end) of a cutter. Face milling is done either with an inserted tooth face-milling cutter (Fig. 70-17) or with a shell end mill (Fig. 72-1).

Bevels and **chamfers** are flat surfaces cut at an angle to the main workpiece surfaces. A bevel extends from side to side, completely removing the perpendicular edge. A chamfer removes only a part of the perpendicular edge.

Bevels and chamfers are cut by using **angle cutters** (Fig. 72-2), by using plain cutters or end mills with the workpiece held at the desired angle (Fig. 72-1), or by positioning the head of a vertical milling machine to the desired angle (Fig. 72-3). Angular positioning of the workpiece may also be done with a swivel vise, a tilting or universal vise, or by using a fixture as in Figure 72-4.

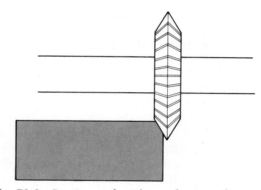

Fig. 72-2 *Cutting a chamfer with an angle cutter.*

Fig. 72-1 *Face-milling a flat angular surface with a shell end mill.* (Clausing)

Fig. 72-3 *Milling a chamfer with the head of a vertical milling machine set at the desired angle.* (Clausing)

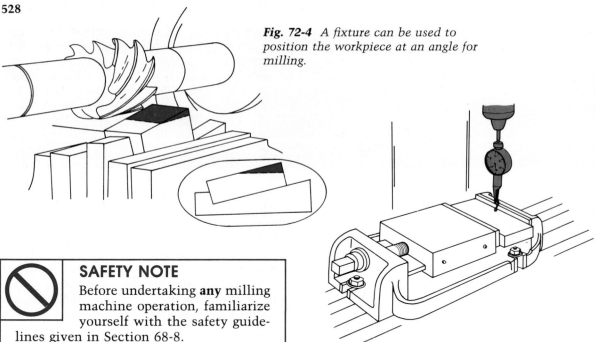

Fig. 72-4 *A fixture can be used to position the workpiece at an angle for milling.*

Procedure for Milling

1. Remove any burrs or surface irregularities on the workpiece by filing or grinding.
2. Mount a vise on the milling table after wiping clean both the table and the bottom of the vise. For maximum holding power, mount the workpiece in the vise with its longest dimension parallel to the vise jaws (Fig. 72-3). If the entire top of the workpiece is to be milled, the vise need not be precisely aligned with the worktable. However, for milling the end of the workpiece square with its sides, the vise jaws must be aligned either perpendicular or parallel to the machine column with a **dial indicator** (Fig. 72-5).
3. Obtain a sharp cutter of the type and size desired, and install it tightly in the proper position, using the correct arbor or adapter. **Be sure to wipe all mating surfaces clean before installing the cutter.**
4. Wipe the vise and workpiece clean. Also clean the **parallels** if they are to be used. Then mount the workpiece in the vise, seating it tightly against the parallels with a lead hammer. **When the workpiece is properly seated, the parallels cannot be moved by hand.**

Fig. 72-5 *Aligning the vise square with the machine column using a dial indicator. Adjust the vise until the dial indicator gives a constant reading across the entire vise jaw.*

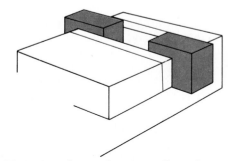

Fig. 72-6 *In order to clamp small workpieces securely that cannot be centered in the vise, place a block of the same size on the opposite side of the vise.*

When possible, center the workpiece in the vise so that the jaws remain parallel when tightened. Small workpieces that must extend from one side of the vise can only be held securely when balanced with a piece of the same size on the opposite side of the vise (Fig. 72-6).

5. Determine the correct rpm for the cutter and set the machine as near that speed as possible.
6. Determine and set the machine for the correct feed rate.
7. Position the workpiece so that the surface to be milled is centered in relation to the cutter.
8. Start the machine and check the directions of cutter rotation and table feed. **The cutter teeth must point in the same direction as the desired spindle rotation.** Stop the machine and correct if necessary.
9. Restart the machine and slowly advance the workpiece by hand-cranking the table until the workpiece just touches the cutter. Then stop the cutter rotation and back the workpiece away so as to position the cutter at the starting side of the cut. Adjust the table the amount desired for the **rough cut. Always leave 0.010″ to 0.030″ [0.25 to 0.76 mm] for a finish cut.** Lock all directions of table movement except the direction in which the cut will be made.
10. Start the cutter rotation and advance the workpiece to the cutter by hand-cranking the table. Then engage the power feed and let the cut proceed about ⅛″ [3 mm].

11. Stop the feed and cutter rotation. Back the workpiece away from the cutter so the workpiece can be measured. If the size of the workpiece is as planned, start the machine and finish the rough cut. Otherwise, adjust the machine before completing the cut.
12. At the end of the rough cut, stop the machine and adjust the rpm and feed rate for the finish cut, unless the rough cut was a heavy cut. In this case, start the machine and feed the workpiece past the cutter about ¼″ [6.35 mm] **at the same setting used for the rough cut.** A small amount of additional material may be removed, indicating the amount that the cutter had sprung away from its normal centerline during the rough cut. After carrying out this procedure, stop the cutter and measure the workpiece.
13. With the machine adjusted for the finish cut, start the cutter and again allow the cut to proceed about ⅛″ (3 mm). Stop the cutter, measure the workpiece, and make any adjustments in the depth of cut before completing the cut.

REVIEW REVIEW REVIEW REVIEW REVIEW

WORDS TO KNOW

bevel	dial indicator	finish cut	rough cut
chamfer	face milling	plain milling	

REVIEW QUESTIONS

1. Name two ways of milling broad, flat surfaces.
2. How is a bevel different from a chamfer?
3. Name three ways of milling bevels and chamfers.
4. What device makes possible precision alignment of the milling vise parallel to an axis of table travel?
5. After a heavy milling cut, what should be done before adjusting the machine for the finish cut?

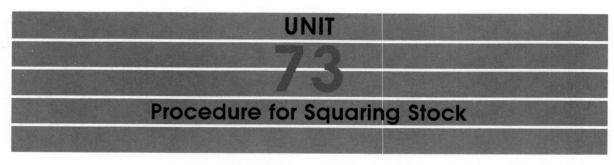

UNIT 73

Procedure for Squaring Stock

Sometimes all six surfaces of a rectangular workpiece must be machined so that opposite surfaces are accurately parallel, and adjacent surfaces are accurately at 90° to each other. This is known as **squaring stock.** The order in which the surfaces are machined is illustrated in Figure 73-1. The procedures for machining the surfaces are given below.

The First Broad Surface

Prepare the machine and use the procedure given in Unit 72.

The First Long Edge

1. Place the machined broad surface against the stationary vise jaw. Support it on a parallel if necessary.
2. Place a round rod of about ¼" [6.35 mm] diameter between the movable vise jaw and the workpiece (Fig. 73-2). Position the rod halfway between the bottom of the workpiece and the top of the vise jaw. Tighten the vise and seat the workpiece with a lead hammer.

   Use of the round rod assures that the machined surface will align itself parallel with the stationary vise jaw.
3. Mill off the top edge, using the basic procedure given in Unit 72.

The Second Long Edge

1. Loosen the vise, remove the workpiece, and file off the sharp edges.
2. Place the machined edge down in the vise, tighten the vise, and seat the workpiece with a lead hammer.
3. Proceed as for machining the first edge, but finish the width of the workpiece to the desired size.

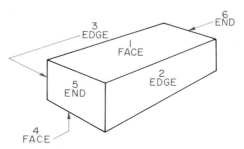

Fig. 73-1 *The order for machining surfaces when squaring a block.*

The Second Broad Surface

1. Place the workpiece in the vise with the finished broad surface down. Support it on parallels if necessary, and tighten it securely.
2. Proceed as in Unit 72, and finish the thickness of the workpiece to the desired size.
3. Remove the workpiece from the vise and file off the sharp edges.

The First End

1. To machine the ends square, the workpiece may be held vertically if it is strong enough not to bend under the pressure of cutting. Use a square to align the workpiece in the vise (Fig. 73-3).

   Long, thin workpieces should be positioned horizontally, broad surface down, for vertical milling (Fig. 73-4A). For horizontal milling, place the workpiece horizontally on edge, and use a vertical cut to square the end (Fig. 73-4B).
2. Remove just enough material to fully machine the end.

The Second End

1. Turn the stock end-for-end and retighten it in the vise.
2. Proceed as for machining the first end, but finish the workpiece to the desired length.
3. Remove the workpiece from the vise and remove the sharp edges with a file.

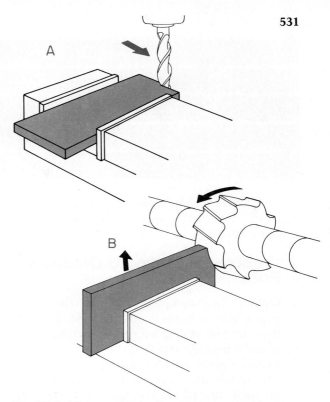

Fig. 73-4 *Two methods of squaring the ends of long, thin workpieces.*

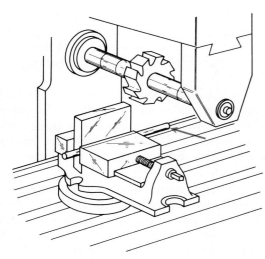

Fig. 73-2 *Stock positioned in a vise for machining the first edge. Placing a round rod between the workpiece and the moveable jaw assures that the first face will be pressed tightly against the fixed vise jaw.*

Fig. 73-3 *Using a square to align a workpiece vertically in the vise.*

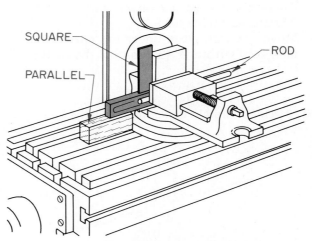

REVIEW REVIEW REVIEW REVIEW REVIEW

REVIEW QUESTIONS

1. What does "squaring stock" mean?
2. List the order in which the six surfaces of a block should be machined for squaring.

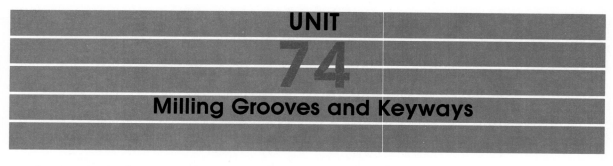

UNIT 74

Milling Grooves and Keyways

A groove or a keyway may be cut with a plain milling cutter, an end mill, or a Woodruff key cutter.

Procedure for Cutting a Groove in a Block

1. Obtain the workpiece, file off the sharp edges, and mount it in the vise. Be sure that the vise is aligned parallel with an axis of milling table travel.
2. Install a plain or side-milling cutter of suitable width and diameter if using a horizontal mill. Install an end mill of correct diameter if using a vertical mill.
3. Determine the correct cutter rpm and feed rate, and set the machine accordingly. Check for the proper directions of cutter rotation and table feed.
4. Move the workpiece under the cutter and raise it to within ⅛" [3.2 mm] of the cutter.

5. Locate the cutter where the groove is to be milled by measuring from the side of the workpiece with a steel rule or a depth micrometer (Fig. 74-1). Set the transverse table lock.
6. Start the cutter rotating and raise the table until the workpiece just touches the cutter. Then move the workpiece out from under the cutter, and raise the table the amount desired for the first cut. Set the vertical table lock.
7. Start the machine and feed the workpiece into the cutter by hand about ⅛" [3.2 mm]. Stop the cutter rotation, back the workpiece away, and check the position of the cut. Correct the position of the cut if necessary, then finish the cut (Fig. 74-2).
8. Make any additional cuts needed to machine the groove to the correct depth and width.

Fig. 74-1 *Locating the cutter for machining a groove.*

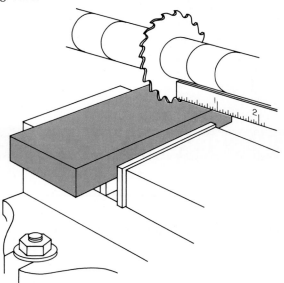

Fig. 74-2 *Machining a groove with a plain milling cutter.*

Procedure for Milling a T-slot or Dovetail Groove

1. Proceed as for cutting a plain groove as described above. Machine the groove to the dimensions of the vertical part of the T-slot, or the center part of the dovetail groove.
2. Install a T-slot or dovetail cutter of correct size. Determine the correct rpm and feed rate and set the machine.
3. Carefully align the T-slot or dovetail cutter, and set all table locks except for the direction of cut.
4. Start the cutter rotation and feed the workpiece into the cutter by hand. Stop and check the cutter position when the full cutter diameter has entered the workpiece.
5. Make any necessary corrections in the cutter position, then finish the cut (Figs. 74-3 and 74-4).

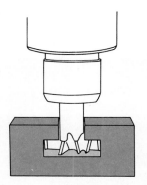

Fig. 74-3 *Cutting the horizontal part of a T-slot on a vertical milling machine.*

Fig. 74-4 *Milling a dovetail on a vertical milling machine.*

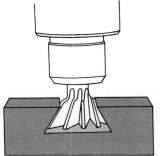

Procedure for Milling a Plain Keyway in a Shaft

1. Obtain the workpiece and mount it securely (Fig. 74-5).
2. Install a cutter of correct dimensions.
3. Raise the table until the cutter has passed the diameter of the workpiece. Using a strip of paper as a feeler gage between the cutter and the side of workpiece, move the workpiece slowly toward the cutter until you feel a pull on the paper (Fig. 74-6).

Fig. 74-5 *Milling a keyway in a shaft held in a vise.*

Fig. 74-6 *Using a piece of paper as an aid in locating a cutter against the side of the workpiece. To center the cutter, move the workpiece one-half its diameter plus one-half the cutter width plus the thickness of the paper.*

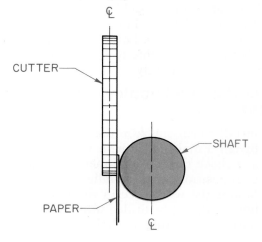

4. Lower the table until the cutter is about ⅛″ [3.2 mm] above the workpiece.
5. Center the cutter over the workpiece by moving the workpiece under the cutter an amount equal to half the workpiece diameter or width **plus** half the cutter width **plus** the thickness of the paper (Fig. 74-6).
6. Start the cutter and raise the workpiece until it just touches the cutter.

7. Back the workpiece away from the cutter, and raise the table the amount required for the size of the keyway being cut. Consult a handbook for machinists for standard keyway dimensions.
8. Advance the workpiece to the cutter, engage the power feed, and make the cut. At the end of the cut, stop the cutter and back the workpiece away. Measure the cut and make a second cut if necessary.

REVIEW REVIEW REVIEW REVIEW REVIEW

REVIEW QUESTIONS

1. List three kinds of cutters used for milling plain grooves.
2. Describe the procedure for milling T-slots and dovetails.
3. Describe how to center a cutter over a round shaft for cutting a keyway.

UNIT 75

Drilling and Boring Operations

Vertical milling machines are often used for drilling and other hole-machining operations. The micrometer dials on the table handwheels make it possible to locate the centers of holes very accurately.

Procedure for Locating and Drilling Holes

1. Install a drill chuck in the spindle.
2. Install a dial indicator in the drill chuck and check the vise alignment and the vertical position of the spindle.
3. Mount the workpiece in the vise so that holes will not be drilled into the vise bottom or supporting parallels.

4. Install an **edge finder** in the drill chuck. Position the end of the edge finder about ¼″ [6.35 mm] below the top surface of the workpiece (Fig. 75-1).
5. Set the spindle speed at about 600 rpm, and release the micrometer dials on the handwheels.
6. Start the machine and move the table in the longitudinal direction until the end of the workpiece contacts the side of the edge finder and makes it jump off-center (Fig. 75-2).
7. Move the edge finder above the top surface of the workpiece. Set the longitudinal micrometer dial for zero, then move it

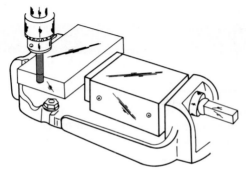

Fig. 75-1 *Using an edge finder to locate the center of a hole from the end of a workpiece.*

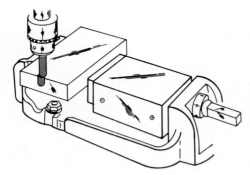

Fig. 75-2 *The end of the edge finder jumps off-center when it contacts the workpiece.*

half the edge finder diameter (usually .250″ [6.35 mm]) plus the distance the center of the hole is located from the end of the workpiece. Set the longitudinal table lock.

8. Move the workpiece in the transverse direction far enough to position the end of the edge finder ¼″ [6.35 mm] below the top surface of the workpiece.

9. Repeat steps 6 and 7 to locate the center of the hole in the transverse direction. Set the transverse table lock and stop the machine.

10. Remove the edge finder from the drill chuck.

11. Install a center drill in the drill chuck and drill a center hole.

12. Follow the center drill with drills and other drilling tools as required. **To provide room for tool changing, raise the quill or lower the table. DO NOT MOVE THE WORKPIECE LONGITUDINALLY OR TRANSVERSELY.**

13. After finishing the first hole, release the table locks and use the micrometer dials to position the workpiece accurately for the next hole. Remember to reset the table locks before center-drilling and drilling each hole.

Procedure for Boring

1. Using the procedure described above, locate and drill a hole about ¹⁄₁₆″ [1.6 mm] smaller than the diameter of the hole desired.

2. Install a boring head (Figs. 56-12 and 75-3).

3. Install a boring tool of suitable size in the boring head.

4. Adjust the boring head until the boring tool touches the side of the drilled hole. Withdraw the boring tool from the hole and adjust the boring head to enlarge the diameter by about .020″ [0.5 mm].

5. Start the machine, engage the power feed, and bore the hole about ⅛″ [3.2 mm] deep. Stop the machine, withdraw the boring tool, and measure the hole diameter.

6. If the hole is not oversize, start the machine and finish boring the hole.

7. Stop the machine, withdraw the boring bar, and measure the hole.

8. Adjust the boring head for the finish cut, start the machine, and bore the hole about ⅛″ [3.2 mm] deep. Then stop the machine and measure the hole.

9. Adjust the boring head, if necessary, to make the hole the correct diameter. Then continue with the finishing cut.

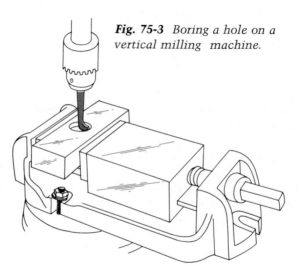

Fig. 75-3 *Boring a hole on a vertical milling machine.*

REVIEW   REVIEW   REVIEW   REVIEW   REVIEW

REVIEW QUESTIONS

1. Describe how an edge finder is used for precision hole location.
2. How much undersize should a hole be drilled if it is to be finished to size by boring?
3. How is a boring head able to bore holes of different sizes?

UNIT

76

Dividing or Indexing Operations

The dividing, or **indexing,** head is used in milling operations to divide a circle into any number of equal parts (Fig. 76-1). One of the most common types of dividing heads is the **universal spiral dividing** head shown in Figure 76-2. Indexing is necessary to machine square or hexagonal bolt heads, to cut gears and splines, and to cut flutes in reamers, taps, and other cutting tools. Indexing as a function means that the dividing head spindle is rotated a certain angle. The size of the angle is determined by the number of holes, or spaces on the circle of holes on the index plate, that the dividing head index plate is moved.

The main parts of a universal dividing head are shown in Figure 76-2A and B. The **index crank** is attached to a worm shaft that has a **worm gear** on the end inside the dividing head. The **work spindle** has a **40-tooth worm wheel** on the end inside the dividing head. The worm wheel meshes with the worm gear on its shaft. Thus, when the index crank is turned 40 complete turns, the work spindle turns one complete turn or 360°. Or, one turn of the index crank causes the work spindle to revolve through 9° ($40 \times 9° = 360°$).

The **index plunger pin** fits into a hole in the **index plate** and holds the crank in position so that the spindle cannot turn. Thus, the index plunger pin must be withdrawn from the hole before the crank can be turned.

Fig. 76-1 *Using a dividing head to space holes evenly around a circle.*

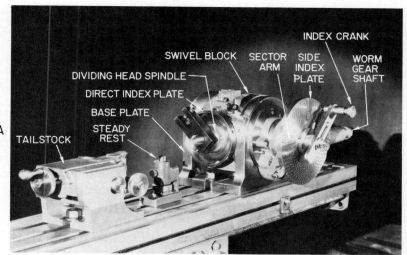

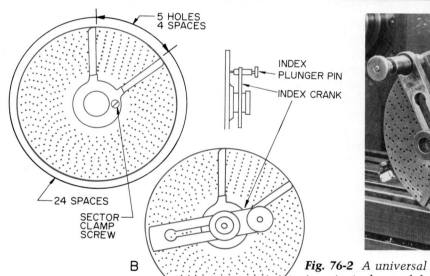

Fig. 76-2 *A universal spiral dividing head with its principal parts labeled.* (Cincinnati Milacron)

The **plate stop** holds the index plate in position so that it cannot turn. However, the index plate must turn for operations involving the machining of a helix (spiral).

As was explained in Section 69-2, the workpiece in a dividing head operation can be mounted on a lathe mandrel, which is held between the **spindle center** and the center of a tailstock (Fig. 69-4). Short workpieces may be mounted in a 3-jaw universal chuck (Fig. 69-5).

76-1 Direct Indexing

Direct indexing is the simplest form of indexing, but its use is limited. Each dividing head has a **direct index plate** attached to its spindle so that the ratio of its movement is 1:1 with the spindle. Direct index plates have 24 equally spaced holes.

The 24-hole direct indexing plate can be used for dividing a circle into 24, 12, 8, 6, 4, 3, or 2 equal divisions. Dividing the number of equal spaces desired into 24 gives the number of holes that must be indexed. For example, to cut a square on the end of a shaft: 24 ÷ 4 = 6. Indexing 6 holes for each cut will produce the desired square.

Angles in multiples of 15° can also be indexed. Dividing 15 into the angle desired gives the number of holes to be indexed for moving the number of degrees desired. For example: 120° ÷ 15 = 8 holes.

For direct indexing, first retract the index plunger pin from the index plate. Next, rotate the index plate through the number of spaces desired by turning the index crank. Then, reinsert the plunger pin in the hole in the index plate. On some dividing heads, it is possible to disengage the worm gear attached to the index crank. When the **quick index plunger pin** is withdrawn, the direct index plate can be moved by hand without turning the index crank, which provides faster indexing. After each desired turn of the direct index plate, the quick index plunger pin must be engaged to hold the plate in position.

76-2

Plain Indexing

Plain indexing, also called **simple indexing,** makes it possible to index many divisions not possible by the direct indexing method. Divisions of 5, 7, 9, 11, 13, and many other numbers of equally spaced divisions can be indexed by the plain indexing method.

The worm shaft must be engaged with the work spindle for plain indexing. The work spindle is turned by withdrawing the index plunger pin and turning the index crank. The plunger pin is then set again while the workpiece is milled.

The index plate has several circles of holes. A different number of holes is equally spaced on each **hole circle.** Some dividing heads have holes on each side of the index plate. The plate may be reversed for the desired hole circle. An index plate of the type in

Figure 76-2 has the following circles of equally spaced holes:

One side—
24-25-28-30-34-37-38-39-41-42-43
Other side—
46-47-49-51-53-54-57-58-59-62-66

Two **sector arms** are located on the front of the index plate. The arms can be swiveled freely around the plate. A **lock screw** is used to lock the two arms apart for a space representing a fraction of a hole circle. It is possible this way to index a fractional part of a revolution with the index crank.

The following formula can be used to determine the number of revolutions of the index crank for a desired number of equally spaced divisions:

$$T = \frac{40}{N}$$

Where:

T = Number of turns, or fractional part of turns, of the index crank

40 = Number of teeth on the worm wheel

N = Number of divisions desired

Example: Determine the number of revolutions of the index crank for indexing each tooth space for an 18-tooth spur gear.

Solution:

$$T = \frac{40}{18}$$

$$T = 2\frac{4}{18} = 2\frac{2}{9} \text{ turns}$$

The fractional part of a revolution of the index crank is established between the two sector arms. To determine the distance that the arms must be set apart, select a circle with a number of holes that is divisible by the denominator of the fraction. Using the above example, the number 54 is divisible by 9 (54 ÷ 9 = 6, or 1/9 = 6/54). Thus 2/9 = 12/54. The sector arms are then spaced with 12 spaces between holes on the 54-hole circle. (**NOTE:** This is the space between 13 holes. It is the number of spaces between holes that is important. It is like counting the spaces between the fingers of your hand. You have four spaces between five fingers.)

During the indexing for the 18-tooth gear above, each gear tooth is indexed 2¹²⁄₅₄ revolutions. That is, 2 complete turns of the index crank, plus the ¹²⁄₅₄ revolution between the sector arms.

76-3 Angular Indexing

Plain indexing can also be used for indexing angles. For each turn of the index crank, the workpiece will rotate through ¼₀th of a circle or 9° (360° ÷ 40 = 9°). Therefore, to find the number of index crank turns needed to index for a given angle, simply divide the angle desired by 9.

Example: Index for two holes to be drilled 45° apart.

Solution:
$$T = 45 \div 9 = 5$$

After drilling the first hole, the index crank would be turned 5 full turns.

Other more complex methods of indexing are sometimes necessary. These are described in handbooks for machinists.

REVIEW REVIEW REVIEW REVIEW REVIEW

WORDS TO KNOW

angular indexing	index plunger pin	sector arms	worm gear
direct indexing	plain indexing	simple indexing	worm shaft
direct index plate	plate stop	universal spiral	worm wheel
index crank	quick index plunger	dividing head	
index plate	pin	work spindle	

REVIEW QUESTIONS

1. What is the purpose of a dividing or indexing head?
2. List the number of equal divisions that can be obtained by direct indexing.
3. How does plain, or simple, indexing differ from direct indexing?
4. What dividing head feature makes it possible to keep track of less than full turns of the index crank?
5. Using plain indexing, calculate the number of index crank turns required to divide a circle into 15 equal parts.
6. Using plain indexing, calculate the number of index crank turns required to mill two flats 135° apart.

Theresa Ruggeri found her special place in metalworking by accident. When her young daugher entered pre-school, she began to look for an opportunity to increase the family income. Nearby was a small, specialized broaching plant that would hire women. She applied for a job, was hired, and has enjoyed working there ever since.

Although Theresa had not had any metalwork training in high school, she did have qualities that were important in learning to operate broaching machinery. She could think in an orderly manner, so she had little difficulty in learning operations involving a series of steps. She accepted the fact that the work would sometimes be oily and messy. And she was patient with the routine. Often a broaching machine will turn out 50,000 identical pieces!

Theresa became efficient at running both the vertical and horizontal broaching machines used to make automotive parts, dental tools, and aircraft components. Then she was taught to operate a machine that de-burrs parts made by the broaches. Removing ragged edges is crucial to the correct functioning of many parts.

Theresa has been at the plant for 10 years now and does inspection work in addition to operating machinery. The plant has a friendly, family-like atmosphere. Another benefit for Theresa is the satisfaction of knowing that her high-quality work really makes a difference wherever the broached parts are used.

Theresa Ruggeri
Broaching Machine
Operator

UNIT
77
Shaping and Planing Machines

Shaping and planing machines cut by moving either the tool or the workpiece back and forth in a straight line, with a cutting stroke and a return stroke.

Both machines use a single-point cutting tool. A shaper cuts by moving the workpiece across the path of a cutting tool that moves back and forth (Fig. 77-1). A planer moves the tool across the path of the workpiece that goes back and forth (Fig. 77-2).

Horizontal shapers (Fig. 77-3) are used primarily for machining flat surfaces, which may be horizontal, vertical, or angular. **Vertical shapers** (Fig. 77-4), also known as **slotters,** are used more for machining keyways, splines (a series of grooves cut around a circular part), and other shapes in the hubs (center parts) of large gears, pulleys, and flywheels.

The size of a shaper is usually described by the maximum length of stroke and the type of cutting it will do: light-, medium (standard), or heavy-duty. The maximum stroke lengths for shapers vary from 7" [178 mm] to 36" [914 mm]. On most shapers the following adjustments can be made manually, without the machine being turned on:

1. tool-slide position
2. horizontal table movement
3. table elevation
4. length of stroke
5. position of stroke
6. cutting speed selection
7. feed adjustment.

The workpiece must be held securely in position for machining on the machine table. In most cases a machine vise bolted to the top or side of the table is used, along with fixtures such as precision parallels.

Planers and shapers require many strokes of the tool or workpiece to complete the cutting operation. Because milling machines can remove metal at a more rapid rate, they have almost completely replaced shapers and planers for production work. However, shaper cutting tools are easy to grind and maintain.

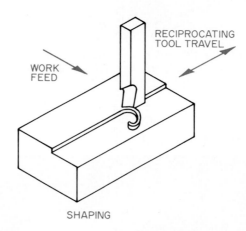

Fig. 77-1 *The basic principles of shaping.*

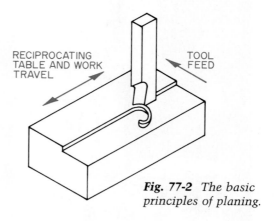

Fig. 77-2 *The basic principles of planing.*

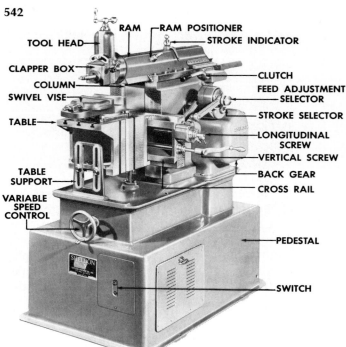

Fig. 77-3 *A 12" (305 mm) horizontal shaper with its principal parts labeled.* (Sheldon Machine Co., Inc.)

Fig. 77-4 *A vertical shaper.*

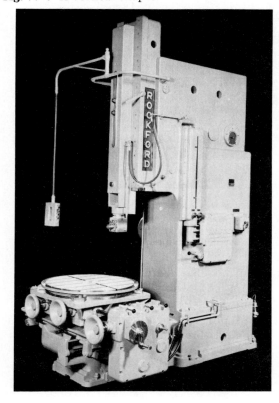

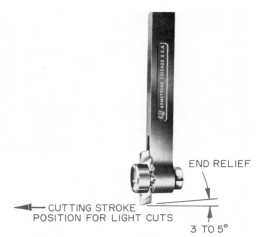

Fig. 77-5 *A shaper and planer toolholder. Cutting tools should have a 3° to 5° end relief.*

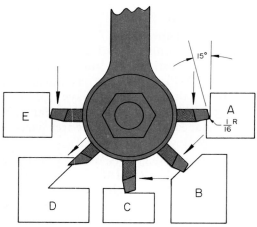

Fig. 77-6 *Various tool positions in a shaper and planer swivel-head toolholder. (A) Vertical cut. (B) Angular cut. (C) Horizontal cut. (D) Angular dovetail cut. (E) Vertical cut.*

Consequently, the shaper is still used in some maintenance machine shops, tool-and-die shops, and school shops.

A standard shaper and planer toolholder (Fig. 77-5) holds the cutting tool parallel to the shank of the toolholder and perpendicular to the surface of the work. Any desired back-rake angle must be ground on the tool bit.

With the shaper and planer toolholder, the tool may be rotated to five different positions for various kinds of cuts (Fig. 77-6).

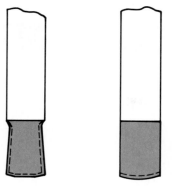

SQUARE-NOSE
FINISHING TOOL   ELLIPTICAL-NOSE
FINISHING TOOL

Fig. 77-7 *Tools for finishing cuts on shapers and planers.*

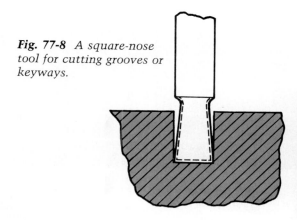

Fig. 77-8 *A square-nose tool for cutting grooves or keyways.*

Fig. 77-9 *A large double-housing planer.* (Rockford Machine Tool Co.)

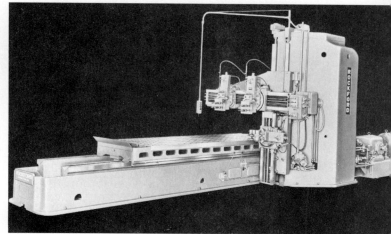

Fig. 77-10 *A large open-side planer.* (Rockford Machine Tool Co.)

Shaper tool bits are ground in a manner similar to lathe tool bits. Roughing tools (Fig. 77-6A, B, and C), finishing tools (Fig. 77-7), square-nose tools (Fig. 77-8) and dovetail tools (Fig. 77-6D) are some of the common shapes. A left-hand tool is most often used.

Planers are used mostly for machining workpieces that are too large for shapers. **Double-housing planers** (Fig. 77-9) have two vertical columns. A cross-rail from column to column carries the tool head, so that it can be fed across the moving workpiece. **Open-side planers** (Fig. 77-10) support the cross-rail from a single vertical column. Workpieces can overhang the table of this planer on the open side. The basic procedures and principles used in machining with a shaper also apply to planer operations.

Do not attempt to operate a shaper until after your instructor has:

1. demonstrated its proper setup and operation.
2. explained the operator and machine safety rules for using a shaper.
3. given you permission to set up the shaper.
4. approved your setup before starting the machine.

REVIEW REVIEW REVIEW REVIEW REVIEW

WORDS TO KNOW

cross-rail	horizontal shaper	single-point tool	tool-head assembly
double-housing planer	open-side planer	slotter	vertical shaper

REVIEW QUESTIONS

1. Name two kinds of shapers and the kind of machining done by each kind.
2. Name two kinds of planers.
3. How are planers different from shapers?

UNIT
78
Broaching Machines

Broaching machines, like shapers, cut by moving the tool in a straight line, with a cutting stroke and a return stroke. Broaching machines, however, usually complete the cutting operation in one stroke of the tool. These machines use specially designed cutting tools called **broaches** (Fig. 78-1).

Broaches contain rows of cutting edges or teeth, each of which removes a small amount of material. Each tooth is a few thousandths of an inch (hundredths of a millimeter) ''higher'' than the tooth ahead of it (Fig. 78-2). The depth of the cut, the pitch (distance from tooth to tooth), and other design features of a broach depend on the material and design of the workpiece.

Fig. 78-1 *Pull-type broaches. Note the tiny broach in the man's right hand.* (Apex Broach & Machine Co.)

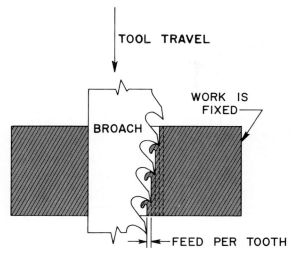

Fig. 78-2 *Action on a broaching tool.*

Fig. 78-4 *Examples of parts shaped partly by surface broaching.* (Apex Broach & Machine Co.)

Fig. 78-3 *A keyway broach cutting an internal keyway in a gear.* (DuMont)

Fig. 78-5 *A horizontal broaching machine.* (Apex Broach & Machine Co.)

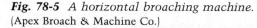

Most broaching machines pull the broach through or across the workpiece. Some short broaches may be pushed through the work. **Internal broaching** is done inside a hole in the workpiece. It is used especially for forming holes of complex shapes. Keys, splines, gear teeth, and holes with irregular shapes are often machined by broaching (Fig. 78-3). **Surface or external broaching** is done on the outside of the workpiece. Figure 78-4 shows several parts with features made by surface broaching.

Broaching machines are of two types, according to the direction of the broaching tool movement: **horizontal** or **vertical** (Fig. 78-5 (p. 545) and Fig. 78-6). On some machines the broach is fixed in position and the workpiece moves. Vertical machines may either pull up or pull down the broach. To reduce idle time the return stroke in broaching machines is often two or more times as fast as the cutting stroke.

Broaching can be used to machine complex parts that would be too costly to produce by other methods. It is rapid, accurate, and leaves a smooth finish. Broaching is widely used in manufacturing automotive parts and many other metal products that are made in large quantities.

Broaching Comes to the Rescue

T E C H N O L O G I E S   A N D   P R A C T I C E S

Imagine an executive planning session where the design drawings for a new five-cycle washing machine are presented. The design looks good, but a small detail is causing a big problem. The special piece that is critical for shifting speeds will take four separate milling operations. The cost of producing this one "widget" would make the final price of the washer too high to be competitive.

The head manufacturing engineer suggests that they broach the part. In the beginning, it would mean a greater investment (the special broaching equipment needed). But in the long run, each "widget" would cost less. The savings to the company—and the customer—would be considerable.

By the end of the session, the executives decide on broaching.

Any metal that can be machined can be broached. And almost any shape that can be made with a straight-line cutting motion can be made with a broaching tool.

Tooling is the heart of the broaching process. Most broaches are made to fit the special needs of a single customer. The broach designed to machine our "widget" would be useless to a manufacturer of gears for diesel trains.

What the planning session executives liked most about broaching was its low cost for their high-production needs. The savings come from the fewer sharpening times per parts broached as compared with other machining methods. In a job in which a milling cutter has to be sharpened every 5,000 parts, a broach might have to be sharpened only every 80,000 parts. There are big savings in setup time, too. One broaching setup can take the place of 15 milling setups.

If large quantities of parts are needed, broaching is the ideal machining method. Odd-shaped "widgets" never have to hold up production.

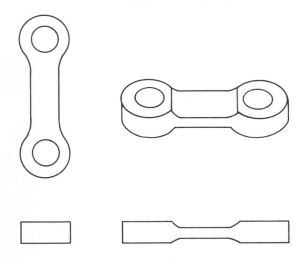

Fig. 78-6 *A vertical broaching machine.* (Apex Broach & Machine Co.)

REVIEW   REVIEW   REVIEW   REVIEW   REVIEW

Words to know

broach   internal broaching   surface broaching   vertical broaching
horizontal
  broaching

Review questions

1. Name the two general kinds of broaching operations.
2. What are the different kinds of broaching machines?
3. How is cutting done on broaching machines?
4. What are the advantages of the broaching process?
5. For what kind of production is broaching best suited?

PART

19

Precision Grinding

William Collins is approaching the end of a four-year apprenticeship and will soon be a journeyman precision grinder. He was introduced to grinding during his two years of vocational machining in high school. On the job, however, he has developed a much fuller knowledge of tool and cutter grinding.

As he moved through his apprenticeship, William discovered that learning precision grinding requires much patience and practice. He had to familiarize himself with the properties of metals and the procedures for sharpening a wide variety of metal-cutting tools. He also had to become acquainted with the industry codes for marking grinding wheels.

Choosing the correct wheel for the job is one of the major decisions William must make. He works with carbide, hardened steel, and stainless steel tools, and he must pick the right grade of wheel and grain size for each metal. Depending on the type of milling cutter, reamer, or tap to be ground, he decides to use certain cup or disc wheels.

How the workpiece is positioned on the grinding machine is also important. William must calculate how much to offset the center of the tool from the center of the grinding wheel. To work efficiently, he must also determine the best point to begin grinding.

While William always enjoyed working with machinery, he faced some real challenges during his apprenticeship. He learned that difficult machining problems could be solved by patiently working out the correct procedure. William knows that the end of his training period does not mean the end of learning or decision-making. But now he is well-equipped to deal with whatever may arise.

William Collins
Tool and Cutter Grinder

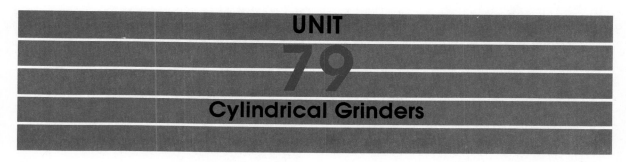

UNIT 79
Cylindrical Grinders

Grinding is a machining process that removes metal from the workpiece either with a grinding wheel, an abrasive belt, a disc, or some other form of abrasive.

The term **grinding** is used when a relatively small amount of metal is removed, as in tool sharpening and in finishing hardened steel workpieces to size. The use of abrasive tools for rapid removal of large amounts of metal to produce a workpiece of desired shape and size is referred to as **abrasive machining.**

79-1 Introduction to Precision Grinding

Grinding operations can be classified under two headings—precision and nonprecision. **Nonprecision** grinding involves the removal of metal that usually cannot be removed efficiently in any other way and that does not require accuracy. Examples include reshaping cold chisels and center punches, snagging the rough spots from castings, and grinding excess metal from welds. Nonprecision grinding is usually done on a pedestal grinder or with a portable grinder.

Precision grinding requires grinding that is accurate to specified size limits.

Grinding many kinds of machine parts to tolerances of plus or minus 0.0001" [0.0025 mm] is a common industrial requirement. Special parts for precision instruments and gages are sometimes ground to tolerances of plus or minus 0.000020" (20 microinches, or 20 millionths of one inch [0.00051 mm]). Precision grinding, therefore, makes it possible to machine to closer tolerances than with other common chip-machining operations.

Many parts are rough-machined first, then machined to size by grinding. Parts that are heat-treated often become warped or change size during heat-treatment. After heat treatment, they usually are too hard to be machined by conventional methods. They must, therefore, be machined to final size by grinding.

Machines are made for many kinds of precision grinding operations. **Cylindrical grinders** used for grinding round surfaces are discussed in this unit. **Tool and cutter grinders** are discussed in Unit 80. **Surface grinders** used for grinding flat surfaces are discussed in Units 81 and 82.

79-2 Cylindrical Grinding

Cylindrical grinding is the grinding of parts with a cylindrical or conical (tapered) shape.

The relationship between the grinding wheel and the workpiece for cylindrical grinding operations is shown in Figure 79-1. Roughing cuts vary from 0.001" to 0.004" [0.025 to 0.10 mm] deep, depending upon the shape and size of the workpiece and the size and rigidity of the machine. Finishing cuts usually vary from 0.0002" to 0.001" [0.005 to 0.025 mm] deep.

There are several types of cylindrical grinding machines. **Plain cylindrical grinding** machines can only grind cylindrical surfaces and shallow tapers (Fig. 79-2). **Universal cylindrical grinding** machines are much more versatile. The machine table can be swiveled for grinding long tapers (Fig. 79-3). The headstock

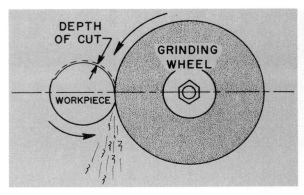

Fig. 79-1 *The relationship of the grinding wheel and the workpiece in cylindrical grinding.*

Fig. 79-3 *Grinding a taper on a universal cylindrical grinding machine with the table swiveled.* (Brown and Sharpe Mfg. Co.)

Fig. 79-2 *Grinding a small part in a plain cylindrical grinding machine.* (Henry Felde Tool & Machine Co.)

may be swiveled for grinding steep tapers. It also can be swiveled 90° for **face-grinding** flat surfaces (Fig. 79-4).

For cylindrical grinding of long parts, the workpiece is mounted between the **headstock** and **footstock centers,** similar to mounting work between centers on a lathe (Fig. 79-3). Short workpieces are held in a chuck mounted on the headstock as shown in Figures 79-4 and 79-5.

79-3 Internal Grinding

Internal grinding produces a smooth and accurate surface in a cylindrical hole (Fig. 79-5). The internal surface may be ground straight or tapered.

For production purposes, special internal grinding machines are used. However, in most small machine shops, internal grinding is done with an **internal grinding attachment** on a universal cylindrical grinding machine (Fig. 79-5).

79-4 Centerless Grinding

This is a form of cylindrical grinding. It is done without using center holes or a chuck for holding the workpiece while grinding. Center-

Fig. 79-4 *A universal cylindrical grinding machine with its headstock swiveled 90 degrees for face grinding.* (Brown and Sharpe Mfg. Co.)

Fig. 79-5 *Internal grinding on a universal cylindrical grinding machine with an internal grinding attachment.* (Brown and Sharpe Mfg. Co.)

Fig. 79-6 *A centerless grinding machine grinding a piece of tubing.* (Cincinnati Milacron)

less grinding is done with a **centerless grinding machine** (Fig. 79-6). The relationship of the workpiece, the regulating wheel, and the grinding wheel on centerless grinding machines is shown in Figure 79-7. Straight or tapered objects such as spindles, piston pins, roller bearings, and lathe centers are ground by this method. **Form grinding** may also be done with centerless grinders.

79-5

Form Grinding

In form grinding, the face of the grinding wheel is cut to the form or profile of the shape to be ground. When the workpiece is ground, it takes on the shape of the grinding wheel face (Fig. 79-8).

Grinding wheels are available with faces having standard shapes for grinding fillets, rounded corners, and grooves. For other nonstandard form-grinding operations, the face of the grinding wheel is cut to the desired shape with a diamond dressing tool.

Fig. 79-7 *In centerless grinding the combined notion of the grinding wheel and the regulating wheel cause the workpiece to rotate as it is supported in place by the workrest blade.*

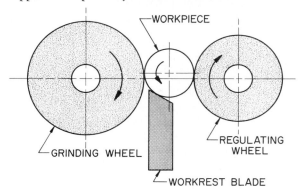

WORKPIECE

GRINDING WHEEL

REGULATING WHEEL

WORKREST BLADE

Fig. 79-8 *Abrasive machining a worm screw from a solid workpiece by form-grinding.* (Norton Co.)

REVIEW   REVIEW   REVIEW   REVIEW   REVIEW

Words to Know

abrasive machining	footstock	nonprecision	surface grinder
centerless grinder	form grinding	grinding	tool and cutter
cylindrical grinding	internal grinding	plain cylindrical	grinder
face grinding	internal grinding	grinder	universal cylindrical
	attachment	precision grinding	grinder
		regulating wheel	

Review Questions

1. Explain the difference between grinding and abrasive machining.
2. Explain the difference between nonprecision and precision grinding.
3. What is the main advantage of precision grinding?
4. How do plain and universal grinders differ?
5. What is internal grinding?
6. What is centerless grinding?
7. Explain how form grinding is done.

UNIT

80

Tool and Cutter Grinders

Tool and cutter grinding is the sharpening of milling cutters, counterbores, reamers, taps, and similar metal-cutting tools. Tool and cutter grinding machines are especially designed for this purpose.

Cutting tools must be sharp in order to cut efficiently. When they become dull, surface finish quality rapidly worsens, workpiece size changes, and increased horsepower is required to make them cut.

The tool and cutter grinding machine setup for sharpening a plain-tooth helical milling cutter is shown in Figure 80-1. Figure 80-2 shows the setup for sharpening a form-relieved milling cutter, which is used for machining curved surfaces. Figure 80-3 shows the arrangement for sharpening an end milling cutter. Tool and cutter grinding may be done with either of two types of grinding wheels, the **disc wheel** and the **cup wheel.** The use of a particular wheel depends on the kind of tool or cutter to be sharpened.

The setup for disc wheel grinding. Figure 80-4 shows the arrangement of the cutter, tooth rest, and grinding wheel for sharpening cutters with a disc wheel. The **tooth rest** is set at the same height as the cutter centerline. The amount of offset between the centerlines of the grinding wheel and the cutter determines the clearance angle ground on the cutter.

Fig. 80-2 The setup for grinding the face of teeth on form-relieved milling cutters. (Cincinnati Milling Machine Co.)

Fig. 80-3 The setup for grinding an end mill with helical teeth. (Cincinnati Milling Machine Co.)

Fig. 80-1 Grinding a plain helical milling cutter on a tool and cutter grinder. (Cincinnati Milling Machine Co.)

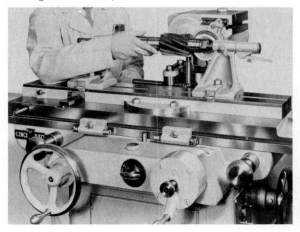

The setup for cup wheel grinding. Figure 80-5 shows the arrangement of the tooth rest, cutter, and grinding wheel for sharpening cutters with a cup wheel. The tooth rest is set the necessary distance below the cutter centerline for the desired clearance angle. Recommended clearance angles and offset amounts may be found in handbooks for machinists.

TECHNOLOGIES AND PRACTICES

New Machines for a New Industry

To some turn-of-the-century Americans, the new-fangled motor car was a nuisance. To others, the automobile provided a stimulus to create new production methods and machinery. After 1900, many companies made cars by assembling parts manufactured by other companies. Competition between the parts manufacturers was strong. One person who met the challenge of this competition was Massachusetts engineer Charles H. Norton.

During the late 1800's, Norton worked for a company noted for its grinding machines. At that time, these tools were used only for finishing. By the time a workpiece came to a grinder, it was already cut to within 0.002" [.508 mm] of its final size. Norton designed a more accurate machine for the firm, but it was still considered a precision finishing tool.

In 1890, Norton became a partner in a Detroit tool-making firm. Soon afterwards, he saw the need for manufacturing auto parts faster and more accurately. He got the idea for a precision production grinder that would do away with many separate machining operations. It would be able to take a workpiece from the rough machined stage, remove excess metal, and quickly finish it to a precise form. Other metal cutting, such as turning and filing, would be bypassed.

To accomplish this operation, Norton used a grinding wheel with a two-foot diameter, which was unusual at the time. He continued development despite ridicule and produced a heavy production grinder in 1900.

The 1903 Norton grinder cut crankshaft machining time from five hours to 15 minutes. A grinder introduced in 1911 turned out one-piece camshafts. Up to that time, the shafts had been assembled from several separate parts.

Large-scale mass production of automobiles would have been difficult, if not impossible, without precision grinding machines. The "horseless carriage" was here to stay, thanks to the perseverance of Charles Norton.

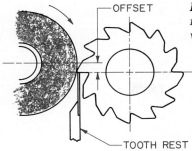

Fig. 80-4 *The arrangement of the tooth rest, cutter, and grinding wheel for disc wheel sharpening.*

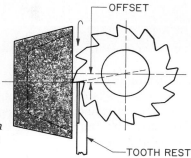

Fig. 80-5 *The arrangement of the tooth rest, cutter, and grinding wheel for cup wheel sharpening.*

REVIEW REVIEW REVIEW REVIEW REVIEW

Words to Know

cup wheel grinding　　disc wheel grinding　　tool and cutter grinding　　tooth rest

Review Questions

1. Name several kinds of tools that may be resharpened on a tool and cutter grinder.
2. What two grinding wheel shapes are commonly used for sharpening milling cutter teeth?
3. How is the clearance angle established when resharpening milling cutters with a disc wheel? Cup wheel?

UNIT
81

Surface-Grinding Machines

Surface grinding produces a smooth, true, flat surface on parts. Also, when the face of the grinding wheel is shaped to some special contour, form grinding may be done with a surface grinding machine.

81-1 Surface-grinding Machines

Surface-grinding machines can be classified as those with **horizontal spindles** (Figs. 81-1 and 81-2) and those with **vertical spindles** (Figs. 81-3 and 81-4).

Horizontal-spindle surface grinders are most common in small machine shops, tool-and-die shops, maintenance shops, and school shops. With this machine, the workpiece is mounted on the table, usually on a **magnetic chuck** (Fig. 81-5), in a vise (Fig. 81-6), or bolted to the table (Fig. 81-11).

One kind of horizontal-spindle surface grinder is equipped with a **reciprocating table,** which can move back and forth, or **reciprocate,** longitudinally. This may be done with power or manual feed. As the table reciprocates, it is fed crosswise under the grinding wheel (Fig. 81-7). The wheel takes a new cut each time the table reverses direction.

Some horizontal-spindle surface-grinding machines are equipped for handfeeding only (Fig. 81-1). Others are equipped with automatic power feeds for longitudinal and cross feeding (Fig. 82-1). These machines can also be fed manually with the table handwheels.

Fig. 81-2 *A surface grinder with a horizontal spindle and rotary table attachment.* (Harig Products, Inc.)

Fig. 81-1 *A handfeed surface grinder with a wet-grinding attachment.* (Brown & Sharpe Mfg. Co.)

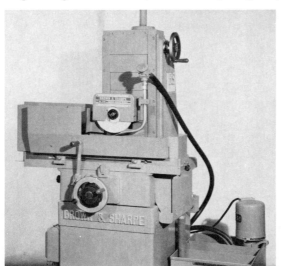

Fig. 81-3 *A surface grinder with a vertical spindle and reciprocating table.* (Harig Products, Inc.)

Fig. 81-4 *Surface grinding a large steel block on a large vertical spindle grinding machine with a rotary table.* (Norton Company)

Fig. 81-5 *A surface grinder equipped with a magnetic chuck.* (Brown & Sharpe Mfg. Co.)

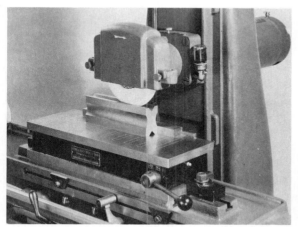

Fig. 81-6 *Surface grinding a workpiece held in a machine vise.* (Brown & Sharpe Mfg. Co.)

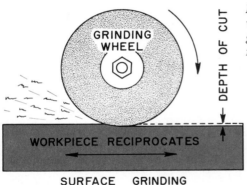

Fig. 81-7 *The relationship of the grinding wheel and the workpiece on a surface grinder with a horizontal spindle and reciprocating table.*

A second kind of horizontal-spindle surface grinder is equipped with a **rotary table** (Fig. 81-2). The rotary table is mounted on top of a longitudinal table. The workpiece is mounted on a magnetic chuck, which revolves on the rotary table underneath the grinding wheel. As grinding takes place, the longitudinal table is fed in either direction under the grinding wheel.

Vertical-spindle surface-grinding machines have the grinding wheel mounted on a vertical spindle. Workpieces to be ground are mounted on the table, which may be reciprocating (Fig. 81-3) or revolving (Fig. 81-4). Vertical-spindle machines provide a larger area of contact between the grinding wheel and the workpiece. Therefore, they grind more rapidly than horizontal-spindle machines. For this reason, they are widely used for production grinding, where many parts must be ground rapidly. Since more heat is also created, a cutting fluid is used while grinding with machines of this type.

Size

The size of surface-grinding machines is designated by the size of the **working area** of the table. A size 6″ × 18″ [152 × 457 mm] machine, as shown in Figure 82-1, has a table with a working area of 6″ [152 mm] cross travel and 18″ [457 mm] longitudinal table travel. The maximum height of workpieces that may be ground is also an important dimension in describing the size of a surface grinder.

81-2 Holding Work for Surface Grinding

Workpieces of various shapes and sizes can be mounted on the surface-grinding machine in many ways. The following methods are suggested.

By using a magnetic chuck (Fig. 81-5): A magnetic chuck with approximately the same working area as the machine table is mounted on the table. Workpieces made of magnetic materials can be held securely by this method.

SAFETY NOTE

If the workpiece has only small areas in contact with the chuck, flat pieces of steel should be placed on the chuck against both ends of the workpiece. The extra flat pieces help hold the work securely in position.

By using a machine vise: A machine vise may be bolted to the machine table (Fig. 81-6). This is a safe way to hold workpieces too small to be held on a magnetic chuck. It is also useful for grinding angular surfaces. A dial indicator or a surface gage can be used for positioning the workpiece surface horizontally.

By using a swivel vise: The vise (Fig. 81-8) is bolted to the table and the workpiece is clamped in the vise. The vise is then positioned at the desired angle.

By using a tilting vise (Fig. 81-9): This vise can be placed on a magnetic chuck and tilted to any desired angle, from horizontal to the 90° vertical position. This method works well for grinding angular surfaces. It also works well for grinding vertical surfaces on parts of unusual shape, as in Figure 81-9.

Fig. 81-8 *Surface grinding a workpiece held in a swivel vise.* (Manual High School, Roger Bean)

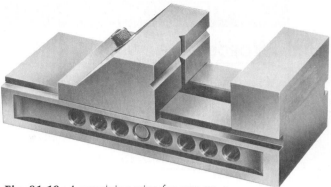

Fig. 81-10 *A precision vise for use on a magnetic chuck.*

Fig. 81-9 *Surface grinding a workpiece held in a tilting vise.* (Brown & Sharpe Mfg. Co.)

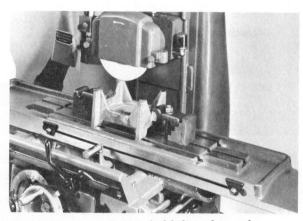

Fig. 81-11 *A workpiece held directly on the worktable with clamps and step blocks.*

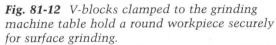

Fig. 81-12 *V-blocks clamped to the grinding machine table hold a round workpiece securely for surface grinding.*

By using a precision vise: A precision vise (Fig. 81-10) can be placed on a magnetic chuck for holding small workpieces securely and accurately. Round parts can also be held in the V-grooves in the vise jaw.

By clamping directly to the table: A workpiece can be positioned, aligned, and clamped to the machine table using standard workpiece-holding accessories (Fig. 81-11).

By using V-blocks: Round workpieces can be clamped on V-blocks for grinding. The V-blocks can be clamped to the table (Fig. 81-12) or they can be held in position with a magnetic chuck.

REVIEW · REVIEW · REVIEW · REVIEW · REVIEW

WORDS TO KNOW

horizontal spindle	reciprocating table	surface grinding	tilting vise
magnetic chuck	rotary table	swivel vise	vertical spindle
precision vise			

REVIEW QUESTIONS

1. List several kinds of surfaces that can be ground on surface-grinding machines.
2. Describe the difference between a reciprocating table and a rotary-table surface-grinding machine.
3. How is the size of a surface-grinding machine designated?
4. List four kinds of vises that can be used for holding workpieces on a surface grinder.
5. List three methods of holding a workpiece on a surface grinder, other than using vises.

UNIT 82

Surface Grinding with Horizontal-Spindle Surface-Grinding Machines

Horizontal-spindle surface-grinding machines are most commonly used in small commercial shops, tool-and-die shops, and school shops. The parts and controls on horizontal-spindle grinding machines are designed somewhat differently by various machine manufacturers. However, the principles involved in the operation of many machines of this type are the same.

82-1 Operating Features

A horizontal-spindle surface-grinding machine equipped for both handfeeding and power feeding is shown in Figure 82-1. A close-up of hand and power feed controls is shown in Figure 82-2.

Fig. 82-1 *A 6" × 18" (152 × 457 mm) surface grinding machine with controls for both hand feed and hydraulic power feed.* (Brown and Sharpe Mfg. Co.)

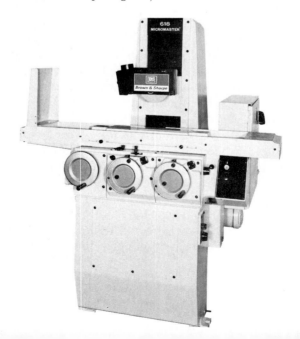

Grinding Wheel Elevation

The grinding wheel is mounted on a horizontal spindle that may be raised or lowered with the **elevating handwheel.** The handwheel generally has graduations that make it possible to adjust the wheel elevation in increments of 0.0002″ [0.005 mm]. Machines of the type shown in Figure 82-2 also have an auxiliary **fine-feed adjusting knob** that adjusts the wheel elevation in increments of 0.0001″ [0.0025 mm].

Wheel rpm

The maximum rpm indicated on the grinding wheel always should be equal to or higher than the rpm of the wheel spindle.

SAFETY NOTE

If the spindle rpm exceeds the maximum indicated rpm for the wheel, the wheel may fly apart and injure someone.

On machines with V-belt drive and step pulleys, the rpm can be changed as necessary for smaller or larger grinding wheels. Most surface-grinding machines, however, are designed to operate at one standard speed. For example, a spindle speed of approximately 3450 rpm is often used on machines that use a 7″ [178 mm] diameter grinding wheel. This gives a cutting speed of 6319 feet per minute [1926 mpm].

Table Feed

The table travels longitudinally (to the right or left), and crosswise (towards or away from the column).

Longitudinal table travel may be handfed with the **table handwheel.** The table is fed crosswise by hand with the cross-feed handwheel.

On machines equipped with power feed, the rate of longitudinal table travel can be adjusted. Table speed should be slower for finishing cuts than for roughing cuts. The amount of cross feed also can be adjusted. Lighter cross feeds are used for finishing cuts than for roughing cuts.

The controls used for changing the rate of longitudinal table feed and the rate of cross feed are somewhat different on each kind of machine (Fig. 82-2). Therefore, it is always best to have your instructor show you how to use the various controls before using the machine for the first time. The procedures for us-

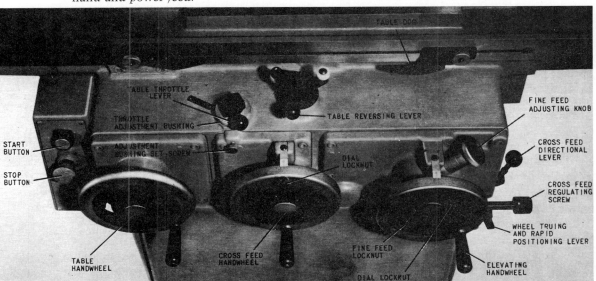

Fig. 82-2 *The operating controls on a surface grinding machine equipped with hand and power feed.*

ing the feed controls and other controls are included in the handbook provided by the manufacturer of the machine.

Table dogs (Fig. 82-2) are provided for setting the length of table travel. As the table travels, the dogs contact the table reversing lever, thus causing the table to travel in the opposite direction.

Cross feeds may be set from 0.010″ to 0.250″ [0.25 to 6.4 mm] on machines equipped with automatic cross-feed mechanisms. However, for average roughing cuts on smaller machines, a cross feed of 0.050″ to 0.100″ [1.27 to 2.54 mm] is satisfactory. For finishing cuts, the cross feed should be less, usually from 0.030″ to 0.050″ [0.76 to 1.27 mm]. **Never use cross feeds of more than one-half the width of the wheel.** The cross-feed handwheel has 0.0002″ [0.005 mm] graduations for accurately setting the amount of cross feed.

Depth of Cut

The depth of cut may vary according to the following:
1. Whether the cut is a roughing or a finishing cut.
2. Whether grinding is done wet or dry.
3. The rigidness of the machine and the rigidness of the setup.

Deep roughing cuts produce a rougher surface than shallow finishing cuts. Surface finish is better with wet grinding than with dry grinding. For average conditions, roughing cuts from 0.002″ to 0.003″ [0.05 to 0.08 mm] should be used. Finishing cuts of 0.001″ [0.025 mm] or less produce good results.

Wet or Dry Grinding

During grinding, abrasive grains fracture from the wheel, and fine metal chips are produced. For dry grinding, a **vacuum exhaust attachment** is recommended. This attachment collects the abrasive grit and dust and keeps the machine and the work area clean.

A **wet-grinding attachment** (Fig. 81-1, 82-1) is used for grinding with a cutting fluid. Use of cutting fluid carries away heat, thus, heavier cuts can be taken. Cutting fluid also improves surface finish, increases grinding wheel life, and carries grit and grinding dust away.

 SAFETY NOTE
Never turn on the cutting fluid while the grinding wheel is stopped. The porous wheel will absorb cutting fluid and will become unbalanced. If the wheel is used in this condition, it may be thrown out of true. It may also crack or break.

Therefore, turn the wheel on before turning the coolant on. Turn the coolant off before turning the wheel off.

An emulsifiable (soluble) oil solution, in which the oil and water mix completely, is recommended for grinding ferrous metals. A solution composed of 40 parts water and 1 part emulsifiable oil is recommended. Cutting fluids for use with other metals are listed in Table 50-2.

 82-2 Grinding Wheel Selection

The following kinds of straight grinding wheels are recommended for surface-grinding with horizontal-spindle reciprocating-table surface grinders:

Material	Kind of Grinding Wheel
Soft Steel	23A46—J8VBE
Cast Iron	32A46—18VBE (or)
	37C36—KVK
Hardened Steel	32A46—H8VBE
General-Purpose	23A46—H8VBE
Nonferrous Metals	37C36—KVK

For more specific grinding wheel recommendations, consult a standard handbook for machinists, a manufacturer's catalog, or a manufacturer's sales representative.

82-3 Truing and Dressing the Wheel

When a grinding wheel becomes dull, loaded, or out of shape, it must be **dressed** and **trued. Dressing** means to sharpen a wheel. **Truing** means to cut the wheel so that there will be no high spots when the wheel is running. Truing also refers to forming a wheel to a particular shape, such as a convex or concave shape. A diamond tool is used for dressing or truing grinding wheels.

Procedure for Truing or Dressing

1. Put on safety goggles.
2. Mount the grinding wheel on the spindle.
3. Select a wheel-truing fixture and fasten it to the magnetic chuck or the table. The diamond-point tool should be placed ahead of the vertical centerline of the wheel. It should also be inclined slightly in the direction of wheel travel. This procedure will prevent the diamond dressing tool from gouging or digging into the grinding wheel.
4. Start the machine. With the elevating handwheel, lower the wheel until it just touches the diamond-point tool.
5. With the cross-feed handwheel, move the table so that the diamond cuts across the wheel.
6. Lower the wheel 0.0005" [0.01 mm] for each additional cut until the wheel is true. If the machine is equipped with a wet-grinding attachment, a cutting fluid should be used while truing or dressing the wheel.

Shaping the Wheel

It is sometimes necessary to grind a special shape or form, such as a rounded fillet, a V-groove, or some irregular surface. In such cases, it is necessary to cut or true the grinding wheel to conform to the shape that is to be ground. For example, a V-shaped groove is being ground in Figure 81-5. For this purpose, the grinding wheel must be ground to the shape of the V-groove. A **radius and wheel truing attachment** can be used for shaping wheels.

82-4 Procedure for Surface Grinding

Following is the preliminary procedure to be followed in setting up for surface grinding. When the preliminary procedure has been completed, the specific procedures for manual-feed machines or power-feed machines should be followed.

Preliminary Procedure

1. Select a grinding wheel that is recommended for the kind of material to be ground. Use only a wheel with cardboard discs on each side that are in good condition. **Make sure that the maximum rpm indicated for the wheel is equal to or higher than the spindle rpm.** Test the wheel to see that it is sound. Do this by striking it lightly with a light hammer. A clear ring indicates that the wheel is sound and has no cracks.
2. Mount the grinding wheel on the wheel spindle and tighten the wheel snugly.
3. True the wheel as explained above.
4. Remove all burrs or nicks from the workpiece with a file.
5. Wipe dust or dirt from the machine table, magnetic chuck, or other work-holding tools or accessories. Then mount the workpiece on the machine.
6. Lubricate the machine with the proper machine oil before using it.
7. Protect your eyes by wearing approved safety goggles or face shield.

Procedure for Manual Feeding

1. Complete the preliminary steps of procedure, steps 1 through 7, listed above.
2. On machines equipped with power feed, the power-feed mechanisms should be disengaged for manual operation. On the machine shown in Figure 82-2, this is done by turning the **table throttle lever** to the off position. The power cross feed must also be **disengaged.** This is done with the **cross-feed directional lever.** Then the table handwheel and cross-feed handwheel can be engaged for manual operation.

With the **table handwheel** and the **cross-feed handwheel,** move the workpiece under the grinding wheel. Turn the machine on. With the **elevating handwheel,** lower the grinding wheel until it is just above the workpiece.

3. With the cross-feed handwheel, feed the workpiece outward (away from the column) until the far side of the wheel extends beyond the work a distance equal to ¾ the width of the wheel face. Thus ¼ the width of the wheel is above the work. Lower the grinding wheel until it just touches the workpiece, then move the table to the left or right until the wheel clears the end of the workpiece by about 1″ [25 mm].

4. With the elevating handwheel, lower the grinding wheel 0.002″ to 0.003″ [0.05 to 0.08 mm] for a roughing cut. Allow sufficient material for a final finishing cut of 0.0005″ to 0.001″ [0.01 to 0.025 mm] depth. Lock the grinding head in position with the **locking screw,** if the machine is so equipped. Turn on the cutting fluid or the vacuum exhaust, as desired.

5. With the table handwheel, feed the table longitudinally under the grinding wheel at a steady rate until the workpiece has passed beyond the grinding wheel about 1″ [25 mm].

6. With the cross-feed handwheel, feed the work crosswise one complete turn, about 0.100″ [2.54 mm], for the next cut.

7. Continue grinding as in steps 5 and 6 until the entire surface has been ground.

8. Measure the thickness of the workpiece. If more roughing cuts are necessary, continue grinding as in steps 4 through 7. However, cross-feed each additional cut in the direction opposite to the previous cut. This causes the wheel to wear off more evenly.

   If additional roughing cuts are not necessary, make a finishing cut. Use a cross feed of 0.030″ to 0.050″ [0.76 to 1.27 mm].

   When the work has been ground to the specified dimension, turn off the coolant, stop the machine, remove the workpiece, and clean the machine and accessories. Return all tools and accessories to their proper place.

9. Remove sharp burrs and edges with a file so that you do not get cut by them.

Procedure for Power Feeding

1. Complete the preliminary steps of procedure, 1 through 7, listed above.
2. Perform Steps 2 and 3 of the Procedure for Manual Feeding above.
3. Bring the right-hand **table dog** against the right side of the **table-reversing lever.** Fasten the dog in position by tightening the clamping bolt.
4. Move the table to the right until the end of the workpiece has passed the grinding wheel a distance of at least 1″ [25 mm].
5. Bring the left-hand table dog against the left side of the table-reversing lever. Fasten the dog in position by tightening the clamping bolt.
6. With the elevating handwheel, lower the grinding wheel 0.002″ to 0.003 ″ [0.05 to 0.08 mm] for a roughing cut. Allow sufficient material for a final finishing cut of 0.0005″ to 0.001″ [0.01 to 0.25 mm] depth. Lock the grinding head with the locking screw, if the machine is so equipped. Turn on the cutting fluid or the vacuum exhaust, as desired.
7. Set the power cross-feed mechanism for a feed of about 0.100″ [2.54 mm] for roughing cuts.
8. Engage the automatic longitudinal table-feed mechanism. On the machine in Figure 82-2, this is done with the **table throttle lever.**
9. Engage the automatic cross-feed mechanism for automatic feed in the proper direction. On the machine in Figure 82-2, this is done with the **cross-feed directional lever.**

 SAFETY NOTE

Even when work seems well clamped, it often pulls loose. When this happens, shut off the machine and step away from it.

10. When the cut has been completed, disengage the automatic longitudinal table feed and the automatic cross feed.

11. Bring the table to one side, against the table dog, so that the end of the workpiece is at least 1" [25 mm] beyond the grinding wheel.

12. Measure the workpiece. If additional roughing cuts are necessary, proceed as in steps 6 through 11 above. However, for each additional cut, feed the table crosswise in the direction opposite to the direction of feed for the previous cut. This procedure causes the wheel to wear more evenly.

If additional roughing cuts are not necessary, make a finishing cut. Finishing cuts should be 0.001" [0.025 mm] or less in depth. Use a cross-feed of 0.030" to 0.050" [0.76 to 1.27 mm].

13. When the workpiece has been ground to the specified dimension, turn off the coolant, stop the machine, remove the workpiece, and clean the machine and accessories. Place all tools and accessories in the proper place.

14. Remove sharp burrs or edges with a file so that you do not get cut by them.

REVIEW   REVIEW   REVIEW   REVIEW   REVIEW

WORDS TO KNOW

cross feed
cross-feed
  handwheel
cross-feed
  directional lever
dressing a grinding
  wheel

elevating
  handwheel
fine-feed adjusting
  knob
manual feed
power feed

radius and wheel
  truing attachment
table dogs
table handwheel
table-reversing lever
table throttle lever

truing a grinding
  wheel
vacuum exhaust
  attachment
wet-grinding
  attachment

REVIEW QUESTIONS

1. Name the control that raises and lowers the grinding wheel on a surface grinder.
2. What are table dogs used for on surface-grinding machines?
3. How much cross-feed should be used for roughing cuts on horizontal-spindle surface-grinding machines?
4. How much cross feed should be used for finishing cuts on a horizontal-spindle surface-grinding machine?
5. List several factors that must be considered in determining the depth of cut for surface grinding.
6. For average conditions, what should be the depth of a rough cut when surface grinding? Finishing cut?
7. What are the advantages of wet grinding?
8. On machines equipped with coolant systems, explain why the coolant should always be turned on after turning on the grinding wheel, and turned off before stopping the grinding wheel.
9. What kind of cutting fluid is recommended for wet-grinding of ferrous metals?
10. What code-numbered grinding wheel is recommended for surface-grinding hardened steel?
11. Explain the difference in meaning between truing and dressing a grinding wheel.
12. Describe how to check a grinding wheel for cracks.

PART

20

Modern Machining Processes

Since he was small, Carl Cataldo has been unusually curious about how things work. When he was twelve years old, he made his first telescope. Shortly after that he began making and flying model airplanes. The one process that has always appealed to him is imagining something, creating it, and "seeing it fly." He is doing just that today on a far larger scale.

After high school, where Carl's courses were heavy on math and science, he became a journeyman toolmaker and then earned a BS degree in Mechanical Engineering. He immediately looked for a job where he could make something fly. For the last ten years Carl has worked for one of the largest aerospace manufacturers in the industry. Due to his many abilities, he has been promoted several times and is now a Technical Specialist in Producibility.

Much of Carl's work centers on designing aircraft parts. These are often delicate and require special handling. An example of one such project was the aileron piece of a high-performance plane. It was seven feet long, and had to be very lightweight. A honeycomb core was the solution. However, the core could not be machined by conventional milling so electrical discharge machining (EDM) was used. Using a copper platen as an electrode, EDM produced an acceptable finished surface. Then an adhesive could be applied to bond (fasten) the outer skin for the aileron.

Carl has found that working with aircraft design brings him close to many, nontraditional things—cutting plastic with a thin stream of water or slicing titanium with a stream of water and powdered garnet. He admits it sometimes seems like magic. For students wondering about the possibilities of all these new materials and processes, Carl says most positively, "Don't ever be afraid of the future."

Carl Cataldo
*Technical Specialist in
Producibility*

Charles Zilch

UNIT
83
Electrical Discharge Machining (EDM)

Electrical discharge machining (EDM) removes metal by causing electricity to arc between the tool and the workpiece. The arcing is repetitive and carefully controlled. During cutting, both the tool and the workpiece are submerged in a **dielectric** (insulating) fluid (Fig. 83-1). EDM is valued for its ability to machine complex shapes in metals of any hardness. It is widely used in making injection and compression molds for rubber and plastic molding, molds for die-casting metals, and dies for forging and metal stamping (Fig. 83-2). It can also remove broken taps and studs and drill holes as small as 0.002″ [0.05 mm]. Because no tool pressures are involved, it is useful for machining delicate workpieces such as metal honeycomb structures. A disadvantage is that only materials that can conduct electricity can be machined.

Types of EDM machines. There are two types of EDM machines, those that use **solid electrodes** and those that use a **traveling wire**

electrode. The solid electrode machines range in size from small bench-top models to machines capable of handling huge workpieces. Figure 83-3 shows an EDM solid electrode machine of medium size. Basic machines of this type can only plunge a nonrotating tool directly into a workpiece. More versatile machines provide tool orbiting to equalize wear, lead screws to permit tapping of holes, and power feed to permit sawing and slotting.

Traveling wire electrode machines (Fig. 83-4) use a reel of round wire as an electrode. This enables cutting in any direction, and any profile shape can be cut. These machines have revolutionized the cutting of blanking dies for sheet metal stamping. Die blocks may be hardened before cutting, and the shape cut exactly to size. Both punch and die are now made from the same block, the clearance being determined by the diameter of the wire used for cutting.

Fig. 83-1 *The basic components of an EDM system.*

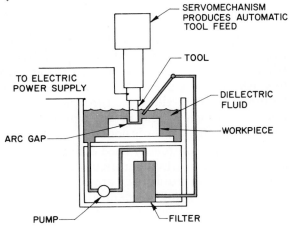

Fig. 83-2 *EDM handles intricate molds with ease. Use of EDM eliminates tool marks and much hand polishing.* (Elox Corporation)

Fig. 83-3 *A solid electrode (ram type) EDM machine of medium size. (Raycon Corporation)*

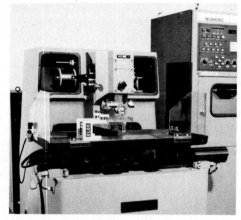

Fig. 83-4 *A traveling wire electrode EDM machine.*

EDM electrodes (tools). Electrode materials, which must conduct electricity, include high-purity graphite, brass, copper, copper-graphite, tungsten and several tungsten alloys, and zinc alloys. The EDM process causes much greater tool wear than conventional machining processes. Often, several identical tools must be made, one or more for roughing cuts, and one or more for making finishing cuts. Sometimes **stepped tools** can accomplish the same results as several tools (Fig. 83-5).

Metal removal rate is directly related to amperage (electric current) settings. Low amperage settings produce slow rates of metal removal and good finishes, while high amperage settings produce higher rates of metal removal and poorer finishes. Finishes of 30 to 150 microinches (30-150 millionths of an inch [0.75 to 3.75 micrometers]) are normal, but with care, a 10 microinch [0.25 micrometer] finish is possible.

Since a gap must exist between the tool and the workpiece, the tool produces a cavity slightly larger than itself. This size difference is referred to as tool **overcut** and generally amounts to only a few thousandths of an inch (hundredths of a millimeter). The overcut can be as small as .0002" [0.005 mm].

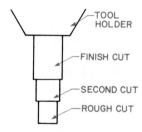

Fig. 83-5 *A stepped EDM electrode can sometimes be used in place of several electrodes.*

Dielectric fluids. To obtain uniform cutting action and good finishes, a flow of **dielectric fluid** must be directed through the arc gap to wash away the chips. The fluid stream may be directed along the tool, through a hollow tool, or through a hole in the workpiece opposite from the point of tool entry.

The most commonly used dielectric fluids are low-viscosity (thin) petroleum oils, such as kerosene. Other fluids used are de-ionized water, silicone oils, and ethylene glycol/water solutions.

REVIEW REVIEW REVIEW REVIEW REVIEW

WORDS TO KNOW

EDM	dielectric fluid	solid electrodes	traveling wire
electrical discharge	overcut	stepped tool	electrode
machining			

REVIEW QUESTIONS

1. Explain the EDM process and list its advantages and disadvantages.
2. How do the two types of EDM machines differ? Describe the kind of work done by each.
3. Name several kinds of materials used for making EDM electrodes.
4. What is the unique property of a dielectric fluid?
5. Name several dielectric fluids used in EDM work.
6. Why are stepped cutting tools sometimes used in EDM?
7. How is the quality of surface finish controlled in EDM?

UNIT
84

Electrochemical Machining (ECM)

Electrochemical machining (ECM) is based on the same principles as electroplating (see Unit 46). However, instead of depositing metal on the workpiece, ECM reverses the process so that metal is **depleted,** or removed, from the workpiece. The basic components of an ECM system are shown in Figure 84-1.

In ECM, the tool becomes the cathode (negative electrode) and the workpiece becomes the anode (positive electrode). A gap between the tool and workpiece of from .001" to .010" [0.025 to 0.25 mm] is maintained. The gap provides space for the flow of **electrolyte,** and keeps the electrical circuit from shorting. A low-voltage, high-amperage direct current passes from the workpiece to the tool through the electrolyte. The current causes metal particles to be dissolved from the workpiece into the electrolyte by electrochemical action **(electrolysis).**

The electrolyte is pumped through the gap between the tool and workpiece at high pressures. As a result, the dissolved metal particles are washed away and filtered out. This process prevents them from being deposited on the tool.

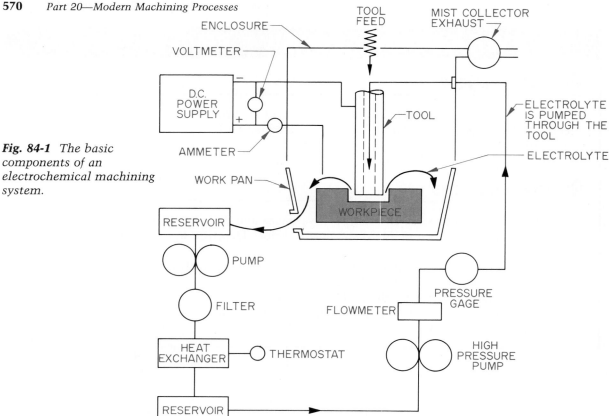

Fig. 84-1 *The basic components of an electrochemical machining system.*

With the ECM process, accuracy and tool life are very good for these reasons: (1) the tool never touches the workpiece, (2) it receives no buildup of metal from the workpiece, and (3) it is worn very little by the flow of electrolyte. ECM **electrodes** are most commonly made of copper alloys, type 316 stainless steel, and titanium. Copper and brass tools are best except for thin tools requiring great stiffness.

ECM can machine any metal that conducts electricity, regardless of hardness. Absence of any tool pressure on the workpiece makes the process ideal for machining thin materials and fragile workpieces.

ECM excels in machining metals that are difficult to machine, especially when holes or cavities of complex shape must be made. No burrs are produced by ECM. The finishes are bright and smooth and ordinarily do not require polishing. However, the metal removal rates of ECM are low compared to conventional machining methods. Thus, ECM is not often used on metals that have good machinability.

Electrochemical deburring (ECD) is an adaptation of ECM. It uses tooling designed for the removal of burrs and sharp edges left on parts machined by conventional methods (Fig. 84-2).

Electrochemical grinding (ECG) applies the principles of ECM to the conventional grinding process (Fig. 84-3). The grinding wheels used must be made with an **electrically conductive bond.** ECG removes metal as much as 80% faster than conventional grinding without an appreciable loss in accuracy or surface finish. Only about 10% of conventional grinding wheel pressure is necessary. Also, since 90% of the metal is removed by electrolysis, wheel wear and the need for wheel dressing are sharply reduced.

ECG is preferred for grinding carbide tools because cutting edges can be ground in a single pass. Smooth, burr-free cutting edges are produced. Wheel wear is reduced to 15% of that which takes place with conventional grinding.

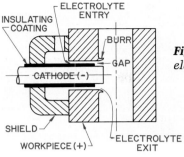

Fig. 84-2 *The tooling arrangement for electrochemical deburring.*

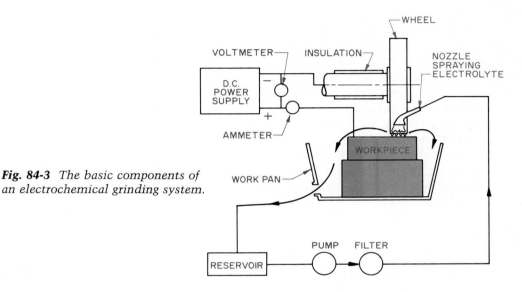

Fig. 84-3 *The basic components of an electrochemical grinding system.*

REVIEW   REVIEW   REVIEW   REVIEW   REVIEW

WORDS TO KNOW

anode	ECG	electrochemical	electrode (tool)
cathode	ECM	grinding	electrolysis
ECD	electrochemical	electrochemical	electrolyte
	deburring	machining	

REVIEW QUESTIONS

1. How is electrochemical machining similar to electroplating?
2. What prevents the buildup of metal on the tool in ECM?
3. List the main advantages of ECM.
4. What is meant by electrochemical deburring?
5. How does the electochemical grinding process differ from conventional grinding?
6. What are the main advantages of ECG?

UNIT

85

Electron Beam Machining (EBM)

Electron beam machining (EBM) uses the same equipment as electron beam welding, which was discussed earlier in Unit 26. For machining, the equipment is operated at different power settings than for welding. Machining is accomplished by focusing a high-speed beam of electrons on the workpiece (Fig. 85-1). Sufficient heat is produced to **vaporize** any known material, but the amount of metal removed is very small.

EBM is used chiefly for drilling very small holes and cutting narrow slots in hard-to-machine materials up to ¼" [6.35 mm] thick. Holes as small as 0.0005" [0.0125 mm] and slots as narrow as 0.001" [0.025 mm] can be made in any material.

EBM is most efficient when done in a vacuum. This permits electron beams of full power as small as 0.001" [0.025 mm] to be focused on spots equally small. The beam may be directed into several patterns within a ¼"

[6.35 mm] square by a **magnetic deflection coil** (Fig. 85-1). This allows drilling of closely spaced patterns of holes at a single location, drilling of holes of different sizes and shapes, and cutting of slots of various widths and shapes (Fig. 85-2).

The disadvantages of EBM include the need for highly trained operators, high equipment costs, slow cycle times, and limits on workpiece size due to the size of the vacuum chamber. The process also produces X-rays, thus requiring X-ray shielding of the work area. An EBM machine is shown in Figure 26-42.

Fig. 85-1 *The basic components of an electron beam machining system.*

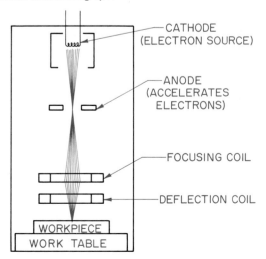

Fig. 85-2 *The patterns of electron beam movement produced by magnetic deflection coils.*

BEAM DEFLECTION SYSTEM
FREQUENCY .005 TO 15,000 CPS

TYPE	WAVE FORM	BEAM PATTERN		
		X	Y	XY
SINE WAVE	OSCILLATION			
SINE-COSINE WAVE	CIRCLE GENERATION			
SQUARE WAVE	OSCILLATION			
DITHER	CIRCLE/ON CIRCLE			
D.C.	OFFSET ANY ABOVE PATTERN			

REVIEW   REVIEW   REVIEW   REVIEW   REVIEW

WORDS TO KNOW

EBM	electron beam	magnetic deflection	vaporize
electron beam	welding	coil	
machining			

REVIEW QUESTIONS

1. How is electron beam machining accomplished?
2. How is electron beam machining related to electron beam welding?
3. Describe the kind of machining best done by EBM.
4. List the main advantages and disadvantages of EBM.

UNIT

86

Laser Beam Machining (LBM)

Laser beam machining (LBM), like laser beam welding (discussed in Unit 26), uses a concentrated beam of light as its tool. For machining instead of welding, different power settings are used. Lasers can machine any known material. The intense heat of the laser beam removes the material to be machined mainly by **vaporization.** The rate of metal removal, however, is relatively small, which limits laser use to hole-drilling and cutting of relatively thin materials.

Two types of lasers are in common use. **Solid-state lasers** (Fig. 86-1) are capable only of short bursts of power. **Gas lasers** (Fig. 86-2) produce a continuous laser beam.

Fig. 86-1 *The basic components of a solid laser system.*

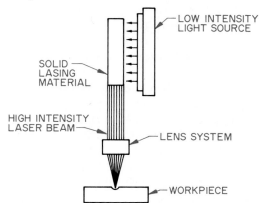

Fig. 86-2 *The basic components of a gas laser system.*

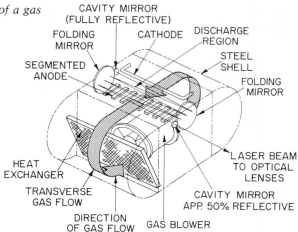

Fig. 86-3 *A solid laser machining and welding system.* (Control Laser)

Fig. 86-4 *This magnified photo of a jet engine component shows the precision that can be achieved through laser drilling. Each of the round holes is .017" in diameter. Each of the holes was drilled in 1 second.* (Coherent General, Inc.)

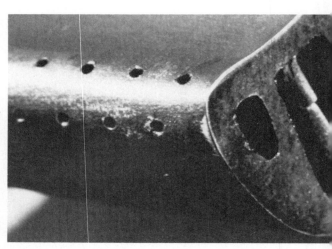

Solid-state lasers are best suited to hole-drilling, or to spot-welding and heat-treating. Laser-drilled holes are slightly tapered, but have clean edges with little spatter. The power source of the solid-state laser can be finely regulated, thus permitting precise control of hole sizes. A cheap way to drill holes up to 0.020" [0.5 mm] diameter in thin, flat material is with a laser. Laser-drilling of holes up to 0.050" [1.25 mm] is also economical if the holes enter on slanted or curved surfaces, or are in difficult-to-reach spots. Figure 86-3 shows a general-purpose laser welding and machining system.

Presently, **carbon dioxide lasers** are most efficient in converting electricity into laser power (Fig. 86-2). Gas lasers operate basically the same way as solid-state lasers, except that a gas serves to create a continuous, highly concentrated laser beam. This makes the gas laser best suited to continuous cutting, welding, or heat-treating.

Laser cutting systems that use oxygen to increase their cutting capacity are now in service. They are capable of making fast, clean cuts in mild steel up to ½" [12.7 mm] thick (Fig. 86-4). These systems are also used for partial cutting operations such as scribing and engraving, and for heat-treating and welding.

SAFETY NOTE
To protect against possible injury from reflected laser beams, beam paths are enclosed with guards, and workers must wear laser-proof safety glasses.

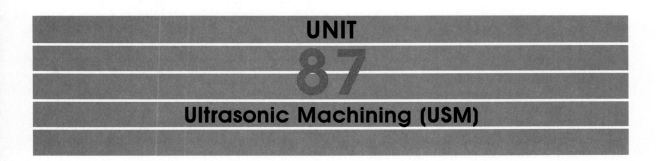

Words to know

carbon dioxide laser	laser beam	laser beam welding	solid-state lasers
gas lasers	machining	LBM	vaporization

Review questions

1. How is laser beam machining related to laser beam welding?
2. By what process do laser beams machine metal?
3. What kinds of machining are solid-state lasers used for? Why?
4. What kind of machining are gas lasers used for? Why?
5. What technique is used to increase the cutting power of lasers?

UNIT
87
Ultrasonic Machining (USM)

In ultrasonic **machining** (USM), also known as **impact grinding,** fine abrasive particles suspended in a **fluid (usually water) are** directed into a gap **between the** tool and the workpiece (Fig. 87-1). **The tool vibrates a few** thousandths of an inch (**hundredths of a mil**limeter) at an ultrasonic **frequency** of 20,000 or more cycles per second. **This** movement causes the abrasive **particles to bombard the** workpiece with high **velocity, thus** grinding the workpiece to the **shape** of the tool.

The abrasive **particles** may be boron carbide, silicon carbide, **or aluminum oxide. Grit** sizes used range **from 280 to 800 mesh, de**pending on the desired **degree** of accuracy **and** quality of finish.

Tools are usually **made** of soft steel **or** brass and must be a **mirror image** of the shape

Fig. 87-1 *The basic components of an ultrasonic machining system.*

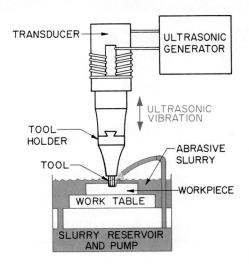

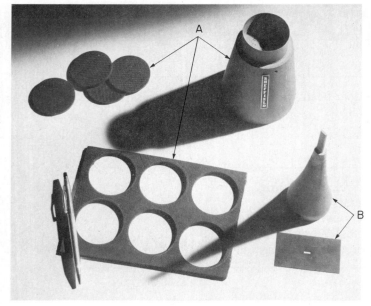

Fig. 87-2 *Examples of ultrasonic machining:*
(A) Blanking tool, workpiece, and blanked discs;
(B) Slotting tool and slotted workpiece.

to be machined. Tool wear is high due to the abrasive cutting action. One or more roughing tools and a finishing tool are usually needed for each job. The tools are usually fastened to their toolholders by brazing. A tolerance of .002" [0.05 mm] is easily held and .0005" [0.01 mm] is possible by using finer abrasive grits. Finishes are good, in the vicinity of 20 microinches [0.5 microns] for ordinary work.

A major advantage of the USM process is that it can machine materials that cannot be machined by EDM, ECM, or ECG because they don't conduct electricity. Glass, ceramic materials, metal oxides, and precious and semi-precious gems are nonconducting materials that can be readily machined by USM. This process is also valued for its ability to machine carbides, tough alloys, and hardened steels. Soft materials such as carbon, graphite, and plastics are cut as readily as hard materials.

The process is very versatile, enabling any shape to be produced in a workpiece for which a tool can be made (Fig. 87-2).

REVIEW   REVIEW   REVIEW   REVIEW   REVIEW

WORDS TO KNOW

impact grinding	ultrasonic	USM
ultrasonic frequency	machining	

REVIEW QUESTIONS

1. Explain how cutting is accomplished in ultrasonic machining.
2. Name several kinds of abrasives used for ultrasonic machining.
3. Name two metals commonly used for making tools for ultrasonic machining.
4. What is the main disadvantage of ultrasonic machining?
5. What are the main advantages of ultrasonic machining?

UNIT 88

Chemical Machining (CHM)

Chemical machining (CHM) shapes metal by using strong **acid** or **alkaline solutions** to dissolve away unwanted metal. There are two types of chemical **machining**: (1) chemical blanking, used for cutting out parts from thin sheet metals, and (2) **chemical milling**, used for removal of metal from heavier material.

Chemical blanking. An accurate drawing of the part to be made is the first step in chemical blanking. This drawing may be up to 20 times as large as the part. The drawing is then reduced photographically to make a negative of the exact size of the part. The sheet metal to be machined is prepared with an acid-resisting, light-sensitive coating called a **photoresist**. The negative of the drawing is used to make a contact print directly on the coated surface. The exposed sheet metal is then placed in a chemical solution that dissolves away the light-exposed portions, leaving the workpiece blanked to accurate size and shape (Fig. 88-1).

Other methods of **applying the acid-resistant coating, also called **masking,** include **silkscreen** and **offset printing.** Chemical blanking technology is widely used in making printed circuit boards and integrated circuits.

Chemical milling. Chemical milling is used mostly in the aerospace industries. It is the most efficient way of removing unwanted weight from large, complex aircraft frame parts (Fig. 88-2).

The procedure for chemical milling begins with cleaning the metal. Next, masking of **neoprene rubber** or **vinyl plastic** is sprayed or flowed on and cured by baking. The masking is then cut and peeled away from areas to be chemically milled. The part is placed in a tank of the chemical-milling solution until the unwanted metal is dissolved away. Rinsing with clean water and demasking are then done.

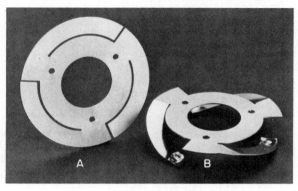

Fig. 88-1 *A typical part cut by chemical blanking: (A) the part as blanked from the sheet; (B) the part bent to final shape.*

Fig. 88-2 *A large airframe section that has been chemically milled to reduce its weight without loss of strength.*

Chemical milling is **very simple** and does not require highly skilled labor or expensive equipment. Other advantages are:

1. It does not cold-work (mechanically stress) the metal as conventional machining does.
2. Very large parts can be machined.
3. Any number of workpiece surfaces can be machined at the same time.
4. Removal of metal from complex surfaces is easily accomplished.
5. Since there are no mechanical cutting pressures involved, thin and delicate workpieces can be safely machined.

 SAFETY NOTE
Extreme care must be taken when mixing or working with chemical-machining solutions. Concentrated acids and alkalis instantly cause burns to clothing and skin. Etching solutions are less dangerous but are still very hazardous. A full-face shield, rubber gloves, rubber apron, and rubber boots must be worn for complete protection against splashes and spills. An emergency shower should be nearby, and adequate ventilation must be provided to carry off toxic fumes.

REVIEW   REVIEW   REVIEW   REVIEW   REVIEW

WORDS TO KNOW

acid solution	chemical machining	masking	photoresist
alkaline solution	chemical milling	neoprene rubber	silk-screen printing
chemical blanking	CHM	offset printing	vinyl plastic

REVIEW QUESTIONS

1. How is metal removal accomplished in chemical machining?
2. Explain the difference between chemical blanking and chemical milling.
3. What kinds of parts are made by chemical blanking? Chemical milling?
4. Name two masking materials used in chemical milling.
5. List the main advantages of chemical milling.
6. What personal safety precautions mut be taken during chemical machining?

UNIT

89

Miscellaneous Machining Processes

Metalworking research is constantly developing new methods to solve special problems. Some recent advanced machining techniques are briefly described in this unit.

Abrasive jet machining (AJM) uses abrasive grains propelled by a high-velocity stream of air as the cutting tool (Fig. 89-1). The abrasive grains bombard the workpiece at nearly the speed of sound, but since the abrasive grains are very small, material removal is very slow. Aluminum oxide and silicon carbide abrasives are usually used.

AJM is used mostly for cleaning and deburring, etching of glass and ceramics, and trimming of electrical resistors. It is also used for scribing and cutting hard, brittle semiconductor materials. Accurate cuts as narrow as 0.005" [0.127 mm] are possible. In many cases,

AJM is the only way of deburring and finishing holes and surfaces inside of parts.

Abrasive flow machining (AFM) is also known as **abrasive flow deburring.** It is used mainly for deburring, rounding sharp edges, and surface polishing. In this process an **abrasive slurry** is pumped back and forth across the edges or surfaces to be machined. Workpieces are placed in a fixture that restricts the abrasive flow to the parts that need machining (Fig. 89-2). Aluminum oxide and silicon carbide abrasives of 20 to 60 grit are usually used.

Plasma arc machining (PAM) is done with a cutting torch that produces an extremely hot jet of **ionized gas** called **plasma.** Temperatures of 20,000 to 50,000° F [11,100 to 27,760° C] are obtained by heating a gas with an electric arc inside a specially designed water-cooled torch (Fig. 89-3). The PAM process is used mainly for cutting shapes of steel, aluminum, and other metals that cannot be cut with oxyacetylene torches or lasers. PAM can cut stainless steel as thick as 5 inches [127 mm] and aluminum as thick as 6 inches [152 mm]. Plasma arc cutting systems are also built into some turret punching machines for use in making large cutouts.

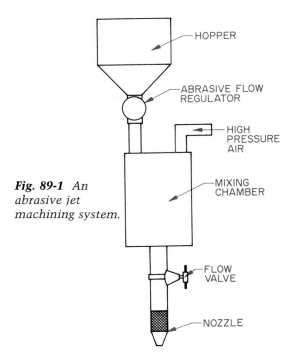

Fig. 89-1 An abrasive jet machining system.

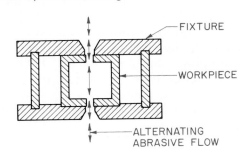

Fig. 89-2 A fixture for deburring holes with abrasive flow machining.

Water jet cutting is a very new process that is done with a fine stream of water under extremely high pressure. Pressures up to 60,000 psi [413.69 MPa] are used with stream diameters ranging from 0.003″-0.020″ [0.076-0.51 mm]. This creates a water jet with a velocity of up to 3400 ft/second [1036 M/second] that has tremendous cutting power. A complete water jet cutting system is shown in Figure 89-4.

Filtered water is used for cutting most nonmetallic materials. For most metalcutting, however, abrasives are added to the stream of water after it leaves the nozzle. Both ferrous and nonferrous metals can be cut, including such extremely tough materials as titanium up to 2″ [50.8 mm] thick.

Advantages of waterjet cutting include:

1. smooth, burr-free cuts as narrow as 0.003″ [0.076 mm].

Stretching It to the Limit

TECHNOLOGIES AND PRACTICES

Building a plastic model airplane is much easier than making the real thing. Traditional production of a beam frame for a B-1 bomber requires 104 separate components. However, a new metalworking process—superplastic forming—is making aircraft construction much simpler. This type of non-traditional machining is growing in importance in the aerospace industry.

"Superplasticity" is the capability of a metal to be stretched without weakening or breaking when heated under pressure. Titanium, a metal commonly used in aerospace products, has this capability. It can be stretched as much as 200%. This means that large structures once made of many titanium parts can often be redesigned into one-piece structures. These stretch-formed pieces do not require drilling or fastening. Production is thus simplified and some assembly procedures are eliminated. The photographs at the right show the differ-

ence between a structure assembled the old way and the same part formed by the new method.

Superplastic forming begins with the placing of sheet metal between two dies. The upper die is flat and has holes drilled in it. The lower die is in the shape of the product. These dies are clamped together. Then argon gas is pumped into spaces in the upper die. Argon prevents the surface of the hot metal from being contaminated by impurities in the air. It also provides the pressure needed to carry out the forming process.

The entire die casing is then placed in a press and heated between 1650° and 1750°F. The metal now reaches its superplastic state. Gas pressure is slowly increased in the upper die to provide the slow strain needed for the process. As pressure in the upper die is increased, argon is slowly released from the lower die. During this procedure, the titanium is pressed into the shape of the lower die cavity.

There are factors in superplastic forming that must be precisely controlled, such as temperature and pressure. But on the whole, this process is simpler than traditional methods. Although aircraft construction is still not as simple as putting together a plastic model, superplastic forming has made it easier and more economical.

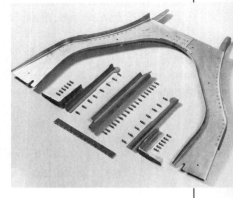

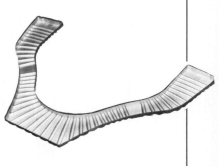

2. cool cutting with no **grain or** metallurgical damage to metals.
3. cutting speeds of up to 1000 inches/minute [25.4 M/minute], depending on the thickness and kind of **material being cut.**

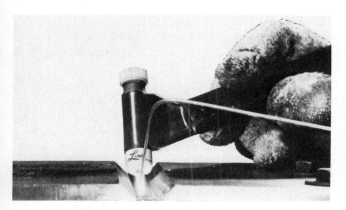

Fig. 89-3 *A plasma arc cutting torch.* (Union Carbide Corporation, Linde Division)

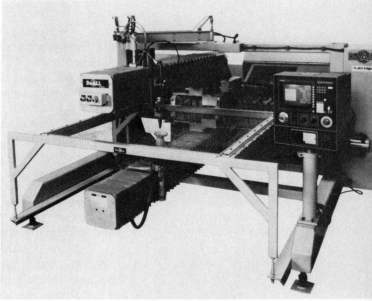

Fig. 89-4 *A complete water jet cutting system. The basic components are a water filtration unit, a computer controlled water intensifier unit, a CNC motion control system, and a cutting head assembly.* (DoAll)

REVIEW   REVIEW   REVIEW   REVIEW   REVIEW

Words to know

abrasive flow deburring	AJM ionized gas	abrasive jet machining	plasma arc machining
abrasive flow machining	PAM AFM	abrasive slurry plasma	water jet cutting

Review questions

1. Explain the **abrasive** jet machining process.
2. What kind of **work** is abrasive jet machining used for?
3. Explain the **abrasive** flow machining process.
4. What kind of **work** is abrasive flow **machining** used for?
5. Explain the **plasma** arc process.
6. What kind of **work** is the plasma arc **process** best suited for?
7. When water jet cutting is used for cutting metals, what is added to the steam of water to speed the **cutting?**
8. Name three **advantages** of water jet cutting.

Although he held an engineering degree and had a broad background in mathematics, James Bailey required further training when he was hired as the Computer Numerical Control (CNC) Coordinator for a Michigan manufacturing company. He was sent to two different machine-building schools for several weeks of specialized study. At one, he acquired a basic knowledge of numerical control. At the other, he learned manual programming for such equipment as lathes and milling machines. He also learned how to set up numerically controlled machining centers.

James notes that his abilities and the needs of the company are a good match. At the plant, which produces testing equipment for the automotive industry, he does a wide variety of programming. Some of the work, such as programming parts to be run on a lathe, is relatively routine. But when he is challenged by a part that requires complex curve and angle programming, his interest in the project becomes quite intense. With numerical control, James can improve the production rate of a machine up to four times its normal output. Increasing the efficiency of machine tools is one of the most enjoyable parts of his job.

For those interested in working with numerical control, he suggests a basic knowledge of metalworking machinery and computer programming. James teaches some trade courses at a junior college. There he finds that many students are "terrified" by trigonometry, another basic requirement for the job. He advises them to relax and move gradually through the course. They will find that it is not nearly as difficult as they had imagined. Perseverance can lead them into a creative, challenging, and fast-growing part of industry.

James Bailey
CNC Coordinator

UNIT
90
Principles of Automation

The term **automation** comes from the word **automatic,** which means **self-acting** or **self-adjusting.** Automated machines, processes, or systems of manufacturing generally possess the following characteristics:

1. They operate with little or no human help.
2. They detect, or sense, the need for a corrective adjustment in the process or operation.
3. They make the required corrective adjustments with little or no human assistance.

The true concept of automation is **continuous automatic production.** This method of production, in some applications, can automatically produce the part(s) and inspect, assemble, test, and package the product in one continuous flow (Fig. 90-1).

Feedback

Automatic machines, processes, or systems use a principle called **feedback.** This is a way for a system or operation to automatically correct or adjust its performance. Information about the process or operation is detected and reported (fed back) to an adjusting control. Understanding the following terms or devices used in automated systems will help you understand the meaning of feedback.

Output is the work produced by a machine operation or process. The output may be either a product or a service, such as a machined part or the opening of a door.

Input consists of the commands, data, or standards specifying the output. This may be information such as size dimensions, position location, machine speed, weight, temperature.

Sensors are electronic, mechanical, or other kinds of instruments or devices that detect and report conditions of the products or services. Sensors may measure size, weight, temperature, color, pressure, or chemical composition. Sensors feed information back to the control center.

Fig. 90-1 *This automated, flexible machining line can run continuously unmanned. It is controlled by a host computer. Six machining centers are linked to an automated stacker crane storage and retrieval system. The parts are delivered to the machining system by the stacker crane and automatically unloaded onto the machines. They are then picked up and returned to the storage area when machining has been completed.* (Cross & Trecker)

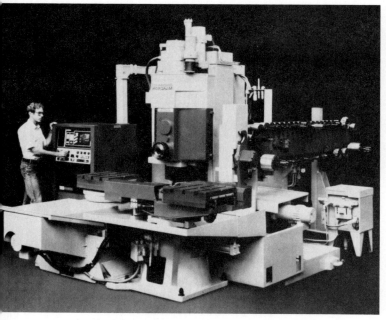

Fig. 90-2 *This machining process is being controlled by a computer.* (Cincinnati Milacron)

Fig. 90-3 *This programmable controller is designed for large-scale operations.* (Allen-Bradley)

The **control center** compares the output with the input commands or data. It then gives the necessary instructions to the machine—to stop, continue, or change speed or direction. Thus, the control center actually regulates, or controls, the automated machine or process. In complex automated machines or systems, the control center is either an **electronic computer** (Fig. 90-2) or a **controller** that can be programmed (Fig. 90-3). In simple automatic machines or processes, the control center may be a simple electrical on/off switch.

Feedback Control Loop

Engineers use the term "feedback control loop" to describe how an automated machine or process is controlled. The term **loop** refers to the flow of information through the automated system. A feedback control system may have an **open loop** or a **closed loop.**

The heating system in a home is a good example of a simple automated **closed-loop system.** The system includes a furnace, a **thermostat,** a thermometer and an electrical circuit with a contact switch (Fig. 90-4). The desired temperature (input), for example 68°F [20°C], is set on the thermostat. When the

temperature falls below 68°F [20°C], the thermostat sensor closes a switch in the electrical circuit to the furnace. Electricity starts the furnace, and the furnace produces heat (output). When the thermostat senses that the temperature in the room has risen to the desired input temperature setting (feedback), it opens the switch in the electrical circuit and thus shuts off the furnace. In this simple system, the thermostat is both the sensor and the control center. The thermometer is only a "readout" device to show the performance of the heating system to the homeowner. Similar closed-loop systems are used for the automatic operation of air-conditioning systems, hot water heaters, refrigerators, and many kinds of machines (Fig. 90-5).

As you have seen, a closed-loop system is one in which measurement of the output is fed back to a control center and compared with the input. In an **open-loop system,** no corrective adjustment automatically takes place as a result of the feedback. Instead, a signal such as a light or horn warns an operator to make the necessary corrective adjustments. Because closed-loop feedback systems are capable of making the corrective adjustments, they are used in most automated machines or processes.

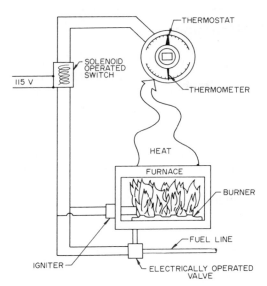

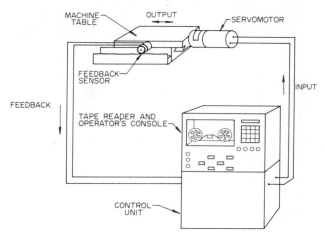

Fig. 90-4 *A simple closed loop feedback system. The machine (furnace) produces a product (heat) that is measured by the thermostat. The thermostat controls the furnace by activating the switch, which either starts or stops the furnace. As a result, the furnace maintains a constant temperature.*

Fig. 90-5 *A closed loop machine control system. When the servomotor moves the table to the desired position, the sensor signals the control unit to stop the servomotor.*

Automatic Material Handling

Advanced manufacturing systems often involve continuous automatic handling of materials. These systems are used in such continuous process industries as steelmaking, papermaking, chemical processing, and petroleum refining. Unit-processing, however, also uses automatic material handling, as in stamping automobile fenders, machining engine blocks, printing sheets of paper, and filling milk cartons (Fig. 90-6).

The Future of Automation in Metalworking

Continuous automatic production, from refining ore to assembling products, has long been an engineer's dream. Before long it will be achieved with robots, computerized numerically controlled machines, and highly automated production lines. People will be needed, however, to design, make, install, and service automated systems. While automation is bringing many changes in metalworking, it is also creating employment opportunities.

Fig. 90-6 *This AGV (Automatically Guided Vehicle) is being used to transport packaged goods within the manufacturing plant.* (Jervis P. Webb Co.)

True "Metal" Workers

Many of us have seen or heard of the fantastic robots Ar-too Dee-too and C3PO of the movie *Star Wars.* These metal people were always on hand in case the hero got into trouble and needed expert mechanical advice, calculations, or a special tool. It may be some time before we have robots like these. But you may be interested to know that robots already are performing many important tasks in industry.

Industrial robots first appeared on factory assembly lines in the early 1960s. These special machines took over the jobs that were monotonous, uncomfortable, or dangerous for humans. Robot welders, for example, did some of the more difficult work in automobile plants.

Robot welders don't look anything like humans. The first ones, which did point-to-point spot welding, resembled large, straight arms. They were programmed to produce an electric current every few seconds. If something went wrong and the workpiece wasn't in place, the robot would produce the current anyway. One of the first obvious improvements was to add a camera "eye," so the robot could "see" what was—or wasn't—in front of it.

Later robot welders, equipped with more sensors, could tell if they were about to go off the programmed track. They could then correct themselves before making mistakes. This self-correction, called a "feedback loop" or "adaptive control," is as close as a machine can come to reacting in a human way.

The latest robot welders, using tiny computers called "microprocessors," can copy the detailed techniques of human hand welding.

Robot welders now being designed have movable "wrists" and "fingers," do laser-beam welding, and can sense the soundness of their welds. Robot "metal-workers" have made automobile manufacture more efficient. They may not have the capabilities of the *Star Wars* robots—yet. But their functions make them reliable co-workers in our factories. And they will play an increasing role in raising production rates.

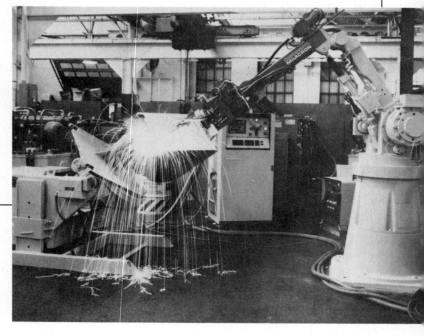

REVIEW REVIEW REVIEW REVIEW REVIEW

WORDS TO KNOW

automatic	feedback	open-loop system	regulator
automation	feedback control	output	self-acting
closed-loop system	loop	programmable	self-adjusting
computer	input	controller	sensors
control center			

REVIEW QUESTIONS

1. What is meant by the term **automation?**
2. List three characteristics that automated machines or systems possess.
3. What is meant by the term **output** as it applies to automated systems?
4. What is meant by the term **input** as it applies to automated systems?
5. What is meant by the term **sensor** as it applies to automated systems?
6. What is the function of a computer, controller, or regulator in an automated system?
7. What is the meaning of the term **feedback control loop** in an automated system?
8. Explain how the feedback control loop for an automatic heating system works.
9. Explain the difference between open-loop and closed-loop feedback systems.

UNIT

91

Introduction to Numerical Control (N/C)

Numerical control (N/C) is a programmable control system for automatically operating machine tools and other manufacturing equipment (Fig. 91-1). An N/C program must be written to provide the instructions to the **machine control unit (MCU)** for performing the desired series of tasks. N/C programs consist of coded instructions that use ordinary numbers, letters of the alphabet, and common symbols used in mathematics and punctuation. The coded instructions are converted into electrical signals that control the operation of electric motors and other devices that run the machine.

Numerical control is a proven system for providing automatic operation of machines. Most new metalworking machine tools are now provided with N/C controls. In addition, N/C is being used to control some assembly machines, robots, and lasers.

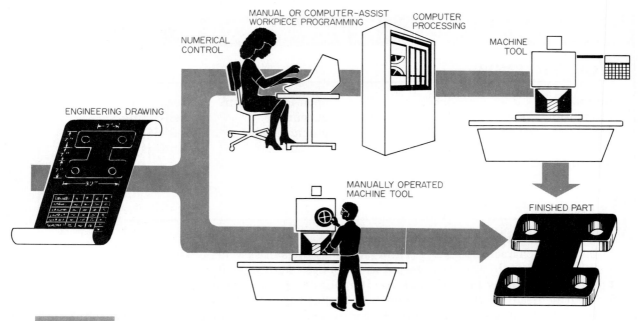

Fig. 91-1 *The major steps in manufacturing parts by numerical control, compared with the steps in manufacturing by manual control.*

<table>
<tr><td>91-1</td></tr>
</table>

91-1 Numerical Control Systems

Numerically coded instructions to a machine may be provided by punched tape (Fig. 91-2), or magnetic tape or disc. The present trend, however, is to provide instructions directly from a computer.

Direct numerical control (DNC) systems use a large computer capable of controlling many machines at the same time. **Computer numerical control (CNC)** systems use a **microcomputer** for the operation of each machine. Communication between the machine and the computer is through the MCU at each machine. This arrangement allows program corrections and changes to be made quickly at each machine at any time, instead of waiting for new tapes to be made. An N/C machine with a CNC control unit is shown in Figure 91-3.

91-2 Advantages of Numerical Control

The following are the most important advantages of using N/C machines:

1. N/C machines consistently produce accurate work without the need for expensive jigs to guide the tools. Usually, only simple workholding fixtures are needed with N/C machines. Thus, N/C greatly reduces the record keeping and storage space formerly needed for large quantities of jigs.
2. One N/C machine can often do the work of several conventional machines. The **machining center** in Figure 91-4 is an example. This machine, which automatically changes tools, saves floor space. It also reduces the need to move parts from one machine to another.
3. N/C programs can be prepared much faster than jigs can be designed and built, which greatly reduces **lead time.** Lead time is the time needed for planning and tooling-up to make a product or part. Also, design changes can be made quickly by changing the N/C program.
4. Because N/C is accurate and reliable, fewer parts are spoiled because of human error. This also reduces the amount of inspection needed for quality control.

E.I.A. STANDARD CODING
FOR
I INCH WIDE, EIGHT TRACK TAPE

TAPE PUNCH	8 EL	7 X	6 O	5 CH	4 8	·	3 4	2 2	1 1
0									
1									
2									
3									
4									
5									
6									
7									
8									
9									
a									
b									
c									
d									
e									
f									
g									
h									
i									
j									
k									
l									
m									
n									
o									
p									
q									
r									
s									
t									
u									
v									
w									
x									
y									
z									
· (PERIOD)									
, (COMMA)									
/									
+ (PLUS)									
— (MINUS)									
SPACE									
DELETE									
CARR. RET. OR END OF BLOCK									
BACK SPACE									
TAB									
END OF RECORD									
LEADER									
BLANK TYPE									
UPPER CASE									
LOWER CASE									

Fig. 91-2 *The Electronics Industries Association (EIA) standard code for 1" (25.4 mm) wide 8-track tape. The code represented by the punched tape uses the binary number system.*

Fig. 91-3 *This CNC machine control system relies on the power of a microcomputer.* (Clausing)

Fig. 91-4 *An automatic tool-changing N/C machining center can replace several manually operated machines.* (DeVlieg Machine Co.)

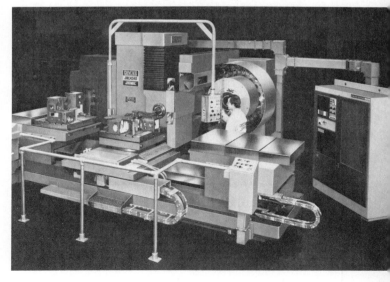

5. Since N/C provides a standard method of making each part, management has better control of production schedules and production costs.

6. N/C is ideal for small quantity repeat orders. Once written, N/C programs can be stored indefinitely on tape or other memory devices. When needed, they can be returned quickly to the machine for re-use. A stored N/C program eliminates the need to replan the job and greatly reduces lead time.

91-3 The Basis for N/C Measurement

A system of **rectangular coordinates** called the **Cartesian coordinate system** (Fig. 91-5) is the basis for N/C measurements. It provides a way of identifying the **axis** (path) of motion, X, Y, or Z, and the **direction** of motion, + or −. The X, Y, and Z axes and their respective planes XY, XZ, and YZ are at 90° to each other. **The Z axis is always assigned to the machine spindle.** Therefore, for vertical-spindle machines, such as drill presses and vertical milling machines (Fig. 91-6), the Z axis is vertical. For horizontal-spindle machines, such as lathes and horizontal-spindle milling machines, the Z axis is horizontal (Fig. 91-7).

Once a reference point and a unit of measurement has been established, any point in space or on a workpiece can be accurately located by specifying its coordinates. This method of location is illustrated in Figure 91-5. Using the intersection of the X, Y, and Z planes as the fixed reference point (0), Point A has coordinates of X + 4, Y + 2, and Z + 3. Point B has coordinates of X + 4, Y − 3, and Z − 2.

Fig. 91-5 *The Cartesian coordinate system used in N/C programming.*

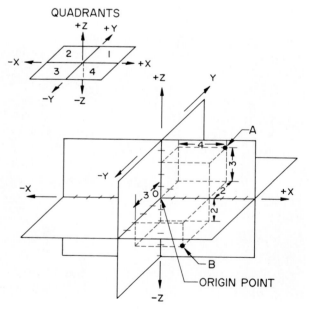

Notice that the XY plane is divided into **quadrants.** Many N/C systems are designed so that all points on an object are in the first quadrant. With these systems, all positions are designated positive (+). When the object is located this way, the positive (+) sign may be omitted in the program. For example, the coordinates for Point A in Figure 91-5 would be written as X4, Y2, Z3. Figure 91-8 outlines a rectangular block positioned in the first quadrant. The position of each of its corners, labeled A through H, is given in the accompanying chart. Study the diagram until you understand the method of describing the location of these points.

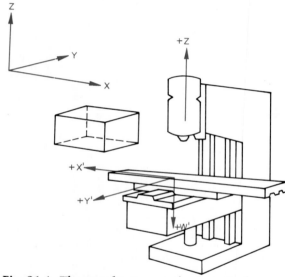

Fig. 91-6 *The coordinate axes for a vertical milling machine of the column and knee type.*

Fig. 91-7 *The coordinate axes for a horizontal spindle turret lathe.*

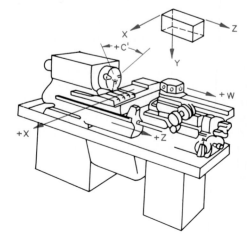

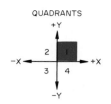

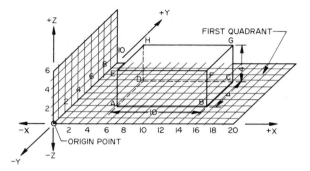

POINT	X	Y	Z
A	5	3	0
B	15	3	0
C	15	7	0
D	5	7	0
E	5	3	4
F	15	3	4
G	15	7	4
H	5	7	4

Fig. 91-8 *A rectangular block positioned in the first quadrant. The chart shows the coordinate position of each corner.*

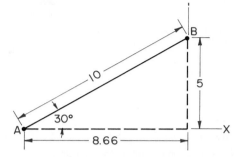

Fig. 91-9 *N/C contouring systems produce angular movement by programming the X and Y movements required. The program "X + 8.66 Y + 5" moves the tool 10 units along a 30° path.*

91-4 Kinds of Numerical Control

There are two main kinds of N/C systems: (1) point-to-point, and (2) contouring.

Point-to-Point N/C. A point-to-point N/C system is basically a positioning system. Its primary purpose is to move a tool or workpiece from one programmed point to another. Point-to-point N/C systems are suitable for hole-machining operations such as drilling, countersinking, counterboring, reaming, and tapping. Hole-punching machines, spot welding machines, and assembly machines also use point-to-point N/C systems.

Most point-to-point N/C systems also permit straight-line cutting such as the milling of slots or grooves. Straight-line cuts in either the X or Y axis may be programmed, and 45° angles are cut by moving both the X and Y axes drive motors at the same time. Programming of other angles and curves is possible, but it is not practical with point-to-point N/C systems.

Contouring N/C. Contouring N/C systems are capable of directing the tool or workpiece to move at any angle, and also along curved paths. Many contouring N/C machines, such as lathes and vertical milling machines, are of the **two-axis** type. These machines can cut continuous path contours in the XY plane. **Three-axis** machines are capable of cutting movements in all three axes at the same time. Such movement is required for machining three-dimensional shapes in die and mold cavities.

Most contouring N/C systems can only move the tool or workpiece in straight lines parallel to the machine axes. Therefore, to produce angular or circular movement, the machine control unit must calculate and order movements in each axis. These movements must match as closely as possible the angle or curve desired. Angular movement is produced by programming the amount of movement required in the X and Y axes (Fig. 91-9). A circular path is produced by determining the amount of X and Y movement required and locating the center of the arc (Fig. 91-10). Both angles and curves are cut by breaking the angle of curve into a series of straight lines (chords) that fit to the degree of accuracy required (Fig. 91-11). The X and Y coordinates of each line must then be calculated and programmed. This task is greatly simplified by using computer-assisted N/C programming languages.

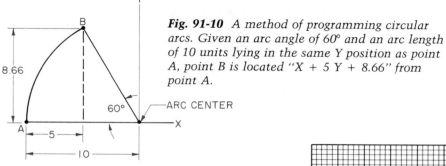

Fig. 91-10 *A method of programming circular arcs. Given an arc angle of 60° and an arc length of 10 units lying in the same Y position as point A, point B is located "X + 5 Y + 8.66" from point A.*

Fig. 91-11 *In N/C machining, angles and curves are actually cut by a series of short, straight-line cuts parallel to the machine axes. Because the size of each move is so small, the machined surface is smooth and continuous.*

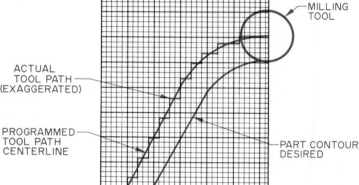

91-5 Production Steps in N/C Machining

The steps involved in machining parts on N/C machine tools are listed below.

1. The designer, usually an engineer, determines the part specifications and makes a sketch of the part and any necessary workholding fixtures.
2. The designer, or a design technician, then uses a computer-aided drafting and design (CADD) system to create computer drawings of the part and fixtures.
3. "Hard-copy" drawings on paper or film are made on a computer-driven drafting plotter or printer after the CADD drawings are checked by the engineer.
4. The N/C programmer studies the part drawing and determines the best sequence of machining operations to be used for making the part.
5. The **N/C programmer** than prepares the N/C program. The program must contain the correct step-by-step instructions for each machining operation. Machining cycle codes, tool or workpiece movement in each axis, spindle speeds, feed rates, coolant flow, and tool changes must all be correctly programmed.

The program is prepared in one of the following ways:

a. **Manual programming.** A handwritten **program manuscript** is prepared, then a punched tape of the program is made by typing out the program on a computer terminal or typewriter equipped with a tape punch.

b. **N/C computer-language programming.** In this type of programming, a handwritten program manuscript is first written, using an N/C computer language such as APT or Compact II. This program is then entered into a computer that automatically converts it into the standard N/C program needed to run the machine (Fig. 91-12). The N/C program may be stored in computer memory, on magnetic tape or disc, on punched tape, or sent electronically to a machine with a computer numerical control unit (see below).

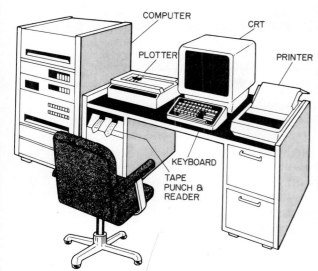

Fig. 91-12 *A complete system for N/C computer-language assisted N/C programming.*

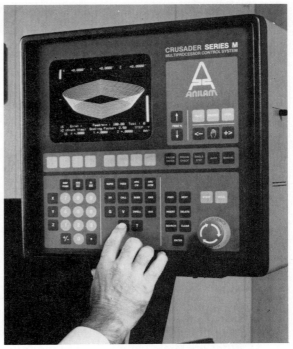

Fig. 91-13 *Most new N/C machines are being equipped with CNC controls such as the one shown here.* (Anilam Electronics Corporation)

c. **CNC (computer numerical control)** programming. CNC machine control systems are designed to use a microcomputer as the central control unit (Fig. 91-13). Programming is basically the same as manual programming, but the power of the computer is used to simplify the programming. Some CNC's are known as **manual data input (MDI)** systems because the program must be entered manually through the control panel. Other CNC's allow both MDI and program input from a remote tape reader or another computer.

6. The program is next checked for accuracy by the programmer. The first time a new program is run, the programmer and the machine operator make a **dry run.** This is a test run of the program without a workpiece in position, so that if the program contains gross errors, no damage will occur to the expensive machine and cutting tools. If program errors are found, they are corrected and another dry run is made. This procedure is repeated until the program appears to be correct.

7. Test runs of the program are then made with a workpiece in position. In some cases, test runs are made using machinable wax or plastic materials that are less costly than most metals. The workpiece is accurately measured to determine whether any of its dimensions are incorrect. If necessary, further adjustments are made in the program.

8. When a program has been approved for production, it is delivered to the machine or the machine operator along with a part drawing and a program manuscript. The program manuscript contains machine setup and operation instructions that must be carried out in order to machine the part successfully. On more complex N/C machines, all of the machining is done automatically. On simple N/C machines, the operator may need to make tool changes, adjust feed rates and spindle speeds, set tool depth stops, and turn coolant on and off.

REVIEW   REVIEW   REVIEW   REVIEW   REVIEW

WORDS TO KNOW

axis of motion
Cartesian
  coordinate system
computer numerical
  control (CNC)
computer numerical
  control
  programming
contouring N/C
  system

direct numerical
  control (DNC)
dry run
lead time
manual data input
  (MDI)
machine control
  unit (MCU)
machining center
manual programmer
microcomputer

N/C (numerical
  control)
N/C computer-
  language
  programming
N/C programmer
point-to-point N/C
  system
program manuscript
quadrants

rectangular
  coordinates
three-axis machines
two-axis machines
X axis
Y axis
Z axis

REVIEW QUESTIONS

1. List several ways of providing instructions to N/C machines.
2. How do DNC and CNC systems differ? How are they the same?
3. What are the advantages of using N/C machines?
4. Explain how the Cartesian coordinate system works. Which axis is always assigned to the machine spindle?
5. Make a sketch showing the orientation of the X, Y, and Z axis for a vertical milling machine.
6. Name the two main kinds of N/C systems and explain how they differ.
7. Explain how N/C machines actually cut angles and curves.
8. List the main production steps for N/C machining.
9. Name the three methods of N/C programming.
10. Explain the difference between dry runs and test runs and tell why each is necessary.

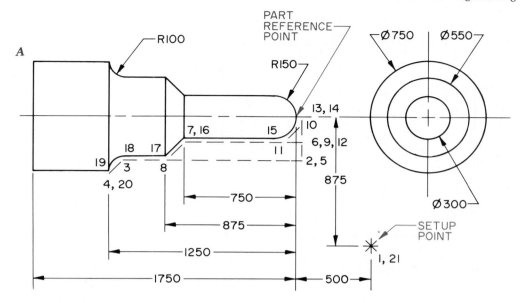

A

B

N	G	X	Z	I	K	F	M	Remarks
00	95						03	Feed in inches/revolution
01	92	1750	500					Absolute programming/setup location
02	00	570	50			*		Rapid feed to location
03	01	570	−1150			15		First rough cut
04	01	770	−1250			15		Second rough cut
05	00	570	50					Rapid feed to location
06	00	360	50					Rapid feed to location
07	01	360	−750			15		Third rough cut
08	01	610	−875			15		Fourth rough cut
09	00	360	50					Rapid feed to location
10	00	200	50					Rapid feed to location
11	01	350	−100					Fifth rough cut
12	00	350	50					Rapid feed to location
13	00	0	50					Rapid feed to location
14	01	0	0			5		Position to begin finishing cut
15	03	300		0	150	5	99	Turn end radius
16	01	300	−750			5		Turn 300 diameter
17	01	550	−875			5		Turn angle
18	01	550	−1150			5		Turn 550 diameter
19	02	750	−1250	100	0	5	99	Turn 100 radius
20	00	800	−1250					Rapid feed out
21	00	1750	500					Rapid feed to setup point
22							30	Program end

*The rapid feed rate is fixed and does not require programming.

Fig. 92-3 *(A) A cylindrical part with units added for absolute dimensioning. Note the difference between the part reference point and the setup point. (This machine has no machine reference point.) (B) The absolute program for the part.*

Fig. 92-4 *A small N/C lathe designed especially for instructional use. (Emco Maier Inc.)*

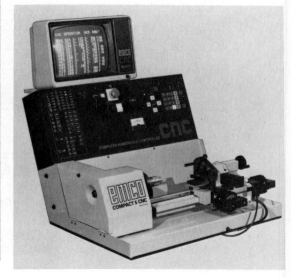

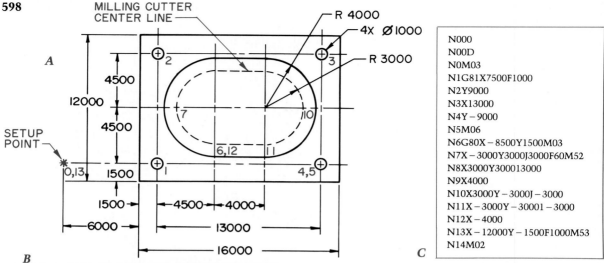

Fig. 92-5 *(A) The drawing of the part shown in Figure 92-1A with units added for incremental dimensioning. (B) The incremental N/C program manuscript for the part. (C) The typewritten printout of the N/C word-address program for machining the part as it would appear after punching a tape of the program.*

N	G	X	Y	I	J	F	M	EOB	Instructions
N000								EOB	1000 dia drill
N00	D							EOB	
N0							03	EOB	
N1	81	7500				1000		EOB	
N2			9000					EOB	
N3		13000						EOB	
N4			−9000					EOB	
N5							06	EOB	Change to 2000 dia end mill
N6	80	−8500	1500				03	EOB	
N7		−3000	3000		3000	60	52	EOB	
N8		3000	3000	3000				EOB	
N9		4000						EOB	
N10		3000	−3000		−3000			EOB	
N11		−3000	−3000	−3000				EOB	
N12		−4000						EOB	
N13		−12000	−1500			1000	53	EOB	
N14							02	EOB	

The part reference point is located at the lower left corner of the **workpiece.** The machine reference point is located at the lower left corner of the **drawing.** The distance between the two (6000 units each on the X and Y axes) must be added to all part dimensions to obtain the correct absolute programming dimensions.

Most absolute N/C systems are designed so that the part is always located in the first quadrant of the coordinate system (Fig. 91-5). All coordinate positions, then, are positive numbers. **When most N/C systems are programmed, the plus sign and decimal points may be omitted.** (Section 92-3 explains how fractional or decimal figures are changed into coordinate numbers.) Compare Figures 92-1A and 92-3A with their programs (Figs. 92-1B and 92-3B) to become familiar with the absolute dimensioning system.

Incremental dimensioning system. The part drawings in Figures 92-5A and 92-6A are dimensioned by the incremental method. With this method, the distance between points on a part is given without reference to a fixed point. The programmed dimensions for each tool movement are measured from the position of the tool at the starting point of each move. Compare Figure 92-5A with the program given in Figure 92-5B and Figure 92-6A with the program in 92-6B. You will see that some negative moves are required. Incremental programming requires all moves in the negative direction to be preceded with the minus (−) sign, such as X-8500 in line (block) N6 of Figure 92-5B.

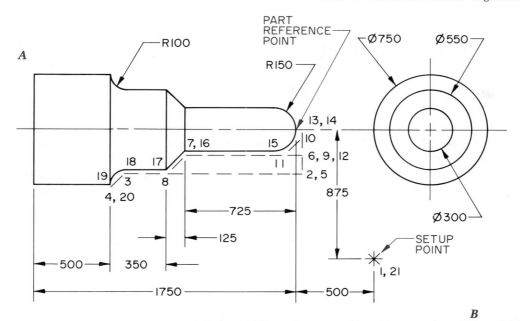

Fig. 92-6 *(A) A cylindrical part with units added for incremental dimensioning. (B) The incremental N/C program manuscript for the part.*

N	G	X	Z	I	K	F	M	Remarks
00	91						03	Incremental programming
01	95							Feed in inches/revolution
02	00	−590	−450			*		Rapid feed to location
03	01	0	−1200			15		First rough cut
04	01	−100	−100			15		Second rough cut
05	00	−100	−1300					Rapid feed to location
06	00	−105	0					Rapid feed to location
07	01	0	−800			15		Third rough cut
08	01	125	−125			15		Fourth rough cut
09	00	−125	925					Rapid feed to location
10	00	−130	−25					Rapid feed to location
11	01	125	−125					Fifth rough cut
12	00	0	125					Rapid feed to location
13	00	−175	0					Rapid feed to location
14	01	0	−25			5		Position to begin finishing cut
15	03	150	−150	0	−150	5	99	Turn end radius
16	01	0	−600			5		Turn 300 diameter
17	01	125	−125			5		Turn angle
18	01	0	−275			5		Turn 550 diameter
19	02	100	−100	100	0	5	99	Turn 100 radius
20	00	25	0					Rapid feed out
21	00	475	1750					Rapid feed to setup point
22							30	Program end

*The rapid feed rate is fixed and does not require programming.

92-2 N/C Programming Codes

Instructions are provided to N/C control systems with the use of one of two **Binary Coded Decimal Systems:** (1) the Electronics Industries Association (EIA) code (Fig. 91-2), or (2) the American Society for Computer Information Interchange (ASCII) code. EIA-coded N/C programs will not run on ASCII-coded machine control units, and vice versa. However, control units are now being built to accept tapes with either code.

92-3 N/C Language

N/C program format. Most N/C systems use either a **word address format** or a **tab sequential format.** "Words" consist of a letter followed by the numerical data, such as N1G81X2250Y500F1000 (five words). Each letter identifes a different machine function. In the tab sequential format, the numerical data are separated by a space, or tab, code. The space serves like a divider in a file. The same information given in the word address form above would appear as 1 81 2250 500 1000 in tab sequential format.

Tab sequential programming information must be written in a fixed sequence according to the way the machine control unit is wired. The number of tab codes, or spaces, preceding the numerical data determines which machine function will be activated. Word address programming does not have to be entered in a fixed sequence. The common practice, however, is to list the data in the sequence shown in the programming examples.

Information blocks. An N/C program is made up of blocks of coded information. A block of information consists of the information on each line of a program manuscript (Figs. 92-1B, 92-3B, 92-5 and 92-6B). An **end-of-block** (EOB) **code** must separate the blocks of information.

The programming system may be either full-block or variable-block. **Full-block programming** requires information to be written in each category of each block of the program (columns G-M of each program). This type of system cannot remember information from one block to another. Figures 92-3B and 92-6B are examples of full block programming. **Variable-block programming** systems can remember information that is the same for succeeding blocks in the program. For example, if a move is required only in the Y axis, the system can remember the coordinate in the X axis from the last move. This feature greatly reduces programming time. The information in the programs in Figures 92-1B, and 92-5B is in variable-block form.

Information within a block. A block of information for a two-axis contouring N/C program includes:

1. sequence number (N)
2. preparatory function (G)
3. X dimension
4. Y dimension (for a milling machine) or a Z dimension (for a lathe)
5. I dimension
6. J dimension
7. feed rate (F)
8. miscellaneous function (M).

More sophisticated machines also use an S number to program spindle speed, and a T number for automatic tool changing.

Sequence number. The sequence number identifies each block of information on the program. Most machine control units have a sequence number readout that displays the number of the operation being performed. A letter such as N or H is used as an address for the sequence number.

Preparatory functions. G-code numbers are used to program the N/C machine for a certain type of operation, such as an automatic drilling cycle, or a milling cycle. Examples of G-codes are shown in Table 92-1. G-code numbers may differ for different N/C machines.

X, Y, Z, I, and J coordinate dimensions. Coordinate dimensions are written in terms of the smallest unit of movement for which the N/C system is designed. Inch systems are usually programmed in units of 0.001″ or 0.0001″. Metric systems are usually programmed in units of 0.02 or 0.01 mm. Thus, for a 0.001″ system, 3¼″ would be written 3250. 5⁄16″ would have to be rounded off to 312 or 313 (instead of 3125), since the system cannot move less than 0.001″. For a 0.02 mm system, 28.6 mm would be written 2860. 19.05 mm would have to be written as 1904 or 1906, since the system cannot move in units less than 0.02 mm.

Table 92-1

Examples of N/C Preparatory Function Codes

Cycle code	Cycle name
Compact 5 lathe codes	
G00	Rapid feed
G01	Linear interpolation
G02	Circular interpolation (CCW viewed from top of lathe tool)
G03	Circular interpolation (CW viewed from top of lathe tool)
G22	Program end
G78	Threading cycle
G84	Longitudinal turning cycle
G91	Incremental programming
G92	Tool offset with absolute programming
G94	Feed rate in inches/minute (mm/minute)
G95	Feed rate in inches/revolution (mm/rev.)
Milling machine codes	
G78	Mill stop
G79	Mill
G80	Cancel
G81	Drill
G82	Dwell
G84	Tap
G85	Bore

X, Y, and **Z** are used in word address programming to identify moves in those axes. (The **Z** axis is omitted on programs for two-axis systems.) **I** and **J** are used in contour programming to locate the center of the arc or circle being programmed. **I** identifies the distance to center in the **X** axis; **J** identifies the distance to center in the **Y** axis. In incremental programming, the center location is measured from the center of the tool at the beginning of the contour move (Fig. 92-5B). In absolute programming, the coordinates of the center from the machine reference point are given (see Fig. 92-1B).

Feed rate. The feed rate can be programmed on most N/C machines. High feed rates are used for rapid tool or workpiece movements between machining operations. Slower feed rates must be used during machining operations. Feed rates for machining may be in inches per minute, mm per minute, or m per minute. For drilling and lathe turning, units of 0.001″ per revolution or 0.02 mm per revolution are used. Some inch/minute systems use units of 1⁄10 of an inch, such as 3.5″/min. Since decimals are omitted in the program, this would be written as 35.

Miscellaneous functions. M-codes are referred to as **on-off** machine functions. They regulate spindle motion, tool changes, and other functions. Examples of M-codes are given in Table 92-2. M-codes may differ for different N/C machines, but attempts are being made to standardize all code numbers.

Table 92-2

Examples of Miscellaneous Function Codes

Code #	Function
M02	End of program
M03	Spindle ON
M05	Spindle OFF
M06	Tool change
M52	Advance spindle
M53	Retract spindle
M56	Tool inhibit
M57	Index turret depth stop

92-4 Manual N/C Program-Writing Procedure

1. The first step in N/C programming is to decide how the workpiece will be held for machining. Workholding fixtures sometimes are obstacles to machine moves. Therefore, N/C programs must be carefully written to prevent collisions between fixtures and cutting tools.
2. The location of the workpiece on the machine should next be decided. For milling machines, **locate the workpiece so that all machining operations can be performed within the travel limits of the machine.** For lathes, **be sure a sufficient length of stock is provided so that the workpiece can be machined without tools colliding with the chuck.**
3. Select a safe and convenient **setup point.** It should be far enough away from the workpiece so that sharp tools do not endanger the operator when he or she is loading or unloading a workpiece.
4. The most efficient machining sequence should then be determined, and the workpiece drawing numbered accordingly.
5. Write the N/C program. Zero's may be used to number the program blocks before the first tool or workpiece move. In this way the block numbers on the program will be the same as the sequence numbers for machine operations on the part drawing.

   The first line of every N/C program should contain only an EOB code, which is necessary for carrying out the **rewind stop** command given on the next line of the program. The second line of every program should have only a rewind stop code and an EOB code. When using punched tape, the rewind stop command turns off the rewinding motor when the tape is rewound to the beginning of the program. Rewind stop codes differ for different N/C systems. In the program examples given in Figures 92-1B and 92-5B the letter **D** is used.

   Most N/C systems do not require use of a positive (+) sign. **To determine whether a move is positive or negative,**

write the program as though the tool were doing the moving, not the workpiece.

   All programs are finished with an **end-of-program code,** followed by the final EOB code. This will automatically rewind the tape or otherwise return the program to the starting point, ready to run the next part.
6. After the program has been written, it should be checked for obvious mistakes. All N/C programs should start and stop at the setup point (sometimes called home). Therefore, incremental program moves are self-checking, since the sum of all positive moves in each axis should cancel the sum of all negative moves.

Figure 92-1B gives the program for the part shown in Figure 92-1A, which uses absolute dimensioning. It is written in word address, variable block format, with the part located in the first quadrant. Figure 92-5B gives the N/C program for the same part with incremental dimensioning (Fig. 92-5A). This program is also written in word address, variable block format. Incremental programming requires the use of minus (−) signs to signal moves in the negative direction.

Figure 92-3B gives the N/C program for the part shown in Fig. 92-3A, which uses absolute dimensioning. It is written in word address, full block format, the format required for the lathe pictured in Figure 92-4. **Note that in absolute mode, the workpiece diameter is programmed.** Also, with the setup point given, Z moves to the left of the end of the workpiece require a minus sign.

Fig. 92-6B gives the N/C program for the same lathe part with incremental dimensioning (Fig. 92-6A). Note that in incremental programming, Z moves to the left of the setup point, and X moves toward the center of the spindle require a minus sign.

92-5 Punching the N/C Tape

N/C tapes are made on tape-punching typewriters or computer terminals such as shown in Figure 91-12. After turning on machines like that shown in Figure 91-12, the tape punch is turned on next. The operator then types the information on the N/C program manuscript in the same order as it was written. As each key is struck, its corresponding pattern of holes is punched in the tape. It is not necessary to leave spaces between information categories in word address program tapes. This feature saves typing and shortens the tape. After the tape is punched, it may be run through the typewriter's tape reader, which causes the typewriter to print out the information contained on the tape. The printout provides a means of checking the accuracy of the program tape.

The typewritten program obtained while punching the tape for the word address program in Figure 92-5B appears in Figure 92-5C (EOB codes do not print).

REVIEW REVIEW REVIEW REVIEW REVIEW

WORDS TO KNOW

absolute dimensions	incremental	N/C computer	variable-block
binary coded	dimensions	language	system
decimal systems	information block	on-off functions	word address format
computer-assisted	machine reference	part reference point	
programming	point	rewind stop code	
end-of-block code	manual	setup point (home)	
end-of-program code	programming	tab sequential	
full-block system		format	

REVIEW QUESTIONS

1. How do absolute and incremental dimensioning differ?
2. What is the difference between the part reference point and the machine table reference point? From which point must all tool movements be measured for absolute programming?
3. In incremental programming, what symbol is used to program a move in the negative direction?
4. How do word address and tab sequential formats differ? What advantages does word address programming have?
5. What code is used to separate blocks of information?
6. How do full-block and variable-block programming systems differ?
7. What are G-code numbers used for in N/C programming?
8. Explain the use of "I" and "J" in word address programming.
9. How are feed rates for milling operations specified?
10. What functions are M-code numbers used for? Give several examples.
11. What should be considered when deciding where to locate the setup point for a particular operation?
12. Explain how incremental programs are partly self-checking.

PART

22

Inspection and Testing

Four years ago, Larry Taylor began as an inspection trainee at a large aeronautics plant. He had studied metalworking at a junior college, and had worked as a welder and machinist. Today Larry is an associate engineer in the quality assurance department.

Larry provides advice and assistance to plant employees to insure that high-quality manufacturing is done. He checks everything from "womb to tomb," that is, from the initial design to the finished product. Beginning with the standard stock, he determines whether metal shipped from the supplier meets design specifications. He then follows its progress through the stages of production, and makes sure that machinists are using tools correctly to meet manufacturing standards.

Using micrometers, optical comparators, and coordinate measuring machines, Larry sees that every part produced is within strict dimension limits. He may "dig" inside a completed turbine engine to satisfy himself that the parts are secure. Or he may test the working parts of landing gear. If any product is unsatisfactory, he orders it scrapped, reworked, or redesigned.

Larry feels that high schools should introduce students to the new possibilities of a career such as his. More and more courses and degrees are being offered in quality assurance. He advises interested students to assess their own capabilities, set reasonable goals, and then be prepared to move up slowly in the field.

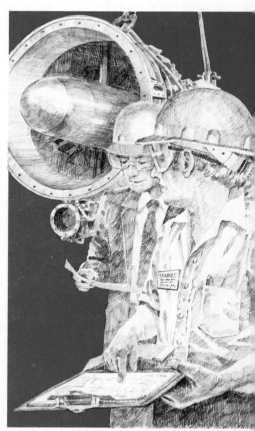

Larry discovered himself that becoming a quality assurance engineer is not an "overnight" process. He has attained one goal. And he knows that there will be more accomplishments to strive for as he continues in metalworking.

Larry Taylor
Associate Engineer
Quality Assurance

UNIT
93

Inspection Tools and Equipment

The quality of manufactured products is controlled through a program of inspection and statistical process control (SPC). The technique of SPC is to monitor each production process by inspecting a sample of the product at regular intervals. The degree of precision required and the reliability of the production process determine how often and how large the sample should be. The regular inspection of production samples provides necessary information on whether the production equipment requires adjustment. If it does, technicians determine how it should be adjusted to prevent or minimize the production of defective parts.

Inspection is usually done by specially trained inspectors. Inspection may be done either at work stations in the plant or in special inspection rooms (Fig. 93-1).

Fig. 93-1 An inspection room.

Accurate inspection then, is critical to the success of SPC and the manufacture of quality products at lowest cost. A complete inspection program includes examination of the following:

1. materials
2. measurements
3. finish
4. performance.

Parts that do not pass inspection are either reworked or scrapped. Measuring instruments used in inspection must also be inspected regularly.

93-1 The Need for Accuracy in Measurements

Parts must be made within specified size limits to assure their interchangeability. **Interchangeability** is the manufacture of parts to such accuracy that any part of a product can be replaced with a like part taken from another identical product of the same make and model. It also means that **replacement parts** will fit and perform as well as the original parts.

With high accuracy in manufacturing, parts of a product can be made at different locations so that all parts will fit together properly when shipped to an assembly point. For example, automobile parts are often made hundreds and even thousands of miles away from the assembly plant. Bodies are made in one plant, frames in another, engines in another, wheels in another, and so on. Therefore, it is necessary to make quantities of each part for a product as near alike as possible. Only in this way can parts be selected at random with the assurance that they will assemble and perform properly.

93-2 Standards for Measurement

A standard is necessary so that an inch or a meter is the same length in all parts of the world. The International Bureau of Weights and Measures, established in 1875 near Paris, France has defined the length of the meter as 1,650,763.73 wavelengths of orange light emitted by Krypton-86 atoms in an electrical discharge. The **International Inch,** as defined in terms of metric units [2.54 centimeters], can be stated in terms of wavelengths of Krypton light as follows:

$$1'' = 0.0254 \text{ meters} \times 1,650,763.73$$
$$\text{wavelengths per meter}$$
$$1'' = 41,929.3987 \text{ wavelengths}$$

Light waves do not vary significantly with temperature changes and changes in atmospheric conditions. Therefore, measurement by this exact method may be duplicated in any part of the world.

93-3 Gage Blocks, A Practical Standard

Precision **gage blocks** (Fig. 93-2) are used as a **practical standard** for measurement in industrial plants the world over. Gage blocks are solid, simple-looking blocks of hardened steel, tungsten carbide, or a special ceramic. They are made to precise sizes and have extremely flat polished surfaces. Gage blocks are precise to within a few **millionths of an inch** (hundred-thousandths of a millimeter).

The best known gage blocks were invented by Carl E. Johansson in Sweden in 1895. They became known the world over as **Johansson gage blocks,** or **Jo-blocks.** Today gage blocks are manufactured by several companies according to three grades of accuracy: Classes 1, 2, and 3. These are U.S. Federal quality classifications based on allowable tolerances for **length, flatness, parallelism,** and **surface finish.** The length tolerances for blocks up to one inch, or metric blocks up to 10 mm, measured at a temperature of 68°F [20°C] are as follows:

	Inch	Metric
Class 1:	± 0.000 002"	± 0.00005 mm
Class 2:	+ 0.000 004"	+ 0.00010 mm
	− 0.000 002"	− 0.00005 mm
Class 3:	+ 0.000 008"	+ 0.00020 mm
	− 0.000 004"	− 0.00010 mm

Class 1 gage blocks, called **laboratory** or **master** gages, are usually used in temperature-controlled laboratories as references to check the accuracy of other gages. Class 2 gage blocks, called **inspection-grade** gages, are used for inspection of finished parts and may also be used for setting **working gages.** Class 3 gage blocks are often called **working blocks.** They are used constantly by machinists and tool-and-die makers. Working blocks are essential for accurately laying out lines and hole centers, checking the accuracy of other measuring tools, and precisely setting cutting or measuring tools (Fig. 93-3).

Gage blocks may be joined by squeezing them together with a twisting motion called wringing. This forces all the air from between the blocks. Because the blocks are so flat and smooth, the blocks stick tightly together because of **adhesion.** The adhesion is strong enough to support considerable weight.

Fig. 93-2 *A set of gage blocks.* (The L.S. Starrett Co.)

Fig. 93-3 *Using gage blocks with a planer gage to establish the gaging height of a dial indicator.*

Fig. 93-4 *Using a telescoping gage to measure an inside diameter.*

93-4 Inspection Tools and Gages

Many kinds of inspection gages are available. Some are designed for general use and can be used for a number of measuring and gaging purposes within a broad range of sizes. Some are designed for special gaging purposes within a very narrow size range. Others are designed to gage only one size. Commonly used gages are described in the following paragraphs.

Nonindicating mechanical gages, also called **attribute gages,** can determine only whether a part dimension is within preset limits; they do not measure the actual part size.

Adjustable gases are designed for general use. They can be adjusted within a certain range of sizes. Several gages of this type include the **planer gage** (Fig. 93-3), the **telescoping gage** (Fig. 93-4), **small hole gages** (Fig. 93-5), and **dial-indicating** type gages (Figs. 93-17 through 93-24). The adjustable **snap gage** (Fig. 93-9) can be used for gaging various dimensions within a limited size range.

Fig. 93-5 *Using a small hole gage to measure the width of a groove.*

Fixed gages are usually made for gaging only one size. A few of the common fixed gages include **caliper-type snap gages** (Fig. 93-6); **ring gages** (Fig. 93-11); **plug gages** (Fig. 93-14); **thread gages** (Fig. 93-15); and **reference gages** (Fig. 93-7).

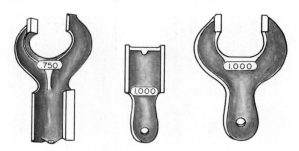

Fig. 93-6 *Fixed snap gages.*

Fig. 93-7 *Reference gages.*

Reference gages are made of hardened steel and are used to test or check inspection gages. Reference gages are also called master gages. Inspection gages are checked with the reference gages to determine whether they are worn, damaged, or out of adjustment. Micrometers can also be checked in this manner.

93-5 Go and Not-Go Gages

Go and not-go gages are often called **limits gages.** They are **double gages** because they have two gaging points or surfaces. One tests the upper size limits and the other tests the lower size limit of a part being gaged. There are several types of go and not-go gages, including snap gages, ring gages, and plug gages.

The principles involved in testing parts with go and not-go gages can be understood by studying Figure 93-8. The figure shows a cy-

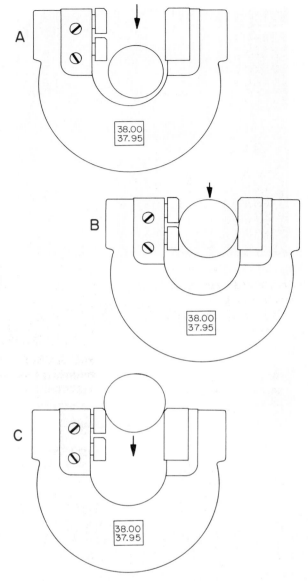

Fig. 93-8 *Testing a part with a limits gage. (A) The part is too small. (B) The part is satisfactory. (C) The part is too large.*

lindrical part being tested with a **limits snap gage.** The upper gaging point is the **go** point, while the lower one is the **not-go** point. If the part is within specified size limits, it will pass through the go point or surface, but it will not pass through the not-go point or surface.

93-6

Snap Gages

Snap gages are used for checking the outside diameter, length, or thickness of parts. They are used in a manner similar to the way a **caliper** is used. Hence, snap gages are often called **caliper gages.** Snap gages are available in a wide variety of styles and sizes. They may be fixed (Fig. 93-6), adjustable (Fig. 93-9), or dial-indicating (Fig. 93-23).

Adjustable snap gages may be supplied **set** and **sealed** at specific limits by the manufac-

turer. Gages are also available **unset** and **unsealed.** The **button anvils** on these gages may then be adjusted to the desired size with gage blocks, as in Figure 93-9.

Limits snap gages are available with **gaging rolls,** instead of anvils, for testing the pitch diameter of screw threads (Fig. 93-10).

93-7

Ring Gages

A ring gage is a hardened steel ring or collar. Three kinds of ring gages are used:
1. plain ring gages (Fig. 93-11)
2. tapered ring gages (Fig. 93-12)
3. thread ring gages (Fig. 93-13).

Plain ring gages are used to test the external dimension limits of straight round parts.

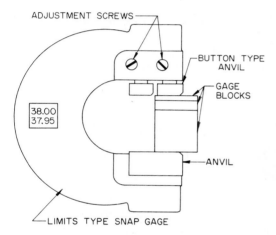

Fig. 93-9 *Setting the size of an adjustable limits snap gage with gage blocks.*

Fig. 93-11 *Plain ring gages.* (Greenfield Tap and Die Corp.)

Fig. 93-10 *A roll-threat snap gage.* (Greenfield Tap and Die Corp.)

Fig. 93-12 *Tapered ring gages test the size and fit of male tapers. Tapered plug gages test the size and fit of tapered holes.* (Brown & Sharpe Mfg. Co.)

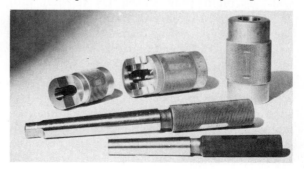

Fig. 93-13 *Go and not-go thread ring gages with their holder.* (Greenfield Tap and Die Corp.)

Fig. 93-14 *A double end plain plug gage.*

Fig. 93-15 *A double end thread plug gage.*

The **not-go** ring, identified by the groove around the outside diameter, is used to check the minimum size limit. The **go** ring is used to check the maximum size limit. The go ring should pass over a part that is inside specified size limits, with little or no interference. The not-go ring should not pass over the part. If both rings pass over the part, it is undersize. If neither does, it is oversize.

Tapered ring gages have a tapered hole. They are used for testing the size and fit of a taper, such as the tapered shank on a drill or reamer.

Thread ring gages of the go and not-go type in Figure 93-13 are used for checking the fit and the pitch diameter limits of external screw threads.

Plug Gages

Three kinds of plug gages are in common use: (1) plain plug gages; (2) tapered plug gages; and (3) thread plug gages. Plug gages of special design are also made for checking square holes or holes of special shape.

Plain plug gages (Fig. 93-14) are accurate cylinders that are used to check the size limits of straight cylindrical holes. The go gage should enter the hole with little or no interference. If great pressure is necessary, the hole is too small. The not-go gage should not enter the hole. If it does, the hole is too large.

Tapered plug gages (Fig. 93-12) are used for checking the size, amount of taper, and the fit of tapered holes. This type of gage is used to test the tapered hole in drill sleeves, in machine tool spindles, and in various kinds of tool adapters.

Thread plug gages (Fig. 93-15) are used for checking the size limits and the fit of internal screw threads.

93-9 Standard Mechanical Gages

Standard mechanical gages are used for measuring common materials, shapes, and tools.

The **radius gage,** also known as the **fillet gage,** is used to measure the radius of rounded corners (Fig. 61-4).

Drill gages, used to check the sizes of unmarked drills, are described in Unit 54.

The **screw-pitch gage** is used to check the pitch of screw threads. It is described in Unit 19.

Sheet metal and wire gages are used for measuring standard sheet metal and wire sizes. They are described in Unit 29.

Two uses of the **center gage** are given in Units 16 and 67.

The **thickness gage,** also called a **feeler gage,** is made up of thin steel blades of different thicknesses. The blades are used to measure small gaps between parts (Fig. 93-16).

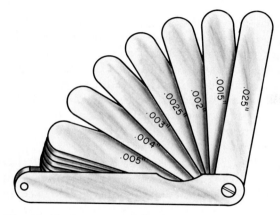

Fig. 93-16 *One type of thickness or feeler gage.*

Fig. 93-17 *(A) A balanced-type dial indicator with 0.0001" (0.000025 mm) graduations. (B) A continuous-type dial indicator.* (The L.S. Starrett Co.)

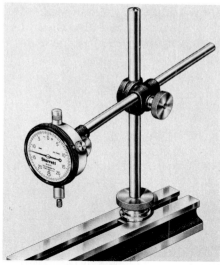

A

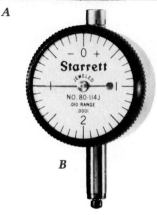

B

93-10 Dial-Indicating Mechanical Gages

Inspectors, machinists, and toolmakers use a variety of dial-indicating gages and measuring instruments. A **dial indicator** looks somewhat like a watch (Fig. 93-17). The dial indicator provides an actual measurement of the amount of error, in size or alignment, for a part being checked (Fig. 93-18).

The graduations on dial gages vary in size. They may be marked in thousandths of an inch (0.001"), in ten-thousandths of an inch (0.0001"), or to the nearest 50 millionths of an inch (0.00005"). The dial indicator in Figure 93-17 has 0.0001" graduations. The numbered graduations are thousandths of an inch and the shorter graduations between them are ten-thousandths of an inch.

Metric dial indicators are marked in hundredths of a millimeter [0.01 mm], or in two-thousandths of a millimeter [0.002 mm].

Fig. 93-18 *Checking the height of a machined part with a dial indicator mounted on a surface gage base.* (The L.S. Starrett Co.)

Two types of dial gages are in common use. The **balanced type** (Fig. 93-17) is numbered in both directions starting with zero. This type is most common on inspection-type gages. The **continuous-reading type** (Fig. 93-19) is numbered continuously starting at zero.

Dial Indicator Set

The dial indicator shown in Figure 93-18 is mounted on a column that is clamped in the T-slot of a steel **surface-gage base.** It is used as a gage for checking the thickness of parts.

When using a dial indicator in this way, the operator must first set the indicator to the basic thickness of the part to be gaged or tested. Setting is done with the use of gage blocks or other measurement standards (Fig. 93-3). At the basic thickness, or **gaging height,** the dial should be set at **zero.** The spindle of the dial indicator should be in the middle of its travel range so as to enable the dial hand to rotate in either direction through the desired measuring range.

A **universal dial indicator set** (Fig. 93-19) is used for many kinds of testing and measuring applications. With the accessories provided, it may be mounted on a surface-gage base, clamped to flat or round surfaces, or it may be mounted in the tool post on a lathe. With the **hole-testing attachment,** holes can be accurately centered in a lathe chuck or on other machine tools (Fig. 93-20).

Universal dial indicators such as that shown in Figure 93-21A are small, convenient to use, and versatile. They are often used in conjunction with a vernier height gage for inspection work (Fig. 93-21B).

Dial-indicating depth gages (Fig. 93-22) are used for gaging the depths of grooves, shoulders, keyways, holes, and similar recesses. Extension points make it possible to increase the measuring depths.

Dial-indicating snap gages (Fig. 93-23) are used for gaging the diameters of parts. The gage shows whether the parts are within the size limits specified and also the amount the part is over or under the basic size.

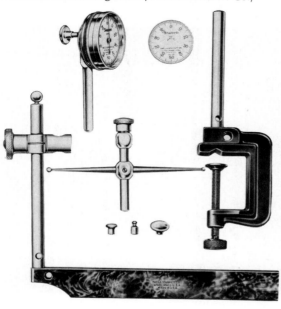

Fig. 93-19 *A universal dial indicator with a continuous-reading dial.* (The L.S. Starrett Co.)

Fig. 93-20 *Using a dial indicator with a hole testing attachment to center a part in a lathe.* (Brown & Sharpe Mfg. Co.)

Dial Comparator

A dial comparator (Fig. 93-24), used for gaging thickness, determines whether parts are within the limits specified. Before a part is gaged, the comparator is set to the specified limits, usually with gage blocks. Gaging will then show the comparison between the set limits and the actual size of the part. The table may be raised or lowered for parts of various thicknesses. The contact point is raised or lowered through its range with the lifting lever at the top.

Fig. 93-22 *A dial-indicating depth gage with extension rods.* (MTI Corporation)

Fig. 93-21 *(A) A small universal dial indicator commonly used for setup and inspection work. (B) Using a small universal dial indicator with a vernier height gage to inspect a part.* (The L.S. Starrett Co.)

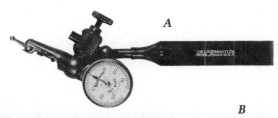

A

B

Fig. 93-23 *Using a dial-indicating snap gage to measure a part during precision grinding.* (Federal Products Corp.)

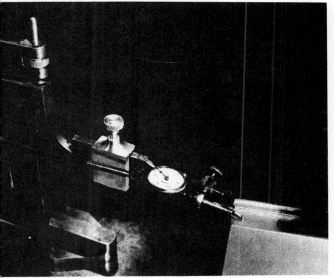

LIFTING LEVER

MOVABLE
TABLE

Fig. 93-24 *A dial comparator.* (Federal Products Corp.)

Fig. 93-25 *Air gages.* (Bendix)

Fig. 93-26 *Using an electronic gage for inspecting a part.* (DoAll)

93-11 Air and Electronic Gages

Air and electronic gages are essentially comparators that are preset to measure a particular size. They also indicate the exact amount the part is over or under size.

Air gages operate by measuring either the volume of air lost or the drop in pressure resulting from the air escaping between the gaging head and the part. The gage is calibrated to read directly in thousandths, ten-thousandths, or even millionths of an inch, or in hundredths or thousandths of a millimeter. Air gages use either a dial gage or a glass tube in which either the height of a rubber float or the height of a column of fluid indicates the size of the part (Fig. 93-25).

Electronic gages use a **stylus,** or a probe, such as used on dial indicators, in a gage head to contact the workpiece (Fig. 93-26). The me-

chanical motion of the stylus is converted to an electrical signal that moves a needle on an electric meter. The electric meter reads directly to the desired degree of accuracy. Electronic gages are capable of detecting size differences as small as one millionth of an inch [25 millionths of a millimeter].

Air and electronic gages are also useful for checking flatness, parallelism, straightness, roundness (circularity), and concentricity (concentric parts have a common center or common axis).

93-12 Optical Inspection Tools

Magnifying glasses aid accurate reading of vernier calipers, scales, and other finely graduated instruments. Illuminating magnifying glasses are often used in assembly and inspection of small parts.

Microscopes are used for many inspection jobs, including evaluation of material samples, measurement of surface imperfections, and measurement of miniature parts.

An **optical comparator** (Fig. 93-27) projects onto a screen an enlarged, shadow-like profile of the object being inspected. Here both its size and shape are compared to a master draw-

ing. The optical comparator is especially useful for checking small, irregularly shaped objects that cannot easily be measured with conventional tools. Flexible parts (such as springs and soft rubber or plastic objects) may distort under the pressure of ordinary measuring tools. However, they can easily be inspected with the optical comparator. The accuracy of gear tooth shape and screw thread form and pitch are also easily checked in this manner.

An **optical flat** is a disc or rectangle of polished quartz with precision-ground flat surfaces (Fig. 93-28A). It is used with a monochromatic (one-color) light, usually helium light. The light passes through the optical flat onto the surface of the part being inspected. The light produces dark band patterns on the surface of the part that tell how flat the part is, how parallel it is to another surface, or what its size is as compared to the specified size (Fig. 93-28B). When optical flats are used with helium light, each dark band becomes a measurement of 11.6 millionths of an inch [0.295 micrometers] (Fig. 93-29).

Fig. 93-27 *An optical comparator with the image of a part projected on its screen.*

93-13 Coordinate Measuring Machines

Coordinate measuring machines (Fig. 93-30) provide a new method of inspecting parts without using traditional measuring tools and gages. **Sensing probes** are used to contact the workpiece wherever measurements need to be made. The machine senses the movement of the probe in the X, Y, and Z axes (Fig. 91-5) and continuously displays its position with **digital readouts**. This enables accurate measurements of height, width, length, parallelism, hole diameters, hole positions, and squareness. When coupled to a computer, the coordinate measuring machine can also quickly check angles and irregular shapes. **Numerically controlled** coordinate measuring machines can be programmed for completely automatic inspection of parts. (Numerical control is explained in Unit 91.)

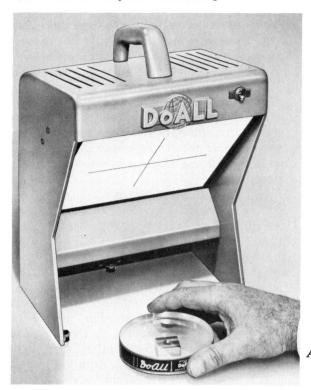

1. *The flat surface is out of parallel in one axis.*

2. *The flat surface is out of parallel in both axes.*

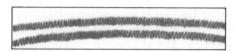

3. *A convex surface.*

A   *B*

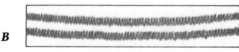

4. *A concave surface.*

Fig. 93-28 *(A) Using an optical flat with helium light to measure the flatness of a part. (B) The band patterns produced by an optical flat show surface characteristics.* (DoALL Company)

Fig. 93-29 *The surface that faces the work is the functioning part of an optical flat. It is transparent and can also reflect light. Therefore, all light waves that strike this surface are, in effect, split in two longitudinally. One part is reflected back by the surface of the flat. The other part passes through and is reflected back by the surface under inspection, as illustrated. Whenever the reflected split portions of two light waves cross each other (interfere), they become visible and produce dark bands. This happens whenever the distance between the reflecting surfaces is one-half of a wave length or multiples thereof.*

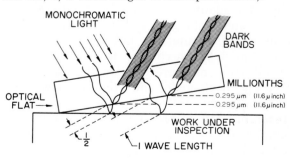

Fig. 93-30 *Inspecting a part with a coordinate measuring machine. Digital readouts display the movement of the sensing probe in each axis, enabling rapid and accurate inspection of parts.*

93-14 Surface Finish Measurement

The quality of the machined finish is extremely important to the service life of parts that slide or roll against each other. If the surface on a bearing is too rough it will rapidly wear out. If its surface is too smooth it cannot hold enough lubricant to keep it from rapidly wearing out. It is the responsibility of design engineers to specify the finish quality necessary for the correct functioning of parts. Machinists and inspectors, then, must have equipment for checking the quality of surface finish.

One method of checking surface quality is comparison with a **surface finish comparator** (Fig. 93-31). Comparison is made by sense of touch. The inspector drags a fingernail first over the standard specimen and then over the surface being checked. This provides a quick approximation of surface finish quality.

Accurate measurement of surface finish quality is made with an electrical instrument called a **surface finish indicator** (Fig. 93-32). With this instrument, a **tracer head** that houses a diamond-tipped stylus is drawn over the surface being measured. The mechanical movement of the stylus is converted to an electrical signal. The signal, in turn, moves a needle on an electric meter. The meter scale is marked to read in millionths of an inch or millionths of a meter, the units of measure used for indicating surface finish quality. Table 93-1 shows the range of surface roughness produced by different production methods.

93-15 Care of Inspection Equipment

Gages and other inspection equipment are very expensive. They should be kept very clean and handled and stored away with the greatest care.

Many gages have to be protected from heat and cold. For example, the warmth of your hand will expand or warp the gage and thus change its size. A gage lying in the sunlight will change in the same way. Rubber or wooden handles are often put on gages to protect them from hand warmth during gaging of a piece of work. Rooms in which inspection is done and in which gages are stored are often kept at 68°F [20°C].

A gage that has been dropped on the floor or otherwise bumped should be inspected before using again. Gages become worn after they have been used to inspect many pieces and should, therefore, be inspected from time to time.

Fig. 93-31 A surface finish comparator.

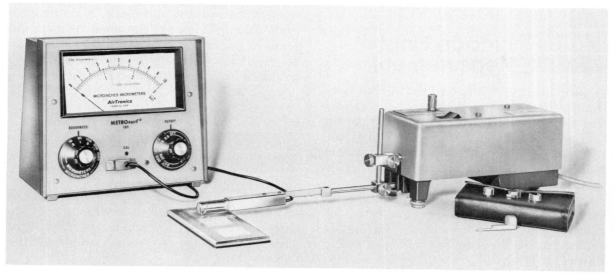

Fig. 93-32 *A surface finish indicator with a motor driven stylus.*

Table 93-1

Surface Roughness Produced by Common Production Methods

Process	ROUGHNESS AVERAGE R_a — microinches μin. (Micrometers μm)												
	2000 (50)	1000 (25)	500 (12.5)	250 (6.3)	125 (3.2)	63 (1.6)	32 (0.80)	16 (0.40)	8 (0.20)	4 (0.10)	2 (0.05)	1 (0.025)	0.5 (0.012)
Flame cutting													
Snagging													
Sawing													
Planing, shaping													
Drilling													
Chemical milling													
Elect. discharge mach.													
Milling													
Broaching													
Reaming													
Electron Beam													
Laser													
Electrochemical													
Boring, turning													
Barrel finishing													
Electrolytic grinding													
Roller burnishing													
Grinding													
Honing													
Electro-polish													
Polishing													
Lapping													
Superfinishing													

The ranges shown above are typical of the processes listed.
Higher or lower values may be obtained under special conditions.

Key ▬ Average Application
▨ Less Frequent Application

REVIEW   REVIEW   REVIEW   REVIEW   REVIEW

WORDS TO KNOW

adhesion
adjustable gages
air gage
attribute gage
caliper gage
coordinate
  measuring
  machine
dial comparator
dial-indicating
  depth gage
dial-indicating snap
  gage
dial indicator
  balanced type
  continuous-
    reading type
digital readout

drill gage
electronic gage
fixed gages
gage blocks
gaging height
go or not-go gage
hole-testing
  attachment
inspection
inspection-grade
  gage blocks
interchangeability
Jo-blocks
laboratory or master
  gages
limits gages
mechanical gages
negative allowance

nonindicating
optical comparator
optical flat
plain plug gage
plain ring gage
planer gage
positive allowance
practical standard
radius gage or fillet
  gage
reference gage
roll-thread snap
  gage
screw-pitch gage
sensing probe
small-hole gage
snap gage
stylus

surface finish
  comparator
surface finish
  indicator
surface-gage base
tapered plug gage
tapered ring gage
telescoping gage
thickness or feeler
  gage
thread plug gage
thread ring gage
tracer head
universal dial
  indicator set
working blocks
working gages
wringing

REVIEW QUESTIONS

1. What factors are inspected for the purpose of controlling the quality of manufactured metal products?
2. What is meant by "interchangeability of parts"? Why is it important? How is it made possible?
3. What is the length of the International Inch in terms of metric units?
4. What is used as the practical standard of precision measurement in industrial plants all over the world?
5. List the three classes of gage blocks, and state the kind of work done with each class.
6. Describe how gage blocks are assembled for use.
7. Telescoping and small-hole gages are used for making what kinds of measurements?
8. What are master gages used for? What is another name for them?
9. Describe how go and not-go gages are used.
10. Describe a common snap gage and tell how it is used.
11. What is a ring gage? Name three kinds.
12. What is a plug gage? Name three kinds.
13. What is a radius gage used for?
14. Describe a thickness gage and tell what it is used to measure.
15. List two types of dial gages, and explain how their graduations are numbered.
16. How is the gaging height established for a dial comparator?
17. Describe how air gages differ from mechanical gages.
18. What kind of inspection are optical comparators well suited for?
19. Describe three properties of a surface that can be checked with an optical flat.
20. Explain how coordinate measuring machines are used to inspect parts.

UNIT
94

Destructive and Nondestructive Testing

Testing is an essential part of the manufacturing process. It is carried out to determine whether materials, components, and assemblies meet product design specifications. The most common types of tests are described below.

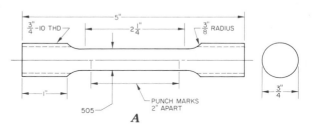

A

94-1 Destructive Testing

Destructive testing is performed to determine whether metals meet strength, fatigue, ductility, and corrosion resistance specifications.

Strength Testing

The two most common strength tests are the **tensile** and **impact** tests.

Tensile strength is the ability of a material to resist forces tending to pull it apart. The tensile strength of materials is expressed as the number of pounds or kilograms of pulling force required to break a sample having a cross-section of one square inch [645.2 sq. mm].

Tensile tests are usually done with samples made to standard specimen sizes of less than a square inch (Fig. 94-1A). A typical tensile testing machine is shown in Figure 94-1B.

B

C

Fig. 94-1 *(A) One size of standard tensile test specimen. (B) A tensile testing machine. Machine jaws grip the specimen on each side and pull until the specimen breaks. The dial shows how much force was required. (C) The specimen is broken when the pulling force exceeds the specimen's ultimate tensile strength.* (Howard Davis, USX Corporation)

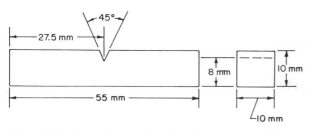

Fig. 94-2 *V-notch standard test specimen used for Charpy or Izod impact tests.*

Fig. 94-3 *Using an impact testing machine to make a Charpy impact test. The machine can also be used to do Izod impact tests.* (Tinius Olsen)

Impact tests are made to determine the shock resistance or toughness of a metal. The **impact resistance** of a metal is expressed in terms of the number of foot-pounds or meter-kilograms of force required to break a sample of standard size.

The two standard impact tests, **Charpy** and **Izod,** use test specimens of the same size (Fig. 94-2). The method of testing differs, however. In the Izod test, the specimen is held vertically at one end, and a hammer blow is directed against the notched side of the specimen. In Charpy testing, the specimen is supported at both ends in a horizontal position, and the direction of the hammer blow is from the side opposite the notch. An impact testing machine is shown in Figure 94-3.

Fatigue Testing

Fatigue failure of a metal occurs as the result of repeated application of small bending loads. The repeated bending causes embrittlement of the metal, which can lead to cracking and failure.

Fatigue tests are most often made using a standard test specimen of round cross section (Fig. 94-4). The test specimen is mounted in the fatigue testing machine so that the specimen is bent (Fig. 94-5). This places the metal fibers under compression on the inside of the bend and under tension on the outside. The specimen is then rotated at high speed until it fails. The number of revolutions or bending cycles which the metal can tolerate before failure is known as the **fatigue limit.**

Ductility Testing

Bend tests are used to test the ductility of welds, and also of sheet and bar stock. **Guided-bend testers** are used for testing welds of solid strip and pipe. A standard **test** is used for testing the ductility of sheet metal.

Corrosion Testing

Corrosion testing of metals is done both in the laboratory and in the field to test the resistance of metals to corrosive liquids or atmospheres.

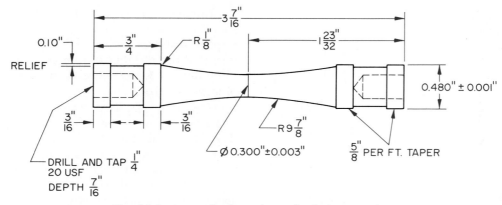

Fig. 94-4 *A standard specimen for fatigue testing.*

Laboratory corrosion tests include (1) the **total immersion test,** in which the metal is submerged throughout the test, (2) the **alternate immersion test,** in which the metal is alternately immersed and withdrawn, and (3) the **salt spray test,** which is done in a closed chamber containing moist salt air.

Field corrosion tests are done to determine corrosion resistance in environmental conditions which are expected in actual service. Tests are commonly made in industrial, marine, and desert atmospheres, as well as in soils and in sea water.

94-2 Nondestructive Testing

Nondestructive inspection techniques enable inspectors to check properties critical to the safe performance of metal parts without causing damage to the parts themselves. Nondestructive testing is concerned with **hardness testing** and **testing for cracks and flaws.**

These tests are made on parts at certain stages during their manufacture so that defec-

Fig. 94-5 *Schematic drawing of a fatigue testing machine.*

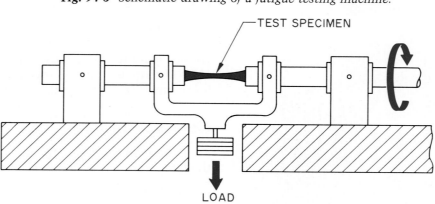

tive parts can be rejected as early as possible. Parts are also tested after a period of time in service as a means of discovering and eliminating those with **fatigue cracks.** The aircraft industry does a great deal of nondestructive inspection of engine and airframe parts, both during new construction and during overhaul.

Hardness Testing

The hardness of metals is designated by a **hardness number** from a **hardness scale.** Different hardness-testing instruments use different scales. Three of the most common types of hardness-testing instruments are:

1. the Rockwell Hardness Tester
2. the Brinell Hardness Tester
3. the Shore Scleroscope Hardness Tester.

The Rockwell hardness tester functions according to the depth of penetration made in metal by a specific kind of penetrator point forced by a given load (Fig. 94-6 and Table 94-1). The hardness is indicated directly by a hardness number that is read from either a dial or a digital readout (Fig. 94-7). This number is based on the difference between the depth of penetration caused by a **minor** load and that caused by a **major** load as they are applied to the penetrator. Deep penetration indicates a softer metal.

Table 94-1

Rockwell Hardness Scales

Scale or prefix	Type of penetrator	Major loads in kgs	Dial hardness numbers
Standard Scales			
B	1.5 mm (1/16″) Ball	100	Red
C	Diamond	150	Black
Special Scales			
A	Diamond	60	Black
D	Diamond	100	Black
E	3.2 mm (1/8″) Ball	100	Red
F	1.5 mm (1/16″) Ball	60	Red
G	1.5 mm (1/16″) Ball	150	Red
H	3.2 mm (1/8″) Ball	60	Red
K	3.2 mm (1/8″) Ball	150	Red
Superficial Hardness Scales			
15N	Diamond	15	N (Green)
30N	Diamond	30	N (Green)
45N	Diamond	45	N (Green)
15T	1.5 mm (1/16″) Ball	15	T (Green)
30T	1.5 mm (1/16″) Ball	30	T (Green)
45T	1.5 mm (1/16″) Ball	45	T (Green)

Fig. 94-7 *A motorized combination tester for standard Rockwell and Rockwell Superficial hardness testing.* (Wilson Instrument Division)

Fig. 94-6 *Penetrators used on the Rockwell Hardness Tester (A) The 120° diamond point. (B) The 1/16″ (1.5 mm) diameter ball point.*

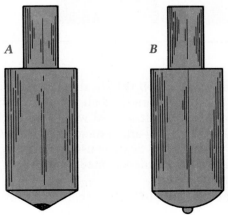

Inspecting Inside and Out

The inspection of metal products can present a manufacturer with some particularly difficult problems. An inspector, for example, quickly becomes bored while inspecting small, complex parts. He or she may easily miss defects. Other kinds of products may have internal flaws, which can't be seen. And how do you effectively inspect objects such as large tanks for pressurized gas?

These problems are now being solved with a variety of electronic inspection systems.

Many companies are using visual image scanners. A TV camera or laser scanner hooked up to a computer imitates the human "eyeballing" approach. The scanner "feeds" an image of the part into the computer, where it is compared with models of good and bad parts stored in the computer's memory. Visual scanning is now being used to improve coordinate measuring machines. Cameras magnify microscopic parts

to 80 times their size for close inspection.

In ultrasonic inspection, high-frequency sound waves are used to inspect metal products for internal flaws. With this system, parts must be submerged in a liquid, which acts as a sound-wave conductor. Automotive steering parts, for example, are tested while in oil. Each part passes through a row of probes that shoot ultrasonic pulses into it. When a pulse hits a flaw, it bounces back to a sensor. A horn and a light signal that the part is being rejected.

Sound is also involved, in another way, in acoustic

emission testing. In this type of non-destructive inspection, stresses are placed on the metal part. As force is applied, the noise produced is monitored by electronic sensors. Technicians are able to tell whether a part "sounds" right. Acoustic emission is used extensively in the testing of large pressure-tight metal structures, such as the butane tank pictured at the right.

Electronics is bringing about a revolution in quality assurance inspection. With its help, inspectors are finding that once-difficult problems can be easily solved.

Rockwell hardness testers of several types are available. They may be the stationary type (Fig. 94-7) or the portable type (Fig. 94-8). Testers are available for testing according to the standard **Rockwell Hardness Scales** only or for testing according to the **Rockwell Superficial Hardness Scales** only. Some testers can be used for testing hardness according to either scale.

The **Rockwell-B** (RB) Scale requires use of a 1/16" [1.5 mm] diameter ball penetrator made of hardened steel. It is used with a minor load of 10 kg [22.05 lbs] and a major load of 100 kg [220.5 lbs]. The RB Scale is used for testing the hardness of unhardened steel, cast iron, and nonferrous metals.

The **Rockwell-C** (RC) Scale requires the use of a diamond-point penetrator called a

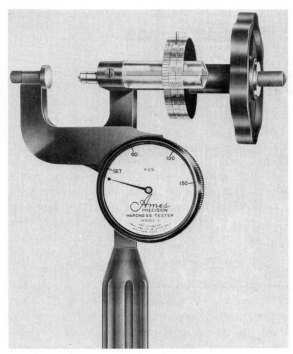

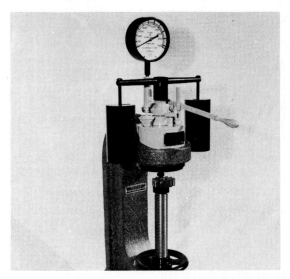

Fig. 94-9 *A Brinell hardness tester.* (Pittsburgh Instrument and Machine Co.)

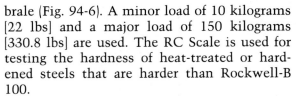

Fig. 94-8 *A portable Rockwell hardness tester.*

brale (Fig. 94-6). A minor load of 10 kilograms [22 lbs] and a major load of 150 kilograms [330.8 lbs] are used. The RC Scale is used for testing the hardness of heat-treated or hardened steels that are harder than Rockwell-B 100.

Of the various Rockwell Hardness Scales, the RB and RC are the most widely used. In Rockwell Superficial Hardness Tests, lighter loads are applied and a smaller dent is made in the surface of metal being tested. Superficial hardness tests are useful for measuring the hardness of very thin metal parts and case-hardened parts that cannot properly be measured with the Rockwell B scale.

The Brinell hardness tester (Fig. 94-9) forces a hard ball into a smooth metal surface. The ball is 10 mm [0.394"] in diameter. For standard Brinell (BHN) Hardness Tests on steel, a load of 3000 kg [6600 lbs.] is applied. The load is applied steadily and is held for a minimum period of 15 seconds for steel and 30 seconds for nonferrous metals.

The diameter of the dent made by the ball determines the Brinell Hardness Number. The diameter of the dent is measured with a microscope that has a special measuring lens. The diameter of the dent is converted to a hardness number by using a comparison chart that is supplied with the testing machine.

Brinell testers work best on metals that are not extremely hard. These include nonferrous metals, soft steels, and medium-hard steels. The Brinell hardness of steel generally ranges from about BHN 150 for soft, low-carbon steel to BHN 739 for hardened, high-carbon steel. On very hard steels, the dent is so small that it is difficult to see or measure.

The Shore Scleroscope Hardness Tester (Fig. 94-10) operates on the **rebound principle.** It measures the height to which a diamond-tipped hammer rebounds after being dropped on a metal surface being tested. Harder metals cause the hammer to rebound higher, thus indicating higher hardness values.

In contrast to the Rockwell and Brinell testers, Scleroscope Testers are essentially **nonmarring,** particularly on harder metals. A

Fig. 94-10 *A Shore Scleroscope hardness tester.* (Shore Instrument and Mfg. Co.)

small dent may appear on softer metals. The hardness number is read directly from a vertical column or a dial.

Testing hardness with a file. The approximate hardness of steel may be tested with the **arris** (corner) of a file. **Do not test the hardness of hardened steel with the flat surface of the file, or you will dull and ruin the teeth.** You can make a rough estimate of the hardness of steel tested with the arris of a file as follows:

Rockwell C Hardness Number	Action of File on Steel
20	File removes metal easily with slight pressure
30	File starts to resist cutting metal
40	File cuts metal with difficulty
50	File barely cuts metal with great difficulty
57	File glides over metal without cutting

Tests for Detecting Cracks and Flaws

Several techniques are used to reveal surface cracks and hidden flaws in castings, welds, and even rolled or forged metals. Five methods described here are:

1. fluorescent penetrant inspection
2. magnetic particle inspection
3. radiographic inspection
4. ultrasonic inspection
5. eddy current inspection.

Fluorescent Penetration Inspection

This technique uses a **fluorescent penetrating oil** or **dye penetrant.** The oil is brushed or sprayed on the part (Fig. 94-11), or the part is dipped in the oil. After being wiped dry, the part is dusted with an absorbent powder, which draws the fluorescent penetrating oil out of any cracks that are present. When the part is placed under **ultraviolet light,** the cracks appear in bright fluorescent color.

A similar method, called Spotcheck® (marketed by the Magnaflux Corporation), uses a dye penetrant. However, the developer used with this method causes the cracks to appear in regular light without the need for ultraviolet light. Fluorescent penetrants cannot detect flaws that do not break through the surface.

Fig. 94-11 *Spraying a pump impeller for fluorescent penetrant inspection.* (Magnaflux Corporation)

Magnetic Particle Inspection

In magnetic particle inspection (Fig. 94-12), the part is first magnetized. It is then either dusted with fine iron powder or coated with a solution in which iron particles are suspended. Flaws in the workpiece cause the lines of magnetic force to become distorted and break through the surface. There they attract concentrations of the iron particles, which reveal defects in the metal. This method can detect only those flaws that break through or are just below the surface.

Radiographic Inspection

In radiographic inspection, the workpiece is exposed to **X-ray** or **gamma ray** radiation. The resultant image is viewed on a fluoroscope or on film. A defect will show up on the screen or film as a dark area (Fig. 94-13). X-rays are very sensitive and are capable of inspecting any thickness of almost any kind of material. Internal flaws such as **voids** (holes) in castings are readily detected. Cracks, however, are not readily revealed by radiography.

Gamma radiation, because of its greater penetrating power, is more effective than X-ray radiation in inspecting thick sections. It is also less expensive, and its equipment is more portable.

Ultrasonic Inspection

In ultrasonic inspection, high-frequency sound waves are introduced into the workpiece. The sound waves reflect from the workpiece surfaces and from any internal defects. The process measures both the workpiece thickness (Fig. 94-14) and the exact depth of

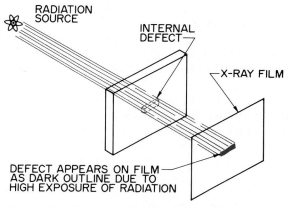

Fig. 94-13 *The principle of radiographic inspection.*

Fig. 94-14 *The principle of ultrasonic inspection, a method of locating an internal defect.*

Fig. 94-12 *Magnetic particle inspection.*

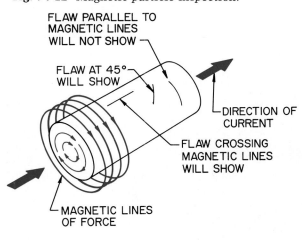

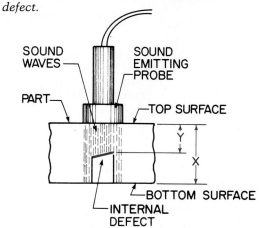

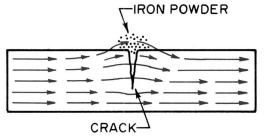

flaws. For convenience in detecting flaws, the sound beam is converted to an electrical signal, which is then shown graphically on an oscilloscope screen (Fig. 94-15). Considerable skill is required in the use and interpretation of ultrasonic inspection equipment.

Eddy Current Inspection

Eddy current inspection can be used only to inspect materials that conduct electricity. An electric coil is placed around, in, or near the part being inspected. It is then energized with alternating current, which produces a magnetic field. The coil's magnetic field causes **eddy currents** (circular-turning electrical currents) to be produced in the part. The flow of the eddy currents is opposite to the flow of electricity in the coil. The opposing currents produce changes in the coil's magnetic field. These changes are converted to voltages that can be read on a meter (Fig. 94-16).

Eddy current inspection is very sensitive and very fast. It can be used for finding cracks and flaws, variations in thickness, and differ-

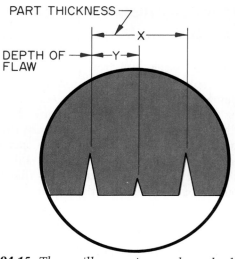

Fig. 94-15 *The oscilloscope image shows both part thickness and the depth of the internal flaw.*

ences in alloys and heat treatment. However, since eddy currents only form on the surface, only defects at or near the surface can be found with this method.

Fig. 94-16 *An eddy current tester.*

REVIEW REVIEW REVIEW REVIEW REVIEW

WORDS TO KNOW

alternate immersion
  test
arris
bend test
brale
Brinell Hardness
  Tester
Charpy test
cup-drawing test
destructive testing
eddy current
  inspection
fatigue cracks
fatigue failure

fatigue limit
fatigue testing
field corrosion test
fluorescent
  penetrant
  inspection
gamma ray
  radiation
guided-bend tester
hardness number
hardness scale
impact resistance
impact testing
Izod test

laboratory corrosion
  test
nondestructive
  inspection
penetrator
radiographic
  inspection
rebound principle
Rockwell Hardness
  Test
Rockwell
  Superficial
  Hardness Tester
salt spray test

Shore Scleroscope
  Hardness Tester
Spotcheck®
tensile testing
total immersion
  test
ultrasonic
  inspection
ultraviolet light
X-ray radiation

REVIEW QUESTIONS

1. Describe how a tensile test is made.
2. Name the two kinds of impact tests and describe how they are different.
3. Describe how a fatigue test is made.
4. Name several uses for bend tests.
5. What is the purpose of a cup-drawing test?
6. Name the three kinds of laboratory corrosion tests.
7. Why are field corrosion tests conducted?
8. Tell what is meant by "nondestructive inspection," and give several reasons why it is necessary.
9. How is the hardness of metals specified or designated?
10. List two types of Rockwell hardness testers.
11. What kinds of metal are Rockwell-C tests generally done on?
12. What kinds of metal are generally tested according to the Rockwell-B scale?
13. What kind of parts are tested on the Rockwell Superficial Hardness Tester?
14. Explain how a Brinell hardness test is made.
15. What kinds of metal do Brinell hardness testers work best on?
16. Explain how a Shore Scleroscope Hardness Tester operates.
17. What is the major advantage in using the Shore Scleroscope tester?
18. Describe the fluorescent penetrating oil inspection process. How does it differ from the Spotcheck process?
19. How does the magnetic particle inspection process work?
20. What kind of flaws can be detected by dye penetrant and magnetic particle inspection?
21. Explain the radiographic inspection process.
22. Describe the ultrasonic inspection process.
23. List several uses for eddy current inspection.

PART

23

Making Metal Products

Jim Mendoza is a plant engineer in the machining division of a large automobile manufacturer. He says his career began when he got interested in drawing and machines while in junior high school. He works almost every day with automated material-handling equipment. But he does more than that. He gets involved in designing products, helping develop new products, and quality control. This variety is what he likes most.

Jim Mendoza has seen a lot of changes in manufacturing since he entered a tool-and-die apprentice program over 30 years ago. At smaller, less specialized shops, Jim learned something about all parts of the tool-and-die industry. Later, when he moved to a bigger company, he felt he needed more training, so he enrolled in an engineering program. With a choice of programs, he chose plant engineering over electrical and mechanical engineering.

Plant engineering and tool-and-die operations are becoming more complicated. They are more and more automated. Robots are used in more applications. Computers are everywhere. Products are manufactured more quickly. Closer tolerances are possible.

But, Jim emphasizes, the most important skill is the one that got him interested in manufacturing long ago, when he was in eighth grade—drawing. Someone who likes drawing and knows how computers are used in industry can have a great career in metals manufacturing, perhaps as a plant engineer like Jim Mendoza.

A plant engineer, Jim insists, should like "hands-on" work that changes all the time. "You'll never learn it all," he says. "In this field there's always a new challenge," says Jim.

Jim Mendoza
Plant Engineer

Charles Zilch

UNIT
95
Development of Manufacturing Technology

The invention of the steam engine by James Watt in England in 1776 is accepted as the beginning of the industrial revolution. However, the beginning of modern manufacturing methods for producing metal products is credited to two early gun manufacturers, the Americans Eli Whitney and Simeon North. Both have been credited with the use of interchangeable parts in manufacturing. In reality, however, only North used interchangeable parts in manufacturing.

95-1 Interchangeable Parts

Whitney, better known for his invention of the cotton gin, obtained a contract from the United States Government in 1798 to manufacture 12,000 muskets. He suggested to the government that he would be able to create a manufacturing system that would be able to make parts so alike as to be **interchangeable.** Only in this way could replacement parts be made and stored to keep the muskets in repair. This problem had plagued armies since the invention of firearms.

Interchangeable gun parts would be identical in size and shape. Thus, the parts of one gun could be interchanged, or replaced, with identical spare parts. Whitney was not successful in developing the use of interchangeable parts. The muskets he manufactured were made almost entirely by hand. Also, the records of Whitney's company make no mention of machinery that could be used for the mass production of gun parts.

The concept of interchangeable parts depends on the use of jigs and fixtures for accurately locating and holding parts during drill-ing, filing, and other shaping operations (see Figs. 49-11 and 49-12). (A jig or fixture is a mechanical device like a brace or frame, often with clamps, that holds a workpiece in the correct position during machining.) The concept of interchangeable parts also involves the principle of **division of labor.** This ensures that each worker is trained to become expert at one kind of skill needed to manufacture the product.

In 1799, Simeon North obtained a contract from the U.S. Government for 500 pistols. In 1800, he obtained a contract for 1500 pistols, and other contracts followed (Fig. 95-1). By 1813 the goal of interchangeability must have been achieved, because in that year interchangeability was a condition of the contract North received for 20,000 pistols. In 1818, North introduced the first known true milling machine.

As the success of North became known, his methods were adopted by other manufacturers. Soon this became the standard way of producing products in quantity. An outstanding example of the benefits of using his meth-

Fig. 95-1 In 1915, Simeon North was the first to manufacture the United States guns with interchangeable parts. Manufacturing tolerances, however, were not precise by today's standards. (American Precision Museum)

ods occurred in the manufacture of clocks. Before adopting North's methods, Eli Terry, an American, produced less than a hundred wooden clock movements and dials each year for a retail price of $25. Beween 1807 and 1810, after adopting North's methods, he produced four thousand clock movements and dials for a retail price of $4. By 1840, Chauncy Jerome, a former employee of Terry's, was making 40,000 clocks with brass movements per year. His clocks sold for $1.40 each.

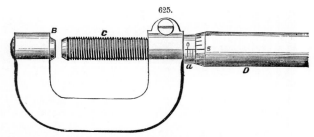

Fig. 95-2 *An early Brown and Sharpe micrometer.* (North Wind Picture Archives)

95-2 Precision Metalworking Machines

Further development of metal manufacturing technology required the invention and production of accurate and reliable machine tools. Without precision machine tools, production machinery for making low-cost consumer products could not be built. The invention of the change-gear screw cutting lathe by Henry Maudslay in 1797 pointed the way. Other machine tools came in a steady stream during the 19th century:

1. The metal cutting planer before 1814 by the Englishman Mathew Murray.
2. The milling machine by Simeon North in 1818.
3. The gear cutting machine by Richard Roberts in England in 1821.
4. The shaper by James Naysmith in England in 1836.
5. The power feed drill press in 1840 by James Naysmith.
6. The turret lathe by Stephen Fitch, an American, in 1845.
7. The multiple spindle drill press by Andrew Shanks, an American, in 1860.
8. The automatic lathe by Christopher Spencer, an American, in 1873.
9. The universal grinding machine in 1876 by Joseph Brown, an American.
10. The surface grinder in 1880 by the Americans Joseph Brown and Lucien Sharpe.
11. The multiple spindle automatic lathe by Christopher Spencer in 1891.

By the end of the 19th century, all of the basic machine tools had been invented and developed to an advanced, complex degree. The development of precision measuring tools largely made this possible. James Watt's early micrometer was improved upon by the Frenchman Palmer, and again by the Americans Brown and Sharpe (Fig. 95-2). The first vernier calipers were made by David Brown in 1851. Gage blocks were invented by Carl Johansson in 1895. Ever since then, they have provided practical standards of precision measurement that are still the standard today (see Fig. 93-2).

By 1920, the development of electric power had brought better lighting to the workplace. It also permitted each machine to have its own drive motor of proper size, rather than powered by belt from an **overhead line shaft** (Fig. 95-3). This development provided unlimited flexibility in machine placement, and made possible more efficient plant layout and work flow. The quieter, safer, more efficient workplaces improved **productivity.**

By this time, cutting tools of high speed steel had also become available, providing a three-fold increase in cutting speeds. Today, cutting tools of carbide, ceramic, and synthetic diamond have replaced high speed steel for most production work. These cutting tools have further increased cutting speeds 300-800%. They also make it possible to cut much harder materials.

To keep pace with cutting tool development, machines are now built more ruggedly to withstand high cutting forces. Spindle speeds have been increased and more powerful drive motors are provided.

Fig. 95-3 *Leather belts driven by overhead line shafts powered early machine tools.* (North Wind Picture Archives)

Development of Automatic Machines and Automation for Manufacture of Parts

95-3

The development of automatic machines is a direct outgrowth of the development of clocks. Mechanical clocks are, after all, self-regulating, automatic machines for telling time. At the beginning of the Industrial Revolution, clocks had already been in use for hundreds of years. Water-powered clocks were made in China between 800 and 1100 A.D. Weight-driven clocks appeared in Europe in 1300 A.D. Spring-driven clocks appeared after 1550 A.D., and spring-driven pendulum clocks were first made in Holland in 1657.

James Watt provided one of the earliest examples of automatic machine operation when he invented the **fly-weight governor.** Its purpose was to automatically regulate the speed of his stationary steam engines (Fig. 95-4). By 1820, machine tools were provided with power feed to automatically drive their cutting tools. In 1842, John Howe, an American, succeeded in constructing a fully automatic machine for making straight pins used in sewing (Fig. 95-5).

The first automatic lathe was invented by Christopher Spencer in 1873, who also invented the first multiple spindle automatic lathe in 1891. These machines were automatically regulated by the use of screws, gears, and cams. 5, 6, and 8 spindle automatic lathes were later developed (see Fig. 58-6). Even today, they are the most efficient machines for mass producing precision cylindrical parts. They can make many parts at a rate of less than 10 seconds apiece.

Fig. 95-4 *The fly-weight governor, invented by James Watt to regulate the speed of his steam engines.* (North Wind Picture Archives)

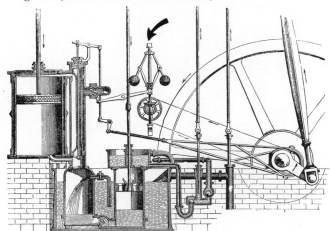

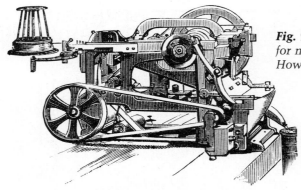

Fig. 95-5 *This fully automatic machine for making straight pins was built by John Howe in 1842.* (North Wind Picture Archives)

For high volume production of complex auto parts such as engine blocks and transmission cases, special stand-alone machines that could rapidly perform each type of machining operation were first made. However, this required a large amount of manual labor to move the workpieces from machine to machine. Not only was this very time-consuming, but the handling also damaged some parts.

Today, special **transfer machines** automatically perform all the machining operations required, and automatically transfer or move the workpiece from one machining station to the next (Fig. 95-6). Many of these machines are highly automated, with sensing devices that adjust the machine for tool wear, sense tool breakage, and automatically replace broken tools.

The term **"automation"** was first used in 1947 by Delmar Harder, a Ford Motor Company vice president, to describe self-regulating manufacturing machines. Automated machines that can manufacture only one product are referred to as **hard automation.**

By 1955, the fist N/C (numerically controlled) machine tools had become available, and in 1958 the first **flexible manufacturing system** was created. This consisted of three N/C machines, one each for milling, drilling and tapping, and boring.

The drilling and tapping machine was the only one that was equipped with an automatic tool-changer. The three machines were linked together with work-handling equipment, and the entire system was under tape control.

This system was very crude by today's standards. Although the machine control units (MCU's) used the same electronic technology as early computers, they were **hard wired;** that is, they were not programmable at the machine. As a result, much machine time was lost in checking and correcting initial machining programs.

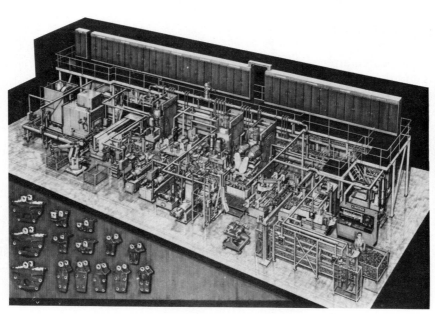

Fig. 95-6 *This flexible transfer line machines the family of fourteen truck spring baskets shown at the lower left. The production rate is more than 200 units per hour.* (Cross & Trecker)

Today, most N/C machine tools use CNC (computer numerical control) MCU's that permit program correction to be made at each machine (Fig. 91-13). CNC units also eliminate the use of punched tape. They can also be linked directly to a large mainframe computer for **direct numerical control** (DNC) of machine tools (Fig. 95-7).

Today's N/C machines used in flexible manufacturing systems are normally equipped with **broken tool sensors** and automatic tool changers. In addition, **electronic probes** are used for workpiece identification and location, selection of the correct program to machine the part, and inspection of the part to correct the program automatically for tool wear (Fig. 95-8).

Since flexible manufacturing systems use general purpose N/C machines, they do not compete with hard automation because their rate of production is much slower. However, they are now rapidly being adopted for manufacturing low volume, repeat order parts (Fig. 95-9). Because flexible manufacturing machines are programmable, they can be used for producing many different parts. For this reason, they are referred to as **soft automation**.

Fig. 95-8 *An electronic probe used on N/C machines for automatic inspection and adjustment of the machine for tool wear.* (Cincinnati Milacron)

Fig. 95-9 *Flexible manufacturing systems are groups of N/C machines connected with automatic part handling devices. Workpieces are automatically loaded and unloaded from machines, and transferred between machines.* (Cross & Trecker)

Fig. 95-7 *Computer numerical control (CNC) units eliminate the need for punched tape, and can send and receive programs directly to or from a host computer for direct numerical control (DNC).* (Cincinnati Milacron)

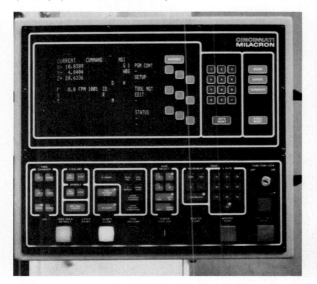

95-4 Development of Product Assembly Methods

From the early days of mass-production manufacturing, each product or product component was completely assembled by one individual. This practice changed after Henry Ford adopted the use of the moving assembly line in 1913, and proved its efficiency for assembling large numbers of complex products. His first assembly line for magnetos reduced the assembly time from 18 to 5 minutes. Assembly of the entire automobile chassis, which had taken 12½ hours, took only a little over 1½ hours on an assembly line (Fig. 95-10). In 1912, before adoption of the assembly line, he produced 181,000 cars and trucks for sale at $600 each. By 1925, he was producing almost 2,000,000 a year at a price of $290 each.

Fig. 95-11 *MacIntosh computers are assembled on automatic assembly lines.* (Apple Computer Company)

Today, assembly lines are used in all industries, and fully automatic assembly of many product components is common (Fig. 95-11). Robots are also being used in increasing numbers for assembly because they provide a flexible assembly system that can be quickly adapted to product changes (Fig. 95-12).

Fig. 95-10 *Henry Ford's first auto assembly line reduced assembly time from 12-1/2 hours to 1-1/2 hours.* (From The Collections of Henry Ford Museum & Greenfield Village)

Fig. 95-12 *Assembly of circuit boards using robots is more efficient than using manual labor.* (Apple Computer Company)

Fig. 95-13 *Before undertaking any project, it is essential to establish a plan of procedure.* (Manual High School, Roger Bean)

95-5 Computer-Aided Manufacturing and Computer-Integrated Manufacturing

Computer-aided manufacturing (CAM) means using computers for one or more manufacturing tasks. At first, the high cost of computers limited their use to large companies, which used them mostly for data processing (record keeping). As company managers realized the power of computers, computer experts developed software—instructional programs for computers—for other manufacturing applications. Soon, large companies were using computers for such CAM applications as design and drafting, engineering, automated warehousing, process control, inventory control, and purchasing. Today, powerful microcomputers and CAM software are available at such low cost that they are used by even small companies.

Computer-integrated manufacturing (CIM) means using computers for controlling every manufacturing task. Each computer in the CIM system gathers data and reports it to a main computer, where it is automatically grouped together category by category and further analyzed. This information is used by supervisors and managers to detect possible problems. If necessary, orders to avoid or correct problems are then given. The goal of CIM is to provide completely self-regulating factories, which may make completely unmanned factories possible in the future.

REVIEW   REVIEW   REVIEW   REVIEW   REVIEW

WORDS TO KNOW

automation
broken tool sensors
CAM
cams
CIM
computer-aided
  manufacturing
computer-integrated
  manufacturing

direct numerical
  control
DNC
division of labor
electronic probe
flexible assembly
  system

flexible
  manufacturing
  system
fly-weight governor
hard automation
hard wired
interchangeable

moving assembly
  line
overhead line shaft
productivity
soft automation
transfer machines
uniformity system

REVIEW QUESTIONS

1. Name the invention that started the industrial revolution. Who was its inventor? What year was it invented?
2. Who was the first to manufacture a product in the United States using interchangeable parts?
3. What is meant by division of labor?
4. How did adoption of mass production methods affect the price of clocks?
5. Who invented the change gear screw cutting lathe? In what year was it invented?
6. By what date had all the basic machine tools been invented?
7. When were the first gage blocks invented? Who was the inventor?
8. What is a line shaft, and how did it power machines in early factories?
9. Name three cutting tool materials that have replaced high speed steel for most production machining today.
10. The development of what mechanical device led to the development of automatic machines.
11. How did James Watt regulate the speed of his stationary steam engines?
12. What product did John Howe's automatic machine produce?
13. What devices are used to control the most efficient multiple spindle automatic lathes?
14. How do transfer machines speed up production?
15. What does automation mean?
16. What is meant by hard automation? Soft automation?
17. What is a flexible manufacturing system?
18. List three uses for electronic probes.
19. For what kind of manufacturing are flexible manufacturing systems best suited?
20. What year was the moving assembly line adopted by Henry Ford? Compare how it affected the cost of his cars and trucks between 1912 and 1925.
21. Why are robots being used in increasing numbers for assembly?
22. Explain how CAM differs from CIM.

UNIT 96

Industrial Organization

The successful operation of a company requires knowledge and skillful decision making in seven areas of activity: (1) research and development; (2) production; (3) marketing; (4) finance and control; (5) personnel administration; (6) secretarial and legal; and (7) external relations. In most companies, responsibility for carrying out these activities is divided among several employees. The purpose of an **organization structure** is to identify the people responsible for the different aspects of company operations, and to establish a clear **line of authority.**

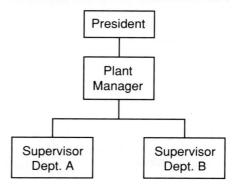

Fig. 96-1 *A line organization chart is commonly used by small companies.*

96-1 Line Organization

Line organization is so called because the positions listed on the **organization chart** fall in a vertical line (Fig. 96-1). This is the simplest form of organization, and it is used by most small companies. With this organization, the president, who is either the owner or a major partner, must make all or most company decisions. There is no staff to provide aid and reduce the work load of managing all aspects of company operations.

96-2 Line and Staff Organization

As a company grows, it is impossible for one person to manage all aspects of company operations. Therefore, a staff of specialists are hired and made responsible for specific areas of company operations. The specialists report directly to the president and are given titles such as vice president, director, or manager. The president, however, retains overall responsibility for operation of the company. This type of organization is called a **line and staff organization** and is used by all large companies (Fig. 96-2).

96-3 Company Organization and Control Devices

For efficient company operation, it is very important that: (1) a clear line of authority be established, (2) the responsibilities of each manager be clearly stated, and (3) policies and procedures be established for carrying out all company operations.

As we have already seen, the organization chart is used to identify the managers responsible for each aspect of company operation. It also establishes a line of authority for decision making in the company. However, an organization chart provides only a skeleton of company organization.

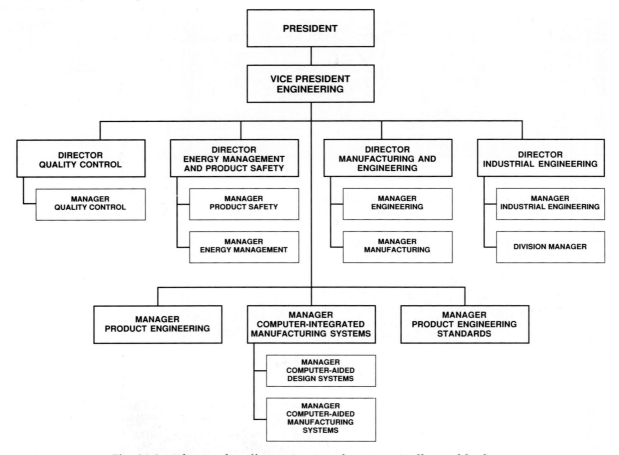

Fig. 96-2 *A line and staff organization chart is typically used by large companies.*

The **organization manual** is the document, often a loose-leaf note book, that provides the facts about the positions on the organization chart. This manual provides a detailed outline of the duties and responsibilities of each job on the chart. In this way, everyone knows exactly what their job is, and what their scope of authority is. The organization manual helps to avoid overlapping duties between employees and the resultant confusion that can occur. It is also a valuable aid in hiring and training new employees, because it provides a written record of what is required to carry out each job.

While the organization manual tells **what** each job involves, it does not tell **how** each task is to be carried out. For this purpose, a **standard practice manual** must be provided. The standard practice manual provides company policy and standard operating procedures for carrying out all aspects of company operations. It should include information on policies and procedures for hiring, wage levels, standards of performance, promotion, vacation, dismissal of employees, requisitioning, ordering, receiving of supplies and materials, admission and supervision of visitors, and use of company vehicles.

The standard practice manual helps assure that all employees in the company follow approved company policies. It is also useful for employee training.

It is very important that the above documents be kept up to date, so that they provide current information. Otherwise, valuable time and effort can be lost in directing communications to the wrong people and in following outdated policies and procedures.

REVIEW   REVIEW   REVIEW   REVIEW   REVIEW

WORDS TO KNOW

line and staff organization	line organization	organization manual	standard practice manual
line of authority	organization chart	organization structure	

REVIEW QUESTIONS

1. List the seven areas of activity that require knowledge and skillful decision making for the successful operation of a company.
2. What is the purpose of an organization structure?
3. How does a line organization differ from a line and staff organization?
4. What is the purpose of an organization chart?
5. Why is an organization manual needed?
6. How does a standard practice manual help in the operation of a company?

UNIT 97

Product Engineering

Before a new product can be made, it must be designed, developed, and tested. This process is often repeated until the designers and engineers are satisfied with the appearance and performance of the product. This activity is carried out by a product development team of people who are skilled in the engineering sciences, drafting, and art.

Mechanical engineers are responsible for selecting the most suitable materials and manufacturing processes for producing the product. They select materials on the basis of their mechanical, electrical, and chemical properties and their cost. They choose manufacturing processes on the basis of their ability to produce reliable, accurate parts at lowest cost.

Mechanical engineers then use **CADD (computer-aided** and **drafting design)** systems to create the mechanical design of the product components (Fig. 97-1). Each product component can then be tested for weak spots, using **CAE (computer-aided engineering)** software. By using CAE for testing, engineers save the cost of hundreds of hours of actual testing, which is very expensive. For consumer products, a **product designer** skilled in art uses a CADD system to provide an attractive design for the product (Fig. 97-2).

After the product is designed, drafters produce working drawings of each part. Today, drafters often use a CADD system to prepare the drawings. The system usually involves a computer-driven drafting plotter to make originals and copies of the drawings on paper or film (Fig. 97-3). Copies of the drawings may also be reproduced in quantity on drafting room copy machines.

A **prototype,** a full-size working model, of the product is then made. Engineers and product designers use a prototype:

(1) to learn possible difficulties in constructing the product;
(2) to provide a model for study of its design; and
(3) to provide a model for performance testing (Fig. 97-4).

In many cases, several prototypes are made to test the construction and performance features of different product designs.

When the engineers are satisfied with the product's appearance and performance, changes in the working drawings are made where necessary, and the product is approved for manufacture.

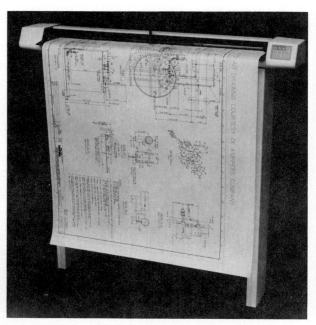

Fig. 97-3 *Computer-driven drafting machines are used to make paper drawings of parts designed on CAD systems. (Houston Instruments)*

Fig. 97-1 *A mechanical engineer designing a product component using a CAD system. (Rohr Industries)*

Fig. 97-2 *A product designer using a CAD system to design a product. (General Motors)*

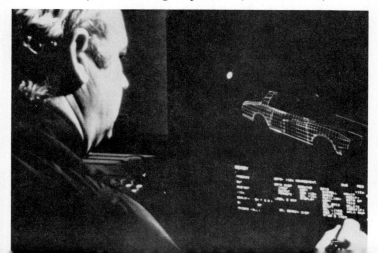

Fig. 97-4 *Prototype of new model auto being tested. (General Motors)*

REVIEW   REVIEW   REVIEW   REVIEW   REVIEW

WORDS TO KNOW

CADD
computer-aided
  design
	CAE
	computer-aided
	  engineering
		mechanical
		  engineer
		product designer
			prototype

REVIEW QUESTIONS

1. What are the three stages involved in creating a new product?
2. Who is responsible for selecting the materials and manufacturing processes for a new product?
3. List four factors that are considered when selecting materials for a new product.
4. What factors are considered when selecting the manufacturing processes for a new product?
5. How is CAE used in producing new products?
6. Who is responsible for creating the design of consumer products?
7. What person usually produces the working drawings for a new product?
8. Using a CADD system, how are the first paper working drawings made?
9. What is a prototype, and why is it made?
10. Why are several prototypes sometimes made?

UNIT

98

Manufacturing Process Design

Manufacturing process design is concerned with determining the most economical method for producing the product. This work is done by process or manufacturing engineers. Three basic factors are involved in manufacturing process design: (1) the quantity of the product to be manufactured; (2) the quality of the product; and (3) equipment that is available or can be purchased.

98-1   Manufacturing Quantities of a Product

Product volume greatly determines the process selected for production. In general, **as product volume increases, the production cost per unit decreases.** Using a special bolt as an example, the following manufacturing processes would be used according to the quantity desired:

Quantity	Process
1-10	A manually operated lathe or an N/C lathe
11-100	An N/C lathe or a manually operated turret lathe
101-15,000	An N/C automatic screw machine
15,001-100,000	A cam controlled automatic screw machine
over 100,000	A cold heading machine

Similar examples could be provided for parts to be made by casting, forging, or stamping.

In general, **as the desired quality of a product increases, the cost to produce it increases.** Higher quality often requires use of higher cost materials—for example, the use of an alloy tool steel for a screwdriver blade instead of plain carbon steel. Higher quality often requires closer tolerances in part size and shape, which requires better equipment or a more expensive process. Investment casting, for example, can produce parts to closer tolerances of size and shape, but it is a more expensive process than sand casting. Furthermore, high quality usually requires better finishing materials or methods, or both. A chrome plated finish is far more expensive than a painted finish. All of the above high quality features result in an increased **rejection rate.** This requires more parts to be reworked or scrapped, which raises production costs.

In most cases, the process or manufacturing engineer attempts to design the manufacturing process so that it uses existing equipment. This plan usually results in the lowest cost for producing the product, because expensive new equipment need not be purchased. The process engineer, however, must always investigate whether the product can be made at a lower cost by using new equipment that is more productive, or a new process. Another possibility to be considered is the "make or buy decision"; that is, whether the product can be purchased at lower cost than it can be made by the company.

98-2 Economic Manufacturing Lot Size

For many products, production equipment can produce parts at a rate far exceeding daily demand. It is necessary, therefore, to produce these parts in "lots" of an economical size. The **economical manufacturing lot size** depends on many factors such as:
(1) the rate at which the parts can be produced,
(2) the rate at which the parts are used,
(3) the cost of carrying the parts in inventory, and
(4) the cost of producing the parts.

The rate at which the part is used, together with the time needed to produce a replacement lot, is of great importance. There must always be enough parts in stock to meet usage levels, plus a reserve quantity.

The cost to manufacture the part is next in importance. The **larger the lot size, the lower the cost per unit.** However, a larger lot size requires a greater expenditure for material, labor, material handling and storing, and higher insurance and tax costs. Also, money taken out of savings and invested in larger lot sizes cannot earn interest. If a business loan is obtained, interest charges add to the overall cost.

For example, suppose a company plans to use an N/C automatic lathe to make 100 of the special bolts mentioned above. The estimated setup time and cost to prepare the machine and tools would be 2 hours at $50 per hour, or $100. This results in a **setup cost** of $1 per bolt. For 1000 bolts, the setup cost would be reduced to $.10 per bolt, and for 10,000 bolts, the setup cost would be only $.01 per bolt. If the cost of making each bolt is $.35 for material and $1.80 for all other costs except setup, the cost per bolt is $2.15.

For a lot size of 100 bolts, the total cost would be $50 for setup plus $215 for the bolts or $265, which amounts to $2.65 per bolt. For 1000 bolts, the total cost would be $2150 + $50 = $2200, or $2.20 per bolt. For 10,000 bolts, the total cost would be $21,500 + $50 = $21,550, or $2.16 per bolt.

98-3 Determining Economic Manufacturing Lot Size

The most economical quantity of parts to be made may be determined by the following formula:

economic lot size

$$= \sqrt{\frac{M \times U \times S \times 560}{C \times (M - U) \times F}} \text{ where:}$$

M = number of parts that can be made per day

U = number of parts needed per day

S = total cost of setup in dollars

C = total cost of material, labor, and overhead per part, not including setup

F = decimal fraction by which the cost of the part is increased if kept in storage for one year. For example, if C = $.90, the interest rate is 6%, and storage cost is $.01 per part per year, then for storing one part for one year the cost would be increased .90 × .06 + .01 = $.064, or 7% (.064 ÷ .90).

Using the special bolts as an example, if M = 1440, U = 50, S = $100, C = $.90, and F = .07 (7%), then

economic lot size

$$= \sqrt{\frac{1440 \times 50 \times 100 \times 560}{.90 \, (1440 - 50) \times .07}}$$

$$= \sqrt{\frac{4,032,000,000}{87.57}}$$

$$= \sqrt{46,043,165}$$

$$= 6785.5 \text{ or } 6786 \text{ bolts.}$$

With a usage rate of 50 per day, annual usage would be 50 × 260 working days per year or 13,000 bolts. At a production rate of 1440 per day, a production run would require 4.71 days (6786 ÷ 1440). This would provide a supply of bolts for 135 working days (6786 ÷ 50), or 27 weeks (135 ÷ 5).

98-4 Types of Manufacturing

Products made in quantity are made either by intermittent or continuous manufacturing. **Continuous manufacturing** is used for very high volume production. It uses continuously moving assembly lines like those used in automobile and appliance manufacturing (Fig. 98-1).

Intermittent manufacturing is used when demand for the product is much lower than the rate of production. In this case, economic lot sizes are determined and produced. Intermittent manufacturing also includes **job-lot** manufacturing, in which parts are made to customer order. Job-lot manufacturing is used mostly in the production of expensive machines and equipment, and for repair parts and special tooling (Fig. 98-2).

Fig. 98-1 *Continuous manufacturing of refrigerators using a moving assembly line.* (General Electric)

Fig. 98-2 *A high-speed cold header such as this is sometimes used in job-lot manufacturing.* (National Machinery Company)

98-5 Process Design Communications and Records

Process or manufacturing engineers are responsible for selecting the manufacturing methods and the type of machines to be used. They also decide the best sequence of operations (step-by-step procedure) for making each part, sub-assembly, and final assembly of the product.

The **working drawing** is the most important of the communication and record forms. Before any work can begin, approved working drawings must be obtained for each part from the product engineering department (Fig. 98-3). Each part drawing is then studied, and a list is made of the operations required for manufacturing the part.

The operations are then arranged in the sequence for the most economical manufacture of the part, and are recorded on a **standard process sheet** (Fig. 98-4). It is very important that the operation descriptions be clear, but they should be as brief as possible. This work is usually done by manufacturing engineers or technologists who are expert in the processes required to make the part.

The standard process sheet also contains the following information:

(1) the part number and name
(2) the sub-assembly and assembly numbers
(3) the kind and quantity of material required
(4) the kind of machine on which it is made
(5) the setup time and production rate
(6) the standard tooling package numbers.

A master file of all standard process sheets is kept in the process engineering department. This file provides the knowledge needed for manufacture of the company's products, and is therefore one of the company's most valuable assets.

Fig. 98-3 *Working drawing of a pin.* (John Deere)

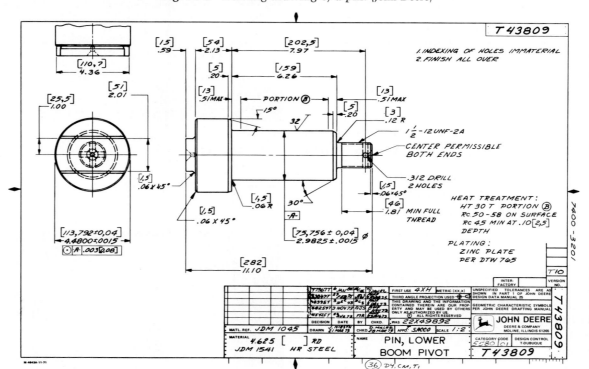

```
TXJDS           Mon Feb 15 08:34:15 1988           1

   T43809          0100      JOB DETAIL SHEET AS OF 01 JUN 1987        PG 1
                                                              STD.HRS.
   OPER   DEPT  MACH.CODE              LG       ACTS          /100 PCS
   0100   15    10157                   9       0.3700         0.4800

   PCS/CYCLE    6.                                          \TSM:  1.636

   REASON CHANGE: NEW STANDARD ENGR: GRIMES
      TX02563    :
   PART DIMENSION: MATERIAL: JDM 1541 HRS
                 : WIDTH: 4.625    LGTH: 11.10    WGT: 25.800  LBS.

   000010 M401      LOAD (6  ) PARTS; (1 ) PER TRIP         D   1/   1   0.079
   000020 TXA501    LOAD PART(S) TO BASKET OR CONVEYOR FROM D   6/   1   0.642
                    CONTAINER
   000030 M402      PUSH LOADED BASKET TO POWER CONVEYOR    D   1/   1   0.040
   000040 M403      WALK TO UNLOAD END                      D   1/   1   0.035
                    UNLOAD (6  ) PARTS; (1 ) PER TRIP
   000050 TXA507    PLACE ASIDE PART(S) FROM BASKET OR      D   6/   1   0.642
                    CONVEYOR TO CONTAINER
   000060 AA1139    POSITION CARDBOARD IN BOTTOM OF         D   1/   1   0.014
                    CONTAINER ONLY
   000070 A118      TALLY COUNT                             D   1/   1   0.040
   000080 CL100ATX  CHANGE LOADS                            D   6/   1   0.144

   THE APPROVED METHOD IS AS SHOWN ON THIS FORM AND NO CHANGE IN METHOD
   MAY BE MADE BY THE EMPLOYEE WITHOUT SECURING APPROVAL OF THE
   COMPANY AS INDICATED BY THE ISSUANCE OF A REVISION.
```

Fig. 98-4 *Standard process sheet for making the pin shown in Fig. 98-3.*
(John Deere)

REVIEW REVIEW REVIEW REVIEW REVIEW

WORDS TO KNOW

continuous manufacturing
economical manufacturing lot size
intermittent manufacturing
job-lot manufacturing
manufacturing process design
product volume
rejection rate
sequence of operations
setup cost
standard process sheet
working drawing

REVIEW QUESTIONS

1. List the three basic factors involved in manufacturing process design.
2. Explain how product volume is related to production cost per unit.
3. How does increased product quality affect production cost per unit?
4. What is meant by economical manufacturing lot size?
5. What is meant by setup cost?
6. How is economical manufacturing lot size determined?
7. For what kind of production volume is continuous manufacturing used? Intermittent manufacturing? Job-lot manufacturing?
8. What is the most important communication and record form used in process design?
9. List the information that a standard process sheet contains.

UNIT 99

Product Marketing

Marketing is the function of industry that is concerned with sales and distribution of the finished product. There are six main functions of marketing:

(1) marketing research
(2) product planning
(3) distribution
(4) advertising
(5) sales, and
(6) product servicing.

Marketing research for existing products is done to find out who the customers are, how satisfied they are with the product, and to obtain suggestions for product improvement. For new products, marketing research is done to find out how well consumers like the product, and also its name, method of packaging, and price.

Marketing research data is obtained in three ways:

(1) research of company sales and service records
(2) taking a survey of present and potential customers, and
(3) test marketing the product.

Marketing research provides important information about the products that customers need or want. This information is needed for:

(1) determining new product acceptance
(2) making improvements to existing products
(3) developing new product ideas.

Product planning is a marketing function that is concerned with making product improvements, adding new products, and discontinuing old products. It is responsible for developing **sales forecasts** for each product in each sales territory, which directly affects production scheduling and product distribution.

Distribution involves those activities needed to get the product to the customer. Three channels of distribution are used:

(1) through wholesalers
(2) direct to the user, and
(3) through manufacturer's agents.

Distribution usually includes warehousing the product, inventory control, and shipping.

Wholesalers purchase the product in large quantities and resell the product to retailers in standard package quantities (Fig. 99-1). Retailers then display and sell the individual products to the consumer. Most consumer goods are sold this way.

Selling direct to the user eliminates the wholesaler and retailer from the distribution system. This can result in lower cost to the consumer, greater profit for the manufacturer, or both. All forms of **advertising** are used for direct sales, including personal contact by salespersons, telephone soliciting, and television, radio, magazine, newspaper, and billboard ads.

Fig. 99-1 *Wholesalers buy the product from the manufacturer and sell it to retailers. Most consumer goods are sold this way.* (Wilkins Pipe & Supply, Roger Bean)

ADS Solves a Manufacturing Problem

A few years ago Mc-Donnell Douglas Aircraft Company faced a difficult situation. Wings for aircraft that McDonnell Douglas was building each required the drilling of 6,000 fastener holes. That drilling took 600 person hours per wing to complete—three shifts a day for nine days. Now it takes three shifts a day for only five days. Soon it may take only three days. The reason for this reduction in time is McDonnell Douglas' new wing Automated Drilling System (ADS).

ADS is a gentle giant: it does large-scale work, but it is very precise and produces high-quality detail too. Its two gantry-type direct numerical control machine tools travel over a work pit 108 feet long and 16 feet deep. They work together to drill one wing or, if need be, separately to drill two wings at the same time.

After a wing is scanned by a high-precision, solid-state camera to determine where each hole should be drilled, the wing skin is bolted into place for drilling. A laser bar code reader monitors the drilling tools that are in use, and tool speeds are adjusted by the system automatically. Each hole takes about 35 seconds to drill.

The wing Automated Drilling System was built for McDonnell Douglas by Ingersoll Milling Machine Company. The system is so complex that it required a CAD/CAM system to design and manufacture it. This $4.5-million system is a success because of its speed and precision, and also because of its flexibility and the impressive size of its work envelope.

Experts believe that new work cells like ADS will improve not only manufacturing efficiency but also the product designs themselves. Ultimately, better tooling will mean *both* faster work *and* better-designed products.

Manufacturer's agents sell products of several non-competing companies in a limited sales territory. Many industrial and some consumer goods are sold this way. For example, an agent may offer machine tools made by one company, cutting tools by another, cutting fluids from a third, etc.

Advertising informs possible customers of a company's products. Its single purpose is to persuade consumers to purchase the product. Television, radio, newspapers, magazines, and direct mail are the most widely used advertising media. The success of a product, however, is determined by customer satisfaction with the product, not by advertising.

The sale of company products is carried out by salespersons employed by a sales department. Some salespersons work from a company office. They receive and process mail or telephone orders, and may also phone possible customers to try to sell directly. Other salespersons call personally on regular and possible customers in their sales territory. To be successful, salespersons need to be trained in sales methods, and should know all about the products they sell.

Product service is that function of marketing concerned with servicing the product to keep it operating properly, and repairing it when necessary. Many of today's products are highly technical and require specially trained workers to do correct service and repair (Fig. 99-2). This kind of employment is growing rapidly; in fact, more people in the United States are now employed in service industries than in manufacturing.

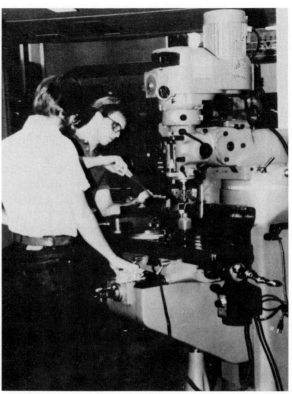

Fig. 99-2 *Product service is important in maintaining customer satisfaction. Here, production equipment is being repaired by company servicepersons.* (DoALL)

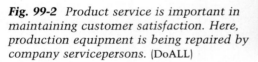

REVIEW   REVIEW   REVIEW   REVIEW   REVIEW

Words to know

advertising	marketing	product service	wholesalers
distribution	manufacturer's agent	sales forecasts	

Review questions

1. List the six functions of marketing.
2. List the three methods of obtaining market research data.
3. List the three types of information obtained by marketing research.
4. Explain how marketing is concerned with product planning.
5. What three channels of distribution are used by manufacturers?
6. Why doesn't the success of a product depend on advertising?
7. Give three ways company salespersons are used to sell products.
8. Why is product service a rapidly growing area of employment?

UNIT
100

Production Planning and Quality Control

In large companies the functions of production planning and quality control are usually carried on by separate departments in the manufacturing division. However, these functions are normally an important part of any manufacturing organization, regardless of whether a company is large, middle-sized, or small.

100-1 Production Planning

Production planning is concerned with establishing the routes and schedules for manufacturing the product. The plan for processing the materials in the plant involves the functions of routing, loading, scheduling, and dispatching. A purchasing department is responsible for obtaining the supplies and materials needed to make the product.

Routing is the function of determining the route the material must take through the plant. In **generalized routing,** the route is established to buildings or departments, which then do their own routing. In **detailed routing,** the route specifies the work station or machine to be used for each step in the manufacturing process. Routing information is obtained either from the standard process sheet (Fig. 98-4), the **flow process sheet** (Fig. 100-1), or a separate form used for this purpose.

Loading is the function of calculating the time required to process a job lot, and charging it against available production time. In **generalized loading,** the time is charged to a building or a department. In **detailed loading,** the time is charged to the work station or machine. This information is recorded on a **loading chart,** which then provides a record of the

planned use of each work station and machine (Fig. 100-2). To reduce the number of record forms, this function is often combined with scheduling.

Scheduling is planning when the work is to be done. **Schedule charts** are used to provide a record of the time that each department, work station, or machine takes to perform its function (Fig. 100-3). These charts show the planned use; that is, how much work is ahead for each productive unit and when each job is to be completed (Fig. 100-4). Schedule charts must be continually updated to reflect actual completion times and to record new orders.

Dispatching is authorizing the start of a manufacturing operation. Authorization is provided with a **job ticket,** which is issued by the production control department or by the local departmental dispatcher. The job ticket is one of the most important paper forms in the production control system. When filled out after the job is completed, it provides a written record of the number of parts processed and the actual production time required. It provides the information needed to determine accurate production costs, which are necessary for determining a profitable price.

100-2 Quality Control

An overall program of quality control must be concerned with three aspects of quality:

(1) product design quality
(2) conformance with (meeting) design specifications
(3) product performance quality.

Flow Process Sheet

Flow Chart No._____   _____ Of _____

PRODUCT_____   PART NAME _____   PART #_____

OPERATION/PROCESS_____

CHARTER BY_____   DATE _____

SYMBOLS   ⇨ TRANSPORTATION   **D** DELAY
○ OPERATION   ☐ INSPECTION   ▽ STORAGE

Oper. No.	Chart Symbol	Process Description	Time in Min.	Distance in Feet
	○ ⇨ ☐ **D** ▽			
	○ ⇨ ☐ **D** ▽			
	○ ⇨ ☐ **D** ▽			
	○ ⇨ ☐ **D** ▽			
	○ ⇨ ☐ **D** ▽			
	○ ⇨ ☐ **D** ▽			
	○ ⇨ ☐ **D** ▽			
	○ ⇨ ☐ **D** ▽			
	○ ⇨ ☐ **D** ▽			
	○ ⇨ ☐ **D** ▽			
	○ ⇨ ☐ **D** ▽			
	○ ⇨ ☐ **D** ▽			
	○ ⇨ ☐ **D** ▽			
	○ ⇨ ☐ **D** ▽			
	○ ⇨ ☐ **D** ▽			
	○ ⇨ ☐ **D** ▽			
	○ ⇨ ☐ **D** ▽			
	○ ⇨ ☐ **D** ▽			

Fig. 100-1 *An example of a flow process sheet used for analyzing and recording the flow of product through a plant.*

Fig. 100-2 *A loading chart showing the work available for each machine each week (light lines), and the work backlog (blue lines).*

Loading Chart

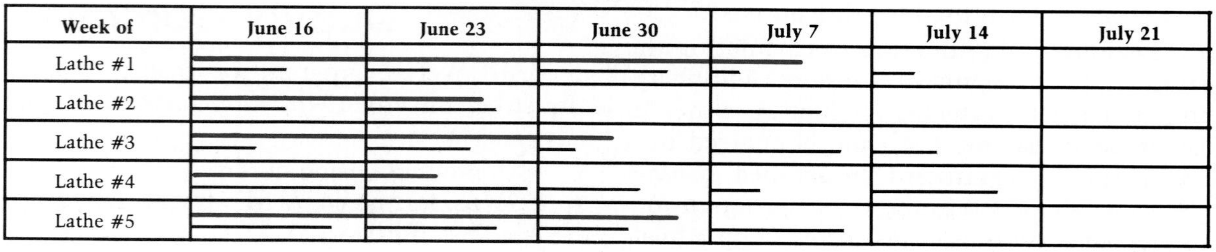

Week of	June 16	June 23	June 30	July 7	July 14	July 21
Lathe #1						
Lathe #2						
Lathe #3						
Lathe #4						
Lathe #5						

Milling Department

Week of	May 5	May 12	May 19	May 26	June 2	June 9
Mill #1	Job 135	Job 140		Job 157		
Mill #2	Job 136			Job 141		
Mill #3	Job 137		Job 142		Job 158	
Mill #4	Job 138		Job 143	Job 159		
Mill #5	Job 139			Job 144		

Fig. 100-3 *A Gantt-type machine scheduling chart. The chart shows planned starting and completion time for each job scheduled for each machine (dark lines), time scheduled for maintenance (x), and the percentage of the job completed (light lines). Performance is indicated at the end of the week of May 19, as shown by the V shaped mark. Note that all machines are on or ahead of schedule except Mill #2.*

Part #300 Mounting Bracket

	Feb.	Mar.	Apr.	May	June	July	Aug.
Engineering							
Tooling							
Procurement							
Manufacturing							
Part 301							
Part 302							
Part 303							
Part 304							
Assembly							

Fig. 100-4. *A Gantt-type chart for scheduling a product with several parts. The status of the project is indicated as of the end of May. Note that incomplete tooling has delayed production of part #304, and also the start of assembly.*

Quality of design is the responsibility of the product engineering department (see Unit 97). An old saying states "quality begins on the drawing board." What this means is that no amount of quality control can make up for a poorly designed product. The appearance and performance of a product are a direct result of the design and specifications that the product designers and engineers establish.

Quality of conformance with design specifications is primarily an inspection function. This involves inspection of **purchased materials and parts** to make sure that they meet quality standards established by the product design department. It also involves inspection of the **work-in-process.** Much unofficial inspection is performed by production workers in the normal course of carrying out their work. Official inspection, however, is carried out by qualified inspectors either at the various work stations and machines or in an inspection room (see Fig. 93-1).

The amount, or numbers, of the product that is inspected depends on the complexity of the product, and critical requirements of its performance. Products involving human safety usually receive 100% inspection. Many products, however, are inspected by **statistical sampling.** In this method, only a small percentage of the product needs to be inspected. However, the sample selected at random provides effective quality control for the whole production run.

Increasingly, production machines are being equipped with automatic measuring devices. They measure critical dimensions and automatically adjust the machine when necessary. The accuracy of machines so equipped greatly reduces the amount of inspection needed.

Statistical process control (SPC) is used to reduce the percentage of rejects and lower production costs. In SPC, a sample of parts is periodically measured at each machine and analyzed statistically to determine whether the machine needs adjustment. Special electronic measuring tools are used to transmit the measurements taken to a computer (Fig. 100-5). The computer automatically makes a statistical analysis of the measurements and produces the SPC charts that indicate whether the machine is performing correctly or needs adjustment.

Finally, **finished goods inspection** must be made by qualified inspectors (Fig. 100-6). The items checked at this stage include critical part dimensions, tests for correct operation, and finish quality. Final inspection should be careful and complete to prevent a faulty product from being sent to a customer.

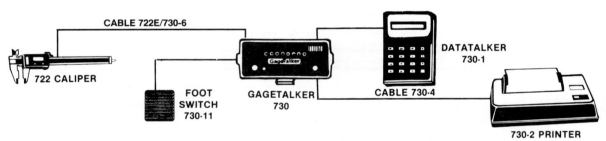

Fig. 100-5 *This electronic vernier caliper can transmit measurements to a computer, where they are automatically analyzed statistically. It produces a computer printout of measurement data for a part.* (L.S. Starrett Co.)

Fig. 100-6 *A product must undergo final inspection before packaging and shipping.* (Manual High School, Roger Bean)

REVIEW REVIEW REVIEW REVIEW REVIEW

WORDS TO KNOW

dispatching
finished goods
  inspection
flow process chart

job ticket
loading
purchased goods
  inspection

routing
scheduling
statistical process
  control

statistical sampling
work-in-process

REVIEW QUESTIONS

1. What are the two main responsibilities of production planning?
2. Explain the difference between generalized and detailed routing.
3. What information is contained on flow process sheets?
4. What is the function of loading?
5. What information is recorded on schedule charts?
6. What is meant by dispatching?
7. Tell what a job ticket is used for, and why it is important.
8. What three aspects of quality are included in an overall quality control program?
9. List three kinds of product inspection that must be done to assure product quality.
10. Why is 100% inspection used for some products?
11. Explain how statistical process control works.

UNIT
101

Metalworking in the Manufacturing Laboratory

Manufacturing has become a regular course offering in many technology curriculums in public schools. It is also an activity that is practiced by the Junior Achievement and Junior Engineer programs. Their objective is to acquaint those interested in engineering and business with the ways products are manufactured and marketed. A well equipped school laboratory provides an excellent facility for learning how products are manufactured (Fig. 101-1).

101-1 Getting Organized

The first step in starting a manufacturing activity is to form a company or corporation and elect or appoint the company officers. An organization chart should then be made to identify the person responsible for each of the seven areas of manufacturing activity dis-

Fig. 101-1 *A well-equipped school laboratory is an excellent facility for learning how products are manufactured.* (Manual High School, Roger Bean)

Fig. 101-2 *Product ideas obtained from class members are listed on the chalkboard.* (Manual High School, Roger Bean)

cussed in Unit 96. This chart is also needed to establish a clear line of authority (see Figures 96-1 and 96-2).

An organization manual should then be prepared that provides a detailed outline of the duties and responsibilities of each job on the organization chart. A standard practice manual is then written to establish how each task in each job is to be carried out. The instructor should then provide training materials and sessions to prepare the managers to carry out their duties.

101-2 Product Selection and Marketing

The final decision on the product selected for manufacturing rests with your instructor. However, some instructors like to have the class help decide the product to be produced. You may be shown examples or photographs of the kind and quality of products previous classes have manufactured. Product ideas may then be obtained from class members and listed on the chalkboard (Fig. 101-2). The class should then discuss both the good points and manufacturing difficulties of each product so as to eliminate the impractical product ideas. Class members can then vote to determine the product to be manufactured.

The product marketing group helps in the search and selection of the product to be manufactured. Estimates of the cost of each product should be made to help the selection process. After the product has been selected, the possible customers should be surveyed to determine preference for the product design, performance features, choice of material, color, and kind of finish.

If production is limited to provide the product only to the class members, the marketing function is greatly simplified. However, if the product is to be sold outside of class, plans must be made and carried out to package, advertise, distribute, and sell the product.

The sale price for the product is determined by adding a **profit percentage** to all the production and overhead costs. **Production costs** include material, labor, expendable tools, and machine time. **Overhead costs** include cost for light, heat, electricity, water, factory rent, taxes, and also engineering, supervision, and marketing costs.

It is very difficult to make a profit with low production quantities unless the product is very simple, and tooling, labor, and overhead costs are very low. The **breakeven point** is the number of products that must be sold before a profit can be made. It can be determined by constructing a **breakeven chart** (Fig. 101-3).

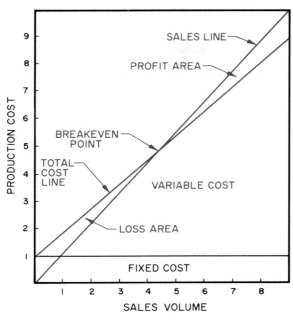

Fig. 101-3 *Breakeven charts determine how many products must be produced in order to begin making a profit.*

Fig. 101-4 *Production drawings being made on a CAD system.* (Richwoods High School, Roger Bean)

101-3 Product Engineering

The product engineering group, in consultation with the instructor, develops the product design and specifications, and produces the preliminary working drawings. A **prototype** of the product is then made under close supervision of the product engineers and instructor. Any difficulties in producing the prototype should be carefully noted. Using this information, the product engineering group decides whether changes should be made in the product design, production methods, or choice of materials used.

After the final design of the product has been approved, the product engineering group makes the **production drawings** for each part (Fig. 101-4). The product engineers then prepare a standard process sheet for each part, listing the correct **operational sequence** for producing the part (Fig. 101-5). A standard process sheet should also be made for each subassembly, for the final assembly, and for packaging.

Fig. 101-5 *Standard process sheets must be prepared and checked.* (Manual High School, Roger Bean)

Special tooling such as work-holding, inspection, and assembly fixtures, and drill jigs should then be designed, produced, and tested for accuracy.

Tool Tray Flow Chart Data

Ends	Sides & Bottom	Handle
⇨ deliver material to shear	⇨ deliver material to shear	⇨ deliver material to shear
◯ cut to length	◯ cut to length	◯ cut to length
◯ cut to width	◯ cut to width	◯ cut to width
☐ inspect	☐ inspect	☐ inspect
⇨ to notcher	⇨ to notcher	⇨ to notcher
◯ cut angles	◯ notch V's	◯ notch corners
☐ inspect	◯ clip corners	☐ inspect
⇨ to assembly	☐ inspect	⇨ to bar folder
	⇨ to bar folder	◯ bend end tabs
	◯ bend hems	⇨ to box & pan brake
	◯ bend seams	◯ bend sides
	☐ inspect	☐ inspect
	⇨ to box & pan brake	⇨ to assembly
	◯ bend sides	
	☐ inspect	
	⇨ to assembly	

◯ spot weld ends to tray
◯ spot weld handle to tray
⇨ to deburring station
◯ remove all sharp edges
☐ inspect
⇨ to finishing department
◯ degrease with solvent

◯ allow to air dry
◯ apply primer
▽ allow to air dry
◯ apply finish coat of paint
▽ allow to air dry
☐ inspect
◯ package
⇨ to storage or ship to customer

Fig. 101-6 *Flow process sheets are prepared to document the path each part takes through the factory.*

101-4 Production Planning

The production planning group then prepares a flow process sheet, or a routing sheet, to establish the path each part must take through the "factory" (Fig. 101-6). A flow process sheet should also be made for each subassembly, final assembly, and packaging.

Loading or schedule charts, and sometimes both, are then prepared to plan when and on what equipment the work will be done (Fig. 101-7). Job tickets are then prepared to authorize the start of work on each part. All production work should be carefully tracked to obtain accurate production times and quantities so that accurate production costs can be calculated.

The kind and quantity of each type of worker needed is then determined. Students may then be permitted to apply for the type of job they want, or they may be assigned jobs on the basis of their known skills.

101-5 Manufacturing

Manufacturing can begin after the production engineering, planning, and production tooling have been completed. Each work station must first be prepared with the necessary tooling. Standard process sheets should be provided at each work station, and workers should be trained to perform each operation.

Production Schedule Chart

Product: Tool Tray	Monday	Tuesday	Wednesday	Thursday	Friday
Sides & bottom	——————	——————			
Ends	————	——————			
Handle		———	———		
Assemble			————	—————	
Finish				——————	—————

Fig. 101-7 *A schedule chart should be made for producing the product.*

When actual production begins, production supervisors should check on each worker to be sure the work is being done safely and properly. Official inspection should also be done to make sure that product quality standards are being met.

A **pilot production run** (trial run) is usually made, in order to find out where production problems may occur. If problems are found, they must be corrected before full-scale production can be successful.

101-6 Review of the Manufacturing Exercise

At the conclusion of the manufacturing exercise, the instructor and class may review the entire learning experience step-by-step to emphasize the principles of manufacturing. You may be asked to suggest better ways of carrying out the manufacturing experience should other classes make the same product again.

REVIEW REVIEW REVIEW REVIEW REVIEW

WORDS TO KNOW

breakeven point	profit percentage	operational	production drawings
breakeven chart	prototype	sequence	production costs
pilot production run		overhead costs	

REVIEW QUESTIONS

1. What is the first step in undertaking a manufacturing activity?
2. What tool of organization is used to show what each company officer is responsible for, and also to show the company line of authority?
3. What is a product prototype and why is it made?
4. How many standard process sheets are required for producing the product ready for sale?
5. How many flow process sheets are required for producing the product ready for sale?
6. What is a pilot production run and why is it used?
7. How is the sale price of a product determined?
8. List the production costs involved in manufacturing.
9. List the overhead costs involved in manufacturing.
10. What is meant by the breakeven point? How is it determined?

PART

24

Product Suggestions

The following products, some simple and some more difficult, have been selected to provide experience with basic metalworking processes. In construction a product must often be planned so as to use the machinery in your school shop and materials that are readily available. The construction notes for each product are given as a recommended construction sequence. These may need to be altered to suit available equipment and materials. Be sure to consult your instructor about design changes or alternate ways of making a product.

Before beginning work on a product, review Unit 10; then, plan your product, work out the best construction procedure, and get approval from your instructor.

Dimensions on drawings and in materials lists are in inches. Dimension tables with metric dimensions are included to provide practice in using dimensions in millimeters.

The products and the processes used in their construction are listed below:

1. Dinner Bell Triangle and Striker: layout, hacksawing, chamfering, bending.
2. Wall Bracket: layout, hacksawing, flaring (cold forging); grinding or filing; bending; center punching; drilling; brazing, welding, or riveting; painting.
3. Record Rack: sawing, filing or grinding, bending, drilling, riveting, painting.
4. Hanging or Standing Candle Holder: layout, hacksawing, bending, forming, brazing or welding, painting.
5. Sit-up Bar: layout, hacksawing, bending, drilling, facing, turning, welding, painting.
6. Fireplace Tools: layout, hacksawing, bending, forging, drilling, tapping, threading, riveting if desired, brazing or welding, patternmaking, mold making, casting, filing, painting.
7. Flower Pot Holder: layout, hacksawing, bending, filing, welding or brazing, or drilling and riveting, painting.
8. Dog Stake: layout, hacksawing, drilling, reaming if necessary, bending, brazing and welding.
9. Screwdriver: (A) Blade: layout, hacksawing, center drilling, knurling, facing, chamfering, forging, grinding, filing, heat treating, abrasive polishing. (B) Handle: band sawing, facing, chamfering, drilling, turning.
10. Cold Chisel: layout, hacksawing, forging, grinding, filing, heat treating, abrasive polishing.
11. Scratch Pad Holder: layout, cutting (squaring shear, plain notcher, jeweler's saw), filing, bending (bar folder, box and pan brake), finishing (wire wheel or buffing).

12. Kitchen Canister Scoop: layout, cutting, bending, filing, rolling, grooved seaming, soldering, lacquering.
13. Dustpan: layout, cutting (squaring shear, tab and plain notcher), bending (bar folder, box and pan brake), filing, spot welding, riveting, painting if desired.
14. Mailbox: layout, cutting (squaring shear, plain notcher), bending (bar folder, box and pan brake), filing, spot welding, soldering, abrasive polishing, painting.
15. Toolbox and Tray: layout, cutting (squaring shear, tab and plain notcher), bending (bar folder, box and pan brake), filing, rod bending (vise and hammer), spot welding, painting.
16. Night Table or Dresser Lamp: (A) Cast Parts: patternmaking, mold making, casting, hacksawing, drilling, finishing (filing, wire brushing, painting). (B) Tubing: hacksawing, facing, filing, painting. (C) 1/8" Pipe: hacksawing, filing.

17. Coasters: cutting (ring and circle shear or tin snips), metal spinning (forming, edge trimming), polishing.
18. Meat Tenderizer: sawing, facing, straight, taper, and concave radius turning, chamfering, grooving, knurling, tapping, threading, center drilling, drilling, milling 60° grooves, filing, draw filing or belt grinding.
19. Soft Hammer: turning, facing, grooving, threading, milling, filing.
20. Tic-Tac-Toe Game Peg: N/C lathe programming, turning, grooving, chamfering, cutoff.
21. Tic-Tac-Toe Game Board: N/C mill programming, milling, drilling, finishing (filing, abrasive polishing, buffing).
22. Parcheesi Game Piece: N/C lathe programming, radius, taper, and straight turning, chamfering, cutoff.

One other product, the Desk-Top Pencil Holder, is included in Unit 10, "Product Planning."

Note: All dimensions are in inches.

1. Dinner Bell Triangle and Striker

Materials: Hot Rolled Steel
1 Pc ⅜ Dia. × 33½
1 Pc 5/16 Dia. × 10

Construction Notes:
1. Enlarge pattern to full size with 1″ squares.
2. Chamfer ends of rods.
3. Bend eye of triangle to match pattern.
4. Bend 60-degree angles.
5. Bend closed eye of striker.

Dimension Table

inch	mm
33½	851
10	254
½	13
⅜	10
5/16	8

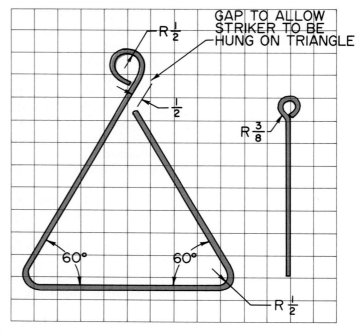

SCALE: $\frac{3″}{16} = 1″$

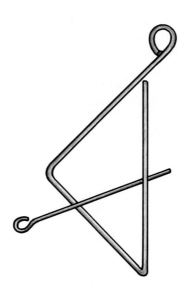

Product prepared by Donald G. Marquardt

2. Wall Bracket

Materials: Hot Rolled Steel
Part A: ⅛ × ¾ × 15
Part B: ⅛ × ¾ × 10½
Part C: ⅛ × ¾ × 9½

Construction Notes:

1. Enlarge pattern to 1″ squares.
2. Flare ends of pieces as desired before bending. File or grind off sharp edges as necessary.
3. Curve ends of Parts A and C to match pattern with hammer and stake or jig.
4. Drill ³⁄₁₆″ holes ¾″ from each end of 10½″ strip for mounting bracket on wall.
5. Braze or weld edges of strips together.

Finish: Flat black paint.

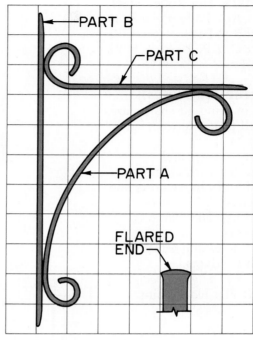

SCALE: $\frac{1''}{4}$ = 1″

Dimension Table

inch	mm	inch	mm
15	381	¾	19
10½	267	³⁄₁₆	5
9½	241	⅛	3

3. Record Rack

Materials: Hot Rolled Steel
Support A: 2 Pc ⅛ × ¾ × 38
Support B: 2 Pc ⅛ × ¾ × 30
Support C: 2 Pc ⅛ × ¾ × 22
Legs: 2 Pc ⅛ × ¾ × 12

Construction Notes:

1. File or grind off sharp edges on all pieces to rounded corners.
2. Bend supports and assemble with clamps.
3. Drill holes in supports and fasten with ¼″ rivets.
4. Bend legs and clamp to supports.
5. Drill holes and attach legs with ¼″ rivets.

Finish: Flat black paint.

Dimension Table

inch	mm	inch	mm
38	965	8	203
30	762	4	102
22	559	1	25
20	508	¾	18
12	305	¼	6
9	229	⅛	3

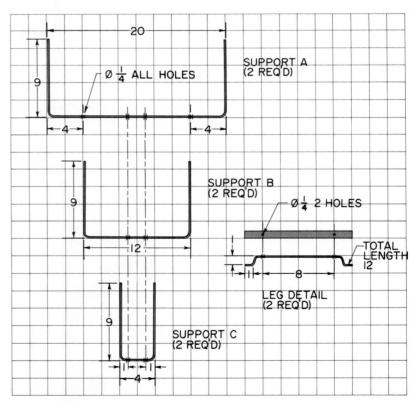

SCALE: $\frac{3″}{16}$ = 2″

Product prepared by Robert W. Todd

4. Hanging or Standing Candle Holder

Materials:

Arms: ¼ × ¼ × 24 Hot
    Rolled Steel, 3 Pc
Eye: ¼ × ¼ × 4 Hot Rolled
    Steel
Disk: 3½ Dia. × 20 ga. Cold
    Sheet Steel (Heavier
    metal may be
    substituted.)

Construction Notes:

1. Draw bending pattern full
   size with 1″ squares and
   bend three arms to fit
   pattern.
2. Bend hanging eye around 1″
   Dia. rod.
3. Cut 3½″ disk and hammer
   edge up slightly over stake.
4. Assemble three arms 120
   degrees apart from each
   other and weld or braze at
   top. May be easier to
   assemble if bottom is held
   in jig.
5. Weld or braze hanging eye
   on top of assembly.
6. Braze candle disk centered
   on three bottom curves of
   arms.

Dimension Table

inch	mm	inch	mm
24	610	2	51
4	102	1	25
3½	89	¼	6

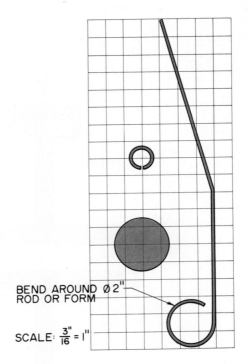

BEND AROUND ⌀2″
ROD OR FORM

SCALE: $\frac{3″}{16}$ = 1″

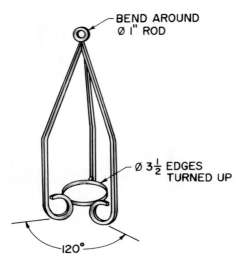

BEND AROUND
⌀1″ ROD

⌀ 3½ EDGES
TURNED UP

120°

Product prepared by Donald G. Marquardt

5. Sit-up Bar

Materials:
Hot Rolled Steel
1 Pc ⅛ × 1 × 13
1 Pc ⅛ × 1 × 10
1 Pc 14 gage, 4 × 6¼
1 Pc 14 gage, 1⅞ Dia.
1 Pc ⅝ Dia. × ¹³⁄₃₂ Cold
Rolled Steel
1 Pc 11 × ¾ Black Iron Pipe
(OD 1.05)
1 thumbscrew, ⁵⁄₁₆-18 × 1½
with 4 std. nuts to fit
2 rubber chair boots 1″ Dia.

Dimension Table

inch	mm	inch	mm
13	330	1	25
11	279	¾	19
10	254	⅝	16
8	203	¹³⁄₃₂	10
6¼	159	¹¹⁄₃₂	9
5	127	⁵⁄₁₆	8
4	102	¼	6
2¼	57	.24	6
2	51	³⁄₁₆	5
1⅞	48	⅛	3
1½	38	¹⁄₁₆	2

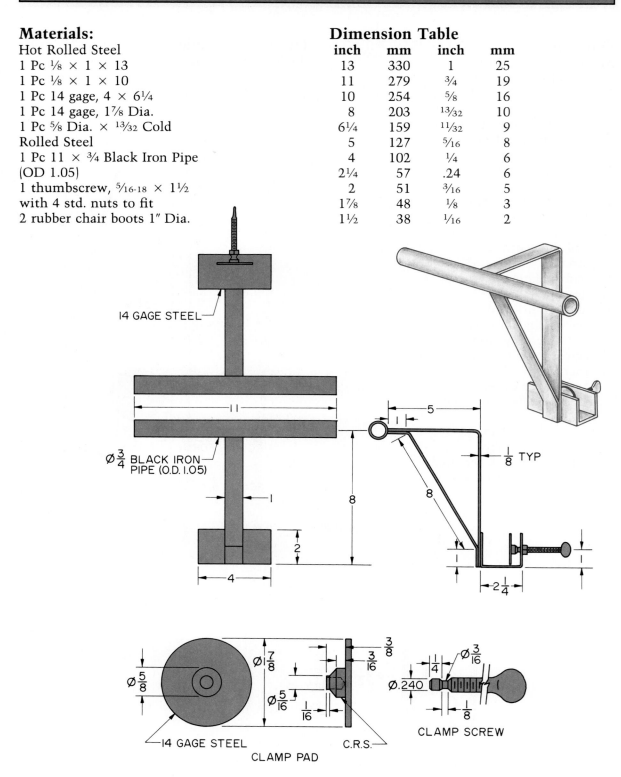

14 GAGE STEEL

Ø¾ BLACK IRON PIPE (O.D. 1.05)

⅛ TYP

CLAMP PAD

14 GAGE STEEL

C.R.S.

CLAMP SCREW

Sit-up Bar *(continued)*

Construction Notes:

Clamp

1. Cut 14-gage sheet for the clamp body. CAUTION: 14-gage is too thick to be cut on most sheet metal squaring shears; band sawing is recommended.
2. Lay out and drill an $\frac{11}{32}''$ hole for the clamp screw.
3. Bend into a U shape as shown.
4. Braze a standard $\frac{5}{16}$-18 nut into position over the $\frac{11}{32}''$ hole.

Clamp screw

If a collet is not available to hold the screw for machining, use three nuts to hold the screw in a universal chuck as:

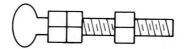

Tighten nuts together to keep screw from turning inside the nuts.

Clamp pad

Assemble the 14-gage disc and the CRS swivel by brazing.

Clamp assembly

1. Screw the $\frac{5}{16}$-18" thumbscrew through the nut of the clamp.
2. Slide the clamp pad onto the end of the screw.
3. Insert a block of steel $\frac{3}{4}''$ × 2" × 4" in the clamp and tighten it with the clamp screw.
4. Mount the clamp in a machinist's vise so that when the vise is tightened the $\frac{3}{4}''$ block of steel will push against the clamp pad.
5. Using a pin punch and a ballpeen hammer, reduce the diameter of the $\frac{1}{16}''$ flange on the pad swivel enough to prevent it coming off the clamp screw.

Bar and Support

1. Bend right-angle and diagonal pieces. Weld as shown.
2. For final assembly, weld bar, support, and clamp as shown.

6. Fireplace Tools

Materials:

Fireplace or Stove Tongs
Top Handles: 2 Pc $\frac{3}{16} \times \frac{5}{8} \times$ 21½ Hot Rolled Steel
Bottom Tongs: 2 Pc $\frac{3}{16} \times \frac{5}{8}$ × 14 Hot Rolled Steel
Rivets: $\frac{3}{16}$ Dia. × $\frac{5}{8}$ Solid Iron Round-head (4)
Spacers: $\frac{3}{16}$ Flat Washers (4)

Fireplace Poker, Shovel, and Stand
Poker Handle: $\frac{3}{8}$ Dia. × 30¼ Hot Rolled Steel
Poker End: $\frac{3}{8}$ Dia. × 3 Hot Rolled Steel
Shovel Handle: $\frac{3}{8}$ Dia. × 28 Hot Rolled Steel
Stand Handle: $\frac{3}{8}$ Dia. × 32¾ Hot Rolled Steel
Stand Arm: $\frac{3}{8}$ Dia. × 14 Hot Rolled Steel
Stand Base: $\frac{3}{4} \times 5 \times 7$ Cast Aluminum
Shovel: $6 \times 7 \times 16$-gage Cold Steel Sheet
Jam Nut: $\frac{3}{8}$-16 NC

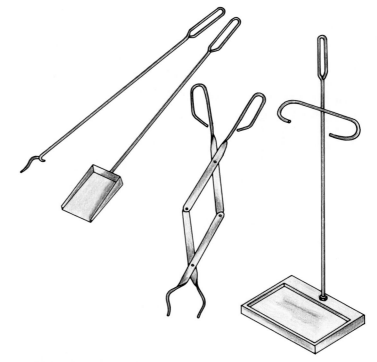

Construction Notes:

Fireplace or Stove Tongs
1. Enlarge details full-size to use for bending pattern.
2. Form handles around 1⅜" Dia. rod.
3. Make 90-degree twists where specified.
4. Form tong ends.
5. Drill holes as specified.
6. Assemble with washers and set rivets snugly enough to remove looseness but still allow fairly easy arm movement. $\frac{3}{16}$" bolts and nuts may be substituted for rivets.

Fireplace Poker, Shovel, and Stand
1. Enlarge details full-size to use for bending patterns.
2. Cut pieces as specified.
3. Cold-bend handles around $\frac{3}{4}$" Dia. rod or form. Handles may be separate machined pieces; for example, brass.
4. Bend end of poker shank to fit pattern.
5. Hot-forge curled poker end to fit pattern. Braze or weld to bend in poker shank.
6. Hot-forge end of shovel shank. Bend and flatten.
7. Bend corners of shovel and braze or weld.
8. Braze, weld, or rivet shank to shovel.
9. Bend stand arm around 3" Dia. form.
10. Make casting pattern and cast base as specified. Base may be made of heavy sheet steel if desired.
11. Thread base and stand handle as specified and assemble.

Dimension Table

inch	mm	inch	mm
32¾	832	1⅜	35
30¼	768	1⅛	28
28	711	1	25
14	356	¾	19
7	178	$\frac{11}{16}$	17
6¼	159	⅝	16
6	152	½	13
5	127	⅜	9
4	102	$\frac{5}{16}$	8
3¾	95	¼	6
3½	89	$\frac{13}{64}$	5
3	76	$\frac{3}{16}$	5
2⅝	67	⅛	3
1½	38	$\frac{1}{16}$	2

Fireplace Tools *(continued)*

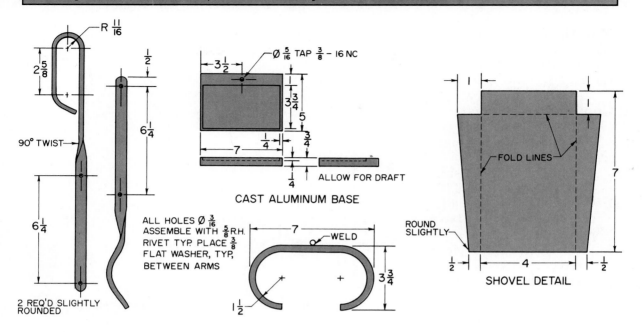

R $\frac{11}{16}$

$2\frac{5}{8}$

90° TWIST

$6\frac{1}{4}$

$6\frac{1}{4}$

2 REQ'D SLIGHTLY ROUNDED

STOVE TONGS

$\frac{1}{2}$

Ø $\frac{5}{16}$ TAP $\frac{3}{8}$ – 16 NC

$3\frac{1}{2}$

$3\frac{3}{4}$

5

$\frac{3}{4}$

$\frac{1}{4}$

7

$\frac{1}{4}$

ALLOW FOR DRAFT

CAST ALUMINUM BASE

ALL HOLES Ø $\frac{3}{16}$
ASSEMBLE WITH $\frac{5}{8}$ R.H.
RIVET TYP. PLACE $\frac{3}{8}$
FLAT WASHER, TYP,
BETWEEN ARMS

7

WELD

$3\frac{3}{4}$

$1\frac{1}{2}$

STAND ARM DETAIL

1

1

FOLD LINES

7

ROUND SLIGHTLY

$\frac{1}{2}$

4

$\frac{1}{2}$

SHOVEL DETAIL

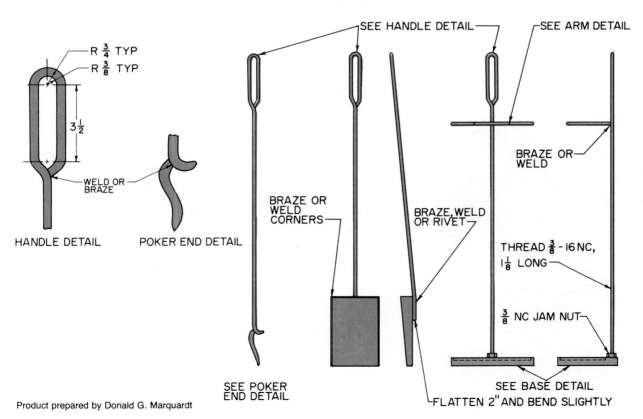

R $\frac{3}{4}$ TYP

R $\frac{3}{8}$ TYP

$3\frac{1}{2}$

WELD OR BRAZE

HANDLE DETAIL

POKER END DETAIL

SEE HANDLE DETAIL

SEE ARM DETAIL

BRAZE OR WELD CORNERS

BRAZE, WELD OR RIVET

BRAZE OR WELD

THREAD $\frac{3}{8}$ – 16 NC, $1\frac{1}{8}$ LONG

$\frac{3}{8}$ NC JAM NUT

SEE POKER END DETAIL

FLATTEN 2" AND BEND SLIGHTLY

SEE BASE DETAIL

Product prepared by Donald G. Marquardt

7. Flower Pot Holder

Materials: Band Iron
Part A: 2 Pc ⅛ × ½ × 17
Part B: 1 Pc ⅛ × ½ × 12⅜
Part C: 2 Pc ⅛ × ½ × 5¾

Construction Notes:

1. Draw pattern full size using 1" squares. (Change diameter of round pot holder to fit different size of flower pot if desired.)
2. Cut pieces to lengths, file rough edges, and bend to fit plan.
3. Weld, braze, or rivet pieces together as directed by instructor.

Dimension Table

inch	mm	inch	mm
17	432	3⅜	86
12⅜	314	½	13
5¾	146	¹⁄₁₆	2

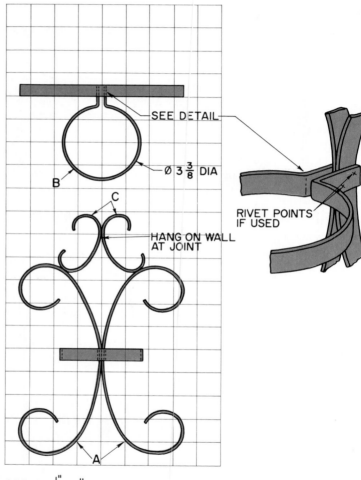

RIVET POINTS
IF USED

SEE DETAIL

B

Ø 3⅜ DIA

C

HANG ON WALL
AT JOINT

A

SCALE: ¼" = 1"

Product prepared by Donald G. Marquardt

8. Dog Stake

Materials:
Cold Rolled Steel ¾ Dia. ×
13½
Black Pipe ¾ Inside Dia. × 4
Steel Rod ¼ Dia. × 4
⅛ × 1½ cotter pin

Construction Notes:
1. Use V-block and drill press to drill hole in stake for cotter pin.
2. Make washers by cutting ¼″ slices of black pipe.
3. Ream or drill inside of black pipe part if necessary to get free fit on stake.
4. Braze lower washer to shaft from bottom side only.
5. Bend ¼″ steel rod to form eye for dog chain.
6. Weld ¼″ steel rod to 3″ pivot section of black pipe.

Dimension Table
inch	mm	inch	mm
13½	343	¾	19
9	229	¼	6
4	102	³⁄₁₆	5
3	75	⅛	3
1	25		

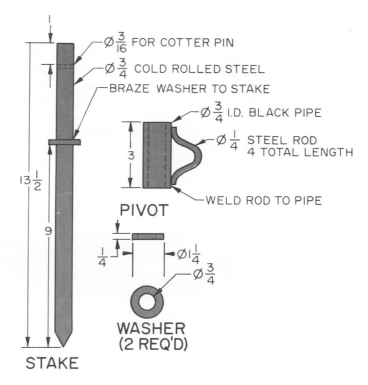

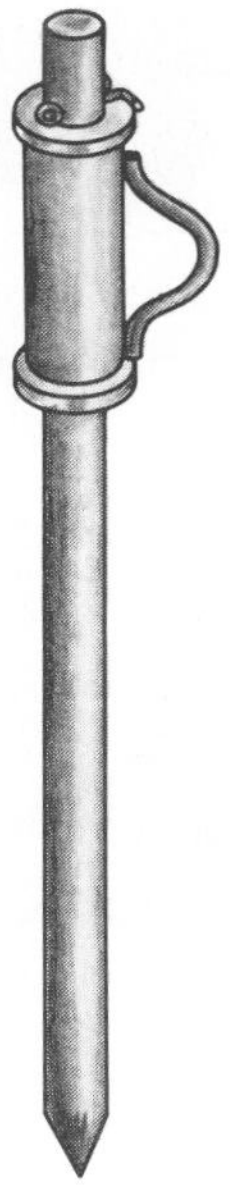

Ø³⁄₁₆ FOR COTTER PIN
Ø¾ COLD ROLLED STEEL
BRAZE WASHER TO STAKE
Ø¾ I.D. BLACK PIPE
Ø¼ STEEL ROD 4 TOTAL LENGTH
WELD ROD TO PIPE
13½
9
3
PIVOT
¼
Ø1¼
Ø¾
WASHER (2 REQ'D)
STAKE

Product prepared by Robert W. Todd

9. Screwdriver

Materials:
¼ Dia. 1045 steel rod
1 Dia. screwdriver handle stock

Construction Notes:

A. Blade
1. Cut a piece of ¼ Dia. steel rod 6″ long.
2. Knurl 2″ of one end of the rod.
3. Hot forge the opposite end of the rod to form the rough blade shape.
4. Grind, file, and abrasive polish the blade to the finished size and shape.
5. Harden and temper the blade.
6. Polish the blade with abrasive cloth.

B. Handle
1. Cut a piece of screwdriver handle stock 4⅛″ long.
2. Center it in a 4-jaw lathe chuck, then face off and chamfer the end.
3. Rechuck the handle, then face off to length, drill, chamfer, and turn the groove to size and shape.

C. Assembly
1. Clamp the blade horizontally in a vise equipped with soft jaws so that the knurled end is completely exposed.
2. Heat the handle in a 300°F oven until it becomes pliable.
3. Using heat resistant gloves, remove the handle from the oven and force it onto the blade.
4. If the handle has become distorted during assembly, straighten it out so that it will be properly shaped when it becomes cold and rigid.

Dimension Table

inch	mm	inch	mm
6	152	½	13
4	102	⅜	10
2	51	¼	6
1¼	32	⅛	3
1	25	1/32	0.8
¾	19		

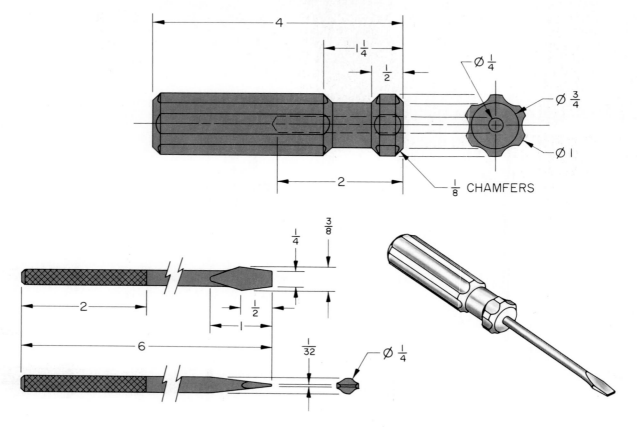

10. Cold Chisel

Materials:
½ Dia. × 6 Octagonal or Hexagonal Tool Steel. Alternate—Recycled Auto Sway Bar.

Construction Notes:
1. Heat bottom third of chisel blank to 1550-1975°F [843-1079°C] (bright red to light yellow).
2. Forge taper 1½″ long and ³⁄₁₆″ thick at end.
3. Finish as desired. If chisel is to be draw-filed, allow it to cool slowly after last forging. One taper surface should be filed to view colors during tempering.
4. Harden cutting edge by heating tapered portion to 50°-100° above the critical temperature for the metal used, then quenching.
5. Grind cutting edge to 60° included angle; also round ends very slightly.
6. Grind chamfer on head. Round striking surface slightly.
7. Reclean one tapered surface.
8. Heat tapered end until cutting edge reaches about 545°F [285°C] (violet color) and quench.
9. Make test cuts with chisel on low-carbon steel.

Dimension Table

inch	mm
6	152
1½	38
⁵⁄₈	16
½	13
³⁄₁₆	5

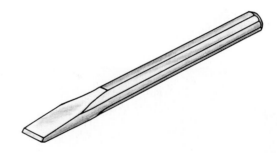

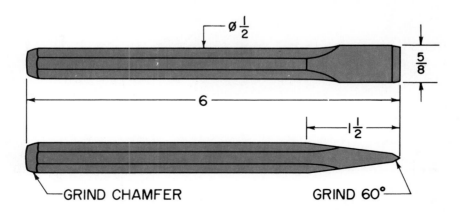

GRIND CHAMFER   GRIND 60°

Product prepared by Donald G. Marquardt

11. Scratch Pad Holder

Material:

0.032 3003-H14 aluminum, or
half-hard brass or copper sheet

Construction Notes:

1. Lay out and cut to size and
   shape.
2. Deburr edges with a file.
3. Bend the sides.
4. Finish as desired.

Dimension Table

inch	mm	inch	mm
7¼	184	4 ·	102
6¼	159	1¼	32
6	152	1	25
5¼	133	¾	19
4¼	108		

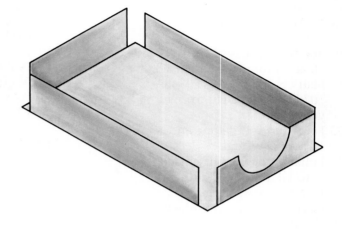

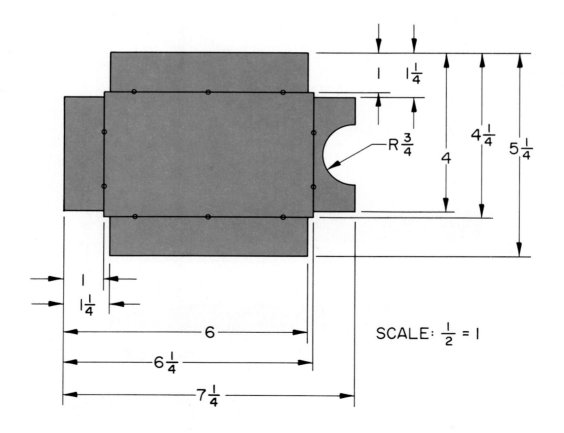

SCALE: $\frac{1}{2}$ = 1

12. Kitchen Canister Scoop

Materials:
Tin Plate or Brass, 28 or 30 gage

Construction Notes:
1. Lay out pattern. Use aviation snips without blade serrations to cut curved lines for the body and back. Lightly file off sharp edges.
2. Cut, roll, and seam the body.
3. Cut, hem, and shape the handle.
4. Using solder sparingly, attach the back and handle to the body.

Finish: Lacquer or leave unfinished.

Dimension Table

inch	mm	inch	mm
$6^{27}/_{32}$	174	¾	19
3	76	½	13
2¾	70	⅜	10
2½	64	¼	6
2	51	³/₁₆	5
1	25	⅛	3

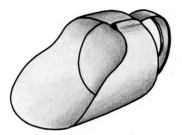

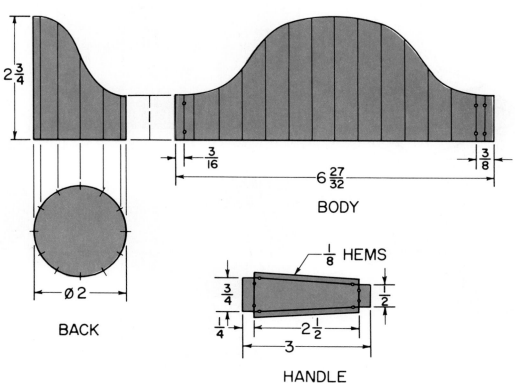

BODY

BACK

HANDLE

SCALE: $\frac{3}{8}$ = 1"

13. Dustpan

Material:
26 Gage Galvanized Steel

Construction Notes:
1. Lay out, cut, and fold the dust pan body first.
2. Spot weld the top and back of the body to the sides. If spot-welder is unavailable, consult instructor about attaching with blind rivets or solder.
3. Lay out, cut, and fold the handle.
4. Attach the handle with spot welds or pull-stem rivets.
5. File off sharp edges.

Finish: Unfinished or painted as desired. May be decorated with decals to suit.

Dimension Table

inch	mm	inch	mm
15	381	3¼	83
14	357	2	51
11	279	1½	38
7½	191	1	25
6¼	159	½	13
5	127	⅜	10
4	102	¼	6

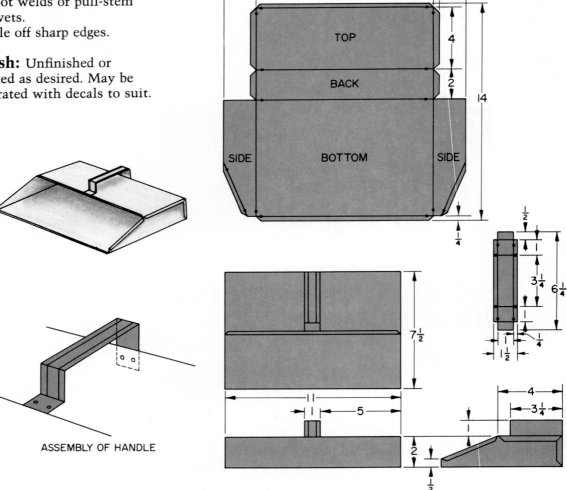

ASSEMBLY OF HANDLE

14. Mailbox

Materials:
26 Gage Steel
12″ piano hinge
Small sheet of copper or brass

Construction Notes:
1. Lay out and cut the back, bottom, and front. Fold as shown.
2. Lay out and cut the side pieces.
3. Attach the side pieces by spot welding.
4. Lay out, cut, and fold the cover. Lightly file off sharp edges.
5. Spot weld the hinge to the body.
6. Spot weld the hinge to the cover.
7. Cut and attach a decorative brass or copper panel to the front by soldering.

Finish: Polish the decorative panel, then cover it with masking tape while painting the body with black enamel.

Dimension Table:

inch	mm	inch	mm
18⁵⁄₁₆	465	6½	165
16	406	6	152
15½	395	5¼	133
15	382	5	127
14½	368	4½	114
14	356	3½	84
8	203	½	13
6⁹⁄₁₆	167	¼	6

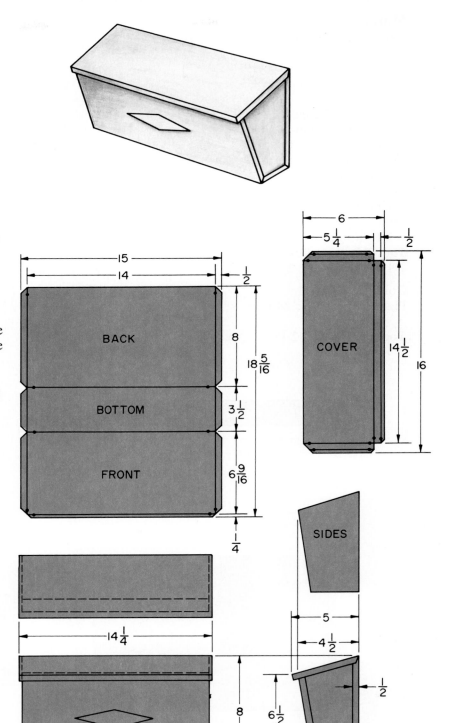

15. Toolbox and Tray

Materials:

Galvanized or Cold Rolled
Steel Bottom and Sides:
   1 Pc 26 gage × 19 × 19
Half lids: 2 Pc 26 gage × 5⅜
   × 19
Ends: 2 Pc 22 gage × 7 × 8
Tool Tray Bracket:
   2 Pc 22 gage × 1¼ × 8
Handle Mounting Clips:
   4 Pc 22 gage × ½ × 1⅝
Tool Tray Bottom and Sides:
   1 Pc 26 gage × 12 × 18½
Tool Tray Ends:
   2 Pc 22 gage × 3¼ × 7¾
Tool Tray Handle:
   1 Pc 22 gage × 2 × 19

Cold Rolled Steel:
Piano Hinge: 2 Pc 24 gage × 1
   × 18
Toolbox Handle: 2 Pc ¼ Dia.
   × 9¼

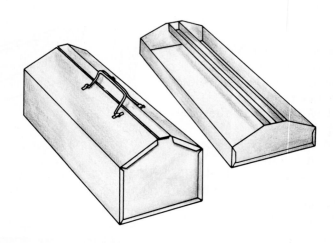

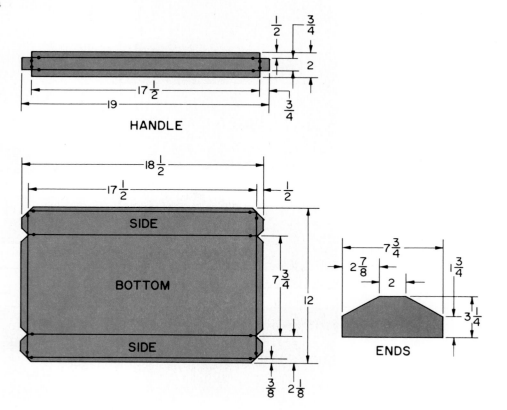

HANDLE

SIDE

BOTTOM

SIDE

ENDS

Toolbox and Tray *(continued)*

Construction Notes:

Half Lid: Hem should be towards inside of box. File off sharp edges.

Ends: Attach tool tray brackets to ends before assembling with sides and bottom. File off sharp edges.

Handle Mounting Clips: Make 90-degree bends ½" from each end, then wrap around ¼" rod to form loop for handle.

Handles: Make bends ½" from each end first. Then make bends 2¼" from ½" bends to form U shape. Finish by bending 40 degrees, ¾" from top of handle.

Tool Tray: Hems should be towards inside of tray. File off sharp edges on sides and handle.

Assembly: Spot-weld throughout.

Finish: Plain or painted.

Dimension Table

inch	mm	inch	mm
19	483	3⅜	86
18½	470	3	76
18	457	2⅞	73
17½	445	2¼	57
12	305	2⅛	54
9¼	235	2	51
8	203	1¾	44
7¾	197	1⅝	41
7	178	1⅜	35
5½	140	1¼	32
5⅜	137	1	25
5¼	133	¾	19
3¾	95	½	13
3½	90	⅜	10
3¼	83	¼	6

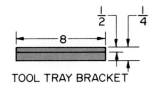

TOOL TRAY BRACKET

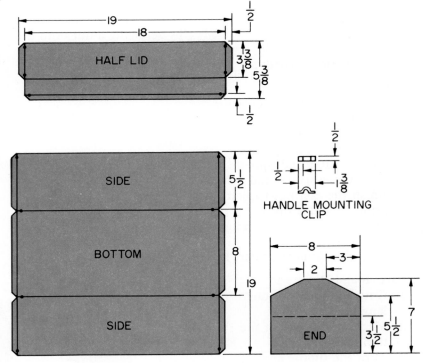

HALF LID

SIDE

BOTTOM

SIDE

HANDLE MOUNTING CLIP

END

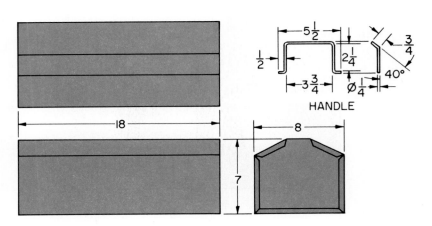

HANDLE

16. Lamp

Materials:

Parts A, C, and E: Aluminum castings

Part B: 1½ OD, 1⅜ ID aluminum tubing 6⅛ long

Part D: 2½ OD, 2⅜ ID aluminum tubing 2⅜ long

Part F: ⅛ Dia. × 11 threaded pipe, lock washers, and two nuts

Construction Notes:

Parts A, C, and E:

1. Turn hardwood patterns for each part.
2. Ram molds and make castings for each part.
3. Cut off gates and runners from the castings, and finish the castings by belt grinding and filing.
4. Drill the ²⁷⁄₆₄″ hole through each casting.
5. Drill the ¼″ hole in Part E.

Parts B and D:

1. Cut the tubing to rough length.
2. Machine one end of the tubing.
3. Turn the tubing around and machine it to length.
4. Polish the tubing with steel wool or fine abrasive cloth.

Assembly:

1. Place a lockwasher and nut on one end of the threaded ⅛″ pipe.
2. Slide the parts on the threaded pipe, beginning with Part E.
3. Adjust the threaded pipe so that ⅜″ projects from the top of Part A.
4. Fasten the parts together by screwing a nut onto the top of Part A.

Finishing:

1. Wash the lamp with solvent to degrease it; then wipe it dry with a clean cloth.
2. Apply two coats of a zinc chromate primer; sand lightly between coats.
3. Apply two coats of enamel; sand lightly between coats.

Final Assembly:

1. Screw the lamp socket base onto the top of the threaded pipe.
2. Attach the lamp cord to the lamp socket terminals. IMPORTANT: HAVE THIS STEP CHECKED BY YOUR INSTRUCTOR.
3. Thread the lamp cord through the pipe and out the hole in Part E; attach the socket to the socket base.
4. Attach a plug to the lamp cord. IMPORTANT: HAVE THIS STEP CHECKED BY YOUR INSTRUCTOR.
5. Screw a light bulb into the lamp socket.
6. Attach the lamp shade.

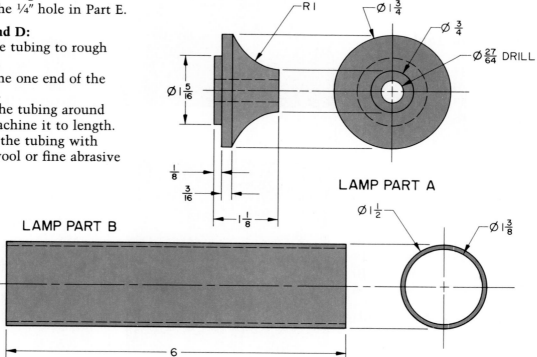

LAMP PART A

LAMP PART B

Lamp (*continued*)

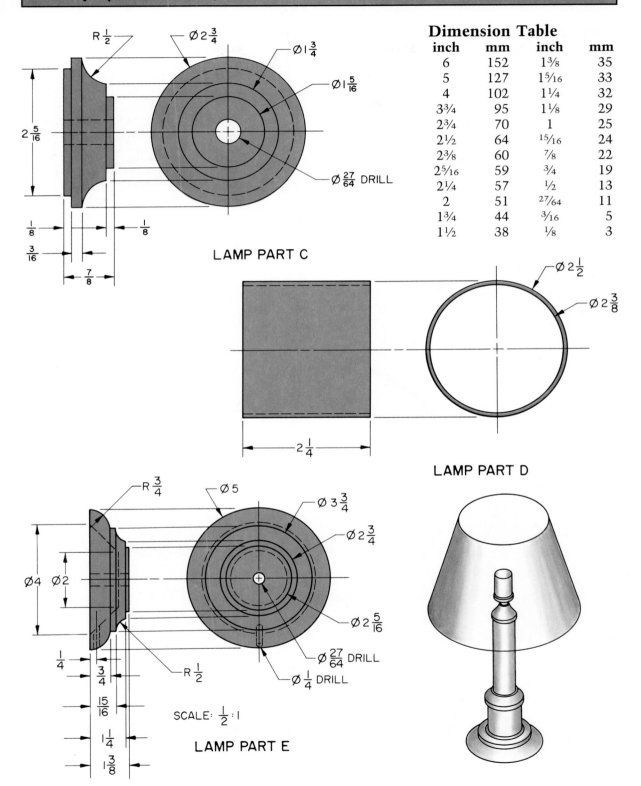

Dimension Table

inch	mm	inch	mm
6	152	1³⁄₈	35
5	127	1⁵⁄₁₆	33
4	102	1¹⁄₄	32
3³⁄₄	95	1¹⁄₈	29
2³⁄₄	70	1	25
2¹⁄₂	64	¹⁵⁄₁₆	24
2³⁄₈	60	⁷⁄₈	22
2⁵⁄₁₆	59	³⁄₄	19
2¹⁄₄	57	¹⁄₂	13
2	51	²⁷⁄₆₄	11
1³⁄₄	44	³⁄₁₆	5
1¹⁄₂	38	¹⁄₈	3

LAMP PART C

LAMP PART D

LAMP PART E

SCALE: ¹⁄₂ : 1

17. Coaster

Material:
0.040 thick 1100-0 aluminum sheet
Blank diameter is approximately 3½

Dimension Table

inch	mm
3	76
¼	6
³⁄₃₂	2

Construction Notes:
1. Carefully center the blank on the spinning chuck and tighten it in place.
2. Using a slow rpm, carefully form the bottom of the coaster enough to trap it on the chuck.
3. Trim the blank round and to size, then trim the sharp edges.
4. Spin the blank down to the chuck.
5. Finish as desired.

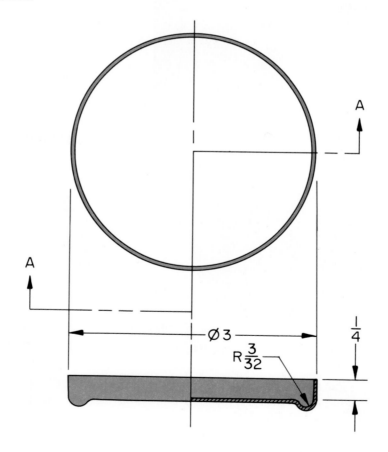

18. Meat Tenderizer

Materials: Aluminum
Handle: 1 Pc $\frac{7}{8}$ Dia $\times$ 10$\frac{1}{2}$
Head: 1 Pc 1$\frac{3}{4}$ $\times$ 1$\frac{3}{4}$ $\times$ 2$\frac{5}{8}$

Construction Notes:
Handle
1. Center-drill both ends if the taper must be turned between centers, one end if a taper attachment is used.
2. Knurl the handle.
3. Turn the diameters on the mallet end, including the $\frac{3}{4}$" shoulder diameter. Chamfer the end and turn the threads. Leave the center hole in the threaded end.
4. Use a $\frac{1}{16}$" radius tool to cut a groove on the taper side of the shoulder to a $\frac{9}{16}$" diameter.
5. Turn the taper.
6. Mark the handle length. Protect the knurl from damage by wrapping the chuck jaws with pieces of 1100-0 aluminum sheet.
7. Machine off the excess. Chamfer the end $\frac{1}{8}$" $\times$ 45°.

Head
1. Use the lathe to face off the block to length.
2. Use a 60-degree double-angle cutter to mill the grooves. Mill parallel grooves on one side. On the other side, mill two sets of grooves at right angles. File off sharp edges.
3. Drill and tap the hole.
4. Draw-file or abrasive-belt grind the flat sides of the head.

Dimension Table

inch	mm	inch	mm
10$\frac{1}{2}$	267	$\frac{3}{4}$	19
9	229	$\frac{9}{16}$	14
4$\frac{1}{4}$	108	$\frac{1}{2}$	13
3$\frac{3}{4}$	95	$\frac{29}{64}$	12
2$\frac{5}{8}$	67	$\frac{7}{16}$	11
2$\frac{1}{2}$	64	.175	5
1$\frac{3}{4}$	44	.150	4
1$\frac{3}{8}$	35	$\frac{1}{8}$	3
1$\frac{1}{4}$	32	$\frac{1}{16}$	2
$\frac{7}{8}$	22		

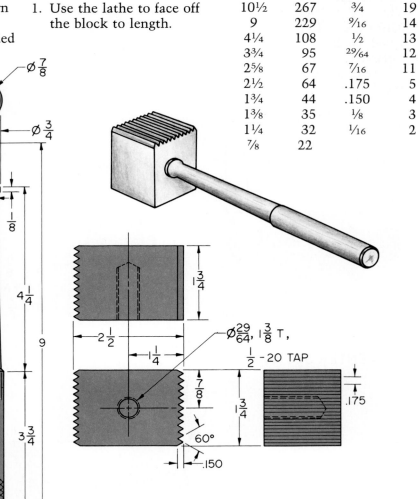

19. Soft Hammer

Materials:
1 Dia. cold rolled steel, brass, and cellulose butyrate rod
8 oz. wood ballpeen hammer handle

Construction Notes:

Center section
1. Face off and turn the ½" diameter on one end.
2. Thread the ½ diameter.
3. Turn the part around, face it to length, and turn the ½" diameter.
4. Thread the ½" diameter.
5. Mill the slot to receive the wood handle.
6. Enlarge each side of the slot with a file as shown in the drawing.

End Caps
1. Face off and chamfer one end.
2. Turn the part around, then face it off to length.
3. Drill and tap the hole.

Assembly
1. Screw the end caps on the center section.
2. Fit the handle to the slot in the head.
3. Drive in the wedges to secure it to the handle.

Dimension Table

inch	mm	inch	mm
2½	64	$^{29}/_{64}$	12
1½	38	$^{7}/_{16}$	11
1	25	$^{13}/_{32}$	10
¾	19	$^{3}/_{8}$	10
⅝	16	$^{5}/_{16}$	8
½	13	$^{1}/_{16}$	2

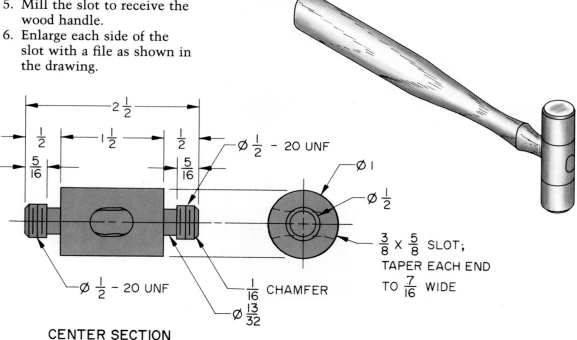

CENTER SECTION

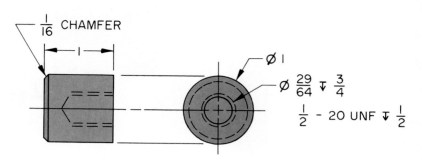

END CAPS

20. Pegs for Tic-Tac-Toe Game

Materials:
⅜ Dia. 2011-T3 aluminum and type 360 brass rod

Construction Notes:
1. Write the N/C program for turning the peg.
2. Prepare right hand and straight turning tools, and a cutoff tool.
   A. If the lathe has a turret, install the tools in the turret.
   B. Determine the straight and cutoff tool offsets in relation to the right hand turning tool.
3. Enter the N/C program in the lathe control unit.
4. Check the program accuracy by making a dry run or using the N/C program tool path graphics.
5. Make any program corrections needed.
6. Install a ⅜″ diameter rod in the lathe, leaving 1⅛″ projecting from the chuck or collet.
7. Using the manual lathe controls, face off the end of the rod with the right hand turning tool.
8. Locate the right hand turning tool at the setup location.
9. Make a test part and check its dimensions.
10. Make any program corrections needed before machining additional parts.

Dimension Table

inch	mm
.850	21.59
.683	17.35
.516	13.11
.370	9.40
.350	8.89
.270	6.86
.190	4.83
.030	0.76

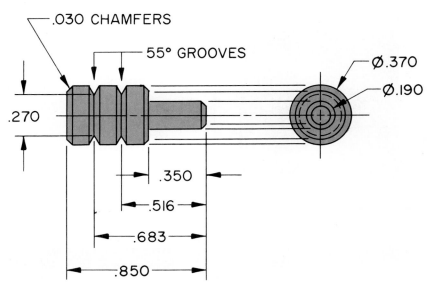

21. Tic-Tac-Toe Game Board

Material:
⅜ black acrylic sheet

Construction Notes:
1. Layout 3⅛″ squares on the acrylic sheet.
2. Cut out the squares on the band saw, or jig saw.
3. Machine the squares to size using the side of a very sharp end milling cutter.
4. Remove the sharp edges with a file.
5. Install the #7 drill and ³⁄₁₆″ end mill in their toolholders and determine their offsets.
6. Write the N/C program for drilling and milling the part.
7. Check the accuracy of the program by making a dry run or using the N/C tool path graphics.
8. Make any program corrections needed.
9. Make a test part and check its dimensions.
10. Make any program corrections needed to produce an accurate part before machining additional parts.

Dimension Table

inch	mm
3	76
1	25
½	13
⅜	10
#7	5.11
³⁄₁₆	4.76

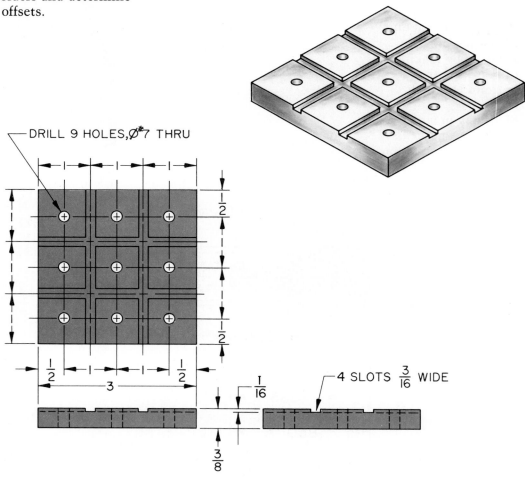

DRILL 9 HOLES, ⌀#7 THRU

4 SLOTS ³⁄₁₆ WIDE

22. Parcheesi Game Piece

Materials:
⅝ Dia. rods of 2011-T3 aluminum, type 360 brass, and plastic

Construction Notes:
1. Write the N/C program for turning the part.
2. Prepare a right hand turning tool and a cutoff tool.
   A. If the lathe has a turret, install the tools in the turret.
   B. Determine the cutoff tool offsets in relation to the right hand turning tool.
3. Enter the N/C program in the lathe control unit.
4. Check the program accuracy by making a dry run or using the N/C program tool path graphics.
5. Make any program corrections needed.
6. Install the ⅝" diameter rod in lathe, leaving 1¼" projecting from the chuck or collet.
7. Using the manual controls, face off the end of the rod with the right hand turning tool.
8. Locate the right hand turning tool at the setup location.
9. Make a test part and check its dimensions.
10. Make any program corrections needed to produce an accurate part before machining additional parts.

Dimension Table

inch	mm
.875	22.23
.770	19.56
.610	15.49
.250	6.35
.200	5.08
.150	3.81
¹⁄₆₄	.40

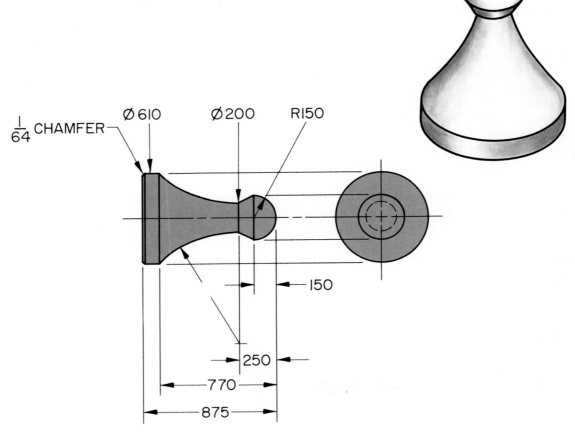

GLOSSARY

abrasive—very hard, tough material crushed and ground into grains; used to cut away metal in grinding, polishing, and buffing

absolute dimensioning system—a numerical control system in which all tool movements are measured and programmed from the machine reference point

allowance—the amount of acceptable clearance between mating parts; allowance may be **positive (sliding fit)** or **negative (force fit)**

alloy—a metal formed by melting and mixing two or more pure metals

alloy steels—alloys made of steel and one or more elements intentionally added to obtain properties not found in plain carbon steels

angle plate—a piece of metal with two surfaces at 90° to each other; used with clamps to hold a workpiece for layout or machining

annealing—a heat-treatment process that removes hardness from metals by relieving internal stress

anode—the positively charged electrode

arbor—a machine shaft that supports a cutting tool

attribute gage—also **nonindicating mechanical gage;** a gage that shows only whether a part dimension is within preset limits

automation—the working of machines, equipment, or processes without direct control by an operator

axis—an imaginary line through the center of an object around which the object can rotate

backlash—wear in screw or gear mechanisms that may result in slippage, reaction (end play), and objectionable vibration

back-rake—the angle of the cutting tool face with a horizontal line extending from the end of the cutting edge toward the shank; measured vertically

base metal—1) in welding, the metal of pieces to be joined; 2) in alloys, the basic metal to which other elements are added

basic oxygen process (BOP)—a steelmaking process in which pure oxygen under high pressure is used to speed the chemical reactions for producing steel from pig iron and scrap

bevel—a flat surface cut at an angle to the main work surface, extending from side to side

blade pitch—the distance from a point on one saw tooth to the same point on a neighboring tooth

blank—1) in sheet metalworking, a flat piece of metal of the size and shape needed to make a particular object; 2) any piece of metal that is ready to be cut or stamped into a finished form (for example, a gear blank)

brazing—a method of joining metals, similar to hard soldering; uses nonferrous filler rods at temperatures above 800°F [427°C]

break even chart—a chart, usually a graph, that shows how many products must be manufactured before the company makes any profit

break even point—the number of products that must be sold before a profit can be made

brittleness—a measure of how easily a metal will break when bent

buffing—polishing a metal surface to a smooth, bright finish by rubbing it with a wheel to which a fine abrasive compound has been applied

burnishing—a metal-finishing process in which metal is made smooth and bright by rubbing with hardened steel tools

cam—a machine part mounted on a rotating shaft that is used to change rotary (turning) motion to straight-line, often back-and-forth, motion *carburizing*—in case-hardening, applying a carbonaceous substance to the surface of steel and soaking the steel to produce a surface layer of iron carbide

Cartesian coordinate system—a system of locating points in 3-dimensions; includes the X, Y, and Z *axes* and four *quadrants* within which points are plotted

case-hardening—heat-treatment in which the surface of the metal hardens while the core remains soft

casting—1)the making of metal objects by pouring liquid metal into molds and letting it harden; 2) an object made by this method

cast iron—re-melted and re-cast pig iron; has a carbon content of 1.7% to 6%

cathode—a negatively charged electrode

center drill—also *combination drill and countersink;* a tool used to make hole centers for guiding drills and to make bearing surfaces for lathe centers

centerless grinding—a form of cylindrical grinding done without using center holes or a chuck to support the workpiece

chamfer—to cut part of an edge of a workpiece at an angle smaller than 90°

charge—1) (noun) metal that is to be melted in a furnace; 2) (verb) to place metal into a furnace to be melted

chemical milling (CHM)—shaping metal by using strong acid or alkaline solutions to dissolve unwanted metal

cladding—a metal-plating process in which a thin layer of corrosion-resistant metal is bonded to another metal

closed dies—forging dies made to the size and shape of the object desired

closed-loop system—an automated system in which the feedback loop is completely closed

collet—1) the body of a threading die; holds the cutters and a guide; 2) a small, self-centering lathe chuck

compound rest—a sliding fixture attached to the cross-slide on the lathe carriage; holds the toolpost

compressive strength—resistance to the force tending to crush material by squeezing

computer-aided design (CAD)—the use of a computer to assist in the creation or modification of the design of a product. Most CAD software will operate a printer or a plotter so that a hard copy (paper drawing) of the product can be made. CADD is the acronym or abbreviation used for "computer-aided design and drafting."

computer-aided engineering (CAE)—the use of a computer to solve engineering problems by graphical or mathematical methods

computer-aided manufacturing (CAM)—the use of computers for one or more manufacturing tasks, particularly with computer numerically controlled (CNC) machine tools and transfer machines. CAM applications may include design and drafting, engineering, automated warehousing, process control, inventory control, and purchasing.

computer-integrated manufacturing (CIM)—a broad system that uses computers for controlling every manufacturing task, CIM usually involves several computers that gather and report data to a main computer to be automatically summarized and analyzed. The goal of CIM is a completely self-regulated, unmanned factory.

computer numerical control (CNC)—a numerical control system with a microcomputer for each machine.

continuous manufacturing—a system for making very large quantities of a product, usually with assembly line techniques such as in the manufacture of automobiles and appliances

contouring N/C system—a numerical control system capable of directing the tool or workpiece to move at any angle and along curved paths

cope—in sand casting, the top half of a flask

corrosion resistance—the ability of a metal to withstand harmful effects of gradual chemical action

corundum—a natural abrasive, aluminum oxide

crocus—a fine, soft, red abrasive of iron oxide

cross feed—1) in lathe work, movement of the cutting tool across the end of the workpiece; 2) in milling or surface grinding, movement of the table toward or away from the column

cross-slide—a fixture attached to the lathe carriage that holds the compound rest and can be moved in and out

curing—hardening or setting

cutting speed—the distance a point on the tool or workpiece moves in one minute, expressed in feet or meters per minute

decimal equivalent—the equivalent, in the decimal system, of a common fraction; for example, ½" = .500"

density—a measure of the weight of a material for a given amount of it (for example, a cubic foot of water weighs 62.5 lbs.; a cubic foot of gold weighs 1205.6 lbs.

depth of cut—the distance a cutting tool is advanced into the workpiece at a right angle to the piece

dial indicator—an instrument used in setup and inspection work that shows on a dial the amount of error in size or alignment of a part

die—1) a tool used for cutting external threads; 2) a tool used to stamp forms from metal in forging or sheet metalwork; 3) a device through which steel is drawn; 4) a mold used in die-casting

die casting—a casting process in which molten metal is forced under pressure into a mold

dimension—a measurement

dimension limits—the acceptable upper and lower limits set by designers for a given dimension

direct numerical control (DNC)—a numerical control system using one large computer to control many machines at once

dispatching—the function of starting and controlling a manufacturing operation; usually done with a job ticket issued by the production control group or departmental dispatcher

dividing head—a milling machine accessory used to divide a circular metal object into a number of equal parts

down milling—also *climb milling;* feeding the workpiece in the same direction as cutter rotation

draft—the angle of taper of the sides of a sand casting pattern; may be *positive* (easily removed without damaging the mold), *negative* (requiring special construction to remove without damaging the mold), or *zero* (no taper)

drag—in sand casting, the bottom half of a flask

drawing—1) in sheet metalwork, forming an object by stamping flat metal with a die; 2) pulling cold steel through a die to produce a smaller diameter *(cold drawing)*

dress—to sharpen a grinding wheel

drill jig—a device that holds the workpiece and guides the drill in drilling operations

dry-sand mold—a sand casting mold made of a mixture of sand and oil; it is baked hard before using

ductility—a measure of a metal's ability to be bent, rolled, or otherwise changed in shape without breaking; refers especially to stretching or drawing

eccentric—having a different center

economical manufacturing lot size—the lowest quantity of a part that can be manufactured, stored in inventory, and sold at a profit

elastic limit—the maximum load per square inch or square centimeter that can be applied to a metal without changing its shape permanently

electric arc furnace—a steelmaking furnace that uses an electric arc between carbon electrodes and the metal to produce extremely high temperatures

electric induction furnace—a furnace for melting metal; heat is produced by a rapidly expanding and collapsing magnetic field

electrode—1) in an electric circuit, any structure that acts as the negative or positive pole; 2) in welding, a metal rod that electricity flows through

electrolyte—a fluid that conducts electricity

electronic probe—an electronic device used for identifying, locating, and selecting workpieces, machine programs, and tools used with numerically controlled machines in flexible manufacturing systems. The probe may also inspect parts in production to correct the NC program automatically for tool wear.

electroplating—a metal-finishing process in which a thin layer of metal is deposited by electrochemical means

emery—a natural abrasive composed of corundum and iron oxide

emulsifiable oil—also *soluble* or *water-soluble* oil; a cutting fluid made by adding oil and other ingredients to water

end cutting-edge angle—on a lathe tool bit, the angle formed by the end cutting-edge and a line drawn 90° to the side of the shank

end milling cutter—also *end mill;* a milling cutter designed to mill slots, shoulders, curved edges, keyways, and pockets where arbor-type cutters cannot be used

end-relief—also *front clearance;* the angle ground on the front of a lathe tool bit that allows it to cut into the workpiece

etching—1) applying dilute acid solution to metal to provide a dull, slightly roughened surface; 2) marking or decorating metal by using acid to eat into the metal

extrusion—forming a specific shape of metal product by pushing heating metal through a die opening

facing—in lathework, cutting across the end of a workpiece, usually to machine a flat surface

feed—1) the movement of a cutting tool into the workpiece; 2) the movement of a workpiece into the cutting tool

feedback—in automated systems, a signal of output that is received by a sensor, which then compares it with a specified input

feedback control loop—the cyclical flow of information through an automated system

feed rate—a measure of feed given in distance per unit of time, such as inches or mm per minute

ferrous metal—a metal that contains iron

fillet—1) a radius, or curve, at the angular intersection of two surfaces; 2) in sand casting, a piece of wax, leather, wood, or plastic glued to inside pattern corners

fixture—a workpiece-holding device used for quick supporting and clamping of pieces for machining

flash—in casting or forging, the excess metal edge that forms at the parting line between the halves of a die or mold

flexible manufacturing system—usually a group of numerically-controlled or computer numerically-controlled machine tools that can be programmed to produce a variety of products

flow process sheet—a sheet showing the routing information for manufacturing a product. It shows the order of work stations or machines that are used in each step in manufacturing the product.

flutes—grooves cut into the bodies of milling cutters, drills, and reamers

flux—a chemical substance used in soldering, welding, and casting to clean metal of oxides and other impurities

force fit (FN)—a fit between mating parts that involves interference, or *negative clearance*

free carbon—carbon that is not chemically combined with other elements but is scattered throughout a metal's grain structure

fusibility—a measure of a metal's ability, when in its liquid state, to join easily with another liquid metal; related to *weldability*

galvanizing—protecting iron and steel from rust by coating with zinc

gate—in sand casting, the part of the gating system through which metal flows into the mold cavity

glazed—worn smooth and dull, as with grinding wheels

grade—in reference to grinding wheels, a measure of the looseness or tightness with which abrasive grains are held together

grain—the arrangement of particles in metal; similar to the grain of wood

gram (g)—a standard measure of weight in the S.I. metric system; equal to 0.035 ounce

graphite—a soft, iron-gray, smooth form of carbon; used as a lubricant

hand of cut—the direction of a milling cut; either *right-hand* (counterclockwise cutter rotation) or *left-hand* (clockwise cutter rotation)

hand of cutter—the direction that a milling cutter must rotate to cut; either *right-hand* (counterclockwise) or *left-hand* (clockwise)

hand of helix—the direction of the helical flutes on milling cutters, drills, and reamers; either *right-hand* (twist to right) or *left-hand* (twist to left)

hard automation—an automated production line or a group of automated machines that can manufacture only one product

hardenability—the measure of a metal's ability to harden uniformly and completely to its center

hardening—a heat-treatment process in which steels are hardened by heating slowly to a certain hardening temperature, then cooling rapidly in a solution

hardness—the resistance of a metal to penetration

hard soldering—soldering or brazing using silver-alloy solders at temperatures above 800°F

headstock—a major lathe component housing the motor-driven spindle that holds and turns the workpiece

heat treatment—heating and cooling metals in their solid state in order to change their properties

high-carbon steel—also **carbon tool steel;** steel with a carbon content of .60% to 1.50%

high-speed steel (HSS)—also **high-speed tool steel;** a group of alloy steels used extensively for cutting tools; carbon content of 0.70% to 1.50%

I.D.—abbreviation for inside diameter

incremental dimensioning system—an N/C dimensioning system in which the distance between points is based on the position of the tool at the start of each move, not in relation to a fixed reference point

indexing—1) in dividing head operations, moving a workpiece so that equally spaced divisions can be machined; 2) on turret-type machines, revolving the turret to use a different tool

information block—the data contained in one line of an N/C program manuscript

input—in automated systems, the commands or other data that specify the output

intermittent manufacturing—a system for making economic-lot quantities of a product for which the demand is lower than the rate of production; includes job-lot manufacturing of expensive machines and equipment, repair parts, and special tooling made to the customer's order

investment mold—also **lost-wax mold;** a casting mold made by melting a wax pattern out of a hardened plaster or ceramic covering

jig—a device that holds metal to be cut or bent and guides the tool used

Jo blocks—precision blocks of hardened steel, tungsten carbide, or ceramic used as practical standards for setting gages

job lot—the manufacturing quantity of a part, usually a small number, made especially to fill a customer's order

job ticket—a form used in the production control system to authorize the start of the manufacturing of a product; contains blanks for entering the written record of the number of products or parts processed, the actual production time required, and other information necessary for determining production costs

kerf—the cut made by a saw

key—a small piece of metal that is inserted into both a **keyway** in a shaft and a slot in a gear or pulley to keep the gear or pulley from turning on the shaft

kilogram (kg)—a standard measure of weight in the S.I. metric system; equal to 2.2 pounds

knurling—raising a pattern of points or ridges on a surface so it can be gripped better

laser—a device that generates an extremely concentrated beam of light that is capable of vaporizing any known material; used in **laser beam machining, laser beam welding,** etc.

lathe center—a lathe accessory with a 60° cone point; inserted into a lathe headstock or tailstock to support a workpiece

layout—the transfer of information from a working drawing to metal surfaces by marking lines, circles, and arcs

lead of thread—the distance a screw thread moves along its axis in one revolution

lead screw—on a lathe, the long screw that is driven by the end gears; supplies power to the carriage

limits gage—also **go and not-go gage;** a gage that tests the upper size limit and the lower size limit

line and staff organization—a more complex form of organizing people in larger companies or organizations. A staff of specialists, who assist and report directly to the president, are responsible for specific operations. In some companies they may have few if any line responsibilities.

linear measurement—straight-line measurement

line organization—the simplest form of organizing people for doing a job, commonly used in small companies, single departments, and small units of the armed forces. The positions on an organization chart usually fall in a vertical line extending from the president or leader who must make most of the important company or organization decisions.

lip angle—the angle at which the lips of a drill are ground

lip clearance—in drills, the angle ground behind the cutting edges, measured from the workpiece surface; allows lips to cut into metal

live center—1) headstock center that turns with the spindle 2) tailstock center that turns on ball bearings

loading—calculating the time required to process a job lot so it can be charged against available production time

low-carbon steel—steel with 0.5-.30% carbon content

longitudinal feed—1) lathework: movement of the cutting tool along the workpiece, parallel to the lathe bed; 2) milling and grinding machines: movement of the table horizontally to the right or left

M—the abbreviation for Mega in the S.I. metric system; meaning one million

machinability—a measure of a metal's ability to be cut, or **machined**

machine reference point—in N/C operations using absolute dimensioning, the point from which all tool movements are measured and programmed; built into the N/C machine by the manufacturer

magneto—an electrical generator with permanent magnets that is used to generate current for the engine in an internal-combustion machine

major diameter—the largest diameter of a straight external or internal thread

malleability—a measure of a metal's ability to be hammered or rolled into shape without breaking

mandrel—1) a solid steel bar with a slight taper; used in lathework to hold cylindrical parts accurately in relation to a hole in the part; 2) the stem in pull-stem rivets

marketing—a word that includes all of the functions people do in moving, promoting, and selling products from the time they come from the manufacturer until they are bought and used by consumers. This usually includes storing, transporting, advertising, displaying, and selling a product.

mechanical properties—the characteristics of metals when they are acted on by outside forces; for example, hardness and ductility

medium-carbon steel—steel with a carbon content of .30% to .60%

metal fatigue—a condition of metal resulting from repeated stress; causes failure under loads that are below the metal's tensile strength

metallurgist—an engineer trained in metals theory and the technology of obtaining and using metals

meter (m)—a standard measurement of length in the S.I. metric system (the International System of Units); equal to 1,000 millimeters or 39.37 inches

metric ton (t)—a standard measure of weight in the S.I. metric system; equal to 1.1 U.S. tons

MIG/metal inert gas/welding—a gas-metal arc welding process using a consumable wire electrode that is fed through a welding gun

mill—1) (noun) a factory where molten metal is cast into products such as ingots, slabs, blooms, and billets, or where these products are shaped further into bars, rods, etc.; 2) (verb) to cut metal with a multiple-tooth cutting tool called a **mill**, or **milling cutter**

millimeter (mm)—a standard measure of length in the S.I. system; equal to 0.03937"

minor diameter—also **root diameter**; the smallest diameter of a straight external or internal thread

mold—a hollow form in which molten metal is cast

N/C—abbreviation for numerical control

nitriding—in case-hardening, applying a nitrogenous substance to steel to produce a thin surface layer of iron nitride

nonferrous metal—metal that does not contain iron

normalizing—a process of heat-treatment process that relieves internal stress and removes the effects of other heat-treatment processes

nose angle—on a lathe tool bit, the angle formed by the side cutting-edge and the end cutting-edge

numerical control (N/C)—a system used in automated machining to control machine operations by numerically coded electronic impulses to working parts

O.D.—abbreviation for outside diameter

open dies—forging dies with flat, V-shaped, or slightly convex surfaces; metal is squeezed between these surfaces, but the dies do not enclose it

open-loop system—an automated system in which no provision is made to report to the control system whether commands have been properly carried out

operational sequence—the step-by-step manufacturing procedure necessary for producing a product

organization chart—a schematic diagram that shows the organization of a company, government, or military unit. It identifies the managers or leaders responsible for each aspect of company operations and the line of authority for decision making.

organization manual—a printed manual, often a looseleaf book, that provides a detailed outline of the duties and responsibilities of each job on an organization chart

output—in automated systems, work performed by a machine operation

overhead costs—costs such as light, heat, electricity, water, factory rent, taxes, engineering, supervision, and marketing costs in running a company that usually must be paid even if no products are produced

oxyacetylene welding—a welding process using a burning mixture of oxygen and acetylene as the heat source

parallel line development—pattern development used in sheet metalworking for objects with parallel sides

parting plane—also **parting line;** in sand casting, the line at which the two halves of the flask meet when assembled

part reference point—the point on a workpiece chosen by an N/C programmer from which all tool movement will be measured

Pascal (Pa)—a standard measurement of pressure in the S.I. metric system; equal to 0.0000145 pound per square inch

peen—1) (noun) the ball-, wedge-, or cone-shaped part of a peening hammer; 2) (verb) to hammer with the peen to make a roughened texture

physical properties—characteristics of metals when they are not being acted upon by outside forces such as machining or heat treating; color, density, and weight are examples of these

pickling—soaking a metal in acid to remove scale

pig iron—crude iron from the blast furnace; about 93% pure iron, 3-5% carbon, and other elements

pilot production run—a trial manufacturing run, in which a small quantity of products are produced to determine where production problems may occur. The problems must be solved before full-scale production can be scheduled.

pitch diameter—on a straight thread, the diameter on a thread profile where the widths of the thread and groove are equal

pitch of thread—the distance from one point on a screw thread to the same point on the next thread

plain milling—machining a flat surface with a plain milling cutter mounted on a horizontal milling machine arbor

point-to-point N/C system—an N/C system in which the tool or workpiece moves in straight lines from one programmed point to another

powder metallurgy (P/M)—the production of metal parts by compressing metal powders in precision dies or molds

production drawings—the detailed part and assembly drawings of a product that are necessary for its manufacture; also called working drawings

proof circle—in drilling, a scribed circle smaller than the hole to be drilled; used to determine accurate drill positioning

prototype—a full-size, working model of a product, sometimes one-of-a-kind, used to test product design, construction, and performance features

psi—abbreviation for pounds per square inch

punching—in sheet metalwork, a punch press operation that produces forms by removing unwanted metal

pyrometer—a temperature-indicating instrument used to measure high temperatures

quenching—cooling hot metal suddenly by plunging in water, brine, or oil, or allowing it to air-cool

radial line development—in sheet metalworking, a type of pattern development used for objects such as cones and pyramids

radius gage—also **fillet gate**; gage used to measure the radius of rounded corners

rake angle—on fluted cutting tools, the angle between the flute and the workpiece; may be **positive** (less than 90°) or **negative** (greater than 90°); helps to curl metal chips

raker set—a tooth set with one tooth bent to the right, one to the left, and one straight tooth in between

rate of taper—the rate at which a workpiece is to be tapered on a lathe; expressed in inches per foot or millimeters per meter

reference cut—in machining, the first cut, from which other cutting measurements are taken

reference gage—also **master gage**; a fixed gage made of hardened steel; used to test the accuracy of inspection gages and micrometers

research—careful study or examination to discover and determine the meaning of new facts and how to solve problems by using them. Research in industry often involves determining the need for a product in the marketplace (market research) and how the product should be manufactured to meet the need (product research)

riser—in sand casting, a vertical channel connected to the mold cavity; used to control casting shrinkage

robot—an automatic machine that performs functions ordinarily done by human beings and which may be programmed to perform different tasks

root—on a screw thread, the bottom surface that joins two adjoining sides

routing—determining the route that the material for making and assembling a product must take through the plant or factory

runner—in sand casting, a horizontal channel through which metal flows from the sprue to the gate

running fit (RC)—a close fit between two parts with enough clearance so that one can rotate freely without wobbling

SAW (submerged arc welding)—an arc welding process in which the arc is submerged under a mound of granular flux; bare filler wire is fed automatically

scheduling—planning when the work is to be done for manufacturing a product

screw plate—a set of threading tools that includes dies, taps, and the tools needed to use them

setover screws—screws on the lathe tailstock used to align the tailstock with the headstock

setup costs—the cost of labor and other related one-time charges to organize and prepare the machines and tools for manufacturing a product

setup point—also **home**; in N/C work, a point chosen by the operator as the starting and ending point for the N/C program

shear strength—resistance to cutting or slicing forces

shim—a small thin piece of metal used between mating parts to provide the proper fit

shrink fit (FN)—a force fit in which a part with an opening is heated, fitted to a mating part, then allowed to cool, thus shrinking onto the second part

side-rake—the angle formed between a lathe tool face and a horizontal plane; measured at a right angle to the shank

side-relief—also **side clearance**; the angle ground between a lathe tool flank and the original side; allows the side cutting-edge to enter the workpiece

sintering—bonding powdered metals by heating a mixture of them to high temperatures below their melting points

slag—by-product of metal purification, welding, and casting; contains dirt, scale, and impurities

sliding fit (RC)—a close fit between two parts with enough clearance so that one can slide freely without wobbling

smelting—the separation of a pure metal from its ore by melting in contact with a flux

snagging—removal of flash and other casting imperfections with a utility grinder

soft automation—See **flexible manufacturing system.**

soft soldering—a soldering method using solder with a melting point of less than 800°F [427°C]

software—a computer term that refers to the programs that control the operation of the computer, and which direct the computer to perform specific functions

solder—1) (verb) to join metals with a nonferous filler metal that has a melting point lower than the metals to be joined; 2) (noun) the filler metal used in soldering

spindle—on metalworking machines, a revolving shaft that holds and drives the cutting tool or workpiece

sprue—in sand casting, the vertical hole through which molten metal flows from the pouring basin to the runner and gate

stainless steel—an alloy of iron, chromium, and nickel or manganese; highly corrosion-resistant

standard practice manual—a printed manual or booklet that describes company policy and standard procedures for carrying out all aspects of company operations

standard process sheet—a document containing the sequence of operations for the most economical manufacture of a part

statistical process control (SPC)—a quality control procedure used to reduce the percentage of rejects and to lower production costs. A sample of parts is periodically measured at each machine and then analyzed statistically to determine whether the machine needs adjustment.

statistical sampling—a quality control procedure which requires inspection of only a small percentage of the quantity of a product being manufactured

straddle milling—using two side-milling cutters to machine two parallel sides at the same time

stretchout—in sheet metalworking, a pattern that shows the size and shape of the flat sheet needed to make an object

superheat—in casting operations, the number of degrees above its melting point at which metal is poured

surface plate—a large iron or granite plate used as a flat surface on which to place a workpiece for layout

surface speed—the rotation speed of a cutting tool or workpiece measured at its rim, or *circumference*

tailstock—a movable fixture opposite the headstock on a lathe; has a spindle used to support one end of a workpiece, and in which to hold drilling tools

tailstock setover—in taper turning, the amount that the tailstock is offset from the headstock

tang—1) the pointed end of a file that fits into the handle; 2) the flattened end of a drill shank that fits into a slot in a drill sleeve or into a drillpress spindle

tap—a tool used to cut internal threads

tap drill—a drill used to make a hole before tapping

tempering—1) heat-treating metal to relieve internal stress and increase toughness; 2) in green-sand molding, mixing sand with water or oil so that it will pack properly

template or templet—a pattern used for laying out the shape of workpieces or for marking holes, arcs, etc.

tensile strength—resistance to the force tending to pull material apart

thread class—a category that designates the fit between mating internal and external threads

TIG (tungsten inert gas welding)—a welding process using a non-consumable tungsten electrode and an inert gas shield of argon or helium; also *GTAW (gas tungsten arc welding)*

tolerance—acceptable variation in a part dimension; the difference between the upper and lower dimension limits

toolpost—the part of the lathe compound rest that holds the toolholder

tool steel—plain and alloy steel of medium and high carbon content used for making tools

tooth pitch—a measure of the spacing between saw blade teeth; expressed as number of teeth per inch or the distance between adjacent teeth in millimeters

tooth set—the way saw teeth are bent to one side or the other to make a kerf wider than the thickness of the saw blade

torque—a turning or twisting force applied to a bolt or shaft

torsional strength—resistance to twisting forces

toughness—a measure of a metal's ability to withstand sudden shock without breaking *(fracturing)*

transfer machine—a production machine that automatically performs machining or other operations and automatically transfers the workpiece from one machining station or workstation to the next

transverse feed—on column-and-knee milling machines, table movement toward or away from the column; see **cross feed**

triangulation—a type of pattern development in sheet metalworking used for objects with irregular shapes

tripoli—an abrasive used in buffing; made of weathered, decomposed limestone

truing—cutting a grinding wheel to eliminate high spots during running

tungsten carbide—one of the hardest alloys; produced by sintering tungsten, cobalt, and carbon

turning—a lathe operation in which the tool cuts along the outside diameter of the workpiece

turret—a machine fixture that holds multiple tools and can be revolved *(indexed)* to present a specific tool

turret drill press—a multiple-tool drill press; the desired tool is brought into position by revolving a turret

turret lathe—a lathe equipped with a turret holding multiple tools for performing several different lathe operations

ultrasonic frequency—a frequency above the limit of human hearing (20,000 cycles per second)

Unified Form Thread—also **Unified Screw Thread**; a screw thread form used in the U.S., Canada, and Great Britain

universal spiral attachment—a milling machine accessory for machining of spiral surfaces or grooves

up milling—also **conventional milling**; feeding the workpiece against the direction of cutter rotation

vaporization—changing of a substance from its solid state to a gaseous state by heat

variable-speed drive—a drive system consisting of a belt and a pulley whose effective size can be varied to provide a continuous range of speeds

V-blocks—steel blocks with V-shaped grooves; used to hold round workpieces for layout or machining

vernier—a scale added to a measuring tool that enables it to make finer measurements

vertical feed—in knee-and-column milling machines, the up or down movement of the knee and the table

viscosity—a measure of the stiffness, or thickness, of a fluid

wavy set—a tooth set in which several teeth are bent to the right and several to the left, alternately

ways—the precision-machined V-shaped and flat tracks of the lathe bed on which the carriage and tailstock slide

welding—joining pieces of metal together by using enough temperature, pressure, or a combination of both to cause metal from both pieces to flow and blend together

white lead—a poisonous compound of lead; it is mixed with linseed oil to make a high-pressure lubricant

wholesale—the sale of goods or products in quantity, usually to a retail merchant for resale to consumers

word address form—a method of coding N/C instructions. Each word consists of a letter, which identifies a different machine function, followed by numerical data.

work-hardening—the hardening that occurs in metal during cold working

work-in-process—the quantity of a product on the factory floor in its various stages of production at any given time

wrought iron—pig iron from which most of the carbon has been removed; contains about 0.04% carbon

INDEX